# Lecture Notes in Computer Science 10833

Commenced Publication in 1973
Founding and Former Series Editors:
Gerhard Goos, Juris Hartmanis, and Jan van Leeuwen

More information about this series at http://www.springer.com/series/7409

Flavio Ferrarotti · Stefan Woltran (Eds.)

# Foundations of Information and Knowledge Systems

10th International Symposium, FoIKS 2018
Budapest, Hungary, May 14–18, 2018
Proceedings

 Springer

*Editors*
Flavio Ferrarotti
Software Competence Center Hagenberg
Hagenberg im Mühlkreis
Austria

Stefan Woltran (iD)
Vienna University of Technology
Vienna
Austria

ISSN 0302-9743                    ISSN 1611-3349  (electronic)
Lecture Notes in Computer Science
ISBN 978-3-319-90049-0          ISBN 978-3-319-90050-6  (eBook)
https://doi.org/10.1007/978-3-319-90050-6

Library of Congress Control Number: 2018940148

LNCS Sublibrary: SL3 – Information Systems and Applications, incl. Internet/Web, and HCI

Printed on acid-free paper

This Springer imprint is published by the registered company Springer International Publishing AG
part of Springer Nature
The registered company address is: Gewerbestrasse 11, 6330 Cham, Switzerland

# Preface

This volume contains the articles that were presented at the 10th International Symposium on Foundations of Information and Knowledge Systems (FoIKS 2018) held in Budapest, Hungary, during May 14–18, 2018.

The FoIKS symposia provide a biennial forum for presenting and discussing theoretical and applied research on information and knowledge systems. The goal is to bring together researchers with an interest in this subject, share research experiences, promote collaboration, and identify new issues and directions for future research. Speakers are given sufficient time to present their ideas and results within the larger context of their research. Furthermore, participants are asked in advance to prepare a first response to a contribution of another author in order to initiate discussion.

Previous FoIKS symposia were held in Linz (Austria) in 2016, Bordeaux (France) in 2014, Kiel (Germany) in 2012, Sofia (Bulgaria) in 2010, Pisa (Italy) in 2008, Budapest (Hungary) in 2006, Vienna (Austria) in 2004, Schloss Salzau near Kiel (Germany) in 2002, and Burg/Spreewald near Berlin (Germany) in 2000. FoIKS took up the tradition of the conference series Mathematical Fundamentals of Database Systems (MFDBS), which initiated East–West collaboration in the field of database theory. Former MFDBS conferences were held in Rostock (Germany) in 1991, Visegrád (Hungary) in 1989, and Dresden (Germany) in 1987.

FoIKS 2018 solicited original contributions on foundational aspects of information and knowledge systems. This included submissions that apply ideas, theories, or methods from specific disciplines to information and knowledge systems. Examples of such disciplines are discrete mathematics, logic and algebra, model theory, information theory, complexity theory, algorithmics and computation, statistics, and optimization. Suggested topics included, but were not limited to, the following:

- Big data: models for data in the cloud, programming languages for big data, query processing
- Database design: formal models, dependencies, and independencies
- Dynamics of information: models of transactions, concurrency control, updates, consistency preservation, belief revision
- Information fusion: heterogeneity, views, schema dominance, multiple source information merging, reasoning under inconsistency
- Integrity and constraint management: verification, validation, consistent query answering, information cleaning
- Intelligent agents: multi-agent systems, autonomous agents, foundations of software agents, cooperative agents, formal models of interactions, negotiations and dialogue, logical models of emotions
- Knowledge discovery and information retrieval: machine learning, data mining, formal concept analysis and association rules, text mining, information extraction

- Knowledge representation, reasoning, and planning: non-monotonic formalisms, probabilistic and non-probabilistic models of uncertainty, graphical models and independence, similarity-based reasoning, preference modeling and handling, computation models of argument, argumentation systems
- Logics in databases and AI: classical and non-classical logics, logic programming, description logic, spatial and temporal logics, probability logic, fuzzy logic
- Mathematical foundations: discrete structures and algorithms, graphs, grammars, automata, abstract machines, finite model theory, information theory, coding theory, complexity theory, randomness
- Security in information and knowledge systems: identity theft, privacy, trust, intrusion detection, access control, inference control, secure Web services, secure Semantic Web, risk management
- Semi-structured data and XML: data modeling, data processing, data compression, data exchange
- Social computing: collective intelligence and self-organizing knowledge, collaborative filtering, computational social choice, Boolean games, coalition formation, reputation systems
- The Semantic Web and knowledge management: languages, ontologies, agents, adaptation, intelligent algorithms, ontology-based data access
- The WWW: models of Web databases, Web dynamics, Web services, Web transactions and negotiations, social networks, Web mining

The call for papers resulted in the submission of 40 articles. Each one was carefully reviewed by at least three international experts. In total, fourteen articles were accepted for long presentation and six articles were accepted for short presentation. This volume contains versions of these articles that have been revised by their authors according to the comments provided in the reviews. After the conference, authors of a few selected articles were asked to prepare extended versions of their articles for publication in a special issue of the journal *Annals of Mathematics and Artificial Intelligence*.

During this symposium we had the opportunity to celebrate Prof. Klaus-Dieter Schewe's 60th birthday. FoIKS itself is one of the many successful initiatives of Prof. Klaus-Dieter Schewe. He is the chair of the FoIKS Steering Committee and continues to be a major driving force behind the symposium. As a token of appreciation, Prof. Klaus-Dieter Schewe received a Festschrift with contributions from his former students, collaborators, and colleagues – most are researchers whose academic careers have been strongly influenced by him.

We wish to thank all authors who submitted papers and all conference participants for fruitful discussions. We are grateful to our keynote speakers Gerd Brewka, Laura Kovács, Sebastian Link, David Pearce, and Bernhard Thalheim. We would like to thank the Program Committee members and additional reviewers for their timely expertise in carefully reviewing the submissions. The support of the conference provided by the *Artificial Intelligence Journal* (AIJ), the Association for Logic Programming (ALP), the European Association for Theoretical Computer Science (EATCS), and by the Vienna Center for Logic and Algorithms (VCLA) is gratefully acknowledged. We thank the Software Competence Center Hagenberg for hosting the FoIKS Website and specially Senén González for redesigning and maintaining it. Last but not least, special thanks go to the local organization team: Tiziana Del Viscio, Dezsõ Miklós, and Attila Sali, for their support and for being our hosts during the wonderful days at the Alfréd Rényi Institute of Mathematics in Budapest.

May 2018                                    Flavio Ferrarotti
                                            Stefan Woltran

# Conference Organization

FoIKS 2018 was organized by the Alfréd Rényi Institute of Mathematics.

## Program Chairs

Flavio Ferrarotti     Software Competence Center Hagenberg, Austria
Stefan Woltran     TU Wien, Austria

## Program Committee

| | |
|---|---|
| Yamine Ait Ameur | IRIT/INPT-ENSEEIHT, France |
| Pablo Barceló | Universidad de Chile, Chile |
| Kim Bauters | Bristol University, UK |
| Christoph Beierle | University of Hagen, Germany |
| Leopoldo Bertossi | Carleton University, Canada |
| Philippe Besnard | CNRS/IRIT, France |
| Nicole Bidoit | Université Paris Sud, LRI (UMR 8623), France |
| Meghyn Bienvenu | CNRS, University of Montpellier, Inria, France |
| Joachim Biskup | Technische Universität Dortmund, Germany |
| Marina De Vos | University of Bath, UK |
| Michael Dekhtyar | Tver State University, Russia |
| Dragan Doder | IRIT, Université Paul Sabatier, France |
| Thomas Eiter | Vienna University of Technology, Austria |
| Christian Fermüller | Vienna University of Technology, Austria |
| Flavio Ferrarotti | Software Competence Centre Hagenberg, Austria |
| Marc Gyssens | Universiteit Hasselt, Belgium |
| Edward Hermann Haeusler | PUC-Rio, Brazil |
| Martin Homola | Comenius University, Bratislava, Slovakia |
| Anthony Hunter | University College London, UK |
| Gabriel Istrate | West University of Timişoara, Romania |
| Gyula Y. Katona | Budapest University of Technology and Economics, Hungary |
| Gabriele Kern-Isberner | Technische Universität Dortmund, Germany |
| Attila Kiss | Eötvös Loránd University, Hungary |
| Ioannis Kokkinis | Technische Universität Dortmund, Germany |
| Sébastien Konieczny | CRIL - CNRS, France |
| Julia Kontinen | University of Helsinki, Finland |
| Nicola Leone | University of Calabria, Italy |
| Sebastian Link | The University of Auckland, New Zealand |
| Thomas Lukasiewicz | University of Oxford, UK |

| | |
|---|---|
| Sofian Maabout | LaBRI. University of Bordeaux, France |
| Andrea Marino | University of Pisa, Italy |
| Jorge Martinez-Gil | Software Competence Center Hagenberg, Austria |
| Henri Prade | IRIT - CNRS, France |
| Elena Ravve | ORT-Braude College, Israel |
| Sebastian Rudolph | TU Dresden, Germany |
| Attila Sali | Alfréd Rényi Institute of Mathematics, Hungary |
| Vadim Savenkov | Vienna University of Economics and Business, Austria |
| Klaus-Dieter Schewe | Software Competence Center Hagenberg, Austria |
| Thomas Schwentick | Technische Universität Dortmund, Germany |
| Kostyantyn Shchekotykhin | Alpen-Adria Universität Klagenfurt, Austria |
| Csaba István Sidló | Hungarian Academy of Sciences, Hungary |
| Guillermo Ricardo Simari | Universidad del Sur in Bahia Blanca, Argentina |
| Mantas Simkus | Vienna University of Technology, Austria |
| Bernhard Thalheim | Christian Albrechts University Kiel, Germany |
| Alex Thomo | University of Victoria, Canada |
| Mirek Truszczynski | University of Kentucky, USA |
| Gyorgy Turan | University of Illinois at Chicago, USA |
| José María Turull Torres | Universidad Nacional de La Matanza, Argentina |
| Dirk Van Gucht | Indiana University, USA |
| Jonni Virtema | Hasselt University, Belgium |
| Qing Wang | The Australian National University, Australia |
| Stefan Woltran | Vienna University of Technology, Austria |

## Additional Reviewers

| | |
|---|---|
| Leila Amgoud | Silvia Miksch |
| David A. Mix Barrington | Nysret Musliu |
| Alex Baumgartner | Alexandre Rademaker |
| Senén González | Gábor Rácz |
| Matthias Hofer | Kai Sauerwald |
| Markus Kröll | Patrik Schneider |
| Martin Lackner | Josef Widder |
| Marco Maratea | |

## Local Organization Chair

Attila Sali              Alfréd Rényi Institute of Mathematics, Hungary

## Local Organization Team

Tiziana Del Viscio
Dezsõ Miklós

## Sponsors

*Artificial Intelligence Journal* (AIJ)
Association for Logic Programming (ALP)
European Association for Theoretical Computer Science (EATCS)
Vienna Center for Logic and Algorithms (VCLA)

# Keynote Speakers

# Computational Models of Argument: A New Perspective on Persisting KR Problems

Gerhard Brewka

University of Leipzig, Germany

**Short Biography:** Gerhard Brewka is a Professor of Intelligent Systems at Leipzig University, Germany. His research focuses on knowledge representation, in particular logic programming, nonmonotonic reasoning, preference and inconsistency handling, and computational models of argumentation. He served as President of EurAI (formerly ECCAI), the European Association of AI, and of Knowledge Representation Inc. In 2002, Brewka was awarded a EurAI Fellowship. He is a member of the IJCAI Board of Trustees and was Conference Chair of IJCAI-16 in New York.

**Summary:** In the last two decades the area of knowledge representation and reasoning (KR) has seen a steady rise of interest in the notion of argument, an old topic of study in philosophy. This interest was fueled by a certain dissatisfaction with existing approaches, especially to default reasoning and inconsistency handling, and by the demands of applications in legal reasoning and several related fields.

The ultimate goal of computational argumentation is to enable the development of computer-based systems capable to support – and to participate in – argumentative activities. To achieve this goal one has to come up with models which formally capture the way we usually come to conclusions and make decisions, namely by

1  constructing arguments for and against various options,
2  establishing relationships among the arguments, most notably the attack relation, and
3  identifying interesting subsets of the arguments which represent coherent positions based on these relations.

In the talk we will highlight some of the main ideas and key techniques that have been developed in the field and show how they address issues of representing knowledge, handling inconsistencies, and reasoning by default. We will mainly focus on Abstract Dialectical Frameworks (ADFs) which substantially generalize the well-known and widely used Dung Frameworks. In particular, we will demonstrate how the operator-based techniques underlying ADFs allow us to turn directed graphs with arbitrary edge labels, which are widely used to visualize argumentation and reasoning scenarios, into full-fledged knowledge representation formalisms with a whole range of precisely defined semantics.

# Automated Reasoning for Systems Engineering

Laura Kovács

TU Wien, Austria

**Short Biography:** Laura Kovács is a full professor at the Faculty of Informatics of Vienna University of Technology (TU Wien). She also holds a part-time professor position at the Department of Computer Science and Engineering of the Chalmers University of Technology. She has a diploma in computer science and math from the West University of Timisoara, Romania and a PhD with highest distinction in computer science from the Research Institute of Symbolic Computation (RISC-Linz) of the Johannes Kepler University Linz, Austria. Prior to her appointment to Vienna, she was an associate professor at Chalmers.

In her research, Laura Kovács deals with the design and development of new theories, technologies, and tools for program analysis, with a particular focus on automated assertion generation, symbolic summation, computer algebra, and automated theorem proving. She is the co-developer of the Vampire theorem prover. In 2014, she received the Wallenberg Academy Fellowship and an ERC Starting Grant.

**Summary:** Automated reasoning, and in particular first-order theorem proving, is one of the earliest research areas within artificial intelligence and formal methods. It is undergoing a rapid development thanks to its successful use in program analysis and verification, semantic Web, database systems, symbolic computation, theorem proving in mathematics, and other related areas. Breakthrough results in all areas of theorem proving have been obtained, including improvements in theory, implementation, and the development of powerful theorem proving tools.

In this talk I give a brief overview on the main ingredients of automated theorem proving, and focus on recent challenges and developments in the area. Further, I will discuss recent applications of theorem proving in rigorous systems engineering.

# Old Keys that Open New Doors

Sebastian Link

University of Auckland, New Zealand

**Short Biography:** Sebastian is a full professor at the Department of Computer Science in the University of Auckland. His research interests include conceptual data modeling, semantics in databases, foundations of mark-up languages, and applications of discrete mathematics to computer science. Sebastian received the Chris Wallace Award for Outstanding Research Contributions in recognition of his work on the semantics of SQL and XML data. Sebastian has published more than 150 research articles. He is a member of the editorial board of the journal Information Systems.

## Summary

Keys enforce Codd's integrity for entities,
Giving fast access to data since the seventies.
The issue of missing information remains fundamental,
Better notions of keys will prove to be instrumental.

We review keys on classical relations,
Recalling the simplest of all axiomatisations.
An extremal cardinality a non-redundant family retains,
Whenever it lives up to Sperner's anti-chains.
Armstrong relations are built after an anti-key hunt,
The discovery by hypergraph transversals is simply elegant.

As nulls in applications do require some finesse,
We review key sets that have high expressiveness.
Establishing an axiomatisation that is binary,
We show implication to be complete for coNP.
Armstrong relations do not necessarily exist,
The discovery of keys sets as an open problem we enlist.

Key sets with singletons avoid the likely intractability curtain,
Leading to keys that hold in every world so certain.
We look at possible and certain keys together with NOT NULL,
Which lead to problems that are anything but dull.
Implication is easily characterised axiomatically and algorithmically,
The structure and computation of Armstrong relations is captured non-trivially.
Extremal families occupy two levels with some gaps,
The discovery can use transversals in two steps.

We briefly summarise keys on data with veracities,
considering probabilities, possibilities, and contextualities.
Concluding with problems for minds that are bright,
We hope the talk sparks research with heaps of insight.

# The Logical Basis of Knowledge Representation in Answer Set Programming

David Pearce

Universidad Politécnica de Madrid, Spain

**Short Biography:** David Pearce studied Philosophy, Logic and Scientific Method at the Universities of Sussex and Oxford, obtaining his D Phil (Sussex) in 1980. From 1982–94 he worked at the Philosophy Institute of the Free University Berlin as a Lecturer and later Heisenberg Research Fellow. From 1992–94 he was Acting Professor at the Universities of Göttingen and Heidelberg. In 1994 he moved to the German AI Research Centre (DFKI) in Saarbrücken, where until 2000 he coordinated one of the founding European Networks of Excellence: Compulog Net. From 2000–2002 he worked at the Future and Emerging Technologies Unit of the European Commission in Brussels where he was involved in the management and supervision of EU research programmes. He then moved to Madrid as Ramón y Cajal Research Fellow at the Rey Juan Carlos University, later becoming professor in the Technical University of Madrid in 2009. From 2011–14 he coordinated the EU funded action: the European Network for Social Intelligence (SINTELNET).

David Pearce has worked mainly in the areas of Logic and Knowledge Representation, with a special interest in nonmonotonic reasoning and logic programming. He has made numerous contributions to the field of Answer Set Programming (ASP). In the late 1980s, together with Gerd Wagner, he introduced the concept of strong negation into logic programming. From 1995 onwards he developed Equilibrium Logic as a new logical foundation for ASP. In 2001, together with Vladimir Lifschitz and Agustín Valverde, he initiated the study of strongly equivalent logic programs which opened up a new research area in nonmonotonic reasoning and KRR that is still active today. His current research interests include combining Artificial Intelligence with Social Ontology. Pearce was elected ECCAI (now EurAI) Fellow in 2014.

**Summary:** In this talk I give an introduction to the underlying logic of Answer Set Programming. The basis is a non-classical, intermediate logic and its non-monotonic extension, known as *equilibrium logic*. Together they provide an alternative to the standard paradigm of two-valued, classical logic. In view of the origins of answer set programming, it seems appropriate to call this new approach *stable reasoning*. The talk will focus on the intuitive meaning of the main logical definitions, and explain their effect with some example programs. I will also discuss some of the main extensions of the basic language that may be useful for knowledge representation.

# Revisiting the Database Constraints Theory

Bernhard Thalheim

Christian-Albrechts-University at Kiel, Germany

**Short Biography:** Prof. Dr.rer.nat.habil. Bernhard Thalheim (Director, Department of Computer Science, Faculty of Engineering at Christian-Albrechts University Kiel, Germany) (MSc, PhD, DSc) is full professor at Christian Albrechts University in Germany. His major research interests are database theory, logic in databases, and systems development methodologies, in particular for web information systems. He has published more than 300 refereed publications, edited more than 30 conference volumes, co-founded three international conferences, and has been programme committee chair for almost three dozen international conferences such as MFDBS, ER, FoIKS, ASM, SDKB, NLDB and ADBIS. He got several international awards, e.g. the Kolmogorov professorship at Lomonossow University Moscow and the P. P. Chen award of Elsevier. He has been an associated professor at Dresden University of Technology, a visiting professor at Kuwait University, Alpen-Adria University Klagenfurt and others, and a full professor at Rostock University and Brandenburg University of Technology at Cottbus.

**Summary:** The theory of database constraints has been developed for a long time within the relational database modelling setting. The 80ies brought a large body of knowledge and led to the impression that the theory development is completed. A typical example is normalisation theory that has been developed inside the relational understanding. It must already be reconsidered for the table database modelling setting. Cardinality constraints defined in an entity-relationship modelling setting were the most essential addition to the theory of relational constraints. It seems that the theory of object-relational constraints is still a lacuna. Therefore, monographs and textbooks remain to be on the level of the early 90ies as far as constraints are considered. Database technology brought however powerful and sophisticated systems. So, the constraints that might be supported without loss of performance are far richer. Database applications need more sophisticated constraints. So, the paper presents some solutions for constraint enhancement, constraint handling, structure optimisation, and database modelling at the conceptual level. It completes with open problems.

# Contents

# Papers of Invited Talks

# Old Keys that Open New Doors

Sebastian Link

Department of Computer Science, University of Auckland, Auckland, New Zealand
s.link@auckland.ac.nz

Keys enforce Codd's integrity for entities,
Giving fast access to data since the seventies.
The issue of missing information remains fundamental,
Better notions of keys will prove to be instrumental.

We review keys on classical relations,
Recalling the simplest of all axiomatisations.
An extremal cardinality a non-redundant family retains,
Whenever it lives up to Sperner's anti-chains.
Armstrong relations are built after an anti-key hunt,
The discovery by hypergraph transversals is simply elegant.

As nulls in applications do require some finesse,
We review key sets that have high expressiveness.
Establishing an axiomatisation that is binary,
We show implication to be complete for coNP.
Armstrong relations do not necessarily exist,
The discovery of keys sets as an open problem we enlist.

Key sets with singletons avoid the likely intractability curtain,
Leading to keys that hold in every world so certain.
We look at possible and certain keys together with NOT NULL,
Which lead to problems that are anything but dull.
Implication is easily characterised axiomatically and algorithmically,
The structure and computation of Armstrong relations is captured non-trivially.
Extremal families occupy two levels with some gaps,
The discovery can use transversals in two steps.

We briefly summarise keys on data with veracities,
considering probabilities, possibilities, and contextualities.
Concluding with problems for minds that are bright,
We hope the talk sparks research with heaps of insight.

© Springer International Publishing AG, part of Springer Nature 2018
F. Ferrarotti and S. Woltran (Eds.): FoIKS 2018, LNCS 10833, pp. 3–13, 2018.
https://doi.org/10.1007/978-3-319-90050-6_1

# 1  Motivation

Keys are a core enabler for data management. They are fundamental for under-standing the structure and semantics of data. Given a collection of entities, a key is a set of attributes whose values uniquely identify an entity in the collection. Keys form the primary mechanism to enforce entity integrity within database systems [9,31]. Keys are fundamental in many classical areas of data manage-ment, including data modeling, database design, indexing, transaction process-ing, and query optimization. Knowledge about keys enables us to (i) uniquely ref-erence entities across data repositories, (ii) minimize data redundancy at schema design time to process updates efficiently at run time, (iii) provide better selec-tivity estimates in cost-based query optimization, (iv) provide a query optimizer with new access paths that can lead to substantial speedups in query processing, (v) allow the database administrator to improve the efficiency of data access via physical design techniques such as data partitioning or the creation of indexes and materialized views, and (vi) provide new insights into application data. Mod-ern applications raise the importance of keys even further. They can facilitate the data integration process, help with the detection of duplicates and anomalies, provide guidance in repairing and cleaning data, and provide consistent answers to queries over dirty data. The discovery of keys from data is one of the core activities in data profiling.

*Purpose and organisation.* The purpose of this paper is to look at different notions of keys over incomplete relations. The paper also provides a point of ref-erence to various computational problems associated with integrity constraints in general, and keys in particular. The paper is not meant to provide an overview of the state of the art solutions to these computational problems, but merely to provide some motivation for their study and the points of entry for such research. The computational problems are motivated and stated in Sect. 2. The notions of candidate keys, unique constraints, key sets, possible and certain keys are exemplified in Sect. 3. The recent class of embedded uniqueness constraints is briefly discussed in Sect. 4. A short overview about the literature on these com-putational problems is given in Sect. 5. Some other classes of keys in different models of data are referenced in Sect. 6. Some open problems are discussed in Sect. 7.

# 2  Computational Problems

The effective use and maintenance of keys (and any class of integrity constraints) makes it necessary to investigate several computational problems.

In practice, data administrators can benefit from knowing how complex the maintenance of their database can grow. For example, it is useful to know how large a non-redundant family of keys over a schema with $n$ attributes can be, and which of these families attain such extreme cardinality. Here, non-redundancy of the family $\Sigma$ means that none of the keys $\sigma \in \Sigma$ is implied by the remaining keys $\Sigma \setminus \{\sigma\}$ in the family. That is, for every $\sigma \in \Sigma$ there is some relation that satisfies all the keys in $\Sigma \backslash \{\sigma\}$ but violates $\sigma$. Non-redundancy is an important property in practice, guaranteeing that no resources are wasted in redundantly validating the satisfaction of any keys when a database is updated. That is, the maximum cardinality of non-redundant families of keys also represents the worst possible number of keys that must necessarily be validated whenever updates occur. More positively, this number can also be interpreted as the best possible number of keys from which query optimisations may result.

| Name: | EXTREMAL |
| --- | --- |
| Input: | A relation schema $R$ with $n$ attributes |
| Problem: | Which non-redundant families of keys over $R$ |
| | Attain maximum cardinality? |

The EXTREMAL problem subsumes the problem of determining what the maximum cardinality of a non-redundant family of keys actually is. The problem also assumes that we know what a non-redundant family of keys constitutes. In other words, we already know for any given set $\Sigma \cup \{\varphi\}$ of keys when $\Sigma$ implies $\varphi$. This is known as the IMPLICATION PROBLEM, and asks on input $\Sigma \cup \{\varphi\}$ whether every relation that satisfies all elements of $\Sigma$ also satisfies $\varphi$. The IMPLICATION PROBLEM gains its practical motivation from minimising the costs in the processing of updates and queries. Indeed, when validating whether a given update results in a relation that satisfies a given set of keys, then this set should be non-redundant. Otherwise, we would incur unnecessary overheads. Similarly, when processing a query we might be able to save time by knowing that the underlying relation satisfies some key because it is implied by the set of keys that the relation is known to satisfy. A simple example is the removal of a superfluous DISTINCT clause because the set of attributes forms a super key.

| Name: | IMPLICATION |
| --- | --- |
| Input: | Set $\Sigma \cup \{\varphi\}$ of keys |
| Problem: | Does $\Sigma$ imply $\varphi$? |

Another fundamental problem is the correct acquisition of keys, that is, which keys actually express business rules that hold on a given application domain? For this problem, business analysts must often work together with domain experts, but need to overcome a communication barrier: analysts understand database concepts but not necessarily the domain, while domain experts understand the domain but not necessarily database concepts. Sample data has been found very valuable in addressing this mismatch in expertise [28,30]. The sample should satisfy all the keys that are currently perceived meaningful by the analysts but violate any key that they currently perceive meaningless. This amounts to saying that the sample constitutes an *Armstrong relation* for the set of keys currently perceived to be meaningful [13]. The idea is that analysts and domain experts inspect the sample together. If there is some key that is incorrectly perceived to be meaningless, then the sample violates this actually meaningful key and the domain expert should be able to notice this violation in the sample and point it out to the analyst, who can then include the key in the set of meaningful ones. An iteration of this process should lead to a more complete set of meaningful keys. This approach motivates the problem of computing an Armstrong relation for a given set of keys, that is, a relation that satisfies every key in the given set but violates every key that is not implied by the given set.

| Name: | ARMSTRONG |
|---|---|
| Input: | Set $\Sigma$ of keys |
| Problem: | How can we compute an Armstrong relation for $\Sigma$? |

Note that the ARMSTRONG problem assumes that Armstrong relations actually exist. This is not the case for arbitrary classes of integrity constraints [13], but it is true for keys over complete relations. Our acquisition problem actually motivates related computational problems. Instead of pointing out flaws, the domain expert may want to apply changes to the given sample data to rectify perceived problems with it. In this case, the business analyst faces the task of having to extract which keys are satisfied by the modified data sample. The same problem occurs whenever we want to know which keys are satisfied by a given data set. This problem is known as the discovery problem, and constitutes an important task in data profiling [1].

| Name: | DISCOVERY |
|---|---|
| Input: | A relation $r$ |
| Problem: | What is the set of keys that $r$ satisfies? |

Indeed, the combination of solutions to the ARMSTRONG and DISCOVERY problems does not just offer computational support towards the acquisition of meaningful keys, but is also helpful in the cleaning of data [44]. Given a relation $r$, one may compute an *informative Armstrong sample* $r' \subseteq r$, that is, a 'small' subset of $r$ that satisfies the same keys as $r$. A team of data scientists may now investigate the sample $r'$ and apply updates to $r'$ that resolve instances of dirty data. These updates are propagated to the original relation $r$, and the process is iterated until the team is happy with the newly generated sample $r'$ as well as the set $\Sigma$ of keys that hold on the sample (and therefore on the modified entire data set). The point here is that the informative Armstrong samples provide a more targeted representation of the constraints on which the data scientists can spot problems with the data more easily and respond appropriately. Indeed, the improvement in data quality goes hand in hand with an improvement in the acquisition of business rules: violations of business rules guide the data repairs and data repairs lead to the discovery of business rules [44].

# 3 Candidate Keys, Key Sets, Possible and Certain Keys

Due to the demand in real-life applications, data models have been extended to accommodate missing information [17, 35]. The industry standard for data management, SQL, allows occurrences of a null marker to model any kind of missing value. Occurrences of the null marker mean that no information is available about an actual value of that row on that attribute, not even whether the value exists and is unknown nor whether the value does not exist. Codd's principle of entity integrity suggests that every entity should be uniquely identifiable [9]. In SQL, this has led to the notion of a *primary key*, which is a distinguished candidate key.

## 3.1 Candidate Keys and UNIQUE Constraints

A *candidate key* is a collection of attributes which stipulates uniqueness and completeness. That is, no row of a relation must have an occurrence of the null marker on any columns of the candidate key and the combination of values on the columns of the candidate key must be unique. The class of candidate keys has been investigated in [19]. The requirement to have a primary key over every table in the database is often not achievable in practice. Indeed, it can happen easily that a given relation does not exhibit any candidate key. This is illustrated by the following example.

*Example 1.* Consider the following snapshot of data from an accident ward at a hospital [38]. Here, we collect information about the *name* and *address* of a patient, who was treated for an *injury* in some *room* at some *time*.

| Room | Name | Address | Injury | Time |
|------|------|---------|--------|------|
| 1 | Miller | ⊥ | Cardiac infarct | Sunday, 16 |
| ⊥ | ⊥ | ⊥ | Skull fracture | Monday, 19 |
| 2 | Maier | Dresden | ⊥ | Monday, 20 |
| 1 | Miller | Pirna | Leg fracture | Sunday, 16 |

Evidently, the snapshot does not satisfy any candidate key since each column features some null marker occurrence, or a duplication of some value.

SQL also supports the concept of a unique constraint. For a set $X$ of attributes, unique($X$) is satisfied by a table unless there are two different rows in the table that have matching non-null values. For example, the snapshot in Example 1 violates unique($\{room, name, time\}$), but satisfies unique($\{address\}$) and unique($\{injury\}$). In summary, candidate keys require completeness while unique constraints do not take into account any rows that are incomplete on any of its columns. In particular, unique constraints only identify rows uniquely that are complete on all of its attributes. They are therefore not suitable to enforce entity integrity.

## 3.2   Key Sets

In response, Thalheim proposed the notion of a key set [39]. This notion was investigated further by Levene and Loizou [31]. As the term suggests, a key set is a set of attribute subsets. Naturally, we call each element of a key set a key. A relation satisfies a given key set if for every pair of distinct rows in the relation there is some key in the key set on which both rows have no null marker occurrences and non-matching values on some attribute of the key. The flexibility of a key set over candidate keys can easily be recognized, as a candidate key would be equivalent to a singleton key set, with the only element being the candidate key. Indeed, with a key set different pairs of rows in a relation may be distinguishable by different keys of the key set, while all pairs of rows in a relation can only be distinguishable by the same candidate key. We illustrate the notion of a key set on our running example.

*Example 2.* The relation in Example 1 satisfies no candidate key. Nevertheless, the relation satisfies several key sets. For example, the key set $\{\{injury\}, \{time\}\}$ is satisfied, but not the key set $\{\{injury, time\}\}$.

Unfortunately, it turns out that general key sets do enjoy the nice computational properties that other notions of keys enjoy. For example, the implication problem of key sets is *coNP*-complete and Armstrong relations do not always exist [18]. Singleton key sets are those key sets that contain only singleton keys as elements. They enjoy a simple unary axiomatisation, their implication problem can solved in linear time, and they do enjoy Armstrong relations [18].

## 3.3   Certain and Possible Keys

Interestingly, singleton key sets correspond to so-called *certain keys* [24]. Certain keys are keys that hold over every possible world of an incomplete relation, where a possible world is a complete relation that results by independently replacing null marker occurrences in the given incomplete relation by some domain value or the null marker 'N/A' (not applicable, that is, a domain value does not exist). Similarly, *possible keys* are keys that hold over some possible world of an incomplete relation. The combined class of possible and certain keys together with NOT NULL constraints has been studied in [24].

*Example 3.* Consider the following possible worlds of the snapshot from Example 1.

| Room | Name | Address | Injury | Time |
|------|------|---------|--------|------|
| 1 | Miller | Radebeul | Cardiac infarct | Sunday, 16 |
| N/A | Schmidt | Radebeul | Skull fracture | Monday, 19 |
| 2 | Maier | Dresden | Arm fracture | Monday, 20 |
| 1 | Miller | Pirna | Leg fracture | Sunday, 16 |
| Room | Name | Address | Injury | Time |
| 1 | Miller | Radebeul | Cardiac infarct | Sunday, 16 |
| 3 | Schmidt | Radeberg | Skull fracture | Monday, 19 |
| 2 | Maier | Dresden | Cardiac infarct | Monday, 20 |
| 1 | Miller | Pirna | Leg fracture | Sunday, 16 |

The worlds show that the keys $\{address\}$ and $\{injury\}$ are possible, but not certain. It is also simple to observe that the key $\{injury, time\}$ is certain because the only null marker occurrence in *injury* appears together with a *time* value that is unique. Similarly, the key $\{room, name, time\}$ is not possible because the first and last tuple will have duplicate values in those columns in every world possible.

## 4 Embedded Uniqueness Constraints

The class of embedded uniqueness constraints was introduced recently [45]. They are expressions of the form $(E, X)$ over relation schemata $R$ such that $X \subseteq E \subseteq R$ holds. They are satisfied by an $R$-relation if the key $X$ is satisfied by the relation $r^E \subseteq r$ that contains those tuples of $r$ which are complete on all the attributes in $E$. Embedded uniqueness constraints allow users to stipulate completeness and uniqueness requirements separately. The unique constraint in SQL, $\texttt{unique}(X)$, is the special case of embedded uniqueness constraints $(E, X)$ where $E = X$. In addition, the satisfaction of embedded uniqueness constraints is independent of the interpretation of null marker occurrences, since their semantics only relies on the complete fragments that are embedded in an incomplete relation. Emphasizing the attributes in $E - X$ we sometimes write $(E - X, X)$ instead of $(E, X)$.

As we have seen, the snapshot of Example 1 does not satisfy the unique constraint $\texttt{unique}(\{time, name, room\})$, but it does satisfy the embedded uniqueness constraint

$$(address, \{time, name, room\}) \, .$$

While solutions to the implication problem and the computation of Armstrong relations were presented in [45], the problem EXTREMAL and DISCOVERY for embedded uniqueness constraints were addressed in [43]. The application of the algorithms for the discovery and computation of Armstrong relations to iterative data cleansing and business rule acquisition is described in a recent demonstration paper at SIGMOD [44].

## 5  Summary

Table 1 shows references to articles that address the computational problems associated with different classes of keys we have discussed in this paper. They discuss state of the art results on these computational problems, but also related problems.

**Table 1.** References to articles that address the computational problems related to various notions of keys

| Problem | Relational keys | Key sets | Possible and certain keys | Embedded uniques |
|---|---|---|---|---|
| EXTREMAL | [4, 10, 12] | [39] | [24] | [43] |
| IMPLICATION | [2, 38] | [18, 39] | [24, 25] | [45] |
| ARMSTRONG | [3, 11, 13, 22, 28, 34, 36, 37, 40] | [18] | [24, 25] | [45] |
| DISCOVERY | [1, 5, 16, 32, 33, 42] | | [24–26] | [43, 44] |

## 6  Other Classes of Keys

Due to the requirements of modern applications, notions of keys have been developed for different models of uncertain data. These include probabilistic keys [7] and possibilistic keys [23]. Addressing needs in data exchange and integration, keys for XML [8, 15, 20, 21] and graphs [14] have emerged. Other classes of keys include conditional keys [6], keys for RDF [29], and description logics [41].

## 7  Open Problems

While much is known about keys over complete relations, there are still open problems in this context. Generally, it is not well understood how minimum-sized Armstrong relations can be generated and what the exact complexity for finding Armstrong relations is. While it was recently shown that the discovery of keys from relations is $W[2]$-complete in the input size [5], the development of discovery algorithms for keys that scale well to data sets with large numbers of columns and rows is a constant challenge. These open problems are at least as challenging for the notions of keys over incomplete relations, for example for embedded uniqueness constraints. While it has been characterized when Armstrong relations exist for a given set of possible and certain keys with NOT

NULL constraints, the exact complexity of deciding whether Armstrong relations exist is unknown. Little is known for keys sets, except for the special case of singleton key sets. The motivation of arbitrarily-sized key sets is not clear, apart from the ability of stipulating completeness and uniqueness requirements in a more flexible manner than for candidate keys. All computational problems for the general class of key sets still leave room for insight. In particular, there is no algorithm yet for the discovery of key sets. There is also no characterisation for the existence of Armstrong relations for key sets, and no algorithm for the computation of Armstrong relations whenever they exist. Challenging problems for embedded uniqueness constraints do include the computation of 'small' Armstrong relations and algorithms for their discovery from large data sets. The inclusion of keys (and other classes of integrity constraints) in computational problems makes solutions more applicable in database practice, but also more challenging. For example, certain query answering under primary key constraints has only been solved recently [27,46], and only for the class of Boolean self-join free conjunctive queries.

# References

1. Abedjan, Z., Golab, L., Naumann, F.: Profiling relational data: a survey. VLDB J. **24**(4), 557–581 (2015)
2. Armstrong, W.W.: Dependency structures of data base relationships. In: IFIP Congress, pp. 580–583 (1974)
3. Beeri, C., Dowd, M., Fagin, R., Statman, R.: On the structure of Armstrong relations for functional dependencies. J. ACM **31**(1), 30–46 (1984)
4. Biskup, J.: Some remarks on relational database schemes having few minimal keys. In: Düsterhöft, A., Klettke, M., Schewe, K.-D. (eds.) Conceptual Modelling and Its Theoretical Foundations. LNCS, vol. 7260, pp. 19–28. Springer, Heidelberg (2012). https://doi.org/10.1007/978-3-642-28279-9_3
5. Bläsius, T., Friedrich, T., Schirneck, M.: The parameterized complexity of dependency detection in relational databases. In: LIPIcs-Leibniz International Proceedings in Informatics, vol. 63. Schloss Dagstuhl-Leibniz-Zentrum fuer Informatik (2017)
6. Bohannon, P., Fan, W., Geerts, F., Jia, X., Kementsietsidis, A.: Conditional functional dependencies for data cleaning. In: Chirkova, R., Dogac, A., Özsu, M.T., Sellis, T.K. (eds.) Proceedings of the 23rd International Conference on Data Engineering, ICDE 2007, The Marmara Hotel, Istanbul, Turkey, 15–20 April 2007, pp. 746–755. IEEE Computer Society (2007)
7. Brown, P., Link, S.: Probabilistic keys. IEEE Trans. Knowl. Data Eng. **29**(3), 670–682 (2017)
8. Buneman, P., Davidson, S.B., Fan, W., Hara, C.S., Tan, W.C.: Keys for XML. Comput. Netw. **39**(5), 473–487 (2002)
9. Codd, E.F.: A relational model of data for large shared data banks. Commun. ACM **13**(6), 377–387 (1970)
10. Demetrovics, J.: On the equivalence of candidate keys with Sperner systems. Acta Cybern. **4**(3), 247–252 (1979)
11. Demetrovics, J., Füredi, Z., Katona, G.O.H.: Minimum matrix representation of closure operations. Discrete Appl. Math. **11**(2), 115–128 (1985)

12. Demetrovics, J., Katona, G.O.H., Miklós, D., Seleznjev, O., Thalheim, B.: Asymptotic properties of keys and functional dependencies in random databases. Theor. Comput. Sci. **190**(2), 151–166 (1998)
13. Fagin, R.: Horn clauses and database dependencies. J. ACM **29**(4), 952–985 (1982)
14. Fan, W., Fan, Z., Tian, C., Dong, X.L.: Keys for graphs. PVLDB **8**(12), 1590–1601 (2015)
15. Ferrarotti, F., Hartmann, S., Link, S., Marin, M., Muñoz, E.: The finite implication problem for expressive XML keys: foundations, applications, and performance evaluation. In: Hameurlain, A., Küng, J., Wagner, R., Liddle, S.W., Schewe, K.-D., Zhou, X. (eds.) Transactions on Large-Scale Data- and Knowledge-Centered Systems X. LNCS, vol. 8220, pp. 60–94. Springer, Heidelberg (2013). https://doi.org/10.1007/978-3-642-41221-9_3
16. Gottlob, G.: Hypergraph transversals. In: Seipel, D., Turull-Torres, J.M. (eds.) FoIKS 2004. LNCS, vol. 2942, pp. 1–5. Springer, Heidelberg (2004). https://doi.org/10.1007/978-3-540-24627-5_1
17. Greco, S., Molinaro, C., Spezzano, F.: Incomplete Data and Data Dependencies in Relational Databases. Synthesis Lectures on Data Management. Morgan & Claypool Publishers, San Rafael (2012)
18. Hannula, M., Link, S.: Automated reasoning about key sets (2018, to appear)
19. Hartmann, S., Leck, U., Link, S.: On Codd families of keys over incomplete relations. Comput. J. **54**(7), 1166–1180 (2011)
20. Hartmann, S., Link, S.: Unlocking keys for XML trees. In: Schwentick, T., Suciu, D. (eds.) ICDT 2007. LNCS, vol. 4353, pp. 104–118. Springer, Heidelberg (2006). https://doi.org/10.1007/11965893_8
21. Hartmann, S., Link, S.: Efficient reasoning about a robust XML key fragment. ACM Trans. Database Syst. **10:34**(2), 1–10:33 (2009)
22. Katona, G.O.H., Tichler, K.: Some contributions to the minimum representation problem of key systems. In: Dix, J., Hegner, S.J. (eds.) FoIKS 2006. LNCS, vol. 3861, pp. 240–257. Springer, Heidelberg (2006). https://doi.org/10.1007/11663881_14
23. Koehler, H., Leck, U., Link, S., Prade, H.: Logical foundations of possibilistic keys. In: Fermé, E., Leite, J. (eds.) JELIA 2014. LNCS (LNAI), vol. 8761, pp. 181–195. Springer, Cham (2014). https://doi.org/10.1007/978-3-319-11558-0_13
24. Köhler, H., Leck, U., Link, S., Zhou, X.: Possible and certain keys for SQL. VLDB J. **25**(4), 571–596 (2016)
25. Köhler, H., Link, S., Zhou, X.: Possible and certain SQL keys. PVLDB **8**(11), 1118–1129 (2015)
26. Köhler, H., Link, S., Zhou, X.: Discovering meaningful certain keys from incomplete and inconsistent relations. IEEE Data Eng. Bull. **39**(2), 21–37 (2016)
27. Koutris, P., Wijsen, J.: Consistent query answering for self-join-free conjunctive queries under primary key constraints. ACM Trans. Database Syst. **42**(2), 9:1–9:45 (2017)
28. Langeveldt, W., Link, S.: Empirical evidence for the usefulness of Armstrong relations in the acquisition of meaningful functional dependencies. Inf. Syst. **35**(3), 352–374 (2010)
29. Lausen, G.: Relational databases in RDF: keys and foreign keys. In: Christophides, V., Collard, M., Gutierrez, C. (eds.) ODBIS/SWDB -2007. LNCS, vol. 5005, pp. 43–56. Springer, Heidelberg (2008). https://doi.org/10.1007/978-3-540-70960-2_3
30. Le, V.B.T., Link, S., Ferrarotti, F.: Empirical evidence for the usefulness of Armstrong tables in the acquisition of semantically meaningful SQL constraints. Data Knowl. Eng. **98**, 74–103 (2015)

31. Levene, M., Loizou, G.: A generalisation of entity and referential integrity in relational databases. ITA **35**(2), 113–127 (2001)
32. Lucchesi, C.L., Osborn, S.L.: Candidate keys for relations. J. Comput. Syst. Sci. **17**(2), 270–279 (1978)
33. Mannila, H., Räihä, K.: Dependency inference. In: Proceedings of 13th International Conference on Very Large Data Bases, VLDB 1987, 1–4 September 1987, Brighton, England, pp. 155–158 (1987)
34. Mannila, H., Raihä, K.: Design by example: an application of Armstrong relations. J. Comput. Syst. Sci. **33**(2), 126–141 (1986)
35. Paredaens, J., Bra, P.D., Gyssens, M., Gucht, D.V.: The Structure of the Relational Database Model. EATCS Monographs on Theoretical Computer Science, vol. 17. Springer, Heidelberg (1989). https://doi.org/10.1007/978-3-642-69956-6
36. Sali, A., Schewe, K.: Keys and Armstrong databases in trees with restructuring. Acta Cybern. **18**(3), 529–556 (2008)
37. Sali, A., Székely, L.: On the existence of Armstrong instances with bounded domains. In: Hartmann, S., Kern-Isberner, G. (eds.) FoIKS 2008. LNCS, vol. 4932, pp. 151–157. Springer, Heidelberg (2008). https://doi.org/10.1007/978-3-540-77684-0_12
38. Thalheim, B.: Dependencies in Relational Databases. Teubner (1991)
39. Thalheim, B.: On semantic issues connected with keys in relational databases permitting null values. Elektronische Informationsverarbeitung Kybernetik **25**(1/2), 11–20 (1989)
40. Thi, V.D.: Minimal keys and antikeys. Acta Cybern. **7**(4), 361–371 (1986)
41. Toman, D., Weddell, G.E.: On keys and functional dependencies as first-class citizens in description logics. J. Autom. Reason. **40**(2–3), 117–132 (2008)
42. Trinh, T.: Using transversals for discovering XML functional dependencies. In: Hartmann, S., Kern-Isberner, G. (eds.) FoIKS 2008. LNCS, vol. 4932, pp. 199–218. Springer, Heidelberg (2008). https://doi.org/10.1007/978-3-540-77684-0_15
43. Wei, Z., Link, S.: Discovering embedded uniqueness constraints (2018, to appear)
44. Wei, Z., Link, S.: DataProf: semantic profiling for iterative data cleansing and business rule acquisition. In: SIGMOD (2018, to appear)
45. Wei, Z., Link, S., Liu, J.: Contextual keys. In: Mayr, H.C., Guizzardi, G., Ma, H., Pastor, O. (eds.) ER 2017. LNCS, vol. 10650, pp. 266–279. Springer, Cham (2017). https://doi.org/10.1007/978-3-319-69904-2_22
46. Wijsen, J.: A survey of the data complexity of consistent query answering under key constraints. In: Beierle, C., Meghini, C. (eds.) FoIKS 2014. LNCS, vol. 8367, pp. 62–78. Springer, Cham (2014). https://doi.org/10.1007/978-3-319-04939-7_2

# Regular Articles

# Concatenation, Separation, and Other Properties of Variably Polyadic Relations

Heba Aamer[1(✉)] and Haythem O. Ismail[1,2]

[1] Department of Computer Science, German University in Cairo, Cairo, Egypt
{heba.aamer,haythem.ismail}@guc.edu.eg
[2] Department of Engineering Mathematics, Cairo University, Cairo, Egypt

**Abstract.** The standard model of relations as sets of $k$-tuples, though well-suited to mathematical discourse, has been criticized as being neither flexible nor natural for commonsense reasoning. The interpretation of predicates in first-order logic is classically limited to the standard model of relations, which makes first-order representation and reasoning conceptually simple, but sometimes far from natural and much less parsimonious when compared to, say, natural language predication. We address these issues by considering a model of relations as sets of variable-length tuples, and by introducing a first-order language where predication is interpreted using said model. Allowing relations to be of variable adicity, introduces new properties that do not make sense in the standard model. By investigating the interaction among these properties, we are lead to efficient, sound, and (sometimes) complete analytical inference mechanisms for the proposed language.

**Keywords:** Variably polyadic relations · Covered relations
Multigrade predicates · Closure · Reasoning

## 1 Introduction

According to the standard model of relations as sets of $k$-tuples, relations are construed as having a fixed number of ordered argument places, each filled by a single entity [13]. Despite the relative simplicity of logical languages which respect this view, e.g. classical first-order logic, the standard model has long been criticized both on philosophical and logical grounds [6,11,12,15,21]. One of the main motivations for criticism is that the model bans relations with variable adicity. While banning variable adicity might be tolerated in mathematical discourse, such is not the case in commonsense situations, where at least two objections are typically raised. The first is based on the apparently unbounded number of arguments that action verbs admit [4,10]. This may be attested to by examples such as the following Kenny-sequence, where not only do the arguments vary in number, but they also vary in the *roles* they play even if they have the same number (cf. (1c) and (1d)).

© Springer International Publishing AG, part of Springer Nature 2018
F. Ferrarotti and S. Woltran (Eds.): FoIKS 2018, LNCS 10833, pp. 17–33, 2018.
https://doi.org/10.1007/978-3-319-90050-6_2

(1)  a. Brutus killed Caesar.
     b. Brutus killed Caesar with a knife.
     c. Brutus killed Caesar with a knife at noon.
     d. Brutus killed Caesar with a knife at Pompey's theater.

This classical objection has well-known classical responses [4,16]. But such responses cannot address the second objection which is based on the observation that some examples, not involving actions, appear to include variably-polyadic relations [14,15]. For example, the relations of being sisters, living together, cooking dinner, or being relatively-prime intuitively exhibit variable adicity:

(2)  a. Sue and Molly are sisters.
     b. Sue, Molly, and Sally are sisters.
     c. Dilip and Gyorgy live together.
     d. Dilip, Gyorgy, and Omar live together.
     e. Dave cooked dinner.
     f. Dave and Tori cooked dinner.
     g. 10 and 21 are relatively prime.
     h. 6, 10, and 15 are relatively prime.

Although sequences (1) and (2) both provide evidence against the standard model of relations, they do so differently. Whereas sequence (1) alludes to the unbounded number of *roles* that arguments of a predicate may play, sequence (2), while maintaining a fixed number of roles, suggests that an unbounded number of individuals may play (what intuitively is) the same role. Consequently, sentences like those in (2) are susceptible to distributive/collective ambiguities.

With such data, logicians and knowledge engineers are faced with serious questions about the proper treatment of predication. To be faithful to the standard view, they should, for example, distinguish the relation of two women's being sisters from the relation of three women's being sisters, hence employing two predicate symbols, a binary sisters$_2$ and a ternary sisters$_3$, respectively. Alternatively, less laborious approaches to *some* of the questions raised by (1) and (2) have been proposed, alluding to logics of plurals [14,15], logics with flexible predicates [21], or logics with "set arguments" [19,20].

Covered relations [9] present a new flexible model of relations as structured sets of structured tuples. It is a variably *polyvalent, polyadic* model, where polyvalency refers to the variable number of roles, while polyadicity refers to the variable number of entities playing each role. In this case, covered relations act as a general framework that addresses the two main objections to classical relations. In this paper, we are primarily interested in certain inference patterns peculiar to a first-order language in which predicates are interpreted as covered relations. Without any loss of generality, and with a considerable simplification of the exposition, we only consider variably (*uni*valent) polyadic (henceforth, VP) relations.

In Sect. 2, definitions of properties of VP relations and proofs of interactions among them are presented. In Sect. 3, we discuss a first-order language where each predicate is associated with a decoration set. This set reflects properties of the VP relation denoted by the predicate. Section 4 presents efficient inference mechanisms for reasoning about VP relations with various properties in the given language. Such mechanisms are proven to be sound and (sometimes) complete.

## 1.1 Terminology

Henceforth, unless otherwise stated, a relation is univalent and VP: A relation $R$ is a set of non-empty tuples (of possibly varying lengths) over some domain $D$. $R$ is $k^\uparrow$-adic if $k = min\{|t| \mid t \in R\}$. Likewise, $R$ is $k^\downarrow$-adic if $\{|t| \mid t \in R\}$ is finite and $k = max\{|t| \mid t \in R\}$. If $R$ is $l^\uparrow$-adic and $u^\downarrow$-adic, then $\boldsymbol{arity}(R) = [l, u] \cap \mathbb{N}$. If the $u^\downarrow$-adicity is undefined, then $\boldsymbol{arity}(R) = [l, \infty[ \cap \mathbb{N}$. If $l = u = k$, $R$ is a classical $k$-adic relation. For a tuple $t$, $t_i$ denotes the element at index $i$ in $t$, where indices are 1-based. For any two indices $i, j$, if $1 \leq i \leq j \leq |t|$, then $\boldsymbol{subseq}(t)_i^j = (t_i, \cdots, t_j)$; otherwise, $\boldsymbol{subseq}(t)_i^j = ()$. $\oplus$ denotes the tuple-appending operator: $t \oplus t' = \tilde{t}$, where $|\tilde{t}| = |t| + |t'|$, $\boldsymbol{subseq}(\tilde{t})_1^{|t|} = t$, and $\boldsymbol{subseq}(\tilde{t})_{1+|t|}^{|t'|+|t|} = t'$. The empty tuple $()$ is the neutral element of $\oplus$. $\boldsymbol{reverse}(t)$ is the result of reversing $t$: $\boldsymbol{reverse}(t) = t'$, with $t_i' = t_{|t|-i+1}$ for every $1 \leq i \leq |t|$. Likewise, $\boldsymbol{rotate}(t)^r$ is the result of rotating $t$ $r$ steps to the right: $\boldsymbol{rotate}(t)^r = \boldsymbol{subseq}(t)_{|t|-(r\%|t|)+1}^{|t|} \oplus \boldsymbol{subseq}(t)_1^{|t|-(r\%|t|)}$. The set $\{\boldsymbol{rotate}(t)^r \mid 1 \leq r \leq |t|\}$ of all rotations of a tuple $t$ is denoted by $\boldsymbol{rotations}(t)$. If $t_i = t_j'$, then $t$ and $t'$ are $(i, j)$-concatenable and $t_i \circ_j t' = \boldsymbol{subseq}(t)_1^i \oplus \boldsymbol{subseq}(t')_{j+1}^{|t'|}$.

## 2   Properties of Variably Polyadic Relations

A relational property which is well understood in the dyadic case is that of symmetry, indicating the insignificance of the order of elements in pairs of the relation. Considering general VP relations, however, uncovers a rich variety of permutability properties [9]. The strongest such property holds if the relation is closed under *all* permutations of its tuples. We reserve the term "symmetric" for this strong property (cf. [2]). Symmetric VP relations are very common, including equivalence relations and the family of relations of the "co-predicates" mentioned in [15]. Special cases of the permutable relations are those which are rotary or reversible.

**Definition 1.** *Let $R$ be a relation.*

- *$R$ is rotary if and only if, for every tuple $t \in R$, $\boldsymbol{rotations}(t) \subseteq R$.*
- *$R$ is reversible if and only if, for every tuple $t \in R$, $\boldsymbol{reverse}(t) \in R$.*

An example of a relation which is both rotary and reversible, but not symmetric, is the simple-polygon relation defined over tuples of points. (Simple polygons are polygons that do not intersect themselves.) If $t = (p1, p2, p3, p4)$ forms a simple polygon, rotating or reversing $t$ still forms a simple polygon, but an arbitrary permutation thereof, e.g. $(p2, p3, p1, p4)$, need not. Similarity relations are reversible but not rotary.

While permutability properties are valid for $k$-adic relations and are not distinctive of variable polyadicity, *separability* and *expandability* properties are peculiar to the VP case.

**Definition 2.** *Let $R$ be a relation.*

- *$R$ is separable if, for every tuple $t \in R$ and every $m \in \mathbf{arity}(R)$ with $m < |t|$, $R$ contains every size-$m$ contiguous sub-sequence of $t$.*
- *$R$ is expandable if, for every tuple $t \in R$ and every $m \in \mathbf{arity}(R)$ with $m > |t|$, $R$ contains every tuple of size $m$, of which $|t|$ is a size-$t$ contiguous sub-sequence.*

Let $St$ be the relation that holds of a sequence of two or more train stations if there is a train which passes by them in the given order. For example, suppose that $t = (s1, s2, s3) \in St$. This means that there is a train which passes by station $s1$ then $s2$ then $s3$. Evidently, the same train passes by any size-2, contiguous sub-sequence of $t$, making $St$ separable. An example of an expandable relation is the symmetric relation *Incons* which holds of tuples of logical clauses which are (classically) inconsistent. *Incons* is evidently expandable due to the monotonicity of classical logic. (Likewise, the relations of sisterhood and relative-primacy from Sect. 1 are examples of symmetric relations which are, respectively, separable and expandable.)

Another interesting property characteristic of VP relations is *concatenability*.

**Definition 3.** *Let $R$ be a relation. $R$ is concatenable if and only if, for every $(i, j)$-concatenable $t$ and $t'$ in $R$, $t_i \circ_j t' \in R$.*

Similarity, for example, is a concatenable (though not transitive) relation. Another example is the relation $Alt = \{t|$ for $1 < i \leq |t|, t_i > 0$ if $t_{i-1} < 0$, otherwise $t_i < 0\}$ of sign-alternating tuples of integers. (This relation is also separable and reversible.) If the $(3, 1)$-concatenable tuples $(1, -2, 3, -4)$ and $(3, -1, 2)$ are in $Alt$, then so is their concatenation $(1, -2, 3, -1, 2)$.

*Note 1.* The definition presented for concatenable relations is pervasive. The definition has no restriction on the length of the tuples unlike separable or expandable relations. In separable or expandable relations, the property is dependent on the arity of the relation. However, this is not the case with concatenable relations.

*Example 1 ((Non-)Concatenable Relation).* Let $R$ be a relation with $3 \in \mathbf{arity}(R)$, and $\{(1, 2, 3), (3, 4, 5)\} \subseteq R$. $R$ is not a concatenable relation according to the definition, in case $\{(1, 2, 3, 4, 5), (3)\} \not\subseteq R$. So if $R$ is concatenable, then it must be the case that $\{1, 5\} \subset \mathbf{arity}(R)$.

In the rest of this section, we make some observations about interesting interdependencies among the presented relational properties. We say that a relation $R$ on domain $D$ is *trivial* if it is either empty or contains every tuple of elements of $D$ with length in $\mathbf{arity}(R)$.

**Observation 1.** *If a relation $R$ is expandable and concatenable, then it is trivial.*

*Proof.* Suppose that $R$ is a non-trivial relation. Thus, there are two tuples $t$ and $t'$ of elements of $D$ such that $t \notin R$, with $|t| \in \mathbf{arity}(R)$, and $t' \in R$. Let $t^l = (t_1) \oplus t'$ and $t^r = t' \oplus t$. Since $R$ is expandable, then both $t^l$ and $t^r$ are in $R$. Now, given that $R$ is concatenable, and that $t^l$ and $t^r$ are $(1, |t'|+1)$-concatenable, then $t^l {}_1\circ_{(|t'|+1)} t^r = \mathbf{subseq}(t^l)_1^1 \oplus \mathbf{subseq}(t^r)_{|t'|+2}^{|t^r|} = (t_1, \cdots, t_{|t|}) = t \in R$. Hence, a contradiction.

**Proposition 1.** *If a relation $R$ is concatenable and rotary, then it is separable.*

*Proof.* Let $t \in R$ and let $s$ be a contiguous subsequence of $t$. Hence, there are tuples $l$ and $r$ such that $t = l \oplus s \oplus r$. Since $R$ is rotary, then the two rotations (of $t$) $t' = s \oplus r \oplus l$ and $t'' = r \oplus l \oplus s$ are also in $R$. Evidently, $t'_{|s|} = t''_{|t''|} = s_{|s|}$. It follows from the concatenability of $R$ that $t'{}_{|s|}\circ_{|t''|}t'' = \mathbf{subseq}(t')_1^{|s|} \oplus \mathbf{subseq}(t'')_{|t''|+1}^{|t''|} = s\oplus() = s \in R$. Thus, $R$ is separable.

**Lemma 1.** *If a relation $R$ is rotary and concatenable, then, for every tuple $t \in R$ with $|t| > 1$, the set of pairs $\{(t_i, t_j)|1 \le i, j \le |t|\} \subseteq R$.*

*Proof.* We prove the lemma by cases.

First, suppose that $i \ne j$. Hence, there are unique tuples $l$, $r$, and $s$ such that $t' = (t_j) \oplus l \oplus (t_i) \oplus r$ and $t'' = s \oplus (t_i)$ are rotations of $t$. (Intuitively, $t'$ is the rotation that starts with $t_j$, while $t''$ is the one that ends with $t_i$.) Since $R$ is rotary, then it contains both $t'$ and $t''$. Moreover, from the concatenability of $R$, and $t_i$'s being a common element of $t'$ and $t''$, $\tilde{t} = t'{}_{|l|+2}\circ_{|t''|}t'' = (t_j) \oplus l \oplus (t_i) \in R$. Again from the rotary property of $R$, the rotation $(t_i, t_j) \oplus l$ of $\tilde{t}$ is also in $R$. Since $R$ is separable (from Proposition 1), it follows that $(t_i, t_j) \in R$.

Now, suppose that $i = j$. Hence, there is a unique, non-empty tuple $s$ such that $t' = (t_i) \oplus s$ is the rotation of $t$ that starts with $t_i$ and $t'' = s \oplus (t_i)$ is the rotation that ends with $t_i$. Since $R$ is rotary, then $R$ contains both $t'$ and $t''$. Further, from the concatenability of $R$, and since the last element in $s$ is common in $t'$ and $t''$, then $\tilde{t} = t'{}_{|t|}\circ_{|s|}t'' = (t_i) \oplus s \oplus (t_i) \in R$. Again from the rotary property, $(t_i, t_i) \oplus s$, which is a rotation of $\tilde{t}$, belongs to $R$. It follows from the separability of $R$ that $(t_i, t_i) \in R$.

**Proposition 2.** *If a relation $R$ is rotary and concatenable, then it is symmetric.*

*Proof (Proof Idea).* Let $t \in R$, with $|t| > 1$, and let $t'$ be some permutation of $t$. By Lemma 1, $\{(t'_i, t'_{i+1})|1 \le i < |t'|\} \subseteq R$. Given the concatenability of $R$, $(t'_1, t'_2) \circ [(t'_2, t'_3) \circ [\cdots \circ (t'_{|t'|-1}, t'_{|t'|}) \cdots]] = t' \in R$.[1] Hence, $R$ is symmetric.

**Observation 2.** *A concatenable relation $R$ is $1^\uparrow$-adic, if*

---

[1] Here we use square brackets for grouping.

1. $R$ is reversible, or
2. $R$ is separable and $|\mathbf{arity}(R)| > 1$.

*Proof.* Suppose that $R$ is concatenable.

1. Let $t \in R$. Since $R$ is reversible, then $t' = \mathbf{reverse}(t) \in R$. Further, given that $R$ is concatenable, and $t$ and $t'$ are $(|t|, 1)$-concatenable, then $t_{|t|} \circ_1 t' = (t_{|t|}) \in R$. Hence, $R$ must be $1^{\uparrow}$-adic.
2. Let $R$ be $l^{\uparrow}$-adic and assume that $l > 1$. Since $|\mathbf{arity}(R)| > 1$, there must be some $t \in R$ with $|t| > l$. Hence, $|t| \geq 3$. From the separability of $R$, $t' = \mathbf{subseq}_2^{l+1}(t)$ and $t'' = \mathbf{subseq}_1^{l}(t)$ both belong to $R$. Further, since $R$ is concatenable, and $t'$ and $t''$ are $(1, 2)$-concatenable, then $t'\,_1\circ_2 t'' = (t_2, \cdots, t_l) \in R$. But then $|(t_2, \cdots, t_l)| = (l - 1) \geq l$. Hence, a contradiction. So it must be that $l \leq 1$. Since $l > 0$, then $l = 1$. $\qquad \blacksquare$

The following definitions and observation will prove useful when presenting later proofs.

**Definition 4.** *A **tuple expression** over a set of tuples $S$ is an expression which has one of the following forms, where $t \in S$, $a$ and $b$ are tuple expressions over $S$, and $i, j \in \mathbb{N}$:*

1. *$t$;*
2. *$(a, b, {}_i\circ_j)$;*
3. *$(a, \mathbf{subseq}_i^j)$; or*
4. *$(a, \mathbf{reverse})$.*

*If a tuple expression is of the form 1, 2, or 3, then it is a **non-reversible expression**; if it is of the form 1, 2, or 4, then it is a **non-separable expression**; if it is both non-reversible and non-separable, then it is a **concatenation-only expression**.*

To each tuple expression, we associate a *degree of concatenation* and a *value*.

**Definition 5.** *If $\mathfrak{e}$ is a tuple expression, then the **degree of concatenation** of $\mathfrak{e}$, denoted $\mathfrak{D}(\mathfrak{e})$, is a natural number inductively defined as follows:*

1. *$\mathfrak{D}(t) = 0$.*
2. *$\mathfrak{D}((a, b, {}_i\circ_j)) = \mathfrak{D}(a) + \mathfrak{D}(b) + 1$.*
3. *$\mathfrak{D}((a, \mathbf{subseq}_i^j)) = \mathfrak{D}(a)$.*
4. *$\mathfrak{D}((a, \mathbf{reverse})) = \mathfrak{D}(a)$.*

**Definition 6.** *If $\mathfrak{e}$ is a tuple expression, then the **value** of $\mathfrak{e}$, denoted $\circledast[\mathfrak{e}]$, is a tuple which is recursively defined as follows:*

1. *$\circledast[t] = t$.*
2. *$\circledast[(a, b, {}_i\circ_j)] = (\circledast[a]\,_i\circ_j \circledast[b])$, if $\circledast[a]$ and $\circledast[b]$ are defined and are $(i, j)$-concatenable; otherwise, it is undefined.*

3. $\circledast[(a, \mathbf{subseq}_i^j)] = \mathbf{subseq}(\circledast[a])_i^j$, *if* $\circledast[a]$ *is defined and* $1 \leq i \leq j \leq |\circledast[a]|$; *otherwise, it is undefined.*

4. $\circledast[(a, \mathbf{reverse})] = \mathbf{reverse}(\circledast[a])$, *if* $\circledast[a]$ *is defined; otherwise, it is undefined.*

*If* $\mathfrak{e}_1$ *and* $\mathfrak{e}_2$ *are tuple expressions, we write* $\mathfrak{e}_1 \equiv \mathfrak{e}_2$ *whenever* $\circledast[\mathfrak{e}_1] = \circledast[\mathfrak{e}_2]$.

*Example 2.* Let $t = (1, 2, 3, 4)$, and $t' = (5, 3, 6, 7)$. If $\mathfrak{e} = (t', (t, \mathbf{reverse}), {}_2 \circ_2)$, then $\circledast[\mathfrak{e}] = (5, 3, 2, 1)$.

$$\begin{aligned}
\circledast[\mathfrak{e}] &= \circledast[(t', (t, \mathbf{reverse}), {}_2\circ_2)] \\
&= (\circledast[t']) \,{}_2\circ_2 (\circledast[(t, \mathbf{reverse})]) \\
&= (\circledast[t']) \,{}_2\circ_2 (\mathbf{reverse}(\circledast[t])) \\
&= (\circledast[t']) \,{}_2\circ_2 (\mathbf{reverse}((1, 2, 3, 4))) \\
&= (5, 3, 6, 7) \,{}_2\circ_2 (4, 3, 2, 1) \\
&= (5, 3, 2, 1)
\end{aligned}$$

Using tuple expressions, we can easily make the following observations about tuple operations.

**Observation 3.** *Let $a$ and $b$ be tuple expressions.*

1. $((a, \mathbf{reverse}), \mathbf{reverse}) \equiv a$.
2. *Provided that* $k \leq l \leq j - i + 1$, $((a, \mathbf{subseq}_i^j), \mathbf{subseq}_k^l) \equiv (a, \mathbf{subseq}_{i+k-1}^{i+l-1})$.
3. $((a, \mathbf{subseq}_i^j), \mathbf{reverse}) \equiv ((a, \mathbf{reverse}), \mathbf{subseq}_{l-j+1}^{l-i+1})$, *where* $l = |\circledast[a]|$.
4. $((a, b, {}_i\circ_j), \mathbf{reverse}) \equiv ((b, \mathbf{reverse}), (a, \mathbf{reverse}), {}_k\circ_l)$, *where* $k = |\circledast[b]| - j + 1$, *and* $l = |\circledast[a]| - i + 1$.
5. *Provided that values of all sub-expressions are defined,* $((a, \mathbf{subseq}_i^j), (b, \mathbf{subseq}_l^r), {}_x\circ_y) \equiv ((a, b, {}_m\circ_k), \mathbf{subseq}_i^{r-k+m})$, *where* $m = i + x - 1$, *and* $k = l + y - 1$.

The following result, though intuitive, is important to be explicitly stated if inductive arguments on the structure of concatenation operations are to be accepted. Intuitively, a tuple $t$ is the result of a sequence of concatenations over a set of tuples $\mathcal{S}$ if $t \in \mathcal{S}_\omega$ where:

- $\mathcal{S}_0 = \mathcal{S}$,
- For every ordinal $\alpha$, $\mathcal{S}_\alpha = \mathcal{S}_{<\alpha} \cup \{t \,{}_i\circ_j t' | t, t' \in \mathcal{S}_{<\alpha}$ and $t$ and $t'$ are $(i, j)$-concatenable tuples$\}$,
- $\mathcal{S}_{<\alpha} = \bigcup_{\beta < \alpha} \mathcal{S}_\beta$, and
- $\mathcal{S}_\omega = \bigcup_\alpha^\infty \mathcal{S}_\alpha$.

**Proposition 3.** *Let $t$ be a tuple. If $t$ is the result of a sequence of concatenations over a set of tuples $\mathcal{S}$, then there is a (finite) concatenation-only expression $\mathfrak{e}$ over $\mathcal{S}$ with $\circledast[\mathfrak{e}] = t$.*

*Proof (Proof Sketch).* *The proof consists of two parts:*

- *Proving that there is a concatenation-only expression $\mathfrak{e}'$ over a set of tuples $\mathcal{S}'$ with $\circledast[\mathfrak{e}'] = t$.*
- *Proving that $\mathcal{S}' \subseteq \mathcal{S}$ and, hence, that $\mathfrak{e}$ can be taken to be $\mathfrak{e}'$.*

**Part 1.** *Suppose that $t^s = (t_1) \oplus r^0$ and $t^e = l^{|t|} \oplus (t_{|t|})$. Further, for $1 \leq i < |t|$, $t^i = l^i \oplus (t_i, t_{i+1}) \oplus r^i$. Evidently, $t^i$ and $t^{i+1}$ are $(|l^i|+2, |l^{i+1}|+1)$-concatenable. Moreover, $t^s$ and $t^1$ are $(1, |l^1|+1)$-concatenable and $t^{|t|-1}$ and $t^e$ are $(|l^{|t|-1}|+2, |t^e|)$-concatenable. To construct $\mathfrak{e}'$, we recursively construct sub-expressions thereof. Let $(\mathfrak{e}^1, \cdots, \mathfrak{e}^{|t|})$ be a sequence of concatenation-only expressions (with $\mathfrak{D}(\mathfrak{e}^i) = i$) defined as:*

- *$\mathfrak{e}^1 = (t^s, t^1, {}_1\circ_{|l^1|+1})$. Thus, $\circledast[\mathfrak{e}^1] = (t_1, t_2) \oplus r^1$.*
- *For $1 < i < |t|$, let $\mathfrak{e}^i = (\mathfrak{e}^{i-1}, t^i, {}_i\circ_{|l^i|+1})$. Thus, $\circledast[\mathfrak{e}^i] = (t_1, \cdots, t_{i+1}) \oplus r^i$.*
- *$\mathfrak{e}^{|t|} = (\mathfrak{e}^{|t|-1}, t^e, {}_{|t|}\circ_{|t^e|})$. Thus, $\circledast[\mathfrak{e}^{|t|}] = (t_1, \cdots, t_{|t|})$.*

*Taking $\mathfrak{e}' = \mathfrak{e}^{|t|}$, and $S' = \{\{t^s, t^e\} \cup \{t^i | 1 \leq i < |t|\}\}$. Then, evidently, $\mathfrak{e}'$ is a concatenation-only expression over $S'$ with $\circledast[\mathfrak{e}'] = t$.*

**Part 2.** *We need to prove that some choices of $r^0, \cdots, r^{|t-1|}$, and $l^1, \cdots, l^{|t|}$ exist such that $S' \subseteq S$. The proof of this part follows from the structure of the concatenation operation and the existence of $t$. Recall that, provided that $t'$ and $t''$ are $(i, j)$-concatenable,*

$$t' \, {}_i\circ_j t'' = \boldsymbol{subseq}(t')_1^i \oplus \boldsymbol{subseq}(t'')_{j+1}^{|t''|}$$

*Accordingly, the tuple resulting from concatenation must have the following properties:*

- *It starts with the first element in $t'$.*
- *It ends with the last element in $t''$.*
- *Every two consecutive elements in the result of the concatenation are originally either found in $t'$ or in $t''$.*

*From the existence of $t$, we know that at least one tuple in $S$ starts with $t_1$. Let that tuple be $t^s$. Similarly, we will find a tuple representing $t^e$. Further, for $1 \leq i < |t|$, since $t_i$ and $t_{i+1}$ exist in $t$ consecutively, then there must be at least one tuple in $S$ that contains $t_i$ immediately followed by $t_{i+1}$. Let that tuple be $t^i$. Thus, $S' \subseteq S$.*

*Example 3 (Infinite Sequence of Concatenations). Let $t = (1, 2, 3)$ and $t' = (3, 4, 5) \in S$. If $\tilde{t} = [[[[[t \, {}_3\circ_1 t'] \, {}_5\circ_3 t'] \, {}_5\circ_3 t'] \, {}_5\circ_3 t'] \cdots]$, then $\tilde{t}$ is the result of an infinite sequence of concatenations over $S$ with $\tilde{t} = (1, 2, 3, 4, 5)$.*

    *Following Proposition 3, one possible concatenation-only expression $\mathfrak{e}$ over $S$ with $\circledast[\mathfrak{e}] = \tilde{t}$ is $(((((t, t, {}_1\circ_2), t, {}_2\circ_3), t', {}_3\circ_1), t', {}_4\circ_2), t', {}_5\circ_3)$.*

## 3  Representing Variably Polyadic Relations

In this section, we describe the syntax and semantics of a language $\mathcal{L}_{VP}$ for representing and reasoning about VP relations. $\mathcal{L}_{VP}$ is a usual first order language, but with *decorated, multigrade* predicates. It is a relatively simple fragment of the language presented in [9], where the simplicity is afforded by restricting ourselves to univalent relations.

**Definition 7.** *An $\mathcal{L}_{\text{VP}}$ predication structure is a quadruple $\mathfrak{P} = \langle \mathbb{P}, \lfloor \cdot \rfloor, \lceil \cdot \rceil, \mathbb{D} \rangle$, where:*

1. $\mathbb{P}$ *is an alphabet, whose symbols are referred to as predicates.*
2. $\lfloor \cdot \rfloor : \mathbb{P} \to \mathbb{N}$, *is a function that maps a predicate symbol to its minimum arity.*
3. $\lceil \cdot \rceil : \mathbb{P} \rightharpoonup \mathbb{N}$, *is a partial function which maps a predicate symbol to its maximum arity, if there is a maximum.*
4. $\mathbb{D} : \mathbb{P} \to 2^{\{\circlearrowright, \leftrightarrow, \Uparrow, \Downarrow, \bowtie, \odot\}}$, *where $\mathbb{D}(P)$ is referred to as the decoration of predicate symbol $P$.*

**Definition 8.** *Let $\mathfrak{P}$ be a predication structure and $D$ a non-empty set. For $P \in \mathbb{P}$, the interpretation $[\![P]\!]^D$ of $P$ is a relation $R$ on $D$, where:*

1. $R$ *is $k^{\uparrow}$-adic with $k = \lfloor P \rfloor$*
2. $R$ *is $k^{\downarrow}$-adic with $k = \lceil P \rceil$, if $\lceil P \rceil$ is defined*
3. *for every $d \in \mathbb{D}(P)$, if $d$ is $\Downarrow$ ($\Uparrow, \circlearrowright, \leftrightarrow, \bowtie, \odot$), then $R$ is separable (respectively expandable, rotary, reversible, symmetric, concatenable).*

In what follows, let $\mathcal{V}$ be a countably-infinite set of variables and $\mathcal{F}$ a finite set of function symbols each with an associated arity. (As usual, arities are indicated by superscripts; $f^0 \in \mathcal{F}$ is referred to as a constant.) The set of terms is defined as usual.

**Definition 9.** *Let $\mathfrak{P} = \langle \mathbb{P}, \lfloor \cdot \rfloor, \lceil \cdot \rceil, \mathbb{D} \rangle$ a predication structure. An $\langle \mathcal{V}, \mathcal{F}, \mathfrak{P} \rangle$-generated atomic formula is a formula of the form*

$$P(\tau_1, \tau_2, \ldots, \tau_n)$$

*where $P \in \mathbb{P}$, $\tau_i$ is a term, for every $1 \le i \le n$, and $\lfloor P \rfloor \le n \le \lceil P \rceil$.*

As usual, given an interpretation of the predicates in an $\mathcal{L}_{\text{VP}}$ predication structure, an atomic formula $P(\tau_1, \tau_2, \ldots, \tau_n)$, where $P$ is a predicate and $\tau_1, \tau_2, \ldots, \tau_n$ are terms, is true just in case $([\![\tau_1]\!]^D, [\![\tau_2]\!]^D, \ldots, [\![\tau_n]\!]^D) \in [\![P]\!]^D$.

For example, consider representing the relation *Alt* of finite, sign-alternating sequences of integers (see Sect. 2). We construct a predication structure with a predicate alternate $\in \mathbb{P}$ such that:

- $\mathbb{D}(\texttt{alternate}) = \{\Downarrow, \odot, \leftrightarrow\}$,
- $\lfloor \texttt{alternate} \rfloor = 1$, and
- $\lceil \texttt{alternate} \rceil$ is undefined.

Now, if an $\mathcal{L}_{\text{VP}}$ theory includes the following atomic sentences:

- alternate$(5, -2, 1, -5, 4, -1)$, and
- alternate$(-1, 1, -3)$.

Then, given the decoration of alternate, a proof theory for $\mathcal{L}_{\text{VP}}$ should allow us to infer, for example, the following atoms:

- alternate$(-1, 1, -5, 4)$,
- alternate$(1, -5)$,
- alternate$(-3, 1, -1)$, and
- alternate$(1, -1, 4)$.

To that end, specialized inference rules for each decoration symbol should be incorporated in our proof theory. One way to efficiently achieve this is to heed Shapiro's advice to implement the inference rules as part of a unification algorithm [20].[2] Although we do not present a complete unification algorithm for $\mathcal{L}_{VP}$ here, we describe algorithms which provide the base cases for such an algorithm.

## 4    Reasoning About Closures

Intuitively, the problem we address is the following: Given a set of atoms with predicate $P$, which other $P$-atoms should we infer given the decoration of $P$? To make this more precise, we introduce some handy notation and terminology. Henceforth, we assume $P$ to be a predicate of some $\mathcal{L}_{VP}$ predication structure. We say that $(\tau_1, \ldots, \tau_n)$ is a $P$-tuple, if $\lfloor P \rfloor \leq n \leq \lceil P \rceil$ and $\tau_i$ is a ground term for every $1 \leq i \leq n$. If $\mathcal{A}$ is a set of $P$-tuples, then $[\![\mathcal{A}]\!] = \{[\![\tau]\!] | \tau \in \mathcal{A}\}$, where $[\![\tau]\!] = ([\![\tau_1]\!], \ldots, [\![\tau_n]\!])$ if $\tau = (\tau_1, \ldots, \tau_n)$. Similar to the classical closures of dyadic relations with respect to common properties such as reflexivity, symmetry, and transitivity, let $[\![\mathcal{A}]\!]^*$ be the closure of $[\![\mathcal{A}]\!]$ with respect to the properties corresponding to $\mathbb{D}(P)$. For example, if $\mathbb{D}(P) = \{\leftrightarrow, \Uparrow\}$, then $[\![\mathcal{A}]\!]^*$ is the reversible, expandable closure of $[\![\mathcal{A}]\!]$. Similarly, we define $\mathcal{A}^* = \{\tau | [\![\tau]\!] \in [\![\mathcal{A}]\!]^*\}$. Our problem can now be stated as follows.

**Problem 1: VP Closure (VPClos)**
**Instance:**    A predicate $P$;
          a set $\mathcal{A}$ of $P$-tuples;
          a $P$-tuple $\tau$
**Question:**    Is $\tau \in \mathcal{A}^*$?

The complexity of deciding **VPClos** varies with the instance, depending on $\mathbb{D}(P)$. In this paper, we are only interested in instances in which the represented relation is concatenable (i.e., $\odot \in \mathbb{D}(P)$). The reason is that all other properties (except symmetry and concatenation), and combinations thereof, yield sub-problems that can be decided by simple variations of common string matching algorithms [3,7,8]. Symmetry with other properties can be done efficiently using set operations [17]. Concatenation, however, does not reduce to simple matching: We need to check if $[\![\tau]\!]$ can be constructed by concatenating two or more tuples in $[\![\mathcal{A}]\!]$. The problem becomes more complex when we consider combining concatenability with other properties.

---

[2] In [20] (also in [19]), Shapiro is interested in special cases of what we refer to as symmetric and separable relations.

Focusing only on concatenable relations, leaves us with thirty two possibilities for $\mathbb{D}(P)$. However, given the results of Sect. 2, these reduce to only five non-trivial cases: $\{\odot\}$, $\{\leftrightarrow, \odot\}$, $\{\Downarrow, \odot\}$, $\{\leftrightarrow, \Downarrow, \odot\}$, and $\{\circlearrowleft, \leftrightarrow, \Downarrow, \bowtie, \odot\}$. Of these, we only discuss the first four in detail.

*Remark 1.* Given the strong properties it exhibits, the fifth case can be accounted for by noting that: (i) due to symmetry, tuples can be replaced by multisets; (ii) due to concatenability, the collection of multisets can be partitioned into blocks corresponding to the connected components of the intersection graph whose nodes are the multisets [5]; and (iii) due to separability, the **VPClos** question can be answered by checking if the query $\tau$ is a subset of the union of the multisets in one of the blocks. This can be efficiently implemented using a disjoint-sets data structure with a union-find algorithm [18].

For the remaining cases, we note that $[\![\mathcal{A}]\!]^*$ can be characterized in terms of the tuple expressions of Sect. 2. In particular, in each case, $[\![\mathcal{A}]\!]^* = \circledast[\mathfrak{E}]$, where $\mathfrak{E}$ is a set of tuple expressions over $[\![\mathcal{A}]\!]$ and $\circledast[\mathfrak{E}]$ is the set of corresponding tuples in $D$ (if defined) values thereof.

1. If $\mathbb{D}(P) = \{\odot\}$, then $\mathfrak{E}$ is the set of concatenation-only expressions.
2. If $\mathbb{D}(P) = \{\leftrightarrow, \odot\}$, then $\mathfrak{E}$ is the set of non-separable expressions.
3. If $\mathbb{D}(P) = \{\Downarrow, \odot\}$ and $\lfloor P \rfloor \neq \lceil P \rceil$, then $\mathfrak{E}$ is the set of non-reversible expressions (cf. Observation 2).
4. If $\mathbb{D}(P) = \{\leftrightarrow, \Downarrow, \odot\}$ and $\lfloor P \rfloor \neq \lceil P \rceil$, then $\mathfrak{E}$ is the set of all (unconstrained) expressions.

It is notable that when $\mathbb{D}(P) = \{\Downarrow, \odot\}$ and $\lfloor P \rfloor = \lceil P \rceil$, then $\circledast[\mathfrak{E}] = \circledast[\mathfrak{F}]$, where $\mathfrak{E}$ is the set of concatenation-only expressions over $[\![\mathcal{A}]\!]$ and $\mathfrak{F}$ is the set of non-reversible expressions over $[\![\mathcal{A}]\!]$. It is easy to show that if $\mathfrak{f} \in \mathfrak{F}$, then $(\mathfrak{f}, \textbf{\textit{subseq}}_i^j)$ is only valid for $i = 1$ and $j = \lfloor P \rfloor = |\circledast[\mathfrak{f}]|$. Consequently, $(\mathfrak{f}, \textbf{\textit{subseq}}_i^j) \equiv \mathfrak{f}$. So this case reduces to case 1. By a similar argument, the case of $\mathbb{D}(P) = \{\leftrightarrow, \Downarrow, \odot\}$ and $\lfloor P \rfloor = \lceil P \rceil$ reduces to case 2.

## 4.1   Concatenable-Only Relations

We first consider relations which are only concatenable; syntactically, $\mathbb{D}(P) = \{\odot\}$. Our solution to such instances of **VPClos** is based on a data structure which we call the *concatenation graph*.[3]

**Definition 10.** *Let $\mathcal{A}$ be a set of P-tuples. The concatenation graph of $\mathcal{A}$, denoted $CG(\mathcal{A})$, is a quadruple $\mathcal{G} = \langle \mathcal{N}, \mathcal{E}, S, E \rangle$ where*

- $\mathcal{N} = \{\tau_i | \tau \in \mathcal{A} \text{ and } 1 \leq i \leq |\tau|\}$ *is the set of nodes,*
- $\mathcal{E}$ *is the set of edges with $(u, v) \in \mathcal{E}$ iff there is some $\tau \in \mathcal{A}$ with $\tau_i = u$, and $\tau_{i+1} = v$ for $1 \leq i < |\tau|$,*

---

[3] Though designed with a different construction and for a totally different purpose, concatenation graphs somewhat resemble the directed acyclic word graphs of [1].

- $S \subseteq \mathcal{N}$ is the set of S-nodes (start nodes) with $u \in S$ iff there is some $\tau \in \mathcal{A}$ with $\tau_1 = u$, and
- $E \subseteq \mathcal{N}$ is the set of E-nodes (end nodes) with $u \in E$ iff there is some $\tau \in \mathcal{A}$ with $\tau_{|\tau|} = u$.

Figure 1 shows a set of P-tuples and the corresponding concatenation graph.

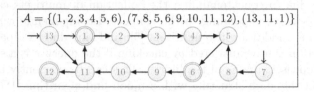

**Fig. 1.** A set $\mathcal{A}$ of P-tuples and $CG(\mathcal{A})$. Nodes with an arrow coming in from nowhere are S-nodes; double-circled nodes are E-nodes

The link between $\mathcal{L}_{VP}$ syntax and semantics is established by the notion of a *C-path* in $CG(\mathcal{A})$

**Definition 11.** *A C-Path in $CG(\mathcal{A})$ is a directed path starting with an S-node and ending with an E-node. If $p = (p_1, \ldots, p_n)$ is a C-path and $t = (\llbracket p_1 \rrbracket, \llbracket p_2 \rrbracket, \ldots, \llbracket p_n \rrbracket)$, we say that $p$ is a C-path of $t$.*

We now prove the following *soundness* result.

**Theorem 1.** *Let $\mathcal{A}$ be a set of P-tuples. If there is a C-path $p$ in $CG(\mathcal{A})$, then there is a concatenation-only expression $\mathfrak{e}$ over $\llbracket \mathcal{A} \rrbracket$, such that $p$ is a C-path of $\circledast[\mathfrak{e}]$.*

*Proof. We prove the existence of $\mathfrak{e}$ by construction.[4] Let $p = (p_1, \ldots, p_m)$. By Definition 11, $p_1$ is an S-node, $p_m$ is an E-node, and there is an edge from $p_i$ to $p_{i+1}$ for every $1 \le i < m$. From the construction of $\mathcal{G}$, there is some $\tau^s \in \mathcal{A}$ with $\tau_1^s = p_1$ and some $\tau^e \in \mathcal{A}$ with $\tau_{|\tau^e|}^e = p_m$. Further, for every $1 \le i < m$, there is some $\tau^i \in \mathcal{A}$ with $\tau_j^i = p_i$ and $\tau_{j+1}^i = p_{i+1}$, for some $1 \le j < |\tau^i|$. (Intuitively, $\tau^i$ is responsible for $i^{th}$ edge in $p$.) Now, let $t^s = \llbracket \tau^s \rrbracket$ and $t^e = \llbracket \tau^e \rrbracket$. Further, for $1 \le i < m$, let $t^i = \llbracket \tau^i \rrbracket = l^i \oplus (\llbracket p_i \rrbracket, \llbracket p_{i+1} \rrbracket) \oplus r^i$. Evidently, $t^i$ and $t^{i+1}$ are $(|l^i| + 2, |l^{i+1}| + 1)$-concatenable. Moreover, $t^s$ and $t^1$ are $(1, |l^1| + 1)$-concatenable and $t^{m-1}$ and $t^e$ are $(|l^{m-1}| + 2, |t^e|)$-concatenable. To construct $\mathfrak{e}$, we recursively construct sub-expressions thereof. Let $(\mathfrak{e}^1, \cdots, \mathfrak{e}^m)$ be a sequence of concatenation-only expressions (with $\mathfrak{D}(\mathfrak{e}^i) = i$) defined as:*

- $\mathfrak{e}^1 = (t^s, t^1, {}_1 \circ_{|l^1|+1})$. *Thus, $\circledast[\mathfrak{e}^1] = (\llbracket p_1 \rrbracket, \llbracket p_2 \rrbracket) \oplus r^1$.*
- *For $1 < i < m$, $\mathfrak{e}^i = (\mathfrak{e}^{i-1}, t^i, {}_i \circ_{|l^i|+1})$. Thus, $\circledast[\mathfrak{e}^i] = (\llbracket p_1 \rrbracket, \cdots, \llbracket p_{i+1} \rrbracket) \oplus r^i$.*
- $\mathfrak{e}^m = (\mathfrak{e}^{m-1}, t^e, {}_m \circ_{|t^e|})$. *Thus, $\circledast[\mathfrak{e}^m] = (\llbracket p_1 \rrbracket, \cdots, \llbracket p_m \rrbracket)$.*

---

[4] The construction of $\mathfrak{e}$ is similar to the one used in proving Proposition 3.

*Taking* $\mathfrak{e} = \mathfrak{e}^m$, *then, evidently,* $\mathfrak{e}$ *is a concatenation-only expression over* $[\![\mathcal{A}]\!]$ *with* $p$ *a C-path of* $\circledast[\mathfrak{e}]$.

A corresponding *completeness* result can only be secured by making the unique names assumption ($[\![\tau]\!] = [\![\tau']\!]$ implies $\tau = \tau'$.) At the cost of our rather simple construction, we can relax the unique names assumption and retain completeness by taking the nodes of concatenation graphs to be, not terms, but equivalence classes thereof. We stand by simplicity though.

**Theorem 2.** *Let* $\mathcal{A}$ *be a set of P-tuples such that, for every* $\tau, \tau' \in \mathcal{A}$, *if* $[\![\tau]\!] = [\![\tau']\!]$ *then* $\tau = \tau'$. *If* $\mathfrak{e}$ *is a concatenation-only expression over* $[\![\mathcal{A}]\!]$ *with* $\circledast[\mathfrak{e}]$ *defined, then there is a C-path of* $\circledast[\mathfrak{e}]$ *in* $CG(\mathcal{A})$.

*Proof. We prove the theorem by strong induction on* $\mathfrak{D}(\mathfrak{e})$.[5]
**Basis.** *Suppose that* $\mathfrak{D}(\mathfrak{e}) = 0$. *Thus, there is some* $t \in [\![\mathcal{A}]\!]$ *such that* $\mathfrak{e} = t = \circledast[\mathfrak{e}]$. *By definition of concatenation graphs, there is a C-path of* $t$ *in* $CG(\mathcal{A})$.
**Induction Hypothesis.** *For some* $0 < k \in \mathbb{N}$, *if* $\mathfrak{e}$ *is a concatenation-only expression over* $[\![\mathcal{A}]\!]$ *with* $\mathfrak{D}(\mathfrak{e}) < k$ *and with* $\circledast[\mathfrak{e}]$ *defined, then there is a C-path of* $\circledast[\mathfrak{e}]$ *in* $CG(\mathcal{A})$.
**Induction Step.** *Let* $\mathfrak{e}$ *be a concatenation-only expression over* $[\![\mathcal{A}]\!]$ *with* $\mathfrak{D}(\mathfrak{e}) = k$. *Since* $k > 0$, *then* $\mathfrak{e} = (a, b, {}_i\circ_j)$, *where* $a$ *and* $b$ *are concatenation-only expressions with* $k = 1 + \mathfrak{D}(a) + \mathfrak{D}(b)$. *By the induction hypothesis,* $t' = \circledast[a]$ *and* $t'' = \circledast[b]$ *have C-paths in* $CG(\mathcal{A})$, *say* $p'$ *and* $p''$, *respectively.* *Let* $t = \circledast[\mathfrak{e}] = t' {}_i\circ_j t'' = \boldsymbol{subseq}(t')_1^i \oplus \boldsymbol{subseq}(t'')_{j+1}^{|t''|}$. *If* $\boldsymbol{subseq}(t'')_{j+1}^{|t''|} = ()$, *then* $t = t'$ *and* $p'$ *is a C-path of* $t$. *Hence, considering* $\boldsymbol{subseq}(t'')_{j+1}^{|t''|} \neq ()$, $t = (t'_1, \cdots, t'_i, t''_{j+1}, \cdots, t''_{|t''|})$. *Given that* $p'$ *and* $p''$ *are C-paths, it follows that* $p'_1$ *is an S-node and* $p''_{|t''|}$ *is an E-node. Moreover, by the unique names assumption,* $p'_i = p''_j$. *Hence, the sequence* $p = (p'_1, \ldots, p'_i, p''_{j+1}, \ldots, p''_{|t''|})$ *is a concatenation path in* $CG(\mathcal{A})$. *But* $t_l = [\![p_l]\!]$, *for* $1 \leq l \leq |p|$. *Thus,* $p$ *is a C-path of* $t$.

According to the results just presented, a simple algorithm for **VPClos** checks whether the query $\tau$ is a C-path in $CG(\mathcal{A})$. The time and space complexity of the algorithm are both determined by the concatenation graph and the length of the query tuple. In particular, both are $O(|\langle \mathcal{A} \rangle| + |\tau|)$ (where $\langle \mathcal{A} \rangle$ is the string encoding of $\mathcal{A}$). To achieve this complexity, one possible model of the concatenation graph is using a hash-table of hash-tables of nodes. So it takes constant time to add an edge to the graph and to check for the existence of edges. This complexity is linear in the size of the input, which, though theoretically good, may be prohibitive for large graphs. Luckily, however, the graph is constructed only once in practice, and successive queries can be answered in time which is only $\Theta(|\tau|)$. This is typically optimal since we got to, at least, read the input query.

---

[5] That this suffices to prove completeness relies on the finite-representation property of concatenation proved in Proposition 3.

## 4.2   Reversible Concatenable Relations

We now consider instances of **VPClos** in which the represented relation is only reversible and concatenable; syntactically, $\mathbb{D}(P) = \{\leftrightarrow, \odot\}$. Thus, $[\![\mathcal{A}]\!]^*$ is a set of values of *non-separable* tuple expressions over $\mathcal{A}$.

**Lemma 2.** *If $\mathcal{A}$ is a set of P-tuples with $\mathbb{D}(P) = \{\leftrightarrow, \odot\}$, then $[\![\mathcal{A}]\!]^* = [\![\mathcal{A}^{\leftrightarrow}]\!]^*$, where $\mathcal{A}^{\leftrightarrow} = \mathcal{A} \cup \{\mathbf{reverse}(\tau) | \tau \in \mathcal{A}\}$.*

*Proof (Proof Sketch). From the fourth clause of Observation 3, a non-separable tuple expression $\mathfrak{e}$ is equivalent to a non-separable expression with the **reverses** pushed all the way inside. Intuitively, we can do all the reversing before all concatenations. Further, from the first clause of Observation 3, such an expression is equivalent to one with no two consecutive **reverses**. Thus, if $\mathfrak{E}$ is the set of non-separable tuple expressions over $[\![\mathcal{A}]\!]$, then each expression in $\mathfrak{E}$ has an equivalent expression in $\mathfrak{F} \subset \mathfrak{E}$, where $\mathfrak{F}$ is the smallest set satisfying the following (with $t \in [\![\mathcal{A}]\!]$):*

1. *If $t \in \mathfrak{E}$, then $t \in \mathfrak{F}$.*
2. *If $(t, \mathbf{reverse}) \in \mathfrak{E}$, then $(t, \mathbf{reverse}) \in \mathfrak{F}$.*
3. *If $\mathfrak{e}_1, \mathfrak{e}_2 \in \mathfrak{F}$, then $(\mathfrak{e}_1, \mathfrak{e}_2, {}_i\circ_j) \in \mathfrak{F}$, for every $i$ and $j$ such that $\circledast[\mathfrak{e}_1]_i = \circledast[\mathfrak{e}_2]_j$.*

*Thus, $[\![\mathcal{A}]\!]^* = \circledast[\mathfrak{F}]$. But it is clear that $\circledast[\mathfrak{F}] = \circledast[\mathfrak{F}^{\leftrightarrow}]$, where $\mathfrak{F}^{\leftrightarrow}$ is identical to $\mathfrak{F}$ with every (sub-)expression of the form $(t, \mathbf{reverse})$ replaced by the tuple $\mathbf{reverse}(t)$. Referring to Observation 3 again, $\circledast[\mathfrak{F}^{\leftrightarrow}] = \circledast[\mathfrak{E}^{\leftrightarrow}]$, where $\mathfrak{E}^{\leftrightarrow}$ is the set of non-separable tuple expressions over $[\![\mathcal{A}^{\leftrightarrow}]\!]$. It follows that $[\![\mathcal{A}]\!]^* = \circledast[\mathfrak{E}] = \circledast[\mathfrak{F}] = \circledast[\mathfrak{F}^{\leftrightarrow}] = \circledast[\mathfrak{E}^{\leftrightarrow}] = [\![\mathcal{A}^{\leftrightarrow}]\!]^*$.*

It is important to note that, in the above proof, the set $\mathfrak{F}^{\leftrightarrow}$ is a set of concatenation-only expressions. Thus, we can reproduce the soundness and completeness results of the previous section by working with $\mathcal{A}^{\leftrightarrow}$ rather than $\mathcal{A}$.

**Theorem 3.** *Let $\mathcal{A}$ be a set of P-tuples with $\mathcal{A}^{\leftrightarrow}$ as defined in Lemma 2.*

1. *If there is a C-path $p$ in $CG(\mathcal{A}^{\leftrightarrow})$, then there is a non-separable expression $\mathfrak{e}$ over $[\![\mathcal{A}]\!]$ such that $p$ is a C-path of $\circledast[\mathfrak{e}]$.*
2. *If, for every $\tau, \tau' \in \mathcal{A}$, $[\![\tau]\!] = [\![\tau']\!]$ implies $\tau = \tau'$ and $\mathfrak{e}$ is a non-separable expression over $[\![\mathcal{A}]\!]$ with $\circledast[\mathfrak{e}]$ defined, then there is a C-path of $\circledast[\mathfrak{e}]$ in $CG(\mathcal{A}^{\leftrightarrow})$.*

*Proof. The proof follows directly from Lemma 2, Theorems 1 and 2.*

The **VPClos**-algorithm for the concatenable-only case can, thus, be readily extended to the reversible-concatenable case but with $CG(\mathcal{A}^{\leftrightarrow})$ as the concatenation graph. $CG(\mathcal{A}^{\leftrightarrow})$ has the following interesting properties. First, if there is an edge from $u$ to $v$, then there is an edge from $v$ to $u$. Second, the $S$-nodes and the $E$-nodes are identical. Hence, $CG(\mathcal{A}^{\leftrightarrow})$ can be replaced by the underlying undirected graph of $CG(\mathcal{A})$ which is identical in size to $CG(\mathcal{A})$.

## 4.3   Separable Concatenable Relations

In this section we consider relations $R$ which are concatenable and separable (and possibly reversible) but not symmetric with $\mathbf{arity}(R) > 1$; syntactically, $\{\Downarrow, \odot\} \subseteq \mathbb{D}(P) \subseteq \{\leftrightarrow, \Downarrow, \odot\}$ and $\lfloor P \rfloor \neq \lceil P \rceil$. Thus, $[\![\mathcal{A}]\!]^*$ is the set of values of tuple expressions over $[\![\mathcal{A}]\!]$ which are either non-reversible or totally unconstrained.

**Lemma 3.** *If $\mathcal{A}$ is a set of P-tuples with $\{\Downarrow, \odot\} \subseteq \mathbb{D}(P) \subseteq \{\leftrightarrow, \Downarrow, \odot\}$ and $\lfloor P \rfloor \neq \lceil P \rceil$, then $[\![\mathcal{A}]\!]^* = [\![\mathcal{A}^\Downarrow]\!]^*$, where $\mathcal{A}^\Downarrow = \mathcal{A} \cup \{(\tau_i)|\tau \in \mathcal{A} \text{ and } 1 \leq i \leq |\tau|\}$.*

*Proof (Proof Sketch). By Clauses 3 and 5 of Observation 3, a tuple expression is equivalent to one in which we pull all **subseqs** all the way outside. Further, Clause 2 indicates that a sequence of **subseqs** reduces to a single one. Thus, if $\mathfrak{E}$ is the set of non-reversible or unconstrained expressions over $[\![\mathcal{A}]\!]$, then every expression in $\mathfrak{E}$ has an equivalent expression in $\mathfrak{F} \subset \mathfrak{E}$, where $\mathfrak{F}$ is the smallest set satisfying the following condition: If $\mathfrak{e}$ is a non-separable expression in $\mathfrak{E}$ then $\mathfrak{e}$ and $(\mathfrak{e}, \mathbf{subseq}_i^j)$, for every $1 \leq i \leq j \leq |\circledast[\mathfrak{e}]|$, are in $\mathfrak{F}$. (Intuitively $\mathfrak{F}$ is the set of tuple expressions equivalent to the ones in $\mathfrak{E}$ with all **subseqs** pulled all the way outside and reduced to single one if more than one is in the expression.) Thus, $[\![\mathcal{A}]\!]^* = \circledast[\mathfrak{F}]$.[6] Hence, it suffices to show that $\circledast[\mathfrak{F}] = [\![\mathcal{A}^\Downarrow]\!]^*$.*

*First, we note that if $\mathfrak{e}$ is a non-separable expression, then $t = \circledast[(\mathfrak{e}, \mathbf{subseq}_i^j)] = [(t_i) \ _1\circ_i \ [\circledast[\mathfrak{e}] \ _j\circ_1 (t_j)]] = \circledast[((t_i), (\mathfrak{e}, (t_j), _j\circ 1), _1\circ_i)]$. Thus, $\circledast[\mathfrak{F}] = \circledast[\mathfrak{F}^\Downarrow]$, where $\mathfrak{F}^\Downarrow$ is the smallest set of expressions satisfying the following:*

1. *If $\mathfrak{e} \in \mathfrak{F}$ is a non-separable expression, then $\mathfrak{e} \in \mathfrak{F}^\Downarrow$.*
2. *If $t \in \mathfrak{F}$ is a tuple, then $\{(t_i)|1 \leq i \leq |t|\} \subset \mathfrak{F}^\Downarrow$. This follows from Observation 2.*
3. *If $\mathfrak{e}_1, \mathfrak{e}_2 \in \mathfrak{F}^\Downarrow$, then $(\mathfrak{e}_1, \mathfrak{e}_2, _i\circ_j) \in \mathfrak{F}^\Downarrow$, for every $i$ and $j$ such that $\circledast[\mathfrak{e}_1]_i = \circledast[\mathfrak{e}_2]_j$.*

*Referring to Observation 3 again, $\circledast[\mathfrak{F}^\Downarrow] = \circledast[\mathfrak{E}^\Downarrow]$, where $\mathfrak{E}^\Downarrow$ is the set of non-separable expressions over $[\![\mathcal{A}^\Downarrow]\!]$. It follows that $[\![\mathcal{A}]\!]^* = \circledast[\mathfrak{E}] = \circledast[\mathfrak{F}] = \circledast[\mathfrak{F}^\Downarrow] = \circledast[\mathfrak{E}^\Downarrow] = [\![\mathcal{A}^\Downarrow]\!]^*$.*

Again, we note that $\mathfrak{F}^\Downarrow$ in the proof is a set of non-separable expressions. Thus, we can employ the methods of Subsects. 4.1 and 4.2 to solve instances of **VPClos** where the represented relation is separable and concatenable; we only need to use $CG(\mathcal{A}^\Downarrow)$ instead of $CG(\mathcal{A})$.

**Theorem 4.** *Let $\mathcal{A}$ be a set of P-tuples with $\lfloor P \rfloor \neq \lceil P \rceil$ and $\mathcal{A}^\Downarrow$ as defined in Lemma 3.*

1. *If there is a C-path $p$ in $CG(\mathcal{A}^\Downarrow)$ (respectively, $CG((\mathcal{A}^\Downarrow)^\leftrightarrow)$), then there is a non-reversible (respectively, unconstrained) expression $\mathfrak{e}$ over $[\![\mathcal{A}]\!]$ such that $p$ is a C-path of $\circledast[\mathfrak{e}]$.*

---

[6] That $\circledast[\mathfrak{F}] \subseteq [\![A]\!]^*$ follows from Observation 2.

2. *If, for every* $\tau, \tau' \in \mathcal{A}$, $\llbracket \tau \rrbracket = \llbracket \tau' \rrbracket$ *implies* $\tau = \tau'$ *and* $\mathfrak{e}$ *is a non-reversible (respectively, unconstrained) expression over* $\llbracket A \rrbracket$ *with* $\circledast[\mathfrak{e}]$ *defined, then there is a C-path of* $\circledast[\mathfrak{e}]$ *in* $CG(\mathcal{A}^{\Downarrow})$ *(respectively,* $CG((\mathcal{A}^{\Downarrow})^{\leftrightarrow}))$.

*Proof.* The proof follows directly from Lemma 3 and Theorems 1, 2, and 3.

Since $\{\Downarrow, \odot\} \subseteq \mathbb{D}(P)$ and $\lfloor P \rfloor \neq \lceil P \rceil$, it follows from Observation 2 that $\lfloor P \rfloor = 1$. So tuples that consists of a single term are valid $P$-tuples. Thus, $S = E = \mathcal{N}$ in $CG(\mathcal{A}^{\Downarrow})$. Hence, searching for a C-path in $CG(\mathcal{A}^{\Downarrow})$ reduces to searching for any directed path in $CG(\mathcal{A})$. Figure 2 displays the undirected concatenation graph of the alternate-theory from Sect. 3, where $\mathbb{D}(\text{alternate}) = \{\leftrightarrow, \Downarrow, \odot\}$. As predicted, $(-1, 1, -5, 4)$, $(1, -5)$, $(-3, 1, -1)$, and $(1, -1, 4)$ have corresponding paths in the graph.

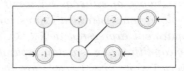

**Fig. 2.** The undirected concatenation graph for the set $\{(-1, 1, -3), (5, -2, 1, -5, 4, -1)\}$ of alternate-tuples

## 5   Conclusion

Variably-polyadic relations are not very popular in logic-based artificial intelligence. However, admitting them into a commonsense ontology is perhaps a reasonable move. $\mathcal{L}_{\text{VP}}$ is an example of a simple first-order language for representing and reasoning about VP relations. It is related to the language presented in [21], but the latter lacks predicate decoration and is more complex due to the inclusion of sequence variables. By considering properties which are peculiar to VP relations, such as concatenation and separation, interesting reasoning problems emerge. We have described efficient inference algorithms for reasoning about these properties, with the resulting proof theory being sound and (sometimes) complete. A natural next step is to consider incorporating the algorithms presented here into a fully-fledged unification algorithm for $\mathcal{L}_{\text{VP}}$. Another challenge, that is highlighted by Observation 2, is to revise the definition of concatenable relations in order to allow having a length limit on the tuples that should belong to the relation; thus giving priority to the length limits. One example motivating this step, consider the relation of increasing tuples of integers. This relation is not concatenable according to the definition presented in the paper. In case we want to think of it as a concatenable relation, it follows from Observation 2 that tuples of single elements must be in the relation. However, it is not very intuitive to say that, for example, (1) is an increasing tuple of integers.

**Acknowledgments.** We thank three anonymous reviewers of FoIKS 2018, for pointing out their insightful remarks that certainly resulted in a more readable (and, at places, more correct) paper.

# References

1. Blumer, A., Blumer, J., Haussler, D., Ehrenfeucht, A., Chen, M.T., Seiferas, J.: The smallest automaton recognizing the subwords of a text. Theoret. Comput. Sci. **40**, 31–55 (1985)
2. Cristea, I., Ştefănescu, M.: Hypergroups and n-ary relations. Eur. J. Comb. **31**(3), 780–789 (2010)
3. Crochemore, M., Rytter, W.: Text Algorithms. Oxford University Press Inc., New York (1994)
4. Davidson, D.: The logical form of action sentences. In: Recher, N. (ed.) The Logic of Decision and Action, pp. 81–95. University of Pittsburgh Press, Pittsburgh (1967)
5. Erdős, P., Goodman, A.W., Pósa, L.: The representation of a graph by set intersections. Can. J. Math. **18**(1), 106–112 (1966)
6. Fine, K.: Neutral relations. Philos. Rev. **109**(1), 1–33 (2000)
7. Graham, S.: String Searching Algorithms, vol. 3. World Scientific, Singapore (1994)
8. Gusfield, D.: Algorithms on Strings, Trees and Sequences: Computer Science and Computational Biology. Cambridge University Press, Cambridge (1997)
9. Ismail, H.O.: Four remarks on relations and predication. In: Arazim, P., Lavicka, T. (eds.) The Logica Yearbook 2016. College Publications, London (2017)
10. Kenny, A.: Action Emotion and Will. Routledge and Kegan Paul, London (1963)
11. Leo, J.: The identity of argument places. Rev. Symbolic Logic **1**, 335–354 (2008)
12. Leo, J.: Modeling relations. J. Philos. Logic **37**, 353–385 (2008)
13. MacBride, F.: Relations. In: Zalta, E.N. (ed.) The Stanford Encyclopedia of Philosophy. Metaphysics Research Lab, Stanford University, Winter 2016 edn. (2016)
14. Morton, A.: Complex individuals and multigrade relations. Noûs **9**(3), 309–318 (1975)
15. Oliver, A., Smiley, T.: Multigrade predicates. Mind **113**(452), 609–681 (2004)
16. Parsons, T.: Events in the Semantics of English. MIT Press, Cambridge (1990)
17. Savnik, I.: Index data structure for fast subset and superset queries. In: Cuzzocrea, A., Kittl, C., Simos, D.E., Weippl, E., Xu, L. (eds.) CD-ARES 2013. LNCS, vol. 8127, pp. 134–148. Springer, Heidelberg (2013). https://doi.org/10.1007/978-3-642-40511-2_10
18. Sedgewick, R., Wayne, K.: Algorithms. Addison-Wesley Professional, Boston (2011)
19. Shapiro, S.C.: SNePS: a logic for natural language understanding and commonsense reasoning. In: Iwańska, Ł.M., Shapiro, S.C. (eds.) Natural Language Processing and Knowledge Representation: Language for Knowledge and Knowledge for Language, pp. 175–195. AAAI Press/The MIT Press, Menlo Park (2000)
20. Shapiro, S.C.: Symmetric relations, intensional individuals, and variable binding. Proc. IEEE **74**(10), 1354–1363 (1986)
21. Taylor, B., Hazen, A.P.: Flexibly structured predication. Logique Anal. **139–140**, 375–393 (1992)

# Compilation of Conditional Knowledge Bases for Computing C-Inference Relations

Christoph Beierle, Steven Kutsch[✉], and Kai Sauerwald

Faculty of Mathematics and Computer Science, FernUniversität in Hagen,
58084 Hagen, Germany
Steven.Kutsch@fernuni-hagen.de

**Abstract.** A conditional knowledge base $\mathcal{R}$ contains defeasible rules of the form "If A, then usually B". For the notion of c-representations, a skeptical inference relation taking all c-representations of $\mathcal{R}$ into account has been suggested. In this paper, we propose a 3-phase compilation scheme for both knowledge bases and skeptical queries to constraint satisfaction problems. In addition to skeptical c-inference, we show that also credulous and weakly skeptical c-inference can be modelled as a constraint satisfaction problem, and that the compilation scheme can be extended to such queries. For each compilation step, we prove its soundness and completeness, and demonstrate significant efficiency benefits when querying the compiled version of $\mathcal{R}$. These findings are also supported by experiments with the software system `InfOCF` that employs the proposed compilation scheme.

## 1 Introduction

Conditionals of the form "if $A$, then usually $B$" establish a plausible (or reasonable, probable, ...) relationship between $A$ and $B$, allowing also for exceptions. A set $\mathcal{R}$ of such conditionals is called a knowledge base. A major question in nonmonotonic reasoning is what such a conditional knowledge base entails (e.g., [9,19,21]). This induces an inference relation saying that $A$ entails $B$ in the context of $\mathcal{R}$, denoted by $A \mathrel{|\!\sim}_{\mathcal{R}} B$. Depending on the semantics chosen, the computation of $\mathrel{|\!\sim}_{\mathcal{R}}$ might involve complex and costly computations. The main idea of compiling a knowledge base $\mathcal{R}$ for answering queries is therefore to transform $\mathcal{R}$ into a compiled form such that it is cheaper to use the compiled version of $\mathcal{R}$ instead of using $\mathcal{R}$ for answering whether an inference holds in the context of $\mathcal{R}$. The potential benefits of using the latter will increase the more queries are asked with respect to $\mathcal{R}$.

In this paper, we propose a compilation scheme for $\mathcal{R}$ tailored towards computing various inference relations based on c-representations [16,17]. Realizing skeptical c-inference takes all c-representations into account and requires to generate and solve a complex constraint satisfaction problem [3]. Employing the 3-phase compilation developed here for skeptical c-inference yields significant

© Springer International Publishing AG, part of Springer Nature 2018
F. Ferrarotti and S. Woltran (Eds.): FoIKS 2018, LNCS 10833, pp. 34–54, 2018.
https://doi.org/10.1007/978-3-319-90050-6_3

benefits when using a compiled version of $\mathcal{R}$; the benefit for answering queries consists of reusing the precompiled results of NP-hard computations. We also develop a new method for realizing credulous and weakly skeptical c-inference [4] and show that the computation scheme can be extended to these inference relations. For all compilation and optimization steps, formal correctness proofs are given.

Darwiche and Marquis [10] detailed different approaches of compiling propositional knowledge bases to easier target languages, that allow for easier and faster inference, but they do not consider conditional knowledge bases. Eiter and Lukasewicz [13] studied the efficiency benefits of adding strict facts to a conditional knowledge base, but the compilation of a knowledge base is not addressed.

After recalling the required background (Sect. 2), the three phases of knowledge base compilation (Sects. 3, 4 and 5) and the compilation of skeptical c-inference is introduced (Sect. 6). Section 7 investigates the compilation benefits and briefly describes an implementation employing our compilation scheme. In Sect. 8, a realization and a compilation of credulous and weakly skeptical c-inference is developed, and in Sect. 9, we conclude and point out further work.

## 2    Background

**Conditional Logic and OCFs.** Let $\Sigma = \{v_1, ..., v_m\}$ be a finite propositional alphabet. From $\Sigma$ we obtain the propositional language $\mathcal{L}$ as the set of formulas of $\Sigma$ closed under negation $\neg$, conjunction $\wedge$, and disjunction $\vee$, as usual. For shorter formulas, we abbreviate conjunction by juxtaposition (i.e., $AB$ stands for $A \wedge B$), and negation by overlining (i.e., $\overline{A}$ is equivalent to $\neg A$). A *literal* is a propositional variable $v_i$ or a negated propositional variable $\overline{v_i}$. A conjunction that mentions every variable in $\Sigma$, is called a complete conjunction over $\Sigma$. Let $\Omega$ denote the set of possible worlds over $\mathcal{L}$; $\Omega$ will be taken here simply as the set of all propositional interpretations over $\mathcal{L}$ and can be identified with the set of all complete conjunctions over $\Sigma$. For $\omega \in \Omega$, $\omega \models A$ means that the propositional formula $A \in \mathcal{L}$ holds in the possible world $\omega$.

A *conditional* $(B|A)$ with $A, B \in \mathcal{L}$ encodes the defeasible rule "if $A$ then normally $B$" and is a trivalent logical entity with the evaluation going back to de Finetti [11]:

$$(B|A)(\omega) = \begin{cases} true & \text{iff } \omega \models AB \quad \text{(verification)} \\ false & \text{iff } \omega \models A\overline{B} \quad \text{(falsification)} \\ undefined & \text{iff } \omega \models \overline{A} \quad \text{(not applicable)} \end{cases}$$

An *ordinal conditional function* (OCF, ranking function) [23] is a function $\kappa : \Omega \to \mathbb{N}_0 \cup \{\infty\}$ that assigns to each world $\omega \in \Omega$ an implausibility rank $\kappa(\omega)$: the higher $\kappa(\omega)$, the more surprising $\omega$ is. OCFs have to satisfy the normalization condition that there has to be a world that is maximally plausible, i.e., $\kappa^{-1}(0) \neq \emptyset$. The rank of a formula $A$ is defined by $\kappa(A) = \min\{\kappa(\omega) \mid \omega \models A\}$. An OCF $\kappa$ *accepts* a conditional $(B|A)$, denoted by $\kappa \models (B|A)$, if the verification of the conditional is less surprising than its falsification, i.e., if $\kappa(AB) < \kappa(A\overline{B})$. This can also be understood as a nonmonotonic inference relation between the premise $A$ and the conclusion $B$: We say that $A$ $\kappa$-entails $B$, written $A \hspace{1pt}\vert\!\sim_\kappa B$, iff $\kappa$ accepts the conditional $(B|A)$; formally, this is given by:

$$A \hspace{1pt}\vert\!\sim_\kappa B \quad \text{iff} \quad \kappa \models (B|A) \quad \text{iff} \quad \kappa(AB) < \kappa(A\overline{B}) \tag{1}$$

Note that $\kappa(AB) < \kappa(A\overline{B})$ is equivalent to $\kappa(AB) - \kappa(A) > 0$, giving us

$$\kappa \models (B|A) \text{ iff } \kappa(AB) - \kappa(A) > 0. \tag{2}$$

The acceptance relation in (1) is extended as usual to a set $\mathcal{R}$ of conditionals, called a *knowledge base*, by defining $\kappa \models \mathcal{R}$ if $\kappa \models (B|A)$ for all $(B|A) \in \mathcal{R}$. This is synonymous to saying that $\kappa$ is *admissible* with respect to $\mathcal{R}$ [15], or that $\kappa$ is a *ranking model* of $\mathcal{R}$. $\mathcal{R}$ is *consistent* iff it has a ranking model; otherwise, $\mathcal{R}$ is called *inconsistent*.

**P-Entailment and System P-Inference.** While $A \hspace{1pt}\vert\!\sim_\kappa B$ as given in (1) defines a nonmonotonic inference relation based on a single ranking function $\kappa$, one can also define an inference relation taking *all* models of a knowledge base $\mathcal{R}$ into account. This yields the notion of *p-entailment* which is a well-established inference in the area of ranking functions.

**Definition 1 (p-entailment [15]).** *Let $\mathcal{R}$ be a knowledge base and let $A, B$ be formulas. Then, $A$ p-entails $B$ in the context of $\mathcal{R}$, written $A \hspace{1pt}\vert\!\sim_\mathcal{R}^p B$, if $A \hspace{1pt}\vert\!\sim_\kappa B$ holds for all $\kappa$ accepting $\mathcal{R}$.*

Nonmonotonic inference relations are usually evaluated by means of properties. In particular, the axiom system P [1] provides an important standard for plausible, nonmonotonic inferences. We refer to Dubois and Prade [12] for the relation between p-entailment and system P:

**Proposition 1 ([12]).** *Let $A$, $B$ be formulas and let $\mathcal{R}$ be a knowledge base. Then $B$ follows from $A$ in the context of $\mathcal{R}$ with the rules of system P if and only if $A$ p-entails $B$ in the context of $\mathcal{R}$.*

So, given a knowledge base $\mathcal{R}$, system P inference is the same as p-entailment.

**C-Representations and C-Inference.** Among the models of $\mathcal{R}$, c-representations are special ranking models obtained by assigning individual impacts to the conditionals in $\mathcal{R}$. The rank of a possible world is then defined as the sum of impacts of falsified conditionals. For an in-depth introduction to c-representations and their use of the principle of conditional preservation we refer to [16,17]. The central definition is the following:

**Definition 2 (c-representation [16,17]).** *A* c-representation *of a knowledge base* $\mathcal{R} = \{(B_1|A_1), \ldots, (B_n|A_n)\}$ *is a ranking function $\kappa$ constructed from integer impacts $\eta_i \in \mathbb{N}_0 = \{0, 1, 2, \ldots\}$ assigned to each conditional $(B_i|A_i)$ such that $\kappa$ accepts $\mathcal{R}$ and is given by:*

$$\kappa(\omega) = \sum_{\substack{1 \leqslant i \leqslant n \\ \omega \models A_i \overline{B}_i}} \eta_i \tag{3}$$

Every c-representation exhibits desirable inference properties [16,17]. C-inference was introduced in [3] as the skeptical inference relation taking all c-representations of $\mathcal{R}$ into account.

**Definition 3 (c-inference, $\mathrel{\vrule height 1.3ex depth 0pt width 0pt}\!\!\sim^{sk}_{\mathcal{R}}$ [3]).** *Let $\mathcal{R}$ be a knowledge base and let $A$, $B$ be formulas. Then $B$ is a (skeptical) c-inference from $A$ in the context of $\mathcal{R}$, denoted by $A \mathrel{\vrule height 1.3ex depth 0pt width 0pt}\!\!\sim^{sk}_{\mathcal{R}} B$, if $A \mathrel{\vrule height 1.3ex depth 0pt width 0pt}\!\!\sim_{\kappa} B$ holds for all c-representations $\kappa$ for $\mathcal{R}$.*

## 3 Phase I: Compiling Knowledge Bases to CSPs

For illustrating the steps and concepts of our compilation scheme, we will use the following as a running example.

*Example 1.* Let $\Sigma = \{b, p, f, w\}$ representing birds, penguins, flying things and winged things, and let $\mathcal{R}_{bird} = \{r_1, r_2, r_3, r_4\}$ be the knowledge base with:

$$
\begin{array}{lll}
r_1 : (f|b) & \quad & \text{birds usually fly} \\
r_2 : (\overline{f}|p) & \quad & \text{penguins usually do no fly} \\
r_3 : (b|p) & \quad & \text{penguins are usually birds} \\
r_4 : (w|b) & \quad & \text{birds usually have wings}
\end{array}
$$

For determining whether a c-inference $A \mathrel{\vrule height 1.3ex depth 0pt width 0pt}\!\!\sim^{sk}_{\mathcal{R}} B$ holds, one has to take into account all c-representations of $\mathcal{R}$ and their behaviour with respect to $A$ and $B$. Our compilation approach will use the following modelling of c-representations as solutions of a constraint satisfaction problem (CSP) that has been employed for computing c-representations using constraint logic programming [6].

**Definition 4 ($CR(\mathcal{R})$ [6]).** *Let $\mathcal{R} = \{(B_1|A_1), \ldots, (B_n|A_n)\}$. The constraint satisfaction problem for c-representations of $\mathcal{R}$, denoted by $CR(\mathcal{R})$, on the constraint variables $\{\eta_1, \ldots, \eta_n\}$ ranging over $\mathbb{N}_0$ is given by the conjunction of the constraints, for all $i \in \{1, \ldots, n\}$:*

$$\eta_i > \min_{\substack{\omega \models A_i B_i \\ \omega \models A_j \overline{B}_j}} \sum_{\substack{j \neq i}} \eta_j - \min_{\substack{\omega \models A_i \overline{B}_i \\ \omega \models A_j \overline{B}_j}} \sum_{\substack{j \neq i}} \eta_j \tag{4}$$

A solution of $CR(\mathcal{R})$ is an $n$-tuple $\overrightarrow{\eta} = (\eta_1, \ldots, \eta_n)$ of natural numbers; $\overrightarrow{\eta}$ induces the ranking function $\kappa_{\overrightarrow{\eta}}$ as given by (3). For a constraint satisfaction problem $CSP$, the set of solutions is denoted by $Sol(CSP)$. Thus, with $Sol(CR(\mathcal{R}))$ we denote the set of all solutions of $CR(\mathcal{R})$.

*Example 2.* With $\Omega_\Sigma$ denoting the set of worlds over $\Sigma = \{b, p, f, w\}$ and $r_i = (B_i|A_i)$ for $i \in \{1, \ldots, 4\}$ the constraint system $CR(\mathcal{R}_{bird})$ is:

$$\eta_1 > \min_{\substack{\omega \in \Omega_\Sigma \\ \omega \models bf}} \sum_{\substack{j \neq 1 \\ \omega \models A_j \overline{B_j}}} \eta_j \quad - \quad \min_{\substack{\omega \in \Omega_\Sigma \\ \omega \models b\overline{f}}} \sum_{\substack{j \neq 1 \\ \omega \models A_j \overline{B_j}}} \eta_j \tag{5}$$

$$\eta_2 > \min_{\substack{\omega \in \Omega_\Sigma \\ \omega \models p\overline{f}}} \sum_{\substack{j \neq 2 \\ \omega \models A_j \overline{B_j}}} \eta_j \quad - \quad \min_{\substack{\omega \in \Omega_\Sigma \\ \omega \models pf}} \sum_{\substack{j \neq 2 \\ \omega \models A_j \overline{B_j}}} \eta_j \tag{6}$$

$$\eta_3 > \min_{\substack{\omega \in \Omega_\Sigma \\ \omega \models pb}} \sum_{\substack{j \neq 3 \\ \omega \models A_j \overline{B_j}}} \eta_j \quad - \quad \min_{\substack{\omega \in \Omega_\Sigma \\ \omega \models p\overline{b}}} \sum_{\substack{j \neq 3 \\ \omega \models A_j \overline{B_j}}} \eta_j \tag{7}$$

$$\eta_4 > \min_{\substack{\omega \in \Omega_\Sigma \\ \omega \models bw}} \sum_{\substack{j \neq 4 \\ \omega \models A_j \overline{B_j}}} \eta_j \quad - \quad \min_{\substack{\omega \in \Omega_\Sigma \\ \omega \models b\overline{w}}} \sum_{\substack{j \neq 4 \\ \omega \models A_j \overline{B_j}}} \eta_j \tag{8}$$

Table 1 details how solutions of $CR(\mathcal{R}_{bird})$ translate to OCFs accepting $\mathcal{R}_{bird}$.

**Table 1.** Verification and falsification for the conditionals in $\mathcal{R}_{bird}$ from Example 2. $\vec{\eta}_1$, $\vec{\eta}_2$ and $\vec{\eta}_3$ are solutions of $CR(\mathcal{R}_{bird})$ and $\kappa_{\vec{\eta}_1}(\omega)$, $\kappa_{\vec{\eta}_2}(\omega)$, and $\kappa_{\vec{\eta}_3}(\omega)$ are their induced ranking functions according to Definition 2.

| $\omega$ | $r_1:$ $(f\|b)$ | $r_2:$ $(\overline{f}\|p)$ | $r_3:$ $(b\|p)$ | $r_4:$ $(w\|b)$ | impact on $\omega$ | $\kappa_{\vec{\eta}_1}(\omega)$ | $\kappa_{\vec{\eta}_2}(\omega)$ | $\kappa_{\vec{\eta}_3}(\omega)$ |
|---|---|---|---|---|---|---|---|---|
| $bpfw$ | $v$ | $f$ | $v$ | $v$ | $\eta_2$ | 2 | 4 | 5 |
| $bpf\overline{w}$ | $v$ | $f$ | $v$ | $f$ | $\eta_2 + \eta_4$ | 3 | 7 | 12 |
| $bp\overline{f}w$ | $f$ | $v$ | $v$ | $v$ | $\eta_1$ | 1 | 3 | 4 |
| $bp\overline{f}\,\overline{w}$ | $f$ | $v$ | $v$ | $f$ | $\eta_1 + \eta_4$ | 2 | 6 | 11 |
| $b\overline{p}fw$ | $v$ | $-$ | $-$ | $v$ | 0 | 0 | 0 | 0 |
| $b\overline{p}f\overline{w}$ | $v$ | $-$ | $-$ | $f$ | $\eta_4$ | 1 | 3 | 7 |
| $b\overline{p}\,\overline{f}w$ | $f$ | $-$ | $-$ | $v$ | $\eta_1$ | 1 | 3 | 4 |
| $b\overline{p}\,\overline{f}\,\overline{w}$ | $f$ | $-$ | $-$ | $f$ | $\eta_1 + \eta_4$ | 2 | 6 | 11 |
| $\overline{b}pfw$ | $-$ | $f$ | $f$ | $-$ | $\eta_2 + \eta_3$ | 4 | 8 | 11 |
| $\overline{b}pf\overline{w}$ | $-$ | $f$ | $f$ | $-$ | $\eta_2 + \eta_3$ | 4 | 8 | 11 |
| $\overline{b}p\overline{f}w$ | $-$ | $v$ | $f$ | $-$ | $\eta_3$ | 2 | 4 | 6 |
| $\overline{b}p\overline{f}\,\overline{w}$ | $-$ | $v$ | $f$ | $-$ | $\eta_3$ | 2 | 4 | 6 |
| $\overline{b}\,\overline{p}fw$ | $-$ | $-$ | $-$ | $-$ | 0 | 0 | 0 | 0 |
| $\overline{b}\,\overline{p}f\overline{w}$ | $-$ | $-$ | $-$ | $-$ | 0 | 0 | 0 | 0 |
| $\overline{b}\,\overline{p}\,\overline{f}w$ | $-$ | $-$ | $-$ | $-$ | 0 | 0 | 0 | 0 |
| $\overline{b}\,\overline{p}\,\overline{f}\,\overline{w}$ | $-$ | $-$ | $-$ | $-$ | 0 | 0 | 0 | 0 |
| impacts: | $\eta_1$ | $\eta_2$ | $\eta_3$ | $\eta_4$ | | | | |
| $\vec{\eta}_1$ | 1 | 2 | 2 | 1 | | | | |
| $\vec{\eta}_2$ | 3 | 4 | 4 | 3 | | | | |
| $\vec{\eta}_3$ | 4 | 5 | 6 | 7 | | | | |

Note that solving $CR(\mathcal{R}_{bird})$ directly requires to solve $2 \cdot |\mathcal{R}_{bird}|$ minimization tasks. The variable $\omega$ in each minimization task runs over the models of a propositional formula, thus each minimization task requires the enumeration of all models of a propositional formula, which may be up to $2^{|\Sigma|}$ many. For each fitting possible world, the involved summation term in turn requires to evaluate $|\mathcal{R}_{bird}| - 1$ propositional formulas with respect to this possible world.

Phase I of the knowledge base compilation scheme for a knowledge base $\mathcal{R}$ transforms $\mathcal{R}$ into $CR(\mathcal{R})$ as given by Definition 4. It has been shown that $CR(\mathcal{R})$ is a sound and complete modelling of all c-representations of $\mathcal{R}$ [3, Proposition 3 and 4]; moreover, $\mathcal{R}$ is consistent iff $CR(\mathcal{R})$ has a solution [3, Corollary 1]. This ensures the correctness of Phase I of the knowledge base compilation.

## 4   Phase II: From $CR(\mathcal{R})$ to Powerset Representations

In general, the transformation of the constraints in $CR(\mathcal{R})$ to a form that allows the use of an automated constraint solver requires several computationally hard calculations, e.g., the enumeration of all models of a propositional formula. The following notion of *PSR terms* provides a concept for representing a compiled form of the subtraction expressions in $CR(\mathcal{R})$ that only involves constraint variables and no propositional worlds.

**Definition 5 (Powerset Representation, PSR term).** *Let $\mathcal{R}$ and $CR(\mathcal{R})$ be as in Definition 4, and let*

$$\eta_i > \underbrace{\min_{\substack{\omega \models A_i B_i}} \sum_{\substack{j \neq i \\ \omega \models A_j \overline{B_j}}} \eta_j}_{V_{min_i}} - \underbrace{\min_{\substack{\omega \models A_i \overline{B_i}}} \sum_{\substack{j \neq i \\ \omega \models A_j \overline{B_j}}} \eta_j}_{F_{min_i}} \tag{9}$$

*be a constraint in $CR(\mathcal{R})$. The* powerset representation *of $V_{min_i} - F_{min_i}$, also called* PSR term, *is the pair $\langle \Pi(V_{min_i}), \Pi(F_{min_i}) \rangle$ with*

$$\Pi(V_{min_i}) = \{ \, \{ \eta_j \mid j \neq i, \; \omega \models A_j \overline{B_j} \} \mid \omega \models A_i B_i \} \tag{10}$$
$$\Pi(F_{min_i}) = \{ \, \{ \eta_j \mid j \neq i, \; \omega \models A_j \overline{B_j} \} \mid \omega \models A_i \overline{B_i} \} \tag{11}$$

*Example 3.* The PSR terms for the four constraints (5)–(8) are:

$$\langle \Pi(V_{min_1}), \Pi(F_{min_1}) \rangle = \langle \{ \{\eta_2\}, \{\eta_2, \eta_4\}, \varnothing, \{\eta_4\} \}, \{\varnothing, \{\eta_4\} \} \rangle \tag{12}$$
$$\langle \Pi(V_{min_2}), \Pi(F_{min_2}) \rangle = \langle \{ \{\eta_1\}, \{\eta_3\}, \{\eta_1, \eta_4\} \}, \{\varnothing, \{\eta_4\}, \{\eta_3\} \} \rangle \tag{13}$$
$$\langle \Pi(V_{min_3}), \Pi(F_{min_3}) \rangle = \langle \{ \{\eta_2\}, \{\eta_2, \eta_4\}, \{\eta_1\}, \{\eta_1, \eta_4\} \}, \{\varnothing, \{\eta_2\} \} \rangle \tag{14}$$
$$\langle \Pi(V_{min_4}), \Pi(F_{min_4}) \rangle = \langle \{ \{\eta_2\}, \{\eta_1\}, \varnothing \}, \{ \{\eta_2\}, \{\eta_1\}, \varnothing \} \rangle \tag{15}$$

Thus, a PSR term $\langle \mathcal{V}, \mathcal{F} \rangle$ is a pair of sets of subsets of the involved constraint variables. The following definition assigns an arithmetic expression to any set of sets of constraint variables. For every set $S$, we will use $\mathcal{P}(S)$ to denote the power set of $S$.

**Definition 6 (represented arithmetic term, $\rho$).** *Let $CV = \{\eta_1, \ldots, \eta_n\}$ be a set of constraint variables and let $M \in \mathcal{P}(CV)$ be an element of the power set of $CV$. The arithmetic expression represented by $M = \{S_1, \ldots, S_r\}$, denoted by $\rho(M)$, is:*

$$\rho(M) = \min\{\sum_{\eta \in S_1} \eta, \ldots, \sum_{\eta \in S_r} \eta\} \tag{16}$$

*Note that $\min \emptyset = \infty$, and if $S = \emptyset$ then $\sum_{\eta \in S} \eta = 0$. We extend the definition of $\rho$ to PSR terms $\langle \mathcal{V}, \mathcal{F} \rangle$:*

$$\rho(\langle \mathcal{V}, \mathcal{F} \rangle) = \begin{cases} \infty & \text{if } \rho(\mathcal{V}) = \infty \text{ and } \rho(\mathcal{F}) = \infty \\ \rho(\mathcal{V}) - \rho(\mathcal{F}) & \text{else} \end{cases} \tag{17}$$

Note that the first case in (17) catches the extreme case of a knowledge base $\mathcal{R}$ containing a conditional of the form $(A|\bot)$. Because such a conditional is never applicable, it is never verified or falsified. Thus, a knowledge base containing $(A|\bot)$ is inconsistent, since no ranking function accepting $(A|\bot)$ exists.

The following proposition states that a subtraction expression occurring in $CR(\mathcal{R})$ can safely be replaced by the arithmetic expressions obtained from its PSR representation.

**Proposition 2.** *Let $\mathcal{R}$ be a knowledge base, $CV$ be the constraint variables occurring in $CR(\mathcal{R})$, and $V_{min} - F_{min}$ be an expression occurring in $CR(\mathcal{R})$. Then for every variable assignment $\alpha : CV \to \mathbb{N}_0$ we have:*

$$\alpha(V_{min}) - \alpha(F_{min}) = \alpha(\rho(\langle \Pi(V_{min}), \Pi(F_{min}) \rangle)) \tag{18}$$

The following example illustrates the relationship between the original constraints in $CR(\mathcal{R}_{bird})$ and the arithmetic terms obtained from the PSR terms through $\rho$ under a given variable assignment $\alpha$.

*Example 4.* We take $V_{min_2}$ and $F_{min_2}$ for which the PSR terms $\Pi(V_{min_2})$ and $\Pi(F_{min_2})$ are given in Example 3. For the variable assignment $\alpha$ with $\alpha(\eta_1) = 1$, $\alpha(\eta_2) = 2$, $\alpha(\eta_3) = 2$, and $\alpha(\eta_4) = 1$ we get

$$\alpha(V_{min_2}) - \alpha(F_{min_2}) = \min\{1, 2, 1 + 1\} - \min\{0, 1, 2\} \tag{19}$$

for the left hand side of (18). For the right hand side of (18) we get:

$$\alpha(\rho(\langle \Pi(V_{min_2}), \Pi(F_{min_2}) \rangle)) \tag{20}$$

$$= \alpha(\rho(\{\{\eta_1\}, \{\eta_3\}, \{\eta_1, \eta_4\}\}) - \rho(\{\emptyset, \{\eta_4\}, \{\eta_3\}\})) \tag{21}$$

$$= \alpha(\min\{\eta_1, \eta_3, \eta_1 + \eta_4\} - \min\{0, \eta_4, \eta_3\}) \tag{22}$$

$$= \min\{1, 2, 1 + 1\} - \min\{0, 1, 2\} \tag{23}$$

Note that, as stated by Proposition 2, the expressions (19) and (23) are equal.

**Definition 7 (Knowledge base compilation Phase II).** *Phase II of the compilation scheme for a knowledge base $\mathcal{R}$ transforms $CR(\mathcal{R})$ into $PSR(\mathcal{R})$ where $PSR(\mathcal{R})$ is obtained from $CR(\mathcal{R})$ by replacing every subtraction expression of the form $V_{min} - F_{min}$ by its PSR term $\langle \Pi(V_{min}), \Pi(F_{min}) \rangle$.*

In order to be able to directly compare the results of the different compilation phases, we will use $\rho(PSR(\mathcal{R}))$ to denote the result of replacing every PSR term $\langle \mathcal{V}, \mathcal{F} \rangle$ in $PSR(\mathcal{R})$ by $\rho(\langle \mathcal{V}, \mathcal{F} \rangle)$. Using this notation, Proposition 2 ensures:

**Proposition 3 (Correctness of knowledge base compilation Phase II).** *For every knowledge base $\mathcal{R}$, we have $Sol(CR(\mathcal{R})) = Sol(\rho(PSR(\mathcal{R})))$.*

In order to ease our notation, in the following we may omit the explicit distinction between a PSR term $\langle \mathcal{V}, \mathcal{F} \rangle$ and its represented subtraction expression $\rho(\langle \mathcal{V}, \mathcal{F} \rangle)$. Likewise, we may omit the distinction between $PSR(\mathcal{R})$ and $\rho(PSR(\mathcal{R}))$.

# 5   Phase III: Optimizing PSR Subtraction Expressions

The powerset representation $\langle \mathcal{V}, \mathcal{F} \rangle$ of a subtraction expression can be optimized. For instance, the minimum of two sums $S_1$ and $S_2$ of non-negative integers is $S_1$ if all summands of $S_1$ also occur in $S_2$. Figure 1 contains a set $\mathcal{T}$ of transformation rules that can be applied to pairs of elements of the powerset of constraint variables, and thus in particular to the PSR representation of a subtraction expression:

(**ss-V**)   removes a set $S'$ that is an element in the first component if it is a superset of another set $S$ in the first component.

(**ss-F**)   removes a set $S'$ that is an element in the second component if it is a superset of another set $S$ in the second component.

(**elem**)   removes an element $\eta$ that is in every set in both the first and the second component from all these sets.

(**∅-V**)   removes all other sets from the first component if it contains the empty set, such that the empty set remains as the only element in $\mathcal{V}$.

(**∅-F**)   removes all other sets from the second component if it contains the empty set, such that the empty set remains as the only element $\mathcal{F}$.

Note that $\mathcal{T}$ is not a minimal set of transformation rules because $(∅\text{-}V)$ and $(∅\text{-}F)$ could be replaced by a finite chain of applications of $(ss\text{-}V)$ and $(ss\text{-}F)$, respectively. We include these two rules because they allow for reductions involving fewer steps.

The following propositions state properties of the transformation rules $\mathcal{T}$ which will be vital when using them for compiling $CR(\mathcal{R})$:

**Proposition 4.** *The transformation system $\mathcal{T}$ is terminating.*

**Proposition 5.** *The transformation system $\mathcal{T}$ is confluent.*

$(ss\text{-}V)$ subset-$V$: $\qquad\qquad \dfrac{\langle \mathcal{V} \cup \{S, S'\},\ \mathcal{F}\rangle}{\langle \mathcal{V} \cup \{S\},\ \mathcal{F}\rangle}$ $\qquad\qquad S \subseteq S'$

$(ss\text{-}F)$ subset-$F$: $\qquad\qquad \dfrac{\langle \mathcal{V},\ \mathcal{F} \cup \{S, S'\}\rangle}{\langle \mathcal{V},\ \mathcal{F} \cup \{S\}\rangle}$ $\qquad\qquad S \subseteq S'$

$(elem)$ element: $\qquad \dfrac{\langle \{V_1 \cup \{\eta\}, \ldots, V_p \cup \{\eta\}\},\ \{F_1 \cup \{\eta\}, \ldots, F_q \cup \{\eta\}\}\rangle}{\langle \{V_1, \ldots, V_p\},\ \{F_1, \ldots, F_q\}\rangle}$

$(\varnothing\text{-}V)$ empty-$V$: $\qquad\qquad \dfrac{\langle \mathcal{V} \cup \{\varnothing\},\ \mathcal{F}\rangle}{\langle \{\varnothing\},\ \mathcal{F}\rangle}$

$(\varnothing\text{-}F)$ empty-$F$: $\qquad\qquad \dfrac{\langle \mathcal{V},\ \mathcal{F} \cup \{\varnothing\}\rangle}{\langle \mathcal{V},\ \{\varnothing\}\rangle}$

**Fig. 1.** Transformation rules $\mathcal{T}$ for optimizing PSR representations of subtractions.

Termination of $\mathcal{T}$ is easy to show, and confluence of $\mathcal{T}$ holds because all critical pairs reduce to a common normal form (cf. [2, 18]).

**Proposition 6 ($\mathcal{T}$ correct).** *Let $\mathcal{R}$ be a knowledge base, $CV$ be the constraint variables occurring in $CR(\mathcal{R})$, and $\langle \mathcal{V}, \mathcal{F}\rangle$ be an expression occurring in $PSR(\mathcal{R})$. Then for every variable assignment $\alpha : CV \to \mathbb{N}_0$ we have:*

$$\alpha(\rho(\langle \mathcal{V},\ \mathcal{F}\rangle)) = \alpha(\rho(\mathcal{T}(\langle \mathcal{V},\ \mathcal{F}\rangle))) \tag{24}$$

*Proof.* It suffices to show that every individual rule in $\mathcal{T}$ is correct.

$(ss\text{-}V)$ The rule $(ss\text{-}V)$ is applicable if in $\mathcal{V}$ there are two sets $S$ and $S'$ such that $S \subseteq S'$. Under $\rho$, this corresponds to a minimization term containing two sums $s = c_1 + \ldots + c_n$ and $s' = c_1 + \ldots + c_n + c_1' + \ldots + c_m'$ for $m \in \mathbb{N}_0$, or $s = s'$. Since for every $\alpha$ it holds that $\alpha(s) \leqslant \alpha(s')$, the sum $s'$ can safely be ignored in the minimization. Hence, the set $S'$ can be removed from $\mathcal{V}$.

$(ss\text{-}F)$ The argument for the correctness of $(ss\text{-}V)$ also holds for $(ss\text{-}F)$.

$(elem)$ The rule $(elem)$ is applicable if there is a $\eta \in CV$ that is an element of every set in $\mathcal{V}$ and $\mathcal{F}$. Under $\rho$, this corresponds to a subtraction expression in which each sum in both minimization terms has a common addend $\eta$. For every variable assignment $\alpha$, the value $\alpha(\eta)$ thus is an addend in both the minimal sum in $\rho(\mathcal{V})$ and the minimal sum in $\rho(\mathcal{F})$. Since the value of the minimal sum in $\rho(\mathcal{F})$ is subtracted from the value of the minimal sum in $\rho(\mathcal{V})$, the common addend $\eta$ can safely be removed from every sum in $\rho(\mathcal{V})$ and $\rho(\mathcal{F})$. This means that $\eta$ can be removed from every set in $\mathcal{V}$ and $\mathcal{F}$.

$(\varnothing\text{-}V)$ **and** $(\varnothing\text{-}F)$ As stated above, $(\varnothing\text{-}V)$ and $(\varnothing\text{-}F)$ can be replaced by a finite chain of applications of $(ss\text{-}V)$ and $(ss\text{-}F)$, respectively. Therefore, their correctness follows from the correctness of $(ss\text{-}V)$ and $(ss\text{-}F)$. $\qquad\square$

Thus, the result of applying $\mathcal{T}$ exhaustively to a PSR term $\langle \mathcal{V}, \mathcal{F}\rangle$ is a simplified PSR term that is equivalent to $\langle \mathcal{V}, \mathcal{F}\rangle$ with respect to all variable assignments.

*Example 5.* Consider the PSR representation $\langle \Pi(V_{min_3}), \; \Pi(F_{min_3}) \rangle$ given in (14) for the subtraction expression in the constraint (7). The following is a possible sequence of applications of rules from $\mathcal{T}$ to (14) where underlining indicates the subexpression to which the given transformation rule is applied:

$$\langle \{\{\underline{\eta_2}\}, \{\eta_2, \eta_4\}, \{\eta_1\}, \{\eta_1, \eta_4\}\}, \; \{\varnothing, \{\underline{\eta_2}\}\} \rangle \xrightarrow{(ss\text{-}V)} \langle \{\{\underline{\eta_2}\}, \{\eta_1\}, \{\eta_1, \eta_4\}\},$$
$$\{\varnothing, \{\underline{\eta_2}\}\} \rangle \xrightarrow{(ss\text{-}V)} \langle \{\{\eta_2\}, \{\eta_1\}\}, \; \{\underline{\varnothing}, \{\eta_2\}\} \rangle \xrightarrow{(\varnothing\text{-}F)} \langle \{\{\eta_2\}, \{\eta_1\}\}, \; \{\varnothing\} \rangle$$

Since $\mathcal{T}$ is confluent, all application sequences for (14) lead to the obtained unique normal form $\mathcal{T}(\langle \Pi(V_{min_3}), \; \Pi(F_{min_3}) \rangle) = \langle \{\{\eta_2\}, \{\eta_1\}\}, \; \{\varnothing\} \rangle$.

For the knowledge base $\mathcal{R}_{bird}{}' = \mathcal{R}_{bird} \cup \{r_5 : (\overline{b}|\top)\}$ the PSR term for the conditional $r_1 : (f|b)$ is:

$$\langle \Pi(V'_{min_1}), \; \Pi(F'_{min_1}) \rangle = \langle \{\{\eta_2, \eta_5\}, \{\eta_2, \eta_4, \eta_5\}, \{\eta_5\}, \{\eta_4, \eta_5\}\}, \; \{\{\eta_5\}, \{\eta_4, \eta_5\}\} \rangle$$

This term can be obtained from $V_{min_1}$ and $F_{min_1}$ given in (12) by adding the impact $\eta_5$ to every set in $V_{min_1}$ and $F_{min_1}$, since the conditional $r_5$ is falsified in every model of both the verification and the falsification of the conditional $r_1$. By applying $\mathcal{T}$ to $\langle \Pi(V'_{min_1}), \; \Pi(F'_{min_1}) \rangle$ we get:

$$\langle \{\{\eta_2, \underline{\eta_5}\}, \{\eta_2, \eta_4, \underline{\eta_5}\}, \{\underline{\eta_5}\}, \{\eta_4, \underline{\eta_5}\}\}, \; \{\{\underline{\eta_5}\}, \{\eta_4, \underline{\eta_5}\}\} \rangle$$
$$\xrightarrow{(elem)} \langle \{\{\underline{\eta_2}\}, \{\eta_2, \eta_4\}, \varnothing, \{\eta_4\}\}, \; \{\underline{\varnothing}, \{\eta_4\}\} \rangle$$
$$\xrightarrow{(\varnothing\text{-}V)} \langle \{\varnothing\}, \; \{\varnothing, \{\underline{\eta_4}\}\} \rangle$$
$$\xrightarrow{(\varnothing\text{-}F)} \langle \{\varnothing\}, \; \{\varnothing\} \rangle$$

Note that the transformation rule (*elem*) is essential to obtain the final term.

We will now apply the optimization method to the constraint system $CR(\mathcal{R})$.

**Definition 8 (Knowledge base compilation Phase III, $CCR(\mathcal{R})$).** *Phase III of the compilation scheme for a knowledge base $\mathcal{R}$ transforms $PSR(\mathcal{R})$ into $CCR(\mathcal{R})$, called the* compilation *of $\mathcal{R}$, where $CCR(\mathcal{R})$ is obtained from $PSR(\mathcal{R})$ by replacing ever PSR term $\langle V, \; \mathcal{F} \rangle$ by its optimized normal form $\mathcal{T}(\langle V, \; \mathcal{F} \rangle)$.*

*Example 6.* $CCR(\mathcal{R}_{bird})$, the compilation of $\mathcal{R}_{bird}$, is given by:

$$\begin{aligned}
\eta_1 &> \langle \{\varnothing\}, \{\varnothing\} \rangle \\
\eta_2 &> \langle \{\{\eta_1\}, \{\eta_3\}, \{\eta_4\}\}, \{\varnothing\} \rangle \\
\eta_3 &> \langle \{\{\eta_2\}, \{\eta_1\}\}, \{\varnothing\} \rangle \\
\eta_4 &> \langle \{\varnothing\}, \{\varnothing\} \rangle
\end{aligned}$$

Similar as before, $\rho(CCR(\mathcal{R}))$ denotes the constraint system obtained from $CCR(\mathcal{R})$ by replacing every PSR term $\langle V, \; \mathcal{F} \rangle$ by $\rho(\langle V, \; \mathcal{F} \rangle)$.

**Proposition 7 (Soundness and completeness of compilation).** *For every knowledge base* $\mathcal{R}$*, the compilation of* $\mathcal{R}$ *is sound and complete, i.e.,*

$$\{\kappa_{\vec{\eta}} \mid \vec{\eta} \in Sol(\rho(CCR(\mathcal{R})))\} = \{\kappa \mid \kappa \text{ is a c-representation of } \mathcal{R}\}.$$

*Proof.* The proof follows from the soundness and completeness of $CR(\mathcal{R})$ [3, Propositions 3 and 4] together with Propositions 3 and 6.     □

The complete knowledge base compilation scheme can now be illustrated by:

$$\mathcal{R} \xrightarrow{\text{Phase I}} CR(\mathcal{R}) \xrightarrow{\text{Phase II}} PSR(\mathcal{R}) \xrightarrow{\text{Phase III}} CCR(\mathcal{R})$$

The next section extends this compilation scheme to queries.

## 6    Compilation for Skeptical C-Inference

For computing a p-entailment $A \mathrel{|\!\sim}_{\mathcal{R}}^{p} B$, a well-known theorem says that this can be reduced to the consistency of the extended knowledge base $\mathcal{R} \cup \{(\overline{B}|A)\}$.

**Proposition 8** ([12,14,15]). *Let* $\mathcal{R}$ *be a knowledge base and let* $A$*,* $B$ *be formulas. Then* $A$ *p-entails* $B$ *in the context of a knowledge base* $\mathcal{R}$ *iff* $\mathcal{R} \cup \{(\overline{B}|A)\}$ *is inconsistent.*

A c-inference $A \mathrel{|\!\sim}_{\mathcal{R}}^{sk} B$, however, can not be reduced to the consistency of an extended knowledge base [3]. Instead, computing a c-inference can be reduced to the solvability of a CSP using the (non-)acceptance constraint for $(B|A)$.

**Definition 9** ($CR_{\mathcal{R}}(B|A)$, $\neg CR_{\mathcal{R}}(B|A)$ [3]). *Let* $(B|A)$ *be a conditional and* $\mathcal{R} = \{(B_1|A_1), \ldots, (B_n|A_n)\}$ *be a knowledge base. The acceptance constraint for* $(B|A)$ *with respect to* $\mathcal{R}$*, denoted by* $CR_{\mathcal{R}}(B|A)$*, is:*

$$\min_{\substack{\omega \models AB}} \sum_{\substack{1 \leqslant i \leqslant n \\ \omega \models A_i \overline{B_i}}} \eta_i \quad < \quad \min_{\substack{\omega \models A\overline{B}}} \sum_{\substack{1 \leqslant i \leqslant n \\ \omega \models A_i \overline{B_i}}} \eta_i \tag{25}$$

$\neg CR_{\mathcal{R}}(B|A)$ *denotes the negation of (25), i.e., it denotes the constraint:*

$$\min_{\substack{\omega \models AB}} \sum_{\substack{1 \leqslant i \leqslant n \\ \omega \models A_i \overline{B_i}}} \eta_i \quad \geqslant \quad \min_{\substack{\omega \models A\overline{B}}} \sum_{\substack{1 \leqslant i \leqslant n \\ \omega \models A_i \overline{B_i}}} \eta_i \tag{26}$$

Note that both $CR_{\mathcal{R}}(B|A)$ and $\neg CR_{\mathcal{R}}(B|A)$ are constraints on the constraint variables $\eta_1, \ldots, \eta_n$ which are used in the CSP $CR(\mathcal{R})$, but they do not introduce any new variables not already occurring in $CR(\mathcal{R})$.

**Proposition 9 (c-inference as a CSP** [3]). *Let* $\mathcal{R} = \{(B_1|A_1), \ldots, (B_n|A_n)\}$ *be a consistent knowledge base and* $A, B$ *formulas. Then the following holds:*

$$A \mathrel{|\!\sim}_{\mathcal{R}}^{sk} B \quad iff \quad CR(\mathcal{R}) \cup \{\neg CR_{\mathcal{R}}(B|A)\} \text{ has no solution.} \tag{27}$$

Like for a knowledge base $\mathcal{R}$, we can apply similar compilation and optimization steps to a query.

**Definition 10 (query compilation, $\neg CCR_{\mathcal{R}}(B|A)$).** *Let $A, B$ be formulas and $\mathcal{R} = \{(B_1|A_1), \ldots, (B_n|A_n)\}$ be a knowledge base. The compilation of a query $A \hspace{0.1em}\sim\hspace{-0.9em}\mid{}^{sk}_{\mathcal{R}} B$, denoted by $\neg CCR_{\mathcal{R}}(B|A)$, is obtained in three phases:*
*Phase I results in $\neg CR_{\mathcal{R}}(B|A)$. Then, Phase II transforms $\neg CR_{\mathcal{R}}(B|A)$ given by $V_q \geqslant F_q$ into*

$$0 \leqslant \langle \Pi(V_q), \ \Pi(F_q) \rangle \tag{28}$$

*denoted by $\neg PSR_{\mathcal{R}}(B|A)$, with*

$$\Pi(V_q) = \{ \, \{\eta_i \mid \omega \models A_i \overline{B_i}\} \mid \omega \models AB \} \tag{29}$$

$$\Pi(F_q) = \{ \, \{\eta_i \mid \omega \models A_i \overline{B_i}\} \mid \omega \models A\overline{B} \} \tag{30}$$

*Phase III yields $\neg CCR_{\mathcal{R}}(B|A)$ by replacing the expression $\langle \Pi(V_q), \Pi(F_q) \rangle$ in $\neg PSR_{\mathcal{R}}(B|A)$ by $\mathcal{T}(\langle \Pi(V_q), \Pi(F_q) \rangle)$.*

*Example 7.* Consider the knowledge base $\mathcal{R}_{bird} = \{(f|b), (\overline{f}|p), (b|p), (w|b)\}$ from Example 1. The query $p \hspace{0.1em}\sim\hspace{-0.9em}\mid{}^{sk}_{\mathcal{R}_{bird}} w$ asking whether penguins have wings in the context of $\mathcal{R}_{bird}$ is compiled in three steps:

I. $\neg CR_{\mathcal{R}_{bird}}(w|p)$:

$$\min_{\omega \models pw} \sum_{\substack{\omega \models A_i \overline{B_i} \\ (B_i|A_i) \in \mathcal{R}_{bird}}} \eta_i \ \ \geqslant \ \ \min_{\omega \models p\overline{w}} \sum_{\substack{\omega \models A_i \overline{B_i} \\ (B_i|A_i) \in \mathcal{R}_{bird}}} \eta_i$$

II. $\neg PSR_{\mathcal{R}_{bird}}(w|p)$:

$$0 \leqslant \langle \{\{\eta_1\}, \{\eta_2\}, \{\eta_3\}, \{\eta_2, \eta_3\}\}, \ \{\{\eta_3\}, \{\eta_1, \eta_4\}, \{\eta_2, \eta_3\}, \{\eta_2, \eta_4\}\}\rangle$$

III. $\neg CCR_{\mathcal{R}_{bird}}(w|p)$:

$$0 \leqslant \langle \{\{\eta_1\}, \{\eta_2\}, \{\eta_3\}\}, \ \{\{\eta_3\}, \{\eta_1, \eta_4\}, \{\eta_2, \eta_4\}\rangle$$

Recall that we make no distinction between $\langle \mathcal{V}, \mathcal{F} \rangle$ and $\rho(\langle \mathcal{V}, \mathcal{F} \rangle)$. This allows us, for instance, to deal with $CCR(\mathcal{R})$ as a constraint system instead of using $\rho(CCR(\mathcal{R}))$ or to write $\neg PSR_{\mathcal{R}}(B|A)$ synonymously for $\rho(\neg PSR_{\mathcal{R}}(B|A))$.

**Proposition 10 (correctness of compiled c-inference).** *Let $\mathcal{R}$ be a consistent knowledge base and $A, B$ formulas. Then the following holds:*

$$A \hspace{0.1em}\sim\hspace{-0.9em}\mid{}^{sk}_{\mathcal{R}} B \quad iff \quad CCR(\mathcal{R}) \cup \{\neg CCR_{\mathcal{R}}(B|A)\} \ has \ no \ solution. \tag{31}$$

*Proof.* Using Proposition 9, the proof is analogous to the proof of Proposition 7.

*Example 8.* Since $CCR(\mathcal{R}_{bird}) \cup \{\neg CCR_{\mathcal{R}_{bird}}(w|p)\}$ has no solution, $p \mathrel{\vert\!\sim}^{sk}_{\mathcal{R}_{bird}} w$ is a c-inference.

As an immediate consequence of the correctness of modelling c-inference as a CSP and of the correctness of compiling knowledge bases and queries we get:

**Proposition 11.** *Let $\mathcal{R} = \{(B_1|A_1), \ldots, (B_n|A_n)\}$ be a consistent knowledge base and $A, B$ be formulas. Then $A \mathrel{\vert\!\sim}^{sk}_{\mathcal{R}} B$ is equivalent to every of the following conditions, regardless how $\mathcal{X}$ is chosen from $\{CR, PSR, CCR\}$:*

$$CR(\mathcal{R}) \cup \{\neg \mathcal{X}_{\mathcal{R}}(B|A)\} \text{ has no solution.} \tag{32}$$

$$PSR(\mathcal{R}) \cup \{\neg \mathcal{X}_{\mathcal{R}}(B|A)\} \text{ has no solution.} \tag{33}$$

$$CCR(\mathcal{R}) \cup \{\neg \mathcal{X}_{\mathcal{R}}(B|A)\} \text{ has no solution.} \tag{34}$$

We will now investigate the benefits of the compilation and optimization.

## 7 Compilation Benefits and Implementation

The main objective of compilation and optimization techniques is to obtain performance gains when executing a compiled and optimized program instead of the uncompiled and non-optimized version. The cost of compilation itself is usually neglected as a program compiled once can be executed arbitrarily often. This also applies to the situation considered in this paper. Since the motto is "compile once, query often" [10], the essential benefits of knowledge base compilation becomes apparent when comparing the costs of querying an uncompiled version of a knowledge base $\mathcal{R}$ on the one hand and the cost of querying the compiled and optimized version of $\mathcal{R}$ on the other hand.

**Compilation Pipeline and the Reasoning Platform InfOCF.** The compilation scheme presented above has been implemented in the reasoning platform InfOCF [5]. InfOCF allows us to load knowledge bases, calculate ranking functions based on system Z [21] or c-representations, and implements a number of different nonmonotonic inference relations. Beside both system P and system Z entailment, it implements serveral inference relations based on c-representations, employing the constraint solver of SICStus Prolog using the library clp(FD) [20]. To make use of compiled knowledge bases, InfOCF implements the compilation pipeline as outlined in Fig. 2. Thus, multiple queries of the form $A \mathrel{\vert\!\sim}^{sk}_{\mathcal{R}} B$ to a knowledge base $\mathcal{R}$ are dealt with by constructing $CCR(\mathcal{R})$ once and then using $CCR(\mathcal{R})$ for answering queries. In the following we investigate the benefits of the Phases I to III of this knowledge base compilation.

$$\mathcal{R} \xrightarrow{\text{Phase I}} CR(\mathcal{R}) \xrightarrow{\text{Phase II}} PSR(\mathcal{R}) \xrightarrow{\text{Phase III}} CCR(\mathcal{R})$$

$$\xrightarrow{\text{CSP solver}} Sol(CCR(\mathcal{R}) \cup \{\neg \mathcal{X}_\mathcal{R}(B|A)\})$$

$$\Big\updownarrow = \text{(Prop. 11)}$$

$$\xrightarrow{\text{CSP solver}} Sol(PSR(\mathcal{R}) \cup \{\neg \mathcal{X}_\mathcal{R}(B|A)\})$$

$$A \vdash^{sk}_\mathcal{R} B \xrightarrow{\text{Phase I}} \neg CR_\mathcal{R}(B|A) \xrightarrow{\text{Phase II}} \neg PSR_\mathcal{R}(B|A) \xrightarrow{\text{Phase III}} \neg CCR_\mathcal{R}(B|A)$$

**Fig. 2.** Overview of the compilation pipelines for compiling knowledge bases $\mathcal{R}$ and queries $A \vdash^{sk}_\mathcal{R} B$ where $\mathcal{X} \in \{CR, PSR, CCR\}$ as in Proposition 11

**Phase I and Phase II.** In the approach presented here answering a query $A \vdash^{sk}_\mathcal{R} B$ involves the construction and solving of the constraint systems $CR(\mathcal{R})$ and $\neg CR_\mathcal{R}(B|A)$. Moreover, this is currently the only known feasible way to compute an answer for the query $A \vdash^{sk}_\mathcal{R} B$. Thus, Phase I of the knowledge base compilation is part of every implementation for skeptical c-inference existing today. The benefit of using the result of Phase I is thus the saving of the costs of transforming $\mathcal{R}$ to $CR(\mathcal{R})$; this is given by a linear function on the size of $\mathcal{R}$ since $CR(\mathcal{R})$ as given in Definition 4 and illustrated in Example 2 can be generated from $\mathcal{R}$ by some form of syntactic translation.

Furthermore, every (currently known) approach to skeptical c-inference requires to solve the constraint system $CR(\mathcal{R})$. As argued in Sect. 3, the constraint system $CR(\mathcal{R})$ can not be processed directly by a standard constraint solver. As illustrated in Example 2, according to the present state of the art several model enumerations and propositional entailment problems are solved in order to transform $CR(\mathcal{R})$ into a form usable by a constraint solver. Such a form is essentially given by the result $PSR(\mathcal{R})$ of our knowledge base compilation scheme. Hence, the benefits of reusing the results of Phase II correspond directly to the cost of constructing $PSR(\mathcal{R})$ from $CR(\mathcal{R})$.

**Proposition 12.** *Let $\Sigma$ be an alphabet with $m$ symbols and $\mathcal{R}$ a knowledge base over $\Sigma$ with $n$ conditionals. Then the complexity of constructing $PSR(\mathcal{R})$ from $CR(\mathcal{R})$ is bounded by $\mathcal{O}(n \cdot 2^m)$ propositional formula evaluations.*

Proposition 12 can be proved by formalizing the following outline. Let $\mathcal{R} = \{(B_1|A_1), \ldots, (B_n|A_n)\}$ and $\eta_i > V_{min_i} - F_{min_i}$ be a constraint in $CR(\mathcal{R})$, where $(B_i|A_i)$ is the corresponding conditional of the constraint and

$$V_{min_i} = \min_{\substack{\omega \models A_i B_i \\ \omega \models A_j \overline{B_j}}} \sum_{j \neq i} \eta_j \quad \text{and} \quad F_{min_i} = \min_{\substack{\omega \models A_i \overline{B_i} \\ \omega \models A_j \overline{B_j}}} \sum_{j \neq i} \eta_j.$$

Constructing $\Pi(V_{min_i})$ can be done by first computing the set $Mod(A_iB_i)$, i.e. checking $\omega \models A_iB_i$ for every world $\omega$ over $\Sigma$, where for a formula $F$, $Mod(F)$ denotes the set of all models of $F$. Then compute for each of the models $\omega$ in $Mod(A_iB_i)$ the set of all conditionals from $\mathcal{R}$ which are falsified by $\omega$. Thus, the costs of both steps are bounded by $\mathcal{O}(n \cdot 2^m)$ propositional formula evaluations. By an analogous argumentation, the cost for computing $\Pi(F_{min_i})$ is also bounded by $\mathcal{O}(n \cdot 2^m)$ propositional formula evaluations. By performing these computations for every constraint of the $n$ constraints in $CR(\mathcal{R})$, we can conclude that the complexity of computing $PSR(\mathcal{R})$ from $CR(\mathcal{R})$ is bounded by $\mathcal{O}(n^2 \cdot 2^m)$ propositional formula evaluations. This can be optimized by pre-computing, for every conditional in $\mathcal{R}$, the sets $Mod(A_i B_i)$ and $Mod(A_i \overline{B_i})$, and solving the prior described steps by table lookups. All in all the cost of the computation of all PSR terms for $CR(\mathcal{R})$ is bounded by $\mathcal{O}(n \cdot 2^m)$ propositional formula evaluations.

Therefore, by Proposition 12, the worst case time complexity for compiling $PSR(\mathcal{R})$ from $CR(\mathcal{R})$ is bounded exponentially in the number of propositional symbols. This bound might not be strict, but the computation is at least as hard as solving a boolean satisfiability problem, which is known to be NP complete since the computation of, e.g., the set of verifying worlds, answers the question whether a verifying model exists or not. Thus, compiling $\mathcal{R}$ to $PSR(\mathcal{R})$ and caching $PSR(\mathcal{R})$ can save up to $n \times 2^m$ formula evaluations for every query.

In InfOCF the compilation of knowledge bases is used to significantly speed up the answering of multiple queries for a single knowledge base. The compilation of a knowledge base $\mathcal{R}$ to $PSR(\mathcal{R})$ is what made investigations possible where complete inference relations are computed by determining the acceptance of every syntactically different conditional, up to semantic equivalence, for skeptical c-inference with respect to $\mathcal{R}$. The number of possible queries grows exponentially with the size of the signature, and quickly grows to several million queries. Calculating $PSR(\mathcal{R})$ for a knowledge base only once allows us to answer several hundred thousand queries easily, while this was simply not feasible without employing the compilation of the knowledge base [8].

To illustrate the practical benefits, we measured the compilation time for the knowledge base $\mathcal{R}_{bird}$ (Example 1) over a series of signatures of increasing size. The original signature $\Sigma = \{b, p, f, w\}$ from Example 1 is extended to $\Sigma_1, \ldots, \Sigma_6$ by adding new propositional variables $a_i$, such that $\Sigma_1 = \{b, p, f, w, a_1\}$, $\Sigma_2 = \{b, p, f, w, a_1, a_2\}$ and so forth, giving us signatures of size 5 to 10. Figure 3 shows the results of our measurements.

Figure 3a shows that the time required for the compilation of knowledge bases and queries grows exponentially with the number of atoms in the signature. The time required for the compilation of the query is consistently one fourth of the time required for the compilation of the knowledge base, since in this example the knowledge base contains four conditionals. Note that these empirical results correspond directly to the observation stated in Proposition 12. The compilation time for the knowledge base ranges from $0.14\,\mathrm{s}$ for a signature size of 5, to $44.26\,\mathrm{min}$ for a signature size of 10.

Figure 3b illustrates that, while the time required to answer multiple queries grows linearly with the number of queries, the absolute time can be drastically reduced by compiling the knowledge base once and reusing $CCR(\mathcal{R})$. For $\mathcal{R}_{bird}$ over the signature $\Sigma_4 = \{b, p, f, w, a_1, a_2, a_3, a_4\}$ and 20 queries, the difference between making use of our compilation and recompiling the knowledge base for every query is $14.78\,\mathrm{min}$.

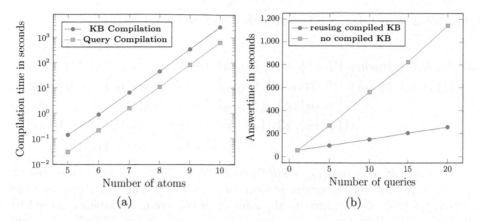

**Fig. 3.** Time measurements with $\mathcal{R}_{bird}$ from Example 1. Part (a) shows the exponential growth (logarithmic scale) of the time required for knowledge base compilation and query compilation. Part (b) shows the answer time for 1 to 20 queries for $\mathcal{R}_{bird}$ over $\Sigma_4$ with $|\Sigma_4| = 8$.

**Phase III.** Proposition 12 implies that the time costs of compiling Phase II can be exponential; corresponding benefits can thus be achieved by reusing the compilation result of Phase II. For studying the effect of Phase III, note that there are knowledge bases for which the minimization terms in $PSR(\mathcal{R})$ contain exponentially many sums. For example, for a knowledge base $\mathcal{R}_n$ of conditional facts of the form $(a_i|\top)$ for $i \in \{1, \ldots, n\}$ (cf. [7]), each conditional is verified and falsified by $2^{n-1}$ possible worlds. Therefore, both $\Pi(V_{min_i})$ and $\Pi(F_{min_i})$ contain $2^{n-1}$ elements.

The constraints in $CCR(\mathcal{R})$ only contain PSR terms in normal form with respect to the transformation system $\mathcal{T}$, i.e. there is no rule in $\mathcal{T}$ that is applicable to a PSR term in $CCR(\mathcal{R})$. Therefore, especially the two rules $(ss\text{-}V)$ and $(ss\text{-}F)$ are not applicable, which implies for every constraint $\eta > \langle \mathcal{V}, \mathcal{F} \rangle$ in $CCR(\mathcal{R})$ that there are no two elements $v_1, v_2 \in \mathcal{V}$ such that $v_1 \subseteq v_2$ holds. The same holds for the set $\mathcal{F}$. Using this fact, we can give an upper bound for the size of the constraints in $CCR(\mathcal{R})$ due to Sperner's Theorem [22], thus indicating the benefits of Phase III compiling $PSR(\mathcal{R})$ to $CCR(\mathcal{R})$.

**Proposition 13.** *For every knowledge base* $\mathcal{R} = \{(B_1|A_1), \ldots, (B_n|A_n)\}$ *and every constraint* $\eta_i > \langle \mathcal{V}, \mathcal{F} \rangle \in CCR(\mathcal{R})$ *it holds that both* $\mathcal{V}$ *and* $\mathcal{F}$ *have at most* $\binom{n}{\lfloor n/2 \rfloor}$ *elements.*

The following Example illustrates the effectiveness of $\mathcal{T}$.

*Example 9.* Consider $\Sigma = \{b, h, l, t, z\}$ and the knowledge base $\mathcal{R}_Z = \{r_1, \ldots, r_7\}$ with $r_1 = (b|z)$, $r_2 = (h|z)$, $r_3 = (h|zb)$, $r_4 = (t|zb)$, $r_5 = (t|zbh)$, $r_6 = (l|zbh)$, and $r_7 = (l|zbht)$. Optimizing the seven PSR terms in $PSR(\mathcal{R}_Z)$ yields:

$$\langle \{\{\eta_2, \eta_3, \eta_4\}, \{\eta_2, \eta_3\}, \{\eta_4, \eta_5, \eta_6\}, \{\eta_6, \eta_7\}, \{\eta_4, \eta_5\}, \varnothing\}, \ \{\{\eta_2\}, \varnothing\}\rangle$$

$$\xrightarrow{\mathcal{T}} \langle \{\varnothing\}, \{\varnothing\}\rangle$$

$$\langle\{\{\eta_1\}, \{\eta_4, \eta_5, \eta_6\}, \{\eta_6, \eta_7\}, \{\eta_4, \eta_5\}, \varnothing\}, \ \{\{\eta_1\}, \{\eta_3, \eta_4\}, \{\eta_3\}\}\rangle$$

$$\xrightarrow{\mathcal{I}} \langle\{\varnothing\}, \ \{\{\eta_1\}, \{\eta_3\}\}\rangle$$

$$\langle\{\{\eta_4, \eta_5, \eta_6\}, \{\eta_6, \eta_7\}, \{\eta_4, \eta_5\}, \varnothing\}, \ \{\{\eta_2, \eta_4\}, \{\eta_2\}\}\rangle \xrightarrow{\mathcal{I}} \langle\{\varnothing\}, \ \{\{\eta_2\}\}\rangle$$

$$\langle\{\{\eta_2, \eta_3\}, \{\eta_6, \eta_7\}, \varnothing\}, \ \{\{\eta_2, \eta_3\}, \{\eta_5, \eta_6\}, \{\eta_5\}\}\rangle \xrightarrow{\mathcal{I}} \langle\{\varnothing\}, \ \{\{\eta_2, \eta_3\}, \{\eta_5\}\}\rangle$$

$$\langle\{\{\eta_6, \eta_7\}, \varnothing\}, \ \{\{\eta_4, \eta_6\}, \{\eta_4\}\}\rangle \xrightarrow{\mathcal{I}} \langle\{\varnothing\}, \ \{\{\eta_4\}\}\rangle$$

$$\langle\{\{\eta_4, \eta_5\}, \varnothing\}, \ \{\{\eta_4, \eta_5\}, \{\eta_7\}\}\rangle \xrightarrow{\mathcal{I}} \langle\{\varnothing\}, \ \{\{\eta_4, \eta_5\}, \{\eta_7\}\}\rangle$$

$$\langle\{\varnothing\}, \ \{\{\eta_6\}\}\rangle \xrightarrow{\mathcal{I}} \langle\{\varnothing\}, \ \{\{\eta_6\}\}\rangle$$

One benefit of optimizing $PSR(\mathcal{R})$ to $CCR(\mathcal{R})$ lies in the space required to persistently store the constraint system for a knowledge base. In Example 9 the size of $CCR(\mathcal{R})$ as measured in the number of constraint variables required to describe every PSR term is almost a quarter of the size of $PSR(\mathcal{R})$. A space reduction of this scale can make a significant difference when storing larger knowledge bases persistently.

## 8   Credulous and Weakly Skeptical C-Inference

In addition to skeptical c-inference $\mathrel{|\!\sim}_{\mathcal{R}}^{sk}$ taking all c-representations of $\mathcal{R}$ into account, further inference relations based on c-representations have been suggested.

**Definition 11 (credulous c-inference, $\mathrel{|\!\sim}_{\mathcal{R}}^{cr}$ [4]).** *Let $\mathcal{R}$ be a knowledge base and let $A$, $B$ be formulas. $B$ is a credulous c-inference from $A$ in the context of $\mathcal{R}$, denoted by $A \mathrel{|\!\sim}_{\mathcal{R}}^{cr} B$, if there is a c-representation $\kappa$ for $\mathcal{R}$ such that $A \mathrel{|\!\sim}_{\kappa} B$.*

Credulous c-inference is a liberal extension of skeptical c-inference since $A \mathrel{|\!\sim}_{\mathcal{R}}^{sk} B$ implies $A \mathrel{|\!\sim}_{\mathcal{R}}^{cr} B$ for any consistent knowledge base $\mathcal{R}$ and any formulas $A, B$. While credulous c-inference has the disadvantage that we might have both, $A \mathrel{|\!\sim}_{\mathcal{R}}^{cr} B$ and $A \mathrel{|\!\sim}_{\mathcal{R}}^{cr} \overline{B}$, *weakly skeptical* c-inference is strictly more liberal than skeptical inference, but less permissive than credulous inference.

**Definition 12 (weakly skeptical c-inference, $\mathrel{|\!\sim}_{\mathcal{R}}^{ws}$ [4]).** *Let $\mathcal{R}$ be a knowledge base and let $A$, $B$ be formulas. $B$ is a weakly skeptical c-inference from $A$ in the context of $\mathcal{R}$, denoted by $A \mathrel{|\!\sim}_{\mathcal{R}}^{ws} B$, if there is a c-representation $\kappa$ for $\mathcal{R}$ such that $A \mathrel{|\!\sim}_{\kappa} B$ and there is no c-representation $\kappa'$ for $\mathcal{R}$ such that $A \mathrel{|\!\sim}_{\kappa'} \overline{B}$.*

The following example shows that weakly skeptical c-inference allows for some desirable inferences that are not possible under skeptical c-inference.

*Example 10.* Let $\mathcal{R}_{bfa} = \{(f|b), (a|b), (a|fb)\}$ be a knowledge base, where $(f|b)$ stands for *birds usually fly*, $(a|b)$ for *birds are usually animals*, and $(a|fb)$ for *flying birds are usually animals*. Consider a bird that lost its ability to fly $(b\overline{f})$. We would expect that this bird is still considered an animal $(a)$. Yet it holds that $b\overline{f} \mathrel{|\!\not\sim}_{\mathcal{R}_{bfa}}^{sk} a$. On the other hand, both $b\overline{f} \mathrel{|\!\sim}_{\mathcal{R}_{bfa}}^{cr} a$ and $b\overline{f} \mathrel{|\!\not\sim}_{\mathcal{R}_{bfa}}^{cr} \overline{a}$ hold. Therefore, from Definition 12 we get $b\overline{f} \mathrel{|\!\sim}_{\mathcal{R}_{bfa}}^{ws} a$.

In [4], a series of properties for weakly skeptical c-inference are proven, but no realization of credulous or weakly skeptical c-inference has been given. In order to show that the compilation scheme developed in this paper can also be applied for computing these inference relations, we will first show that also credulous and weakly skeptical c-inference can be modelled by CSPs.

**Proposition 14 ( $\hspace{0.1em}\hspace{-0.1em}\sim_{\mathcal{R}}^{cr}$ as a CSP).** *Let $\mathcal{R} = \{(B_1|A_1), \ldots, (B_n|A_n)\}$ be a consistent knowledge base and $A, B$ be formulas. Then the following holds:*

$$A \hspace{0.1em}\hspace{-0.1em}\sim_{\mathcal{R}}^{cr} B \quad \text{iff} \quad CR(\mathcal{R}) \cup \{CR_{\mathcal{R}}(B|A)\} \text{ has a solution.} \tag{35}$$

*Proof.* Assume $A \hspace{0.1em}\hspace{-0.1em}\sim_{\mathcal{R}}^{cr} B$ holds, i.e., $\kappa \models (B|A)$ holds for some c-representation $\kappa$ for $\mathcal{R}$. Due to the completeness of $CR(\mathcal{R})$ [3, Proposition 4], there is a solution $\vec{\eta} = (\eta_1, \ldots, \eta_n)$ of $CR(\mathcal{R})$ such that $\kappa = \kappa_{\vec{\eta}}$ and $\kappa_{\vec{\eta}}$ is defined as in Equation (3). Since $\kappa_{\vec{\eta}} \models (B|A)$, we have $\kappa_{\vec{\eta}}(AB) < \kappa_{\vec{\eta}}(A\overline{B})$ and therefore:

$$\min_{\omega \models AB} \kappa_{\vec{\eta}}(\omega) \; < \; \min_{\omega \models A\overline{B}} \kappa_{\vec{\eta}}(\omega) \tag{36}$$

Applying Eq. (3) to (36) yields Eq. (25). Thus, $\vec{\eta}$ is not just a solution of $CR(\mathcal{R})$, but also of $CR(\mathcal{R}) \cup \{CR_{\mathcal{R}}(B|A)\}$.

For the other direction, let $\vec{\eta} = (\eta_1, \ldots, \eta_n)$ be a solution of $CR(\mathcal{R}) \cup \{CR_{\mathcal{R}}(B|A)\}$. Then $\kappa_{\vec{\eta}}$ is a c-representation due to the soundness of $CR(\mathcal{R})$ [3, Proposition 3]. Furthermore, since (25) holds for $\eta_1, \ldots, \eta_n$, we have $\min_{\omega \models AB} \kappa_{\vec{\eta}}(\omega) < \min_{\omega \models A\overline{B}} \kappa_{\vec{\eta}}(\omega)$ implying $A \hspace{0.1em}\hspace{-0.1em}\sim_{\mathcal{R}}^{cr} B$. $\qquad\square$

Also weakly skeptical c-inference $\hspace{0.1em}\hspace{-0.1em}\sim_{\mathcal{R}}^{ws}$ can be characterized by employing CSPs.

**Proposition 15 ( $\hspace{0.1em}\hspace{-0.1em}\sim_{\mathcal{R}}^{ws}$ as a CSP).** *Let $\mathcal{R} = \{(B_1|A_1), \ldots, (B_n|A_n)\}$ be a consistent knowledge base and $A, B$ be formulas. Then the following holds:*

$$A \hspace{0.1em}\hspace{-0.1em}\sim_{\mathcal{R}}^{ws} B \text{ iff } CR(\mathcal{R}) \cup \{CR_{\mathcal{R}}(B|A)\} \text{ has a solution }, \text{ and} \tag{37}$$
$$CR(\mathcal{R}) \cup \{CR_{\mathcal{R}}(\overline{B}|A)\} \text{ has no solution.}$$

*Proof* From the definition of $\hspace{0.1em}\hspace{-0.1em}\sim_{\mathcal{R}}^{ws}$ (Definition 12) and the definition of $\hspace{0.1em}\hspace{-0.1em}\sim_{\mathcal{R}}^{cr}$ (Definition 11) we immediately get that $A \hspace{0.1em}\hspace{-0.1em}\sim_{\mathcal{R}}^{ws} B$ holds if and only if $A \hspace{0.1em}\hspace{-0.1em}\sim_{\mathcal{R}}^{cr} B$ holds and $A \hspace{0.1em}\hspace{-0.1em}\sim_{\mathcal{R}}^{cr} \overline{B}$ does not hold. These two conditions correspond exactly to the two conditions on the right-hand side of (37) due to Proposition 14. $\qquad\square$

Note that in the three Propositions 9, 14, and 15 different versions of constraints and different forms of arriving at negated variants of constraints are used: $CR(\mathcal{R}) \cup \{\neg CR_{\mathcal{R}}(B|A)\}$, $CR(\mathcal{R}) \cup \{CR_{\mathcal{R}}(B|A)\}$ and $CR(\mathcal{R}) \cup \{CR_{\mathcal{R}}(\overline{B}|A)\}$.

**Definition 13** *($PSR_{\mathcal{R}}(B|A)$, $CCR_{\mathcal{R}}(B|A)$). Let $\mathcal{R}, A, B$ and $V_q$ and $F_q$ as in Definition 10. The constraints $PSR_{\mathcal{R}}(B|A)$ and $CCR_{\mathcal{R}}(B|A)$ are given by:*

$$PSR_{\mathcal{R}}(B|A) : \quad 0 > \langle \Pi(V_q), \Pi(F_q) \rangle \tag{38}$$
$$CCR_{\mathcal{R}}(B|A) : \quad 0 > \mathcal{T}(\langle \Pi(V_q), \Pi(F_q) \rangle) \tag{39}$$

Using the constraints from Definition 13, the compilation of credulous and weakly skeptical queries is defined analogously to the compilation of skeptical queries. Hence, also the correctness proof for these compilations is analogue to the proof of Proposition 10:

**Proposition 16 (Correctness of compiling $\vdash^{cr}_{\mathcal{R}}$ and $\vdash^{ws}_{\mathcal{R}}$ ).** *Let $\mathcal{R}$ be a knowledge base and $A, B$ be formulas. Then:*

$$A \vdash^{cr}_{\mathcal{R}} B \quad iff \quad CCR(\mathcal{R}) \cup \{CCR_{\mathcal{R}}(B|A)\} \ has \ a \ solution. \tag{40}$$

$$A \vdash^{ws}_{\mathcal{R}} B \quad iff \quad CCR(\mathcal{R}) \cup \{CCR_{\mathcal{R}}(B|A)\} \ has \ a \ solution \ , \ and \tag{41}$$
$$CCR(\mathcal{R}) \cup \{CCR_{\mathcal{R}}(\overline{B}|A)\} \ has \ no \ solution.$$

Moreover, also Proposition 11 generalizes to credulous and weakly skeptical c-inference since the result of the three compilation phases may be combined as it is the case in (32)–(34). Since we could show that the different types of queries can be compiled using similar structures, the benefits of caching the results of knowledge base compilation as outlined in Sect. 7 also apply to computing the inference relations $\vdash^{cr}_{\mathcal{R}}$ and $\vdash^{ws}_{\mathcal{R}}$. This observation is again supported by our evaluations using InfOCF that implements credulous and weakly skeptical c-inference employing the compilation scheme developed in this paper.

## 9 Conclusions

For inference relations based on c-representations, we developed a 3-phase compilation scheme enabling up to exponential time benefits when using the compiled version of a knowledge base for answering queries. For credulous and weakly skeptical c-inference we presented a new method of realizing them as constraint satisfaction problems and for compiling them. The compilation approach has been implemented in the InfOCF system, exhibiting significant performance gains. Our future work includes investigating compilation techniques for system P inference and other forms of entailments from conditional knowledge bases.

**Acknowledgements.** This work was supported by DFG Grant BE 1700/9-1 of Prof. Dr. Christoph Beierle as part of the priority program "Intentional Forgetting in Organizations" (SPP 1921). Kai Sauerwald is supported by this Grant. We thank the anonymous reviewers for their valuable hints and comments that helped us to improve the paper.

## References

1. Adams, E.: The Logic of Conditionals. D. Reidel, Dordrecht (1975)
2. Baader, F., Nipkow, T.: Term Rewriting and All That. Cambridge University Press, Cambridge (1998)
3. Beierle, C., Eichhorn, C., Kern-Isberner, G.: Skeptical inference based on c-representations and its characterization as a constraint satisfaction problem. In: Gyssens, M., Simari, G. (eds.) FoIKS 2016. LNCS, vol. 9616, pp. 65–82. Springer, Cham (2016). https://doi.org/10.1007/978-3-319-30024-5_4

4. Beierle, C., Eichhorn, C., Kern-Isberner, G., Kutsch, S.: Skeptical, weakly skeptical, and credulous inference based on preferred ranking functions. In: ECAI-2016, vol. 285, pp. 1149–1157. IOS Press (2016)
5. Beierle, C., Eichhorn, C., Kutsch, S.: A practical comparison of qualitative inferences with preferred ranking models. KI **31**(1), 41–52 (2017)
6. Beierle, C., Kern-Isberner, G., Södler, K.: A declarative approach for computing ordinal conditional functions using constraint logic programming. In: Tompits, H., Abreu, S., Oetsch, J., Pührer, J., Seipel, D., Umeda, M., Wolf, A. (eds.) INAP/WLP -2011. LNCS (LNAI), vol. 7773, pp. 175–192. Springer, Heidelberg (2013). https://doi.org/10.1007/978-3-642-41524-1_10
7. Beierle, C., Kutsch, S.: Comparison of inference relations defined over different sets of ranking functions. In: Antonucci, A., Cholvy, L., Papini, O. (eds.) ECSQARU 2017. LNCS (LNAI), vol. 10369, pp. 225–235. Springer, Cham (2017). https://doi.org/10.1007/978-3-319-61581-3_21
8. Beierle, C., Kutsch, S.: Regular and sufficient bounds of finite domain constraints for skeptical c-inference. In: Benferhat, S., Tabia, K., Ali, M. (eds.) IEA/AIE 2017. LNCS (LNAI), vol. 10350, pp. 477–487. Springer, Cham (2017). https://doi.org/10.1007/978-3-319-60042-0_52
9. Benferhat, S., Dubois, D., Prade, H.: Possibilistic and standard probabilistic semantics of conditional knowledge bases. J. Log. Comput. **9**(6), 873–895 (1999)
10. Darwiche, A., Marquis, P.: A knowledge compilation map. J. Artif. Intell. Res. **17**, 229–264 (2002)
11. de Finetti, B.: La prévision, ses lois logiques et ses sources subjectives. Ann. Inst. Henri. Poincaré **7**(1), 1–68 (1937). English translation in Kyburg, H., Smokler, H.E. (eds.) Studies in Subjective Probability, pp. 93–158. Wiley, New York (1974)
12. Dubois, D., Prade, H.: Conditional objects as nonmonotonic consequence relations: main results. In: Proceedings of the Fourth International Conference on Principles of Knowledge Representation and Reasoning, KR 1994, San Francisco, CA, USA, pp. 170–177. Morgan Kaufmann Publishers (1994)
13. Eiter, T., Lukasiewicz, T.: Complexity results for structure-based causality. Artif. Intell. **142**(1), 53–89 (2002)
14. Goldszmidt, M., Pearl, J.: On the Relation Between Rational Closure and System-Z. UCLA, Computer Science Department (1991)
15. Goldszmidt, M., Pearl, J.: Qualitative probabilities for default reasoning, belief revision, and causal modeling. Artif. Intell. **84**(1–2), 57–112 (1996)
16. Kern-Isberner, G.: Conditionals in Nonmonotonic Reasoning and Belief Revision. LNCS (LNAI), vol. 2087. Springer, Heidelberg (2001). https://doi.org/10.1007/3-540-44600-1
17. Kern-Isberner, G.: A thorough axiomatization of a principle of conditional preservation in belief revision. Ann. Math. Artif. Intell. **40**(1–2), 127–164 (2004)
18. Knuth, D.E., Bendix, P.B.: Simple word problems in universal algebra. In: Leech, J. (ed.) Computational Problems in Abstract Algebra, pp. 263–297. Pergamon Press (1970)
19. Lehmann, D.J., Magidor, M.: What does a conditional knowledge base entail? Artif. Intell. **55**(1), 1–60 (1992)
20. Carlsson, M., Ottosson, G., Carlson, B.: An open-ended finite domain constraint solver. In: Glaser, H., Hartel, P., Kuchen, H. (eds.) PLILP 1997. LNCS, vol. 1292, pp. 191–206. Springer, Heidelberg (1997). https://doi.org/10.1007/BFb0033845

21. Pearl, J.: System Z: a natural ordering of defaults with tractable applications to nonmonotonic reasoning. In: Parikh, R. (ed.) Proceedings of the 3rd Conference on Theoretical Aspects of Reasoning About Knowledge, TARK 1990, San Francisco, CA, USA, pp. 121–135. Morgan Kaufmann Publishers Inc. (1990)
22. Sperner, E.: Ein Satz über Untermengen einer endlichen Menge. Math. Z. **27**(1), 544–548 (1928)
23. Spohn, W.: Ordinal conditional functions: a dynamic theory of epistemic states. In: Harper, W., Skyrms, B. (eds.) Causation in Decision, Belief Change, and Statistics, II, pp. 105–134. Kluwer Academic Publishers (1988)

# Characterizing and Computing Causes for Query Answers in Databases from Database Repairs and Repair Programs

Leopoldo Bertossi[✉]

School of Computer Science, Carleton University, Ottawa, Canada
bertossi@scs.carleton.ca

**Abstract.** A correspondence between database tuples as causes for query answers in databases and tuple-based repairs of inconsistent databases with respect to denial constraints has already been established. In this work, answer-set programs that specify repairs of databases are used as a basis for solving computational and reasoning problems about causes. Here, causes are also introduced at the attribute level by appealing to a both null-based and attribute-based repair semantics. The corresponding repair programs are presented, and they are used as a basis for computation and reasoning about attribute-level causes.

## 1 Introduction

Causality appears at the foundations of many scientific disciplines. In data and knowledge management, the need to represent and compute *causes* may be related to some form of *uncertainty* about the information at hand. More specifically in data management, we need to understand why certain results, e.g. query answers, are obtained or not. Or why certain natural semantic conditions are not satisfied. These tasks become more prominent and difficult when dealing with large volumes of data. One would expect the database to provide *explanations*, to understand, explore and make sense of the data, or to reconsider queries and integrity constraints (ICs). Causes for data phenomena can be seen as a kind of explanations.

Seminal work on *causality in databases* introduced in [32], and building on work on causality as found in artificial intelligence, appeals to the notions of counterfactuals, interventions and structural models [28]. Actually, [32] introduces the notions of: (a) a database tuple as an *actual cause* for a query result, (b) a *contingency set* for a cause, as a set of tuples that must accompany the cause for it to be such, and (c) the *responsibility* of a cause as a numerical measure of its strength (building on [19]).

L. Bertossi—Member of the "Millenium Institute for Foundational Research on Data", Chile.

F. Ferrarotti and S. Woltran (Eds.): FoIKS 2018, LNCS 10833, pp. 55–76, 2018.
https://doi.org/10.1007/978-3-319-90050-6_4

Most of our research on causality in databases has been motivated by an attempt to understand causality from different angles of data and knowledge management. In [11], precise reductions between causality in databases, database repairs, and consistency-based diagnosis were established; and the relationships were investigated and exploited. In [12], causality in databases was related to view-based database updates and abductive diagnosis. These are all interesting and fruitful connections among several forms of non-monotonic reasoning; each of them reflecting some form of uncertainty about the information at hand. In the case of database repairs [8], it is about the uncertainty due the non-satisfaction of given ICs, which is represented by presence of possibly multiple intended repairs of the inconsistent database.

Database repairs can be specified by means of *answer-set programs* (or *disjunctive logic programs with stable model semantics*) [15,26,27], the so-called *repair-programs*. Cf. [8,18] for details on repair-programs and additional references. In this work we exploit the reduction of database causality to database repairs established in [11], by taking advantage of repair programs for specifying and computing causes, their contingency sets, and their responsibility degrees. We show that the resulting *causality-programs* have the necessary and sufficient expressive power to capture and compute not only causes, which can be done with less expressive programs [32], but especially minimal contingency sets and responsibilities (which provably require higher expressive power). Causality programs can also be used for reasoning about causes.

As a finer-granularity alternative to tuple-based causes, we introduce a particular form of *attribute-based causes*, namely *null-based causes*, capturing the intuition that an attribute value may be the cause for a query to become true in the database. This is done by profiting from an abstract reformulation of the above mentioned relationship between tuple-based causes and tuple-based repairs. More specifically, we appeal to *null-based repairs* that are a particular kind of *attribute-based repairs*, according to which the inconsistencies of a database are solved by minimally replacing attribute values in tuples by NULL, the null-value of SQL databases with its SQL semantics. We also define the corresponding notions of contingency set and responsibility. We introduce repair (answer-set) programs for null-based repairs, so that the newly defined causes can be computed and reasoned about.

Finally, we briefly show how causality-programs can be adapted to give an account of other forms of causality in databases that are connected to other possible repair-semantics for databases.

This paper is structured as follows. Section 2 provides background material on relational databases, database causality, database repairs, and answer-set programming (ASP). Section 3 establishes correspondences between causes and repairs, and introduces in particular, null-based causes and repairs. Section 4 presents repair-programs to be used for tuple-based causality computation and reasoning.[1] Section 5 presents answer-set programs for null-based repairs and null-based causes. Finally, Sect. 6, in more speculative terms, contains a

---

[1] This section is a revised version of the extended abstract [13].

discussion about research subjects that would naturally extend this work. In order to better convey our main ideas and constructs, we present things by means of representative examples. The general formulation is left for the extended version of this paper.

## 2   Background

### 2.1   Relational Databases

A relational schema $\mathcal{R}$ contains a domain, $\mathcal{C}$, of constants and a set, $\mathcal{P}$, of predicates of finite arities. $\mathcal{R}$ gives rise to a language $\mathfrak{L}(\mathcal{R})$ of first-order (FO) predicate logic with built-in equality, $=$. Variables are usually denoted by $x, y, z, \ldots$, and sequences thereof by $\bar{x}, \ldots$; and constants with $a, b, c, \ldots$, and sequences thereof by $\bar{a}, \bar{c}, \ldots$. An *atom* is of the form $P(t_1, \ldots, t_n)$, with $n$-ary $P \in \mathcal{P}$ and $t_1, \ldots, t_n$ *terms*, i.e. constants, or variables. An atom is *ground*, aka. a *tuple*, if it contains no variables. Tuples are denoted with $\tau, \tau_1, \ldots$. A database instance, $D$, for $\mathcal{R}$ is a finite set of ground atoms; and it serves as a (Herbrand) interpretation structure for language $\mathfrak{L}(\mathcal{R})$ [30] (cf. also Sect. 2.4).

A *conjunctive query* (CQ) is a FO formula of the form $\mathcal{Q}(\bar{x}) : \exists \bar{y}\,(P_1(\bar{x}_1) \wedge \cdots \wedge P_m(\bar{x}_m))$, with $P_i \in \mathcal{P}$, and (distinct) free variables $\bar{x} := (\bigcup \bar{x}_i) \smallsetminus \bar{y}$. If $\mathcal{Q}$ has $n$ (free) variables, $\bar{c} \in \mathcal{C}^n$ is an *answer* to $\mathcal{Q}$ from $D$ if $D \models \mathcal{Q}[\bar{c}]$, i.e. $\mathcal{Q}[\bar{c}]$ is true in $D$ when the variables in $\bar{x}$ are componentwise replaced by the values in $\bar{c}$. $\mathcal{Q}(D)$ denotes the set of answers to $\mathcal{Q}$ from $D$. $\mathcal{Q}$ is a *boolean conjunctive query* (BCQ) when $\bar{x}$ is empty; and when it is *true* in $D$, $\mathcal{Q}(D) := \{true\}$. Otherwise, if it is *false*, $\mathcal{Q}(D) := \emptyset$. A *view* is predicate defined by means of a query, whose contents can be computed, if desired, by computing all the answers to the defining query.

In this work we consider integrity constraints (ICs), i.e. sentences of $\mathfrak{L}(\mathcal{R})$, that are: (a) *denial constraints* (DCs), i.e. of the form $\kappa : \neg \exists \bar{x}(P_1(\bar{x}_1) \wedge \cdots \wedge P_m(\bar{x}_m))$ (sometimes denoted $\leftarrow P_1(\bar{x}_1), \ldots, P_m(\bar{x}_m)$), where $P_i \in \mathcal{P}$, and $\bar{x} = \bigcup \bar{x}_i$; and (b) *functional dependencies* (FDs), i.e. of the form $\varphi : \neg \exists \bar{x}(P(\bar{v}, \bar{y}_1, z_1) \wedge P(\bar{v}, \bar{y}_2, z_2) \wedge z_1 \neq z_2)$. Here, $\bar{x} = \bar{y}_1 \cup \bar{y}_2 \cup \bar{v} \cup \{z_1, z_2\}$, and $z_1 \neq z_2$ is an abbreviation for $\neg z_1 = z_2$.[2] A *key constraint* (KC) is a conjunction of FDs: $\bigwedge_{j=1}^{k} \neg \exists \bar{x}(P(\bar{v}, \bar{y}_1) \wedge P(\bar{v}, \bar{y}_2) \wedge y_1^j \neq y_2^j)$, with $k = |\bar{y}_1| = |\bar{y}_2|$. A given schema may come with its set of ICs, and its instances are expected to satisfy them. If an instance does not satisfy them, we say it is *inconsistent*. In this work we concentrate on DCs, excluding, for example, *inclusion or tuple-generating dependencies* of the form $\forall \bar{x}(\varphi(\bar{x}) \rightarrow \exists \bar{y} \psi(\bar{x}', \bar{y}))$, with $\bar{x}' \subseteq \bar{x}$. See [1] for more details and background material on relational databases.

### 2.2   Causality in Databases

A notion of *cause* as an explanation for a query result was introduced in [32], as follows. For a relational instance $D = D^n \cup D^x$, where $D^n$ and $D^x$ denote the

---

[2] The variables in the atoms do not have to occur in the indicated order, but their positions should be in correspondence in the two atoms.

mutually exclusive sets of *endogenous* and *exogenous* tuples, a tuple $\tau \in D^n$ is called a *counterfactual cause* for a BCQ $\mathcal{Q}$, if $D \models \mathcal{Q}$ and $D \smallsetminus \{\tau\} \not\models \mathcal{Q}$. Now, $\tau \in D^n$ is an *actual cause* for $\mathcal{Q}$ if there exists $\Gamma \subseteq D^n$, called a *contingency set* for $\tau$, such that $\tau$ is a counterfactual cause for $\mathcal{Q}$ in $D \smallsetminus \Gamma$. This definition is based on [28].

The notion of *responsibility* reflects the relative degree of causality of a tuple for a query result [32] (based on [19]). The responsibility of an actual cause $\tau$ for $\mathcal{Q}$, is $\rho(\tau) := \frac{1}{|\Gamma|+1}$, where $|\Gamma|$ is the size of a smallest contingency set for $\tau$. If $\tau$ is not an actual cause, $\rho(\tau) := 0$. Intuitively, tuples with higher responsibility provide stronger explanations.

The partition of the database into endogenous and exogenous tuples is because the latter are somehow unquestioned, e.g. we trust them, or we may have very little control on them, e.g. when obtained from an external, trustable and indisputable data source, etc.; whereas the former are subject to experimentation and questioning, in particular, about their role in query answering or violation of ICs. The partition is application dependent, and we may not even have exogenous tuples, i.e. $D^n = D$. *Actually, in the following we will assume all the tuples in a database instance are endogenous.* (Cf. [11] for the general case, and Sect. 6 for additional discussions.) The notion of cause as defined above can be applied to monotonic queries, i.e. whose sets of answers may only grow when the database grows [11].[3] *In this work we concentrate only on conjunctive queries, possibly with built-in comparisons, such as $\neq$.*

*Example 1.* Consider the relational database $D = \{R(a_4, a_3), R(a_2, a_1), R(a_3, a_3), S(a_4), S(a_2), S(a_3)\}$, and the query $\mathcal{Q} \colon \exists x \exists y (S(x) \wedge R(x, y) \wedge S(y))$. $D$ satisfies the query, i.e. $D \models \mathcal{Q}$.

$S(a_3)$ is a counterfactual cause for $\mathcal{Q}$: if $S(a_3)$ is removed from $D$, $\mathcal{Q}$ is no longer true. So, it is an actual cause with empty contingency set; and its responsibility is 1. $R(a_4, a_3)$ is an actual cause for $\mathcal{Q}$ with contingency set $\{R(a_3, a_3)\}$: if $R(a_4, a_3)$ is removed from $D$, $\mathcal{Q}$ is still true, but further removing the contingent tuple $R(a_3, a_3)$ makes $\mathcal{Q}$ false. The responsibility of $R(a_3, a_3)$ is $\frac{1}{2}$. $R(a_3, a_3)$ and $S(a_4)$ are actual causes, with responsibility $\frac{1}{2}$. $\qquad\square$

## 2.3    Database Repairs

We introduce the main ideas by means of an example. If only deletions and insertions of tuples are admissible updates, the ICs we consider in this work can be enforced only by deleting tuples from the database, not by inserting tuples (we consider updates of attribute-values in Sect. 3.3). Cf. [8] for a survey on database repairs and consistent query answering in databases.

*Example 2.* The database $D = \{P(a), P(e), Q(a, b), R(a, c)\}$ is inconsistent with respect to (w.r.t.) the (set of) *denial constraints* (DCs) $\kappa_1 \colon \neg \exists x \exists y (P(x) \wedge Q(x, y))$, and $\kappa_2 \colon \neg \exists x \exists y (P(x) \wedge R(x, y))$; that is, $D \not\models \{\kappa_1, \kappa_2\}$.

---

[3] E.g. CQs, unions of CQs (UCQs), Datalog queries are monotonic [11, 12].

A *subset-repair*, in short an *S-repair*, of $D$ w.r.t. the set of DCs is a $\subseteq$-maximal subset of $D$ that is consistent, i.e. no proper superset is consistent. The following are S-repairs: $D_1 = \{P(e), Q(a, b), R(a, b)\}$ and $D_2 = \{P(e), P(a)\}$. A *cardinality-repair*, in short a *C-repair*, of $D$ w.r.t. the set of DCs is a maximum-cardinality, consistent subset of $D$, i.e. no subset of $D$ with larger cardinality is consistent. $D_1$ is the only C-repair. □

For an instance $D$ and a set $\Sigma$ of DCs, the sets of S-repairs and C-repairs are denoted with $Srep(D, \Sigma)$ and $Crep(D, \Sigma)$, resp.

## 2.4 Disjunctive Answer-Set Programs

We consider disjunctive Datalog programs $\Pi$ with stable model semantics [23], a particular class of answer-set programs (ASPs) [15]. They consist of a set $E$ of ground atoms, called the *extensional database*, and a finite number of rules of the form

$$A_1 \vee \ldots A_n \leftarrow P_1, \ldots, P_m, \; not \; N_1, \ldots, \; not \; N_k, \qquad (1)$$

with $0 \leq n, m, k$, and the $A_i, P_j, N_s$ are positive atoms. The terms in these atoms are constants or variables. The variables in the $A_i, N_s$ appear all among those in the $P_j$.

The constants in program $\Pi$ form the (finite) Herbrand universe $U$ of the program. The *ground version* of program $\Pi$, $gr(\Pi)$, is obtained by instantiating the variables in $\Pi$ with all possible combinations of values from $U$. The Herbrand base, $HB$, of $\Pi$ consists of all the possible atomic sentences obtained by instantiating the predicates in $\Pi$ on $U$. A subset $M$ of $HB$ is a (Herbrand) model of $\Pi$ if it contains $E$ and satisfies $gr(\Pi)$, that is: For every ground rule $A_1 \vee \ldots A_n \leftarrow P_1, \ldots, P_m, \; not \; N_1, \ldots, \; not \; N_k$ of $gr(\Pi)$, if $\{P_1, \ldots, P_m\} \subseteq M$ and $\{N_1, \ldots, N_k\} \cap M = \emptyset$, then $\{A_1, \ldots, A_n\} \cap M \neq \emptyset$. $M$ is a *minimal model* of $\Pi$ if it is a model of $\Pi$, and no proper subset of $M$ is a model of $\Pi$. $MM(\Pi)$ denotes the class of minimal models of $\Pi$.

Now, take $S \subseteq HB(\Pi)$, and transform $gr(\Pi)$ into a new, positive program $gr(\Pi) \downarrow S$ (i.e. without *not*), as follows: Delete every ground instantiation of a rule (1) for which $\{N_1, \ldots, N_k\} \cap S \neq \emptyset$. Next, transform each remaining ground instantiation of a rule (1) into $A_1 \vee \ldots A_n \leftarrow P_1, \ldots, P_m$. By definition, $S$ is a *stable model* of $\Pi$ iff $S \in MM(gr(\Pi) \downarrow S)$. A program $\Pi$ may have none, one or several stable models; and each stable model is a minimal model (but not necessarily the other way around) [27].

## 3   Causes and Database Repairs

In this section we concentrate first on *tuple-based causes* as introduced in Sect. 2.2, and establish a reduction to tuple-based database repairs. Next we provide an abstract definition of cause on the basis of an abstract repair-semantics. Finally, we instantiate the abstract semantics to define null-based causes from a particular, but natural and practical notion of attribute-based repair.

### 3.1   Tuple-Based Causes from Repairs

In [11] it was shown that causes (as represented by database tuples) for queries can be obtained from database repairs. Consider the BCQ $Q: \exists \bar{x}(P_1(\bar{x}_1) \wedge \cdots \wedge P_m(\bar{x}_m))$ that is (possibly unexpectedly) true in $D: D \models Q$. Actual causes for $Q$, their contingency sets, and responsibilities can be obtained from database repairs. First, $\neg Q$ is logically equivalent to the DC:

$$\kappa(Q): \neg \exists \bar{x}(P_1(\bar{x}_1) \wedge \cdots \wedge P_m(\bar{x}_m)). \tag{2}$$

So, if $Q$ is true in $D$, $D$ is inconsistent w.r.t. $\kappa(Q)$, giving rise to repairs of $D$ w.r.t. $\kappa(Q)$.

Next, we build differences, containing a tuple $\tau$, between $D$ and S- or C-repairs:

(a) $Diff^s(D, \kappa(Q), \tau) = \{D \smallsetminus D' \mid D' \in Srep(D, \kappa(Q)), \tau \in (D \smallsetminus D')\}$,  (3)

(b) $Diff^c(D, \kappa(Q), \tau) = \{D \smallsetminus D' \mid D' \in Crep(D, \kappa(Q)), \tau \in (D \smallsetminus D')\}$.  (4)

**Proposition 1** [11]. For an instance $D$, a BCQ $Q$, and its associated DC $\kappa(Q)$, it holds:

(a) $\tau \in D$ is an actual cause for $Q$ iff $Diff^s(D, \kappa(Q), \tau) \neq \emptyset$.
(b) For each S-repair $D'$ with $(D \smallsetminus D') \in Diff^s(D, \kappa(Q), \tau)$, $(D \smallsetminus (D' \cup \{\tau\}))$ is a subset-minimal contingency set for $\tau$.
(c) If $Diff^s(D\kappa(Q), \tau) = \emptyset$, then $\rho(\tau) = 0$. Otherwise, $\rho(\tau) = \frac{1}{|s|}$, where $s \in Diff^s(D, \kappa(Q), \tau)$ and there is no $s' \in Diff^s(D, \kappa(Q), \tau)$ with $|s'| < |s|$.
(d) $\tau \in D$ is a most responsible actual cause for $Q$ iff $Diff^c(D, \kappa(Q), \tau) \neq \emptyset$.  □

*Example 3* (Example 1 cont.). With the same instance $D$ and query $Q$, we consider the DC $\kappa(Q): \neg \exists x \exists y(S(x) \wedge R(x, y) \wedge S(y))$, which is not satisfied by $D$. Here, $Srep(D, \kappa(Q)) = \{D_1, D_2, D_3\}$ and $Crep(D, \kappa(Q)) = \{D_1\}$, with $D_1 = \{R(a_4, a_3), R(a_2, a_1), R(a_3, a_3), S(a_4), S(a_2)\}$, $D_2 = \{R(a_2, a_1), S(a_4), S(a_2), S(a_3)\}$, $D_3 = \{R(a_4, a_3), R(a_2, a_1), S(a_2), S(a_3)\}$.

For tuple $R(a_4, a_3)$, $Diff^s(D, \kappa(Q), R(a_4, a_3)) = \{D \smallsetminus D_2\} = \{\{R(a_4, a_3), R(a_3, a_3)\}\}$. So, $R(a_4, a_3)$ is an actual cause, with responsibility $\frac{1}{2}$. Similarly, $R(a_3, a_3)$ is an actual cause, with responsibility $\frac{1}{2}$. For tuple $S(a_3)$, $Diff^c(D, \kappa(Q), S(a_3)) = \{D \smallsetminus D_1\} = \{S(a_3)\}$. So, $S(a_3)$ is an actual cause, with responsibility 1, i.e. a most responsible cause.  □

It is also possible, the other way around, to characterize repairs in terms of causes and their contingency sets [11]. Actually this connection can be used to obtain complexity results for causality problems from repair-related computational problems [11]. Most computational problems related to repairs, especially C-repairs, which are related to most responsible causes, are provably hard. This is reflected in a high complexity for responsibility [11] (cf. Sect. 6 for some more details).

## 3.2   Abstract Causes from Abstract Repairs

We can extrapolate and abstract out from the characterization of causes of Sect. 3.1 by starting from an abstract *repair-semantics*, $Rep^S(D, \kappa(Q))$, which identifies a class of intended repairs of instance $D$ w.r.t. the DC $\kappa(Q)$. By definition, $Rep^S(D, \kappa(Q))$ contains instances of $D$'s schema that satisfy $\kappa(Q)$. It is commonly the case that those instances depart from $D$ in some pre-specified minimal way, and, in the case of DCs, the repairs in $Rep^S(D, \kappa(Q))$ are all sub-instances of $D$ [8] (In Sect. 3.3, we will depart from this latter assumption.).

More concretely, given a possibly inconsistent instance $D$, a general class of repair semantics can be characterized through an abstract partial-order relation, $\preceq_D$,[4] on instances of $D$'s schema that is parameterized by $D$.[5] If we want to emphasize this dependence on the *priority relation* $\preceq_D$, we define the corresponding class of repairs of $D$ w.r.t. a set on ICs $\Sigma$ as:

$$Rep^{S^{\preceq}}(D, \Sigma) := \{D' \mid D' \models \Sigma, \text{ and } D' \text{ is } \preceq_D\text{-minimal}\}. \tag{5}$$

This definition is general enough to capture different classes of repairs and in relation to different kinds of ICs, e.g. those that delete old tuples and introduce new tuples to satisfy inclusion dependencies, and also repairs that change attribute values. In particular, it is easy to verify that the classes of S- and C-repairs for DCs of Sect. 2.3 are particular cases of this definition.

Returning to a general class of repairs $Rep^S(D, \kappa(Q))$, assuming that repairs are sub-instances of $D$, and inspired by (3), we introduce:

$$Diff^S(D, \kappa(Q), \tau) := \{D \smallsetminus D' \mid D' \in Rep^S(D, \kappa(Q)), \tau \in (D \smallsetminus D')\}. \tag{6}$$

**Definition 1.** For an instance $D$, a BCQ $Q$, and a class of repairs $Rep^S(D, \kappa(Q))$:

(a) $\tau \in D$ is an *actual* S-*cause* for $Q$ iff $Diff^S(D, \kappa(Q), \tau) \neq \emptyset$.
(b) For each $D' \in Rep^S(D, \kappa(Q))$ with $(D \smallsetminus D') \in Diff^s(D, \kappa(Q), \tau)$, $(D \smallsetminus (D' \cup \{\tau\}))$ is an S-contingency set for $\tau$.
(c) The S-responsibility of an actual S-cause is as in Sect. 2.2, but considering only the cardinalities of S-contingency sets $\Gamma$. □

It should be clear that actual causes as defined in Sect. 3.1 are obtained from this definition by using S-repairs. Furthermore, it is also easy to see that each actual S-cause accompanied by one of its S-contingency sets falsifies query $Q$ in $D$.

---

[4] That is, satisfying reflexivity, transitivity and anti-symmetry, namely $D_1 \preceq_D D_2$ and $D_2 \preceq_D D_1 \Rightarrow D_1 = D_2$.

[5] These general *prioritized repairs* based on this kind of priority relations were introduced in [34], where also different priority relations and the corresponding repairs were investigated.

This abstract definition can be instantiated with different repair-semantics, which leads to different notions of cause. In the following subsection we will do this by appealing to attribute-based repairs that change attribute values in tuples by *null*, a null value that is assumed to be a special constant in $\mathcal{C}$, the set of constants for the database schema. This will allow us, in particular, to define causes at the attribute level (as opposed to tuple level) in a very natural manner.[6]

### 3.3    Attribute-Based Causes

Database repairs that are based on changes of attribute values in tuples have been considered in [7,8,10], and implicitly in [9] to hide sensitive information in a database $D$ via minimal virtual modifications of $D$. In the rest of this section we make explicit this latter approach and exploit it to define and investigate attribute-based causality (cf. also [11]). First we provide a motivating example.

*Example 4.* Consider the database instance $D = \{S(a_2), S(a_3), R(a_3, a_1), R(a_3, a_4), R(a_3, a_5)\}$, and the query $\mathcal{Q}: \exists x \exists y (S(x) \wedge R(x, y))$. $D$ satisfies $\mathcal{Q}$, i.e. $D \models \mathcal{Q}$.

The three $R$-tuples in $D$ are actual causes, but clearly the value $a_3$ for the first attribute of $R$ is what matters in them, because it enables the join, e.g. $D \models S(a_3) \wedge R(a_3, a_1)$. This is only indirectly captured through the occurrence of different values accompanying $a_3$ in the second attribute of $R$-tuples as causes for $\mathcal{Q}$.

Now consider the database instance $D_1 = \{S(a_2), S(a_3), R(null, a_1), R(null, a_4), R(null, a_5)\}$, where *null* stands for the null value as used in SQL databases, which cannot be used to satisfy a join. Now, $D' \not\models \mathcal{Q}$. The same occurs with the instances $D_2 = \{S(a_2), S(null), R(a_3, a_1), R(a_3, a_4), R(a_3, a_5)\}$, and $D_3 = \{S(a_2), S(null), R(null, a_1), R(null, a_4), R(null, a_5)\}$, among others that are obtained from $D$ only through changes of attribute values by *null*.    □

In the following we assume the special constant *null* may appear in database instances and can be used to verify queries and constraints. We assume that all atoms with built-in comparisons, say $null \, \theta \, null$, and $null \, \theta \, c$, with $c$ a non-null constant, are all false for $\theta \in \{=, \neq, <, >, \ldots\}$. In particular, since a join, say $R(\ldots, x) \wedge S(x, \ldots)$, can be written as $R(\ldots, x) \wedge S(x', \ldots) \wedge x = x'$, it can never be satisfied through *null*. This assumption is compatible with the use of NULL in SQL databases (cf. [10, Sect. 4] for a detailed discussion, also [9, Sect. 2]).

Consider an instance $D = \{\ldots, R(c_1, \ldots, c_n), \ldots\}$ that may be inconsistent with respect to a set of DCs. The allowed repair updates are changes of attribute values by *null*, which is a natural choice, because this is a deterministic solution that appeals to *the* generic data value used in SQL databases to reflect

---

[6] Cf. also [10, Sects. 4, 5] for an alternative repair-semantics based on both null- and tuple-based repairs w.r.t. general sets of ICs and their repair programs. They could also be used to define a corresponding notion of cause.

the uncertainty and incompleteness in/of the database that inconsistency produces.[7] In order to keep track of changes, we may introduce numbers as first arguments in tuples, as global, unique tuple identifiers (tids). So, $D$ becomes $D = \{\ldots, R(i; c_1, \ldots, c_n), \ldots\}$, with $i \in \mathbb{N}$. The tid is a value for what we call the 0-th attribute of $R$. With $id(t)$ we denote the id of the tuple $t \in D$, i.e. $id(R(i; c_1, \ldots, c_n)) = i$.

If $D$ is updated to $D'$ by replacement of (non-tid) attribute values by $null$, and the value of the $j$-th attribute in $R$, $j > 0$, is changed to $null$, then the change is captured as the string $R[i; j]$, which identifies that the change was made in the tuple with id $i$ in the $j$-th $position$ (or attribute) of predicate $R$. These strings are collected forming the set:[8]

$$\Delta^{null}(D, D') := \{R[i; j] \mid R(i; c_1, \ldots, c_j, \ldots, c_n) \in D, c_j \neq null, \text{ becomes}$$
$$R(i; c'_1, \ldots, null, \ldots, c'_n) \in D'\}.$$

For example, if $D = \{R(1; a, b), S(2; c, d), S(3; e, f)\}$ is changed into $D' = \{R(1; a, null), S(2; null, d), S(3; null, null)\}$, then $\Delta^{null}(D, D') = \{R[1; 2], S[2; 1], S[3; 1], S[3; 2]\}$.

For database instances with the constant $null$, IC satisfaction is defined by treating $null$ as in SQL databases, in particular, joins and comparisons in them cannot be satisfied through $null$ (cf. [10, Sect. 4] for a precise formal treatment). This is particularly useful to restore consistency w.r.t. DCs, which involve combinations of (unwanted) joins.

*Example 5* (Example 1 cont.). Still with instance $D = \{S(a_2), S(a_3), R(a_3, a_1), R(a_3, a_4), R(a_3, a_5)\}$, consider the DC (the negation of $\mathcal{Q}$) $\kappa : \neg \exists x \exists y (S(x) \wedge R(x, z))$. Since $D \not\models \kappa$, $D$ is inconsistent.

The updated instance $D_1 = \{S(a_2), S(null), R(a_3, a_1), R(a_3, a_4), R(a_3, a_5)\}$ (among others updated with $null$) is consistent: $D_1 \models \kappa$.    □

**Definition 2.** A *null-based repair* of $D$ with respect to a set of DCs $\Sigma$ is a consistent instance $D'$, such that $\Delta^{null}(D, D')$ is minimal under set inclusion.[9] $Rep^{null}(D, \Sigma)$ denotes the class of null-based repairs of $D$ with respect to $\Sigma$.[10] A *cardinality-null-based repair* $D'$ minimizes $|\Delta^{null}(D, D')|$.    □

---

[7] Repairs based on updates of attribute values using other constants of the domain have been considered in [35]. We think the developments in this section could be applied to them.

[8] The condition $c_i \neq null$ in its definition is needed in case the initially given instance already contain nulls.

[9] An alternative, but equivalent formulation can be found in [9].

[10] Our setting allows for a uniform treatment of general and combined DCs, including those with (in)equality and other built-ins, FDs, and KCs. However, for the latter and in SQL databases, it is common that NULL is disallowed as a value for a key-attribute, among other issues. This prohibition, that we will ignore in this work, can be accommodated in our definition. For a detailed treatment of repairs w.r.t. sets of ICs that include FDs, see [10, Sects. 4, 5].

We can see that the null-based repairs are the minimal elements of the partial order between instances defined by: $D_1 \leq_D^{null} D_2$ iff $\Delta^{null}(D, D_1) \subseteq \Delta^{null}(D, D_2)$.

*Example 6.* Consider $D = \{R(1; a_2, a_1), R(2; a_3, a_3), R(3; a_4, a_3), S(4; a_2), S(5; a_3), S(6; a_4)\}$ that is inconsistent w.r.t. the DC

$$\kappa: \neg \exists xy (S(x) \wedge R(x, y) \wedge S(y)).$$

Here, the class of null-based repairs, $Rep^{null}(D, \kappa)$, consists of:

$D_1 = \{R(1; a_2, a_1), R(2; a_3, a_3), R(3; a_4, a_3), S(4; a_2), S(5; null), S(6; a_4)\}$,
$D_2 = \{R(1; a_2, a_1), R(2; null, a_3), R(3; a_4, null), S(4; a_2), S(5; a_3), S(6; a_4)\}$,
$D_3 = \{R(1; a_2, a_1), R(2; null, a_3), R(3; a_4, a_3), S(4; a_2), S(5; a_3), S(6; null)\}$,
$D_4 = \{R(1; a_2, a_1), R(2; a_3, null), R(3; a_4, null), S(4; a_2), S(5; a_3), S(6; a_4)\}$,
$D_5 = \{R(1; a_2, a_1), R(2; a_3, null), R(3; null, a_3), S(4; a_2), S(5; a_3), S(6; a_4)\}$,
$D_6 = \{R(1; a_2, a_1), R(2; a_3, null), R(3; a_4, a_3), S(4; a_2), S(5; a_3), S(6; null)\}$.

Here, $\Delta^{null}(D, D_2) = \{R[2; 1], R[3; 2]\}$, $\Delta^{null}(D, D_3) = \{R[2; 1], S[6; 1]\}$ and $\Delta^{null}(D, D_1) = \{S[5; 1]\}$. The latter is a cardinality-null-based repair.     □

According to the motivation provided at the beginning of this section, we can now define causes appealing to the generic construction in (6), and using in it the class of null-based repairs of $D$. Since repair actions in this case are attribute-value changes, causes can be defined at both the tuple and attribute levels. The same applies to the definition of responsibility. First, inspired by (6), for a tuple $\tau: R(i; c_1, \ldots, c_n) \in D$, we introduce:[11]

$$Diff^{null}(D, \kappa(\mathcal{Q}), R[i; c_j]) := \{\Delta^{null}(D, D') \mid D' \in Rep^{null}(D, \kappa(\mathcal{Q})), \quad (7)$$
$$R[i; j] \in \Delta^{null}(D, D')\}.$$

**Definition 3.** For $D$ an instance and $\mathcal{Q}$ a BCQ, and $\tau \in D$ be a tuple of the form $R(i; c_1, \ldots, c_n)$.

(a) $R[i; c_j]$ is a *null-attribute-based (actual) cause* for $\mathcal{Q}$ iff $Diff^{null}(D, \kappa(\mathcal{Q}), R[i; c_j]) \neq \emptyset$, i.e. the value $c_j$ in $\tau$ is a cause if it is changed into a null in some repair.
(b) $\tau$ is a *null-tuple-based (actual) cause* for $\mathcal{Q}$ if some $R[i; c_j]$ is a *null-attribute-based cause* for $\mathcal{Q}$, i.e. the whole tuple $\tau$ is a cause if at least one of its attribute values is changed into a null in some repair.
(c) The responsibility, $\rho^{a\text{-}null}(R[i; c_j])$, of a *null-attribute-based cause* $R[i; c_j]$ for $\mathcal{Q}$, is the inverse of $min\{|\Delta^{null}(D, D')| \; : \; R[i; j] \in \Delta^{null}(D, D'), \text{and } D' \in Rep^{null}(D, \kappa(\mathcal{Q}))\}$. Otherwise, it is 0.

---

[11] This is not a particular case of (6), because it does not contain full tuples.

(d) The responsibility, $\rho^{t\text{-}null}(\tau)$, of a null-tuple-based cause $\tau$ for $\mathcal{Q}$, is the inverse of $min\{|\Delta^{null}(D, D')| \;\; : \;\; R[i; j] \in \Delta^{null}(D, D'), \text{ for some } j, \text{ and } D' \in Rep^{null}(D, \kappa(\mathcal{Q}))\}$. Otherwise, it is 0. $\qquad\square$

In cases (c) and (d) we minimize over the number of changes in a repair. However, in case (d), of a tuple-cause, any change made in one of its attributes is considered in the minimization. For this reason, the minimum may be smaller than the one for a fixed attribute value change; and so the responsibility at the tuple level may be greater than that at the attribute level. More precisely, if $\tau = R(i; c_1, \ldots, c_n) \in D$, and $R[i; c_j]$ is a null-attribute-based cause, then: $\rho^{a\text{-}null}(R[i; c_j]) \leq \rho^{t\text{-}null}(\tau)$.

*Example 7* (Example 6 cont.). Consider $R(2; a_3, a_3) \in D$. Its projection on its first (non-id) attribute, $R[2; a_3]$, is a null-attribute-based cause since $R[2; 1] \in \Delta^{null}(D, D_2)$. Also $R[2; 1] \in \Delta^{null}(D, D_3)$. Since $|\Delta^{null}(D, D_2)| = |\Delta^{null}(D, D_3)| = 2$, we obtain $\rho^{a\text{-}null}(R[2; 1]) = \frac{1}{2}$. Clearly $R(2; a_3, a_3)$ is a null-tuple-based cause for $\mathcal{Q}$, with $\rho^{t\text{-}null}(R(2; a_3, a_3)) = \frac{1}{2}$. $\qquad\square$

*Example 8* (Example 4 cont.). The instance with tids is $D = \{S(1; a_2), S(2; a_3), R(3; a_3, a_1), R(4; a_3, a_4), R(5; a_3, a_5)\}$. The only null-based repairs are $D_1$ and $D_2$, with $\Delta^{null}(D, D_1) = \{R[3; 1], R[4; 1], R[5; 1]\}$ and $\Delta^{null}(D, D_2) = \{S[2; 1]\}$.

The values $R[3; a_3], R[4; a_3], R[5; a_3], S[2; a_3]$ are all null-attribute-based causes for $\mathcal{Q}$. Notice that $\rho^{a\text{-}null}(R[3; a_3]) = \rho^{a\text{-}null}(R[4; a_3]) = \rho^{a\text{-}null}(R[5; a_3]) = \frac{1}{3}$, while $\rho^{a\text{-}null}(R[3; a_1]) = \rho^{a\text{-}null}(R[4; a_4]) = \rho^{a\text{-}null}(R[5; a_5]) = 0$, that the value ($a_3$) in the first arguments of the $R$-tuples has a non-zero responsibility, while the values in the second attribute have responsibility 0. $\qquad\square$

Notice that the definition of tuple-level responsibility, i.e. case (d) in Definition 3, does not take into account that a same id, $i$, may appear several times in a $\Delta^{null}(D, D')$. In order to do so, we could redefine the size of the latter by taking into account those multiplicities. For example, if we decrease the size of the $\Delta$ by one with every repetition of the id, the responsibility for a cause may (only) increase, which makes sense.

In Sect. 5 we will provide repair programs for null-based repairs, which can be used as a basis for specifying and computing null-attribute-based causes.

## 4 Specifying Tuple-Based Causes

Given a database $D$ and a set of ICs, $\Sigma$, it is possible to specify the S-repairs of $D$ w.r.t. a set $\Sigma$ of DCs, introduced in Sect. 2.3, by means of an answer-set program $\Pi(D, \Sigma)$, in the sense that the set, $Mod(\Pi(D, \Sigma))$, of its stable models is in one-to-one correspondence with $Srep(D, \Sigma)$ [5,18] (cf. [8] for more references). In the following, to ease the presentation, we consider a single denial constraint[12]

$$\kappa: \neg \exists \bar{x}(P_1(\bar{x}_1) \wedge \cdots \wedge P_m(\bar{x}_m)).$$

---

[12] It is possible to consider combinations of DCs and FDs, corresponding to UCQs, possibly with $\neq$, [11].

Although not necessary for S-repairs, it is useful on the causality side having global unique tuple identifiers (tids), i.e. every tuple $R(\bar{c})$ in $D$ is represented as $R(t; \bar{c})$ for some integer $t$ that is not used by any other tuple in $D$. For the repair program we introduce a nickname predicate $R'$ for every predicate $R \in \mathcal{R}$ that has an extra, final attribute to hold an annotation from the set $\{d, s\}$, for "delete" and "stays", resp. Nickname predicates are used to represent and compute repairs.

The *repair-ASP*, $\Pi(D, \kappa)$, for $D$ and $\kappa$ contains all the tuples in $D$ as facts (with tids), plus the following rules:

$$P_1'(t_1; \bar{x}_1, \mathsf{d}) \vee \cdots \vee P_m'(t_n; \bar{x}_m, \mathsf{d}) \leftarrow P_1(t_1; \bar{x}_1), \ldots, P_m(t_m; \bar{x}_m).$$
$$P_i'(t_i; \bar{x}_i, \mathsf{s}) \leftarrow P_i(t_i; \bar{x}_i),\ not\ P_i'(t_i; \bar{x}_i, \mathsf{d}),\ i = 1, \cdots, m.$$

A stable model $M$ of the program determines a repair $D'$ of $D$: $D' := \{P(\bar{c}) \mid P'(t; \bar{c}, \mathsf{s}) \in M\}$, and every repair can be obtained in this way [18]. For an FD, say $\varphi \colon \neg \exists x y z_1 z_2 v w (R(x, y, z_1, v) \wedge R(x, y, z_2, w) \wedge z_1 \neq z_2)$, which makes the third attribute functionally depend upon the first two, the repair program contains the rules:

$$R'(t_1; x, y, z_1, v, \mathsf{d}) \vee R'(t_2; x, y, z_2, w, \mathsf{d}) \leftarrow R(t_1; x, y, z_1, v), R(t_2; x, y, z_2, w),$$
$$z_1 \neq z_2.$$
$$R'(t; x, y, z, v, \mathsf{s}) \leftarrow R(t; x, y, z, v),\ not\ R'(t; x, y, z, v, \mathsf{d}).$$

For DCs and FDs, the repair program can be made non-disjunctive by moving all the disjuncts but one, in turns, in negated form to the body of the rule [5,18]. For example, the rule $P(a) \vee R(b) \leftarrow Body$, can be written as the two rules $P(a) \leftarrow Body, not R(b)$ and $R(b) \leftarrow Body, not P(a)$. Still the resulting program can be *non-stratified* if there is recursion via negation [27], as in the case of FDs, and DCs with self-joins.

*Example 9* (Example 3 cont.).    For the DC $\kappa(\mathcal{Q}) \colon \neg \exists x \exists y (S(x) \wedge R(x, y) \wedge S(y))$, the repair-ASP contains the facts (with tids) $R(1; a_4, a_3), R(2; a_2, a_1),$ $R(3; a_3, a_3), S(4; a_4), S(5; a_2), S(6; a_3)$, and the rules:

$$S'(t_1; x, \mathsf{d}) \vee R'(t_2; x, y, \mathsf{d}) \vee S'(t_3; y, \mathsf{d}) \leftarrow S(t_1; x), R(t_2; x, y), S(t_3; y). \quad (8)$$
$$S'(t; x, \mathsf{s}) \leftarrow S(t; x),\ not\ S'(t; x, \mathsf{d}).\ \text{etc.}$$

Repair $D_1$ is represented by the stable model $M_1$ containing $R'(1; a_4, a_3, \mathsf{s}), R'(2; a_2, a_1, \mathsf{s}), R'(3; a_3, a_3, \mathsf{s}), S'(4; a_4, \mathsf{s}), S'(5; a_2, \mathsf{s})$, and $S'(6; a_3, \mathsf{d})$. □

Now, in order to specify causes by means of repair-ASPs, we concentrate, according to (3), on the differences between $D$ and its repairs, now represented by $\{P(\bar{c}) \mid P(t; \bar{c}, \mathsf{d}) \in M\}$, the deleted tuples, with $M$ a stable model of the repair-program. They are used to compute actual causes and their $\subseteq$-minimal contingency sets, both expressed in terms of tids.

The actual causes for the query can be represented by their tids, and can be obtained by posing simple queries to the program under the *uncertain or brave* semantics that makes true what is true in *some* model of the repair-ASP.[13] In this case, $\Pi(D, \kappa(\mathcal{Q})) \models_{brave} Cause(t)$, where the *Cause* predicate is defined on top of $\Pi(D, \kappa(\mathcal{Q}))$ by the rules: $Cause(t) \leftarrow R'(t; x, y, \mathsf{d})$ and $Cause(t) \leftarrow S'(t; x, \mathsf{d})$.

For contingency sets for a cause, given the repair-ASP for a DC $\kappa(\mathcal{Q})$, a new binary predicate $CauCont(\cdot, \cdot)$ will contain a tid for cause in its first argument, and a tid for a tuple belonging to its contingency set. Intuitively, $CauCont(t, t')$ says that $t$ is an actual cause, and $t'$ accompanies $t$ as a member of the former's contingency set (as captured by the repair at hand or, equivalently, by the corresponding stable model). More precisely, for each pair of not necessarily different predicates $P_i, P_j$ in $\kappa(\mathcal{Q})$ (they could be the same if it has self-joins or there are several DCs), introduce the rule $CauCont(t, t') \leftarrow P_i'(t; \bar{x}_i, \mathsf{d}), P_j'(t'; \bar{x}_j, \mathsf{d}), t \neq t'$, with the inequality condition only when $P_i$ and $P_j$ are the same predicate (it is superfluous otherwise).

*Example 10* (Examples 3 and 9 cont.). The repair-ASP can be extended with the following rules to compute causes with contingency sets:

$$CauCont(t, t') \leftarrow S'(t; x, \mathsf{d}), R'(t'; u, v, \mathsf{d}).$$
$$CauCont(t, t') \leftarrow S'(t; x, \mathsf{d}), S'(t'; u, \mathsf{d}), t \neq t'.$$
$$CauCont(t, t') \leftarrow R'(t; x, y, \mathsf{d}), S'(t'; u, \mathsf{d}).$$
$$CauCont(t, t') \leftarrow R'(t; x, y, \mathsf{d}), R'(t'; u, v, \mathsf{d}), t \neq t'.$$

For the stable model $M_2$ corresponding to repair $D_2$, we obtain $CauCont(1, 3)$ and $CauCont(3, 1)$, from the repair difference $D \setminus D_2 = \{R(a_4, a_3), R(a_3, a_3)\}$. □

We can use extensions of ASP with set- and numerical aggregation to build the contingency set associated to a cause, e.g. the DLV system [29] by means of its DLV-Complex extension [17] that supports set membership and union as built-ins. We introduce a binary predicate *preCont* to hold a cause (id) and a possibly non-maximal set of elements from its contingency set, and the following rules:

$$preCont(t, \{t'\}) \leftarrow CauCont(t, t').$$
$$preCont(t, \#union(C, \{t''\})) \leftarrow CauCont(t, t''), preCont(t, C),$$
$$not \ \#member(t'', C).$$
$$Cont(t, C) \leftarrow preCont(t, C), \ not \ HoleIn(t, C).$$
$$HoleIn(t, C) \leftarrow preCont(t, C), CauCont(t, t'),$$
$$not \ \#member(t', C).$$

The first two rules build the contingency set for an actual cause (within a repair or stable model) by starting from a singleton and adding additional elements

---

[13] As opposed to the *skeptical or cautious* semantics that sanctions as true what is true in *all* models. Both semantics as supported by the DLV system [29].

from the contingency set. The third rule, that uses the auxiliary predicate *HoleIn* makes sure that a set-maximal contingency set is built from a pre-contingency set to which nothing can be added.

The responsibility for an actual cause $\tau$, with tid $t$, as associated to a repair $D'$ (with $\tau \notin D'$) associated to a model $M$ of the extended repair-ASP, can be computed by counting the number of $t'$s for which $CauCont(t, t') \in M$. This responsibility will be maximum within a repair (or model): $\rho(t, M) := 1/(1 + |d(t, M)|)$, where $d(t, M) := \{CauCont(t, t') \in M\}$. This value can be computed by means of the *count* function, supported by DLV [24], as follows:

$$pre\text{-}rho(t, n) \leftarrow \#count\{t' : CauCont(t, t')\} = n,$$

followed by the rule computing the responsibility:

$$rho(t, m) \leftarrow m * (pre\text{-}rho(t, n) + 1) = 1.$$

Or, equivalently, via $1/|d(M)|$, with $d(M) := \{P(t'; \bar{c}, \mathsf{d}) \mid P(t'; \bar{c}, \mathsf{d}) \in M\}$.

Each model $M$ of the program so far will return, for a given tid that is an actual cause, a *maximal-responsibility contingency set within that model*: no proper subset is a contingency set for the given cause. However, its cardinality may not correspond to the (global) *maximum* responsibility for that tuple. Actually, what we need is $\rho(t) := \max\{\rho(t, M) \mid M \text{ is a model}\}$, which would be an off-line computation, i.e. not within the program. Fortunately, this is not needed since each C-repair gives such a global maximum. So, we need to specify and compute only maximum-cardinality repairs, i.e. C-repairs.

C-repairs can be specified by means of repair-ASPs as above [3], but adding *weak-program constraints* [16, 29]. In this case, since we want repairs that minimize the number of deleted tuples, for each database predicate $P$, we introduce the weak-constraint:

$$:\sim P(t; \bar{x}), \ P'(t; \bar{x}, \mathsf{d}).$$

In a model $M$ the body can be satisfied, and then the program constraint violated, but the number of violations is kept to a minimum (among the models of the program without the weak-constraints).[14] A repair-ASP with these weak constraints specifies repairs that minimize the number of deleted tuples; and *minimum-cardinality* contingency sets and maximum responsibilities can be computed, as above.

The approach to specification of causes can be straightforwardly extended via repair programs for several DCs to deal with unions of BCQs (UBCQs), which are also monotonic.

*Example 11.* Consider $D = \{P(a), P(e), Q(a, b), R(a, c)\}$ and the query $\mathcal{Q} := \mathcal{Q}_1 \vee \mathcal{Q}_2$, with $\mathcal{Q}_1 : \exists xy(P(x) \wedge Q(x, y))$ and $\mathcal{Q}_2 : \exists xy(P(x) \wedge R(x, y))$. It generates

---

[14] In contrast, *hard* program-constraints, of the form $\leftarrow Body$, eliminate the models where they are violated, i.e. where *Body* is satisfied. Weak constraints as those above are sometimes denoted with $\Leftarrow P(t; \bar{x}), P'(t; \bar{x}, \mathsf{d})$.

the set of DCs: $\Sigma = \{\kappa_1, \kappa_2\}$, with $\kappa_1 :\leftarrow P(x), Q(x, y)$ and $\kappa_2 :\leftarrow P(x), R(x, y)$. Here, $D \models Q$ and, accordingly, $D$ is inconsistent w.r.t. $\Sigma$.

The actual causes for $Q$ in $D$ are: $P(a), Q(a, b), R(a, c)$, and $P(a)$ is the most responsible cause. $D_1 = \{P(a), P(e)\}$ and $D_2 = \{P(e), Q(a, b), R(a, c)\}$ are the only S-repairs; $D_2$ is also the only C-repair for $D$. The repair program for $D$ w.r.t. $\Sigma$ contains one rule like (8) for each DC in $\Sigma$. The rest is as above in this section.                                                                         □

*Remark 1.* When dealing with a set of DCs, each repair rule of the form (8) is meant to solve the corresponding, local inconsistency, even if there is inter-action between the DCs, i.e. atoms in common, and other inconsistencies are solved at the same time. However, the minimal-model property of stable models makes sure that in the end a minimal set of atoms is deleted to solve all the inconsistencies [18].                                                                    □

## 5    Specifying Attribute-Based Repairs and Causes

*Example 12.* Consider the instance $D = \{P(1, 2), R(2, 1)\}$ for schema $\mathcal{R} = \{P(A, B), R(B, C)\}$. With tuple identifiers it takes the form $D = \{P(1; 1, 2), R(2; 2, 1)\}$. Consider also the DC:[15]

$$\kappa: \ \neg\exists x \exists y \exists z (P(x, y) \land R(y, z)), \tag{9}$$

which is violated by $D$.

Now, consider the following alternative, updated instances $D_i$, each them obtained by replacing attribute values by *null*:

| $D_1$ | $\{P(1; 1, null), R(2; 2, 1)\}$ |
|---|---|
| $D_2$ | $\{P(1; 1, 2), R(2; null, 1)\}$ |
| $D_3$ | $\{P(1; 1, null), R(2; null, 1)\}$ |

The sets of changes can be identified with the set of changed positions, as in Sect. 3.3, e.g. $\Delta^{null}(D, D_1) = \{P[1; 2]\}$ and $\Delta^{null}(D, D_2) = \{R[2; 2]\}$ (remember that the tuple id goes always in position 0). These $D_i$ are all consistent, but $D_1$ and $D_2$ are the only null-based repairs of $D$; in particular they are $\leq_D^{null}$-minimal: The sets of changes $\Delta^{null}(D, D_1)$ and $\Delta^{null}(D, D_2)$ are incomparable under set inclusion. $D_3$ is not $\leq_D^{null}$-minimal, because $\Delta^{null}(D, D_3) = \{P[1; 2], R[2; 2]\} \supsetneq \Delta^{null}(D, D_2)$.                                                                                          □

As in Sect. 4, null-based repairs can be specified as the stable models of a dis-junctive ASP, the so-called *repair program*. We show next these repair programs by means of Example 12.

The repair programs for null-based repairs are inspired by ASP-programs that are used to specify virtually and minimally updated versions of a database

---

[15] It would be easy to consider tids in queries and view definitions, but they do not contribute to the final result and will only complicate the notation. So, we skip tuple ids whenever possible.

$D$ that is protected from revealing certain view contents [9]. This is achieved by replacing direct query answering on $D$ by simultaneously querying (under the certain semantics) the virtual versions of $D$.

When we have more than one DC, notice that, in contrast to the tuple-based semantics, where we can locally solve each inconsistency without considering inconsistencies w.r.t. other DCs (cf. Remark 1), a tuple that is subject to a local attribute-value update (into *null*) to solve one inconsistency, may need further updates to solve other inconsistencies. For example, if we add in Example 12 the DC $\kappa'$: $\neg\exists x\exists y(P(x,y) \wedge R(y,x))$, the updates in repair $D_1$ have to be further continued, producing: $P(1; null, null), R(2; null, null)$. In other words, every locally updated tuple is considered to: "be in transition" or "being updated" only (not necessarily in a definitive manner) until all inconsistencies are solved.

The above remark motivates the annotation constants that repair programs will use now, for null-based repairs. The intended, informal semantics of annotation constants is shown in the following table. (The precise semantics is captured through the program that uses them.)

| Annotation | Atom | The tuple $R(\bar{a})$ ... |
|---|---|---|
| **u** | $R(t; \bar{a}, \mathbf{u})$ | Tuple result of an update |
| **fu** | $R(t; \bar{a}, \mathbf{fu})$ | Final update of a tuple |
| **t** | $R(t; \bar{a}, \mathbf{t})$ | An initial or updated tuple |
| **s** | $R(t; \bar{a}, \mathbf{s})$ | Definitive, stays in the repair |

More precisely, for each database predicate $R \in \mathcal{R}$, we introduce a copy of it with an extra, final attribute (or argument) that contains an annotation constant. So, a tuple of the form $R(t; \bar{c})$ would become an annotated atom of the form $R'(t; \bar{c}, \mathbf{a})$. The annotation constants are used to keep track of virtual updates, i.e. of old and new tuples: An original tuple $R(t; \bar{c})$ may be successively updated, each time replacing an attribute value by *null*, creating tuples of the form $R(t; \bar{c}', \mathbf{u})$. Eventually the tuple will suffer no more updates, at which point it will become of the form $R'(t; \bar{c}'', \mathbf{fu})$. In the transition, to check the satisfaction of the DCs, it will be combined with other tuples, which can be updated versions of other tuples or tuples in the database that have never been updated. Both kinds of tuples are uniformly annotated with $R'(t', \bar{d}, \mathbf{t})$. In this way, several, possibly interacting DCs can be handled. The tuples that eventually form a repaired version of the original database are those of the form $R'(t; \bar{e}, \mathbf{s})$, and are the final versions of the updated original tuples or the original tuples that were never updated.

In $R'(t; \bar{a}, \mathbf{fu})$, annotation $\mathbf{fu}$ means that the atom with tid $t$ has reached its final update (during the program evaluation). In particular, $R(t; \bar{a})$ has already been updated, and $\mathbf{u}$ should appear in the new, updated atom, say $R'(t; \bar{a}', \mathbf{u})$, and this tuple cannot be updated any further (because relevant updateable attribute values have already been replaced by *null* if necessary). For example, consider a tuple $R(t; a, b) \in D$. A new tuple $R(t; a, null)$ is obtained by updating $b$ into $null$. Therefore, $R'(t; a, null, \mathbf{u})$ denotes the updated tuple. If this tuple is not updated any further, it will also eventually appear as $R'(t; a, null, \mathbf{fu})$, indicating it is a final update.[16] (Cf. rules 3. in Example 13.)

The repair program uses these annotations to go through different steps, until its stable models are computed. Finally, the atoms needed to build a repair are read off by restricting a model of the program to atoms with the annotation $\mathbf{s}$. The following example illustrates the main ideas and issues.

*Example 13* (Example 12 cont.). Consider $D = \{P(1, 2), R(2, 1)\}$ and the DC: $\kappa \colon \neg \exists x \exists y \exists z (P(x, y) \wedge R(y, z))$. The repair program $\Pi(D, \{\kappa\})$ is as follows: (it uses several auxiliary predicates to make rules *safe*, i.e. with all their variables appearing in positive atoms in their bodies)

1. $P(1; 1, 2).\ R(2; 2, 1).$ (initial database)

2. $P'(t_1; x, null, \mathbf{u}) \vee R'(t_2; null, z, \mathbf{u}) \leftarrow P'(t_1; x, y, \mathbf{t}),\ R'(t_2; y, z, \mathbf{t}), y \neq null.$

3. $\qquad P'(t; x, y, \mathbf{fu}) \leftarrow P'(t; x, y, \mathbf{u}), not\ aux_{P.1}(t; x, y),\ not\ aux_{P.2}(t; x, y).$

   $aux_{P.1}(t; x, y) \leftarrow P'(t; null, y, \mathbf{u}), P(t; x, z), x \neq null.$

   $aux_{P.2}(t; x, y) \leftarrow P'(t; x, null, \mathbf{u}), P(t; z, y), y \neq null.$ (idem for $R$)

4. $\qquad P'(t; x, y, \mathbf{t}) \leftarrow P(t; x, y).$

   $P'(t; x, y, \mathbf{t}) \leftarrow P'(t; x, y, \mathbf{u}).$ (idem for $R$)

5. $\qquad P'(t; x, y, \mathbf{s}) \leftarrow P'(t; x, y, \mathbf{fu}).$ (idem for $R$)

   $P'(t; x, y, \mathbf{s}) \leftarrow P(t; x, y),\ not\ aux_P(t).$

   $aux_P(t) \leftarrow P'(t; u, v, \mathbf{u}).$

In this program tids in rules are handled as variables. Constant $null$ in the program is treated as any other constant. This is the reason for the condition $y \neq null$ in the body of 2, to avoid considering the join through $null$ a violation of the DC.[17] A quick look at the program shows that the original tids are never destroyed and no new tids are created, which simplifies keeping track of tuples under repair updates. It also worth mentioning that for this particular example, with a single DC, a much simpler program could be used, but we keep the general form that can be applied to multiple, possibly interacting DCs.

Facts in 1. belong to the initial instance $D$, and become annotated right away with $\mathbf{t}$ by rules 4. The most important rules of the program are those in 2. They enforce one step of the update-based repair-semantics in the presence of $null$ and using $null$ (yes, already having nulls in the initial database is not a problem). Rules in 2. capture in the body the violation of DC; and in the head, the intended way of restoring consistency, namely making one of the attributes participating in a join take value $null$.

---

[16] Under null-based repairs no tuples are deleted or inserted, so the original tids stay all in the repairs and none is created.

[17] If instead of (9) we had $\kappa \colon \neg \exists x \exists y \exists z (P(x, y) \wedge R(y, z) \wedge y < 3)$, the new rule body could be $P'(t_1; x, y, \mathbf{t}), R'(t_2; y, z, \mathbf{t}), y < 3$, because $null < 3$ would be evaluated as false.

Rules in 3. collect the final updated versions of the tuples in the database, as those whose values are never replaced by a *null* in another updated version.

Rules in 4. annotate the original atoms and also new versions of updated atoms. They all can be subject to additional updates and have to be checked for DC satisfaction, with rule 2. Rules in 5. collect the tuples that stay in the final state of the updated database, namely the original and never updated tuples plus the final, updated versions of tuples. In this program *null* is treated as any other constant.                                          □

**Proposition 2.** There is a one-to-one correspondence between the *null*-based repairs of $D$ w.r.t. a set of DCs $\Sigma$ and the stable models of the repair program $\Pi(D, \Sigma)$. More specifically, a repair $D'$ can be obtained by collecting the s-annotated atoms in a stable model $M$, i.e. $D' = \{P(\bar{c}) \mid P'(t; \bar{c}, \mathbf{s}) \in M\}$; and every repair can be obtained in this way.[18]                                          □

*Example 14* (Example 13 cont.). The program has two stable models: (the facts in 1. and the *aux*-atoms are omitted)

$$M_1 = \{P'(1; 1, 2, \mathbf{t}), \; R'(2; 2, 1, \mathbf{t}), \underline{R'(2; 2, 1, \mathbf{s})}, P'(1; 1, null, \mathbf{u}), P'(1; 1, null, \mathbf{t}),$$
$$P'(1; 1, null, \mathbf{fu}), \underline{P'(1; 1, null, \mathbf{s})}\}.$$
$$M_2 = \{P'(1; 1, 2, \mathbf{t}), \; R'(2; 2, 1, \mathbf{t}), \underline{P'(1; 1, 2, \mathbf{s})}, R'(2; null, 1, \mathbf{u}), R'(2; null, 1, \mathbf{t}),$$
$$R'(2; null, 1, \mathbf{fu}), \underline{R'(2; null, 1, \mathbf{s})}\}.$$

The repairs are built by selecting the underlined atoms: $D_1 = \{P(1, null), R(2, 1)\}$ and $D_2 = \{P(1, 2), R(null, 1)\}$. They coincide with those in Example 12.                                          □

Finally, and similarly to the use of repair programs for cause computation in Sect. 4, we can use the new repair programs to compute null-attribute-based causes (we do not consider here null-tuple-based causes, nor the computation of responsibilities, all of which can be done along the lines of Sect. 4). All we need to do is add to the repair program the definition of a cause predicate, through rules of the form:

$$Cause(t; i; v) \leftarrow R'(t; \bar{x}, null, \bar{z}, \mathbf{s}), R(t; \bar{x}', v, \bar{z}'), v \neq null,$$

(with $v$ and *null* the body in the same position $i$), saying that value $v$ in the $i$-th position in original tuple with tid $t$ is a null-attribute-based cause. The rule collects the original values (with their tids and positions) that have been changed into *null*. To the program in Example 13 we would add the rules (with similar rules for predicate $R$)

$$Cause(t; 1; x) \leftarrow P'(t; null, y, \mathbf{s}), P(t; x, y').$$
$$Cause(t; 2; y) \leftarrow P'(t; x, null, \mathbf{s}), P(t; x', y).$$

---

[18] The proof of this claim is rather long, and is similar in spirit to the proof that tuple-based database repairs w.r.t. integrity constraints [6,8] can be specified by means of disjunctive logic programs with stable model semantics (cf. [4,14]).

# 6 Discussion

*Complexity.* Computing causes for CQs can be done in polynomial time in data [32], which also holds for UBCQs [11]. In [12] it was established that cause computation for Datalog queries falls in the second level of the polynomial hierarchy (PH). As has been established in [11,32], the computational problems associated to contingency sets and responsibility are at the second level of PH, in data complexity.

On the other side, our repairs programs, and so our causality-ASPs, can be transformed into non-disjunctive, unstratified programs [5,18], whose reasoning tasks are also at the second level of PH (in data) [22]. It is worth mentioning that the ASP approach to causality via repairs programs could be extended to deal with queries that are more complex than CQs or UCQs, e.g. Datalog queries and queries that are conjunctions of literals (that were investigated in [33]).

*Causality Programs and ICs.* The original causality setting in [32] does not consider ICs. An extension of causality under ICs was proposed in [12]. Under it, the ICs have to be satisfied by the databases involved, i.e. the initial one and those obtained by cause and contingency-set deletions. When the query at hand is monotonic,[19] monotonic ICs, i.e. for which growing with the database may only produce more violations (e.g. denial constraints and FDs), are not much of an issue since they stay satisfied under deletions associated to causes. So, the most relevant ICs are non-monotonic, such as inclusion dependencies, e.g. $\forall xy(R(x,y) \rightarrow S(x))$. These ICs can be represented in a causality-program by means of (strong) program constraints. In the running example, we would have, for tuple-based causes, the constraint: $\leftarrow R'(t,x,y,\mathsf{s}), not\ S'(t',x,\mathsf{s})$.[20]

*Negative CQs and Inclusion Dependencies.* In this work we investigated CQs, and what we did can be extended to UCQs. However, it is possible to consider queries that are conjunctions of literals, i.e. atoms or negations thereof, e.g. $\mathcal{Q}: \exists x \exists y (P(x,y) \wedge \neg S(x))$.[21] (Causes for these queries were investigated in [33].) If causes are defined in terms of counterfactual deletions (as opposed to insertions that can also be considered for these queries), then the repair counterpart can be constructed by transforming the query into the unsatisfied *inclusion dependency* (ID): $\forall x \forall y (P(x,y) \rightarrow S(x))$. Repairs w.r.t. this kind of IDs that allow only tuple deletions were considered in [20], and repairs programs for them in [18]. Causes for CQs in the presence of IDs were considered in [12].

*Endogenous and Prioritized Causes and Repairs.* As indicated in Sect. 3.2, different kinds of causes can be introduced by considering different repair-semantics. Apart from those investigated in this work, we could consider *endogenous repairs*,

---

[10] I.e. the set of answers may only grow when the instance grows.

[20] Or better, to make it *safe*, by a rule and a constraint: $aux(x) \leftarrow S'(t',x,\mathsf{s})$ and $\leftarrow R'(t,x,y,\mathsf{s}), not\ aux(x)$.

[21] They should be *safe* in the sense that a variable in a negative literals has to appear in some positive literal too.

which are obtained by removing only (pre-specified) endogenous tuples [11]. In this way we could give an account of causes as in Sect. 2.2, but considering the partition of the database between endogenous and exogenous tuples.

Again, considering the abstract setting of Section 3.2, with the generic class of repairs $Rep^{S^{\preceq}}(D, \Sigma)$, it is possible to consider different kinds of *prioritized repairs* [34], and through them introduce *prioritized actual causes*. Repair programs for the kinds of priority relations $\preceq$ investigated in [34] could be constructed from the ASPs introduced and investigated in [25] for capturing different optimality criteria. The repair programs could be used, as done in this work, to specify and compute the corresponding prioritized actual causes and responsibilities.

*Optimization of Causality Programs.* Different queries, but of a fixed form, about causality could be posed to causality programs or directly to the underlying repair programs. Query answering could benefit from query-dependent, magic-set-based optimizations of causality and repair programs as reported in [18]. Implementation and experimentation in general are left for future work.

*Connections to Belief Revision/Update.* As discussed in [2] (cf. also [8]), there are some connections between database repairs and belief updates as found in knowledge representation, most prominently with [21]. In [3], some connections were established between repair programs and *revision programs* [31]. The applicability of the latter in a causality scenario like ours becomes a matter of possible investigation.

**Acknowledgements.** This research was supported by NSERC Discovery Grant #06148. Part of this work was done while the author was spending a sabbatical at the "Database and Artificial Intelligence" Group of the Technical University of Vienna with support from the "Vienna Center for Logic and Algorithms" and the Wolfgang Pauli Society. The author is extremely grateful for their support and hospitality, and especially to Prof. Georg Gottlob for making the stay possible. Many thanks to the anonymous reviewers for their excellent feedback.

# References

1. Abiteboul, S., Hull, R., Vianu, V.: Foundations of Databases. Addison-Wesley, Boston (1995)
2. Arenas, M., Bertossi, L., Chomicki, J.: Consistent query answers in inconsistent databases. In: Proceedings of PODS, pp. 68–79 (1999)
3. Arenas, M., Bertossi, L., Chomicki, J.: Answer sets for consistent query answers. Theor. Pract. Log. Program. **3**(4&5), 393–424 (2003)
4. Barcelo, P.: Applications of annotated predicate calculus and logic programs to querying inconsistent databases. MSc thesis PUC, Chile (2002). http://people.scs.carleton.ca/~bertossi/papers/tesisk.pdf
5. Barceló, P., Bertossi, L., Bravo, L.: Characterizing and computing semantically correct answers from databases with annotated logic and answer sets. In: Bertossi, L., Katona, G.O.H., Schewe, K.-D., Thalheim, B. (eds.) SiD 2001. LNCS, vol. 2582, pp. 7–33. Springer, Heidelberg (2003). https://doi.org/10.1007/3-540-36596-6_2

6. Bertossi, L.: Consistent query answering in databases. ACM SIGMOD Rec. **35**(2), 68–76 (2006)
7. Bertossi, L., Bravo, L., Franconi, E., Lopatenko, A.: The complexity and approximation of fixing numerical attributes in databases under integrity constraints. Inf. Syst. **33**(4), 407–434 (2008)
8. Bertossi, L.: Database Repairing and Consistent Query Answering. Synthesis Lectures on Data Management. Morgan & Claypool, San Rafael (2011)
9. Bertossi, L., Li, L.: Achieving data privacy through secrecy views and null-based virtual updates. IEEE Trans. Knowl. Data Eng. **25**(5), 987–1000 (2013)
10. Bertossi, L., Bravo, L.: Consistency and trust in peer data exchange systems. Theor. Pract. Log. Program. **17**(2), 148–204 (2017)
11. Bertossi, L., Salimi, B.: From causes for database queries to repairs and model-based diagnosis and back. Theor. Comput. Syst. **61**(1), 191–232 (2017)
12. Bertossi, L., Salimi, B.: Causes for query answers from databases: datalog abduction, view-updates, and integrity constraints. Int. J. Approx. Reason. **90**, 226–252 (2017)
13. Bertossi, L.: The causality/repair connection in databases: causality-programs. In: Moral, S., Pivert, O., Sánchez, D., Marín, N. (eds.) SUM 2017. LNCS (LNAI), vol. 10564, pp. 427–435. Springer, Cham (2017). https://doi.org/10.1007/978-3-319-67582-4_33
14. Bravo, L.: Handling inconsistency in databases and data integration systems. Ph.D. thesis, Carleton University, Department of Computer Science (2007). http://people.scs.carleton.ca/~bertossi/papers/Thesis36.pdf
15. Brewka, G., Eiter, T., Truszczynski, M.: Answer set programming at a glance. Commun. ACM **54**(12), 93–103 (2011)
16. Buccafurri, F., Leone, N., Rullo, P.: Enhancing disjunctive datalog by constraints. IEEE Tran. Knowl. Data Eng. **12**(5), 845–860 (2000)
17. Calimeri, F., Cozza, S., Ianni, G., Leone, N.: An ASP system with functions, lists, and sets. In: Erdem, E., Lin, F., Schaub, T. (eds.) LPNMR 2009. LNCS (LNAI), vol. 5753, pp. 483–489. Springer, Heidelberg (2009). https://doi.org/10.1007/978-3-642-04238-6_46
18. Caniupan-Marileo, M., Bertossi, L.: The consistency extractor system: answer set programs for consistent query answering in databases. Data Know. Eng. **69**(6), 545–572 (2010)
19. Chockler, H., Halpern, J.Y.: Responsibility and blame: a structural-model approach. J. Artif. Intell. Res. **22**, 93–115 (2004)
20. Chomicki, J., Marcinkowski, J.: Minimal-change integrity maintenance using tuple deletions. Inf. Comput. **197**(1–2), 90–121 (2005)
21. Chou, T., Winslett, M.: A model-based belief revision system. J. Autom. Reason. **12**, 157–208 (1994)
22. Dantsin, E., Eiter, T., Gottlob, G., Voronkov, A.: Complexity and expressive power of logic programming. ACM Comput. Surv. **33**(3), 374–425 (2001)
23. Eiter, T., Gottlob, G., Mannila, H.: Disjunctive datalog. ACM Trans. Database Syst. **22**(3), 364–418 (1997)
24. Faber, W., Pfeifer, G., Leone, N., Dell'Armi, T., Ielpa, G.: Design and implementation of aggregate functions in the DLV system. Theor. Pract. Log. Program. **8**(5–6), 545–580 (2008)
25. Gebser, M., Kaminski, R., Schaub, T.: Complex optimization in answer set programming. Theor. Pract. Log. Program. **11**(4–5), 821–839 (2011)

26. Gebser, M., Kaminski, R., Kaufmann, B., Schaub, T.: Answer Set Solving in Practice. Synthesis Lectures on Artificial Intelligence and Machine Learning. Morgan & Claypool Publishers, San Rafael (2012)
27. Gelfond, M., Kahl, Y.: Knowledge Representation and Reasoning, and the Design of Intelligent Agents. Cambridge University Press, Cambridge (2014)
28. Halpern, J., Pearl, J.: Causes and explanations: a structural-model approach: part 1. Br. J. Philos. Sci. **56**, 843–887 (2005)
29. Leone, N., Pfeifer, G., Faber, W., Eiter, T., Gottlob, G., Perri, S., Scarcello, F.: The DLV system for knowledge representation and reasoning. ACM Trans. Comput. Log. **7**(3), 499–562 (2006)
30. Lloyd, J.W.: Foundations of Logic Programming. Springer, Heidelberg (1987). https://doi.org/10.1007/978-3-642-83189-8
31. Marek, V., Truszczynski, M.: Revision programming. Theor. Comput. Sci. **190**(2), 241–277 (1998)
32. Meliou, A., Gatterbauer, W., Moore, K.F., Suciu, D.: The complexity of causality and responsibility for query answers and non-answers. Proc. VLDB Endow. **4**(1), 34–45 (2010)
33. Salimi, B., Bertossi, L., Suciu, D., Van den Broeck, G.: Quantifying causal effects on query answering in databases. In: Proceedings of TaPP (2016)
34. Staworko, S., Chomicki, J., Marcinkowski, J.: Prioritized repairing and consistent query answering in relational databases. Ann. Math. Artif. Intell. **64**(2–3), 209–246 (2012)
35. Wijsen, J.: Database repairing using updates. ACM Trans. Database Syst. **30**(3), 722–768 (2005)

# Inferences from Attribute-Disjoint and Duplicate-Preserving Relational Fragmentations

Joachim Biskup$^{(\boxtimes)}$ and Marcel Preuß

Fakultät für Informatik, Technische Universität Dortmund, Dortmund, Germany
{joachim.biskup,marcel.preuss}@cs.tu-dortmund.de

**Abstract.** The transmission of own and partly confidential data to another agent, e.g., for cloud computing, comes along with the risk of enabling the receiver to infer information he is not entitled to learn. We consider a specific countermeasure against unwanted inferences about associations between data values whose combination of attributes are declared to be sensitive. This countermeasure fragments a relation instance into attribute-disjoint and duplicate-preserving projections such that no sensitive attribute combination is contained in any projection. Though attribute-disjointness is intended to make a reconstruction of original data impossible for the receiver, the goal of inference-proofness will not always be accomplished. In particular, inferences might be based on combinatorial effects, since duplicate-preservation implies that the frequencies of value associations in visible projections equals those in the original relation instance. Moreover, the receiver might exploit functional dependencies, numerical dependencies and tuple-generating dependencies, as presumably known from the underlying database schema. We identify several conditions for a fragmentation to violate inference-proofness. Besides complementing classical results about lossless decompositions, our results could be employed for designing better countermeasures.

**Keywords:** Attribute-disjointness · Cloud computing
Database relation · Confidentiality · Duplicate-preservation
Fragmentation · Frequencies · Functional dependency
Inference-proofness · Numerical dependency · Projection
Sensitive association · Tuple-generating dependency

## 1 Introduction

A data owner might consider to somehow fragment his relational data and to only make the resulting fragments accessible to another agent, which, for a prominent example, might offer some cloud services to the owner. Such a fragmentation then aims at hiding some information about sensitive associations contained in the original data to the service agent. Thus, though in principle being seen as

© Springer International Publishing AG, part of Springer Nature 2018
F. Ferrarotti and S. Woltran (Eds.): FoIKS 2018, LNCS 10833, pp. 77–96, 2018.
https://doi.org/10.1007/978-3-319-90050-6_5

cooperating, the service agent is also perceived as potentially attacking the confidentiality interests of the owner by attempting to infer hidden original information from accessible data and, if applicable, additional background knowledge. Accordingly, the data owner should carefully choose a fragmentation technique and thoroughly investigate whether the resulting fragmentation of his specific data sufficiently satisfies his confidentiality interests.

Our considerations are motivated by the particular proposal of "combining fragmentation and encryption to protect privacy in data storage" [14], a technique which converts a given relation instance and some confidentiality requirements on the schema level into a set of vertical relational fragments all of which might be accessible for an attacker. We focus on three aspects of this proposal:

- The resulting fragmentation is *attribute-disjoint*, i.e., fragments do not share attributes and thus seem to be unrelated. Moreover, regarding internal storage and external display, the sequence of subtuple instances in a fragment is supposed to be fully independent of the sequences in other fragments, and of any sequence of tuple instances in the hidden data as well.
- Each fragment is *duplicate-preserving* and thus, for any values under attributes in the fragment, their frequency (i.e., number of occurrences) in the fragment is equal to their frequency in the hidden underlying relation instance.
- The attacker might see *all* fragments, and thus he is supposed to take advantage of knowing several views on the same hidden data.

Focusing on the enforcement of confidentiality requirements by means of fragmentation, we will purposely ignore all cryptographic aspects and neglect the details of reconstructability of the original data by the data owner. For further simplifying our investigations, we will also assume that none of the attributes get encrypted values:

- The fragmentation is *full*, i.e., it covers all attributes of the original relation.

For this setting, we will discuss various kinds of *successful inference attacks* based on observable *frequencies* of visible data items and on additional background knowledge in the form of *data dependencies* and actual *content data*, in spite of the *attribute-disjointness* at first glance generating unrelated fragments. In doing so, we will present some fundamental assertions about such inferences, together with some complexity considerations. The resulting main contribution will be the identification of both the crucial role of frequencies and the challenge to future research how to block their exploitation.

*Example 1 (Fragmentation with encryption).* This example illustrates the techniques proposed by Ciriani et al. [14] by means of a simple relational schema *Patient* providing attributes ACTION, S(*ocial*)S(*ecurity*)N(*umber*), (*Patient*)NAME, ILLNESS, (*Prescribed*) MEDICATION, HURTBY, and (*Treating*) DOCTOR to record a unique tuple instance for each medical action. Figure 1 shows a relation instance containing 4 tuple instances.

| Patient | ACTION | SSN | NAME | ILLNESS | MEDICATION | HURTBY | DOCTOR |
|---------|--------|-----|------|---------|------------|--------|--------|
| $r_1$ | 1234 | Hellmann | Borderline | MedA | Hellmann | White |
| $r_2$ | 2345 | Dooley | Laceration | MedB | McKinley | Waren |
| $r_3$ | 3456 | McKinley | Laceration | MedB | Dooley | Waren |
| $r_4$ | 3456 | McKinley | Concussion | MedC | Dooley | Waren |

**Fig. 1.** A relation instance for the relational schema *Patient*

| $F_1$ | ACTION | NAME |
|-------|--------|------|
| $r_2$ | Dooley |
| $r_4$ | McKinley |
| $r_3$ | McKinley |
| $r_1$ | Hellmann |

| $F_2$ | ILLNESS | DOCTOR |
|-------|---------|--------|
| | Laceration | Waren |
| | Borderline | White |
| | Concussion | Waren |
| | Laceration | Waren |

| $F_3$ | MEDICATION | HURTBY |
|-------|------------|--------|
| | MedC | Dooley |
| | MedB | Dooley |
| | MedA | Hellmann |
| | MedB | McKinley |

**Fig. 2.** A simplified fragmentation (without encryption related parts needed for reconstruction by the owner) of the relation instance of the schema *Patient*

Suppose that the owner wants to hide values of the singleton attribute set {SSN}, and value combinations for associations expressed by the non-singleton attribute sets {NAME, DOCTOR}, {NAME, MEDICATION}, {NAME, HURTBY}, and {ILLNESS, HURTBY}, respectively. Single values can only be protected by encryption. But value combinations of a sensitive association can be handled by fragmentation, i.e., by distributing the values occurring in an association among different fragments obtained by projections without duplicate removal, under the condition that the fragments do not overlap and, thus, are not obviously linked. One possible option is to partition the attributes of the schema – in this example except SSN – into the mutually disjoint sets {ACTION, NAME}, {ILLNESS, DOCTOR}, and {MEDICATION, HURTBY}. Then, for each of them a fragment is generated that makes the values of the attribute set visible and stores the encryption of all remaining values under a new attribute, say ENC.
In principle, but no longer considered in the remainder, we would have to manage the encrypted parts to enable the data owner to reconstruct the original tuple instances. And we have to suitably scramble the (sub)tuple instances generated for a fragment to block inferences based on their sequence displayed. A possible result, simplified as indicated, is shown in Fig. 2.

Unfortunately, however, though often being helpful, in this example the attribute-disjointness does not guarantee the confidentiality requirements. In fact, while the fragment instances to $F_1$ and $F_2$ contain 4 subtuple instances each, there are 3 occurrences of the value "Waren" under the attribute DOCTOR for $F_2$ but only 2 occurrences of a value *different* from "McKinley" under the attribute NAME for $F_1$. Hence, any matching of the fragment instances must combine at least one of the occurrences of "Waren" with an occurrence of "McKinley". Thus, exploiting the visible frequencies of occurrences in the fragmentation, the occurrence of the value combination (McKinley, Waren) under the attribute combination {NAME, DOCTOR} in the hidden original relation instance is inferrable, violating the confidentiality requirements. In general, besides frequencies we would also have to consider the impact of data dependencies.

After briefly introducing basic definitions in Sect. 2, we will present and discuss fundamental risks of harmful inferences by exploiting first only observable frequencies (Sect. 3) and subsequently additionally background knowledge in the form of data dependencies, in turn inspecting functional dependencies and more general numerical dependencies (Sect. 4) and finally tuple-generating dependencies with a multivalued dependency as a special case (Sect. 5). In the concluding Sect. 6, we point to related work, summarize our achievements, outline future research on blocking inferences of the kind treated, and highlight the connection of our study with the broader topics of inversion of database queries and reasoning under uncertainty.

## 2  Basic Definitions

Abstracting from any application, ignoring encryption related parts and the owner's need for reconstruction, and assuming the covering of all attributes, our investigations will treat fragmentations of the kind defined below using standard terminology [1], together with their impact on the protection of associations.

**Definition 1 (Full attribute-disjoint and duplicate-preserving fragmentation).** *Let $(R(X), \mathcal{SC})$ be a relational schema with attribute set $X$ and data dependencies $\mathcal{SC}$, and $\mathcal{X} = \langle X_1, \dots, X_m \rangle$ be a sequence of attribute sets partitioning $X$, i.e., the sets $X_i$ are nonempty and mutually disjoint subsets of $X$ such that $X = \bigcup_{i=1,\dots,m} X_i$. Then $\mathcal{F} = \langle F_1(X_1), \dots, F_m(X_m) \rangle$ is the fragmentation schema derived from $R(X)$ and $\mathcal{X}$.*

*Furthermore, let $r$ be a relation instance of $(R(X), \mathcal{SC})$, i.e., a finite set of tuples (without duplicates) over the attributes in $X$ satisfying all data dependencies in $\mathcal{SC}$, containing $n$ different tuples. Then, seen as an operator, the fragmentation schema $\mathcal{F}$ generates the fragmentation instance $\mathcal{F}(r) = \langle f_1, \dots, f_m \rangle$ by taking the projections of $r$ on $X_i$, respectively, without removing duplicates and then probabilistically scrambling the order of them regarding storage or display, $f_i = \bar{\pi}^?_{X_i}(r)$, such that each fragment instance $f_i$ has $n$ subtuple instances[1].*

We emphasize that the setting of Definition 1 requires

- the *absence of duplicates* in original relation instances $r$ (meant to be actually stored under the relational schema $(R(X), \mathcal{SC})$ on the one hand, and
- the *suppression of duplicate removal* when generating the fragmentation instances by taking projections according to the fragmentation schema on the other hand.

---

[1] Where appropriate and convenient, we distinguish between a *tuple* and a *tuple instance*: we call an *assignment* of values to some attributes a tuple, whereas we refer to an *occurrence* of a tuple as a tuple instance having in mind that a relation instance allowing duplicates might contain multiple instances of the same tuple.

While the duplicate preservation under fragmentation is essential for the techniques proposed by Ciriani et al. [14], in an alternative approach, technically, we could allow duplicates already in original relation instances. However, most practical applications and both constraint-enforcement and query-answering based on first-order logic usually assume set semantics rather than multiset semantics for original relation instances and, accordingly, so do we.

**Definition 2 (Syntactically protected association).** *Let* $\mathcal{F} = \langle F_1(X_1), \ldots, F_m(X_m) \rangle$ *be the fragmentation schema derived from a relational schema* $(R(X), \mathcal{SC})$ *and a sequence* $\mathcal{X}$ *of attribute sets partitioning* $X$. *Then an attribute set* $C$ *is an* association syntactically protected *by* $\mathcal{F}$ *iff* $C$ *is a non-singleton subset of* $X$ *but not contained in any of the attribute sets* $X_i$.

Unfortunately, as already mentioned before, the syntactic splitting condition of Definition 2 might fail to ensure strong versions of confidentiality. In particular, an actually occurring value combination of an only syntactically protected association might be inferrable by means of considering so-called matchings.

**Definition 3 (Matching-inferrable value combination).** *Let* $\mathcal{F} = \langle F_1(X_1), \ldots, F_m(X_m) \rangle$ *be the fragmentation schema derived from a relational schema* $(R(X), \mathcal{SC})$ *and a sequence* $\mathcal{X}$ *of attribute sets partitioning* $X$. *Let* $\mathcal{F}(r) = f = \langle f_1, \ldots, f_m \rangle$ *be the fragmentation instance generated from the relation instance* $r$ *of* $(R(X), \mathcal{SC})$. *Furthermore, let attribute set* $C$ *be an association syntactically protected by* $\mathcal{F}$. *A subtuple* $\mu$ *over* $C$ *is called a* matching-inferrable value combination *iff it is generated by* each $\mathcal{SC}$-admissible matching $M$ *of the subtuples in* $f$.

*Here, a* matching *is formed by iteratively taking one subtuple instance from each fragment instance* $f_i$ *and combining them until the fragment instances (all having the same number* $n$ *of subtuple instances) are (simultaneously) exhausted. In this way, a matching* $M$ *generates a collection* $M(r)$ *of* $n$ *tuple instances – possibly containing duplicates – over the attributes of* $X$. *Moreover, a matching* $M$ *is called* $\mathcal{SC}$-admissible *if* $M(r)$ *is an instance of* $(R(X), \mathcal{SC})$, *i.e., a set (containing no duplicates) satisfying all data dependencies in* $\mathcal{SC}$.

*Remark 1.* From an attacking observer's point of view, a matching $M$ can be seen as *one* possibility to undo the unknown scrambling of subtuple instances when the fragment instances have been generated. Some possibilities, however, might produce duplicates or result in a violation of data dependencies, and thus have to be discarded. Accordingly, if an attacker can find out that a subtuple $\mu$ over an attribute set $C$ is generated by *all* remaining $\mathcal{SC}$-admissible possibilities, he can conclude that this subtuple can be obtained by undoing the actually employed scrambling and, thus, occurs in the hidden relation instance. Hence, for a deliberately syntactically protected association $C$, such a subtuple would be matching-inferrable: a successful inference from an attacker's point of view, but a security violation from the owner's point of view.

*Remark 2.* More formally, if $C$ is a deliberately syntactically protected association, then an attacking receiver is suspected to be interested in the *certain* part (formalized by *intersection*) of the *projections* on $C$ of the *relation instances* $r'$ of the *schema* $(R(X), \mathcal{SC})$ contained in the *inversion* of the observed *fragmentation instance* $f = \mathcal{F}(r)$ under the *fragmentation schema* $\mathcal{F}$, i.e., to determine

$$\mathcal{F}_{\mathcal{SC}}^{-1,C}(f) = \bigcap \{\, \pi_C(r') \mid r' \text{ is relation instance of } (R(X), \mathcal{SC}) \text{ and } \mathcal{F}(r') = f \}.$$

For the attacker, a conceptual solution is given by the matching procedure sketched above, due to the straightforward equation

$$\mathcal{F}_{\mathcal{SC}}^{-1,C}(f) = \bigcap \{\, \pi_C(M(r)) \mid M(r) \text{ is formed from } \mathcal{F}(r) = f \text{ and } \mathcal{SC}\text{-admissible} \}.$$

In contrast, the data owner would aim at assuring that the visible fragmentation $f$ does not allow any possibilistic inference, i.e., that $\mathcal{F}_{\mathcal{SC}}^{-1,C}(f) = \emptyset$.

*Remark 3.* The data owner's goal to ensure $\mathcal{F}_{\mathcal{SC}}^{-1,C}(f) = \emptyset$ is also equivalent to the notion of *inference-proofness* as employed by the concept of Controlled Interaction Execution [6], under a confidentiality policy suitably expressing the need to hide value combinations over $C$, as elaborated in [10, 11]. Though without referring to particular formal logic, and similarly as in an abstract version of Controlled Interaction Execution [7], the goal roughly says that a suitable logic-based formalization of the setting does not entail any sentence that logically expresses the subtuple $\mu$ over $C$.

## 3   Frequency-Based Inferences Without Dependencies

To start with, we briefly remind a classical result of the theory of relational databases, see [1], that vertically decomposing a relation instance $r$ – *without* duplicates – into covering projections $\pi_{X_i}(r)$ for $i = 1, \ldots, m$ – while *removing* duplicates – might be *lossy*, i.e., the (natural) join $\bowtie_{j=1 \ldots m} \pi_{X_i}(r)$ of the projections might be a *strict superset* of the original relation instance $r$. In this case, in general an observer of the projections cannot decide whether a *specific* tuple generated by the join is spurious, i.e., not contained in the original relation instance. However, if the observer knows the original cardinality, he can easily decide whether or not the join has produced spurious tuples, just by comparing $\|r\|$ with $\| \bowtie_{j=1 \ldots m} \pi_{X_i}(r) \|$. Further we remind that for pairwise disjoint attribute sets $X_i$ the join $\bowtie$ degenerates to the Cartesian product $\times$.

**Lemma 1 (Matching-inferrable binary value combination).** *Let $n$ be the number of (sub)tuple occurrences in a relation instance $r$ and the fragment instances $f_i$ and $f_j$, $i \neq j$, of a relational schema $(R(X), \mathcal{SC})$ with $\mathcal{SC} = \emptyset$ (i.e., without data dependencies) and the fragmentation schema $\mathcal{F} = \langle F_1(X_1), \ldots, F_m(X_m) \rangle$, respectively. Furthermore, let $C \subseteq X_i \cup X_j$ be an association syntactically protected by $\mathcal{F}$. Consider any value combination $\mu = (\mu_i, \mu_j)$ over $C$ such that $\mu_l$ occurs in exactly $c_{\mu_l}$ many subtuple instances of $f_l$, for $l \in \{i, j\}$. Then, the following assertions hold:*

1. If $c_{\mu_i} + c_{\mu_j} > n$, then $\mu$ is matching-inferrable and has at least $c_{\mu_i} + c_{\mu_j} - n$ occurrences in any matching $M$.
2. If $c_{\mu_i} + c_{\mu_j} \leq n$ and $r$ is unique on $X \setminus (X_i \cup X_j)$, i.e., the projection of $r$ on $X \setminus (X_i \cup X_j)$ would not produce duplicates, then $\mu$ is not matching-inferrable.

*Proof.* 1. Assume $c_{\mu_i} + c_{\mu_j} > n$, and consider any matching $M$. For the $c_{\mu_i}$ many subtuple instances of $f_i$ containing $\mu_i$ there are at most $n - c_{\mu_j}$ many subtuple instances in $f_j$ that do not contain $\mu_j$. Hence $c_{\mu_i} - (n - c_{\mu_j}) = c_{\mu_i} + c_{\mu_j} - n \geq 1$ many of the former subtuple instances must be matched with a subtuple instance of $f_j$ containing $\mu_j$.

2. We have to show that there exists an $\mathcal{SC}$-admissible matching $M$ such that $M(r)$ is a set (without duplicates) not containing $\mu$. If $r$ itself does not contain $\mu$, then the matching that exactly undoes the fragmentation has the desired properties. Otherwise, we can remove all occurrences of $\mu = (\mu_i, \mu_j)$ without affecting the fragmentation result: for each tuple with such an occurrence we exchange either the $X_i$- or the $X_j$-component with the respective component of a tuple that contains neither $\mu_i$ nor $\mu_j$. Such a tuple exists by the first assumption that $c_{\mu_i} + c_{\mu_j} \leq n$. Let then $M$ be a matching such that $M(r)$ generates the result of all exchanges. By the uniqueness of $r$ on $X \setminus (X_i \cup X_j)$ according to the second assumption, $M(r)$ has no duplicates.                                    □

*Remark 4 (Impact of duplicate-free relation instances).* Unfortunately, in Lemma 1 the condition $c_{\mu_i} + c_{\mu_j} > n$ is not necessary for $\mu$ being matching-inferrable, as witnessed by the following counterexample. Let $X = \{A_i, A_j\}$ and $r = \{(a, \mu_j), (\mu_i, \mu_j), (a, b)\}$ be a relation instance having $n = 3$ tuples with $a \neq \mu_i$ and $b \neq \mu_j$ and, thus $c_{\mu_i} + c_{\mu_j} = 1 + 2 = 3 = n$. Consider any matching $M$ of the fragments $f_i = \{\{(a), (\mu_i), (a)\}\}$ and $f_j = \{\{(\mu_j), (\mu_j), (b)\}\}$ such that $M(r)$ does not contain $\mu = (\mu_i, \mu_j)$. Then $M$ combines $\mu_i$ with $b$ and, thus, both occurrences of $\mu_j$ with $a$, yielding duplicates. Hence, $\mu$ is matching-inferrable. In contrast, the proof of Lemma 1, assertion 2 shows that the condition $c_{\mu_i} + c_{\mu_j} > n$ would be necessary if we allowed duplicates in original relation instances.

**Theorem 1 (Existence of a matching-inferrable value combination).**
*Let $n$ be the number of (sub)tuple instances in a relation instance $r$ and the fragment instances $f = \langle f_1, \ldots, f_m \rangle$ of a relational schema $(R(X), \mathcal{SC})$ with $\mathcal{SC} = \emptyset$ (i.e., without data dependencies) and the fragmentation schema $\mathcal{F} = \langle F_1(X_1), \ldots, F_m(X_m) \rangle$, respectively. Furthermore, let $C \subseteq X_{i_1} \cup \cdots \cup X_{i_k}$, with $P := \{i \mid C \cap X_i \neq \emptyset\} = \{i_1, \ldots, i_k\} \subseteq \{1, \ldots, m\}$, be an association syntactically protected by $\mathcal{F}$, and $maxc_{i_l}$ the maximal number of occurrences of a subtuple over the attributes of $C \cap X_{i_l}$ in $f_{i_l}$, for $l = i_1, \ldots, i_k$.*
*If[2] $maxc_{i_1} + \cdots + maxc_{i_k} > (k - 1) \cdot n$, then there exists a matching-inferrable value combination $\mu = (\mu_{i_1}, \ldots, \mu_{i_k})$ over $C \cap X_{i_1} \cup \cdots \cup C \cap X_{i_k}$.*

*Proof.* For $k = 2$, the theorem is an immediate consequence of the first assertion of Lemma 1. The general case can be proved by induction on $k$, exploiting the induction hypothesis and again the first assertion of Lemma 1.                    □

---

[2] As discussed above, if we allowed duplicates in original relation instances, the condition would also be necessary.

# 4    Inferences with Numerical Dependencies

Even if we allowed duplicates in original relation instances, in general the condition presented in Theorem 1 would not be necessary for a relational schema $(R(X), SC)$ with nontrivial *data dependencies* in $SC$ such that certain sets of tuple instances over $X$ are not accepted as a relation instance of the schema. In fact, a data dependency might relate the parts of an occurrence of a value combination split among different fragments. Moreover, to exploit such a relationship for an inference attack sometimes the knowledge of the frequencies of potentially combined parts is crucial.

In this section, we restrict our investigations to cardinality constraints in the form of *numerical dependencies* which include *functional dependencies* as a special case. We will consider the class of *tuple-generating dependencies* in the next section. In this study, however, we neither intend to cover the full range of data dependencies considered so far nor to relate the chosen examples exactly to the various versions suggested in the literature. Rather, by means of examples seen to be intuitively representative, we aim to demonstrate the issues of unwanted and sometimes even unexpected inferences enabled by the knowledge of data dependencies. Regarding the comprehensive class of data dependencies we refer the reader to, e.g., the extensive surveys of the rich literature contained in the textbooks [1, 27] and a few original contributions [3–5, 8, 16, 21, 22, 25, 26] selected out of many more works.

*Example 2 (Functional dependency and frequencies).*    Consider the relation instance of the schema *Patient* and the fragmentation shown in Figs. 1 and 2, respectively. The relation instance satisfies the functional dependency MEDICATION $\rightarrow$ ILLNESS. So, we now assume that this semantic constraint has publicly been declared for the schema such that the attacking receiver holds only those relation instances possible that satisfy this functional dependency. The value "MedB" under attribute MEDICATION occurs twice in the fragment instance $f_3$, and thus also in the hidden relation instance. By the semantic constraint, in the hidden relation instance, both occurrences must appear in combination with the same value under attribute ILLNESS, which then must occur at least twice. Since duplicates are preserved, this value must also occur at least twice in the fragment instance $f_2$. Only the value "Laceration" meets this requirement. Thus, seeing the fragment instances and knowing the functional dependency enables to infer that the value combination (Laceration, MedB) over the attribute set {ILLNESS, MEDICATION} occurs in the hidden relation instance, though, in the sense of Definition 2, this attribute set is an association syntactically protected by the fragmentation and the condition of Lemma 1, assertion 1 is not satisfied.

The preceding example is captured by the following proposition. For the sake of simplicity, it is expressed in terms of a functional dependency relating two single attributes $A$ and $B$ of some schema with attribute set $X$. Evidently, for the general case of a functional dependency relating two sets of attributes $Y \subseteq X$ and $Z \subseteq X$, a suitably adapted proposition holds as well.

**Proposition 1 (Inferences by equations on frequencies).** *For $A, B \in X$, let $(R(X), \{A \to B\})$ be a relational schema with the functional dependency $A \to B$ as a single semantic constraint and $r$ a relation instance containing $n$ different tuples. Furthermore, for each value $a$ occurring in $r$ under attribute $A$ let $c_a$ be the number of its occurrences and, similarly, for each value $b$ occurring in $r$ under attribute $B$ let $c_b$ be the number of its occurrences. Then, for all values $b$ occurring in $r$ under attribute $B$ the following equation holds:*

$$\sum_{a \in \pi_A(\sigma_{B=b}(R))} c_a = c_b. \tag{1}$$

*Proof.* Consider any value $b$ occurring in $r$ under attribute $B$. Then $\pi_A(\sigma_{B=b}(R))$ is the set of all values $a$ – without duplicates – such that $(a, b)$ occurs in the relation instance $r$ of $R$. Each such value $a$ occurs $c_a$ many times, and by the functional dependency $A \to B$ each occurrence is together with $b$.    □

If an attacker knows both the fragment $f_A$ showing the column $A$ of $r$ and the fragment $f_B$ showing the column $B$ of $r$, he can exploit the preceding proposition in a straightforward way as follows. Seeing both fragments, the attacker also knows all frequencies $c_a$ and $c_b$. He can then simply attempt to solve the set of equations derived from instantiating the Eq. (1) – with the relation symbol $R$ treated as the unknown item – to infer all possibilities for the hidden relation instance $r$. If there is a unique solution, the attacker has completely inferred the duplicate-preserving $\{A, B\}$-part of the hidden relation instance $r$ from its published fragments $f_A$ and $f_B$. Even otherwise, all solutions might still coincide for a particular value $b$ whose combinations in the hidden relation instance $r$ are then revealed.

We can consider the attacker's task as to solve the following variant of a *packing problem*. We interpret each value $b$ occurring under attribute $B$ in $f_B$ as a container having capacity $c_b$, and each value $a$ occurring under attribute $A$ in $f_A$ as a packet of size $c_a$. Then the attacker has to find all pairs $(a, b)$ that appear in each possible allocation of the packets to the containers such that all containers are completely filled, under the preconditions that (1) the sum over the packet sizes equals the sum over the container capacities and (2) there exists a solution, namely the one induced by the original relation instance.

Our variant is closely related to the NP-complete problem [SR1] BIN PACKING described in [20], where $k$ bins (containers) each of the same capacity $B$ should be filled with a finite set of items (packets) of given sizes. In our variant the bins may have different capacities, the existence of a solution completely filling all bins is known beforehand by the precondition, and we are interested in the allocations common to all solutions. Moreover, another related problem from the field of protection of statistical databases, [SR35] CONSISTENCY OF DATABASE FREQUENCY TABLES, is listed in [20] as being NP-complete. For this problem, a frequency refers to the number of occurrences of a *pair* of values under *any two* different attributes; furthermore, knowledge about value combinations is also not restricted to the content of a fragment. The problem then is

| $F_A$ | A | $F_B$ | B |
|---|---|---|---|
| | $a_1$ | | $b_1$ |
| | $a_1$ | | $b_1$ |
| | $a_2$ | | $b_2$ |
| | $a_3$ | | $b_3$ |

| $F_A$ | A | $F_B$ | B |
|---|---|---|---|
| | $a_1$ | | $b_1$ |
| | $a_1$ | | $b_1$ |
| | $a_1$ | | $b_1$ |
| | $a_1$ | | $b_1$ |
| | $a_2$ | | $b_2$ |
| | $a_2$ | | $b_2$ |
| | $a_2$ | | $b_2$ |
| | $a_3$ | | $b_2$ |

| $F_A$ | A | $F_B$ | B |
|---|---|---|---|
| | $a_1$ | | $b_1$ |
| | $a_1$ | | $b_1$ |
| | $a_1$ | | $b_1$ |
| | $a_1$ | | $b_1$ |
| | $a_1$ | | $b_1$ |
| | $a_2$ | | $b_2$ |
| | $a_2$ | | $b_2$ |
| | $a_2$ | | $b_2$ |
| | $a_3$ | | $b_2$ |

**Fig. 3.** Three fragmentations $(f_A^i, f_B^i)$ of different relation instances of a schema with functional dependency $A \to B$

to decide whether there exist unknown values supplementing the already known ones such that the given frequencies are satisfied. Due to these relationships, we expect that the attacker's task will be of high computational complexity. This expectation is also supported by the formal complexity analysis given in [7] and other works in the field of confidentiality-preserving data publishing, elaborated from the point of view of the defender.

*Example 3 (Functional dependency and frequencies for packing problem).* Given the functional dependency $A \to B$, consider the three fragmentation instances $(f_A^i, f_B^i)$ over the same fragmentation schema $\langle F_A(\{A\}), F_B(\{B\})\rangle$ shown in Fig. 3. Basically, $(f_A^1, f_B^1)$ is an abstract version of Example 2: since "packet" $a_1$ can only be allocated to "container" $b_1$, the value combination $(a_1, b_1)$ must occur twice in the original hidden relation instance underlying this fragmentation; nothing more definite can be inferred about the combinations of $a_2$ and $a_3$ with $b_2$ and $b_3$, respectively. For $(f_A^2, f_B^2)$, "packet" $a_1$ can be allocated to either "container" $b_1$ or "container" $b_2$, and then "packets" $a_2$ and $a_3$ both must be allocated to the container not selected for "packet" $a_1$. Thus, no (definite) inferences are possible at all. For $(f_A^3, f_B^3)$, Lemma 1 already asserts that the value combination $(a_1, b_1)$ is matching-inferrable and hence occurs at least once in the hidden instance underlying this fragmentation, since $c_{a_1} + c_{b_1} = 5 + 5 > 9$; under the presence of the functional dependency, now Proposition 1 implies more, namely that there must be exactly 5 occurrences. In turn, the latter fact together with the observable frequencies imply that $(a_2, b_2)$ occurs 3 times in the hidden instance, and $(a_3, b_2)$ once. Hence, in this case, the duplicate-preserving $\{A, B\}$-part of the hidden instance can be completely reconstructed from the observable fragmentation instances.

Though even more complex, we can extend our considerations to *numerical dependencies* of the form $Y \to_{max}^{min} Z$, where $Y$ and $Z$ are sets of attributes and $1 \leq min \leq max$ are integers. Such a numerical dependency requires that each subtuple $\mu$ over the attributes of $Y$ occurs combined with at least $min$ and at most $max$ different subtuples $\nu$ over the attributes of $Z$. A functional dependency $Y \to Z$ can be seen as a numerical dependency $Y \to_1^1 Z$.

| $R$ | $A$ | $B$ |
|---|---|---|
| | $a_1$ | $b_1$ |
| | $a_1$ | $b_2$ |
| | $a_2$ | $b_1$ |
| | $a_2$ | $b_2$ |
| | $a_3$ | $b_1$ |
| | $a_3$ | $b_2$ |

| $F_A$ | $A$ |
|---|---|
| | $a_1$ |
| | $a_1$ |
| | $a_2$ |
| | $a_2$ |
| | $a_3$ |
| | $a_3$ |

| $F_B$ | $B$ |
|---|---|
| | $b_1$ |
| | $b_1$ |
| | $b_1$ |
| | $b_2$ |
| | $b_2$ |
| | $b_2$ |

**Fig. 4.** A relation instance of a schema with numerical dependency $A \rightarrow_2^2 B$ and (unscrambled) derived fragmentation instances that uniquely determine the set of tuples occurring in the relation instance

*Example 4 (Numerical dependency and frequencies).* Figure 4 illustrates a special case of an inference for a numerical dependency $A \rightarrow_{max}^{min} B$ with $k := min = max$ and a relation instance with $l \cdot k$ tuple occurrences for some number $l$, having $l$ many different values under attribute $A$ and $k$ many different values under attribute $B$. By the dependency, each of the $l$ values under $A$ must occur in the hidden relation instance combined with each value under $B$, and thus the relation instance must be the Cartesian product of the value sets involved.

**Proposition 2 (Inferences by equations on frequencies).** *For $A, B \in X$, let $(R(X), \{A \rightarrow_{max}^{min} B\})$ be a relational schema with the numerical dependency $A \rightarrow_{max}^{min} B$ as a single semantic constraint and $r$ a relation instance containing $n$ tuples. For each value $a$ occurring in $r$ under attribute $A$, let $c_a$ be its frequency, i.e., the number of its occurrences under $A$, and $d_a := \| \pi_B(\sigma_{A=a}(R)) \|$ its diversity, i.e., the number of different values under attribute $B$ occurring together with $a$, and then for each $b \in \pi_B(\sigma_{A=a}(R))$, $c_a^b$ the frequency of $(a, b)$, i.e., the number of its occurrences in $r$. Moreover, for each value $b$ occurring in $r$ under attribute $B$ let $c_b$ be the number of its occurrences under $B$.*

*Then, for all values $a$ occurring in $r$ under attribute $A$ and for all values $b$ occurring in $r$ under attribute $B$ the following equations holds:*

$$c_b = \sum_{a \in \pi_A(\sigma_{B=b}(R))} c_a^b, \tag{2}$$

$$c_a = \sum_{b \in \pi_B(\sigma_{A=a}(R))} c_a^b, \tag{3}$$

$$min \leq d_a \leq max. \tag{4}$$

*Proof.* Equation (2) can similarly be justified as Eq. (1). Equations (3) and (4) are immediate consequences of the definitions of the items involved. □

*Remark 5.* Similarly as discussed for functional dependencies, the attacker's task can be considered as solving the set of equations derived from instantiating the Eqs. (2), (3) and (4) – with the relation symbol $R$ and the values $d_a$ and $c_a^b$ derived from $R$ treated as the unknown items. Again, in general the equations will not have a unique solution and, thus, regarding a syntactically protected association $C$, conceptually only the intersection of the projections on $C$ will deliver a certain inference. Surely, the data owner is interested in blocking such an inference, i.e., in ensuring that the intersection in empty. Evidently, the latter task is computationally highly complex, and so far neither a practical procedure to solve the equations involved nor an efficient and effective method to block their solvability is known to us. Presumably, the best we can hope to achieve is an approximate blocking method, favoring efficiency at the costs of loss of availability or violation of strict confidentiality.

## 5   Inferences with Tuple-Generating Dependencies

We are now addressing the impact of another well-known class of data dependencies, namely *tuple-generating dependencies* which, basically, require that whenever one or more tuples each of a specific form occur together in a relation instance, possibly related by identical components, another tuple partially constructed from selected components of those tuples and some constant symbols has to be present as well. Schema design theory has identified such dependencies as a possible source of redundancy in relation instances and, thus, of options to infer nontrivial information already from parts of an instance. Furthermore, each functional dependency entails a corresponding tuple-generating dependency, and thus studying the latter kind another aspect of the former one will be treated, together with the consequences of extensional background knowledge as expressed by means of constant symbols.

**Definition 4 (Tuple-generating dependencies).** *For a relational schema $(R(X), \mathcal{SC})$ with attribute set $X = \{A_1, \ldots, A_n\}$ and data dependencies $\mathcal{SC}$, an element of $\mathcal{SC}$ is called a* tuple-generating dependency *if it has a representation as an (untyped) sentence (without free variables) of first-order logic (with constant symbols) of the syntactic (implicational) form*

$$(\forall \boldsymbol{x})(\exists \boldsymbol{y})[[\bigwedge_{j=1,\ldots,p} \alpha_j] \implies \beta] \quad \text{such that}$$

1. *for $j = 1, \ldots, p$, the premises $\alpha_j$ are relational atoms of the form $R(t_{j,1}, \ldots, t_{j,n})$ where each term $t_{j,i}$ is either a universally quantified variable contained in $\boldsymbol{x}$ or a constant symbol;*
2. *the conclusion $\beta$ is a relational atom of the form $R(t_{p+1,1}, \ldots, t_{p+1,n})$ where each term $t_{p+1,i}$ is either a universally quantified variable contained in at least one premise (and thus also in $\boldsymbol{x}$) or an existentially quantified variable contained in $\boldsymbol{y}$ or a constant symbol;*
3. *the prefix $(\forall \boldsymbol{x})(\exists \boldsymbol{y})$ comprises exactly the variables occurring in some premise or in the conclusion.*

We start our investigations about the impact of a single tuple-generating dependency by considering two examples.

*Example 5 (Tuple-generating dependency without frequencies).* Consider the fragmentation schema with attribute sets $X_1 = \{A_1, A_3\}$ and $X_2 = \{A_2, A_4\}$ to split the syntactically protected association $C = \{A_3, A_4\}$ for the relational schema with the attributes $A_1$, $A_2$, $A_3$ and $A_4$ and the dependency $\Phi$ defined by

$$(\forall x_1, x_2, x_3, x_4, \bar{x}_1, \bar{x}_2, \bar{x}_3, \bar{x}_4)$$
$$[[R(x_1, \bar{x}_2, x_3, \bar{x}_4) \wedge R(\bar{x}_1, x_2, \bar{x}_3, x_4)] \implies (\exists y_1, y_2) R(y_1, y_2, x_3, x_4)].$$

Having the fragmentation schema in mind, this dependency can be given the following intuitive interpretation: if simultaneously a value combination $(x_1, x_3)$ is visible in the fragment for $X_1$ and a value combination $(x_2, x_4)$ is visible in the fragment for $X_2$, then the value combination $(x_3, x_4)$ occurs in the split association $C$, the intended protection of which would thus be violated. In contrast, lacking the background knowledge that the original relation satisfies $\Phi$, in general an observer could not distinguish whether the value $x_3$ seen in one fragment and the value $x_4$ seen in the other fragment actually occur together in a single tuple under the attributes in $C$ or not. In fact, the relation $\{(a_1, \bar{a}_2, a_3, \bar{a}_4), (\bar{a}_1, a_2, \bar{a}_3, a_4)\}$ would generate the fragments $\{(a_1, a_3, ), (\bar{a}_1, \bar{a}_3)\}$ and $\{(\bar{a}_2, \bar{a}_4), (a_2, a_4)\}$, leaving open which of the two possible matchings is the original one, in particular whether the value combinations $(a_3, a_4)$ and $(\bar{a}_3, \bar{a}_4)$ or the value combinations $(a_3, \bar{a}_4)$ and $(\bar{a}_3, a_4)$ actually occur under the attributes in $C$.

We also note that the inspected tuple-generating dependency $\Phi$ can actually be considered as an *embedded multivalued dependency* for the projection on the attribute set $\{A_3, A_4\}$, shortly denoted by $\emptyset \twoheadrightarrow A_3 | A_4$, requiring that this projection is the Cartesian product of the projection on $\{A_3\}$ with the projection on $\{A_4\}$, and obviously violated by the relation defined above.

Proposition 3 below will treat the kind of situation described in Example 5 more generally. The proposition will present three syntactic conditions regarding the occurrences of terms in a tuple-generating dependency to perform successful inferences about a split association $C$ solely on observing data in the fragments. These conditions are outlined as follows. On the one hand and straightforwardly, ($a$) each non-constant term in the $C$-part of the conclusion has to be determined in at least one premise. On the other hand and somehow more sophistically, the constraints on relevant terms as expressed in the premises have to be restricted ($b$) regarding occurrences of one or more terms within a single premise and ($c$) regarding the occurrences of one term across two or more premises.

In terms of first-order logic, the latter two conditions would allow us to rewrite the tuple-generating dependency using a slightly more general syntactic form where each original premise has been transformed into a derived formula that gets a prefix of existentially quantified variables. Such a purely existential prefix then serves to express an effect that is equivalent to consider only the projection on the attributes of only one of the fragments. For the dependency $\Phi$ considered above, the following rewriting would be suitable:

$(\forall x_1, x_2, x_3, x_4)$

$[[(\exists \bar{x}_2, \bar{x}_4)R(x_1, \bar{x}_2, x_3, \bar{x}_4) \;\wedge\; (\exists \bar{x}_1, \bar{x}_3)R(\bar{x}_1, x_2, \bar{x}_3, x_4)]$

$\implies (\exists y_1, y_2)R(y_1, y_2, x_3, x_4)].$

To formally express and verify the intuition just outlined, we first need to precisely define the notions of an attribute being either *essential* or *isolated*.

**Definition 5.** *Let $\alpha_j$ be a premise of a tuple-generating dependency $\Phi$ over the attribute set $X = \{A_1, \ldots, A_n\}$. Then the set $E_j$ of essential attributes (for $\alpha_j$) is defined as the smallest subset of $X$ with the following properties:*

1. *If $t_{j,i}$ is a constant symbol in $\alpha_j$, then $A_i \in E_j$.*
2. *If $t_{j,i_1}$ is a universally quantified variable multiply occurring in $\alpha_j$ such that $t_{j,i_1} = t_{j,i_2}$ with $i_1 \neq i_2$, then both $A_{i_1} \in E_j$ and $A_{i_2} \in E_j$.*
3. *If $t_{j,i}$ is a universally quantified variable in $\alpha_j$ that also occurs in the C-part of the conclusion $\beta$ of $\Phi$, then $A_i \in E_j$.*

*All remaining attributes are called* isolated *in $\alpha_j$, i.e., we define $I_j = X \setminus E_j$.*

For the simple dependency $\Phi$ considered in Example 5 above, only the third rule applies and thus we get $E_1 = \{A_3\}$ and $E_2 = \{A_4\}$.

**Proposition 3 (Inferences by a single tuple-generating dependency only).** *Let $\mathcal{F} = \langle F_1(X_1), \ldots, F_m(X_m) \rangle$ be the fragmentation schema derived from a relational schema $(R(X), \mathcal{SC})$ with attribute set $X = \{A_1, \ldots, A_n\}$ and a sequence $\mathcal{X}$ of attribute sets partitioning $X$ such that $\mathcal{SC} = \{\Phi\}$ contains the tuple-generating dependency $\Phi = (\forall \boldsymbol{x})(\exists \boldsymbol{y})[[\bigwedge_{j=1,\ldots,p} \alpha_j] \implies \beta]$ as a single semantic constraint. Furthermore, let attribute set $C$ be an association syntactically protected by $\mathcal{F}$, and consider the following assertions:*

1. (a) *In the conclusion $\beta = R(t_{p+1,1}, \ldots, t_{p+1,n})$, for each attribute $A_i \in C$ the term $t_{p+1,i}$ is a constant symbol or a universally quantified variable.*
   (b) *For each premise $\alpha_j$ the set $E_j$ of its essential attributes is fully contained in exactly one attribute set $X_{e(j)}$ of the partition $\mathcal{X}$.*
   (c) *If a universally quantified variable $x$ occurs in two or more premises $\alpha_{j_1}, \alpha_{j_2}, \ldots$, then all occurrences are within the pertinent sets of essential attributes $E_{j_1}, E_{j_2}, \ldots$.*
2. *For all relation instances $r$ of $(R(X), \mathcal{SC})$ satisfying the premises $\sigma[\alpha_1], \ldots, \sigma[\alpha_p]$ of $\Phi$ for some substitution $\sigma$ of the variables in $\boldsymbol{x}$ the generated fragmentation instance $f$ is not inference-proof regarding $C$, i.e., $\mathcal{F}_{\mathcal{SC}}^{-1,C}(f) \neq \emptyset$.*

*Then assertion 1 implies assertion 2.*

*Proof.* Assuming assertion 1, suppose the relation instance $r$ satisfies both the sentence $\Phi$, which has only universally quantified variables in the premises, and the substituted premises $\sigma[\alpha_1], \ldots, \sigma[\alpha_p]$ of $\Phi$ for a suitable substitution $\sigma$ of the variables in $\boldsymbol{x}$. Then there exists a substitution $\tau$ of the variables in $\boldsymbol{y}$ such that $r$ also satisfies the substituted conclusion $\tau[\sigma[\beta]] = \tau[\sigma[R(t_{p+1,1}, \ldots, t_{p+1,n})]]$.

Thus the subtuple $\mu$ over $C$ formed from this conclusion occurs in $r$. According to the assumed assertion 1.(a), the substitution $\tau$ for the existentially quantified variables is not relevant for $\mu$ and thus we actually have $\mu = (\sigma[t_{p+1,i}])_{A_i \in C}$. In the remainder of the proof we will verify that for the fragmentation $\mathcal{F}(r) = f = \langle f_1, \ldots, f_m \rangle$ we have $\mu \in \mathcal{F}_{SC}^{-1,C}(f)$ and thus $\mathcal{F}_{SC}^{-1,C}(f) \neq \emptyset$.

Let $\tilde{r}$ be any relation instance of the relational schema $(R(X), \{\Phi\})$ generating the same fragmentation, i.e., $\mathcal{F}(\tilde{r}) = f$.

For $j = 1, \ldots, p$ define $\mu_j$ to be the $X_{e(j)}$-part of $\sigma[\alpha_j]$, where $e(j)$ is determined by assumption 1.(b) assuring that $\mu_j$ assigns values to all essential attributes of the premise $\alpha_j$. In particular, we have $\mu_j \in f_{e(j)}$.

Furthermore, for any isolated attribute $A_i$ of $\alpha_j$ consider the term $t_{j,i}$. According to property 1 of Definition 5, $t_{j,i}$ is not a constant symbol and, thus, it is a universally quantified variable. Moreover, this variable has no further occurrences within that premise or any other premise or the $C$-part of the conclusion, according to property 2 of Definition 5, the assumed assertion 1.(c) and property 3 of Definition 5, respectively.

Let $\boldsymbol{x}_{iso}$ comprise all those universally quantified variables under isolated attributes, and $\boldsymbol{x}_{ess}$ the remaining ones occurring in the essential parts of the premises. Denoting the restriction of the substitution $\sigma$ to $\boldsymbol{x}_{ess}$ by $\sigma_{ess}$ and observing that $\mu_j \in f_{e(j)} = \bar{\pi}_{X_{e(j)}}^?(\tilde{r})$ (here $\bar{\pi}^?$ signifies a projection in the sense of Definition 1), we conclude that there exists a substitution $\sigma_{iso}$ of the variables $\boldsymbol{x}_{iso}$ such that $\sigma_{iso}[\sigma_{ess}[\alpha_j]] \in \tilde{r}$. By the construction, these tuples comply with the premises of the dependency $\Phi$. Applying $\Phi$ then implies that for some substitution $\bar{\tau}$ of the existentially quantified variables in $\boldsymbol{y}$ also $\bar{\tau}[\sigma_{iso}[\sigma_{ess}[\beta]]] \in \tilde{r}$. By property 3 of Definition 5 and assumed assertion 1.(a) the C-part of the tuple $\bar{\tau}[\sigma_{iso}[\sigma_{ess}[\beta]]]$ only depends on $\sigma_{ess}$ and thus equals $\mu$. Hence $\mu \in \pi_C(\tilde{r})$. $\quad\square$

Proposition 3 describes situations that enable an attacking observer to violate inference-proofness just be logical entailment without additionally exploiting frequencies. The next example tells us that even in situations not captured by Proposition 3 the observation of frequencies might turn out to be harmful.

*Example 6 (Tuple-generating dependency and frequencies).* We reconsider Example 5 above but now assume a more frequently encountered kind of a tuple-generating dependency, namely the *multivalued dependency* shortly denoted by $A_1, A_2 \twoheadrightarrow A_3 | A_4$, having the following formalization in first-order logic:

$$(\forall x_1, x_2, x_3, x_4, \bar{x}_3, \bar{x}_4)$$
$$[[R(x_1, x_2, x_3, x_4) \wedge R(x_1, x_2, \bar{x}_3, \bar{x}_4)] \implies R(x_1, x_2, x_3, \bar{x}_4)].$$

Intuitively, this dependency requires that whenever the value combination $(x_1, x_2)$ under the attributes $A_1$ and $A_2$ occurs both with the value combinations $(x_3, x_4)$ and $(\bar{x}_3, \bar{x}_4)$ under the attributes $A_3$ and $A_4$, then the former value combination also occurs together with $(x_3, \bar{x}_4)$. More generally, this requirement then implies that $(x_1, x_2)$ even occurs together with each element in the Cartesian product of the jointly occurring values under $A_3$ and the jointly occurring

| $R$ | $A_1$ | $A_2$ | $A_3$ | $A_4$ | | $F_{A_1,A_3}$ | $A_1$ | $A_3$ | | $F_{A_2,A_4}$ | $A_2$ | $A_4$ |
|---|---|---|---|---|---|---|---|---|---|---|---|---|
| | $a_1$ | $a_2$ | $a_3$ | $a_4$ | | | $a_1$ | $a_3$ | | | $a_2$ | $a_4$ |
| | $\bar{a}_1$ | $\bar{a}_2$ | $\bar{a}_3$ | $\bar{a}_4$ | | | $\bar{a}_1$ | $\bar{a}_3$ | | | $\bar{a}_2$ | $\bar{a}_4$ |
| | $\bar{a}_1$ | $\bar{a}_2$ | $\bar{a}_3$ | $\dot{a}_4$ | | | $\bar{a}_1$ | $\bar{a}_3$ | | | $\bar{a}_2$ | $\dot{a}_4$ |
| | $\bar{a}_1$ | $\bar{a}_2$ | $\dot{a}_3$ | $\bar{a}_4$ | | | $\bar{a}_1$ | $\dot{a}_3$ | | | $\bar{a}_2$ | $\bar{a}_4$ |
| | $\bar{a}_1$ | $\bar{a}_2$ | $\dot{a}_3$ | $\dot{a}_4$ | | | $\bar{a}_1$ | $\dot{a}_3$ | | | $\bar{a}_2$ | $\dot{a}_4$ |

**Fig. 5.** A relation instance of a schema with multivalued dependency $A_1, A_2 \twoheadrightarrow A_3|A_4$ and derived fragmentation instances for attribute sets $X_1 = \{A_1, A_3\}$ and $X_2 = \{A_2, A_4\}$ that uniquely determine the set of tuples occurring in the relation instance

values under $A_4$. Consequently, for each value combination $(x_1, x_2)$ the number of jointly occurring value combinations $(x_3, x_4)$ is the cardinality of a Cartesian product. More precisely, this number is the arithmetic product of the cardinality of the jointly occurring $x_3$-values and the cardinality of the jointly occurring $x_4$-values. This consequence might enable combinatorial reasoning under the additional provision that the effect of duplicates is appropriately considered, i.e., that in general an observer can directly determine frequencies rather than only cardinalities.

Most notably, such a reasoning might be successful (from the point of view of an attacker) even for the present situation where both the attribute set $\{A_1, A_2\}$ of the dependency's left-hand side and the attribute set $\{A_3, A_4\}$ of the dependency's right hand side – which is the syntactically protected association $C$ – are split by the fragmentation schema.

In fact, Fig. 5 shows such a success as follows. The single occurrence of $(a_1, a_3)$ has to match the single occurrence of $(a_2, a_4)$, since otherwise, to complete the matching, for each fragment there would be only three candidates left to come up with a result of the form $(\bar{a}_1, \bar{a}_2, ., .)$ but the multivalued dependency would require that there are four, a contradiction. Furthermore, each matching of the remaining subtuple instances in the two fragments produces the same four tuples. Thus the original relation instance can be fully reconstructed based on the fragment instances.

# 6 Related Work and Conclusions

Inference analysis and control for information published about database relations have been an important topic in research on confidentiality enforcement since quite a long time, presumably starting with seminal work on information leakage via statistical databases, as, e.g., summarized by Denning [17] as early as 1982, and later continued under a much broader perspective, as more recently surveyed by, e.g., Fung et al. [18]. The particular proposal of fragmenting relational data for ensuring confidentiality has arisen in different forms with the trend of outsourcing data for cloud computing since around ten years. First proposals by Ciriani et al. [12,13] only used fragmentation, but subsequent work of Aggarwal et al. [2], Ciriani et al. [14], Ganapathy et al. [19] and Xu et al. [28] additionally employed encryption.

Initial deeper analysis by Biskup et al. [10, 11] of the actual achievements of fragmentation in the presence of data dependencies – as usually employed for relational databases in practice – pointed to the weakness of the simple syntactic splitting approach. This analysis also led to more semantically oriented refinements, guaranteeing inference-proofness in a strong sense for special classes of data dependencies, but unfortunately in general also increasing the computational complexity of finding appropriate fragmentation schemas. For the specific setting of [14] also underlying our contribution, Ciriani et al. [15] later also provided a refinement and its analysis, considering a non-standard and still weak syntactic notion of functional dependence as an attacking receiver's background knowledge. Their refinement exemplifies a compromise between the conflicting goals involved, effective preservation of confidentiality on the one hand and efficient computation of fragmentations on the other hand.

Our contribution presents an *exploratory study* regarding the former goal when using the setting of [14]. While the authors of [15] only deal with a weak notion of functional dependence between attributes on the schema level, we study the impact of classical, more expressive functional dependencies on the *instance level*, and we extend these investigations to further important classes of *data dependencies*. Moreover, considering the instance level, we identify the crucial role of *preserving duplicates* when fragmenting a relation instance: this feature opens the way for *combinatorial reasoning* to infer hidden information, as far as we are aware for this context neglected in previous work. Once opened, for the first time this way enables us to investigate possible *interferences* of combinatorial reasoning about observable frequencies on the one hand and entailment reasoning about data dependencies known from the database schema and actual data values observed in the fragments on the other hand.

Briefly summarized, these investigations provide initial, hopefully representative insight into conditions that enable or block inferences of information that is intended to be hidden by completely splitting the underlying data, respectively. Though already aiming at covering most of the relevant cases, future work still has to complement the overall picture, ideally in order to come up with a complete characterization of inference options in terms of a condition that is both necessary and sufficient. Based on such a characterization, we could then design a refined fragmentation approach that guarantees inference-proofness just by ensuring that the result does not satisfy that condition. This long-term research project could be elaborated both for single relation instances and, even more ambitiously, for database schemas dealing with all their respective relation instances. We have already explored a first step in such a direction in our study [10], which however deals with a kind of fragmentation that let each observer only see one fragment. In contrast, one peculiarity of our setting as adopted from [14] is that one observer sees all fragments and, thus, might exploit multiple views on the same underlying original data. This situation is well-known to often constitute a threat to confidentiality, as, e.g., treated in [18] for different settings.

From the point of view of database theory, our contribution deals with a specific case of the much more general problem of computing the *inversion* of database queries or, equivalently, *solving equations* in the relational algebra, as studied in [9]. However, we are now deviating from the pure relational model, which treats relations as pure sets allowing no duplicates and incorporating no sequence of their members. Though we assume that the original relation is duplicate-free, we explicitly study the impact of maintaining duplicates in the fragments. Moreover, the inversion of a fragmentation by means of exploring matchings in our sense aims at undoing the deliberate scrambling of data representations. These features also make our settings slightly different from those for the classical studies of *lossless joins*, see, e.g., [1]. While joins more generally deal with overlapping projections, we require attribute-disjointness of the fragments which reduces the join to the Cartesian product and in most practical cases violates losslessness. Nevertheless, for this special case our results provide insight about the detailed *information content* of a lossy operation, see. e.g., [23].

Furthermore, in general inversion generates *uncertainty* about which element of the pre-image has been the actual one and, thus, the challenge arise how to determine the *certain* part of the pre-image contained in all its elements, also known as *skeptical reasoning*, see, e.g., [24]. It would be worthwhile to explore how the rich insight already gathered for this field could be adapted to our problem, which exhibits the following similarities and particularities. First, the space of possibilities is defined by two arguments: in both cases by a set of explicitly expressed data dependencies – and their closure under entailment of course – on the one hand and by visible data either original but incomplete one or by fragmentation derived one, respectively, on the other hand. Second, the aim is either to exactly determine the certain part (which would be the interest of an attacker) or to block all options to gain any certain information, which is the basic task of an owner's protection mechanism.

**Acknowledgment.** We would like to thank Manh Linh Nguyen for stimulating discussions while he has prepared his master thesis on a partial analysis of the approach of fragmentation with encryption to protect privacy in data storage.

# References

1. Abiteboul, S., Hull, R., Vianu, V.: Foundations of Databases. Addison-Wesley, Reading (1995)
2. Aggarwal, G., Bawa, M., Ganesan, P., Garcia-Molina, H., Kenthapadi, K., Motwani, R., Srivastava, U., Thomas, D., Xu, Y.: Two can keep a secret: a distributed architecture for secure database services. In: 2nd Biennial Conference on Innovative Data Systems Research, CIDR 2005, pp. 186–199 (2005). Online Proceedings
3. Armstrong, W.W.: Dependency structures of data base relationships. In: IFIP Congress, pp. 580–583 (1974)
4. Beeri, C., Vardi, M.Y.: Formal systems for tuple and equality generating dependencies. SIAM J. Comput. **13**(1), 76–98 (1984). https://doi.org/10.1137/0213006

5. Benczúr, A., Kiss, A., Márkus, T.: On a general class of data dependencies in the relational model and its implication problem. Comput. Math. Appl. **21**(1), 1–11 (1991)
6. Biskup, J.: Selected results and related issues of confidentiality-preserving controlled interaction execution. In: Gyssens, M., Simari, G. (eds.) FoIKS 2016. LNCS, vol. 9616, pp. 211–234. Springer, Cham (2016). https://doi.org/10.1007/978-3-319-30024-5_12
7. Biskup, J., Bonatti, P.A., Galdi, C., Sauro, L.: Optimality and complexity of inference-proof data filtering and CQE. In: Kutyłowski, M., Vaidya, J. (eds.) ESORICS 2014. LNCS, vol. 8713, pp. 165–181. Springer, Cham (2014). https://doi.org/10.1007/978-3-319-11212-1_10
8. Biskup, J., Link, S.: Appropriate inferences of data dependencies in relational databases. Ann. Math. Artif. Intell. **63**(3–4), 213–255 (2011). https://doi.org/10.1007/s10472-012-9275-0
9. Biskup, J., Paredaens, J., Schwentick, T., Van den Bussche, J.: Solving equations in the relational algebra. SIAM J. Comput. **33**(5), 1052–1066 (2004). https://doi.org/10.1137/S0097539701390859
10. Biskup, J., Preuß, M.: Database fragmentation with encryption: under which semantic constraints and a priori knowledge can two keep a secret? In: Wang, L., Shafiq, B. (eds.) DBSec 2013. LNCS, vol. 7964, pp. 17–32. Springer, Heidelberg (2013). https://doi.org/10.1007/978-3-642-39256-6_2
11. Biskup, J., Preuß, M., Wiese, L.: On the inference-proofness of database fragmentation satisfying confidentiality constraints. In: Lai, X., Zhou, J., Li, H. (eds.) ISC 2011. LNCS, vol. 7001, pp. 246–261. Springer, Heidelberg (2011). https://doi.org/10.1007/978-3-642-24861-0_17
12. Ciriani, V., De Capitani di Vimercati, S., Foresti, S., Jajodia, S., Paraboschi, S., Samarati, P.: Enforcing confidentiality constraints on sensitive databases with lightweight trusted clients. In: Gudes, E., Vaidya, J. (eds.) DBSec 2009. LNCS, vol. 5645, pp. 225–239. Springer, Heidelberg (2009). https://doi.org/10.1007/978-3-642-03007-9_15
13. Ciriani, V., De Capitani di Vimercati, S., Foresti, S., Jajodia, S., Paraboschi, S., Samarati, P.: Keep a few: outsourcing data while maintaining confidentiality. In: Backes, M., Ning, P. (eds.) ESORICS 2009. LNCS, vol. 5789, pp. 440–455. Springer, Heidelberg (2009). https://doi.org/10.1007/978-3-642-04444-1_27
14. Ciriani, V., De Capitani di Vimercati, S., Foresti, S., Jajodia, S., Paraboschi, S., Samarati, P.: Combining fragmentation and encryption to protect privacy in data storage. ACM Trans. Inf. Syst. Secur. **13**(3), 22:1–22:33 (2010). Article no. 22
15. De Capitani di Vimercati, S., Foresti, S., Jajodia, S., Livraga, G., Paraboschi, S., Samarati, P.: Fragmentation in presence of data dependencies. IEEE Trans. Dependable Secur. Comput. **11**(6), 510–523 (2014)
16. Demetrovics, J., Katona, G.O.H., Sali, A.: The characterization of branching dependencies. Discrete Appl. Math. **40**(2), 139–153 (1992). https://doi.org/10.1016/0166-218X(92)90027-8
17. Denning, D.E.: Cryptography and Data Security. Addison-Wesley, Reading (1982)
18. Fung, B.C.M., Wang, K., Fu, A.W.C., Yu, P.S.: Introduction to Privacy-Preserving Data Publishing - Concepts and Techniques. Chapman & Hall/CRC, Boca Raton (2011)
19. Ganapathy, V., Thomas, D., Feder, T., Garcia-Molina, H., Motwani, R.: Distributing data for secure database services. Trans. Data Privacy **5**(1), 253–272 (2012)
20. Garey, M.R., Johnson, D.S.: Computers and Intractability: A Guide to the Theory of NP-Completeness. Freeman, New York (1979)

21. Grant, J., Minker, J.: Inferences for numerical dependencies. Theor. Comput. Sci. **41**, 271–287 (1985). https://doi.org/10.1016/0304-3975(85)90075-1
22. Hartmann, S.: On the implication problem for cardinality constraints and functional dependencies. Ann. Math. Artif. Intell. **33**(2–4), 253–307 (2001). https://doi.org/10.1023/A:1013133428451
23. Kolahi, S., Libkin, L.: An information-theoretic analysis of worst-case redundancy in database design. ACM Trans. Database Syst. **35**(1), 5:1–5:32 (2010). https://doi.org/10.1145/1670243.1670248
24. Libkin, L.: Certain answers as objects and knowledge. Artif. Intell. **232**, 1–19 (2016). https://doi.org/10.1016/j.artint.2015.11.004
25. Sagiv, Y., Delobel, C., Parker Jr., D.S., Fagin, R.: An equivalence between relational database dependencies and a fragment of propositional logic. J. ACM **28**(3), 435–453 (1981). https://doi.org/10.1145/322261.322263
26. Sali Sr., A., Sali, A.: Generalized dependencies in relational databases. Acta Cybern. **13**(4), 431–438 (1998)
27. Thalheim, B.: Entity-Relationship Modeling - Foundations of Database Technology. Springer, Heidelberg (2000). https://doi.org/10.1007/978-3-662-04058-4
28. Xu, X., Xiong, L., Liu, J.: Database fragmentation with confidentiality constraints: a graph search approach. In: Park, J., Squicciarini, A.C. (eds.) 5th ACM Conference on Data and Application Security and Privacy, CODASPY 2015, pp. 263–270. ACM (2015)

# ASP Programs with Groundings of Small Treewidth

Bernhard Bliem[✉]

University of Helsinki, Helsinki, Finland
bernhard.bliem@helsinki.fi

**Abstract.** Recent experiments have shown ASP solvers to run significantly faster on ground programs of small treewidth. If possible, it may
therefore be beneficial to write a non-ground ASP encoding such that
grounding it together with an input of small treewidth leads to a propositional program of small treewidth. In this work, we prove that a class
of non-ground programs called *guarded ASP* guarantees this property.
Guarded ASP is a subclass of the recently proposed class of connection-
guarded ASP, which is known to admit groundings whose treewidth
depends on both the treewidth and the maximum degree of the input.
Here we show that this dependency on the maximum degree cannot be
dropped. Hence, in contrast to connection-guarded ASP, guarded ASP
promises good performance even if the input has large maximum degree.

## 1 Introduction

Answer Set Programming (ASP) is a popular formalism for solving computationally hard combinatorial problems with applications in many domains
[6,13,17,18]. The workflow for using ASP is generally to first encode the problem
at hand in the language of non-ground ASP (i.e., as an ASP program containing
variables). Instances of that problem can then be represented as sets of ground
(i.e., variable-free) *facts*. To solve an instance, we give our problem encoding
together with the input facts to a *grounder*, which produces an equivalent ground
program, and we then call an ASP *solver* to compute the solutions.

The solving step is the main workhorse of this approach, so improving solver
efficiency is of great interest. One possibility of achieving this is to consider
*treewidth* [21], which is a parameter that intuitively measures the cyclicity of
a graph: the smaller the treewidth, the closer the graph resembles a tree. By
representing ground ASP programs as graphs, we can also use treewidth in the
context of ASP. It has turned out that the performance of modern ASP solvers is
heavily influenced by the treewidth of the given ground input program. Indeed,
an empirical evaluation [2] revealed that the solving time increases drastically
when the treewidth of the input increases but the size and the manner of construction of the programs remain the same.

We typically do not encode our problems in ground ASP directly, however,
but use non-ground programs. There are usually different ways to encode a
problem in non-ground ASP. To present one example given in [2], suppose we

© Springer International Publishing AG, part of Springer Nature 2018
F. Ferrarotti and S. Woltran (Eds.): FoIKS 2018, LNCS 10833, pp. 97–113, 2018.
https://doi.org/10.1007/978-3-319-90050-6_6

want to find all vertices that are reachable from a given starting vertex in a given graph. One way to solve this is by defining the transitive closure of the edge relation:

    trans(X,Y) ← edge(X,Y).
    trans(X,Z) ← trans(X,Y), edge(Y,Z).
      reach(X) ← start(X).
      reach(Y) ← start(X), trans(X,Y).

Alternatively, we can avoid defining the transitive closure:

    reach(X) ← start(X).
    reach(Y) ← reach(X), edge(X,Y).

When these programs are grounded together with the input, they behave quite differently not only in terms of the size of the grounding but also in terms of the treewidth of the grounding. Indeed, as we will show in this paper, the second program has a property that guarantees that we can find a grounding of small treewidth whenever the input has small treewidth. Programs without this property, like the one above relying on the transitive closure, do not allow for this in general. Hence, the way a problem is encoded can influence the treewidth of the ground program considerably, and as the experiments in [2] have shown, this may also have a massive impact on the solving performance. Even though both programs above solve the same problem, we can thus expect the second one to have much better performance in practice.

Since the input for the solver is obtained by grounding, the way we encode our problem in ASP may lead to groundings of huge treewidth even if our instances actually have small treewidth. Unfortunately, it is not obvious how to write a non-ground ASP encoding in order to achieve a low-treewidth grounding and the benefits that come with it. Some ASP modeling techniques may be safe in the sense that they keep the treewidth small, while others may excessively increase it. We can usually model a problem in different ways, but it is not clear which one should be preferred in terms of treewidth.

In an attempt to remedy this, the authors of [2] show that under certain conditions we can find groundings that have small treewidth whenever the input has small treewidth: They present a class of non-ground ASP programs called *connection-guarded*, whose intuition is to restrict the syntax in such a way that only a limited form of transitivity can be expressed. As shown in [2], for any fixed connection-guarded program there are groundings whose treewidth only depends on the treewidth and the maximum degree of the input facts. So for any fixed connection-guarded program, as long as the maximum degree of the input is bounded by a constant, we can find a grounding that has bounded treewidth whenever the input has bounded treewidth. It is not clear whether this also works for inputs of unbounded maximum degree. After all, it is conceivable that this can be achieved by means of clever grounding techniques. Sadly, no such techniques are known.

In the current work, we show that there is most likely no hope for that: We prove that for some connection-guarded programs there can be no procedure that produces groundings whose treewidth depends only on the treewidth of the input (unless $P = NP$ or grounding is allowed to take exponential time).

While the class of connection-guarded programs thus does not achieve the goal of preserving bounded treewidth by grounding, we also present a class that does: We prove that a restriction of connection-guarded programs called *guarded programs* allows us to find groundings that preserve bounded treewidth, and we show that we can still express some problems at the second level of the polynomial hierarchy in that class. We also give indications for when a problem cannot be expressed in guarded ASP.

This paper is structured as follows: First we present some preliminary notions on ASP and treewidth in Sect. 2. Next we discuss grounding and recapitulate a formal definition of this process from [2] in Sect. 3. The first part of our main results is presented in Sect. 4, where we show that connection-guarded ASP does not preserve bounded treewidth. The second part of our contributions follows in Sect. 5, where we prove that guarded ASP preserves bounded treewidth and also provide some complexity results. We discuss the significance and consequences of our results in Sect. 6. Finally we conclude in Sect. 7 and hint at possible directions for future research.

## 2 Preliminaries

### 2.1 Answer Set Programming

We briefly review syntax and semantics of ASP. A *program* in ASP is a set of *rules*, which have the following form:

$$a_1 \vee \ldots \vee a_n \leftarrow b_1, \ldots, b_k, \text{not } b_{k+1}, \ldots, \text{not } b_m.$$

The *head* of a rule $r$ is the set denoted by $H(r) = \{a_1, \ldots, a_n\}$, the *positive body* of $r$ is the set $B^+(r) = \{b_1, \ldots, b_k\}$, and the *negative body* of $r$ is the set $B^-(r) = \{b_{k+1}, \ldots, b_m\}$. The *body* of $r$ is now defined as $B(r) = B^+(r) \cup B^-(r)$.

If the head of a rule is empty, then we call the rule a *constraint*. If the body of a rule is empty, then we we may omit the $\leftarrow$ symbol. If the body of a rule is empty and the head consists of a single atom, then we call the rule a *fact*. A program $\Pi$ is called *positive* if the negative body of each rule in $\Pi$ is empty.

All elements of the heads or the bodies of rules are called *atoms*. A *literal* is an atom $a$ or its negated form $\text{not } a$. An atom has the form $p(t_1, \ldots, t_\ell)$, where $p$ is called a *predicate*. The elements $t_1, \ldots, t_\ell$ in an atom are called *terms*. A term is either a *constant* or a *variable*. It is customary to write predicates and constants as (strings starting with) lower-case symbols and variables as (strings starting with) upper-case symbols. We call a program or a part of a program (like atoms, rules, etc.) *ground* if it contains no variables. A predicate is called *extensional* in a program $\Pi$ if it only occurs in rule bodies of $\Pi$. A ground fact is an *input fact* for $\Pi$ if its predicate occurs as an extensional predicate in $\Pi$.[1] We write $\|\Pi\|$ to denote the size of $\Pi$ (in terms of bits required for representing $\Pi$ as opposed to the number of rules).

A rule $r$ is *safe* if every variable that occurs in $r$ occurs in an element of $B^+(r)$. A program is safe if all its rules are safe. We only admit ASP programs that are safe.

We define the semantics of ASP in terms of ground programs. For this, we first show how arbitrary programs can be transformed into ground programs.

For any program $\Pi$, a *ground instance* of a rule $r \in \Pi$ is any rule that can be obtained by replacing the variables in $r$ with constants occurring in $\Pi$. The *ground instantiation* $\mathrm{Ground}(\Pi)$ of a program $\Pi$ is the set of all ground instances of all rules in $\Pi$.

We call every subset $I$ of the atoms occurring in $\mathrm{Ground}(\Pi)$ an *interpretation* of $\Pi$. An interpretation $I$ *satisfies* a rule $r$ in $\mathrm{Ground}(\Pi)$ if it contains an element of $H(r) \cup B^-(r)$ or if $B^+(r)$ contains an element that is not in $I$. We say that $I$ is a *model* of $\Pi$ if it satisfies every rule in $\mathrm{Ground}(\Pi)$. We define $\Pi^I$, called the *reduct* of $\Pi$ w.r.t. $I$, as $\Pi^I = \{H(r) \leftarrow B^+(r) \mid r \in \Pi, \ B^-(r) \cap I = \emptyset\}$. We call $I$ an *answer set* of $\Pi$ if $I$ is a model of $\Pi$ and no proper subset of $I$ is a model of $\Pi$. Two ASP programs are *equivalent* if they have the same answer sets.

Deciding if a ground ASP program has an answer set is complete for $\Sigma_2^P$ [10]. Moreover, for any fixed non-ground ASP program $\Pi$, the problem of deciding whether, given a set $F$ of input facts, $\Pi \cup F$ has an answer set is $\Sigma_2^P$-complete [11].

## 2.2    Treewidth

Treewidth is a parameter that measures the cyclicity of graphs. It can be defined by means of *tree decompositions* [21]. The intuition behind tree decompositions is to obtain a tree $T$ from a (potentially cyclic) graph $G$ by subsuming multiple vertices of $G$ under one node of $T$ and thereby isolating the parts responsible for cyclicity.

**Definition 1.** *A* tree decomposition *of a graph $G$ is a pair $\mathcal{T} = (T, \chi)$ where $T$ is a (rooted) tree and $\chi : \mathrm{V}(T) \to 2^{\mathrm{V}(G)}$ assigns to each node of $T$ a set of vertices of $G$ (called the node's bag), such that the following conditions are met:*

1. *For every vertex $v \in \mathrm{V}(G)$, there is a node $t \in \mathrm{V}(T)$ such that $v \in \chi(t)$.*
2. *For every edge $(u,v) \in \mathrm{E}(G)$, there is a node $t \in \mathrm{V}(T)$ such that $\{u,v\} \subseteq \chi(t)$.*
3. *If a vertex is contained in the bags of two nodes $t, t'$, then it is also contained in the bags of all nodes between $t$ and $t'$.*

---

[1] In the database community, one of the origins of ASP, it is common to call a non-ground ASP program an *intensional database* (IDB) and a set of input facts an *extensional database* (EDB). Readers used to this terminology should note that the term "ASP program" generalizes both concepts. When the distinction between a non-ground program and its input is important, we will make this clear by calling the latter (i.e., the EDB) *input facts*.

accept ∨ reject.

attend(alice) ∨ attend(bob) ← accept.

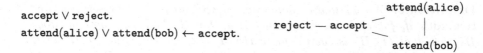

**Fig. 1.** A ground ASP program and its primal graph

*We call* $\max_{t \in V(T)} |\chi(t)| - 1$ *the* width *of* $T$*. The* treewidth *of a graph is the minimum width over all its tree decompositions.*

It is not hard to see that every tree has treewidth 1 and the complete graph with $n$ vertices (often denoted as $K_n$) has treewidth $n - 1$.

In general, constructing an optimal tree decomposition (i.e., a tree decomposition with minimum width) is intractable [1]. However, the problem is solvable in linear time on graphs of bounded treewidth (specifically in time $w^{\mathcal{O}(w^3)} \cdot n$, where $w$ is the treewidth [3]) and there are also heuristics that offer good performance in practice [4,5,9].

We can easily apply the parameter treewidth to ground ASP programs by defining a suitable representation as a graph.

**Definition 2.** *The* primal graph *of a ground ASP program* $\Pi$ *is the graph whose vertices are the atoms occurring in* $\Pi$ *and that has an edge between two atoms if they appear together in a rule in* $\Pi$*. When we speak of the treewidth of a ground program, we mean the treewidth of its primal graph.*

*Example 3.* Figure 1 depicts a ground ASP program and its primal graph. One possible tree decomposition of the primal graph consists of a chain of two nodes, where one bag contains accept and reject, and the other bag contains accept, attend(alice) and attend(bob). Since the largest bag of this tree decomposition has size three, the treewidth of that program is at most two. In fact it is exactly two, since $K_3$ is a subgraph of the primal graph, which means that the treewidth is at least two.

On ground ASP programs, the problem of deciding answer set existence parameterized by the treewidth of the primal graph, is fixed-parameter tractable (FPT; i.e., solvable in time $\mathcal{O}(f(w) \cdot n^c)$, where $f$ is some computable function, $c$ is a constant, and the input has size $n$ and treewidth $w$) [15]. In fact, this problem can even be solved in linear time when the treewidth is bounded by a constant.

As in this work we are interested in the treewidth of groundings in relation to the treewidth of the input of non-ground programs, we also need to define how treewidth can be applied to input facts.

**Definition 4.** *Let* $F$ *be a set of ground facts. We write* $\mathcal{G}(F)$ *to denote the graph whose vertices are the constants occurring in* $F$ *and where there is an edge between two vertices if the respective constants occur together in a fact.*

When we speak of the treewidth or maximum degree of a set $F$ of input facts for a program, we mean the treewidth or maximum degree of $\mathcal{G}(F)$, respectively.

We can now define the property of non-ground programs that is of primary interest in this work.

**Definition 5.** *We say that a (non-ground) ASP program $\Pi$ preserves bounded treewidth if, for each set $F$ of input facts for $\Pi$ there is a ground program $\Pi'$ such that (1) $\Pi'$ is equivalent to $\Pi \cup F$, (2) we can compute $\Pi'$ in time polynomial in $\|\Pi \cup F\|$, and (3) the treewidth of $\Pi'$ is at most $f(\|\Pi\|, w)$, where $f$ is an arbitrary computable function and $w$ is the treewidth of $\mathcal{G}(F)$.*

We say that a class of ASP programs preserves bounded treewidth if every program in the class does.

## 3    Grounding

The naive ground instantiation Ground($\Pi$) of a program $\Pi$, as defined before, is useful for the definition of the ASP semantics, but it blindly instantiates all variables by all possible constants, which is usually not necessary for obtaining an equivalent ground program. Grounders in practice may omit large parts of Ground($\Pi$) in order to keep the grounding as small as possible while preserving equivalence to Ground($\Pi$). The techniques performed by state-of-the-art grounders are quite sophisticated and differ between systems, so we define a simplified notion of grounding for our study.

For a meaningful investigation of the relationship between the treewidth of input facts and the treewidth of the grounding, we need to assume that the grounder does not simply produce the naive ground instantiation, which instantiates each variable with all constants and thus almost always leads to unbounded treewidth. Instead, we use the following definition of grounding from [2], which formalizes the idea that reasonable grounders will not produce rules whose body is obviously false under every answer set. This simplification is so basic that it can be assumed to be implemented by all reasonable grounders. The intuition is that we omit a rule from the naive ground instantiation whenever its positive body contains an atom that cannot possibly be derived.

**Definition 6.** *Let $\Pi$ be an ASP program, let $\Pi^+$ denote the positive program obtained from $\Pi$ by removing the negative bodies of all rules and replacing disjunctions in the heads with conjunctions (that is, we replace a rule $r$ whose head is $h_1 \vee \ldots \vee h_k$ by rules $r_1, \ldots, r_k$ such that $H(r_i) = \{h_i\}$ and the body of $r_i$ is $B^+(r)$). We say that an atom is* possibly true *in $\Pi$ if it is contained in the unique minimal model of $\Pi^+$. We define the* grounding *of $\Pi$, denoted by gr($\Pi$), as the set of all rules $r$ in Ground($\Pi$) such that every atom in $B^+(r)$ is possibly true.*

The following example illustrates this.

*Example 7.* Consider the program $\Pi_E$ from Fig. 2a. Following Definition 6, the program $\Pi_E^+$ looks as depicted in Fig. 2b. The unique minimal model of $\Pi_E^+$ consists of $p(a, b)$, $p(b, c)$, $q(b)$, $q(c)$, $r(a)$ and $r(b)$. This allows us to construct the grounding gr($\Pi_E$) as depicted in Fig. 2c. Note that gr($\Pi_E$) does not contain, for instance, the rule $q(c) \leftarrow p(a, c)$, which is present in Ground($\Pi_E$).

# 4    Connection-Guarded ASP with Unbounded Degrees

The class of connection-guarded ASP programs has been introduced in [2] in order to preserve bounded treewidth by grounding, provided that the maximum degree of the input is also bounded. We briefly recapitulate its definition.

**Definition 8.** *Let $\Pi$ be an ASP program. The* join graph *of a rule $r$ in $\Pi$ is the graph whose vertices are the variables in $r$, and there is an edge between two variables if they occur together in a positive extensional body atom of $r$. We call $\Pi$* connection-guarded *if the join graph of each rule in $\Pi$ is connected.*

For any fixed connection-guarded program $\Pi$, given a set $F$ of input facts such that $\mathcal{G}(F)$ has bounded treewidth and bounded maximum degree, the grounding $\mathrm{gr}(\Pi \cup F)$ has bounded treewidth, as shown in [2]. However, it is easy to see that there are connection-guarded programs such that the notion of grounding from Definition 6 leads to ground programs of unbounded treewidth if the degrees are unbounded.

*Example 9.* The program $\Pi$ consisting of the rule $\mathrm{p}(\mathrm{X},\mathrm{Z}) \leftarrow \mathrm{edge}(\mathrm{X},\mathrm{Y})$, $\mathrm{edge}(\mathrm{Y},\mathrm{Z})$ is connection-guarded, but given a set $F$ of facts describing a star (i.e., tree of height 1) with $n$ vertices, the grounding $\mathrm{gr}(\Pi \cup F)$ has unbounded treewidth because, intuitively, it connects all vertices with each other. (More precisely, the complete graph $K_{n-1}$ is a minor of the primal graph of the grounding, which therefore has treewidth at least $n - 2$.)

While this example shows that, for some connection-guarded programs, grounding as described in Definition 6 may destroy bounded treewidth of the input (if the maximum degree is unbounded), it does not rule out that a more sophisticated notion of grounding may actually preserve bounded treewidth on these programs.

In the rest of this section, we show that this cannot be the case (unless P = NP). We do so by first expressing a problem that is known to be NP-hard on instances of bounded treewidth as a connection-guarded ASP program. Then we prove that P = NP holds if this program preserves bounded treewidth. In other words, the existence of a grounder that runs in polynomial time and preserves bounded treewidth of the input for this program implies P = NP.

|  |  |  |
|---|---|---|
|  |  | p(a,b). |
|  |  | p(b,c). |
| p(a,b). | p(a,b). | q(b) ← p(a,b). |
| p(b,c). | p(b,c). | q(c) ← p(b,c). |
| q(Y) ← p(X,Y). | q(Y) ← p(X,Y). | r(b) ← p(a,b), not q(a). |
| r(X) ← p(X,Y), not q(X). | r(X) ← p(X,Y). | r(c) ← p(b,c), not q(b). |
| (a) Program $\Pi_E$ | (b) Program $\Pi_E^+$ | (c) Grounding $\mathrm{gr}(\Pi_E)$ |

**Fig. 2.** A program $\Pi_E$, its corresponding positive program $\Pi_E^+$ and grounding

**Theorem 10.** *The problem of deciding whether a fixed connection-guarded program $\Pi$ together with a given set $F$ of input facts has an answer set is* NP-*hard. This even holds if the treewidth of $F$ is at most three.*

*Proof.* We reduce from the following NP-complete problem.

---

SUBGRAPH ISOMORPHISM

    Input: Graphs $G$ and $H$

Question: Is there a subgraph of $G$ that is isomorphic to $H$?

---

This problem remains NP-hard even if the treewidth of both $G$ and $H$ is at most two [19].

The connection-guarded program in Fig. 3 encodes SUBGRAPH ISOMORPHISM.[2] We use unary predicates vg and vh to represent the vertices of the input graphs $G$ and $H$, respectively; eg and eh are binary predicates for the respective edges; the binary predicate bridge is used to connect each vertex of $G$ with a new "bridge element", which is in turn connected to each vertex of $H$ also via the bridge predicate; and the binary eq predicate shall be true for all pairs of identical vertices.

The idea behind the bridge predicate is that it allows us to make our encoding connection-guarded in the following way: Whenever we have a rule that contains two variables $X, Y$ that are not connected in the join graph, we can add bridge($X$, b) and bridge(b, $Y$) to the positive body and end up with a connection-guarded program.

Now we define a set $F$ of input facts for an instance $\langle G, H \rangle$ of SUBGRAPH ISOMORPHISM according to the intended meaning of our predicates. We use as constants the vertices of $G$ and $H$ as well as a new constant b. First we add facts $\{vg(v) \mid v \in V(G)\}$ and $\{vh(v) \mid v \in V(H)\}$ to $F$. For the edges, we add facts $\{eg(v, w) \mid (v, w) \in E(G)\}$ and $\{eh(v, w) \mid (v, w) \in E(H)\}$. Finally, we add facts $\{bridge(g, b), bridge(b, h) \mid g \in V(G), h \in V(H)\}$ and $\{eq(v, v) \mid v \in V(G) \cup V(H)\}$. Note that for every fact $eg(x, y)$ or $eh(x, y)$ in $F$ there is also a fact $eg(y, x)$ or $eh(y, x)$, respectively, since the graphs are undirected. It is easy to verify that this encoding is correct, so $H$ is isomorphic to a subgraph of $G$ if and only if $\Pi \cup F$ has an answer set.

The treewidth of $\mathcal{G}(F)$ is the maximum of the treewidth of $G$ and of $H$ plus one: Given tree decompositions $\mathcal{T}_G$ and $\mathcal{T}_H$ of $G$ and $H$, respectively, we can obtain a tree decomposition of $\mathcal{G}(F)$ by taking the disjoint union of $\mathcal{T}_G$ and $\mathcal{T}_H$, adding the bridge element b to every bag and drawing an edge between an arbitrary node from $\mathcal{T}_G$ and an arbitrary node from $\mathcal{T}_H$. $\qquad\square$

---

[2] In practice, we could simplify this encoding substantially by using convenient language constructs provided by ASP systems. For the purpose of this proof, we use our rather restrictive base language. Moreover, note that the positive body of many rules contains atoms whose only purpose is to make the rules connection-guarded. Such redundant atoms could be omitted in practice.

% *Guess a subgraph S of G using predicates* vs/1 *and* es/2.

  vs(X) ← vg(X), not not_vs(X).

 not_vs(X) ← vg(X), not vs(X).

  es(X,Y) ← eg(X,Y), vs(X), vs(Y), not not_es(X,Y).

not_es(X,Y) ← eg(X,Y), vs(X), vs(Y), not es(X,Y).

% *Guess a relation representing an isomorphism using predicate* iso/2.

  iso(G,H) ← vs(G), vh(H), not not_iso(G,H), bridge(G,B), bridge(B,H).

not_iso(G,H) ← vs(G), vh(H), not iso(G,H), bridge(G,B), bridge(B,H).

% *The guessed relation must be a bijection from* V(S) *to* V(H).

    ← iso(G,H1), iso(G,H2), not eq(H1,H2),

    bridge(G,B), bridge(B,H1), bridge(B,H2).

    ← iso(G1,H), iso(G2,H), not eq(G1,G2),

    bridge(G1,B), bridge(G2,B), bridge(B,H).

used(G) ← iso(G,H), bridge(G,B), bridge(B,H).

used(H) ← iso(G,H), bridge(G,B), bridge(B,H).

    ← vg(G), vs(G), not used(G).

    ← vh(H), not used(H).

% *The guessed relation must be an isomorphism.*

  ← iso(G1,H1), iso(G2,H2), es(G1,G2), not eh(H1,H2),

 bridge(G1,B), bridge(G2,B), bridge(B,H1), bridge(B,H2).

  ← iso(G1,H1), iso(G2,H2), eh(H1,H2), not es(G1,G2),

 bridge(G1,B), bridge(G2,B), bridge(B,H1), bridge(B,H2).

**Fig. 3.** An encoding of SUBGRAPH ISOMORPHISM in connection-guarded ASP

The fact that solving connection-guarded ASP is NP-hard (in fact $\Sigma_2^P$-complete) when the non-ground part is fixed has already been demonstrated in [2]. The relevance of Theorem 10 is that it shows this problem to be NP-hard *even if the input has bounded treewidth*.

This is particularly interesting because it allows us to prove that, assuming $P \neq NP$, there cannot be a grounder that runs in polynomial time and preserves bounded treewidth of the input for every connection-guarded program; if there were, we could solve SUBGRAPH ISOMORPHISM on instances of treewidth at most two, which is still NP-hard, in polynomial time: We reduce the problem to connection-guarded ASP as in the proof of Theorem 10. Grounding would then give us a propositional program of bounded treewidth. As ground ASP can be solved in linear time on instances of bounded treewidth [15], this would allow us to solve the problem in polynomial time.

**Theorem 11.** *If the class of connection-guarded ASP programs preserves bounded treewidth, then* $P = NP$.

*Proof.* Suppose connection-guarded ASP preserves bounded treewidth. Then the connection-guarded encoding $\Pi$ of SUBGRAPH ISOMORPHISM from the proof of

Theorem 10 preserves bounded treewidth. In other words, for each set $F$ of facts that encode an instance of SUBGRAPH ISOMORPHISM as described in that proof, there is a ground program $\Pi_F$ such that (1) $\Pi_F$ is equivalent to $\Pi \cup F$, (2) we can compute $\Pi_F$ in time polynomial in $\|\Pi \cup F\|$, and (3) the treewidth of $\Pi_F$ depends only on $\|\Pi\|$ and on the treewidth of $\mathcal{G}(F)$. From the results in [15] it follows that answer set existence for ground programs can be decided in linear time on instances whose primal graph has bounded treewidth. In particular this holds for the ground program $\Pi_F$. Hence we can solve SUBGRAPH ISOMORPHISM in time $\mathcal{O}(f(w) \cdot \|\Pi_F\|)$, where $f$ is some computable function and $w$ is the treewidth of $\Pi_F$. As we can compute $\Pi_F$ in time polynomial in $\|\Pi \cup F\|$, $\|\Pi_F\|$ is polynomial in $\|\Pi \cup F\|$. The program $\Pi$ is the same for every instance, so its size can be considered a constant. Hence $\|\Pi_F\|$ is polynomial in $\|F\|$ and $w$ depends only on the treewidth of $\mathcal{G}(F)$. We have seen in the proof of Theorem 10 that the treewidth of $\mathcal{G}(F)$ depends only on the treewidth of the SUBGRAPH ISOMORPHISM instance. It follows that $w$ is bounded by a constant if the treewidth of the SUBGRAPH ISOMORPHISM instance is bounded by a constant. Therefore SUBGRAPH ISOMORPHISM can be solved in polynomial time on each class of instances of bounded treewidth. As SUBGRAPH ISOMORPHISM is NP-complete on instances whose treewidth is at most two [19], P = NP.                                           □

## 5    Guarded Answer Set Programs

As we have shown in the previous section, connection-guarded ASP does not allow us to preserve bounded treewidth unless the maximum degree of the input is also bounded. In this section, we show that a class of non-ground ASP programs called *guarded ASP* leads to groundings whose treewidth depends only on the treewidth of the input. The notion of guardedness has also appeared, for instance, in the context of the query language Datalog [14].

**Definition 12.** *Let $\Pi$ be an ASP program. We call $\Pi$ guarded if every rule $r$ in $\Pi$ has an extensional atom $A$ in its positive body such that $A$ contains every variable occurring in $r$.*

Clearly every guarded program is connection-guarded. While guarded ASP is not as expressive, it has the advantage of allowing us to achieve what we could not do with connection-guarded ASP: Guarded ASP preserves bounded treewidth.

**Theorem 13.** *If $\Pi$ is a fixed guarded ASP program containing $c$ constants and $k$ predicates of arity at most $\ell$, and $F$ is a set of input facts for $\Pi$ such that $\mathcal{G}(F)$ has treewidth $w$, then the treewidth of the primal graph of $\mathrm{gr}(\Pi \cup F)$ is at most $k \cdot (w + c + 1)^\ell - 1$.*

*Proof.* Let $\mathcal{T}$ be a tree decomposition of $\mathcal{G}(F)$ having width $w$, and let $C$ denote the constants in $\Pi$. We construct a tree decomposition $\mathcal{T}'$ having width $k \cdot (w + c + 1)^\ell - 1$ of a supergraph of the primal graph of $\mathrm{gr}(\Pi \cup F)$. Since the treewidth of a subgraph is at most the treewidth of the whole graph, the statement follows.

We define the tree in $T'$ to be isomorphic to the tree in $T$. Let $N$ be a node in $T$ and $B$ be its bag. We define the bag $B'$ of the corresponding node $N'$ in $T'$ to consist of all atoms $p(x)$ such that $p$ is a predicate occurring in $\Pi$ and $x$ is a tuple of elements of $B \cup C$. The size of $B'$ is then at most $k \cdot (w + c + 1)^\ell$. It remains to show that $T'$ is indeed a tree decomposition of a supergraph of the primal graph of $gr(\Pi \cup F)$.

For every atom $p(x)$ in a rule $r$ of the grounding, we know from guardedness that there is a ground atom $g(y)$ in the positive body of $r$ such that $g$ is extensional and every element of $x$ that is not a constant is also an element of $y$. Since $g$ is extensional, there is a node in $T$ whose bag contains all elements of $y$. By our construction, the bag of the corresponding node in $T'$ contains $p(x)$.

If two atoms $p(x)$ and $q(y)$ occur together in a rule $r$ of the grounding, then from guardedness we infer that $r$ also contains an atom $g(z)$ in the positive body of $r$ such that $g$ is extensional and every element of $x$ or $y$ that is not a constant is also an element of $z$. As before, it follows that the bag of a node in $T$ contains all elements of $x$ and $y$ that are not constants, and the bag of the corresponding node in $T'$ contains both $p(x)$ and $q(y)$.

If the bags of two nodes $N', M'$ of $T'$ both contain an atom $p(x)$, then the bags of the corresponding nodes $N, M$ in $T$ contain all elements of $x$ that are not constants. By the definition of tree decompositions, every bag of each node between $N$ and $M$ in $T$ contains all elements of $x$ that are not constants. Hence, by our construction, the bags of all nodes between $N'$ and $M'$ in $T'$ contain $p(x)$. This proves that $T'$ is a tree decomposition of a supergraph of the primal graph of $gr(\Pi \cup F)$, and its width is at most $k \cdot (w + c)^\ell - 1$.    □

Since the guarded program $\Pi$ and thus $c$, $k$ and $\ell$ are fixed, this shows that the treewidth of the primal graph of $gr(\Pi \cup F)$ is polynomial in the treewidth of the input $F$.

Combining Theorem 13 with the known fixed-parameter tractability of ground ASP parameterized by treewidth, we immediately get the following result:

**Corollary 14.** *For every fixed guarded ASP program $\Pi$, the problem of deciding for a given set $F$ of input facts whether $\Pi \cup F$ has an answer set is fixed-parameter tractable when parameterized by the treewidth of $\mathcal{G}(F)$.*

This is in contrast to connection-guarded ASP. As we have shown in Theorem 10, for fixed connection-guarded programs the answer set existence problem is most likely not FPT when parameterized by the treewidth of the input facts. Yet this problem is FPT when parameterized by both the treewidth and the maximum degree [2]. To complete the picture of the parameterized complexity of the problem with these two parameters, we analyze the remaining case when just the maximum degree is the parameter. We prove that bounded maximum degree alone is also not sufficient for obtaining fixed-parameter tractability, even if the program is guarded.

```
     t(T)  ← verum(T).
     f(F)  ← falsum(F).
t(X) ∨f(X)  ← exists(X).
t(Y) ∨f(Y)  ← forall(Y).
        w ← term(X,Y,Z,Na,Nb,Nc), t(X), t(Y), t(Z), f(Na), f(Nb), f(Nc).
     t(Y)  ← w, forall(Y).
     f(Y)  ← w, forall(Y).
          ← not w.
```

**Fig. 4.** An encoding of QSAT$_2$ in guarded ASP

**Theorem 15.** *It is $\Sigma_2^P$-complete to decide for a fixed guarded program $\Pi$ and a given set $F$ of input facts whether $\Pi \cup F$ has an answer set even if the maximum degree of $\mathcal{G}(F)$ is at most 15.*

*Proof.* For membership, we guess an interpretation $I$ and then check by calling a co-NP oracle whether $I$ is a minimal model of $\mathrm{gr}(\Pi \cup F)^I$. We first show $\Sigma_2^P$-hardness for the case when the maximum degree of $\mathcal{G}(F)$ may be unbounded. Afterwards we show how this construction can be adjusted to obtain degrees of at most 15.

We present a guarded encoding for the well-known $\Sigma_2^P$-complete problem QSAT$_2$. We are given a formula $\exists x_1 \cdots \exists x_k \forall y_1 \cdots \forall y_\ell \, \varphi$, where $\varphi$ is a formula in 3-DNF (i.e., a disjunction of conjunctive terms, each containing at most three literals), and the question is whether there are truth values for the $x$ variables such that for all truth values for the $y$ variables $\varphi$ is true. We assume that each disjunct in $\varphi$ contains exactly three literals, which can be achieved by using the same literal multiple times in a disjunct.

Consider the ASP program in Fig. 4, which is based on the encoding in Sect. 3.3.5 of [16]. The QSAT$_2$ formula is represented as a set $F$ of input facts as follows: We will use each variable in $\varphi$ as a constant symbol, and we introduce new constant symbols t and f. First we put facts verum(t) and falsum(f) into $F$. Then, for each existentially or universally quantified variable $x$, we add a fact exists($x$) or forall($x$), respectively. Finally, for each disjunct $l_1 \wedge l_2 \wedge l_3$ in the formula, we put a fact term($p_1, p_2, p_3, q_1, q_2, q_3$) into $F$, where $p_i$ denotes $v_i$ if $l_i$ is a positive atom $v_i$, otherwise $p_i = $ t, and $q_i$ denotes $v_i$ if $l_i$ is an atom of the form not $v_i$, otherwise $q_i = $ f. The fact term($p_1, p_2, p_3, q_1, q_2, q_3$) thus represents $p_1 \wedge p_2 \wedge p_3 \wedge \neg q_1 \wedge \neg q_2 \wedge \neg q_3$, which is equivalent to the original disjunct. This program is clearly guarded and indeed encodes the QSAT$_2$ problem, as can be seen by the arguments in [16].

This shows $\Sigma_2^P$-hardness of answer set existence for fixed guarded programs. We still have to prove that $\Sigma_2^P$-hardness holds even if the maximum degree of $\mathcal{G}(F)$ is at most 15. For this, we first show that we may assume every variable to occur at most three times in $\varphi$ by a construction that has appeared in [20].

Observe that, for each sequence of variables $z_1, \ldots, z_m$, saying that two variables in this sequence have different truth values is equivalent to saying that

(a) some variable $z_i$ is false but $z_{i+1}$ is true, or (b) $z_m$ is false but $z_1$ is true. With this in mind, we obtain a formula $\varphi'$ from $\varphi$ by replacing every occurrence of an (either existentially or universally quantified) variable $z$ by a new variable $z^i$, where $i$ is the number of the respective occurrence in $\varphi$. (That is, the first occurrence of $z$ in $\varphi$ is replaced by $z_1$, the second by $z_2$, and so on.) To establish the connections between the copies of an old variable, we observe that the following statements are equivalent:

1. There are truth values for the $x$ variables such that, for all truth values for the $y$ variables, $\varphi$ is true.
2. There are truth values for the $x$ variables such that, for all truth values for the $y$ variables and for all truth values for the new copies, the following holds: If every old variable $z$ has the same truth value as all of its copies, then $\varphi'$ is true.
3. There are truth values for the $x$ variables such that, for all truth values for the $y$ variables and for all truth values for the new copies, the following holds: The formula $\varphi'$ is true or, for some old variable $z$ with copies $z^1, \ldots, z^m$, two variables in the sequence $z, z^1, \ldots, z^m$ have different truth values.
4. There are truth values for the $x$ variables such that, for all truth values for the $y$ variables and for all truth values for the new copies, the following formula is true, where $\mathrm{Var}(\varphi)$ denotes the variables occurring in $\varphi$:

$$\varphi' \vee \bigvee_{z \in \mathrm{Var}(\varphi) \text{ with } m \text{ copies}} \left((\neg z \wedge z^1) \vee (\neg z^1 \wedge z^2) \vee \cdots \vee (\neg z^{m-1} \wedge z^m) \vee (\neg z^m \wedge z)\right)$$

Thus we obtain an equivalent formula where each variable occurs at most three times.

In contrast to before, where we showed $\Sigma_2^P$-hardness when the maximum degree of $\mathcal{G}(F)$ may be unbounded, we now need to choose slightly different input facts because the domain elements $\mathsf{t}$ and $\mathsf{f}$ from the previous construction have unbounded degree. Recall that the old construction puts a fact $\mathrm{term}(p_1, p_2, p_3, q_1, q_2, q_3)$ into $F$ for each disjunct in $\varphi$ and that some $p_i$ or $q_j$ may be $\mathsf{t}$ or $\mathsf{f}$ in order to represent the equivalent term $p_1 \wedge p_2 \wedge p_3 \wedge \neg q_1 \wedge \neg q_2 \wedge \neg q_2$. The only thing that matters for $\mathsf{t}$ and $\mathsf{f}$ is that they are always interpreted as true and false, respectively, which the old construction ensures with the facts $\mathrm{verum}(\mathsf{t})$ and $\mathrm{falsum}(\mathsf{f})$. We can thus just use a certain number of copies of $\mathsf{t}$ and $\mathsf{f}$ such that every copy occurs in exactly one fact over the $\mathrm{term}$ predicate and for each copy $x$ we have the respective fact $\mathrm{verum}(x)$ or $\mathrm{falsum}(x)$. Clearly this reduction to ASP is still correct. The maximum degree of $\mathcal{G}(F)$ is at most 15 because every vertex has at most five neighbors from each fact over the $\mathrm{term}$ predicate and every variable occurs in at most three such facts.                    □

## 6   Discussion

Guardedness is evidently a rather strong restriction, even more so than connection-guardedness. Yet, as we have seen in Theorem 15, the restrictions imposed by guardedness do not alleviate the complexity of deciding answer set existence for fixed non-ground programs compared to the general case. Beside the encoding of $\text{QSAT}_2$ that we have presented, there are also several other relevant problems for which there are straightforward encodings in guarded ASP. But clearly there are also many problems that cannot be expressed in guarded ASP under common complexity-theoretic assumptions. As we have seen in Corollary 14, expressing a problem in guarded ASP amounts to a proof that the problem is FPT when parameterized by treewidth. Hence we most likely cannot find a guarded encoding for any problem that is W[1]-hard for treewidth.

We have argued in Theorem 15 that solving guarded ASP is as hard as ASP in general. In other words, every problem in $\Sigma_2^P$ can be reduced in polynomial time to guarded ASP, so one might be confused by our claim that we most likely cannot express any W[1]-hard problem in guarded ASP. After all, there are many problems in $\Sigma_2^P$ that are W[1]-hard when parameterized by treewidth. Note, however, that in general a polynomial-time reduction may increase the treewidth arbitrarily. When talking about the parameterized complexity of problems, we must, however, make sure that our reductions preserve the parameter. So we can indeed find polynomial-time reductions to guarded ASP from some problems that, when parameterized by treewidth, are W[1]-hard, but this requires us to change the problem instances in such a way that the treewidth of the resulting input facts no longer depends only on the treewidth of the original instance.

One may also ask how our result that guarded ASP preserves bounded treewidth relates to grounders in practice. In our investigation of the effect of grounding on the treewidth, we rely on the rather primitive notion of grounding from Definition 6. State-of-the-art grounders, on the other hand, produce groundings whose primal graphs are generally subgraphs of those resulting from our definition of grounding. However, since the treewidth of a subgraph is always at most the treewidth of the whole graph, our result applies also to state-of-the-art grounders.

Moreover, state-of-the-art grounders are capable of solving problems without needing to call an ASP solver if the program has an answer set that is a deterministic consequence of the input, i.e., if no non-deterministic guessing is involved. This is the case, for instance, for Horn programs (that is, ASP programs without negation or disjunction). Our notion of grounding, on the other hand, assumes that the grounder does not propagate deterministic consequences and thus cannot solve such simple problems by itself. This is in fact a reasonable assumption for our purposes: In this work we investigated *syntactic* subclasses of ASP, which means that we are merely interested in the *form* of the non-ground rules. Observe that, for each program that can be solved by the grounder as described before, we can add some rules that force atoms to be guessed. This prevents the grounder from eliminating atoms from rule bodies, and it does not change the form of the original rules. Enforcing the guesses can be done with syntactically very simple (in fact guarded) rules, so *in general* grounders cannot solve guarded programs themselves. (Still, Theorem 13 could of course be slightly extended by allowing for some violations of the guardedness criterion as long as some property of the program guarantees that we can make simplifications that "restore" guardedness.)

Finally, we would like to mention that answer set solving (to be precise, the so-called brave reasoning problem) is still fixed-parameter tractable for guarded (cf. Corollary 14) and even connection-guarded programs when we add weak constraints and aggregates [7] to our language. It is not hard to prove this by translating these constructs into optimization rules and weight rules, respectively, and then invoking the FPT algorithm from [12].

# 7   Conclusion

In this work, we showed that the class of connection-guarded ASP programs does not preserve bounded treewidth (unless $P = NP$). That is, for some connection-guarded programs it is impossible to compute a grounding whose treewidth is "small" whenever the input facts have "small" treewidth (unless grounding is allowed to take exponential time or $P = NP$). At the same time, we have proven that the more restrictive class of guarded ASP programs achieves the goal of preserving bounded treewidth. It may therefore be a good idea to encode problems in guarded ASP whenever possible, since ASP solvers appear to run much faster on groundings of small treewidth. Unsurprisingly, not all problems can be expressed in guarded ASP. In particular, we proved that problems that are not FPT w.r.t. treewidth cannot be expressed in this class. For several problems it is, however, possible to find straightforward guarded encodings (e.g., several standard graph problems such as graph coloring, vertex cover, dominating set, or some reachability-based problems as shown in the example from Sect. 1). Despite the syntactical restrictions imposed by guardedness, ASP solving in this class does not become easier compared to the general case. As we showed, guarded ASP still allows us to express $\Sigma_2^P$-complete problems.

In the future, it may be interesting to investigate the relationship of guarded and connection-guarded ASP to well-known tools for classifying a problem as FPT for the parameter treewidth. In particular, the famous result by Courcelle [8] states that every problem that is expressible in monadic second-order (MSO) logic is FPT w.r.t. treewidth. Similarly, we have seen in Corollary 14 that also every problem that is expressible in guarded ASP is FPT. Since answer-set solving for guarded programs is $\Sigma_2^P$-complete in general (cf. Theorem 15), whereas MSO model checking is PSPACE-complete, guarded ASP seems to be strictly weaker than MSO. We suspect that this still holds if we add aggregates to guarded ASP. For connection-guarded ASP, however, we conjecture that adding aggregates allows us to encode problems that are not expressible in MSO and its known extensions. We thus expect that connection-guarded ASP can be used as a classification tool for getting FPT results when the parameter is the combination of treewidth and maximum degree.

**Acknowledgments.** This work was supported by the Austrian Science Fund (FWF, project Y698) and by the Academy of Finland (grant 312662). Part of this work was done when the author was employed at TU Wien, Vienna, Austria.

# References

1. Arnborg, S., Corneil, D.G., Proskurowski, A.: Complexity of finding embeddings in a k-tree. SIAM J. Algebr. Discrete Methods **8**(2), 277–284 (1987)
2. Bliem, B., Moldovan, M., Morak, M., Woltran, S.: The impact of treewidth on ASP grounding and solving. In: Sierra, C. (ed.) Proceedings of IJCAI 2017, pp. 852–858. AAAI Press (2017)
3. Bodlaender, H.L.: A linear-time algorithm for finding tree-decompositions of small treewidth. SIAM J. Comput. **25**(6), 1305–1317 (1996)
4. Bodlaender, H.L.: Discovering treewidth. In: Vojtáš, P., Bieliková, M., Charron-Bost, B., Sýkora, O. (eds.) SOFSEM 2005. LNCS, vol. 3381, pp. 1–16. Springer, Heidelberg (2005). https://doi.org/10.1007/978-3-540-30577-4_1
5. Bodlaender, H.L., Koster, A.M.C.A.: Treewidth computations I. Upper bounds. Inf. Comput. **208**(3), 259–275 (2010)
6. Brewka, G., Eiter, T., Truszczyński, M.: Answer set programming at a glance. Commun. ACM **54**(12), 92–103 (2011)
7. Calimeri, F., Faber, W., Gebser, M., Ianni, G., Kaminski, R., Krennwallner, T., Leone, N., Ricca, F., Schaub, T.: ASP-Core-2 input language format, Version: 2.03c (2015). https://www.mat.unical.it/aspcomp2013/ASPStandardization
8. Courcelle, B.: The monadic second-order logic of graphs I: recognizable sets of finite graphs. Inf. Comput. **85**(1), 12–75 (1990)
9. Dermaku, A., Ganzow, T., Gottlob, G., McMahan, B., Musliu, N., Samer, M.: Heuristic methods for hypertree decomposition. In: Gelbukh, A., Morales, E.F. (eds.) MICAI 2008. LNCS (LNAI), vol. 5317, pp. 1–11. Springer, Heidelberg (2008). https://doi.org/10.1007/978-3-540-88636-5_1
10. Eiter, T., Gottlob, G.: On the computational cost of disjunctive logic programming: propositional case. Ann. Math. Artif. Intell. **15**(3–4), 289–323 (1995)
11. Eiter, T., Gottlob, G., Mannila, H.: Disjunctive datalog. ACM Trans. Database Syst. **22**(3), 364–418 (1997)
12. Fichte, J.K., Hecher, M., Morak, M., Woltran, S.: Answer set solving with bounded treewidth revisited. In: Balduccini, M., Janhunen, T. (eds.) LPNMR 2017. LNCS (LNAI), vol. 10377, pp. 132–145. Springer, Cham (2017). https://doi.org/10.1007/978-3-319-61660-5_13
13. Gebser, M., Kaminski, R., Kaufmann, B., Schaub, T.: Answer Set Solving in Practice. Synthesis Lectures on Artificial Intelligence and Machine Learning. Morgan & Claypool Publishers, Williston (2012)
14. Gottlob, G., Grädel, E., Veith, H.: Datalog LITE: a deductive query language with linear time model checking. ACM Trans. Comput. Log. **3**(1), 42–79 (2002)
15. Gottlob, G., Pichler, R., Wei, F.: Bounded treewidth as a key to tractability of knowledge representation and reasoning. Artif. Intell. **174**(1), 105–132 (2010)
16. Leone, N., Pfeifer, G., Faber, W., Eiter, T., Gottlob, G., Perri, S., Scarcello, F.: The DLV system for knowledge representation and reasoning. ACM Trans. Comput. Log. **7**(3), 499–562 (2006)
17. Lifschitz, V.: What is answer set programming? In: Fox, D., Gomes, C.P. (eds.) Proceedings of AAAI 2008, pp. 1594–1597. AAAI Press (2008)
18. Marek, V.W., Truszczyński, M.: Stable models and an alternative logic programming paradigm. In: Apt, K., Marek, V.W., Truszczyński, M., Warren, D.S. (eds.) The Logic Programming Paradigm: A 25-Year Perspective, pp. 375–398. Springer, Heidelberg (1999). https://doi.org/10.1007/978-3-642-60085-2_17

19. Matoušek, J., Thomas, R.: On the complexity of finding iso- and other morphisms for partial k-trees. Discrete Math. **108**(1–3), 343–364 (1992)
20. Peters, D.: $\Sigma_2^p$-complete problems on hedonic games, Version: 2. CoRR abs/1509.02333 (2017). http://arxiv.org/abs/1509.02333
21. Robertson, N., Seymour, P.D.: Graph minors. III. Planar tree-width. J. Comb. Theory Ser. B **36**(1), 49–64 (1984)

# Rationality and Context in Defeasible Subsumption

Katarina Britz[1] and Ivan Varzinczak[2,1(✉)]

[1] CSIR-SU CAIR, Stellenbosch University, Stellenbosch, South Africa
abritz@sun.ac.za
[2] CRIL, Univ. Artois & CNRS, Lens, France
varzinczak@cril.fr

**Abstract.** Description logics have been extended in a number of ways to support defeasible reasoning in the KLM tradition. Such features include preferential or rational defeasible concept subsumption, and defeasible roles in complex concept descriptions. Semantically, defeasible subsumption is obtained by means of a preference order on objects, while defeasible roles are obtained by adding a preference order to role interpretations. In this paper, we address an important limitation in defeasible extensions of description logics, namely the restriction in the semantics of defeasible concept subsumption to a single preference order on objects. We do this by inducing a modular preference order on objects from each preference order on roles, and use these to relativise defeasible subsumption. This yields a notion of contextualised rational defeasible subsumption, with contexts described by roles. We also provide a semantic construction for and a method for the computation of contextual rational closure, and present a correspondence result between the two.

## 1 Introduction

Description Logics (DLs) [2] are decidable fragments of first-order logic that serve as the formal foundation for Semantic-Web ontologies. As witnessed by recent developments in the field, DLs still allow for meaningful, decidable extensions, as new knowledge representation requirements are identified. A case in point is the need to allow for exceptions and defeasibility in reasoning over logic-based ontologies [4–6,12,13,15,19,21,23–25,29,30,34,36]. Yet, DLs do not allow for the direct expression of and reasoning with different aspects of defeasibility.

Given the special status of concept subsumption in DLs in particular, and the historical importance of entailment in logic in general, past research efforts in this direction have focused primarily on accounts of defeasible subsumption and the characterisation of defeasible entailment. Semantically, the latter usually takes as point of departure orderings on a class of first-order interpretations, whereas the former usually assume a preference order on objects of the domain.

Recently, we proposed decidable extensions of DLs supporting defeasible knowledge representation and reasoning over ontologies [19,21,22]. Our proposal

© Springer International Publishing AG, part of Springer Nature 2018
F. Ferrarotti and S. Woltran (Eds.): FoIKS 2018, LNCS 10833, pp. 114–132, 2018.
https://doi.org/10.1007/978-3-319-90050-6_7

built on previous work to resolve two important ontological limitations of the preferential approach to defeasibility in DLs—the assumption of a single preference order on all objects in the domain of interpretation, and the assumption that defeasibility is intrinsically linked to arguments or conditionals [18,20].

We achieved this by introducing non-monotonic reasoning features that any classical DL can be extended with in the concept language, in subsumption statements and in role assertions, via an intuitive notion of normality for roles. This parameterised the idea of preference while at the same time introducing the notion of defeasible class membership. Defeasible subsumption allows for the expression of statements of the form "$C$ is usually subsumed by $D$", for example, "Chenin blanc wines *are usually* unwooded". In the extended language, one can also refer directly to, for example, "Chenin blanc wines that *usually have* a wood aroma". We can also combine these seamlessly, as in: "Chenin blanc wines that *usually have* a wood aroma *are usually* wooded". This cannot be expressed in terms of defeasible subsumption alone, nor can it be expressed w.l.o.g. using typicality-based operators [8,26,27] on concepts. This is because the semantics of the expression is inextricably tied to the two distinct uses of the term 'usually'.

Nevertheless, even this generalisation leaves open the question of different, possibly incompatible, notions of defeasibility in subsumption, similar to those studied in contextual argumentation [1,3]. In the statement "Chenin blanc wines are usually unwooded", the context relative to which the subsumption is normal is left implicit—in this case, the style of the wine. In a different context such as consumer preference or origin, the most preferred (or normal, or typical) Chenin blanc wines may not correlate with the usual wine style. Wine $x$ may be more exceptional than $y$ in one context, but less exceptional in another context. This represents a form of inconsistency in defeasible knowledge bases that could arise from the presence of named individuals in the ontology. The example illustrates why a single ordering on individuals does not suffice. It also points to a natural index for relativised context, namely the use of preferential role names as we have previously proposed [19]. Using role names rather than concept names to indicate context has the advantage that constructs to form complex roles are either absent or limited to role composition.

In this paper, we therefore propose to induce preference orders on objects from preference orders on roles, and use these to relativise defeasible subsumption. This yields a notion of contextualised defeasible subsumption, with contexts described by roles. The remainder of the present paper is structured as follows: in Sect. 2, we provide a summary of the required background on $\mathcal{ALC}$, the prototypical description logic and on which we shall focus in the present work. In Sect. 3, we introduce an extension of $\mathcal{ALC}$ to represent both defeasible constructs on complex concepts and contextual defeasible subsumption. In Sect. 4, we address the most important question from the standpoint of knowledge representation and reasoning with defeasible ontologies, namely that of entailment from defeasible knowledge bases. In particular, we present a semantic construction of contextual rational closure and provide a method for computing it. Finally, with Sect. 5 we conclude the paper.

We shall assume the reader's familiarity with the preferential approach to non-monotonic reasoning [31,33,37]. Whenever necessary, we refer the reader to the definitions and results in the relevant literature.

## 2   The Description Logic $\mathcal{ALC}$

The (concept) language of $\mathcal{ALC}$ is built upon a finite set of atomic *concept names* C, a finite set of *role names* R and a finite set of *individual names* I such that C, R and I are pairwise disjoint. With $A, B, \ldots$ we denote atomic concepts, with $r, s, \ldots$ role names, and with $a, b, \ldots$ individual names. Complex concepts are denoted with $C, D, \ldots$ and are built according to the following rule:

$$C ::= \top \mid \bot \mid A \mid \neg C \mid C \sqcap C \mid C \sqcup C \mid \forall r.C \mid \exists r.C$$

With $\mathcal{L_{ALC}}$ we denote the *language* of all $\mathcal{ALC}$ concepts.

The semantics of $\mathcal{L_{ALC}}$ is the standard set theoretic Tarskian semantics. An *interpretation* is a structure $\mathcal{I} := \langle \Delta^{\mathcal{I}}, \cdot^{\mathcal{I}} \rangle$, where $\Delta^{\mathcal{I}}$ is a non-empty set called the *domain*, and $\cdot^{\mathcal{I}}$ is an *interpretation function* mapping concept names $A$ to subsets $A^{\mathcal{I}}$ of $\Delta^{\mathcal{I}}$, role names $r$ to binary relations $r^{\mathcal{I}}$ over $\Delta^{\mathcal{I}}$, and individual names $a$ to elements of the domain $\Delta^{\mathcal{I}}$, i.e., $A^{\mathcal{I}} \subseteq \Delta^{\mathcal{I}}$, $r^{\mathcal{I}} \subseteq \Delta^{\mathcal{I}} \times \Delta^{\mathcal{I}}$, $a^{\mathcal{I}} \in \Delta^{\mathcal{I}}$. Define $r^{\mathcal{I}}(x) := \{y \mid (x,y) \in r^{\mathcal{I}}\}$. We extend the interpretation function $\cdot^{\mathcal{I}}$ to interpret complex concepts of $\mathcal{L_{ALC}}$ in the following way:

$$\top^{\mathcal{I}} := \Delta^{\mathcal{I}}, \quad \bot^{\mathcal{I}} := \emptyset, \quad (\neg C)^{\mathcal{I}} := \Delta^{\mathcal{I}} \setminus C^{\mathcal{I}}$$
$$(C \sqcap D)^{\mathcal{I}} := C^{\mathcal{I}} \cap D^{\mathcal{I}}, \quad (C \sqcup D)^{\mathcal{I}} := C^{\mathcal{I}} \cup D^{\mathcal{I}}$$
$$(\exists r.C)^{\mathcal{I}} := \{x \in \Delta^{\mathcal{I}} \mid r^{\mathcal{I}}(x) \cap C^{\mathcal{I}} \neq \emptyset\}, \quad (\forall r.C)^{\mathcal{I}} := \{x \in \Delta^{\mathcal{I}} \mid r^{\mathcal{I}}(x) \subseteq C^{\mathcal{I}}\}$$

Given $C, D \in \mathcal{L_{ALC}}$, $C \sqsubseteq D$ is called a *subsumption statement*, or *general concept inclusion* (GCI), read "$C$ is subsumed by $D$". $C \equiv D$ is an abbreviation for both $C \sqsubseteq D$ and $D \sqsubseteq C$. An $\mathcal{ALC}$ *TBox* $\mathcal{T}$ is a finite set of subsumption statements and formalises the *intensional* knowledge about a given domain of application. Given $C \in \mathcal{L_{ALC}}$, $r \in$ R and $a, b \in$ I, an *assertional statement* (*assertion*, for short) is an expression of the form $a : C$ or $(a,b) : r$. An $\mathcal{ALC}$ *ABox* $\mathcal{A}$ is a finite set of assertional statements formalising the *extensional* knowledge of the domain. We shall denote statements, both subsumption and assertional, with $\alpha, \beta, \ldots$. Given $\mathcal{T}$ and $\mathcal{A}$, with $\mathcal{KB} := \mathcal{T} \cup \mathcal{A}$ we denote an $\mathcal{ALC}$ *knowledge base*, a.k.a. an *ontology*.

An interpretation $\mathcal{I}$ *satisfies* a subsumption statement $C \sqsubseteq D$ (denoted $\mathcal{I} \Vdash C \sqsubseteq D$) if and only if $C^{\mathcal{I}} \subseteq D^{\mathcal{I}}$. $\mathcal{I}$ satisfies an assertion $a : C$ (respectively, $(a,b) : r$), denoted $\mathcal{I} \Vdash a : C$ (respectively, $\mathcal{I} \Vdash (a,b) : r$), if and only if $a^{\mathcal{I}} \in C^{\mathcal{I}}$ (respectively, $(a^{\mathcal{I}}, b^{\mathcal{I}}) \in r^{\mathcal{I}}$).

An interpretation $\mathcal{I}$ is a *model* of a knowledge base $\mathcal{KB}$ (denoted $\mathcal{I} \Vdash \mathcal{KB}$) if and only if $\mathcal{I} \Vdash \alpha$ for every $\alpha \in \mathcal{KB}$. A statement $\alpha$ is (classically) *entailed* by $\mathcal{KB}$, denoted $\mathcal{KB} \models \alpha$, if and only if every model of $\mathcal{KB}$ satisfies $\alpha$.

For more details on Description Logics in general and on $\mathcal{ALC}$ in particular, the reader is invited to consult the Description Logic Handbook [2].

# 3   Contextual Defeasibility in DLs

In this section, we introduce an extension of $\mathcal{ALC}$ to represent both defeasible constructs on complex concepts and contextual defeasible subsumption. The logic presented here draws on the introduction of defeasible roles [19] and recent preliminary work on context-based defeasible subsumption for $\mathcal{SROIQ}$ [21,22].

## 3.1   Defeasible Constructs

Our previous investigations of defeasible DLs included parameterised defeasible constructs on concepts based on preferential roles, in the form of defeasible value and existential restriction of the form $\forall r.C$ and $\exists r.C$. Intuitively, these concept descriptions refer respectively to individuals whose normal $r$-relationships are only to individuals from $C$, and individuals that have some normal $r$-relationship to an individual from $C$. However, while these constructs allowed for multiple preference orders on (the interpretation of) roles, only a single preference order on objects was assumed. This was somewhat of an anomaly, which we address here by adding context-based orderings on objects that are derived from preferential roles [21]. Briefly, each preferential role $r$, interpreted as a strict partial order on the binary product space of the domain, gives rise to a context-based order on objects as detailed in Definition 3 below.

The (concept) language of *defeasible $\mathcal{ALC}$*, or $d\mathcal{ALC}$, is built according to the following rule:

$$C ::= \top \mid \bot \mid A \mid \neg C \mid C \sqcap C \mid C \sqcup C \mid \forall r.C \mid \exists r.C \mid \forall r.C \mid \exists r.C$$

With $\mathcal{L}_{d\mathcal{ALC}}$ we denote the language of all $d\mathcal{ALC}$ concepts.

The extension of $\mathcal{ALC}$ we propose here also adds contextual defeasible subsumption statements to knowledge bases. Given $C, D \in \mathcal{L}_{d\mathcal{ALC}}$ and $r \in \mathsf{R}$, $C \sqsubseteq_r D$ is a *defeasible subsumption statement* or *defeasible GCI*, read "$C$ is usually subsumed by $D$ in the context $r$". A *defeasible $d\mathcal{ALC}$ TBox $\mathcal{D}$* is a finite set of defeasible GCIs. A *classical $d\mathcal{ALC}$ TBox $\mathcal{T}$* is a finite set of (classical) subsumption statements $C \sqsubseteq D$ (i.e., $\mathcal{T}$ may contain defeasible concept constructs, but not defeasible concept inclusions).

This begs the question of adding some version of "contextual classical subsumption" to the TBox, but, as we shall see in Sect. 3.2, this simply reduces to classical subsumption.

Given a classical $d\mathcal{ALC}$ TBox $\mathcal{T}$, an ABox $\mathcal{A}$ and a defeasible $d\mathcal{ALC}$ TBox $\mathcal{D}$, from now on we let $\mathcal{KB} := \mathcal{T} \cup \mathcal{D} \cup \mathcal{A}$ and refer to it as a *defeasible $d\mathcal{ALC}$ knowledge base* (alias defeasible ontology).

## 3.2   Preferential Semantics

We shall anchor our semantic constructions in the well-known preferential approach to non-monotonic reasoning [31,33,37] and its extensions [7–9,11,16–18], especially those in DLs [15,19,28,35].

Let $X$ be a set and let $<$ be a strict partial order on $X$. With $\min_< X :=$ $\{x \in X \mid$ there is no $y \in X$ s.t. $y < x\}$ we denote the *minimal elements* of $X$ w.r.t. $<$. With $\#X$ we denote the *cardinality* of $X$.

**Definition 1 (Ordered Interpretation).** *An* **ordered interpretation** *is a tuple* $\mathcal{O} := \langle \Delta^\mathcal{O}, \cdot^\mathcal{O}, \ll^\mathcal{O} \rangle$ *such that:*

- $\langle \Delta^\mathcal{O}, \cdot^\mathcal{O} \rangle$ *is an* $\mathcal{ALC}$ *interpretation, with* $A^\mathcal{O} \subseteq \Delta^\mathcal{O}$, *for each* $A \in \mathsf{C}$, $r^\mathcal{O} \subseteq \Delta^\mathcal{O} \times \Delta^\mathcal{O}$, *for each* $r \in \mathsf{R}$, *and* $a^\mathcal{O} \in \Delta^\mathcal{O}$, *for each* $a \in \mathsf{I}$, *and*
- $\ll^\mathcal{O} := \langle \ll^\mathcal{O}_1, \ldots, \ll^\mathcal{O}_{\#\mathsf{R}} \rangle$, *where* $\ll^\mathcal{O}_i \subseteq r^\mathcal{O}_i \times r^\mathcal{O}_i$, *for* $i = 1, \ldots, \#\mathsf{R}$, *and such that each* $\ll^\mathcal{O}_i$ *is a strict partial order and satisfies the smoothness condition* [31].

As an example, suppose $\mathsf{C} := \{A_1, A_2, A_3\}$, $\mathsf{R} := \{r_1, r_2\}$, $\mathsf{I} := \{a_1, a_2, a_3\}$, and $\mathcal{O} = \langle \Delta^\mathcal{O}, \cdot^\mathcal{O}, \ll^\mathcal{O} \rangle$, with $\Delta^\mathcal{O} = \{x_i \mid 1 \leq i \leq 9\}$, $A^\mathcal{O}_1 = \{x_1, x_4, x_6\}$, $A^\mathcal{O}_2 = \{x_3, x_5, x_9\}$, $A^\mathcal{O}_3 = \{x_6, x_7, x_8\}$, $r^\mathcal{O}_1 = \{(x_1, x_6), (x_4, x_8), (x_2, x_5)\}$, $r^\mathcal{O}_2 = \{(x_4, x_4), (x_6, x_4), (x_5, x_8), (x_9, x_3)\}$, $a^\mathcal{O}_1 = x_5$, $a^\mathcal{O}_2 = x_1$, $a^\mathcal{O}_3 = x_2$, and $\ll^\mathcal{O}_1 = \{(x_4 x_8, x_2 x_5), (x_2 x_5, x_1 x_6), (x_4 x_8, x_1 x_6)\}$ and $\ll^\mathcal{O}_2 = \{(x_6 x_4, x_4 x_4), (x_5 x_8, x_9 x_3)\}$. (For the sake of readability, we shall henceforth sometimes write tuples of the form $(x, y)$ as $xy$.) Fig. 1 below depicts the $r$-ordered interpretation $\mathcal{O}$. In the picture, $\ll^\mathcal{O}_1$ and $\ll^\mathcal{O}_2$ are represented, respectively, by the dashed and the dotted arrows. (Note the direction of the $\ll^\mathcal{O}$-arrows, which point from more preferred to less preferred pairs of objects. Also for the sake of readability, we omit the transitive $\ll^\mathcal{O}$-arrows.)

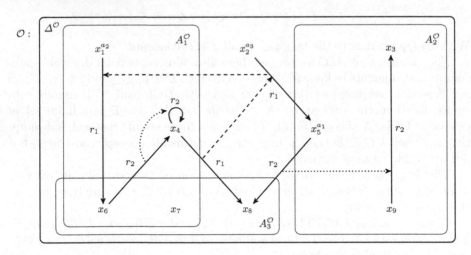

**Fig. 1.** A $d\mathcal{ALC}$ ordered interpretation.

Given $\mathcal{O} = \langle \Delta^\mathcal{O}, \cdot^\mathcal{O}, \ll^\mathcal{O} \rangle$, the intuition of $\Delta^\mathcal{O}$ and $\cdot^\mathcal{O}$ is the same as in a standard DL interpretation. The intuition underlying each of the orderings in $\ll^\mathcal{O}$ is that they play the role of *preference relations* (or *normality orderings*), in a sense similar to that introduced by Shoham [37] with a preference on worlds in a propositional setting and as investigated by Kraus et al. [31,33] and others [11,14,26]: the pairs $(x, y)$ that are lower down in the ordering $\ll_i^{\mathcal{O}}$ are deemed as the most normal (or typical, or expected, or conventional) in the context of (the interpretation of) $r_i$.

In the following definition we show how ordered interpretations can be extended to interpret the complex concepts of the language.

**Definition 2 (Concept Interpretation).** *Let* $\mathcal{O} = \langle \Delta^{\mathcal{O}}, \cdot^{\mathcal{O}}, \ll^{\mathcal{O}} \rangle$, *let* $r \in \mathsf{R}$ *and let* $r_i^{\mathcal{O}|x} := r_i^{\mathcal{O}} \cap (\{x\} \times \Delta^{\mathcal{O}})$ *(i.e., the restriction of the domain of* $r_i^{\mathcal{O}}$ *to* $\{x\}$*). The interpretation function* $\cdot^{\mathcal{O}}$ *interprets* $d\mathcal{ALC}$ *concepts as follows:*

$$\top^{\mathcal{O}} := \Delta^{\mathcal{O}}; \quad \bot^{\mathcal{O}} := \emptyset;$$
$$(\neg C)^{\mathcal{O}} := \Delta^{\mathcal{O}} \setminus C^{\mathcal{O}};$$
$$(C \sqcap D)^{\mathcal{O}} := C^{\mathcal{O}} \cap D^{\mathcal{O}};$$
$$(C \sqcup D)^{\mathcal{O}} := C^{\mathcal{O}} \cup D^{\mathcal{O}};$$
$$(\forall r.C)^{\mathcal{O}} := \{x \mid r^{\mathcal{O}}(x) \subseteq C^{\mathcal{O}}\};$$
$$(\mathbb{\forall} r.C)^{\mathcal{O}} := \{x \mid \min_{\ll_r^{\mathcal{O}}}(r^{\mathcal{O}|x})(x) \subseteq C^{\mathcal{O}}\};$$
$$(\exists r.C)^{\mathcal{O}} := \{x \mid r^{\mathcal{O}}(x) \cap C^{\mathcal{O}} \neq \emptyset\};$$
$$(\mathbb{\exists} r.C)^{\mathcal{O}} := \{x \mid \min_{\ll_r^{\mathcal{O}}}(r^{\mathcal{O}|x})(x) \cap C^{\mathcal{O}} \neq \emptyset\}.$$

If, as in Definition 2, the role name $r$ is not indexed, we use $r$ itself as subscript in $\ll_r^{\mathcal{O}}$. It is not hard to see that, analogously to the classical case, $\mathbb{\forall}$ and $\mathbb{\exists}$ are dual to each other.

**Definition 3 (Satisfaction).** *Let* $\mathcal{O} = \langle \Delta^{\mathcal{O}}, \cdot^{\mathcal{O}}, \ll^{\mathcal{O}} \rangle$, $r \in \mathsf{R}$, $C, D \in \mathcal{L}_{d\mathcal{ALC}}$, *and* $a, b \in \mathsf{I}$. *Define* $\prec_r^{\mathcal{O}} \subseteq \Delta^{\mathcal{O}} \times \Delta^{\mathcal{O}}$ *as follows:*

$$\prec_r^{\mathcal{O}} := \{(x, y) \mid (\exists(x, z) \in r^{\mathcal{O}})(\forall(y, v) \in r^{\mathcal{O}})[((x, z), (y, v)) \in \ll_r^{\mathcal{O}}]\}.$$

*The satisfaction relation* $\Vdash$ *is defined as follows:*

$\mathcal{O} \Vdash C \sqsubseteq D$ *if* $C^{\mathcal{O}} \subseteq D^{\mathcal{O}}$;
$\mathcal{O} \Vdash C \sqsubseteq_r D$ *if* $\min_{\prec_r^{\mathcal{O}}} C^{\mathcal{O}} \subseteq D^{\mathcal{O}}$;
$\mathcal{O} \Vdash a : C$ *if* $a^{\mathcal{O}} \in C^{\mathcal{O}}$;
$\mathcal{O} \Vdash (a, b) : r$ *if* $(a^{\mathcal{O}}, b^{\mathcal{O}}) \in r^{\mathcal{O}}$.

*If* $\mathcal{O} \Vdash \alpha$, *then we say* $\mathcal{O}$ *satisfies* $\alpha$. $\mathcal{O}$ *satisfies a defeasible knowledge base* $\mathcal{KB}$, *written* $\mathcal{O} \Vdash \mathcal{KB}$, *if* $\mathcal{O} \Vdash \alpha$ *for every* $\alpha \in \mathcal{KB}$, *in which case we say* $\mathcal{O}$ *is a model of* $\mathcal{KB}$. *We say* $C \in \mathcal{L}_{d\mathcal{ALC}}$ *is satisfiable w.r.t.* $\mathcal{KB}$ *if there is a model* $\mathcal{O}$ *of* $\mathcal{KB}$ *s.t.* $C^{\mathcal{O}} \neq \emptyset$.

It follows from Definition 3 that, if $\ll_r^{\mathcal{O}} = \emptyset$, i.e., if no $r$-tuple is preferred to another, then $\sqsubseteq_r$ reverts to $\sqsubseteq$. This reflects the intuition that the context $r$ be taken into account through the preference order on $r^{\mathcal{O}}$. In the absence of any preference, the context becomes irrelevant. This also shows why the classical counterpart of $\sqsubseteq_r$ is independent of $r$—context is taken into account in the form of a preference order, but preference has no bearing on the semantics of $\sqsubseteq$.

The following result, of which the proof extends that in the classical case to deal with preferences, will come in handy in Sect. 4.2:

**Lemma 1.** *$d\mathcal{ALC}$ ordered interpretations are closed under disjoint union.*

Lemma 2 below shows that every preferential role interpretation gives rise to a preference order on objects in the domain. Conversely, Lemma 3 shows that every strict partial order on objects in the domain $\Delta^{\mathcal{O}}$ can be obtained from some strict partial order on the interpretation of a new role name as in Definition 3. This means that the more traditional preference order on all objects in the domain is a special case of our proposal.

**Lemma 2.** *Let $\mathcal{O} = \langle \Delta^{\mathcal{O}}, \cdot^{\mathcal{O}}, \ll^{\mathcal{O}} \rangle$, $r \in \mathsf{R}$ and let $\prec_r^{\mathcal{O}}$ be as in Definition 3. Then $\prec_r^{\mathcal{O}}$ is a strict partial order on $\Delta^{\mathcal{O}}$.*

*Proof.* We show that $\prec_r^{\mathcal{O}}$ is (*i*) transitive, (*ii*) irreflexive and (*iii*) antisymmetric.

(i) Suppose $(x, y) \in \prec_r^{\mathcal{O}}$ and $(y, z) \in \prec_r^{\mathcal{O}}$. Then $\exists (x, u) \in r^{\mathcal{O}}$ and $\exists (y, v) \in r^{\mathcal{O}}$ such that $(\forall (z, v') \in r^{\mathcal{O}})[((x, u), (y, v)) \in \ll_r^{\mathcal{O}}$ and $((y, v), (z, v')) \in \ll_r^{\mathcal{O}}]$. Since $\ll_r^{\mathcal{O}}$ is transitive, $(x, z) \in \prec_r^{\mathcal{O}}$. Hence $\prec_r$ is transitive.

(ii) Suppose $(x, x) \in \prec_r^{\mathcal{O}}$, then $\exists (x, y) \in r^{\mathcal{O}}$ such that $((x, y), (x, y)) \in \ll_r^{\mathcal{O}}$, which contradicts the irreflexivity of $\ll_r^{\mathcal{O}}$. Hence $\prec_r^{\mathcal{O}}$ is irreflexive.

(iii) Suppose $(x, y) \in \prec_r^{\mathcal{O}}$ and $(y, x) \in \prec_r^{\mathcal{O}}$. Then $(\exists (x, z) \in r^{\mathcal{O}})(\exists (y, u) \in r^{\mathcal{O}}[((x, z), (y, u)) \in \ll_r^{\mathcal{O}}$ and $((y, u), (x, z)) \in \ll_r^{\mathcal{O}}]$, which contradicts the asymmetry of $\ll$. Hence $\prec_r^{\mathcal{O}}$ is asymmetric (antisymmetric and irreflexive). $\square$

**Lemma 3.** *Let $\mathcal{O} = \langle \Delta^{\mathcal{O}}, \cdot^{\mathcal{O}}, \ll^{\mathcal{O}} \rangle$, and let $\prec$ be a strict partial order on $\Delta^{\mathcal{O}}$. Let $\mathcal{O}'$ be an extension of $\mathcal{O}$ with fresh role name $r \in \mathsf{R}$ added, such that $\mathcal{O}' \Vdash \top \sqsubseteq \exists r.\top$, and $\ll_r^{\mathcal{O}'} := \{((x, z), (y, v)) \mid x \prec y$ and $(x, z), (y, v) \in r^{\mathcal{O}'}\}$. Define $\prec_r^{\mathcal{O}'}$ as in Definition 3. Then $\prec = \prec_r^{\mathcal{O}'}$.*

*Proof.* Suppose $(x, y) \in \prec$. Then $x$ and $y$ are both in the domain of $r^{\mathcal{O}'}$, and $((x, z), (y, v)) \in \ll_r^{\mathcal{O}'}$ for all $(x, z), (y, v) \in r^{\mathcal{O}'}$. Therefore $(x, y) \in \prec_r^{\mathcal{O}'}$. Conversely, suppose $(x, y) \in \prec_r^{\mathcal{O}'}$. Then $(\exists (x, z) \in r^{\mathcal{O}'})(\forall (y, v) \in r^{\mathcal{O}'})[((x, z), (y, v)) \in \ll_r^{\mathcal{O}'}]$. Since $y$ is in the domain of $r^{\mathcal{O}'}$, $(x, y) \in \prec$. $\square$

**Corollary 1.** *Let $\mathcal{O}'$, $\prec$ and $r$ be as in Lemma 3, and let $\sqsubseteq$ be defined by: $\mathcal{O}' \Vdash C \sqsubseteq D$ if and only if $\min_{\prec} C^{\mathcal{O}'} \subseteq D^{\mathcal{O}'}$. Then $\sqsubseteq_r$ has the same semantics as $\sqsubseteq$.*

Corollary 1 states that, in the special case where the domain of a new designated context-providing role includes all objects, contextual defeasible subsumption coincides with defeasible subsumption based on a single preference order. For the more general parameterised case, consider the role hasOrigin, which links individual wines to origins. Wine $y$ is considered more exceptional than $x$ w.r.t. its origin if it has some more exceptional origin link than $x$, and none that are less exceptional.

Contextual defeasible subsumption $\sqsubseteq_r$ can therefore also be viewed as defeasible subsumption based on a preference order on objects in the domain of $r^{\mathcal{O}}$, bearing in mind that, in any given interpretation, it is dependent on $\ll_r^{\mathcal{O}}$. For the remainder of this paper, we use $\mathrel{\reflectbox{$\precsim$}}$ as abbreviation for $\mathrel{\reflectbox{$\precsim$}}_r$, where $r$ is a new role name introduced as in Lemma 3.

This raises the question whether a preference order on objects in the range of $r^{\mathcal{O}}$ could be considered as an alternative. In a more expressive language allowing for role inverses, $\mathrel{\reflectbox{$\precsim$}}_{\mathsf{inv}(r)}$ achieves this goal [21], but in $d\mathcal{ALC}$, this would have to be added as an additional language construct.

**Proposition 1.** *For every $r \in \mathsf{R}$, $\mathrel{\reflectbox{$\precsim$}}_r$ is ampliative and non-monotonic:*

- *Ampliativity: for every $\mathcal{O}$, if $\mathcal{O} \Vdash C \sqsubseteq D$, then $\mathcal{O} \Vdash C \mathrel{\reflectbox{$\precsim$}}_r D$;*
- *Non-monotonicity: it is not generally the case that, for every $\mathcal{O}$, if $\mathcal{O} \Vdash C \mathrel{\reflectbox{$\precsim$}}_r D$, then $\mathcal{O} \Vdash C \sqcap E \mathrel{\reflectbox{$\precsim$}}_r D$ for every $E \in \mathcal{L}_{d\mathcal{ALC}}$.*

The following result, of which the proof is analogous to that in the single-ordering case [12], shows that contextual defeasible subsumption is indeed an appropriate notion of non-monotonic subsumption:

**Lemma 4.** *For every $r \in \mathsf{R}$, $\mathrel{\reflectbox{$\precsim$}}_r$ is a preferential subsumption relation on concepts in that the following rules (a.k.a. KLM-style postulates or properties) hold for every ordered interpretation $\mathcal{O}$, i.e., whenever $\mathcal{O}$ satisfies the rules' antecedent, it satisfies the consequent as well:*

$$\text{(Ref) } C \mathrel{\reflectbox{$\precsim$}}_r C \qquad \text{(LLE) } \frac{C \equiv D,\ C \mathrel{\reflectbox{$\precsim$}}_r E}{D \mathrel{\reflectbox{$\precsim$}}_r E} \qquad \text{(And) } \frac{C \mathrel{\reflectbox{$\precsim$}}_r D,\ C \mathrel{\reflectbox{$\precsim$}}_r E}{C \mathrel{\reflectbox{$\precsim$}}_r D \sqcap E}$$

$$\text{(Or) } \frac{C \mathrel{\reflectbox{$\precsim$}}_r E,\ D \mathrel{\reflectbox{$\precsim$}}_r E}{C \sqcup D \mathrel{\reflectbox{$\precsim$}}_r E} \qquad \text{(RW) } \frac{C \mathrel{\reflectbox{$\precsim$}}_r D,\ D \sqsubseteq E}{C \mathrel{\reflectbox{$\precsim$}}_r E} \qquad \text{(CM) } \frac{C \mathrel{\reflectbox{$\precsim$}}_r D,\ C \mathrel{\reflectbox{$\precsim$}}_r E}{C \sqcap D \mathrel{\reflectbox{$\precsim$}}_r E}$$

We now turn to a class of ordered interpretations that are of special importance in non-monotonic reasoning, namely *modular* interpretations. A strict partial order is called a *modular order* if its set-theoretic complement is a transitive relation.

**Definition 4 (Modular Interpretation).** *A modular interpretation is an ordered interpretation $\mathcal{O} := \langle \Delta^{\mathcal{O}}, \cdot^{\mathcal{O}}, \ll^{\mathcal{O}} \rangle$, where $\ll_r^{\mathcal{O}}$ is modular, for each $r \in \mathsf{R}$.*

We call an ordered model of a knowledge base $\mathcal{KB}$ which is a modular interpretation a *modular model* of $\mathcal{KB}$. It turns out that if the preference order $\ll_r^{\mathcal{O}}$ on the interpretation of $r$ is modular, then the defeasible subsumption $\mathrel{\reflectbox{$\precsim$}}_r$ it induces is also *rational*:

**Lemma 5.** *For every $r \in \mathsf{R}$, $\mathrel{\reflectbox{$\precsim$}}_r$ is a rational subsumption relation on concepts in that every modular interpretation $\mathcal{O}$ satisfies the following rational monotonicity property:*

$$\text{(RM) } \frac{C \mathrel{\reflectbox{$\precsim$}}_r D,\ C \mathrel{\reflectbox{$\not\precsim$}}_r \neg C'}{C \sqcap C' \mathrel{\reflectbox{$\precsim$}}_r D}.$$

The proof of this lemma is along the lines of that for rationality in the single-ordering case [12] and we do not provide it here.

### 3.3   Modelling with Contexts

The motivation for defeasible knowledge bases is to represent defeasible knowledge, and to reason over defeasible ontologies. We conclude this section with an illustration of the different aspects of defeasibility that can be expressed in $d\mathcal{ALC}$. We first consider defeasible existential restriction:

$$\text{Cheninblanc} \sqcap \exists \text{ hasAroma.Wood} \sqsubseteq \exists \text{hasStyle.Wooded}$$

This statement is read: "Chenin blanc wines that normally have a wood aroma are wooded". That is, any Chenin blanc wine that has a characteristic wood aroma, has a wooded wine style. For an example of defeasible subsumption, consider the statement

$$\text{Cheninblanc} \sqsubseteq\!\!\!\sim \exists \text{hasAroma.Floral}$$

where $\sqsubseteq\!\!\!\sim$ is as in Corollary 1, which states that Chenin blanc wines usually have some floral aroma. That is, the most typical Chenin blanc wines all have some floral aroma. Similarly,

$$\text{Cheninblanc} \sqsubseteq\!\!\!\sim \forall \text{hasOrigin.Loire}$$

states that Chenin blanc wines usually come only from the Loire Valley. Now suppose we have a Chenin blanc wine $x$, which comes from the Loire Valley but does not have a floral aroma, and another Chenin blanc wine $y$ which has a floral aroma but comes from Languedoc. No model of this ontology can simultaneously have $x \prec y$ w.r.t. origin and $y \prec x$ w.r.t. aroma. There can therefore be no model that accurately models reality.

This is precisely the limitation imposed by having only a single ordering on objects, as is broadly assumed by preferential approaches to defeasible DLs [14,15,26,28,29], and the motivation for introducing context-based defeasible subsumption. Although the two defeasible statements are not inconsistent, the presence of both rules out certain intended models. In contrast, with contextual defeasible subsumption, both subsumption statements can be expressed *and* $x$ and $y$ can have incompatible preferential relationships in the same model:

$$\text{Cheninblanc} \sqsubseteq\!\!\!\sim_{\text{hasAroma}} \exists \text{hasAroma.Floral}$$
$$\text{Cheninblanc} \sqsubseteq\!\!\!\sim_{\text{hasOrigin}} \forall \text{hasOrigin.Loire}$$

Note that this knowledge base cannot be changed to:

$$\text{Cheninblanc} \sqsubseteq \exists \text{hasAroma.Floral}$$
$$\text{Cheninblanc} \sqsubseteq \forall \text{hasOrigin.Loire}$$

as the latter states that every Chenin blanc wine has a characteristic floral aroma and is usually exclusive to the Loire Valley. This rules out the possibility of a Chenin blanc without a floral aroma, or one that comes only (or just typically) from Languedoc.

We can also add subsumption statements indexed by different contextual roles. For example,

$$\text{Cheninblanc} \sqsubseteq\joinrel\sim \exists\text{hasAcidity.}(\text{Medium} \sqcup \text{High})$$
$$\text{Cheninblanc} \sqsubseteq\joinrel\sim_{\text{hasOrigin}} \exists\text{hasAcidity.High}$$

states that Chenin blanc wines usually have a medium or high acidity, whereas Chenin blanc wines of typical origin have a high acidity.

# 4  Entailment in $d\mathcal{ALC}$

Given a defeasible $d\mathcal{ALC}$ knowledge base $\mathcal{KB}$, we are interested in the reasoning task of *entailment of statements* from $\mathcal{KB}$. That is, given the knowledge specified in $\mathcal{KB}$, how do we decide what other subsumption statements follow from $\mathcal{KB}$? In Sect. 4.1, we first introduce the natural generalisation of entailment to a preferential setting. Thereafter we consider the additional assumption of modularity on preferential models. This serves as motivation for our semantic characterisation of rational entailment in Sect. 4.2.

## 4.1  Preferential Entailment

In order to get to a definition of entailment for $d\mathcal{ALC}$, an obvious starting point is to adopt a Tarskian notion thereof:

**Definition 5 (Preferential Entailment).** *A statement $\alpha$ is preferentially entailed by a defeasible $d\mathcal{ALC}$ knowledge base $\mathcal{KB}$, written $\mathcal{KB} \models_{\text{pref}} \alpha$, if every ordered model of $\mathcal{KB}$ satisfies $\alpha$.*

When assessing how appropriate a notion of entailment is, a task we shall devote time to in this section, the following definitions come in handy, as it will become clear in the sequel:

**Definition 6.** *A defeasible $d\mathcal{ALC}$ knowledge base $\mathcal{KB}$ is called preferential if it is closed under the preferential rules in Lemma 4.*

**Definition 7 (Preferential Closure).** *Let $\mathcal{KB}$ be a defeasible $d\mathcal{ALC}$ knowledge base. With*

$$\mathcal{KB}^*_{\text{pref}} := \bigcap \{\mathcal{KB}' \mid \mathcal{KB} \subseteq \mathcal{KB}' \text{ and } \mathcal{KB}' \text{ is preferential}\}$$

*we denote the preferential closure of $\mathcal{KB}$.*

Intuitively, the preterential closure of a defeasible $d\mathcal{ALC}$ knowledge base $\mathcal{KB}$ corresponds to the 'core' set of statements that hold given those in $\mathcal{KB}$. It provides an alternative, and, in our context, quite convenient, way to look at entailment, as the following result shows:

**Lemma 6.** *Let $\mathcal{KB}$ be a defeasible $d\mathcal{ALC}$ knowledge base and let $\alpha$ be a statement. Then $\mathcal{KB} \models_{\mathsf{pref}} \alpha$ iff $\alpha \in \mathcal{KB}^*_{\mathsf{pref}}$.*

Hence, preferential entailment and preferential closure are two sides of the same coin, mimicking an analogous result for preferential reasoning in both the propositional [31] and the DL [12,15] cases. A further feature of preferential closure (and, therefore, of preferential entailment) is the following:

**Lemma 7.** $\mathcal{KB}^*_{\mathsf{pref}}$ *is preferential.*

In other words, preferential entailment ensures that the set of statements (in particular the $\sqsubseteq_r$-ones) that follow from the knowledge base satisfies the $d\mathcal{ALC}$ versions of the basic KLM-style properties for defeasible reasoning (cf. Lemma 4).

Of course, preferential entailment is not always desirable, one of the reasons being that it is monotonic, courtesy of the Tarskian notion of consequence it relies on (see Definition 5). In most cases, as witnessed by the great deal of work in the non-monotonic reasoning community, a move towards rationality is in order. Thanks to the definitions above and the result in Lemma 5, we already know where to start looking for it:

**Definition 8 (Modular Entailment).** *A statement $\alpha$ is modularly entailed by a defeasible $d\mathcal{ALC}$ knowledge base $\mathcal{KB}$, written $\mathcal{KB} \models_{\mathsf{mod}} \alpha$, if every modular model of $\mathcal{KB}$ satisfies $\alpha$.*

We say a defeasible $d\mathcal{ALC}$ knowledge base $\mathcal{KB}$ is rational if it is closed under the preferential rules in Lemma 4 and the rational mononotonicity rule in Lemma 5.

**Definition 9 (Modular Closure).** *Let $\mathcal{KB}$ be a defeasible $d\mathcal{ALC}$ knowledge base. With*

$$\mathcal{KB}^*_{\mathsf{mod}} := \bigcap \{\mathcal{KB}' \mid \mathcal{KB} \subseteq \mathcal{KB}' \text{ and } \mathcal{KB}' \text{is rational}\}$$

*we denote the modular closure of $\mathcal{KB}$.*

Just as in the preferential case, it turns out modular closure and modular entailment coincide:

**Lemma 8.** *Let $\mathcal{KB}$ be a defeasible $d\mathcal{ALC}$ knowledge base and let $\alpha$ be a statement. Then $\mathcal{KB} \models_{\mathsf{mod}} \alpha$ iff $\alpha \in \mathcal{KB}^*_{\mathsf{mod}}$.*

Unfortunately, modular closure (and modular entailment) falls short of providing us with an appropriate notion of non-monotonic entailment. This is so because it coincides with preferential closure, as the following result, adapted from a well-known similar result in the propositional case [33, Theorem 4.2], shows.

**Lemma 9.** $\mathcal{KB}^*_{\mathsf{mod}} = \mathcal{KB}^*_{\mathsf{pref}}$.

More fundamentally, this means the set of $\sqsubseteq$-statements that are modularly entailed by a knowledge base need not satisfy the rational monotonicity property, since $\mathcal{KB}^*_{\mathsf{mod}}$ (or $\mathcal{KB}^*_{\mathsf{pref}}$) is not, in general, rational. In what follows, we overcome precisely this issue.

## 4.2  Rational Entailment

In this section, we introduce a definition of semantic entailment which, as we shall see, is appropriate in the light of the discussion above. The constructions we are going to present are inspired by the work by Booth and Paris [10] in the propositional case and those by Britz et al. [12] and Giordano et al. [29,30] in a single-ordered preferential DL setting. (We shall give a corresponding proof-theoretic characterisation of such a notion of entailment in Sect. 4.3.)

Let $\mathcal{KB}$ be a defeasible knowledge base and let $\Delta$ be a fixed countably infinite set. We define $\mathcal{O}_{\Delta}^{\mathcal{KB}} := \{\mathcal{O} = \langle \Delta^{\mathcal{O}}, \cdot^{\mathcal{O}}, \ll^{\mathcal{O}} \rangle \mid \mathcal{O} \Vdash \mathcal{KB}$ and $\mathcal{O}$ is modular and $\Delta^{\mathcal{O}} = \Delta\}$. The following result shows that the set $\mathcal{O}_{\Delta}^{\mathcal{KB}}$ characterises modular entailment:

**Lemma 10.** *For every* $\mathcal{KB}$, *every* $C, D \in \mathcal{L}_{d\mathcal{ALC}}$ *and every* $r \in \mathsf{R}$, $\mathcal{KB} \models_{\mathsf{mod}}$ $C \sqsubseteq_r D$ *iff* $\mathcal{O} \Vdash C \sqsubseteq_r D$, *for every* $\mathcal{O} \in \mathcal{O}_{\Delta}^{\mathcal{KB}}$.

Since $\Delta$ is countable, for every $\mathcal{O} \in \mathcal{O}_{\Delta}^{\mathcal{KB}}$, we can partition $\Delta \times \Delta$ into a sequence of layers $(L_0, \ldots, L_n, \ldots)$, where, for each $i \geq 0$, $L_i := \langle L_i^{r_1}, \ldots, L_i^{r_{\#\mathsf{R}}} \rangle$, and such that, for every $x, y \in \Delta$ and every $r \in \mathsf{R}$, $(x, y) \in L_0^r$ iff $(x, y) \in \min_{\ll_r} r^{\mathcal{O}}$ and $(x, y) \in L_{i+1}^r$ iff $(x, y) \in \min_{\ll_r}(r^{\mathcal{O}} \setminus \bigcup_{0 \leq j \leq i} L_j^r)$. (That these constructions are well defined follows from the fact that for every $r \in \mathsf{R}$, $\ll_r$ is smooth.)

**Definition 10 (Height of a pair).** *Let* $\mathcal{O} = \langle \Delta^{\mathcal{O}}, \cdot^{\mathcal{O}}, \ll^{\mathcal{O}} \rangle$, *let* $x, y \in \Delta^{\mathcal{O}}$ *and let* $r \in \mathsf{R}$. *The height of* $(x, y)$ *in* $\mathcal{O}$ *w.r.t.* $r$ *is denoted* $h_{\mathcal{O}}(x, y, r)$ *and is equal to* $i$ *iff* $(x, y) \in L_i^r$.

We can now use the set $\mathcal{O}_{\Delta}^{\mathcal{KB}}$ as a springboard to introduce a version of 'canonical' modular interpretation.

**Definition 11 (Big modular interpretation).** *Let* $\mathcal{KB}$ *be a defeasible knowledge base and define* $\mathcal{O}_{\oplus}^{\mathcal{KB}} := \langle \Delta^{\mathcal{O}_{\oplus}^{\mathcal{KB}}}, \cdot^{\mathcal{O}_{\oplus}^{\mathcal{KB}}}, \ll^{\mathcal{O}_{\oplus}^{\mathcal{KB}}} \rangle$, *where*

- $\Delta^{\mathcal{O}_{\oplus}^{\mathcal{KB}}} := \bigoplus_{\mathcal{O} \in \mathcal{O}_{\Delta}^{\mathcal{KB}}} \Delta^{\mathcal{O}}$, *i.e., the disjoint union of the domains from* $\mathcal{O}_{\Delta}^{\mathcal{KB}}$, *where each* $\mathcal{O} = \langle \Delta^{\mathcal{O}}, \cdot^{\mathcal{O}}, \ll^{\mathcal{O}} \rangle \in \mathcal{O}_{\Delta}^{\mathcal{KB}}$ *has the elements* $x, y, \ldots$ *of its domain renamed as* $x_{\mathcal{O}}, y_{\mathcal{O}}, \ldots$ *so that they are all distinct in* $\Delta^{\mathcal{O}_{\oplus}^{\mathcal{KB}}}$;
- $x_{\mathcal{O}} \in A^{\mathcal{O}_{\oplus}^{\mathcal{KB}}}$ *iff* $x \in A^{\mathcal{O}}$;
- $(x_{\mathcal{O}}, y_{\mathcal{O}'}) \in r^{\mathcal{O}_{\oplus}^{\mathcal{KB}}}$ *iff* $\mathcal{O} = \mathcal{O}'$ *and* $(x, y) \in r^{\mathcal{O}}$;
- $(x_{\mathcal{O}}, y_{\mathcal{O}'}) \ll_r^{\mathcal{O}_{\oplus}^{\mathcal{KB}}} (x'_{\mathcal{O}'}, y'_{\mathcal{O}'})$ *iff* $h_{\mathcal{O}}(x, y, r) < h_{\mathcal{O}'}(x', y', r)$.

The proofs for the two lemmas below follow from the definition of $\mathcal{O}_{\oplus}^{\mathcal{KB}}$:

**Lemma 11.** *For every* $C \subset \mathcal{L}_{d\mathcal{ALC}}$, $x_{\mathcal{O}} \in C^{\mathcal{O}_{\oplus}^{\mathcal{KB}}}$ *iff* $x \in C^{\mathcal{O}}$.

**Lemma 12.** *For every* $r \in \mathsf{R}$, $h_{\mathcal{O}_{\oplus}^{\mathcal{KB}}}(x_{\mathcal{O}}, y_{\mathcal{O}}, r) = h_{\mathcal{O}}(x, y, r)$.

These results, together with the fact that $d\mathcal{ALC}$ modular interpretations are closed under disjoint union (Lemma 1), allow us to show the following:

**Lemma 13.** $\mathcal{O}_{\oplus}^{\mathcal{KB}}$ *is a modular model of* $\mathcal{KB}$.

Given $\mathcal{O}_{\oplus}^{\mathcal{KB}}$, we can then define contextual modular orderings on the domain $\Delta^{\mathcal{O}_{\oplus}^{\mathcal{KB}}}$ in the same way as in Definition 3.

Armed with the definitions and results above, we are now ready to provide an alternative definition of entailment in $d\mathcal{ALC}$:

**Definition 12 (Rational Entailment).** *A statement* $\alpha$ *is rationally entailed by a knowledge base* $\mathcal{KB}$, *written* $\mathcal{KB} \models_{\mathsf{rat}} \alpha$, *if* $\mathcal{O}_{\oplus}^{\mathcal{KB}} \Vdash \alpha$.

That such a notion of entailment indeed deserves its name is witnessed by the following result:

**Lemma 14.** *Let* $\mathcal{KB}$ *be a defeasible knowledge base. For every* $r \in \mathsf{R}$, $\{C \mathbin{\rlap{\sqsubset}{\sim}}_r D \mid \mathcal{O}_{\oplus}^{\mathcal{KB}} \Vdash C \mathbin{\rlap{\sqsubset}{\sim}}_r D\}$ *is rational.*

## 4.3 Computing Contextual Rational Closure

In the remaining of the section, we discuss a known instance of entailment for defeasible reasoning that meets all the requirements of rational entailment. It is a generalisation of the DL version of the propositional *rational closure* studied by Lehmann and Magidor [33], to deal with context-based rational defeasible entailment. We present a proof-theoretic characterisation here, based on the work of Casini and Straccia [24,25]; an alternative semantic characterisation of rational closure in DLs (without contexts) was proposed by Giordano and others [29,30].

Rational closure is a form of inferential closure based on modular entailment $\models_{\mathsf{mod}}$, but it extends its inferential power. Such an extension of modular entailment is obtained formalising what is called the *presumption of typicality* [32, Sect. 3.1]. That is, we always assume that we are dealing with the most typical possible situation compatible with the information at our disposal. We first define what it means for a concept to be *exceptional* in a given context:

**Definition 13 (Contextual Exceptionality).** *A concept* $C$ *is exceptional in the context* $r$ *in the defeasible knowledge base* $\mathcal{KB} = \mathcal{T} \cup \mathcal{D}$ *if* $\mathcal{KB} \models_{\mathsf{mod}} \top \mathbin{\rlap{\sqsubset}{\sim}}_r \neg C$. *A defeasible subsumption statement* $C \mathbin{\rlap{\sqsubset}{\sim}}_r D$ *is exceptional in the context* $r$ *in* $\mathcal{KB}$ *if* $C$ *is exceptional in the context* $r$ *in* $\mathcal{KB}$.

So, a concept $C$ is considered exceptional in a given context in a knowledge base if it is not possible to have a modular model of the knowledge base in which there is a typical individual (i.e., an individual at least as typical as all the others) that is an instance of the concept $C$. Applying the notion of exceptionality iteratively, we associate with every concept $C$ and context $r$ a *rank* in the knowledge base $\mathcal{KB}$, which we denote by $\mathsf{rank}_{\mathcal{KB}}(C, r)$. We extend this to subsumption statements, and associate with every context $r$ and contextual defeasible concept inclusion $C \mathbin{\rlap{\sqsubset}{\sim}}_r D$ a rank, denoted $\mathsf{rank}_{\mathcal{KB}}(C \mathbin{\rlap{\sqsubset}{\sim}}_r D, r)$ and abbreviated as $\mathsf{rank}_{\mathcal{KB}}(C \mathbin{\rlap{\sqsubset}{\sim}}_r D)$:

1. Let $\mathrm{rank}_{\mathcal{KB}}(C, r) = 0$ if $C$ is not exceptional in the context of $r$ and $\mathcal{KB}$, and let $\mathrm{rank}_{\mathcal{KB}}(C \sqsubseteq_r D) = 0$ for every defeasible statement having $C$ as antecedent, with $\mathrm{rank}_{\mathcal{KB}}(C, r) = 0$. The set of statements in $\mathcal{D}$ with rank 0 is denoted as $\mathcal{D}_0^{\mathrm{rank}}$.

2. Let $\mathrm{rank}_{\mathcal{KB}}(C, r) = 1$ if $C$ does not have a rank of 0 in the context of $r$ and it is not exceptional in the knowledge base $\mathcal{KB}^1$ composed of $\mathcal{T}$ and the exceptional part of $\mathcal{D}$, that is, $\mathcal{KB}^1 = \langle \mathcal{T}, \mathcal{D} \setminus \mathcal{D}_0^{\mathrm{rank}} \rangle$. If $\mathrm{rank}_{\mathcal{KB}}(C, r) = 1$, then let $\mathrm{rank}_{\mathcal{KB}}(C \sqsubseteq_r D) = 1$ for every statement $C \sqsubseteq_r D$. The set of statements in $\mathcal{D}$ with rank 1 is denoted $\mathcal{D}_1^{\mathrm{rank}}$.

3. In general, for $i > 0$, a tuple $\langle C, r \rangle$ is assigned a rank of $i$ if it does not have a rank of $i - 1$ and it is not exceptional in $\mathcal{KB}^i = \langle \mathcal{T}, \mathcal{D} \setminus \bigcup_{j=0}^{i-1} \mathcal{D}_j^{\mathrm{rank}} \rangle$. If $\mathrm{rank}_{\mathcal{KB}}(C, r) = i$, then $\mathrm{rank}_{\mathcal{KB}}(C \sqsubseteq_r D) = i$ for every statement $C \sqsubseteq_r D$. The set of statements in $\mathcal{D}$ with rank $i$ is denoted $\mathcal{D}_i^{\mathrm{rank}}$.

4. By iterating the previous steps, we eventually reach a subset $\mathcal{E} \subseteq \mathcal{D}$ such that all the statements in $\mathcal{E}$ are exceptional (since $\mathcal{D}$ is finite, we must reach such a point). If $\mathcal{E} \neq \emptyset$, we define the rank of the statements in $\mathcal{E}$ as $\infty$, and the set $\mathcal{E}$ is denoted $\mathcal{D}_\infty^{\mathrm{rank}}$.

Following on the procedure above, $\mathcal{D}$ is partitioned into a finite sequence $\langle \mathcal{D}_0^{\mathrm{rank}}, \ldots, \mathcal{D}_n^{\mathrm{rank}}, \mathcal{D}_\infty^{\mathrm{rank}} \rangle$ $(n \geq 0)$, where $\mathcal{D}_\infty^{\mathrm{rank}}$ may possibly be empty. So, through this procedure we can assign a rank to every context-based defeasible subsumption statement.

For a concept $C$ to have a rank of $\infty$ corresponds to not being satisfiable in any model of $\mathcal{KB}$, that is, $\mathcal{KB} \models_{\mathrm{mod}} C \sqsubseteq \bot$. Note that this relationship is independent of context:

**Lemma 15.** *Let $C \in \mathcal{L}_{d\mathcal{ALC}}$. Then $\mathrm{rank}_{\mathcal{KB}}(C, r) = \infty$ for all $r \in \mathsf{R}$ if and only iff $\mathcal{KB} \models_{\mathrm{mod}} C \sqsubseteq \bot$.*

Adapting Lehmann and Magidor's construction for propositional logic [33], the contextual rational closure of a knowledge base $\mathcal{KB}$ is defined as follows:

**Definition 14 (Contextual Rational Closure).** *Let $C, D \in \mathcal{L}_{d\mathcal{ALC}}$ and let $r \in \mathsf{R}$. Then $C \sqsubseteq_r D$ is in the rational closure of a defeasible knowledge base $\mathcal{KB}$ if*

$$\mathrm{rank}_{\mathcal{KB}}(C \sqcap D, r) < \mathrm{rank}_{\mathcal{KB}}(C \sqcap \neg D, r) \ \text{ or } \ \mathrm{rank}_{\mathcal{KB}}(C) = \infty.$$

Informally, the above definition says that $C \sqsubseteq_r D$ is in the rational closure of $\mathcal{KB}$ if the ranked models of the knowledge base tell us that, in the context of $r$, some instances of $C \sqcap D$ are more plausible than all instances of $C \sqcap \neg D$.

**Theorem 1.** *Let $\mathcal{KB}$ be a knowledge base having a modular model. For every $C, D \in \mathcal{L}_{d\mathcal{ALC}}$ and every $r \in \mathsf{R}$, $C \sqsubseteq_r D$ is in the rational closure of $\mathcal{KB}$ iff $\mathcal{KB} \models_{\mathrm{rat}} C \sqsubseteq_r D$.*

## 4.4   Rational Reasoning with Contextual Ontologies

The following example shows how ranks are assigned to concepts in a defeasible TBox, and used to determine rational entailment. We first consider only a single context hasE $\in$ R with intuition 'has employment', and then extend the example to demonstrate the strength of reasoning with multiple contexts.

Let $\mathcal{KB} = \mathcal{T} \cup \mathcal{D}$ with $\mathcal{T} = \{$Intern $\sqsubseteq$ Employee, Employee $\sqsubseteq \exists$hasE.$\top\}$ and

$$\mathcal{D} = \left\{ \begin{array}{c} \text{Employee } \sqsubset\!\!\sim_{\text{hasE}} \exists\text{hasID.TaxNo,} \\ \text{Intern } \sqsubset\!\!\sim_{\text{hasE}} \neg\exists\text{hasID.TaxNo,} \\ \text{Intern} \sqcap \text{Graduate } \sqsubset\!\!\sim_{\text{hasE}} \exists\text{hasID.TaxNo} \end{array} \right\}$$

Examining the concepts on the LHS of each subsumption in $\mathcal{D}$, we get that:

1. rank$_{\mathcal{KB}}$(Employee, hasE) $= 0$, since Employee is not exceptional in $\mathcal{KB}$.
2. rank$_{\mathcal{KB}}$(Intern, hasE) $\neq 0$ and rank$_{\mathcal{KB}}$(Intern $\sqcap$ Graduate, hasE) $\neq 0$, since both concepts are exceptional in $\mathcal{KB}$.
3. $\mathcal{KB}^1$ is composed of $\mathcal{T}$ and $\mathcal{D} \setminus \mathcal{D}_0^{\text{rank}}$, which consists of the defeasible subsumptions in $\mathcal{D}$ except for Employee $\sqsubset\!\!\sim_{\text{hasE}} \exists$hasID.TaxNo.
4. rank$_{\mathcal{KB}}$(Intern, hasE) $= 1$, since Intern is not exceptional in $\mathcal{KB}^1$.
5. rank$_{\mathcal{KB}}$(Intern $\sqcap$ Graduate, hasE) $\neq 1$, since Intern $\sqcap$ Graduate is exceptional in $\mathcal{KB}^1$.
6. $\mathcal{KB}^2$ is composed of $\mathcal{T}$ and $\{$Intern $\sqcap$ Graduate $\sqsubset\!\!\sim_{\text{hasE}} \exists$hasID.TaxNo$\}$.
7. Intern $\sqcap$ Graduate is not exceptional in $\mathcal{KB}^2$ and therefore rank$_{\mathcal{KB}}$(Intern $\sqcap$ Graduate, hasE) $= 2$.

There are algorithms to compute rational closure [23, 25, 30] that can readily be adapted to account for context, but one can also apply Definition 14 to determine rational entailment. For example, since rank$_{\mathcal{KB}}$(Intern$\sqcap$Graduate, hasE) $= 2$ but rank$_{\mathcal{KB}}$(Intern $\sqcap \neg$Graduate, hasE) $= 1$, we find that interns are usually not graduates: $\mathcal{KB} \models_{\text{rat}}$ Intern $\sqsubset\!\!\sim_{\text{hasE}} \neg$Graduate.

The context hasE is used to indicate that it is an individual's typicality in the context of employment which is under consideration. Now suppose that $\mathcal{KB}$ in the above example is extended to $\mathcal{KB}' = \langle \mathcal{T}', \mathcal{D}'\rangle$, where $\mathcal{T}' = \mathcal{T}$ and $\mathcal{D}' = \mathcal{D} \cup \{$Millennial $\sqsubset\!\!\sim_{\text{hasE}} \neg$Employee, Millennial $\sqsubset\!\!\sim_{\text{hasQ}}$ Graduate$\}$. The context hasQ is used here to indicate that it is an individual's typicality w.r.t. qualification which is under consideration. The rankings calculated above remain unchanged; in addition, we get rank$_{\mathcal{KB}'}$(Millennial, hasE) $= 0$ and rank$_{\mathcal{KB}'}$(Millennial, hasQ) $= 0$. It now follows that:

- In the context hasQ, millennial interns are usually graduates: $\mathcal{KB}' \models_{\text{rat}}$ Millennial $\sqcap$ Intern $\sqsubset\!\!\sim_{\text{hasQ}}$ Graduate. This follows because rank$_{\mathcal{KB}'}$(Millennial $\sqcap$ Intern $\sqcap$ Graduate, hasQ) $= 0$, whereas rank$_{\mathcal{KB}'}$(Millennial $\sqcap$ Intern $\sqcap \neg$Graduate, hasQ) $= 1$.
- In the context hasE, millennial interns are usually not graduates: $\mathcal{KB}' \models_{\text{rat}}$ Millennial $\sqcap$ Intern $\sqsubset\!\!\sim_{\text{hasE}} \neg$Graduate. This follows because rank$_{\mathcal{KB}'}$(Millennial $\sqcap$ Intern $\sqcap$ Graduate, hasE) $= 2$, whereas rank$_{\mathcal{KB}'}$(Millennial $\sqcap$ Intern $\sqcap \neg$Graduate, hasE) $= 1$.

On the other hand, suppose we were restricted to a single context hasE, i.e., replace hasQ with hasE in $\mathcal{KB}'$ to obtain $\mathcal{KB}''$. We then only get that $\mathcal{KB}'' \models_{\mathsf{rat}}$ Millennial $\sqcap$ Intern $\sqsubseteq_{\mathsf{hasE}} \neg$Graduate.

Which one of these rational entailments is more intuitively correct depends (*sic*) on the context, and can perhaps be understood better by looking at the postulates for non-monotonic reasoning in Lemmas 4 and 5. Looking at models of $\mathcal{KB}'$, in particular $\mathcal{O}_{\oplus}^{\mathcal{KB}'}$, it follows from (RM) that $\mathcal{KB}' \models_{\mathsf{rat}}$ Millennial $\sqcap$ Intern $\sqsubseteq_{\mathsf{hasQ}}$ Graduate. That is, in the context of qualifications, since millennials are usually graduates, so are millennial interns. Also in $\mathcal{KB}'$, applying (RM) to Intern $\sqsubseteq_{\mathsf{hasE}} \neg$Graduate we get Intern $\sqcap$ Millennial $\sqsubseteq_{\mathsf{hasE}} \neg$Graduate. That is, in the context of employment, since interns are usually not graduates, neither are millennial interns.

In contrast, in models of $\mathcal{KB}''$, including the big model $\mathcal{O}_{\oplus}^{\mathcal{KB}''}$, the former deduction is blocked: Applying (RW) to Millennial $\sqsubseteq_{\mathsf{hasE}} \neg$Employee yields Millennial $\sqsubseteq_{\mathsf{hasE}} \neg$Intern. (RM) is now blocked by Millennial $\sqsubseteq_{\mathsf{hasE}} \neg$Intern, hence we cannot conclude that $\mathcal{KB}'' \models_{\mathsf{rat}}$ Millennial $\sqcap$ Intern $\sqsubseteq_{\mathsf{hasE}}$ Graduate.

# 5 Concluding Remarks

In this paper, we have made a case for a context-based notion of defeasible concept inclusion in description logics. We have shown that preferential roles can be used to take context into account, and to deliver a simple, yet powerful, notion of contextual defeasible subsumption. Technically, this addresses an important limitation in previous defeasible extensions of description logics, namely the restriction in the semantics of defeasible concept inclusion to a single preference order on objects. Semantically, it answers the question of the meaning of multiple preference orders, namely that they reflect different contexts.

Building on previous work in the KLM tradition, we have shown that restricting the preferential semantics to a modular semantics allows us to define the notion of rational entailment from a defeasible knowledge base, and to compute the rational closure of a knowledge base as an instance of rational entailment. Future work should consider the implementation of contextual rational closure, as well as the addition of an ABox. Much work is also required on the modelling side once a stable implementation exists. Contextual subsumption provides the user with more flexibility in making defeasible statements in ontologies, but comprehensive case studies are required to evaluate the approach.

**Acknowledgements.** This work is based on research supported in part by the National Research Foundation of South Africa (Grant Number 103345).

# References

1. Amgoud, L., Parsons, S., Perrussel, L.: An argumentation framework based on contextual preferences. In: Proceedings of International Conference on Formal and Applied and Practical Reasoning (FAPR), pp. 59–67 (2000)
2. Baader, F., Calvanese, D., McGuinness, D., Nardi, D., Patel-Schneider, P. (eds.): The Description Logic Handbook: Theory, Implementation and Applications, 2nd edn. Cambridge University Press, Cambridge (2007)
3. Bikakis, A., Antoniou, G.: Defeasible contextual reasoning with arguments in ambient intelligence. IEEE Trans. Knowl. Data Eng. **22**(11), 1492–1506 (2010)
4. Bonatti, P., Faella, M., Petrova, I., Sauro, L.: A new semantics for overriding in description logics. Artif. Intell. **222**, 1–48 (2015)
5. Bonatti, P., Faella, M., Sauro, L.: Defeasible inclusions in low-complexity DLs. J. Artif. Intell. Res. **42**, 719–764 (2011)
6. Bonatti, P., Lutz, C., Wolter, F.: The complexity of circumscription in description logic. J. Artif. Intell. Res. **35**, 717–773 (2009)
7. Booth, R., Casini, G., Meyer, T., Varzinczak, I.: On the entailment problem for a logic of typicality. In: Proceedings of 24th International Joint Conference on Artificial Intelligence (IJCAI) (2015)
8. Booth, R., Meyer, T., Varzinczak, I.: PTL: a propositional typicality logic. In: del Cerro, L.F., Herzig, A., Mengin, J. (eds.) JELIA 2012. LNCS (LNAI), vol. 7519, pp. 107–119. Springer, Heidelberg (2012). https://doi.org/10.1007/978-3-642-33353-8_9
9. Booth, R., Meyer, T., Varzinczak, I.: A propositional typicality logic for extending rational consequence. In: Fermé, E., Gabbay, D., Simari, G. (eds.) Trends in Belief Revision and Argumentation Dynamics. Studies in Logic - Logic and Cognitive Systems, vol. 48, pp. 123–154. King's College Publications, London (2013)
10. Booth, R., Paris, J.: A note on the rational closure of knowledge bases with both positive and negative knowledge. J. Logic Lang. Inform. **7**(2), 165–190 (1998)
11. Boutilier, C.: Conditional logics of normality: a modal approach. Artif. Intell. **68**(1), 87–154 (1994)
12. Britz, K., Casini, G., Meyer, T., Moodley, K., Varzinczak, I.: Ordered interpretations and entailment for defeasible description logics. Technical report, CAIR, CSIR Meraka and UKZN, South Africa (2013). http://tinyurl.com/cydd6yy
13. Britz, K., Casini, G., Meyer, T., Varzinczak, I.: Preferential role restrictions. In: Proceedings of 26th International Workshop on Description Logics, pp. 93–106 (2013)
14. Britz, K., Heidema, J., Meyer, T.: Semantic preferential subsumption. In: Lang, J., Brewka, G. (eds.) Proceedings of 11th International Conference on Principles of Knowledge Representation and Reasoning (KR), pp. 476–484. AAAI Press/MIT Press (2008)
15. Britz, K., Meyer, T., Varzinczak, I.: Semantic foundation for preferential description logics. In: Wang, D., Reynolds, M. (eds.) AI 2011. LNCS (LNAI), vol. 7106, pp. 491–500. Springer, Heidelberg (2011). https://doi.org/10.1007/978-3-642-25832-9_50
16. Britz, K., Varzinczak, I.: From KLM-style conditionals to defeasible modalities, and back. J. Appl. Non-Class. Log. (to appear)
17. Britz, K., Varzinczak, I.: Preferential accessibility and preferred worlds. J. Log. Lang. Inf. (to appear)

18. Britz, K., Varzinczak, I.: Defeasible modalities. In: Proceedings of 14th Conference on Theoretical Aspects of Rationality and Knowledge (TARK), pp. 49–60 (2013)
19. Britz, K., Varzinczak, I.: Introducing role defeasibility in description logics. In: Michael, L., Kakas, A. (eds.) JELIA 2016. LNCS (LNAI), vol. 10021, pp. 174–189. Springer, Cham (2016). https://doi.org/10.1007/978-3-319-48758-8_12
20. Britz, K., Varzinczak, I.: Preferential modalities revisited. In: Proceedings of 16th International Workshop on Nonmonotonic Reasoning (NMR) (2016)
21. Britz, K., Varzinczak, I.: Context-based defeasible subsumption for $d\mathcal{SROIQ}$. In: Proceedings of 13th International Symposium on Logical Formalizations of Commonsense Reasoning (2017)
22. Britz, K., Varzinczak, I.: Towards defeasible $d\mathcal{SROIQ}$. In: Proceedings of 30th International Workshop on Description Logics, vol. 1879. CEUR Workshop Proceedings (2017)
23. Casini, G., Meyer, T., Moodley, K., Sattler, U., Varzinczak, I.: Introducing defeasibility into OWL ontologies. In: Arenas, M., et al. (eds.) ISWC 2015. LNCS, vol. 9367, pp. 409–426. Springer, Cham (2015). https://doi.org/10.1007/978-3-319-25010-6_27
24. Casini, G., Straccia, U.: Rational closure for defeasible description logics. In: Janhunen, T., Niemelä, I. (eds.) JELIA 2010. LNCS (LNAI), vol. 6341, pp. 77–90. Springer, Heidelberg (2010). https://doi.org/10.1007/978-3-642-15675-5_9
25. Casini, G., Straccia, U.: Defeasible inheritance-based description logics. J. Artif. Intell. Res. (JAIR) **48**, 415–473 (2013)
26. Giordano, L., Gliozzi, V., Olivetti, N., Pozzato, G.L.: Preferential description logics. In: Dershowitz, N., Voronkov, A. (eds.) LPAR 2007. LNCS (LNAI), vol. 4790, pp. 257–272. Springer, Heidelberg (2007). https://doi.org/10.1007/978-3-540-75560-9_20
27. Giordano, L., Gliozzi, V., Olivetti, N., Pozzato, G.L.: Reasoning about typicality in preferential description logics. In: Hölldobler, S., Lutz, C., Wansing, H. (eds.) JELIA 2008. LNCS (LNAI), vol. 5293, pp. 192–205. Springer, Heidelberg (2008). https://doi.org/10.1007/978-3-540-87803-2_17
28. Giordano, L., Gliozzi, V., Olivetti, N., Pozzato, G.: $\mathcal{ALC} + T$: a preferential extension of description logics. Fundamenta Informaticae **96**(3), 341–372 (2009)
29. Giordano, L., Gliozzi, V., Olivetti, N., Pozzato, G.: A non-monotonic description logic for reasoning about typicality. Artif. Intell. **195**, 165–202 (2013)
30. Giordano, L., Gliozzi, V., Olivetti, N., Pozzato, G.: Semantic characterization of rational closure: from propositional logic to description logics. Artif. Intell. **226**, 1–33 (2015)
31. Kraus, S., Lehmann, D., Magidor, M.: Nonmonotonic reasoning, preferential models and cumulative logics. Artif. Intell. **44**, 167–207 (1990)
32. Lehmann, D.: Another perspective on default reasoning. Ann. Math. Artif. Intell. **15**(1), 61–82 (1995)
33. Lehmann, D., Magidor, M.: What does a conditional knowledge base entail? Artif. Intell. **55**, 1–60 (1992)
34. Pensel, M., Turhan, A.-Y.: Including quantification in defeasible reasoning for the description logic $\mathcal{EL}_\perp$. In: Balduccini, M., Janhunen, T. (eds.) LPNMR 2017. LNCS (LNAI), vol. 10377, pp. 78–84. Springer, Cham (2017). https://doi.org/10.1007/978-3-319-61660-5_9
35. Quantz, J., Royer, V.: A preference semantics for defaults in terminological logics. In: Proceedings of 3rd International Conference on Principles of Knowledge Representation and Reasoning (KR), pp. 294–305 (1992)

36. Sengupta, K., Krisnadhi, A.A., Hitzler, P.: Local closed world semantics: grounded circumscription for OWL. In: Aroyo, L., Welty, C., Alani, H., Taylor, J., Bernstein, A., Kagal, L., Noy, N., Blomqvist, E. (eds.) ISWC 2011. LNCS, vol. 7031, pp. 617–632. Springer, Heidelberg (2011). https://doi.org/10.1007/978-3-642-25073-6_39
37. Shoham, Y.: Reasoning About Change: Time and Causation from the Standpoint of Artificial Intelligence. MIT Press, Cambridge (1988)

# Haydi: Rapid Prototyping and Combinatorial Objects

Stanislav Böhm⬭, Jakub Beránek$^{(\boxtimes)}$⬭, and Martin Šurkovský⬭

VŠB – Technical University of Ostrava,
17. listopadu 2172/15, 708 00 Ostrava, Czech Republic
{stanislav.bohm,jakub.beranek.st,martin.surkovsky}@vsb.cz

**Abstract.** Haydi (http://haydi.readthedocs.io) is a framework for generating discrete structures. It provides a way to define a structure from basic building blocks and then enumerate all elements, all non-isomorphic elements, or generate random elements in the structure. Haydi is designed as a tool for rapid prototyping. It is implemented as a pure Python package and supports execution in distributed environments. The goal of this paper is to give the overall picture of Haydi together with a formal definition for the case of generating canonical forms.

**Keywords:** Combinatorial objects · Rapid prototyping
Canonical representation

## 1 Introduction

The concept of rapid prototyping helps in verifying the feasibility of an initial idea and reject the bad ones fast. In mathematical world, there are tools like Matlab, SageMath, or R that allow one to build a working prototype and evaluate an idea quickly. This paper is focused on the field of combinatorial objects and provides a prototyping tool that allows to check claims on small instances by search over relevant objects. Haydi (Haystack Diver) is an open-source Python package that provides an easy way of describing such structures by composing basic building blocks (e.g. Cartesian product, mappings) and then enumerating all elements, all non-isomorphic elements, or generating random elements.

The main design goal is to build a tool that is *simple* to use, since building prototypes have to be cheap and fast. There has been an attempt to build a *flexible* tool that describes various structures and reduces limitations for the user. The *reasonable performance* of the solution is also important, but it has a lower priority than the first two goals.

Authors were supported by grants of GACR 15-13784S and SGS No. SP2017/82, VŠB – Technical University of Ostrava, Czech Republic. Computational resources for testing on a super computer were provided by IT4Innovations as project OPEN-8-26.

F. Ferrarotti and S. Woltran (Eds.): FoIKS 2018, LNCS 10833, pp. 133–149, 2018.
https://doi.org/10.1007/978-3-319-90050-6_8

To fulfill these goals, Haydi has been built as a Python package. Python is a well-known programming language and is commonly used as a prototyping language that provides a high degree of flexibility. Since Haydi is written purely in Python, it is compatible with PyPy[1] – a fast Python implementation with JIT compiler. Moreover, Haydi is designed to transparently utilize a cluster of computers to provide a better performance without sacrificing simplicity or flexibility. The distributed execution is built over Dask/distributed[2] and it was tested on Salomon cluster[3].

The goal of this paper is to give the overall picture of Haydi together with a formal definition for the case of generating canonical forms. More detailed and programmer-oriented text can be found in the user guide[4]. Haydi is released as an open source project at https://github.com/spirali/haydi under MIT license.

The original motivation for the tool was to investigate hard instances for equivalence of deterministic push-down automata (DPDAs). We have released a data set containing non-equivalent normed DPDAs [1].

The paper starts with two motivation examples in Sect. 2 followed by covering related works in Sect. 3. Section 4 introduces the architecture of Haydi. Section 5 shows a theoretical framework for generating canonical forms. Section 6 covers a basic usage of distributed computations and used optimizations. The last section shows performance measurements.

## 2     Examples

To give an impression of how Haydi works, basic usage of Haydi is demonstrated on two examples. The first one is a generator for directed graphs and the second one is a generator of finite state automata for the reset word problem.

### 2.1   Example: Directed Graphs

In this example, our goal is to generate directed graphs with $n$ nodes. Our first task is to describe the structure itself: we represent a graph as a set of edges, where an edge is a pair of two (possibly the same) nodes. For the simplicity of outputs, we are going to generate graphs on two nodes. However, this can be simply changed by editing a single constant, namely the number 2 on the second line in following code:

```
>>> import haydi as hd
>>> nodes = hd.USet(2, "n")  # A two-element set with elements {n0, n1}
>>> graphs = hd.Subsets(nodes * nodes)  # Subsets of a cartesian product
```

The first line just imports Haydi package. The second one creates a set of nodes, namely a set of two "unlabeled" elements. The first argument is the

---

[1] https://pypy.org/.

[2] https://github.com/dask/distributed.

[3] https://docs.it4i.cz/salomon/introduction/.

[4] http://haydi.readthedocs.io/.

number of elements, the second one is the prefix of each element name. The exact meaning of *USet* will be discussed further in the paper. For now, it just creates a set with elements without any additional quality, the elements of this set can be freely relabeled. In this example, it provides us with the standard graph isomorphism. The third line constructs a collection of all graphs on two nodes, in a mathematical notation it could be written as "graphs $= \mathcal{P}(\text{nodes} \times \text{nodes})$".

With this definition, we can now iterate all graphs:

```
>>> list(graphs.iterate())
[{}, {(n0, n0)}, {(n0, n0), (n0, n1)}, {(n0, n0), (n0, n1), (n1, n0)},
# ... 3 lines removed ...
n1)}, {(n1, n0)}, {(n1, n0), (n1, n1)}, {(n1, n1)}]
```

or iterate in a way in which we can see only one graph per isomorphic class:

```
>>> list(graphs.cnfs())  # cnfs = canonical forms
[{}, {(n0, n0)}, {(n0, n0), (n1, n1)}, {(n0, n0), (n0, n1)},
{(n0, n0), (n0, n1), (n1, n1)}, {(n0, n0), (n0, n1), (n1, n0)},
{(n0, n0), (n0, n1), (n1, n0), (n1, n1)}, {(n0, n0), (n1, n0)},
{(n0, n1)}, {(n0, n1), (n1, n0)}]
```

or generate random instances (3 instances in this case):

```
>>> list(graphs.generate(3))
[{(n1, n0)}, {(n1, n1), (n0, n0)}, {(n0, n1), (n1, n0)}]
```

Haydi supports standard operations such as *map*, *filter*, and *reduce*. The following example shows how to define graphs without loops, i.e. graphs such that for all edges $(a, b)$ hold that $a \neq b$:

```
>>> no_loops = graphs.filter(lambda g: all(a!=b for (a,b) in g.to_set()))
```

All these constructions can be transparently evaluated as a pipeline distributed across a cluster. Haydi uses Dask/distributed for distributing tasks, the following code assumes that Dask/distributed server runs at `hostname:1234`:

```
# Initialization
>>> from haydi import DistributedContext
>>> context = DistributedContext("hostname", 1234)
# Run a pipeline
>>> graphs.iterate().run(ctx=context)
```

## 2.2  Example: Reset Words

A *reset word* is a word that sends all states of a given finite automaton to a unique state. The following example generates automata and computes the length of a minimal reset word. It can be used for verifying the Černý conjecture on bounded instances. The conjecture states that the length of a minimal reset word is bounded by $(n-1)^2$ where $n$ is the number of states of the automaton [6,7].

First, we describe deterministic automata by their transition functions (a mapping from a pair of state and symbol to a new state). In the following code, n_states is the number of states and n_symbols is the size of the alphabet. We use USet even for the alphabet, since we do not care about the meaning of particular symbols, we just need to distinguish them.

```
# set of states q0, q1, ..., q_{n_states-1}
>>> states = hd.USet(n_states, "q")
# set of symbols a0, ..., a_{a_symbols-1}
>>> alphabet = hd.USet(n_symbols, "a")
# All mappings (states * alphabet) -> states
>>> delta = hd.Mappings(states * alphabet, states)
```

Now we can create a pipeline that goes through all the automata of the given size (one per an isomorphic class) and finds the maximal length among minimal reset words:

```
>>> pipeline = delta.cnfs().map(check_automaton).max(size=1)
>>> result = pipeline.run()
>>> print ("The maximal length of a minimal reset word for an "
...        "automaton with {} states and {} symbols is {}.".
...        format(n_states, n_symbols, result[0]))
```

The function check_automaton takes an automaton (as a transition function) and returns the length of the minimal reset word, or 0 when there is no such a word. It is just a simple breadth-first search on sets of states. The function is listed in Appendix A.

## 3   Related Works

Many complex software frameworks are designed for rapid checking mathematical ideas, for example Maple, Matlab, SageMath. Most of them also contain a package for combinatorial structures, e.g. Combinatorics in SageMath[5], Combstruct in Maple[6].

From the perspective of the mentioned tools, Haydi is a small single-purpose package. But as far as we know, there is no other tool that allows building structures by composition, searching only one structure of each isomorphism class as well as offering simple execution in distributed environment.

Tools focused on the generation of specific structures are on the other side of the spectrum. One example is Nauty [5] that contains Geng for generating graphs, another ones are generators for parity games in PGSolver [3] or automata generator for SageMath [2]. These tools provide highly optimized generators for a given structure.

## 4   Architecture

Haydi is a Python package for rapid prototyping of generators for discrete structures. The main two components are *domains* and *pipelines*. The former is dedicated to defining structures and the latter executes an operation over domains. In this section, both domains and pipelines are introduced. Parts that are related to generating canonical forms are omitted. This is covered separately in Sect. 5.

---

[5]  http://doc.sagemath.org/html/en/reference/combinat/sage/combinat/tutorial.
     html.

[6]  https://www.maplesoft.com/support/help/Maple/view.aspx?path=combstruct.

## 4.1   Domains

The basic structure in Haydi is a *domain* that represents an unordered collection of (Python) objects. On abstract level, domains can be viewed as countable sets with some implementation details. The basic operations with the domains are iterations through their elements and generating a random element. Domains are composable, i.e., more complex domains can be created from simpler ones.

There are six *elementary* domains: Range (a range of integers), Values (a domain of explicitly listed Python objects), Boolean (a domain containing **True** and **False**), and NoneDomain (a domain containing only one element: **None**). Examples are shown in Fig. 1. There are also domains **USet** and **CnfValues**; their description is postponed to Sect. 5, since it is necessary to develop a theory to explain their purpose.

```
>>> import haydi as hd
>>> hd.Range(4)   # Domain of four integers
<Range size=4 {0, 1, 2, 3}>
>>> hd.Values(["Haystack", "diver"])
<Values size=2 {'Haystack', 'diver'}>
```

**Fig. 1.** Examples of elementary domains

New domains can be created by composing existing ones or applying a transformation. There are the following compositions: *Cartesian product, sequences, subsets, mappings,* and *join*. Examples are shown in Fig. 2, more details can be found in the user guide. There are two transformations *map* and *filter* with the standard meaning. Examples are shown in Fig. 3.

```
>>> import haydi as hd
>>> a = hd.Range(2)
>>> b = hd.Values(("a", "b", "c"))
>>> hd.Product((a, b))   # Cartesian product
<Product size=6 {(0, 'a'), (0, 'b'), (0, 'c'), (1, 'a'), ...}>
>>> a * b   # Same as above
<Product size=6 {(0, 'a'), (0, 'b'), (0, 'c'), (1, 'a'), ...}>
>>> hd.Subsets(a)   # Subsets of 'a'
<Subsets size=4 {{}, {0}, {0, 1}, {1}}>
>>> hd.Mappings(a, a)   # Mappings from 'a' to 'a'
<Mappings size=4 {{0: 0; 1: 0}, {0: 0; 1: 1}, {0: 1; 1: 0}, ...}>
>>> hd.Sequences(a, 3)   # Sequences of length 3 over 'a'
<Sequences size=8 {(0, 0, 0), (0, 0, 1), (0, 1, 0), (0, 1, 1), ...}>
>>> hd.Join((a, b))   # Join 'a' and 'b', can be also written as 'a + b'
<Join size=5 {0, 1, 'a', 'b', 'c'}>
```

**Fig. 2.** Examples of domain compositions

```
>>> a = hd.Range(5)
>>> a.map(lambda x: x * 10)
<MapTransformation size=5 {0, 10, 20, 30, 40}>
```

**Fig. 3.** Examples of domain compositions

## 4.2  Pipeline

Domains in the previous section describe a set of elements. Pipelines provide a way how to work with elements in these sets. Generally, a pipeline provides methods for generating and iterating elements and optionally applying simple "map & reduce" transformations.

The pipeline creates a stream of elements from a domain by one of the three methods. We can apply transformations on elements in the stream. The pipeline ends by a reducing action. The schema is shown in Fig. 4. The pipeline consists of:

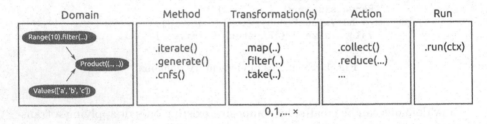

**Fig. 4.** The pipeline schema

**Method.** It specifies how to take elements from the domain into the stream. Haydi provides three options: `iterate()`, `generate(n)`, and `cnfs()`. Method `iterarate()` iterates all elements of a given domain, `generate(n)` creates $n$ random elements of the domain (by default with the uniform distribution over all elements), and `cnfs()` iterates over canonical forms (Sect. 5).

**Transformations.** Transformation modifies/filters elements in a stream. There are three pipeline transformations: `map(fn)` – applies the function `fn` on each element that goes through the pipeline, `filter(fn)` – filters elements in the pipeline according to the provided function, `take(count)` – takes only first `count` elements from the stream. The reason why transformations on domains and in pipeline are distinguished is described in https://haydi.readthedocs.io/en/latest/pipeline.html#transformations.

**Actions.** Action is a final operation on a stream of elements. For example there are: `collect()` – creates a list form of the stream, `reduce(fn)` – applies binary operation on elements of the stream, `max()` – takes maximal elements in the stream.

**Run().** The previous operations declare the pipeline, which is an immutable representation of a computational graph. The `run()` method actually executes the pipeline. The optional `ctx` (context) parameter specifies how should the computation be performed (serially or in a distributed way on a cluster).

The examples of pipelines are shown in Fig. 5. Not all parts of a pipeline have to be specified, if some of them are missing, defaults are used; the default method is `iterate()` and the default action is `collect()`.

```
>>> domain = hd.Range(5) * hd.Range(3)
# Iterate all elemenets and collect them
>>> domain.iterate().collect().run()
[(0, 0), (0, 1), (0, 2), (1, 0), (1, 1), (1, 2), (2, 0),
 (2, 1), (2, 2), (3, 0), (3, 1), (3, 2), (4, 0), (4, 1), (4, 2)]
# The same as above, since iterate() and collect() is default
>>> domain.run()
[(0, 0), (0, 1), (0, 2), (1, 0), (1, 1), (1, 2), (2, 0),
 (2, 1), (2, 2), (3, 0), (3, 1), (3, 2), (4, 0), (4, 1), (4, 2)]
# Generate three elements
>>> domain.generate(3).run()
[(3, 2), (4, 0), (1, 2)]
# Take elements that are maximal in first component
>>> domain.max(lambda x: x[0]).run()
[(4, 0), (4, 1), (4, 2)]
```

**Fig. 5.** Examples of pipelines

# 5    Generating Canonical Forms

In many cases, when we want to verify a property of a discrete structure, we are not interested in the names of the elements in the structure. For example, in the case of graphs we usually want to see only one graph for each isomorphic class. Another example can be finite-state automata; in many cases we are not especially interested in names of states and actual symbols in the input alphabet. For example, in Černý conjecture, the minimal length of reset words is not changed when the alphabet is permuted. On the other hand, symbols in some other problems may have special meanings and we cannot freely interchange them.

Haydi introduces `haydi.USet` as a simple but expressive mechanism for describing what permutations we are interested in. It serves to define partitions of atomic objects. Each partition creates a set of atomic objects that can be freely interchanged with one another; we call these partitions *Unlabeled sets*. They then establish semantics to what structure should be preserved when isomorphisms on various structures are defined.

Haydi allows to iterate a domain in a way where we see only one element for each isomorphic class. It is implemented as an iteration through *canonical forms* (CNFS).

In this section, a simple theoretical framework is built. It gives a formal background to this feature. Paragraphs starting with *"Abstract:"* are meant as part of a theoretical description. Paragraphs starting with *"Haydi:"* describe the implementation of the framework in Haydi.

*Abstract:* Let $\mathcal{A}$ be a set of all atomic objects whose structure is not investigated any further. The set of objects $\mathcal{O}$ is the minimal set with the following properties:

- $\mathcal{A} \subseteq \mathcal{O}$     (atoms)
- If $o_i \in \mathcal{O}$ for $i \in \{1, 2, \ldots, n\}$ then $\{o_1, o_2, \ldots, o_n\} \in \mathcal{O}$     (finite sets)
- If $o_i \in \mathcal{O}$ for $i \in \{1, 2, \ldots, n\}$ then $(o_1, o_2, \ldots, o_n) \in \mathcal{O}$     (finite sequences)

It is assumed that type of each object (atom, sequence, and set) can always be determined. Therefore, it is assumed that sequences and sets are not contained in atoms.

Function atoms : $\mathcal{O} \to 2^{\mathcal{A}}$ that returns the atoms contained in an object is defined as follows:

- atoms$(o) = \{o\}$ if $o \in \mathcal{A}$
- atoms$(o) = \bigcup_{i \in \{1, \ldots, n\}}$ atoms$(o_i)$ if $o = \{o_1, \ldots, o_n\}$ or $o = (o_1, \ldots, o_n)$

*Haydi:* The used Python instantiation of the definitions is the following: $\mathcal{A}$ contains None, True, False, all instances of types int (integers) and str (strings) and instances of the class haydi.Atom. Except for the last one, they are Python built-in objects; the last one is related to unlabeled sets and will be explained later. Sequences in $\mathcal{O}$ are identified with Python tuples, sets with haydi.Set (analogous to standard set). Haydi also contains the type haydi.Map (analogous to dict) for mappings. In the theoretical framework, mappings were not explicitly distinguished, as they can be considered sets of pairs. For sets and maps, standard python objects are not directly used for performance reasons[7]; however, both haydi.Set and haydi.Map can be directly transformed into their standard Python counter-parts.

Note: Generally, domains in Haydi may contain any Python object; however, domains that support iterating over CNFS impose some restrictions that will be shown later. Since the theoretical framework is built just for CNFS, its formalization to Python is mapped in a way that respects these limitations from the beginning. For this reason, $\mathcal{O}$ is not identified with all Python objects. The Python incarnation of $\mathcal{O}$ is called *basic objects*.

Now we established an isomorphism between objects. We define that two objects are isomorphic if they can be obtained one from another by permuting its atoms. To control permutations, partitioning of atoms is introduced and permutation of atoms is allowed only within its "own" class. These classes are defined through uset, that is an abbreviation of "unlabeled set".

---

[7] Built-in classes set and dict are optimized for lookups; however, Haydi needs fast comparison methods as will be seen later. haydi.Set and haydi.Map are stored in a sorted state to enable this.

*Abstract:* Let us fix a function uset : $\mathcal{A} \rightarrow 2^{\mathcal{A}}$ in the following way:

- $\forall a \in \mathcal{A} : a \in \mathsf{uset}(a)$
- $\forall a, b \in \mathcal{A} : \mathsf{uset}(a) = \mathsf{uset}(b) \vee \mathsf{uset}(a) \cap \mathsf{uset}(b) = \emptyset$

Obviously uset partitions $\mathcal{A}$ into disjoint classes.

Let $\mathcal{P}$ be a set of all bijective functions from $\mathcal{A}$ to $\mathcal{A}$ such that for each $\pi \in \mathcal{P}$ holds $\forall a \in \mathcal{A} : \pi(a) \in \mathsf{uset}(a)$.

Applying $\pi \in \mathcal{P}$ to an object $o \in \mathcal{O}$ (written as $o^{\pi}$) is defined as follows:

- $o^{\pi} = \pi(o)$ if $o \in \mathcal{A}$
- $o^{\pi} = \{o_1^{\pi}, \ldots, o_n^{\pi}\}$ if $\{o_1, \ldots, o_n\} = o$
- $o^{\pi} = (o_1^{\pi}, \ldots, o_n^{\pi})$ if $(o_1, \ldots, o_n) = o$

Let $o_1, o_2 \in \mathcal{O}$ then $o_1$ and $o_2$ are *isomorphic* (written as $o_1 \equiv o_2$) if there exists $\pi \in \mathcal{P}$ such that $o_1 = o_2^{\pi}$.

*Haydi:* All integers, strings, `None`, `True`, and `False` have a singleton unlabeled set, i.e., $\mathsf{uset}(a) = \{a\}$. Therefore, all objects that contain only these atoms always form their own "private" isomorphic class. For example: (`"abc"`, 1) cannot be isomorphic to anything else since string `"abc"` and integer 1 cannot be replaced, because for each $\pi \in \mathcal{P}$ holds $\pi(\text{"abc"}) = \text{"abc"}$ and $\pi(1) = 1$.

The only way to create a non-singleton unlabeled set is to use domain `haydi.USet` (Unlabled set) that creates a set of atoms belonging to the same unlabeled set; in other words, if $X$ is created by `haydi.USet` then for each $o \in X$ holds $\mathsf{uset}(o) = X$.

```
>>> a = hd.USet(3, "a")
>>> list(a)
[a0, a1, a2]
```

The first argument is the size of the set, and the second one is the name of the set that has only informative character. The name is also used as the prefix of element names, again without any semantical meaning. Elements of `USet` are instances of `haydi.Atom` that is a wrapper over an integer and a reference to the `USet` that contains them.

Method `haydi.is_isomorphic` takes two objects and returns `True` iff the objects are isomorphic according to our definition. Several examples are shown in Fig. 6.

## 5.1   Canonical Forms

Haydi implements an iteration over canonical forms as a way to obtain exactly one element for each isomorphic class. We define a canonical form as the smallest element from the isomorphic class according to a fixed ordering.

*Abstract:* We fix a binary relation $\leq$ for the rest of the section such that $\mathcal{O}$ is well-ordered under $\leq$. As usual, we write $o_1 < o_2$ if $o_1 \leq o_2$ and $o_1 \neq o_2$. A *canonical form* of an object $o$ is $\mathsf{cf}(o) = \min\{o' \in \mathcal{O} \mid o \equiv o'\}$. We denote $\mathcal{C} = \{o \in \mathcal{O} \mid o = \mathsf{cf}(o)\}$ as a set of all canonical forms.

```
>>> a0, a1, a2 = hd.USet(3, "a")
>>> b0, b1 = hd.USet(2, "b")
>>> hd.is_isomorphic(a0, a2)
True
>>> hd.is_isomorphic(b1, b0)
True
>>> hd.is_isomorphic(a0, b0)
False
>>> hd.is_isomorphic((a0, b0), (a2, b1))
True
>>> hd.is_isomorphic((a0, a0), (a0, a2))
False
```

**Fig. 6.** Isomorphism examples

*Haydi:* Canonical forms can be generated by calling `cnfs()` on a domain. Figure 7 shows simple examples of generating CNFS. In case 1, we have only two results (a0, a0) and (a0, a1); the former represents a pair with the same two values and the latter represents a pair of two different values. Obviously, we cannot get one from the other by applying any permutation, and all other elements of Cartesian product a * a can be obtained by permutations. This fact is independent of the size of a (as it has at least two elements). In case 2, the result is two elements, since we cannot permute elements from different usets. The third case shows canonical forms of a power set of a, as we see there is exactly one canonical form for each size of sets.

```
>>> a = hd.USet(3, "a")
>>> b = hd.USet(2, "b")
>>> list((a * a).cnfs())    # 1
[(a0, a0), (a0, a1)]
>>> list((a + b).cnfs())    # 2
[a0, b0]
>>> list(hd.Subsets(a).cnfs())    # 3
[{}, {a0}, {a0, a1}, {a0, a1, a2}]
```

**Fig. 7.** CNFS examples

Generating CNFS is limited in Haydi to *strict* domains that have the following features:

1. A strict domain contains only basic objects (defined at the beginning of this section).
2. A strict domain is closed under isomorphism.

The first limitation comes from the need of ordering. The standard comparison method `__eq__` is not sufficient since it may change between executions. To ensure deterministic canonical forms[8], Haydi defines `haydi.compare` method.

---

[8] In Python 2, instances of different types are generally unequal, and they are ordered consistently but arbitrarily. Switching to Python 3 does not help us, since comparing incompatible types throws an error (e.g. $3 < (1, 2)$), hence standard comparison cannot serve as ordering that we need for basic objects.

This method is responsible for deterministic comparison of basic objects and provides some additional properties that are explained later. The second condition ensures that canonical forms represent all elements of a domain. Usually these conditions do not present a practical limitation. Elementary domains except for `haydi.Values` are always strict and standard compositions preserve strictness. Elementary domain `haydi.CnfsValues` allows to define a (strict) domain through canonical elements, hence it serves as a substitute for `haydi.Values` in a case when a strict domain from explicitly listed elements is needed.

## 5.2    The Algorithm

This section describes implementation of the algorithm that generates canonical forms. A naïve approach would be to iterate over all elements and filter out non-canonical ones. Haydi avoids the naïve approach and makes the generation of canonical forms more efficient. It constructs new elements from smaller ones in a depth-first search manner. On each level, relevant extensions of the object are explored, and non-canonical ones are pruned. The used approach guarantees that all canonical forms are generated, and each will be generated exactly once, hence the already generated elements do not need to be remembered (except the current branch in a building tree).

This approach was already used in many applications and extracted into an abstract framework (e.g. [4]). The main goal of this section is to show correctness of the approach used in Haydi and not to give an abstract framework for generating canonical elements, since it was done before. However, the goal is not to generate a specific kind of structures, but provide a framework for their describing, therefore, a rather abstract approach must still be used.

Let us note that the algorithm is not dealing here with efficiency of deciding whether a given element is in a canonical form. In our use cases, most elements are relatively small, hence all relevant permutations are checked during checking the canonicity of an element. Therefore, the implementation in Haydi is quite straightforward. It exploits some direct consequences of Proposition 1 that allow the algorithm to reduce the set of relevant permutations and in some cases immediately claim non-canonicity.

The used approach is based on the following two propositions. The first says that an object cannot be canonical if it contains "gaps" in atoms occurring in the object. The second shows that new elements can only be constructed from existing canonical forms and still all of them are reached.

At the beginning, let us introduce some properties of the ordering given by `haydi.compare` which allow the propositions to be established. On the abstract level, the following properties for ordering $\leq$ are assumed where $o, o' \in \mathcal{O}$:

- Tuples of the same length are lexicographically ordered.
- If $o = \{o_1, \ldots, o_n\}$ where $o_1 < \cdots < o_n$ and $o' = \{o'_1, \ldots, o'_n\}$ where $o'_1 < \cdots < o'_n$ then $o \leq o'$ if $(o_1, \ldots, o_n) \leq (o'_1, \ldots, o'_n)$.

A set $X \subseteq \mathcal{A}$ *contains a gap* if there exists $a \in X$ such that there is $a' \in \mathcal{A} \setminus X$ and $a' \in \mathsf{uset}_{\downarrow}(a)$ where $\mathsf{uset}_{\downarrow}(a) = \{a' \in \mathsf{uset}(a) \mid a' < a\}$.

**Proposition 1.** *If $o \in \mathcal{O}$ and* atoms($o$) *contains a gap, then $o$ is not a canonical form.*

Proposition 1 is a direct consequence of the following claim:

**Proposition 2.** *If $o \in O$ and $a', a \in \mathcal{A}$ such that $a' \in$ uset$_{\downarrow}(a), a \in$* atoms($o$)$, a' \notin$ atoms($o$) *and $\pi \in \mathcal{P}$ is a permutation that only swaps $a$ and $a'$ then $o^{\pi} < o$.*

*Proof.* The proposition is proved by induction on the structure of $o$; let $a, a', \pi$ be as in the statement of the proposition: If $o$ is an atom then directly $o = a, o^{\pi} = a'$ and $a' < a$ from assumptions. Now assume that $o = (o_1, \ldots, o_n)$ and the proposition holds for all $o_i, i \in \{1, \ldots, n\}$. From assumptions we get that each $o_i$ does not contain $a'$ and there is the minimal index $f \in \{1, \ldots, n\}$ such that $o_f$ contains $a$. Hence $o_i = o_i^{\pi}$ for all $i \in \{1, \ldots, f - 1\}$ and $o_f^{\pi} < o$ by the induction assumption. Since tuples are lexicographically ordered it follows that $o^{\pi} < o$. Similar ideas apply also for sets.    □

Let us define function parent $: \mathcal{O} \to \mathcal{O} \cup \{\bot\}$ (where $\bot$ is a fresh symbol) that gives rise to a search tree. The function returns a "smaller" object from which the object may be constructed. The function returns $\bot$ for "ground" objects (atoms, empty tuples/sets).

$$\text{parent}(o) = \begin{cases} \bot & \text{if } o \in \mathcal{A} \cup \{(), \{\}\} \\ (o_1, \ldots, o_n) & \text{if } o = (o_1, \ldots, o_{n+1}) \\ o \setminus \{x\} & \text{if } o \text{ is a non-empty set and } x = \max o \end{cases}$$

**Proposition 3.** *For each $o \in \mathcal{O}$ holds:*

1. *Exists $n \in \{1, 2, \ldots\}$ such that* parent$^n(o) = \bot$.
2. *If $o$ is a canonical form then* parent($o$) *is $\bot$ or a canonical form.*

*Proof.* (1) If $o \in \mathcal{A}$ then $n = 1$, if $o$ is a set/tuple then $n$ is the number of elements in the set/tuple.

(2) Assume that there is $o \in \mathcal{C}$ and $o' = $ parent($o$) $\neq \bot$ and there is $\pi \in \mathcal{P}$ such that $o'^{\pi} < o'$. Since $o' \neq \bot$, $o$ has to be a non-empty tuple or set by definition of parent. If $o$ is a tuple then from the lexicographic ordering of tuples follows that $o^{\pi} < o$ and this is a contradiction. Now we explore the case $o = \{o_1, \ldots o_{n+1}\}$ where $o_i < o_j$ for $i < j$ and $i, j \in \{1, \ldots, n+1\}$. If there is $\{p_1, \ldots p_n\} = o'^{\pi}$ such that $p_i < p_j$ for $i, j \in \{1, \ldots, n\}$ then from fact that $o'^{\pi} < o'$ follows that there has to be $f \in \{1, \ldots, n\}$ such that $p_f < o_f$ and $p_i = o_i < p_f$ for all $i \in \{1, \ldots, f - 1\}$. The last step is to explore what happens when $\pi$ is applied on $o$; let $\{q_1, \ldots q_{n+1}\} = o^{\pi}$ such that $q_i < q_j$ for $i, j \in \{1, \ldots, n+1\}$ and let $k \in \{1, \ldots, n+1\}$ such that $q_k = o_{n+1}^{\pi}$. Since applying $\pi$ on an object is bijective, $k \neq f$. If $f < k$ then it follows that $o_i = p_i = q_i$ for $i \in \{1, \ldots, f - 1\}$ and $q_f = p_f < o_f$ and hence $o^{\pi} < o$. If $k < f$ then $o_i = p_i = q_i$ for $i \in \{1, \ldots, k - 1\}$ and $q_k < q_{k+1} = p_k = o_k$ and hence $o^{\pi} < o$.    □

Proposition 3.1 shows that parent defines a tree where: $\perp$ is the root; non-root nodes are elements from $\mathcal{O}$; 3.2 shows that each canonical form can be reached from the root by a path that contains only canonical forms. Moreover, the elements "grow" with the distance from the root.

This serves as a basis for the algorithm generating canonical forms of elements from a domain. It recursively takes an object and tries to create a bigger one, starting from $\perp$. On each level, it checks whether the new element is canonical, if not, the entire branch is terminated. The way of getting a bigger object from a smaller one, depends on the specific domain, what type of objects are generated and by which elements the already found elements are extended. Since domains are composed from smaller ones, Haydi iterates the elements of a subdomain to gain possible "extensions" to create a new object; such extensions are then added to the existing object to obtain a possible continuation in the tree. Since subdomains are also strict domains, only through canonical elements of the subdomain is iterated and new extensions are created by applying permutations on the canonical forms. Once it is clear that the extension leads to an object with a gap, then such a permutation is omitted. Therefore, it is not necessary to go through all of the permutations.

Example:

```
>>> a = hd.USet(1000, "a")
>>> b = a * a
<Product size=1000000 {(a0, a0), (a0, a1), (a0, a2), (a0, a3), ...}>
>>> list(b.cnfs())
[(a0, a0), (a0, a1)]
```

The domain in variable b has one million of elements; however, only two of them are canonical forms. Haydi starts with an empty tuple, then it asks for canonical forms of the subdomain a that is a set containing only a0. The only permutation on a0 that does not create a gap after adding into empty tuple is identity, so the only relevant extension is a0. Therefore, only (a0,) is examined as a continuation. It is a canonical form, so the generation continues. Now the second domain from Cartesian product is used, in this particular example, again canonical forms of a is used. At this point the only no-gap (partial) permutations are identity and swap of a0 and a1, hence possible extensions are a0 and a1. Extending (a0,) give us (a0, a0) and (a0, a1) as results.

The approach is similar when sets are generated. The only thing that needs to be added for this case is a check that the extending object is bigger (w.r.t. $\leq$) than previous ones, to ensure that the current object is the actual parent of the resulting object.

# 6   Distributed Computations

Haydi was designed to enable parallel computation on cluster machines from the beginning. Dask/distributed[9] serves as the backend for computations. The code that uses this feature was already shown at the end of Sect. 2.1.

---

[9] https://github.com/dask/distributed.

Haydi contains a scheduler that dynamically interacts with Dask/distributed scheduler. Haydi's scheduler gradually takes elements from a pipeline and assigns them to Dask/distributed. Haydi calculates an average execution time of recent jobs and the job size is altered to having neither too small jobs nor too large with respect to job time constraints.

Haydi chooses a strategy to create jobs in dependence on a chosen method of a domain exploration. The simplest strategy is for randomly generated elements; the stream in the pipeline induces independent jobs and the scheduler has to care only about collecting results and adhering to a time constraint (that may be specified in run method).

In the case of iterating over all elements, there are three supported strategies: strategy for domains that support *full slicing*, for domains with *filtered slicing*, and a generic strategy for domains without slicing. The last one is a fallback strategy where Haydi scheduler itself generates elements, these elements with the rest of the pipeline are sent as jobs into Dask/distributed.

The full slicing is supported if the number of elements in a domain is known and an iterator over the domain that skips the first $n$ elements can be efficiently created. In this case, the domain may be sliced into disjunct chunks of arbitrary sizes. Haydi scheduler simply creates lightweight disjoint tasks to workers in form "create iterator at $i$ steps and process $m$ elements" without transferring explicit elements of domains. All built-in domains support full slicing as long as the filter is not applied.

If a domain is created by applying a filter, both properties are lost generally, i.e., the exact number of elements, and an efficient iterator from the $n$-th item. However, if the original domain supports slicing it is possible to utilize this fact. Domains can be sliced as if there was no filter present in domain or subdomains at all, while allowing to signalize that some elements were skipped. Note, the filtered elements cannot be silently swallowed, because the knowledge of how many elements were already generated in the underlying domain would be lost. In such a case it could not be possible to ensure that the iterations go over disjunct chunks of a domain. The iterators that allow to signalize that one or more elements were internally skipped are called "skip iterators". The ability to signalize skipping more elements at once allows to implement efficient slicing when filter domains are used in composition. For example, assume a Cartesian product of two filtered domains, where consecutive chunks of elements are dropped when a single element is filtered in a subdomain. This strategy usually works well in practice for domains when elements dropped by the filter are spread across the whole domain.

If canonical forms are generated, then the goal is to build a search tree. One job assigned to Dask/distributed represents a computation of all direct descendants of a node in a search tree. In the current version, it is quite a simple way of distributed tree search and there is a space for improvements; it is the youngest part of Haydi.

# 7    Performance

The purpose of this section is to give a basic impression of Haydi's performance. For comparison the two examples from Sects. 2.1 ad 2.2 are used.

First of all, Haydi is compared with other tools. This comparison is demonstrated on the example of generating directed graphs. Geng [5] is used as a baseline within the comparison, since it is a state of the art generator for graphs. In order to simulate a prototyping scenario a special version is included. This version loads graphs generated by Geng into Python. The loading process is done using the Networkx[10] library and a small manual wrapper. Moreover, the results of two other experiments are included. Both experiments summarize graphs generated by SageMath, in the first case SageMath uses Geng as the backend while in the other one it uses its own graph implementation Cgraph. Haydi was executed with Python 2.7.9 and PyPy 5.8.0. Geng 2.6r7 and SageMath 8.0 were used. Experiments were executed on a laptop with Intel Core i7-7700HQ (2.8 GHz). Source codes of all test scripts can be found in the Haydi's git repository. The results are shown in Table 1. In all cases, except the last one, the goal was to generate all non-isomorphic graphs with the given number of vertices without any additional computation on them. The last entry generates all possible graphs (including isomorphic ones) and runs in parallel on 8 processes.

**Table 1.** Performance of generating graphs

| Tool/# of vertices | 5 | 6 | 7 | 8 |
|---|---|---|---|---|
| Geng (without loading to Python) | <0.01 s | <0.01 s | <0.01 s | 0.01 s |
| Geng + manual parser | <0.01 s | 0.03 s | 0.05 s | 0.11 s |
| Geng + Networkx | 0.27 s | 0.28 s | 0.28 s | 0.94 s |
| SageMath (Geng backend) | 0.17 s | 0.18 s | 0.26 s | 2.17 s |
| SageMath (Cgraph backend) | 0.09 s | 0.55 s | 6.59 s | 139.76 s |
| Haydi canonicals (Python) | 0.53 s | 11.55 s | Timeout | Timeout |
| Haydi canonicals (PyPy) | 0.34 s | 5.46 | Timeout | Timeout |
| Haydi parallel `iterate()` (PyPy) | 3.27 s | 3.49 s | 70.99 s | Timeout |

Timeout is 200 s

It is obvious that Haydi cannot compete with Geng in generating graphs. Geng is hand-tuned for this specific use case, in contrast to Haydi that is a generic tool. On the other hand, the Haydi program that generates graphs can be simply extended or modified to generate different custom structures while modifying Geng would be more complicated.

The second benchmark shows strong scaling of parallel execution of the reset word generator from Sect. 2.2 for six vertices and two alphabet characters for variants where `cnfs()` was replaced by `iterate()`, since the parallelization of

---
[10] https://networkx.github.io/.

cnfs() is not fully optimized, yet. The iterated domain supports the full slicing mode. The experiment was executed on the Salomon cluster (Table 2).

**Table 2.** Performance of iterate() on Salomon

| Nodes (24 CPUs/node) | Time | Strong scaling |
|---|---|---|
| 1 | 3424 s | 1 |
| 2 | 1908 s | 0.897 |
| 4 | 974 s | 0.879 |
| 8 | 499 s | 0.858 |

The last note on performance: we have experimented with several concepts of the tool. The first version was a tool named Qit[11], that shares similar ideas in API design with Haydi. It also has Python API, but generates C++ code behind the scene that is compiled and executed. Benchmarks on prototypes showed it was around 3.5 times faster than pure Python version (executed in PyPy); however, due to C++ layer, Qit was less flexible than the current version Haydi and hard to debug for the end user. Therefore, this version was abandoned in favor of the pure-python version to obtain a more flexible environment for experiments and prototyping. As the problems encountered in generation of combinatorial objects are often exponential, 3.5× speedup does not compensate inflexibility.

## A     Function check_automaton

```
from haydi.algorithms import search
# Let us precompute some values that will be repeatedly used
init_state = frozenset(states)
max_steps = (n_states**3 - n_states) / 6
# Known result is that we do not need more than (n^3 - n) / 6 steps
def check_automaton(delta):
        # This function takes automaton as a transition function and
        # returns the minimal length of reset word or 0 if there
        # is no such word
        def step(state, depth):
                # A step in bread-first search; gives a set of states
                # and return a set reachable by one step
                for a in alphabet:
                        yield frozenset(delta[(s, a)] for s in state)
        delta = delta.to_dict()
        return search.bfs(
                init_state,     # Initial state
                step,           # Function that takes a node and
                                # returns the followers
                lambda state, depth: depth if len(state) == 1 else None,
                # Run until we reach a single state
                max_depth=max_steps,    # Limit depth of search
                not_found_value=0)      # Return 0 when we exceed
                                        # depth limit
```

---

[11] https://github.com/spirali/qit.

# References

1. Böhm, S., Beránek, J., Šurkovský, M.: NDPDA - data set. Technical report, VŠB - Technical University of Ostrava, Czech Republic (2017). http://verif.cs.vsb.cz/sb/data/ndpda_pairs-2017-12.pdf
2. Heuberger, C., Krenn, D., Kropf, S.: Automata in SageMath - combinatorics meet theoretical computer science. Discret. Math. Theoret. Comput. Sci. **18**(3) (2016). http://dmtcs.episciences.org/1475
3. Lange, M., Friedmann, O.: The PGSolver collection of parity game solvers. Technical report, Ludwig-Maximilians-Universität-München (2009)
4. McKay, B.D.: Isomorph-free exhaustive generation. J. Algorithms **26**(2), 306–324 (1998). https://doi.org/10.1006/jagm.1997.0898
5. McKay, B.D., Piperno, A.: Practical graph isomorphism, II. J. Symb. Comput. **60**, 94–112 (2014). http://www.sciencedirect.com/science/article/pii/S0747717113001193
6. Černý, J.: Poznámka k. homogénnym experimentom s konečnými automatmi. Mat. Fyz. Cas SAV **14**, 208–215 (1964)
7. Volkov, M.V.: Synchronizing automata and the Černý conjecture. In: Martín-Vide, C., Otto, F., Fernau, H. (eds.) LATA 2008. LNCS, vol. 5196, pp. 11–27. Springer, Heidelberg (2008). https://doi.org/10.1007/978-3-540-88282-4_4

# Argumentation Frameworks with Recursive Attacks and Evidence-Based Supports

Claudette Cayrol, Jorge Fandinno[✉], Luis Fariñas del Cerro,
and Marie-Christine Lagasquie-Schiex

IRIT, Université de Toulouse, CNRS, Toulouse, France
{ccayrol,jorge.fandinno,luis,lagasq}@irit.fr

**Abstract.** The purpose of this work is to study a generalisation of Dung's abstract argumentation frameworks that allows representing positive interactions (called *supports*). The notion of support studied here is based in the intuition that every argument must be supported by some chain of supports from some special arguments called *prima-facie*. The theory developed also allows the representation of both *recursive attacks* and *supports*, that is, a class of attacks or supports whose targets are other attacks or supports. We do this by developing a theory of argumentation where the classic role of *attacks* in defeating arguments is replaced by a subset of them, which is extension dependent and which, intuitively, represents a set of "valid attacks" with respect to the extension. Similarly, only the subset of "valid supports" is allowed to support other elements (arguments, attacks or supports). This theory displays a conservative generalisation of Dung's semantics (complete, preferred and stable) and also of their principles (conflict-freeness, acceptability and admissibility). When restricted to finite non-recursive frameworks, we are also able to prove a one-to-one correspondence with Evidence-Based Argumentation (EBA). When supports are ignored a one-to-one correspondence with Argumentation Frameworks with Recursive Attacks (AFRA) semantics is also established.

## 1 Introduction

Argumentation has become an essential paradigm for knowledge representation and, especially, for reasoning from contradictory information [2,18] and for formalizing the exchange of arguments between agents in, *e.g.*, negotiation [3]. Formal abstract frameworks have greatly eased the modelling and study of argumentation. For instance, a Dung's argumentation framework (AF) [18] consists of a collection of arguments interacting through an attack relation, enabling to determine "acceptable" sets of arguments called *extensions*.

J. Fandinno—The second author is funded by the Centre International de Mathématiques et d'Informatique de Toulouse (CIMI) through contract ANR-11-LABEX-0040-CIMI within the program ANR-11-IDEX-0002-02.

© Springer International Publishing AG, part of Springer Nature 2018
F. Ferrarotti and S. Woltran (Eds.): FoIKS 2018, LNCS 10833, pp. 150–169, 2018.
https://doi.org/10.1007/978-3-319-90050-6_9

Two natural generalisations of Dung's argumentation frameworks consist in allowing positive interactions (usually expressed by a support relation) and allowing high-order attacks (that target other attacks or supports). These generalisations are not only for the "pleasure" to develop more complex concepts; they mainly allow the representation of richer argumentation problems. Here is an example in the legal field, borrowed from [4].

*Example 1.* The prosecutor says that the defendant has intention to kill the victim (argument $b$). A witness says that she saw the defendant throwing a sharp knife towards the victim (argument $a$). Argument $a$ can be considered as a support for argument $b$. The lawyer argues back that the defendant was in a habit of throwing the knife at his wife's foot once drunk. This latter argument (argument $c$) is better considered attacking the support from $a$ to $b$, than arguments $a$ or $b$ themselves. Now the prosecutor's argumentation seems no longer sufficient for proving the intention to kill. This example is represented as a recursive framework in Fig. 1.                                                                         □

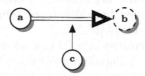

**Fig. 1.** An acyclic recursive framework where supports (resp. attacks) are represented by double (resp. simple) arrows ended with a white (resp. black) triangle. Circles with solid border represent prima-facie arguments while dashed border ones represent standard arguments.

Positive interaction between arguments has been first introduced in [20,31]. In [13], the support relation is left general so that the bipolar framework keeps a high level of abstraction. The associated semantics are based on the combination of the attack relation with the support relation which results in new complex attack relations. However, there is no single interpretation of the support, and a number of researchers proposed specialized variants of the support relation (deductive support [7], necessary support [25,26], evidential support [27,28]). Each specialization can be associated with an appropriate modelling using an appropriate complex attack. These proposals have been developed quite independently, based on different intuitions and with different formalizations. [14] presents a comparative study in order to restate these proposals in a common setting, the bipolar argumentation framework (see also [15] for another survey)

We follow here an evidential understanding of the support relation [27] that allows to distinguish between two different kinds of arguments: *prima-facie* and *standard arguments*. *Prima-facie* arguments were already present in [31] as those that are justified whenever they are not defeated. On the other hand, *standard arguments* are not directly assumed to be justified and must inherit support from prima-facie arguments through a chain of supports. For instance, in Example 1, arguments $a$ and $c$ are considered as prima-facie arguments while $b$ is regarded as a standard argument. Hence, while $a$ and $c$ can be accepted as in Dung's argumentation, $b$ must inherit support from $a$: this holds if $c$ is not accepted, but does not otherwise. Indeed, in the latter, the support from $a$ to $b$ is defeated by $c$.

Concerning frameworks with interactions between arguments and other interactions, a first version has been introduced in [21], then studied in [5] under the name of AFRA (Argumentation Framework with Recursive Attacks). This version describes abstract argumentation frameworks in which the interactions can be either attacks between arguments or attacks from an argument to another attack. In this case, as for the bipolar case, a translation of an AFRA into an equivalent AF can be defined by the addition of some new arguments and the attacks they produce or they receive. A generalization of AFRA has been proposed in [16] in order to take into account supports on arguments or on interactions. These frameworks are called ASAF (Attack-Support Argumentation Frameworks). As for an AFRA, a translation of an ASAF into an equivalent AF is proposed by the addition of arguments and attacks. More recently, alternative acceptability semantics have been defined in a direct way for argumentation frameworks with recursive attacks [10,11].

In this paper, we are interested in a framework with high-order attacks and supports, with an evidential understanding of these supports. So, we apply the notion of prima-facie, not only to arguments, but also to interactions (attacks and supports). The intuition is that prima-facie elements (arguments, attack or supports) are elements that do not have to be supported. More precisely, we study a semantics for argumentation frameworks with recursive attacks *and* evidential supports, based on the following intuitive principles:

**P1** The role played in Dung's argumentation frameworks by attacks in defeating arguments is now played by a subset of these attacks, which is extension dependent and represents the "valid attacks" with respect to that extension.

**P2** The notion of acceptability for prima-facie (and supported) arguments (resp. attacks or supports) is as in recursive frameworks without supports.

**P3** Non-prima-facie arguments (resp. attacks or supports) can only be "accepted" (resp. be "valid") if there is a chain of "valid supports" rooted in some prima-facie arguments. These "valid supports" are also extension dependent.

**P4** It is a conservative generalisation of Dung's framework for the notions of conflict-free, admissible, complete, preferred, and stable extensions.

The paper is organized as follows: the necessary background is given in Sect. 2; new semantics for recursive and evidence-based frameworks are proposed in Sect. 3; a comparison with existing frameworks is given in Sects. 4, 5 and 6; and we conclude in Sect. 7. Proofs of formal results can be found in [12].

## 2    Background

We next give preliminaries about the works the paper is based on. We first review some basic background about Dung's abstract argumentation frameworks [18], the recursive framework of [11] and Evidence-Based Argumentation (EBA) frameworks [27, 30].

### 2.1    Dung's Argumentation

**Definition 1 (D-framework).** *A Dung's abstract argumentation framework* (d-framework *for short*) *is a pair* $\mathbf{dAF} = \langle \mathbf{A,R} \rangle$ *where* $\mathbf{A}$ *is a set of arguments and* $\mathbf{R} \subseteq \mathbf{A} \times \mathbf{A}$ *is a relation representing attacks over arguments.*    □

**Definition 2 (Defeated/acceptable argument).** *Let* $\mathbf{dAF} = \langle \mathbf{A,R} \rangle$ *be a d-framework and* $E \subseteq \mathbf{A}$, *an argument* $a \in \mathbf{A}$ *is said to be:*

1. *defeated w.r.t.* $E$ *iff* $\exists b \in E$ *such that* $(b,a) \in \mathbf{R}$, *and*
2. *acceptable w.r.t.* $E$ *iff for every argument* $b \in \mathbf{A}$ *with* $(b,a) \in \mathbf{R}$, *there is* $c \in E$ *such that* $(c,b) \in \mathbf{R}$.    □

To obtain shorter definitions we will also use the following notations:

$$Def(E) \stackrel{\text{def}}{=} \{ \, a \in \mathbf{A} \mid \exists b \in E \text{ s.t. } (b,a) \in \mathbf{R} \, \}$$
$$Acc(E) \stackrel{\text{def}}{=} \{ \, a \in \mathbf{A} \mid \forall b \in \mathbf{A}, (b,a) \in \mathbf{R} \text{ implies } b \in Def(E) \, \}$$

respectively denote the set of all defeated and acceptable arguments w.r.t. $E$.

**Definition 3 (Semantics).** *Given a d-framework* $\mathbf{dAF} = \langle \mathbf{A,R} \rangle$, *a set of arguments* $E \subseteq \mathbf{A}$ *is said to be:*

1. conflict-free *iff* $E \cap Def(E) = \varnothing$,
2. admissible *iff it is conflict-free and* $E \subseteq Acc(E)$,
3. complete *iff it is conflict-free and* $E = Acc(E)$,
4. preferred *iff it is* $\subseteq$-*maximal admissible,*
5. stable *iff it is conflict-free and* $E \cup Def(E) = \mathbf{A}$.    □

**Theorem 1 (From [18]).** *Given a d-framework* $\mathbf{dAF} = \langle \mathbf{A,R} \rangle$, *the following assertions hold:*

1. *every complete set is also admissible,*
2. *every preferred set is also complete, and*
3. *every stable set is also preferred.*    □

*Example 2.* Consider the d-framework corresponding to Fig. 2. The argument $a$ is accepted w.r.t. any set $E$ because there is no argument $x \subset \mathbf{A}$ such that $(x,a) \in \mathbf{R}$. Furthermore, $b$ is defeated and non-acceptable w.r.t. the set $\{a\}$. Then, it is easy to check that $\{a\}$ is stable (and, thus, conflict-free, admissible, complete and preferred). The empty set $\varnothing$ is admissible, but not complete; and the set $\{b\}$ is conflict-free, but not admissible.

**Fig. 2.** A d-framework

## 2.2  Recursive Argumentation

Let us here recall the necessary background from [11], where high-order attacks are called "recursive".

**Definition 4 (RAF).** *A recursive argumentation framework (RAF) is a tuple* $\langle \mathbf{A}, \mathbf{K}, s, t \rangle$ *where* $\mathbf{A}$ *is a set of arguments,* $\mathbf{K}$ *is a set disjunct from* $\mathbf{A}$, *representing attack names,* $s$ *is a function from* $\mathbf{K}$ *to* $\mathbf{A}$, *mapping each interaction to its source,* $t$ *is a function from* $\mathbf{K}$ *to* $(\mathbf{A} \cup \mathbf{K})$ *mapping each interaction to its target.*

Acceptability semantics are defined by replacing the notion of extension (set of arguments) by a pair of a set of arguments and a set of attacks, called a "structure". The intuition is the fact that two arguments may be conflicting depends on the validity of the attack between them. So it would not be sound to give a definition of a set of arguments being conflict-free, independently of a set of attacks. More generally, the classic role of attacks in defeating arguments is played by a subset of attacks, which is extension dependent, and represents the valid attacks with respect to the extension.

**Definition 5 (Structure).** *A structure on* $\langle \mathbf{A}, \mathbf{K}, s, t \rangle$ *is a pair* $U = (S, \Gamma)$ *such that* $S \subseteq \mathbf{A}$ *and* $\Gamma \subseteq \mathbf{K}$.  □

Intuitively, $S$ represents the set of arguments that are accepted w.r.t. the structure $U$ while $\Gamma$ represents the set of attacks that are valid w.r.t. $U$.

**Definition 6 (Defeat/Inhibition/Acceptability).** *Given* $U = (S, \Gamma)$ *a structure on* $\langle \mathbf{A}, \mathbf{K}, s, t \rangle$. *Let* $a \in \mathbf{A}$ *and* $\alpha \in \mathbf{K}$.
1. *a is defeated wrt* $(S, \Gamma)$ *iff* $\exists \beta \in \Gamma$ *such that* $s(\beta) \in S$ *and* $t(\beta) = a$,
2. *α is inhibited wrt* $(S, \Gamma)$ *iff* $\exists \beta \in \Gamma$ *such that* $s(\beta) \in S$ *and* $t(\beta) = \alpha$.
*Def(U) (resp. Inh(U)) will denote the set of arguments (resp. attacks) that are defeated (resp. inhibited) wrt the structure* $U$.
3. *a is acceptable wrt* $U$ *iff* $\forall \beta \in \mathbf{K}$ *such that* $t(\beta) = a$, *either* $\beta \in Inh(U)$ *or* $s(\beta) \in Def(U)$.
4. *α is acceptable wrt* $U$ *iff* $\forall \beta \in \mathbf{K}$ *such that* $t(\beta) = \alpha$, *either* $\beta \in Inh(U)$ *or* $s(\beta) \in Def(U)$.
*Acc(U) will denote the set of all acceptable arguments and attacks wrt* $U$.  □

Then, semantics are defined as follows:

**Definition 7 (Semantics).** *A structure* $U = (S, \Gamma)$ *on* $\langle \mathbf{A}, \mathbf{K}, s, t \rangle$ *is:*
1. *conflict-free iff* $S \cap Def(U) = \varnothing$ *and* $\Gamma \cap Inh(U) = \varnothing$;

2. *admissible iff it is conflict-free and* $\forall x \in (S \cup \Gamma)$*, $x$ is acceptable wrt $U$;*
3. *complete iff it is conflict-free and* $Acc(U) = S \cup \Gamma$*;*
4. *stable iff it is conflict-free and satisfies:*
     *(a)* $\forall a \in \mathbf{A} \setminus S$*, $a \in Def(U)$ and*
     *(b)* $\forall \alpha \in \mathbf{K} \setminus \Gamma$*, $\alpha \in Inh(U)$;*
5. *preferred iff it is a* $\subseteq$*-maximal[1] admissible structure.*    □

It has been proved in [11] that every complete structure is admissible, every preferred structure is also complete and every stable structure is also preferred.

## 2.3  Evidence-Based Argumentation

We recall the formal definition of EBA frameworks. We follow here the definitions from [30] which correct some technical flaws from [27].

**Definition 8 (Evidence-Based Argumentation framework).** *An Evidence-Based Argumentation framework (EBAF) is a tuple* $\mathbf{EBAF} = \langle \mathbf{A}, \mathbf{R}_a, \mathbf{R}_e \rangle$ *where $\mathbf{A}$ represents a set of arguments,* $\mathbf{R}_a \subseteq (2^{\mathbf{A}} \setminus \varnothing) \times \mathbf{A}$ *is an attack relation and* $\mathbf{R}_e \subseteq (2^{\mathbf{A}} \setminus \varnothing) \times \mathbf{A}$ *is a support relation. A special argument $\eta \in \mathbf{A}$ is distinguished satisfying that there is no $(B, \eta) \in \mathbf{R}_a \cup \mathbf{R}_e$ for any set $B$ nor there is $(B, a) \in \mathbf{R}_a$ with $\eta \in B$. We say that $\mathbf{EBAF}$ is (in)finite iff $\mathbf{A}$ is (in)finite.* □

The special argument $\eta$ serves as a representation of the prima-facie arguments. Note that the attack relation is not a binary relation. Instead, there can be an attack from a *set of arguments* to another argument, something which is not the case in d-frameworks.

**Definition 9 (Evidential Support).** *An argument $a \in \mathbf{A}$ is e-supported by a set $B \subseteq \mathbf{A}$ iff the two following conditions hold:*
1. $a = \eta$*, or*
2. *there is a non-empty $C \subseteq B$ s.t. $(C, a) \in \mathbf{R}_e$ and every $c \in C$ is e-supported by $B \setminus \{a\}$.*    □
*$B$ is said to be a minimal e-support for $a$ iff there is no $C \subset B$ such that $a$ is e-supported by $C$.*    □

Note that $\eta$ is e-supported by any set $B \subseteq \mathbf{A}$.

**Definition 10 (Evidence-Supported Attack).** *A pair $(B, a)$ is said to be an* evidence-supported attack *(e-attack) iff (i) there is $(C, a) \in \mathbf{R}_a$ with $C \subseteq B$ and (ii) all elements in $C$ are e-supported by $B$. $(B, a)$ is said to be a minimal e-attack if there is no e-attack $(C, a)$ with $C \subset B$.*    □

We will say that $B$ e-supports $a$ or that $(B, a)$ is an e-support when $a$ is e-supported by $B$ and that $B$ e-attacks $a$ when $(B, a)$ is an e-attack.

---

[1] Where $U = (S, \Gamma) \subseteq U' = (S', \Gamma')$ iff $(S \cup \Gamma) \subseteq (S' \cup \Gamma')$.

**Definition 11 (Acceptability).** *Given some framework* $\mathbf{EBAF} = \langle \mathbf{A}, \mathbf{R}_a, \mathbf{R}_e \rangle$, *an argument* $a \in \mathbf{A}$ *is said to be* acceptable *w.r.t. a set* $E \subseteq \mathbf{A}$ *iff the following two conditions are satisfied:*

1. *a is e-supported by $E$, and*
2. *for every minimal e-attack $(B, a)$, it holds that $E$ e-attacks some $b \in B$.*    □

**Definition 12 (Semantics).** *A set of arguments* $E \subseteq \mathbf{A}$ *is said to be*

1. self-supporting *iff all arguments $a \in E$ are e-supported by $E$,*
2. conflict-free *iff, for every $a \in E$, there is no $B \subseteq E$ such that $(B, a) \in \mathbf{R}_a$,*
3. admissible *iff it is conflict-free and all arguments $a \in E$ are acceptable w.r.t. $E$,*
4. complete *iff it is admissible and all acceptable arguments w.r.t. $E$ are in $E$,*
5. preferred *iff it is a $\subseteq$-maximal admissible set,*
6. stable *iff it is self-supporting, conflict-free and any argument $a \notin E$ which is e-supported by $\mathbf{A}$ satisfies that $E$ e-attacks either $a$ or every minimal e-support $B$ of $a$.*    □

# 3    Recursive Evidence-Based Argumentation

In this section, we extend the semantics proposed for recursive attacks in [11] with the purpose of handling evidence-based supports.

## 3.1    Recursive Evidence-Based Argumentation Frameworks

**Definition 13 (Recursive Evidence-Based Argumentation Framework).** *An* (evidence-based recursive) argumentation framework $\mathbf{AF} = \langle \mathbf{A}, \mathbf{K}, \mathbf{S}, \mathbf{s}, \mathbf{t}, \mathbf{P} \rangle$ *is a sextuple where* $\mathbf{A}$, $\mathbf{K}$ *and* $\mathbf{S}$ *are three (possible infinite) pairwise disjunct sets respectively representing arguments, attacks and supports names, and where* $\mathbf{P} \subseteq \mathbf{A} \cup \mathbf{K} \cup \mathbf{S}$ *is a set representing the* prima-facie *elements that do not need to be supported. Functions* $\mathbf{s} : (\mathbf{K} \cup \mathbf{S}) \longrightarrow 2^{\mathbf{A}}$ *and* $\mathbf{t} : (\mathbf{K} \cup \mathbf{S}) \longrightarrow (\mathbf{A} \cup \mathbf{K} \cup \mathbf{S})$ *respectively map each attack and support to its source and its target.*    □

As in EBAFs, the source of attacks and supports is a set of arguments. It is obvious that any attack $(a, b)$ in a d-framework can be represented by assigning to it some name $\alpha$ that satisfies $\mathbf{s}(\alpha) = \{a\}$ and $\mathbf{t}(\alpha) = b$. It is also worth mentioning that, from an evidential point of view, every argument and attack of a d-framework is prima-facie. That is, given some $\mathbf{dAF} = \langle \mathbf{A}, \mathbf{R} \rangle$, we can build a corresponding recursive framework $\mathbf{AF} = \langle \mathbf{A}, \mathbf{K}, \mathbf{S}, \mathbf{s}, \mathbf{t}, \mathbf{P} \rangle$ where $\mathbf{K}$ is a set of names of the same cardinality of $\mathbf{R}$, where $\mathbf{S} = \varnothing$ is the empty set of supports, $\mathbf{s}$ and $\mathbf{t}$ map each attack name to its corresponding source and target, and the set of prima-facie elements $\mathbf{P} = \mathbf{A} \cup \mathbf{K}$ includes all arguments and attacks.

*Example 3.* In particular, the d-framework associated with Fig. 2 corresponds to the $\mathbf{AF} = \langle \mathbf{A}, \mathbf{K}, \mathbf{S}, \mathbf{s}, \mathbf{t}, \mathbf{P} \rangle$ with $\mathbf{A} = \{a, b\}$, $\mathbf{K} = \{\alpha\}$, $\mathbf{s}(\alpha) = \{a\}$, $\mathbf{t}(\alpha) = b$ and $\mathbf{P} = \{a, b, \alpha\}$.    □

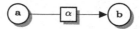

**Fig. 3.** An AF with named attack.

Note also that, different from EBAFs, the set **P** may contain several prima-facie elements (arguments, attacks and supports). This is not a substantial difference, but allows that any graph representing a d-framework has the same semantics when interpreted in our framework. For instance, Fig. 3 depicts the framework of Fig. 2 making explicit the attack name. Note that we use squares in the middle of the arrows to represent attack and support names. As with arguments, a solid border denotes prima-facie elements while a dashed border denotes standard elements. By following this notation every graph within Dung's theory preserves the same semantics, something which is in accordance with principle P4. Note also that, in contrast with EBAFs, we do not assume any constraint on the prima-facie elements, they can be attacked or supported (though supporting prima-facie elements do not make any semantical difference from not doing so).

*Example 4.* As an illustration of frameworks with recursive attacks and supports, consider the argumentation frameworks $\mathbf{AF}_1 = \langle \mathbf{A}_1, \mathbf{K}_1, \mathbf{S}_1, \mathbf{s}_1, \mathbf{t}_1, \mathbf{P}_1 \rangle$ and $\mathbf{AF}_2 = \langle \mathbf{A}_2, \mathbf{K}_2, \mathbf{S}_2, \mathbf{s}_2, \mathbf{t}_2, \mathbf{P}_2 \rangle$ where $\mathbf{A}_1 = \{a, b, c\}$, $\mathbf{K}_1 = \{\beta\}$, $\mathbf{S}_1 = \{\alpha\}$, $\mathbf{A}_2 = \{a, b, c, d\}$, $\mathbf{K}_2 = \{\alpha, \beta\}$, $\mathbf{S}_2 = \{\gamma, \delta\}$, functions $\mathbf{s}_1, \mathbf{t}_1, \mathbf{s}_2$ and $\mathbf{t}_2$ satisfy

$$\mathbf{s}_1(\alpha) = \{a\} \qquad \mathbf{t}_1(\alpha) = b$$
$$\mathbf{s}_1(\beta) = \{c\} \qquad \mathbf{t}_1(\beta) = \alpha$$
$$\mathbf{s}_2(\alpha) = \{a\} \quad \mathbf{t}_2(\alpha) = b \quad \mathbf{s}_2(\gamma) = \{c\} \quad \mathbf{t}_2(\gamma) = \alpha$$
$$\mathbf{s}_2(\beta) = \{a\} \quad \mathbf{t}_2(\beta) = b \quad \mathbf{s}_2(\delta) = \{d\} \quad \mathbf{t}_2(\delta) = \beta$$

and $\mathbf{P}_1 = \{a, c, \alpha, \beta\}$, and $\mathbf{P}_2 = \{a, b, c, d, \gamma, \delta\}$. These two frameworks can be respectively depicted as the graphs in Figs. 4a and b. It is worth to note that Fig. 4a is just the result of naming attacks and supports in Fig. 1. On the other hand, Fig. 4b represents a framework with two attacks between $a$ and $b$ that hold in different contexts: $\alpha$ and $\beta$ are two standard attacks that are respectively supported by different prima-facie arguments, $c$ and $d$ respectively, that represent those different contexts.                                               □

*Example 5.* Consider the following four arguments:[2]

(a) "The Bible says that God is all good",

---

[2] This example is a slight variation of the one discussed in [24]. Having at our disposal supports allows us to explicitly represent the implicit support in "The Bible says that God is all good, so God is all good" which was there expressed as a single argument.

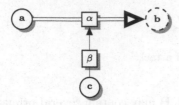
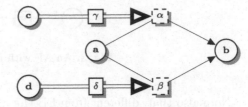

(a) The graph of Fig.1 with attack and support names

(b) A recursive framework representing attacks in different contexts

**Fig. 4.** Recursive frameworks with prima-facie elements

(b) "God is all good",
(c) "The Bible was written by human beings",
(d) "Human beings are not infallible".

Argument (a) may be considered as a support $\alpha$ for argument (b), while (c) and (d) taken together may be considered as an attack $\beta$ to the support $\alpha$. Indeed, arguments (c) and (d), alone or together, contradict neither (a) nor (b). Moreover, (c) alone (resp. (d) alone) does not attack $\alpha$. We must take (c) and (d) together in order to attack $\alpha$. This example can be formalised as $\mathbf{AF}_3 = \langle \mathbf{A}_3, \mathbf{K}_3, \mathbf{S}_3, \mathbf{s}_3, \mathbf{t}_3, \mathbf{P}_3 \rangle$ where $\mathbf{A}_3 = \{a, b, c, d\}$, $\mathbf{K}_3 = \{\beta\}$, $\mathbf{S}_3 = \{\alpha\}$, and $\mathbf{P}_3 = \mathbf{A}_3 \backslash \{b\} = \{a, c, d\}$.

$$\mathbf{s}_3(\alpha) = \{a\} \qquad\qquad \mathbf{t}_3(\alpha) = b$$
$$\mathbf{s}_3(\beta) = \{c, d\} \qquad\qquad \mathbf{t}_3(\beta) = \alpha$$

□

It is worth to mention that the reason to use explicit names for attacks and supports in Definition 13 instead of just relations is twofold. First, this allows the existence of several attacks or supports between the same elements that can be used to represent different contexts as illustrated in Example 4. The second reason is due to the possible existence of cycles of attacks or supports, which has no trivial finite representation as a relation: for instance, attack $\alpha$ in Fig. 5 would correspond to the infinite object $(\{a\}, (\{b\}, (\{c\}, (\{a\}, \ldots))))$.

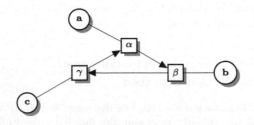

**Fig. 5.** A cyclic recursive framework

## 3.2    Semantics of Recursive Evidence-Based Argumentation Frameworks

We generalize next the notion of structure introduced in [11], which will allow us to characterise which arguments are regarded as "acceptable," and which attacks and supports are regarded as "valid," with respect to some argumentation framework. The notion of structure is analogous to the notion of set of arguments and it will be the basis of defining the corresponding argumentation semantics for recursive frameworks.

**Definition 14 (Structure).** *A triple* $\mathfrak{A} = \langle E, \Gamma, \Delta \rangle$ *is said to be a* structure *of some* $\mathbf{AF} = \langle \mathbf{A}, \mathbf{K}, \mathbf{S}, \mathbf{s}, \mathbf{t}, \mathbf{P} \rangle$ *iff it satisfies:* $E \subseteq \mathbf{A}$, $\Gamma \subseteq \mathbf{K}$ *and* $\Delta \subseteq \mathbf{S}$. $\square$

Intuitively, the set $E$ represents the set of "acceptable" arguments w.r.t. the structure $\mathfrak{A}$, while $\Gamma$ and $\Delta$ respectively represent the set of "valid attacks" and "valid supports" w.r.t. $\mathfrak{A}$. Any attack[3] $\alpha \in \overline{\Gamma}$ is understood as non-valid and, in this sense, it cannot defeat the element that it is targeting. Similarly, any support $\beta \in \overline{\Delta}$ is understood as non-valid and it cannot support the element that it is targeting.

For the rest of this section we assume that all definitions and results are relative to some given framework $\mathbf{AF} = \langle \mathbf{A}, \mathbf{K}, \mathbf{S}, \mathbf{s}, \mathbf{t}, \mathbf{P} \rangle$. We extend now the definition of defeated arguments (Definition 2) using the set $\Gamma$ instead of the attack relation $\mathbf{R}$: given a structure of the form $\mathfrak{A} = \langle E, \Gamma, \Delta \rangle$, we define:

$$Def_X(\mathfrak{A}) \stackrel{\text{def}}{=} \{ x \in X \mid \exists \alpha \in \Gamma, \ \mathbf{s}(\alpha) \subseteq E \text{ and } \mathbf{t}(\alpha) = x \} \tag{1}$$

with $X \in \{ \mathbf{A}, \mathbf{K}, \mathbf{S} \}$. In other words, an element $x$ is defeated w.r.t. $\mathfrak{A}$ iff there is a "valid attack" w.r.t. $\mathfrak{A}$ that targets $x$ and whose source is "acceptable" w.r.t. $\mathfrak{A}$. It is interesting to observe that we may define the *attack relation* associated with some structure $\mathfrak{A} = \langle E, \Gamma, \Delta \rangle$ as follows:

$$\mathbf{R}_{\mathfrak{A}} \stackrel{\text{def}}{=} \{ (\mathbf{s}(\alpha), \mathbf{t}(\alpha)) \mid \alpha \in \Gamma \} \tag{2}$$

and that, using this relation, we can rewrite (1) as:

$$Def_X(\mathfrak{A}) \stackrel{\text{def}}{=} \{ x \in X \mid \exists B \subseteq E \text{ s.t. } (B, x) \in \mathbf{R}_{\mathfrak{A}} \} \tag{3}$$

Now, it is easy to see that our definition for $Def_{\mathbf{A}}(\mathfrak{A})$ can be obtained from Dung's definition of defeat (Definition 2) just by replacing the attack relation $\mathbf{R}$ by the attack relation $\mathbf{R}_{\mathfrak{A}}$ associated with the structure $\mathfrak{A}$ and $\exists b \in E$ by $\exists B \subseteq E$, or in other words, by replacing the set of all attacks in the argumentation framework by the set of the "valid attacks" w.r.t. the structure $\mathfrak{A}$, as stated in P1; and allowing the source of attacks to be, not just arguments, but sets of them.

---

[3] By $\overline{\Gamma} \stackrel{\text{def}}{=} \mathbf{K} \backslash \Gamma$ we denote the set complement of $\Gamma$ w.r.t. $\mathbf{K}$. Similarly, by $\overline{\Delta} \stackrel{\text{def}}{=} \mathbf{S} \backslash \Delta$ we denote the set complement of $\Delta$ w.r.t. $\mathbf{S}$.

By $Def(\mathfrak{A}) \stackrel{\text{def}}{=} Def_{\mathbf{A}}(\mathfrak{A}) \cup Def_{\mathbf{K}}(\mathfrak{A}) \cup Def_{\mathbf{S}}(\mathfrak{A})$, we will denote the set of all defeated arguments. By $\overline{Def_X}(\mathfrak{A}) \stackrel{\text{def}}{=} X \backslash Def_X(\mathfrak{A})$ with $X \in \{\mathbf{A}, \mathbf{K}, \mathbf{S}\}$, we denote the non-defeated arguments (resp. attacks, supports) w.r.t. $\mathfrak{A}$. Furthermore, by $\overline{Def}(\mathfrak{A}) \stackrel{\text{def}}{=} (\mathbf{A} \cup \mathbf{K} \cup \mathbf{S}) \backslash Def(\mathfrak{A})$, we denote the set of all non-defeated elements.

*Example 4 (cont'd).* Consider the framework corresponding to Fig. 4a, and the structure $\mathfrak{A} = \langle E, \Gamma, \Delta \rangle$ with $E = \{a, c\}$, $\Gamma = \{\beta\}$ and $\Delta = \varnothing$. Then, we have that $Def(\mathfrak{A}) = \{\alpha\}$. □

Let us now introduce the notion of *supported elements* w.r.t. a structure. Intuitively, it should be noted that the prima-facie elements (arguments, attacks, supports) of a given framework are supported for any structure. Then, a standard element is supported if there exists a chain of supported supports, leading to it, which is rooted in prima-facie arguments. Formally, given some framework $\mathbf{AF} = \langle \mathbf{A}, \mathbf{K}, \mathbf{S}, \mathbf{s}, \mathbf{t}, \mathbf{P} \rangle$ and some structure $\mathfrak{A} = \langle E, \Gamma, \Delta \rangle$, the set of supported elements $Sup(\mathfrak{A})$ is recursively defined as follows[4]:

$$Sup(\mathfrak{A}) \stackrel{\text{def}}{=} \mathbf{P} \cup \{\, \mathbf{t}(\alpha) \mid \exists \alpha \in \Delta \cap Sup(\mathfrak{A}')\, , \mathbf{s}(\alpha) \subseteq E \cap Sup(\mathfrak{A}')\, \} \qquad (4)$$

with[5] $\mathfrak{A}' = \mathfrak{A} \backslash \{\mathbf{t}(\alpha)\}$. By $Sup_X(\mathfrak{A}) \stackrel{\text{def}}{=} Sup(\mathfrak{A}) \cap X$ with $X \in \{\mathbf{A}, \mathbf{K}, \mathbf{S}\}$, we respectively denote the set of all supported arguments, attacks and supports.

*Example 4 (cont'd).* Consider the framework corresponding to Fig. 4a, and the structure $\mathfrak{A} = \langle E, \Gamma, \Delta \rangle$ with $E = \{a, b, c\}$, $\Gamma = \varnothing$ and $\Delta = \{\alpha\}$. Let us prove that $b \in Sup(\mathfrak{A})$. Note that $b = \mathbf{t}(\alpha)$ with $\alpha \in \Delta$. So we have to prove that $\alpha$ and $a \in \mathbf{s}(\alpha) = \{a\}$ both belong to $Sup(\mathfrak{A} \backslash \{b\})$. That is true since $\alpha$ and $a$ both belong to $\mathbf{P}$.

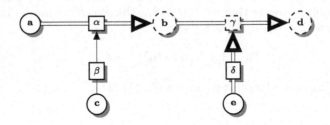

**Fig. 6.** A recursive framework with prima-facie elements

*Example 6.* As a further example, consider the framework corresponding to the graph depicted in Fig. 6 and let $\mathfrak{A} = \langle E, \Gamma, \Delta \rangle$ be a structure with $E = \{a, b, c, d, e\}$, $\Gamma = \varnothing$ and $\Delta = \{\alpha, \gamma, \delta\}$. Then, we have that $Sup(\mathfrak{A}) =$

---

[4] Note that $E = \varnothing$ and $\Delta = \varnothing$ act as base cases, because $E = \varnothing$ (resp. $\Delta = \varnothing$) implies $Sup(\mathfrak{A}) = \mathbf{P}$.

[5] By abuse of notation, we write $\mathfrak{A} \backslash T$ instead of $\langle E \backslash T, \Gamma \backslash T, \Delta \backslash T \rangle$ with $T \subseteq (\mathbf{A} \cup \mathbf{K} \cup \mathbf{S})$.

$\{a, b, c, d, e, \alpha, \beta, \gamma, \delta\}$. Note that $a$, $c$, $e$, $\alpha$, $\beta$ and $\delta$ are supported because they are prima-facie elements. It is also easy to see that $b$ is supported as in the previous example and that $\gamma$ is supported through $\delta$ by $e$. So, $b$ and $\gamma$ both belong to $Sup(\mathfrak{A}\backslash\{d\})$. Hence, $d$ is also supported.    □

Now, drawing on the notion of supported elements w.r.t. a given structure $\mathfrak{A}$, we are able to define the *supportable* elements w.r.t. $\mathfrak{A}$. Intuitively, an element is considered as being still supportable as long as there exists some non-defeated support with all its source elements non-defeated and regarded, in its turn, as supportable. Formally, an element $x$ is supportable w.r.t. $\mathfrak{A}$ iff $x$ is supported w.r.t. $\mathfrak{A}' = \langle \overline{Def_A(\mathfrak{A})}, \mathbf{K}, \overline{Def_S(\mathfrak{A})} \rangle$. Elements that are defeated or that are unsupportable cannot be accepted. In this sense, by $UnAcc(\mathfrak{A}) \overset{\text{def}}{=} Def(\mathfrak{A}) \cup \overline{Sup(\mathfrak{A}')}$ we denote the *unacceptable* elements w.r.t. $\mathfrak{A}$. Moreover, we say that an attack $\alpha \in \mathbf{K}$ is *unactivable*[6] iff either it is unacceptable or some element in its source is unacceptable, that is,

$$UnAct(\mathfrak{A}) \overset{\text{def}}{=} \{ \alpha \in \mathbf{K} \mid \alpha \in UnAcc(\mathfrak{A}) \text{ or } \mathbf{s}(\alpha) \cap UnAcc(\mathfrak{A}) \neq \varnothing \}$$

**Definition 15 (Acceptability).** *An element $x \in \mathbf{A} \cup \mathbf{K} \cup \mathbf{S}$ is said to be acceptable w.r.t. a structure $\mathfrak{A}$ iff (i) $x \in Sup(\mathfrak{A})$ and (ii) every attack $\alpha \in \mathbf{K}$ with $\mathbf{t}(\alpha) = x$ is unactivable, that is, $\alpha \in UnAct(\mathfrak{A})$.*    □

By $Acc(\mathfrak{A})$, we denote the set containing all arguments, attacks and supports that are acceptable with respect to $\mathfrak{A}$.

It is worth to note that, intuitively, an element is acceptable iff it is supported and, in addition, every attack against it can be considered as unactivable because either some argument in its source or itself has been regarded as unacceptable.

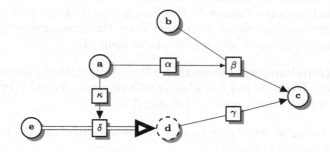

**Fig. 7.** Argumentation framework corresponding to Example 7.

*Example 7.* Consider the argumentation framework of Fig. 7, and the structure $\mathfrak{A} = \langle \{a, b, c, e\}, \{\alpha, \kappa, \gamma\}, \varnothing \rangle$. We have that $c$ is acceptable w.r.t. $\mathfrak{A}$. Note that there are two attacks against $c$: $\beta$ is defeated through $\alpha$ by $a$, while $\gamma$ is unactivable because $d$ is unsupportable since $\delta$ is defeated by $\kappa$.    □

---

[6] Intuitively, such an attack cannot be "activated" in order to defeat the element that it is targeting.

We also define the following order relations that will help us defining preferred structures: for any pair of structures $\mathfrak{A} = \langle E, \Gamma, \Delta \rangle$ and $\mathfrak{A}' = \langle E', \Gamma', \Delta' \rangle$, we write $\mathfrak{A} \sqsubseteq \mathfrak{A}'$ iff $(E \cup \Gamma \cup \Delta) \subseteq (E' \cup \Gamma' \cup \Delta')$. As usual, we say that a structure $\mathfrak{A}$ is $\sqsubseteq$-maximal iff every $\mathfrak{A}'$ that satisfies $\mathfrak{A} \sqsubseteq \mathfrak{A}'$ also satisfies $\mathfrak{A}' \sqsubseteq \mathfrak{A}$.

**Definition 16.** *A structure $\mathfrak{A} = \langle E, \Gamma, \Delta \rangle$ is said to be:*

1. self-supporting *iff* $(E \cup \Gamma \cup \Delta) \subseteq Sup(\mathfrak{A})$,
2. conflict-free *iff* $X \cap Def_Y(\mathfrak{A}) = \varnothing$ *for any* $(X, Y) \in \{(E, \mathbf{A}), (\Gamma, \mathbf{K}), (\Delta, \mathbf{S})\}$,
3. admissible *iff it is conflict-free and* $E \cup \Gamma \cup \Delta \subseteq Acc(\mathfrak{A})$,
4. complete *iff it is conflict-free and* $Acc(\mathfrak{A}) = E \cup \Gamma \cup \Delta$,
5. preferred *iff it is a $\sqsubseteq$-maximal admissible structure*,
6. stable[7] *iff* $(E \cup \Gamma \cup \Delta) = \overline{UnAcc(\mathfrak{A})}$. □

*Example 4 (cont'd).* The framework of Fig. 4a has a unique complete, preferred and stable structure $\mathfrak{A} = \langle \{a, c\}, \{\beta\}, \varnothing \rangle$. Note that $\alpha$ cannot be accepted because it is defeated by $c$ through $\beta$, while $b$ cannot be accepted because, now, it lacks support.

*Example 6 (cont'd).* The framework of Fig. 6 has also a unique complete, preferred and stable structure $\mathfrak{A} = \langle \{a, c, e\}, \{\beta\}, \{\gamma, \delta\} \rangle$. As above, $\alpha$ cannot be accepted because it is defeated by $c$ through $\beta$ which implies that $b$ and $d$ cannot be accepted because of lack of support. $\gamma$ is acceptable because it is supported through $\delta$ by $e$ and not attacked. □

*Example 7 (cont'd).* $\mathfrak{A} = \langle \{a, b, c, e\}, \{\alpha, \kappa, \gamma\}, \varnothing \rangle$ is the unique complete, preferred and stable structure w.r.t. the framework of Fig. 7. □

We show now that, as in Dung's argumentation theory, there is also a kind of Fundamental Lemma for argumentation frameworks with recursive attacks and evidence-based supports. Intuitively, this lemma says that elements of an admissible structure continue to be acceptable when the structure is "reasonably" extended, that is extended with an acceptable element.

**Lemma 1 (Fundamental Lemma).** *Let $\mathfrak{A} = \langle E, \Gamma, \Delta \rangle$ be an admissible structure and $x, y \in Acc(\mathfrak{A})$ be any pair of acceptable elements. Then,[8] (i) $\mathfrak{A}' = \mathfrak{A} \cup \{x\}$ is an admissible structure, and (ii) $y \in Acc(\mathfrak{A}')$.* □

Moreover, admissible structures form a complete partial order with preferred structures as maximal elements:

**Proposition 1.** *The set of all admissible structures forms a complete partial order with respect to $\sqsubseteq$. Furthermore, for every admissible structure $\mathfrak{A}$, there exists a preferred one $\mathfrak{A}'$ such that $\mathfrak{A} \sqsubseteq \mathfrak{A}'$.* □

The following result shows that the usual relation between extensions also holds for structures.

---

[7] Note also this already implies conflict-freeness.

[8] By abuse of notation, we write $\mathfrak{A} \cup T$ instead of $\langle E \cup (T \cap \mathbf{A}), \Gamma \cup (T \cap \mathbf{K}), \Delta \cup (T \cap \mathbf{S}) \rangle$ with $T \subseteq (\mathbf{A} \cup \mathbf{K} \cup \mathbf{S})$.

**Theorem 2.** *The following assertions hold:*

1. *every admissible structure is also self-supporting,*
2. *every complete structure is also admissible,*
3. *every preferred structure is also complete, and*
4. *every stable structure is also preferred.*                                   □

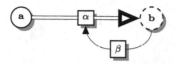

**Fig. 8.** A cyclic recursive framework

*Example 8.* As a further example, consider the framework corresponding to Fig. 8. This framework has a unique complete and preferred structure $\mathfrak{A} = \langle\{a\}, \{\beta\}, \varnothing\rangle$, but no stable one. Note that $\alpha$ and $b$ are neither acceptable nor unacceptable w.r.t. $\mathfrak{A}$: $\alpha$ is not unacceptable because it is supportable (it is prima-facie) and it is not defeated ($b$ is not in the structure) and it is not acceptable because it is attacked by $b$, which is still not unacceptable. Similarly, $b$ is not unacceptable because it is still supportable through $\alpha$, but it is not supported (and, thus not acceptable) because $\alpha$ is not in the structure.                □

## 4    Relation with Recursive Argumentation Frameworks

As mentioned in Sect. 3, our framework is a conservative generalisation of the Recursive Argumentation Framework (RAF) defined in [11] with the addition of supports and joint attacks. RAF's attacks are similar to Dung's attacks with the only difference that they may target, not only arguments, but also other attacks. Hence, translating RAF's (or Dung's) attacks into joint attacks is trivial: every attack with source $a$ is replaced by an attack with the singleton set $\{a\}$ as its source. On the other hand, like Dung's frameworks, RAFs do not encompass the notion of support. From an evidential point of view it is as every argument or attack was externally supported, or in other words, as attacks and arguments were prima-facie. In this sense, every $\mathbf{RAF} = \langle\mathbf{A},\mathbf{K},\mathbf{s},\mathbf{t}\rangle$ can be translated into a corresponding recursive evidence-based argumentation framework of the form $\mathbf{AF} = \langle\mathbf{A},\mathbf{K},\mathbf{S},\mathbf{s}',\mathbf{t},\mathbf{P}\rangle$ with $\mathbf{S} = \varnothing$ (no supports), where every element is considered as prima-facie, that is $\mathbf{P} = \mathbf{A}\cup\mathbf{K}$, and where $\mathbf{s}'$ satisfies $\mathbf{s}'(\alpha) = \{\mathbf{s}(\alpha)\}$ for every attack $\alpha \in \mathbf{K}$. It is easy to check that a structure $\langle E, \Gamma\rangle$ is conflict-free (resp. admissible, complete, preferred, stable) w.r.t. some $\mathbf{RAF}$ iff $\langle E, \Gamma, \varnothing\rangle$ is conflict-free (resp. admissible, complete, preferred, stable) w.r.t. its corresponding $\mathbf{AF}$. Furthermore, there is a one-to-one correspondence between complete, preferred and stable structures in RAF's and their corresponding Dung's extensions, so this correspondence is also carried over to our argumentation frameworks with evidence-based support. In [11], it also has been shown that there is a one-to-one correspondence between RAF and AFRA [5], which is also carried over to our frameworks (when we restrict ourselves to frameworks without supports). Note that AFRA has been extended with supports in [16,17] and called Attack-Support Argumentation Framework (ASAF). However, ASAF supports are understood as necessary conditions for their targets instead. This is quite different from the evidential understanding followed here as shown by the following example.

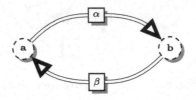

**Fig. 9.** A framework with a cycle of supports

*Example 9.* According to ASAF, the set $\{a, b, \alpha, \beta\}$ is a complete, preferred and stable w.r.t. the framework of Fig. 9. On the other hand, in our framework, $\langle \{a, b\}, \varnothing, \{\alpha, \beta\} \rangle$ is not admissible (and, thus, not complete, preferred nor stable) because neither $a$ nor $b$ are supported by a chain rooted in some prima-facie argument.    □

## 5    Relation with Dung's Argumentation Frameworks

It is also worth to mention that the one-to-one correspondence between RAF (or either AFRA or ASAF) and Dung's frameworks is not directly applicable to conflict-free or admissible sets as illustrated by the following example:

*Example 2 (cont'd).* Consider the argumentation framework corresponding to Fig. 3. According to Dung's theory, this framework has three conflict-free sets, namely $\varnothing$, $\{a\}$ and $\{b\}$, which respectively correspond to the structures: $\langle \varnothing, \{\alpha\}, \varnothing \rangle$, $\langle \{a\}, \{\alpha\}, \varnothing \rangle$ and $\langle \{b\}, \{\alpha\}, \varnothing \rangle$. On the other hand, $\langle \{a, b\}, \varnothing, \varnothing \rangle$ is a conflict-free structure because the attack $\alpha$ is not considered valid. Similarly, $\{a, b\}$ is a conflict-free set according to AFRA or ASAF.    □

The difference between Dung's argumentation frameworks and these three semantics for recursive attacks, illustrated by the above example, can be explained by the fact that, in Dung's theory, every attack is considered as "valid" in the sense that it may affect its target. In [11], it has been shown that a one-to-one correspondence with Dung's theory, for conflict-free and admissible sets, can be recovered by adding a kind of reinstatement principle on attacks, which forces all attacks that cannot be defeated to be "valid". The following extends the definition of d-structure from [11] to the case of supports by strengthening the notion of structure according to the above intuition:

**Definition 17 (D-structure).** *Given some framework* $\mathbf{AF} = \langle \mathbf{A}, \mathbf{K}, \mathbf{S}, \mathbf{s}, \mathbf{t}, \mathbf{P} \rangle$, *a structure* $\mathfrak{A} = \langle E, \Gamma, \Delta \rangle$ *is said to be a d-structure iff it satisfies* $(Acc(\mathfrak{A}) \cap \mathbf{K}) \subseteq$

$\Gamma$ and $(Acc(\mathfrak{A}) \cap \mathbf{S}) \subseteq \Delta$. Then, a conflict-free (resp. admissible, complete, preferred or stable) d-structure is a conflict-free (resp. admissible, complete, preferred, stable) structure which is also a d-structure.    □

As a direct consequence of Definition 16 and Theorem 2, we have:

**Observation 1.** *Every complete (resp. preferred or stable) structure is also a d-structure.*    □

It is easy to check that a structure $\langle E, \Gamma \rangle$ is a d-structure w.r.t. some **RAF** (as defined in [11]) iff $\langle E, \Gamma, \varnothing \rangle$ is a d-structure w.r.t. its corresponding **AF**. Hence, the following result is an immediate consequence of Theorem in [11]:

**Theorem 3.** *Let* $\mathbf{AF} = \langle \mathbf{A}, \mathbf{K}, \mathbf{S}, \mathbf{s}, \mathbf{t}, \mathbf{P} \rangle$ *be some non-recursive framework with* $\mathbf{S} = \varnothing$, $\mathbf{P} = \mathbf{A} \cup \mathbf{K}$, *and that satisfies* $|\mathbf{s}(\alpha)| = 1$ *and* $\mathbf{t}(\alpha) \in \mathbf{A}$, *for all* $\alpha \in \mathbf{K}$. *Then, a d-structure* $\mathfrak{A} = \langle E, \mathbf{K}, \varnothing \rangle$ *is conflict-free (resp. admissible, complete, preferred or stable) w.r.t.* $\mathbf{AF}$ *(Definition 17) iff it is conflict-free (resp. admissible, complete, preferred or stable) w.r.t.* $\mathbf{dAF} = \langle \mathbf{A}, \mathbf{R_{AF}} \rangle$ *(Definition 3) with the relation* $\mathbf{R_{AF}} \overset{\text{def}}{=} \{ (a, \mathbf{t}(\alpha)) \mid \alpha \in \mathbf{K} \text{ and } \mathbf{s}(\alpha) = \{a\} \}$.    □

Theorem 3 formalises how any d-framework can be represented as an **AF**: in particular, in these frameworks, all elements are prima-facie $\mathbf{P} = \mathbf{A} \cup \mathbf{K}$ (so supports are not needed $\mathbf{S} = \varnothing$). Furthermore, an attack only targets arguments, $\mathbf{t}(\alpha) \in \mathbf{A}$ for all $\alpha \in \mathbf{K}$, and the source is a single argument, represented by the restriction to singleton sets $|\mathbf{s}(\alpha)| = 1$.

## 6  Relation with Evidence-Based Argumentation Frameworks

As mentioned in the introduction, (non-recursive) EBAFs were first introduced in [27]. When we are restricted to non-recursive frameworks, the major difference between EBAFs and our frameworks comes from the way in which the notion of acceptability is defined. In both cases, every acceptable argument must also be supported but while, in EBAFs, acceptability relies on what is called *evidence-supported attack* (*e-attack* for short), in our theory, it relies on the idea that arguments are *unacceptable* if they cannot be supported or are defeated. Intuitively, an e-attack is a pair $(B, a)$ where $B$ groups together the arguments necessary to attack $a$ and all the arguments necessary to support all those arguments. Then, acceptability is defined requiring defence against e-attacks instead of standard attacks. In this sense, an EBAF can be understood as a (possibly exponential in size) Dung's framework in which arguments are self-supporting sets and attacks are the e-attacks [28].

Let us start by defining the non-recursive framework that corresponds to some EBAF with finite set of arguments.

**Definition 18.** *Given an* **EBAF** $= \langle \mathbf{A}, \mathbf{R}_a, \mathbf{R}_e \rangle$, *by* $\mathbf{AF_{EBAF}} = \langle \mathbf{A}, \mathbf{K}, \mathbf{S}, \mathbf{s}, \mathbf{t}, \mathbf{P} \rangle$ *we denote the argumentation framework where* $\mathbf{K}$ *and* $\mathbf{S}$ *are two (disjunct) sets with the same cardinality as* $\mathbf{R}_a$ *and* $\mathbf{R}_e$, *respectively;* $\mathbf{P} = \mathbf{K} \cup \mathbf{S} \cup \{\eta\}$ *and functions* $\mathbf{s}$ *and* $\mathbf{t}$ *map each attack and support name to their corresponding source and target,[9] that is, they satisfy:*

$$\mathbf{R}_a = \{ (\mathbf{s}(\alpha), \mathbf{t}(\alpha)) \mid \alpha \in \mathbf{K} \}$$
$$\mathbf{R}_e = \{ (\mathbf{s}(\beta), \mathbf{t}(\beta)) \mid \beta \in \mathbf{S} \}$$

*Given a set* $E \subseteq \mathbf{A}$, *by* $\mathfrak{A}_E \stackrel{\text{def}}{=} \langle E, \mathbf{K}, \mathbf{S} \rangle$ *we denote its corresponding structure.* $\square$

**Observation 2.** *Since there are no attacks against other attacks or supports, every d-structure w.r.t. some* $\mathbf{AF_{EBAF}}$ *is of the form* $\mathfrak{A}_E$ *for some set of arguments* $E \subseteq \mathbf{A}$. $\square$

In order to establish the existence of a one-to-one correspondence between finite EBAFs and non-recursive argumentation frameworks in our theory, let us define $\text{struct}_{\mathbf{EBAF}}(\cdot)$ as the function mapping any set of arguments $E$ into the structure $\mathfrak{A}_E = \langle E, \mathbf{K}, \mathbf{S} \rangle$.

**Theorem 4.** *Let* **EBAF** *be some finite EBA framework. Then, the function* $\text{struct}_{\mathbf{EBAF}}(\cdot)$ *is a one-to-one correspondence between its self-supporting (resp. conflict-free, admissible, complete, preferred or stable) sets according to Definition 12 and the self-supporting (resp. conflict-free, admissible, complete, preferred or stable) d-structures of its corresponding framework* $\mathbf{AF_{EBAF}}$. $\square$

The above result holds for the finite case. That immediately rises the question whether this correspondence can be generalised to non-finite frameworks. The following example answers this question in a negative way.

*Example 10.* Let **EBAF** $= \langle \mathbf{A}, \mathbf{R}_a, \mathbf{R}_e \rangle$ be some EBAF with a set of arguments $\mathbf{A} = \{\eta, a, b, c_1, c_2 \dots\}$, a set of attacks $\mathbf{R}_a = \{(\{a\}, b)\}$ and a set of supports

$$\mathbf{R}_e = \{(\{\eta\}, b)\} \cup \{(\{\eta\}, c_1), (\{\eta\}, c_2), \dots\}$$
$$\cup \{(\{c_1, c_2, \dots, \}, a), (\{c_2, \dots\}, a), \dots\}$$

Let $E = \mathbf{A} \backslash \{a\}$ be a set of arguments. It is easy to see that every argument is supported according to Definition 9 and, thus, that $a$ and all $c_i$ are acceptable because there is no attack against them. This implies that $b$ is not acceptable because it is attacked by $a$ which is supported and not defeated and, thus, that $E$ is not admissible. On the other hand, according to Definition 11, argument $b$ is also acceptable w.r.t. $E$. Just note that, for every e-attack $(C, b)$ against $b$, the set $C$ must include $a$ and infinitely many $c_i$'s and thus, there is always some e-attack $(C', b)$ against $b$ with $C' = C \backslash \{c_i\}$ and $c_i \in C$. Hence, there is no minimal e-attack against $b$, which immediately implies that $b$ is acceptable and that $E$ is admissible. $\square$

---

[9] In other words, for a given $(C, a) \in \mathbf{R}_a$, if $\alpha$ denotes the associated name in $\mathbf{K}$, we have $s(\alpha) = C$ and $t(\alpha) = a$.

It is worth to note that Example 10 can be also used to show that some usual results of abstract argumentation framework are not satisfied for non-finite EBAFs. In particular, the following example illustrates that neither the Fundamental Lemma nor the usual relations between semantics are satisfied:

*Example* 10 *(cont'd).* Note that $a$ is acceptable w.r.t. the admissible set $E$, but $E \cup \{a\}$ is not conflict-free (and, thus, not admissible) because $a$ attacks $b$. This is a counterexample to the Fundamental Lemma. Furthermore, this also implies that $E$ is a preferred set, though it is not a complete one, so the usual relations among semantics are not satisfied.                                                                    □

## 7   Conclusion

In this work we have extended Dung's abstract argumentation framework with recursive attacks and supports. One of the essential characteristics of this extension is that semantics are given with respect to the notion of "valid attacks and supports" which respectively play a role analogous to attacks in Dung's frameworks and supports in Evidence-Based Argumentation (EBA). The bases for this extension were first settled in [11], where semantics for frameworks with recursive attacks without supports were studied. The notions of "grounded attack/support" and "valid attack/support" have been introduced in [9] and encoded through a two-step translation into a meta-argumentation framework.[10] In the first step, a meta-argument is associated to an attack, and a support relation is added from the source of the attack to the meta-argument. In the second step, a support relation is encoded by the addition of a new meta-argument and new attacks. So [9] uses a method for flattening a recursive framework. As a consequence, extensions contain different kinds of argument. In contrast, we propose a theory where valid attacks remain explicit, and distinct from arguments, within the notion of structure.

It is worth mentioning that this extension is a conservative extension with respect to Dung's approach (when d-structures are considered) and that we have proved a one-to-one correspondence with finite EBA frameworks. We have also shown that non-finite EBA frameworks do not satisfy the Fundamental Lemma nor the usual relations among semantics. In this sense, our approach is an alternative semantics for non-finite frameworks with evidence-based supports that satisfies these properties. In addition, with restricted frameworks without supports, we inherit, from [11], a one-to-one correspondence with AFRA-extensions [5] in the case of the complete, preferred and stable semantics.

For a better understanding of the recursive frameworks, future work should include the study of other semantics (stage, semi-stable, grounded and ideal), extending our approach by taking into account other bipolar interactions [16,32],

---

[10] Note that meta-argumentation frameworks have been often used for flattening complex argumentation frameworks (such as bipolar or recursive ones, see for instance [5,9,16]). More generally, meta-level argumentation is concerned with using arguments to reason over arguments (see for instance [22,23]).

and enriching the translation proposed by [6,8,19,29] from Dung's framework into propositional logic and ASP, in order to capture RAF. This is the best way for encoding these frameworks (either directly, or by a flattening process) in order to obtain efficient practical implementations that could be tested in the ICCMA competition (see [1]).

# References

1. ICCMA competition. http://argumentationcompetition.org/2017/
2. Amgoud, L., Cayrol, C.: A reasoning model based on the production of acceptable arguments. Ann. Math. Artif. Intell. **34**, 197–216 (2002)
3. Amgoud, L., Maudet, N., Parsons, S.: Modelling dialogues using argumentation. In: Proceedings of ICMAS, pp. 31–38 (2000)
4. Arisaka, R., Satoh, K.: Voluntary manslaughter? a case study with meta-argumentation with supports. In: Kurahashi, S., Ohta, Y., Arai, S., Satoh, K., Bekki, D. (eds.) JSAI-isAI 2016. LNCS (LNAI), vol. 10247, pp. 241–252. Springer, Cham (2017). https://doi.org/10.1007/978-3-319-61572-1_16
5. Baroni, P., Cerutti, F., Giacomin, M., Guida, G.: AFRA: argumentation framework with recursive attacks. Int. J. Approx. Reason. **52**(1), 19–37 (2011)
6. Besnard, P., Doutre, S.: Checking the acceptability of a set of arguments. In: Delgrande, J.P., Schaub, T. (eds.) Proceedings of NMR, pp. 59–64 (2004)
7. Boella, G., Gabbay, D.M., van der Torre, L., Villata, S.: Support in abstract argumentation. In: Proceedings of COMMA, Frontiers in Artificial Intelligence and Applications, vol. 216, pp. 111–122. IOS Press (2010)
8. Carballido, J.L., Nieves, J.C., Osorio, M.: Inferring preferred extensions by pstable semantics. Intel. Artif.: Revista Iberoam. de Intel. Artif. **13**(41), 38–53 (2009)
9. Cayrol, C., Cohen, A., Lagasquie-Schiex, M.-C.: Towards a new framework for recursive interactions in abstract bipolar argumentation. In: Proceedings of COMMA, Frontiers in Artificial Intelligence and Applications, vol. 287, pp. 191–198. IOS Press (2016)
10. Cayrol, C., Fandinno, J., Fariñas del Cerro, L., Lagasquie-Schiex, M.-C.: Valid attacks in argumentation frameworks with recursive attacks. Technical report IRIT/RR-2017-16-FR, IRIT (2017)
11. Cayrol, C., Fandinno, J., Fariñas del Cerro, L., Lagasquie-Schiex, M.-C.: Valid attacks in argumentation frameworks with recursive attacks. In: Proceedings of Commonsense reasoning, CEUR workshop, vol. 2052 (2017)
12. Cayrol, C., Fandinno, J., Fariñas del Cerro, L., Lagasquie-Schiex, M.-C.: Argumentation frameworks with recursive attacks and evidence-based supports. Technical report IRIT/RR-2018-01-FR, IRIT (2018)
13. Cayrol, C., Lagasquie-Schiex, M.-C.: On the acceptability of arguments in bipolar argumentation frameworks. In: Godo, L. (ed.) ECSQARU 2005. LNCS (LNAI), vol. 3571, pp. 378–389. Springer, Heidelberg (2005). https://doi.org/10.1007/11518655_33
14. Cayrol, C., Lagasquie-Schiex, M.-C.: Bipolarity in argumentation graphs: towards a better understanding. Int. J. Approx. Reason. **54**(7), 876–899 (2013)
15. Cohen, A., Gottifredi, S., Garcia, A.J., Simari, G.R.: A survey of different approaches to support in argumentation systems. Knowl. Eng. Rev. **29**, 513–550 (2014)

16. Cohen, A., Gottifredi, S., García, A.J., Simari, G.R.: An approach to abstract argumentation with recursive attack and support. J. Appl. Log. **13**(4), 509–533 (2015)
17. Cohen, A., Gottifredi, S., García, A.J., Simari, G.R.: On the acceptability semantics of argumentation frameworks with recursive attack and support. In: Proceedings of COMMA, Frontiers in Artificial Intelligence and Applications, vol. 287, pp. 231–242. IOS Press (2016)
18. Dung, P.M.: On the acceptability of arguments and its fundamental role in nonmonotonic reasoning, logic programming and n-person games. Artif. Intell. **77**(2), 321–358 (1995)
19. Egly, U., Gaggl, S.A., Woltran, S.: Answer-set programming encodings for argumentation frameworks. Argum. Comput. **1**(2), 147–177 (2010)
20. Karacapilidis, N.I., Papadias, D.: Computer supported argumentation and collaborative decision making: the HERMES system. Inf. Syst. **26**(4), 259–277 (2001)
21. Modgil, S.: Reasoning about preferences in argumentation frameworks. Artif. Intell. **173**(9–10), 901–934 (2009)
22. Modgil, S., Bench-Capon, T.J.M.: Metalevel argumentation. J. Log. Comput. **21**(6), 959–1003 (2011)
23. Müller, J., Hunter, A., Taylor, P.: Meta-level argumentation with argument schemes. In: Liu, W., Subrahmanian, V.S., Wijsen, J. (eds.) SUM 2013. LNCS (LNAI), vol. 8078, pp. 92–105. Springer, Heidelberg (2013). https://doi.org/10.1007/978-3-642-40381-1_8
24. Nielsen, S.H., Parsons, S.: A generalization of Dung's abstract framework for argumentation: arguing with sets of attacking arguments. In: Maudet, N., Parsons, S., Rahwan, I. (eds.) ArgMAS 2006. LNCS (LNAI), vol. 4766, pp. 54–73. Springer, Heidelberg (2007). https://doi.org/10.1007/978-3-540-75526-5_4
25. Nouioua, F., Risch, V.: Bipolar argumentation frameworks with specialized supports. In: Proceedings of ICTAI, pp. 215–218. IEEE Computer Society (2010)
26. Nouioua, F., Risch, V.: Argumentation frameworks with necessities. In: Benferhat, S., Grant, J. (eds.) SUM 2011. LNCS (LNAI), vol. 6929, pp. 163–176. Springer, Heidelberg (2011). https://doi.org/10.1007/978-3-642-23963-2_14
27. Oren, N., Norman, T.J.: Semantics for evidence-based argumentation. In: Besnard, P., Doutre, S., Hunter, A. (eds.) Proceedings of COMMA, Frontiers in Artificial Intelligence and Applications, vol. 172, pp. 276–284. IOS Press (2008)
28. Oren, N., Reed, C., Luck, M.: Moving between argumentation frameworks. In: Baroni, P., Cerutti, F., Giacomin, M., Simari, G.R. (eds.) Proceedings of COMMA, Frontiers in Artificial Intelligence and Applications, vol. 216, pp. 379–390. IOS Press (2010)
29. Osorio, M., Nieves, J.C., Santoyo, A.: Complete extensions as Clark's completion semantics. In: Proceedings of MICCS, pp. 81–88 (2013)
30. Polberg, S., Oren, N.: Revisiting support in abstract argumentation systems. In: Parsons, S., Oren, N., Reed, C., Cerutti, F. (eds.) Proceedings of COMMA, Frontiers in Artificial Intelligence and Applications, vol. 266, pp. 369–376. IOS Press (2014)
31. Verheij, B · Deflog: on the logical interpretation of prima facie justified assumptions. J. Log. Comput. **13**(3), 319–346 (2003)
32. Villata, S., Boella, G., Gabbay, D.M., van der Torre, L.: Modelling defeasible and prioritized support in bipolar argumentation. Ann. Math. Artif. Intell. **66**(1–4), 163–197 (2012)

# A Decidable Multi-agent Logic
# with Iterations of Upper and Lower
# Probability Operators

Dragan Doder[1], Nenad Savić[2(✉)], and Zoran Ognjanović[3]

[1] Université Paul Sabatier – CNRS, IRIT, 118 Route de Narbonne,
31062 Toulouse CEDEX 9, France
dragan.doder@irit.fr
[2] Institute of Computer Science, University of Bern, Neubrueckstrasse 10,
3012 Bern, Switzerland
savic@inf.unibe.ch
[3] Mathematical Institute of Serbian Academy of Sciences and Arts,
Kneza Mihaila 36, 11000 Belgrade, Serbia
zorano@mi.sanu.ac.rs

**Abstract.** We present a propositional logic for reasoning about higher-order upper and lower probabilities. The main technical result is the proof of decidability of the introduced logical system. We also show that the axiomatization for the corresponding logic without iterations of operators, which we developed in our previous work, is also complete for the new class of models presented in this paper.

**Keywords:** Probabilistic logic · Upper and lower probabilities
Decidability · Completeness theorem

## 1 Introduction

In the last few decades, uncertain reasoning has become an active topic of investigation for researchers in the fields of computer science, artificial intelligence and cognitive science. One particular line of research concerns the formalization in terms of logic. The frameworks designed for reasoning about uncertainty often use probability-based interpretation of knowledge or belief. In the first of those papers [28] motivated by development of an expert system in medicine, Nilsson tried to give a logic with probabilistic operators as a well-founded framework for uncertain reasoning. The question of providing an axiomatization and decision procedure for Nilsson's logic attracted the attention of other researchers in the field, and triggered investigation about formal systems for probabilistic reasoning [6–9, 11, 16, 25, 29–32].

However, in many applications, sharp numerical probabilities appear too simple for modeling uncertainty. In order to model some situations of interest, various imprecise probability models are developed [4, 5, 23, 26, 35–37, 39]. Some of

© Springer International Publishing AG, part of Springer Nature 2018
F. Ferrarotti and S. Woltran (Eds.): FoIKS 2018, LNCS 10833, pp. 170–185, 2018.
https://doi.org/10.1007/978-3-319-90050-6_10

those approaches use sets of probability measures instead of one fixed measure, and the uncertainty is represented by two boundaries, called *lower probability* and *upper probability* [14,22]. Halpern and Pucella [13] give the following example: a bag contains 100 marbles, 30 of them are red and the remaining 70 are either blue or yellow, but we do not know their exact proportion. Obviously, we can assign exact probability 0.3 to the event that a randomly picked ball from the bag is red. On the other hand, for each possible probability $p$ for picking a blue ball, we know that the remaining probability for yellow one is 0.7-$p$. This way we obtain a set of possible probability measures $P$. Based on $P$ we can define the following two functions: the upper probability and the lower probability measure, which assign to an event $X$ the supremum (resp. the infimum) of the probabilities assigned to $X$ by the measures in $P$. Formally, if the uncertainty about probabilities is modeled by a set $P$ of probability measures defined on given algebra $H$, then the lower probability measure $P_\star$ and the upper probability measure $P^\star$ are defined by $P_\star(X) = \inf\{\mu(X) \mid \mu \in P\}$ and $P^\star(X) = \sup\{\mu(X) \mid \mu \in P\}$, for every $X \in H$. Those two functions are related by the formula $P_\star(X) = 1 - P^\star(X^c)$.

Those probability notions were previously formalized in the logic developed in [13], where lower and upper probability operators are applied to propositional formulas, and in [33], where first-order logic is considered (a formula is a Boolean combination of formulas in which lower and upper probability operators are applied to first-order sentences).

In this paper, we use the papers [13,33] as a starting point and generalize them in a way that we reason not only about lower and upper probabilities an agent assigns to a certain event, but also about her uncertain belief about other agent's imprecise probabilities. Thus, we introduce separate lower and upper probability operators for different agents, and we allow nesting of the operators, similarly as it has been done in [7], in the case of simple probabilities[1]. Our preliminary research on the topic is published in [34], where we axiomatized a first-order logic with nesting of lower and upper probability operators. However, since that logic extends standard first-order logic, it is obviously undecidable. To overcome that problem, in this paper we present a propositional variant of this logic, which we denote by ILUPP[2]; we prove that the logic is decidable and we propose a sound and strongly complete axiomatization for the logic.

Our language contains the upper and lower probability operators $U^a_{\geq r}$ and $L^a_{\geq r}$, for every agent $a$ and every rational number $r$ from the unit interval (we also introduce the operators with other types of inequalities, like $U^a_{=r}$). Consider the following example, essentially taken from [34]. *Suppose that an agent a is planning to visit a city based on the weather reports from several sources, and she decides to take an action if the probability of rain is at most $\frac{1}{10}$, according to all reports she considers. Since she wishes to go together with b, she should*

---

[1] For a discussion on higher-order probabilities we refer the reader to [10].

[2] The notation is motivated by the logic LUPP from [34], where $LUP$ stands for "lower and upper probability", while the second $P$ indicates that the logic is propositional. We add $I$ to denote iteration of upper and lower operators.

*be sure with probability at least $\frac{9}{10}$ that $b$ (who might consult different weather reports) has the same conclusion about the possibility of rain.* In our language, this situation can be formalized as

$$U^a_{\leq \frac{1}{10}} Rain \wedge L^a_{\geq \frac{9}{10}} (U^b_{\leq \frac{1}{10}} Rain),$$

where *Rain* is a primitive proposition of the corresponding language. The appropriate modal semantics consists of a specific class of Kripke models, in which every world is equipped with sets of probability measures (one set for each agent).

Our main technical result is that the satisfiability problem for ILUPP logic is decidable. In the proof, we combine the method of filtration [15] and a reduction to linear programming. In the first part of the proof, we show that a formula $\alpha$ is satisfiable in a world $w$ of an ILUPP model if and only if it is satisfiable in a finite model, i.e., a model with a finite number of worlds, bounded by a number which is a function of the length of $\alpha$, and such that the sets of probabilitiy measures are finite in every world of the model. Note that, while in a standard modal framework this is enough to prove decidability, since for every natural number $k$ there are only finitely many modal models with $k$ worlds, this is not the case for our logic. Indeed, since our models involve sets of probability measures, for every finite set of $k$ worlds, there are uncountably many probability measures defined on them, and uncountably many models with $k$ worlds. However, in the second part of the proof we use a reduction to linear programming to solve the probabilistic satisfiability in a finite number of steps.

We also propose a sound and strongly complete axiomatization of the logic. Interestingly, we use the same axiomatization that we used in [33] for the logic LUPP, and we show that it is also complete for the richer logic ILUPP. Of course, the instances of the axiom schemata are different, because the sets of formulas of ILUPP is larger, due to nesting of lower and upper probability operators, and due to the presence of more agents. Also, the definition of the syntactical consequence (proof) $\vdash$ is different, due to the different interpretation of classical formulas. Since the class of formulas and the class of models are different, the proof techniques are modified. In order to achieve completeness, we use a Henkin-like construction, following some of our earlier developed methods [17, 19, 20, 29, 32, 33].

The interesting situation that one axiomatic system is sound and complete for more than one class of models is not an exception. For example, modal system $K$ is also sound and complete with respect to the class of all irreflexive models [15].

The paper is organized as follows: in Sect. 2 we introduce the set of formulas of the logic ILUPP and we define the corresponding semantics. Then, in Sect. 3 we prove that the satisfiability problem for the logic ILUPP is decidable. In Sect. 4 we provide an axiomatic system for the logic, and we prove that the axiomatization is strongly complete. Finally, Sect. 5 contains some concluding remarks.

## 2    The Logic ILUPP

In this section we introduce the syntax and the semantics of the logic ILUPP.

## 2.1 Syntax

Let $\Sigma = \{a, b, \dots\}$ be a finite, non-empty set of agents. Let $S = \mathbb{Q} \cap [0, 1]$ and let $\mathcal{L} = \{p, q, r, \dots\}$ be a denumerable set of propositional letters. The language of the logic ILUPP consists of:

- the elements of set $\mathcal{L}$,
- classical propositional connectives $\neg$ and $\wedge$,
- the list of upper probability operators $U^a_{\geq s}$, for every $a \in \Sigma$ and every $s \in S$,
- the list of lower probability operators $L^a_{\geq s}$, for every $a \in \Sigma$ and every $s \in S$.

**Definition 1 (Formula).** *The set $For_{\text{ILUPP}}$ of formulas is the smallest set containing all elements of $\mathcal{L}$ and that is closed under following formation rules: if $\alpha, \beta$ are formulas, then $L^a_{\geq s}\alpha$, $U^a_{\geq s}\alpha$, $\neg\alpha$ and $\alpha \wedge \beta$ are formulas as well. The formulas from $For_{\text{ILUPP}}$ will be denoted by $\alpha, \beta, \dots$*

Intuitively, $U^a_{\geq s}\alpha$ means that according to an agent $a$, upper probability that a formula $\alpha$ is true is greater or equal to $s$ and analoguosly $L^a_{\geq s}\alpha$ means that according to an agent $a$ lower probability that a formula $\alpha$ is true is greater or equal to $s$.

Note that we use conjunction and negation as primitive connectives, while $\vee$, $\rightarrow$ and $\leftrightarrow$ are introduced in the usual way. We also use abbreviations to introduce other types of inequalities:

- $U^a_{<s}\alpha$ is $\neg U^a_{\geq s}\alpha$, $U^a_{\leq s}\alpha$ is $L^a_{\geq 1-s}\neg\alpha$, $U^a_{=s}\alpha$ is $U^a_{\leq s}\alpha \wedge U^a_{\geq s}\alpha$, $U^a_{>s}\alpha$ is $\neg U^a_{\leq s}\alpha$,
- $L^{\bar{a}}_{<s}\alpha$ is $\neg L^{\bar{a}}_{\geq s}\alpha$, $L^{\bar{a}}_{\leq s}\alpha$ is $U^{\bar{a}}_{\geq 1-s}\neg\alpha$, $L^{\bar{a}}_{=s}\alpha$ is $L^{\bar{a}}_{\leq s}\alpha \wedge L^{\bar{a}}_{\geq s}\alpha$, $L^{\bar{a}}_{>s}\alpha$ is $\neg L^{\bar{a}}_{\leq s}\alpha$.

For example, the expression

$$p \wedge U^a_{=0.9}L^b_{=0.3}(p \vee q)$$

is a formula of our language.

## 2.2 Semantics

The semantics for the logic ILUPP is based on the possible-world approach. Every world is equipped with an evaluation function on propositional letters, and one generalized probability space for each agent.

**Definition 2 (ILUPP-structure).** *An ILUPP-structure is a tuple $\langle W, LUP, v \rangle$, where:*

- *$W$ is a nonempty set of worlds,*
- *$LUP$ assigns, to every $w \in W$ and every $a \in \Sigma$, a space, such that $LUP(a, w) = \langle W(a, w), H(a, w), P(a, w) \rangle$, where:*
  - *$\emptyset \neq W(a, w) \subseteq W$,*
  - *$H(a, w)$ is an algebra of subsets of $W(a, w)$, i.e. a set of subsets of $W(a, w)$ such that:*

– $W(a, w) \in H(a, w)$,
– if $A, B \in H(a, w)$, then $W(a, w) \setminus A \in H(a, w)$ and $A \cup B \in H(a, w)$,
- $P(a, w)$ is a set of finitely additive probability measures defined on $H(a, w)$, i.e. for every $\mu(a, w) \in P(a, w)$, $\mu(a, w) : H(a, w) \longrightarrow [0, 1]$ and the following conditions hold:
  * $\mu(a, w)(W(a, w)) = 1$,
  * $\mu(a, w)(A \cup B) = \mu(a, w)(A) + \mu(a, w)(B)$, whenever $A \cap B = \emptyset$.
– $v : W \times \mathcal{L} \longrightarrow \{true, false\}$ provides for each world $w \in W$ a two-valued evaluation of the primitive propositions.

Now we define satisfiability of the formulas from $For_{\mathsf{ILUPP}}$ in the worlds of ILUPP-structures. As we mentioned in the introduction, for any set $P$ of probability measures defined on given algebra $H$, the lower probability measure $P_\star$ and the upper probability measure $P^\star$ are defined by

– $P_\star(X) = \inf\{\mu(X) \mid \mu \in P\}$ and
– $P^\star(X) = \sup\{\mu(X) \mid \mu \in P\}$,

for every $X \in H$. It is easy to check that

$$P_\star(X) = 1 - P^\star(X^c), \tag{1}$$

for every $X \in H$. In the context of the definition of an ILUPP-structure, we will denote $P_\star(a, w)([\alpha]^a_{M,w}) = \inf\{\mu([\alpha]^a_{M,w}) \mid \mu \in P(a, w)\}$ and $P^\star(a, w)([\alpha]^a_{M,w}) = \sup\{\mu([\alpha]^a_{M,w}) \mid \mu \in P(a, w)\}$, where $[\alpha]^a_{M,w} = \{u \in W(a, w) \mid M, u \models \alpha\}$.

**Definition 3 (Satisfiability relation).** *For every* ILUPP *structure* $M = \langle W, LUP, v \rangle$ *and every* $w \in W$, *the satisfiability relation* $\models$ *fulfills the following conditions:*

– *if* $p \in \mathcal{L}$, $M, w \models p$ *iff* $v(w)(p) = true$,
– $M, w \models \neg\alpha$ *iff it is not the case that* $M, w \models \alpha$,
– $M, w \models \alpha \wedge \beta$ *iff* $M, w \models \alpha$ *and* $M, w \models \beta$,
– $M, w \models U^a_{\geq s}\alpha$ *iff* $P^\star(a, w)([\alpha]^a_{M,w}) \geq s$,
– $M, w \models L^{\overline{a}}_{\geq s}\alpha$ *iff* $P_\star(a, w)([\alpha]^a_{M,w}) \geq s$.

We will omit $M$ when it's clear from context. The possible problem with the previous definition is that it might happen that for some $M$, $w$, $a$ and $\alpha$ the set $[\alpha]^a_{M,w}$ doesn't belong to $W(a, w)$. For that reason, we will consider only so called measurable structures.

**Definition 4 (Measurable structure).** *The structure* $M$ *is measurable if for every* $a \in \Sigma$ *and every* $w \in W$, $H(a, w) = \{[\alpha]_w \mid \alpha \in For_{\mathsf{ILUPP}}\}$. *The class of all measurable structures of the logic* ILUPP *will be denoted by* $\mathsf{ILUPP}_{Meas}$.

**Definition 5 (Satisfiability of a formula).** *A formula* $\alpha \in For_{\mathsf{ILUPP}}$ *is satisfiable if there is a world* $w$ *in an* $\mathsf{ILUPP}_{Meas}$-*model* $M$ *such that* $w \models \alpha$; $\alpha$ *is valid if it is satisfied in every world in every* $\mathsf{ILUPP}_{Meas}$-*model* $M$. *A set of formulas* $T$ *is satisfiable if there is a world* $w$ *in an* $\mathsf{ILUPP}_{Meas}$-*model* $M$ *such that* $w \models \alpha$ *for every* $\alpha \in T$.

# 3   Decidability

In this section, we prove our main technical result. Recall the satisfiability problem: given an ILUPP-formula $\alpha$, we want to determine if there exists a world $w$ in an ILUPP$_{Meas}$-model $M$ such that $w \models \alpha$. Decidability for ILUPP will be proved in two steps:

- first, we show that an ILUPP-formula is satisfiable iff it is satisfiable in a measurable structures with a finite number of worlds,
- second, we show that we can consider only finite measurable structures, i.e., measurable structure with finite number of worlds and with finite sets of probability measures in every world and for every agent, and
- third, we reduce the satisfiability problem in those finite models to a decidable linear programming problem.

In the first part of the proof, we will use the method of filtration [15]. Like the previous papers on the logical formalization of upper and lower probabilities [13,33], we also use the characterization theorem by Anger and Lembcke [2]. It uses the notion of $(n, k)$-cover.

**Definition 6 ($(n, k)$-cover).** *A set $A$ is said to be covered $n$ times by a multiset $\{\{A_1, \ldots, A_m\}\}$ of sets if every element of $A$ appears in at least $n$ sets from $A_1, \ldots, A_m$, i.e., for all $x \in A$, there exists $i_1, \ldots, i_n$ in $\{1, \ldots, m\}$ such that for all $j \leq n$, $x \in A_{i_j}$. An $(n, k)$-cover of $(A, W)$ is a multiset $\{\{A_1, \ldots, A_m\}\}$ that covers $W$ $k$ times and covers $A$ $n + k$ times.*

Now we can state the characterization theorem.

**Theorem 1 (Anger and Lembcke [2]).** *Let $W$ be a set, $H$ an algebra of subsets of $W$, and $f$ a function $f : H \longrightarrow [0, 1]$. There exists a set $P$ of probability measures such that $f = P^\star$ iff $f$ satisfies the following three properties:*

*(1) $f(\emptyset) = 0$,*
*(2) $f(W) = 1$,*
*(3) for all natural numbers $m, n, k$ and elements $A_1, \ldots, A_m$ in $H$, if the multiset $\{\{A_1, \ldots, A_m\}\}$ is an $(n, k)$-cover of $(A, W)$, then $k + nf(A) \leq \sum_{i=1}^{m} f(A_i)$.*

Let $SF(\alpha)$ denote the set of all subformulas of a formula $\alpha$, i.e.

$$SF(\alpha) = \{\beta \mid \beta \text{ is a subformula of } \alpha\}.$$

**Theorem 2.** *If a formula $\alpha$ is satisfiable, then it is satisfiable in an ILUPP$_{Meas}$-model with at most $2^{|SF(\alpha)|}$ worlds.*

*Proof.* Suppose that a formula $\alpha$ holds in some world of the model $M = \langle W, LUP, v \rangle$ and let $k = |SF(\alpha)|$. By $\approx$, we will denote an equivalence relation over $W^2$, such that

$$w \approx u \text{ if and only if for every } \beta \in SF(\alpha), w \models \beta \text{ iff } u \models \beta.$$

Since there are finitely many subformulas of $\alpha$, we know that the quotient set

$$W_{/\approx} = \{C_{w_i} \mid w_i \in W\}$$

is finite, where

$$C_{w_i} = \{u \in W \mid u \approx w_i\}$$

is the class of equivalence of $w_i$. More precisely,

$$|W_{/\approx}| \leq 2^k.$$

Next, from each class of equivalence $C_{w_i}$, we choose an element $w_i$.
Consider a tuple $\overline{M} = \langle \overline{W}, \overline{LUP}, \overline{v} \rangle$, where:

- $\overline{W} = \{w_1, w_2, \dots\}$,
- For every $a$ and for every $w_i$ $\overline{LUP}(a, w_i) = \langle \overline{W}(a, w_i), \overline{H}(a, w_i), \overline{P}(a, w_i) \rangle$ is
  defined as follows:
  - $\overline{W}(a, w_i) = \{w_j \in \overline{W} \mid (\exists u \in C_{w_j}) u \in W(a, w_i)\}$
  - $\overline{H}(a, w_i) = 2^{\overline{W}(a, w_i)}$
  - $\overline{P}(a, w_i)$ is any set of finitely additive measures, such that for every
    $D \in \overline{H}(a, w_i)$, $\overline{P}^{\star}(a, w_i)(D) = P^{\star}(a, w_i)(\bigcup_{w_j \in D}(C_{w_j} \cap W(a, w_i)))$
- $\overline{v}(w_i)(p) = v(w_i)(p)$, for every primitive proposition $p \in \mathcal{L}$.

First, we have to prove that $\overline{P}^{\star}(a, w_i)$ satisfies the conditions $(1) - (3)$ from
Theorem 1, which will guarantee the existence of sets $\overline{P}(a, w_i)$, for every agent
$a$ and each $w_i \in \overline{W}$.

(1) $\overline{P}^{\star}(a, w_i)(\emptyset) = P^{\star}(a, w_i)(\bigcup_{w_j \in \emptyset}(C_{w_j} \cap W(a, w_i))) = P^{\star}(a, w_i)(\emptyset) = 0$;
(2) $\overline{P}^{\star}(a, w_i)(\overline{W}(a, w_i)) = P^{\star}(a, w_i)(\bigcup_{w_j \in \overline{W}(a, w_i)}(C_{w_j} \cap W(a, w_i))) =$
   $= P^{\star}(a, w_i)(W(a, w_i)) = 1$;
(3) Let $\{\{D_1, \dots, D_m\}\}$ be an $(n, k)$-cover of $(D, \overline{W}(a, w_i))$. That means:
   (i) every element from $D$ appears in at least $n + k$ sets from $D_1, \dots, D_m$;
   (ii) every element from $\overline{W}(a, w_i)$ appears in at least $k$ sets from $D_1, \dots, D_m$.
   Therefore,
   (iii) every element from $(\bigcup_{u \in D}(C_u \cap W(a, w_i))$ appears in at least $n + k$ sets
        from $\bigcup_{u \in D_1}(C_u \cap W(a, w_i)), \dots, \bigcup_{u \in D_m}(C_u \cap W(a, w_i))$;
   (iv) every element from $W(a, w_i)$ appears in at least $k$ sets from
        $\bigcup_{u \in D_1}(C_u \cap W(a, w_i)), \dots, \bigcup_{u \in D_m}(C_u \cap W(a, w_i))$.
   Hence, by definition, we obtain that a multiset

$$\{\{ \bigcup_{u \in D_1}(C_u \cap W(a, w_i)), \dots, \bigcup_{u \in D_m}(C_u \cap W(a, w_i))\}\}$$

is an $(n, k)$-cover of

$$(\bigcup_{u \in D}(C_u \cap W(a, w_i)), W(a, w_i)).$$

Hence, using the fact that $P^\star(a, w_i)$ is an upper probability, from Theorem 1, we have that

$$k + nP^\star(a, w_i)(\bigcup_{u \in D}(C_u \cap W(a, w_i))) \le \sum_{j=1}^{m} P^\star(a, w_i)(\bigcup_{u \in D_j}(C_u \cap W(a, w_i))),$$

and therefore

$$k + n\overline{P}^\star(a, w_i)(D) \le \sum_{j=1}^{m} \overline{P}^\star(a, w_i)(D_j).$$

Using induction on the complexity of a formula from the set $SF(\alpha)$, we can prove that for every $w \in \overline{W}$ and every $\beta \in SF(\alpha)$,

$$M, w \models \beta \quad \text{if and only if} \quad \overline{M}, w \models \beta.$$

If a formula is a propositional letter or obtained using Boolean connectives, the claim is trivial. So, let us consider the case when $\beta = U_{\ge s}^a \gamma$:

$$M, w \models U_{\ge s}^a \gamma \qquad \text{iff}$$
$$P^\star(a, w)(\{u \in W(a, w) \mid M, u \models \gamma\}) \ge s \qquad \text{iff}$$
$$P^\star(a, w)(\bigcup_{M, u \models \gamma} C_u \cap W(a, w)) \ge s \qquad \text{iff (ind. hyp)}$$
$$\overline{P}^\star(a, w)(\{u \in \overline{W}^\star(a, w) \mid \overline{M}, u \models \gamma\}) \ge s \qquad \text{iff}$$
$$\overline{M}, w \models U_{\ge s}^a \gamma.$$

Using the Eq. (1) and the fact that $\overline{P}^\star(a, w)$ is an upper probability, the case when $\beta = L_{\ge s}^a \gamma$ can be proved analogously. $\qquad \square$

In the second part of the proof, we use the following result of Halpern and Pucella [13].

**Theorem 3** ([13]). *Let $P$ be a set of probability measures defined on an algebra $H$ over a finite set $W$. Then there exists a set $P'$ of probability measures such that, for each $X \in H$, $P^*(X) = (P')^*(X)$. Moreover, there is a probability measure $\mu_X \in P'$ such that*

$$\mu_X(X) = P^*(X).$$

As a direct consequence of Theorems 2 and 3, we obtain the following result.

**Lemma 1.** *If a formula $\alpha$ is satisfiable, then it is satisfiable in an $\mathsf{ILUPP}_{Meas}$-model with at most $2^{|SF(\alpha)|}$ worlds and for every agent $a \in \Sigma$ and every $w \in W$, $H(a, w) = 2^{W(a, w)}$ and*

$$|P(a, w)| = |H(a, w)|.$$

*Furthermore, for each $X \in H(a, w)$, there exists a $\mu_X \in P(a, w)$ such that*

$$\mu_X(a, w)(X) = P^*(a, w)(X).$$

With this lemma we are ready to prove the decidability result for the ILUPP logic.

**Theorem 4.** *Satisfiability problem for* ILUPP$_{Meas}$ *is decidable.*

*Proof.* Let $M = \langle W, LUP, v \rangle$ be an ILUPP$_{Meas}$-model and $\alpha$ an arbitrary formula. Also, let

$$SF(\alpha) = \{\beta_1, \ldots, \beta_k\}.$$

In every $w \in W$, exactly one of the formulas of the following form:

$$\pm\beta_1 \wedge \cdots \wedge \pm\beta_k$$

holds, where $\pm\beta_i$ denotes $\beta_i$ or $\neg\beta_i$. We will call that formula a characteristic formula for a world $w$ (characteristic formula for a world $w_i$ will be denoted by $\alpha_i$).

By Lemma 1, we know that there exists an ILUPP$_{Meas}$-model $\overline{M}$ with

(1) at most $2^k$ worlds and
(2) at most $2^{2^k}$ probabilistic measures (for any agent and any world),

such that $\alpha$ holds in some world of the model $\overline{M}$ iff $\alpha$ holds in some world of a model $M$.

For every $l \leq 2^k$, we will consider models with

- $l$ worlds, $w_1, \ldots, w_l$, and
- for every agent $a$ and every world $w$, sets of probability measures $P(a, w)$, such that $|P(a, w)| = 2^{|W(a,w)|}$, for every $W(a, w) \subseteq \{w_1, \ldots w_l\}$.

In each of these worlds, exactly one characteristic formula holds. So, for each $l$, we will consider all possible sets of $l$ characteristic formulas such that:

(a) Let $\alpha_i$ be a characteristic formula. In $\alpha_i$ we replace every occurrence of a formula starting with a probabilistic operator with an atomic proposition (all the occurrences of the same formula are assigned the same atomic proposition). Then we obtain a propositional formula, $\alpha_i'$. Using any algorithm for propositional satisfiability we check whether $\alpha_i'$ is satisfiable. If $\alpha_i'$ passes the test, then $\alpha_i$ is further considered for probabilistic tests (as in the paper). If $\alpha_i'$ does not pass the test, then $\alpha_i$ is no longer considered;
(b) At least one formula contains $\alpha$.

For each choice, and each world $w_i$, we will consider following set of linear equalities and inequalities (by $\beta \in (\alpha_j)^+$ we will denote that $\beta$ is a conjunct in $\alpha_j$ and by $\beta \in (\alpha_j)^-$ we will denote that $\neg\beta$ is a conjunct in $\alpha_j$):

(1) $\mu(a, w_i)(\{w_j\}) \geq 0$, for each $\mu(a, w_i) \in P(a, w_i)$ and $j = 1, \ldots, l$;
(2) $\sum\limits_{w_j \in W(a,w_i)} \mu(a, w_i)(\{w_j\}) = 1$, for every $\mu(a, w_i) \in P(a, w_i)$;
(3) $\sum\limits_{w_j \in X} \mu_X(a, w_i)(\{w_j\}) \geq \sum\limits_{w_j \in X} \mu_Y(a, w_i)(\{w_j\})$, for every $X, Y \subseteq W(a, w_i)$;

(4)   $\displaystyle\sum_{w_j:\beta\in(\alpha_j)^+}\mu_X(a,w_i)(\{w_j\})\geq s$, if $U^a_{\geq s}\beta\in\alpha_i$, $X=\{w_j\mid\beta\in(\alpha_j)^+\}$;

(5)   $\displaystyle\sum_{w_j:\beta\in(\alpha_j)^+}\mu_X(a,w_i)(\{w_j\})< s$, if $\neg U^a_{\geq s}\beta\in\alpha_i$, $X=\{w_j\mid\beta\in(\alpha_j)^+\}$;

(6)   $\displaystyle\sum_{w_j:\beta\in(\alpha_j)^-}\mu_X(a,w_i)(\{w_j\})\leq 1-s$, if $L^a_{\geq s}\beta\in\alpha_i$, $X=\{w_j\mid\beta\in(\alpha_j)^-\}$;

(7)   $\displaystyle\sum_{w_j:\beta\in(\alpha_j)^-}\mu_X(a,w_i)(\{w_j\})> 1-s$, if $\neg L^a_{\geq s}\beta\in\alpha_i$, $X=\{w_j\mid\beta\in(\alpha_j)^-\}$.

- First inequality states that all the measures must be nonnegative.
- Second equality assures that the probability of the set of all possible worlds has to be equal to 1.
- Third inequality corresponds to the fact that $\mu_X(a,w)(X)=P^*(a,w)(X)$ and therefore

$$\mu_X(a,w)(X)\geq\mu(a,w)(X),\text{ for all }\mu(a,w)\in P(a,w).$$

- For the fourth and fifth inequality, note that if $X=\{w_j\mid\beta\in(\alpha_j)^+\}$

$$\sum_{w_j:\beta\in(\alpha_j)^+}\mu_X(a,w_i)(\{w_j\})=P^*(a,w_i)([\beta]^a_{w_i}),$$

so these inequalities reflect the appropriate constraints.
- In order to understand sixth and seventh inequality, first recall the equality connecting upper and lower probabilty:

$$P^*([\neg\beta]^a_{w_i})=1-P_*([\beta]^a_{w_i}).$$

Next, note that if $X=\{w_j\mid\beta\in(\alpha_j)^-\}$

$$\sum_{w_j:\beta\in(\alpha_j)^-}\mu_X(a,w_i)(\{w_j\})=P^*(a,w_i)([\neg\beta]^a_{w_i}).$$

Consequently, if

$$P_*([\beta]^a_{w_i})\geq s,$$

then

$$P^*([\neg\beta]^a_{w_i})\leq 1-s,$$

and similarly for the case when $P_*([\beta]^a_{w_i})<s$.

The equations and inequalities 1–7 form a finite system of linear equalities and inequalities and it is well known that solving this system is decidable. If for some fixed $l$ and fixed choice of characteristic formulas, and each choice of subsets $W(a,w)$ of considered sets of worlds (for every agent $a$ and every considered world $w$), corresponding system is solvable, then in each world, probabilistic space can be defined. Moreover, in every world $w$ of the model, the characteristic formula of the world holds in $w$. Since $\alpha$ belongs to at least one of the corresponding characteristic formulas, we have that $\alpha$ is satisfiable.

If the test fails, and there is another possibility of choosing $l$ and/or the set of $l$ worlds and/or subsets $W(a, w)$ of chosen sets of worlds, we continue with the procedure. Otherwise, if for any $l$, any choice of characteristic formulas and any choice of subsets $W(a, w)$, appropriate system is not solvable, using Lemma 1, we conclude that $\alpha$ is not $\mathsf{ILUPP}_{Meas}$-satisfiable.

Note that in the previously described method we consider only finitely many systems of linear equation and inequalities. Therefore, the satisfiability problem is decidable. □

## 4 A Complete Axiomatization

Having settled the decidability issue the for the logic ILUPP, we turn to the problem of developing an axiomatic system for the logic ILUPP. That system will be denoted by $Ax_{\mathsf{ILUPP}}$.

### 4.1 The Axiomatization $Ax_{\mathsf{ILUPP}}$

We start with the observation that, like any other real-valued probabilistic logic, ILUPP is not compact. Indeed, consider the set of formulas $T = \{\neg U_{=0}\alpha\} \cup \{U_{<\frac{1}{n}}\alpha \mid n$ is a positive integer $\}$. Obviously, every finite subset of $T$ is $\mathsf{ILUPP}_{Meas}$-satisfiable, but the set $T$ is not. Consequently, any finitary axiomatic system would be incomplete [38]. In order to achieve completeness, we use two infinitary rules of inference, with countably many premises and one conclusion.

In order to axiomatize upper and lower probabilities, we need to completely characterize them with a small number of properties. There are many complete characterizations in the literature, and the earliest appears to be by Lorentz [24]. We will use Theorem 1 from the previous section.

For the logic ILUPP, we use a minor modification of the axiomatic system for the logic LUPP in [33].

*Axiom schemes*

(1) all instances of the classical propositional tautologies
(2) $U_{\leq 1}^a \alpha \wedge L_{\leq 1}^a \alpha$
(3) $U_{\leq r}^{\bar{a}} \alpha \to \bar{U}_{<s}^a \alpha, \; s > r$
(4) $U_{<s}^{\bar{a}} \alpha \to U_{\leq s}^a \alpha$
(5) $(U_{\leq r_1}^a \alpha_1 \wedge \cdots \wedge U_{\leq r_m}^a \alpha_m) \to U_{\leq r}^a \alpha$, if $\alpha \to \bigvee_{J \subseteq \{1,\ldots,m\}, |J|=k+n} \bigwedge_{j \in J} \alpha_j$ and $\bigvee_{J \subseteq \{1,\ldots,m\}, |J|=k} \bigwedge_{j \in J} \alpha_j$ are tautologies, where $r = \frac{\sum_{i=1}^m r_i - k}{n}, \; n \neq 0$
(6) $\neg(U_{\leq r_1}^a \alpha_1 \wedge \cdots \wedge U_{\leq r_m}^a \alpha_m)$, if $\bigvee_{J \subseteq \{1,\ldots,m\}, |J|=k} \bigwedge_{j \in J} \alpha_j$ is a tautology and $\sum_{i=1}^m r_i < k$
(7) $L_{=1}^a(\alpha \to \beta) \to (U_{\geq s}^a \alpha \to U_{\geq s}^a \beta)$

*Inference Rules*

(1) From $\alpha$ and $\alpha \to \beta$ infer $\beta$

(2) From $\alpha$ infer $L^a_{\geq 1}\alpha$

(3) From the set of premises

$$\{\alpha \to U^a_{\geq s-\frac{1}{k}}\beta \mid k \geq \frac{1}{s}\}$$

infer $\alpha \to U^a_{\geq s}\beta$

(4) From the set of premises

$$\{\alpha \to L^a_{\geq s-\frac{1}{k}}\beta \mid k \geq \frac{1}{s}\}$$

infer $\alpha \to L^a_{\geq s}\beta$.

The axioms 5 and 6 together capture the third condition from the Theorem 1 (see [33]). The rules 3 and 4 are infinitary rules of inference and intuitively state that if an upper/lower probability is arbitrary close to a rational number $s$ then it is at least $s$.

Now we define some proof theoretical notions.

- $\vdash \alpha$ ($\alpha$ is a theorem) iff there is an at most denumerable sequence of formulas $\alpha_1, \alpha_2, \ldots, \alpha$, such that every $\alpha_i$ is an axiom or it is derived from the preceding formulas by an inference rule;
- $T \vdash \alpha$ ($\alpha$ is derivable from T) if there is an at most denumerable sequence of formulas $\alpha_1, \alpha_2, \ldots, \alpha$, such that every $\alpha_i$ is an axiom or a formula from the set $T$, or it is derived from the preceding formulas by an inference rule, with the exception that Inference Rule 2 can be applied only to the theorems;
- $T$ is *consistent* if there is at least one formula $\alpha \in For_{ILUPP}$ that is not deducible from $T$, otherwise $T$ is inconsistent;
- $T$ is *maximal consistent* set if it is consistent and for every $\alpha \in For_{ILUPP}$, either $\alpha \in T$ or $\neg\alpha \in T$;
- $T$ is *deductively closed* if for every $\alpha \in For_{ILUPP}$, if $T \vdash \alpha$, then $\alpha \in T$.

Note that $T$ is inconsistent iff $T \vdash \bot$. Also, it is easy to check that every maximal consistent set is deductively closed.

It is easy to check that the axiomatic system $Ax_{ILUPP}$ is sound with respect to the class of $ILUPP_{Meas}$-models.

## 4.2 Completeness

We prove that the axiomatization $Ax_{ILUPP}$ is complete, using a Henkin-like construction. Due to the presence of infinitary rules, the standard completion technique (Lindenbaum's theorem) has to be modified in the following way: if the current theory is inconsistent with the current formula and that formula can be derived by one of infinitary inference rules, than one of the premises must be blocked.

The proof of completeness is a direct combination of the proof techniques presented in our papers [33, 34]. Thus, here we only present a sketch of the proof, and for details and the completion of the proof we refer the reader to [33, 34].

**Theorem 5 (Strong completeness).** *If $\alpha$ is a formula, and $T$ is a set of formulas of the logic* ILUPP, *then* $T \vdash \alpha$ *iff* $T \models \alpha$.

*Sketch of the Proof.* First we point out that the theorem follows from soundness of the axiomatic system $Ax_{\text{ILUPP}}$, and the following usual formulation of strong completeness:

Every consistent set of formulas $T$ is satisfiable.

Let us prove this statement. First, we will extend $T$ to a maximal consistent set $T^*$. We assume an enumeration $\alpha_0, \alpha_1, \ldots$ of all formulas. Then we define the chain of sets $T_i$, $i = 0, 1, 2, \ldots$ and the set $T^*$ in the following way:

(1) $T_0 = T$,
(2) for every $i \geq 0$,
    (a) if $T_i \cup \{\alpha_i\}$ is consistent, then $T_{i+1} = T_i \cup \{\alpha_i\}$, otherwise
    (b) if $\alpha_i$ is of the form $\beta \to U^a_{\geq s}\alpha$, then $T_{i+1} = T_i \cup \{\neg\alpha_i, \beta \to \neg U^a_{\geq s-\frac{1}{n}}\alpha\}$,
       for some positive integer $n$, so that $T_{i+1}$ is consistent, otherwise
    (c) if $\alpha_i$ is of the form $\beta \to L^a_{\geq s}\alpha$, then $T_{i+1} = T_i \cup \{\neg\alpha_i, \beta \to \neg L^a_{\geq s-\frac{1}{n}}\alpha\}$,
       for some positive integer $n$, so that $T_{i+1}$ is consistent, otherwise
    (d) $T_{i+1} = T_i \cup \{\neg\alpha_i\}$.
(3) $T^* = \bigcup_{i=0}^{\infty} T_i$.

The proof that $T^*$ is a maximal consistent set is based on the following observations:

– Natural numbers $(n)$, from the steps 2(b) and 2(c) of the construction exist; this follows from Deduction Theorem, which holds in ILUPP logic (the deduction theorem can be proved using the implicative form of the two infinitary inference rules, and the fact that the application of Rule 2 is restricted to theorems only).
– Each $T_i$ is consistent, by construction.
– $T^*$ does not contain all the formulas, by construction, using the fact that all $T_i$'s are consistent.
– For every formula $\alpha$, either $\alpha \in T^*$ or $\neg\alpha \in T^*$, by construction (steps (1) and (2)).
– For every formula $\alpha$, if $T^* \vdash \alpha$, then $\alpha \in T^*$ (the proof of this fact is by the induction on the length of the inference).
– By the last two facts, $T^*$ is a deductively closed set, and $T^*$ does not contain all the formulas, so it is consistent. Therefore, $T^*$ is a maximal consistent set.

Now we define the canonical model $M_{Can} = \langle W, LUP, v \rangle$ such that:

– $W = \{w \mid w$ is a maximal consistent set of formulas$\}$,
– for every world $w$ and every propositional letter $p$, $v(w)(p) = true$ iff $p \in w$,
– for every $a \in \Sigma$ and $w \in W$, $LUP(a, w) = \langle W(a, w), H(a, w), P(a, w) \rangle$ is defined in the following way:
    • $W(a, w) = W$,

- $H(a, w) = \{\{u \mid u \in W(a, w), \alpha \in u\} \mid \alpha \in For_{\mathsf{ILUPP}}\}$,
- $P(a, w)$ is any set of probability measures such that
  $P^\star(a, w)(\{u \mid u \in W(a, w), \alpha \in u\}) = \sup\{s \mid U_{\geq s}\alpha \in w\}$.

We have the following properties of $M_{Can}$:

- For every formula $\alpha$ and every $w \in W$, $\alpha \in w$ iff $M_{Can}, w \models \alpha$ (the proof is on the complexity of the formula $\alpha$).
- For every $a \in \Sigma$, every $w \in W$ and every formula $\alpha$, $\{u \mid u \in W(a, w), \alpha \in u\} = [\alpha]_w^a$. (this follows from the previous item).
- $M_{Can}$ is a well defined measurable structure (the proof that $P^\star(a, w)$ is an upper probability measure follows from Theorem 1 and the axioms 5 and 6).

Recall that we extended $T$ to the maximal consistent set $T^*$. We showed that for every formula $\alpha$, and every $w \in W$, $w \models \alpha$ iff $\alpha \in w$. Since $T^* \in W$, we obtain $M_{Can}, T^* \models T$. □

# 5    Conclusion

In this paper we present the proof-theoretical analysis of a logic which allows making statements about upper and lower probabilities. The introduced formalism can be used for reasoning not only about lower and upper probabilities an agent assigns to a certain event, but also about her uncertain belief about other agent's imprecise probabilities. The language of ILUPP is a modal language which extends propositional logic with the unary operators $U_{\geq r}^a$ and $L_{\geq r}^a$, where $a$ is an agent and $r$ ranges over the unit interval of rational numbers. The corresponding semantics $\mathsf{ILUPP}_{Meas}$ consists of the measurable Kripke models with sets of finitely additive probability measures attached to each possible world.

We prove that the satisfiability problem for ILUPP logic is decidable. In the proof, we use the method of filtration [15] to show that if a formula is satisfiable in a world $w$ of an ILUPP structure, then it is satisfiable in a finite structure. We also use a reduction to linear programming to deal with infinitely many probability measures definable on finite algebras, and to solve the satisfiability problem in a finite number of steps.

We also prove that the proposed axiomatic system $Ax_{\mathsf{ILUPP}}$ is strongly complete with respect to the class of $\mathsf{ILUPP}_{Meas}$-models. Since the logic is not compact, the axiomatization contains infinitary rules of inference. In [33] it is shown that the same axiomatic system (the only difference is that in [33] only one agent is considered) is sound and complete for a class of $\mathsf{LUPP}_{Meas}$-models. This situation is not an exception. For example, modal system $K$ is sound and complete with respect to the class of all modal models, but also with respect to the class of all irreflexive models [15].

We propose two topics for future work. First, we will try to prove decidability for the logic ILUPP by employing a tableau procedure. Such a method is developed in [21] for a probabilistic logic with iterations of standard probability operators. We believe that a similar tableaux method can be applied for

ILUPP. Finally, the upper and lower probabilities are just one approach in development of imprecise probability models. In future work, we also wish to logically formalize dierent imprecise probabilities.

**Acknowledgments.** This work was supported by the SNSF project 200021_165549 Justifications and non-classical reasoning, by the Serbian Ministry of Education and Science through projects ON174026, III44006 and ON174008, and by ANR-11-LABX-0040-CIMI.

# References

1. Abadi, M., Halpern, J.Y.: Decidability and expressiveness for first-order logics of probability. Inf. Comput. **112**, 1–36 (1994)
2. Anger, B., Lembcke, J.: Infinitely subadditive capacities as upper envelopes of measures. Zeitschrift fur Wahrscheinlichkeitstheorie und Verwandte Gebiete **68**, 403–414 (1985)
3. Cintula, P., Noguera, C.: Modal logics of uncertainty with two-layer syntax: a general completeness theorem. In: Kohlenbach, U., Barceló, P., de Queiroz, R. (eds.) WoLLIC 2014. LNCS, vol. 8652, pp. 124–136. Springer, Heidelberg (2014). https://doi.org/10.1007/978-3-662-44145-9_9
4. de Cooman, G., Hermans, F.: Imprecise probability trees: bridging two theories of imprecise probability. Artif. Intell. **172**(11), 1400–1427 (2008)
5. Dubois, D., Prade, H.: Possibility Theory. Plenum Press, New York (1988)
6. Fagin, R., Halpern, J., Megiddo, N.: A logic for reasoning about probabilities. Inf. Comput. **87**(1–2), 78–128 (1990)
7. Fagin, R., Halpern, J.: Reasoning about knowledge and probability. J. ACM **41**(2), 340–367 (1994)
8. Fattorosi-Barnaba, M., Amati, G.: Modal operators with probabilistic interpretations I. Stud. Log. **46**(4), 383–393 (1989)
9. Frish, A., Haddawy, P.: Anytime deduction for probabilistic logic. Artif. Intell. **69**, 93–122 (1994)
10. Gaifman, H., Haddawy, P.: A theory of higher order probabilities. In: Skyrms, B., Harper, W.L. (eds.) Causation, Chance and Credence. Proceedings of the Irvine Conference on Probability and Causation, vol. 1, pp. 191–219. Springer, Dordrecht (1988)
11. Halpern, J.Y.: An analysis of first-order logics of probability. Artif. Intell. **46**, 311–350 (1990)
12. Halpern, J.Y., Pucella, R.: A logic for reasoning about evidence. J. Artif. Intell. Res. **1**, 1–34 (2006)
13. Halpern, J.Y., Pucella, R.: A logic for reasoning about upper probabilities. J. Artif. Intell. Res. **17**, 57–81 (2002)
14. Huber, P.J.: Robust Statistics. Wiley, New York (1981)
15. Hughes, G.E., Cresswell, M.J.: A Companion to Modal Logic. Methuen, London (1984)
16. Heifetz, A., Mongin, P.: Probability logic for type spaces. Games Econ. Behav. **35**, 31–53 (2001)
17. Ikodinović, N., Ognjanović, Z., Rašković, M., Perović, A.: Hierarchies of probabilistic logics. Int. J. Approx. Reason. **55**(9), 1830–1842 (2014)

18. Ikodinović, N., Rašković, M., Marković, Z., Ognjanović, Z.: A first-order probabilistic logic with approximate conditional probabilities. Log. J. IGPL **22**(4), 539–564 (2014)
19. Ilić-Stepić, A., Ognjanović, Z.: Complex valued probability logics. Publications de l'Institut Mathematique, N.s. tome **95**(109), 73–86 (2014)
20. Ilić-Stepić, A., Ognjanović, Z., Ikodinović, N.: Conditional p-adic probability logic. Int. J. Approx. Reason. **55**(9), 1843–1865 (2014)
21. Kokkinis, I.: The complexity of satisfiability in non-iterated and iterated probabilistic logics. arXiv:1712.00810v1
22. Kyburg, H.E.: Probability and the Logic of Rational Belief. Wesleyan University Press, Middletown (1961)
23. Levi, I.: The Enterprise of Knowledge. MIT Press, London (1980)
24. Lorentz, G.G.: Multiply subadditive functions. Can. J. Math. **4**(4), 455–462 (1952)
25. Meier, M.: An infinitary probability logic for type spaces. Isr. J. Math. **192**(1), 1–58 (2012)
26. Miranda, E.: A survey of the theory of coherent lower previsions. Int. J. Approx. Reas. **48**(2), 628–658 (2008)
27. Milošević, M., Ognjanović, Z.: A first-order conditional probability logic. Log. J. IGPL **20**(1), 235–253 (2012)
28. Nilsson, N.: Probabilistic logic. Artif. Intell. **28**, 71–87 (1986)
29. Ognjanović, Z., Rašković, M.: Some probability logics with new types of probability operators. J. Log. Comput. **9**(2), 181–195 (1999)
30. Ognjanović, Z., Rašković, M.: Some first-order probability logics. Theoret. Comput. Sci. **247**(1–2), 191–212 (2000)
31. Ognjanović, Z., Rasković, M., Marković, Z.: Probability Logics - Probability-Based Formalization of Uncertain Reasoning. Springer, Heidelberg (2016). https://doi.org/10.1007/978-3-319-47012-2
32. Rašković, M., Marković, Z., Ognjanović, Z.: A logic with approximate conditional probabilities that can model default reasoning. Int. J. Approx. Reason. **49**(1), 52–66 (2008)
33. Savić, N., Doder, D., Ognjanović, Z.: Logics with lower and upper probability operators. Int. J. Approx. Reason. **88**, 148–168 (2017)
34. Savić, N., Doder, D., Ognjanović, Z.: A first-order logic for reasoning about higher-order upper and lower probabilities. In: Antonucci, A., Cholvy, L., Papini, O. (eds.) ECSQARU 2017. LNCS (LNAI), vol. 10369, pp. 491–500. Springer, Cham (2017). https://doi.org/10.1007/978-3-319-61581-3_44
35. Shafer, G.: A Mathematical Theory of Evidence. Princeton University Press, Princeton (1976)
36. Walley, P.: Statistical Reasoning with Imprecise Probabilities. Chapman and Hall, London (1991)
37. Walley, P.: Towards a unified theory of imprecise probability. Int. J. Approx. Reason. **24**(2–3), 125–148 (2000)
38. van der Hoek, W.: Some consideration on the logics $P_F D$. J. Appl. Non-Class. Logics **7**(3), 287–307 (1997)
39. Zadeh, L.A.: Fuzzy sets as a basis for a theory of possibility. Fuzzy Sets Syst. **1**, 3–28 (1978)

# Probabilistic Team Semantics

Arnaud Durand[1], Miika Hannula[2], Juha Kontinen[3], Arne Meier[4],
and Jonni Virtema[5]([⌧])

[1] Institut de Mathématiques de Jussieu - Paris Rive Gauche,
CNRS UMR 7586, Université Paris Diderot, Paris, France
durand@math.univ-paris-diderot.fr
[2] Department of Computer Science, University of Auckland, Auckland, New Zealand
m.hannula@auckland.ac.nz
[3] Department of Mathematics and Statistics, University of Helsinki, Helsinki, Finland
juha.kontinen@helsinki.fi
[4] Institut für Theoretische Informatik,
Leibniz Universität Hannover, Hanover, Germany
meier@thi.uni-hannover.de
[5] Databases and Theoretical Computer Science, Hasselt University, Hasselt, Belgium
jonni.virtema@uhasselt.be

**Abstract.** Team semantics is a semantical framework for the study of
dependence and independence concepts ubiquitous in many areas such as
databases and statistics. In recent works team semantics has been generalised to accommodate also multisets and probabilistic dependencies. In
this article we study a variant of probabilistic team semantics and relate
this framework to a Tarskian two-sorted logic. We also show that very
simple quantifier-free formulae of our logic give rise to NP-hard model
checking problems.

## 1 Introduction

Team semantics is the modern approach for the study of logics of dependence
and independence. The systematic development of team semantics began by the
introduction of Dependence Logic in 2007 [20] although the key ingredients of the
new semantics were already introduced by Hodges 1997 [14]. In team semantics,
satisfaction of formulae is defined not via single assignments but via sets of
assignments (teams). Sets of assignments enables one to introduce a multitude
of interesting atoms to the logic such as dependence, independence, and inclusion
atoms:

$$=(x, y), \quad y \perp_x z \text{ and } x \subseteq y$$

that do not make sense with respect to a single assignment. Independence logic,
introduced by Grädel and Väänänen [10], extends first-order logic with independence atoms. The independence atom $y \perp_x z$ holds if the value of $z$ does
not tell us anything new about the value of $y$ when the value of $x$ is fixed. By
viewing a team $X$ with domain $\{x_1, \ldots, x_n\}$ as a database table over attributes
$x_1, \ldots, x_n$, dependence, inclusion, and independence atoms correspond exactly

© Springer International Publishing AG, part of Springer Nature 2018
F. Ferrarotti and S. Woltran (Eds.): FoIKS 2018, LNCS 10833, pp. 186–206, 2018.
https://doi.org/10.1007/978-3-319-90050-6_11

to functional, inclusion, and embedded multivalued dependencies (EMVDs), see, e.g., [12,13,18]. Moreover EMVDs and probabilistic conditional independence $Y \perp Z|X$ have significant connections, confer, e.g., [1,11,21]. Multiteam semantics, introduced by Durand et al. [3], is the multiset analogue of team semantics. This setting enables the logical study of probabilistic dependencies such as the probabilistic conditional independence atoms $y \perp\!\!\!\perp_x z$ that inherit their semantics from the corresponding notion $Y \perp Z|X$ from statistics. One of the advantages of multiteam semantics is that it allowes to study the interplay of atoms such as $=(x, y)$, $y \perp_x z$, and $y \perp\!\!\!\perp_x z$ in a unified framework.

In this paper, we focus on probabilistic team semantics. A probabilistic team is a set of assignments endowed with a probability distribution that maps each assignment of the set to a ratio. There is a vast literature on probabilistic logics but so far only few works study probabilistic team semantics. The teams that arise from applications (e.g., database tables) often contain duplicate rows leading naturally to multiteams (i.e., multiset analogues of teams). Furthermore, finite multiteams can be viewed as probabilistic teams endowed with the counting measure induced by the multiplicities. Importantly, in many applications, duplicate rows can store relevant information; e.g., if a table is used to store an outcome of a poll or a collection of outcomes of measurements. In these cases the interest lies in the distribution of the data and not so much in the size of the sample. Hence it makes sense to abstract from the concrete data (multiteams) to the distribution of data (probabilistic teams). We consider a logic that uses probabilistic independence $y \perp\!\!\!\perp_x z$ and marginal identity atoms $x \approx y$ as primitives in the setting of probabilistic team semantics. These atoms were recently introduced by Durand et al. [3] in the context of multiteam semantics. The marginal identity atom $x \approx y$ expresses that in a team the distribution of values for the variables $x$ coincides with that of $y$. We relate this logic to a natural variant of (two-sorted) existential second-order logic with quantification over rational distributions. We also consider the complexity of model checking and show that very simple formulae using $x \approx y$ give rise to NP-hard model checking problems.

*Example 1.* Consider a database table that lists results of experiments. The data can be regarded either as a multiteam or as the related probabilistic team using the counting measure; both interpretations having its own advantages. Each record corresponds to outcomes of measurements obtained simultaneously in two locations. The table has four attributes Test1 and Test2 that range over the possible types of measurements and Outcome1 and Outcome2 that range over outcomes of the measurements. The probabilistic independence atom Test1 $\perp\!\!\!\perp$ Test2 expresses that the types of measurements are independently picked in the two locations. The marginal identity atom (Test1, Outcome1) $\approx$ (Test2, Outcome2) expresses that the distributions of results are the same in both test sites. The formula Test1 $-$ Test2 $\vee$ (Test1 $\neq$ Test2 $\wedge$ Outcome1 $\perp\!\!\!\perp$ Outcome2) expresses that there is no correlation between outcomes of the different measurements.

*Example 2.* Consider a database table that describes voting behaviour in two different elections by some sample of voters. Attributes of the table are Election1 and Election2 that range over political parties. Each record corresponds to a voting behaviour of a voter in the sample. The table then gives rise to a probabilistic team that approximates the voting behaviour of the population. The complex formula Election1 = Election2 ∨ (Election1 ≠ Election2 ∧ Election1 ≈ Election2) expresses that each party obtained the same portion of swing voters in the second election that it got in the first election.

It is well known that the satisfaction relation of team semantics can be formalised in (existential) second-order logic when the team is encoded by an additional relation. This result gives an upper bound and a "yardstick" for the expressive power of many of the logics studied in the team semantics literature. One of the motivations for the current article is to develop an analogous yardstick of expressivity for logics over multiteams and probabilistic teams. We use a variant of existential second-order logic over two-sorted structures for this purpose whose first sort encodes the first-order structure and whose second sort consists of the closed interval $[0, 1]$ of rational numbers $\mathbb{Q}_{[0,1]}$ over which arithmetic operations of multiplication and sum can be applied. Distributions from the first sort ranging over the second sort $\mathbb{Q}_{[0,1]}$ encode probabilistic teams.

In the second part of the article we consider the complexity of model-checking in probabilistic and multiteam semantics and show that, over multiteams, very simple formulae using $x \approx y$ give rise to NP-hard model checking problems. This result is in drastic contrast with the influential result of Galliani and Hella [7] that inclusion atoms in the ordinary team semantics give rise to a logic equivalent with (a fragment of) the least fixed point logic and accordingly is contained in PTIME. Interestingly our reduction does not work under the slightly different probabilistic interpretation of disjunction. It is an open question whether the data-complexity of $\mathsf{FO}(x \approx y)$ is in PTIME for the probabilistic semantics.

*Previous Work on Probabilistic Team Semantics:* Probabilistic versions of dependence logic (and IF-logic) have been previously studied by Galliani, Mann, Sevenster, and Sandu [5,8,19]. Moreover, Hyttinen et al. [15,16] consider so-called quantum team and measure team logics over probabilistic teams and give complete axiomatisation for them. It is worth noting, as regards to the connectives and quantifiers, our semantics is similar to the one defined by Galliani [5] and that the atoms $y \perp\!\!\!\perp_x z$ and $x \approx y$ were introduced only later by Durand et al. [3] in the multiteam semantics context.

## 2    A Variant of Existential Second-Order Logic with Quantification over Rational Distributions

First-order variables are denoted by $x, y, z$ and tuples of first-order variables by $\boldsymbol{x}, \boldsymbol{y}, \boldsymbol{z}$. The length of the tuple $\boldsymbol{x}$ is denoted by $|\boldsymbol{x}|$, and for two tuples $\boldsymbol{x}, \boldsymbol{y}$ we denote by $\boldsymbol{x} \setminus \boldsymbol{y}$ any tuple that lists those elements of $\boldsymbol{x}$ that do not appear in $\boldsymbol{y}$. By $\mathrm{Var}(\boldsymbol{x})$ we denote the set of variables that appear in the variable sequence $\boldsymbol{x}$. A *vocabulary* $\tau$ is a set of relation symbols and function symbols with prescribed arities. We mostly denote relation symbols by $R$ and function symbols by $f$, and the related arities by $\text{ar}(R)$ and $\text{ar}(f)$, respectively. A vocabulary is *relational* (resp., *functional*) if it consists of only relation (resp., function) symbols. Similarly, a structure is *relational* (resp., *functional*) if it is defined over a relational (resp., functional) vocabulary. We let $\text{Var}_1$ and $\text{Var}_2$ denote disjoint countable sets of first-order and function variables (with prescribed arities), respectively. The set of rational numbers in the closed interval $[0,1]$ is denoted by $\mathbb{Q}_{[0,1]}$. Given a finite set $A$, a function $f: A \rightarrow \mathbb{Q}_{[0,1]}$ is called a *(probability) distribution* if $\sum_{s\in A} f(s) = 1$. In addition, the empty function is a *distribution*.

A relational $\tau$-structure is a tuple $\mathfrak{A} = (A, (R_i^{\mathfrak{A}})_{R_i\in\tau})$, where $A$ is a nonempty set and each $R_i^{\mathfrak{A}}$ is a relation on $A$ (i.e., $R_i^{\mathfrak{A}} \subseteq A^{\text{ar}(R_i)}$). In this paper, we consider structures that enrich finite relational $\tau$-structures by adding $\mathbb{Q}_{[0,1]}$ as a second domain sort and functions that map tuples from $A$ to $\mathbb{Q}_{[0,1]}$.

**Definition 1.** *Let $\tau$ and $\sigma$ be a relational and a functional vocabulary, respectively. A probabilistic $\tau \cup \sigma$-structure is a tuple*

$$\mathfrak{A} = (A, \mathbb{Q}_{[0,1]}, (R_i^{\mathfrak{A}})_{R_i\in\tau}, (f_i^{\mathfrak{A}})_{f_i\in\sigma}),$$

*where $A$ (i.e. the domain of $\mathfrak{A}$) is a finite nonempty set, each $R_i^{\mathfrak{A}}$ is a relation on $A$ (i.e., a subset of $A^{\text{ar}(R_i)}$), and each $f_i^{\mathfrak{A}}$ is a probability distribution from $A^{\text{ar}(f_i)}$ to $\mathbb{Q}_{[0,1]}$ (i.e., a function such that $\sum_{a\in A^{\text{ar}(f_i)}} f_i(a) = 1$).*

Note that if $f$ is a 0-ary function symbol, then $f^{\mathfrak{A}}$ is the constant 1. Next, we define a variant of functional existential second-order logic with numerical terms ($\text{ESOf}_{\mathbb{Q}}$) that is designed to describe properties of the above probabilistic structures. As first-order terms we have only first-order variables. For a set $\sigma$ of function symbols, the set of numerical $\sigma$-terms $i$ is defined via the following grammar:

$$i ::= f(\boldsymbol{x}) \mid i \times i \mid \text{SUM}_{\boldsymbol{x}} i,$$

where $\boldsymbol{x}$ is a tuple of first-order variables from $\text{Var}_1$ and $f \in \sigma$. The value of a numerical term $i$ in a structure $\mathfrak{A}$ under an assignment $s$ is denoted by $[i]_s^{\mathfrak{A}}$. We have the following rules for the numerical terms:

$$[f(\boldsymbol{x})]_s^{\mathfrak{A}} := f^{\mathfrak{A}}(s(\boldsymbol{x})), \qquad [i \times j]_s^{\mathfrak{A}} := [i]_s^{\mathfrak{A}} \cdot [j]_s^{\mathfrak{A}},$$
$$[\text{SUM}_{\boldsymbol{x}} i(\boldsymbol{x}, \boldsymbol{y})]_s^{\mathfrak{A}} := \sum_{a\in A^{|\boldsymbol{x}|}} [i(\boldsymbol{a}, \boldsymbol{y})]_s^{\mathfrak{A}},$$

where $\cdot$ and $\sum$ are the multiplication and sum of rational numbers, respectively. In this context, $i(\boldsymbol{x}, \boldsymbol{y})$ is a numerical term over variables in $\boldsymbol{x}$ and $\boldsymbol{y}$. Note that, in the semantics of $\text{SUM}_{\boldsymbol{x}} i$ the tuple $\boldsymbol{y}$ could be empty. Furthermore let $\tau$ be a relational vocabulary. The set of $\tau \cup \sigma$-formulae of $\text{ESOf}_{\mathbb{Q}}$ is defined via the following grammar:

$$\phi ::= x = y \mid x \neq y \mid i = j \mid i \neq j \mid R(\boldsymbol{x}) \mid \neg R(\boldsymbol{x}) \mid \phi \wedge \phi \mid \phi \vee \phi \mid \exists x\phi \mid \forall x\phi \mid \exists f\psi,$$

where $i$ is a numerical $\sigma$-term, $R \in \tau$ is a relation symbol, $f \in \text{Var}_2$ is a function variable, $\boldsymbol{x}$ is a tuple of first-order variables, and $\psi$ is a $\tau \cup (\sigma \cup \{f\})$-formula of

ESOf$_\mathbb{Q}$. Note that the syntax of ESOf$_\mathbb{Q}$ admits of only first-order subformulae to appear in negation normal form. This restriction however does not restrict the expressiveness of the language.

Semantics of ESOf$_\mathbb{Q}$ is defined via probabilistic structures and assignments analogous to first-order logic; note that first-order variables are always assigned to a value in $A$ whereas functions map tuples from $A$ to $\mathbb{Q}_{[0,1]}$. In addition to the clauses of first-order logic, we have the following semantical clauses:

$$\mathfrak{A} \models_s i = j \Leftrightarrow [i]_s^{\mathfrak{A}} = [j]_s^{\mathfrak{A}}, \qquad\qquad \mathfrak{A} \models_s i \neq j \Leftrightarrow [i]_s^{\mathfrak{A}} \neq [j]_s^{\mathfrak{A}},$$

$$\mathfrak{A} \models_s \exists f \phi \Leftrightarrow \mathfrak{A}[h/f] \models_s \phi \text{ for some probability distribution } h \colon A^{\mathrm{ar}(f)} \to \mathbb{Q}_{[0,1]},$$

where $\mathfrak{A}[h/f]$ denotes the expansion of $\mathfrak{A}$ that interprets $f$ to $h$.

Note that the property of $h$ being a probability distribution can be expressed by the formula $\mathrm{SUM}_x h(\boldsymbol{x}) = 1$ suggesting that it is not vital whether the restriction to probability distributions is in the semantics or not; in this case, however, $\mathbb{Q}_{[0,1]}$ would not suffice as a second sort and the set of (non-negative) rationals should be used instead. Furthermore, for relating ESOf$_\mathbb{Q}$ to our probabilistic team logic this assumption is essential. Recall that the constant 1 is defined by the unique 0-ary function and is thus essentially included in the language. In structures of size at least 2, the constant 0 can be defined by $g(y)$ by the use of the formula[1]

$$\exists g \exists x \exists y \, (x \neq y \wedge g(x) = 1).$$

In order to get some idea of the expressive power of ESOf$_\mathbb{Q}$, we note that the uniformity of a distribution $f$ can be expressed with

$$\phi(f) := \forall \boldsymbol{x}\boldsymbol{y}(f(\boldsymbol{x}) = 0 \vee f(\boldsymbol{y}) = 0 \vee f(\boldsymbol{x}) = f(\boldsymbol{y})).$$

Furthermore, let $\frac{p}{q}$ be an arbitrary rational number. For $k \leq p$, denote by $\hat{k}$ the length $\log(p+1)$ bit sequence that encodes $k$, and denote by $\boldsymbol{y}_{\hat{k}}$ the variable sequence obtained from $\hat{k}$ by replacing bits 0 and 1 with variables $y_0$ and $y_1$, respectively. For $l \leq q - p$, define $\boldsymbol{z}_{\hat{l}}$ analogously in terms of bit sequences of length $\log((q-p)+1)$. For instance, $(y_0, y_0, \ldots, y_0, y_0)$ is $\boldsymbol{y}_{\hat{0}}$ and $(y_0, y_0, \ldots, y_0, y_1)$ is $\boldsymbol{y}_{\hat{1}}$. Let $E := \{\boldsymbol{y}_{\hat{k}}\boldsymbol{z}_{\hat{0}} \mid 1 \leq k \leq p\} \cup \{\boldsymbol{y}_{\hat{0}}\boldsymbol{z}_{\hat{l}} \mid 1 \leq l \leq q - p\}$. Note that $E$ is not part of the syntax of our logic, but is used as a shorthand in the following formula. Now $i(\boldsymbol{x}) = \frac{p}{q}$ can be described by

$$\phi_{\frac{p}{q}}(\boldsymbol{x}) := \exists y_0 y_1 \exists f \big(y_0 \neq y_1 \wedge \bigwedge_{\boldsymbol{y}\boldsymbol{z}, \boldsymbol{y}'\boldsymbol{z}' \in E} f(\boldsymbol{y}\boldsymbol{z}) = f(\boldsymbol{y}'\boldsymbol{z}') \wedge$$

$$\forall \boldsymbol{y}\boldsymbol{z}(\boldsymbol{y}\boldsymbol{z} \notin E \leftrightarrow f(\boldsymbol{y}\boldsymbol{z}) = 0) \wedge i(\boldsymbol{x}) = \mathrm{SUM}_y \boldsymbol{y}\boldsymbol{z}_{\hat{0}}\big).$$

Note that, by construction, $E$ is finite, and consequently $\phi_{\frac{p}{q}}$ is an ESOf$_\mathbb{Q}$-formula.

---

[1] $f(\boldsymbol{x}) = 0$ is always false for probability distributions $f$ in structures of size 1.

# 3    Probabilistic Team Semantics

In this section, we present probabilistic team semantics for probabilistic team logics. Before going to probabilistic semantics, we quickly review the basics of (multi)team semantics.

## 3.1    Team and Multiteam Semantics

Syntactically, team logics are extensions of first-order logic FO given by the grammar rules:

$$\phi ::= x = y \mid x \neq y \mid R(\boldsymbol{x}) \mid \neg R(\boldsymbol{x}) \mid (\phi \wedge \phi) \mid (\phi \vee \phi) \mid \exists x\phi \mid \forall x\phi,$$

where $\boldsymbol{x}$ is a tuple of first-order variables.

Let $D$ be a finite set of first-order variables and $A$ be a nonempty set. A function $s \colon D \to A$ is called an *assignment*. The set $D$ is the *domain* of $s$, and the set $A$ the *codomain* of $s$. For a variable $x$ and $a \in A$, the assignment $s(a/x) \colon D \cup \{x\} \to A$ is equal to $s$ with the exception that $s(a/x)(x) = a$.

A *team* is a finite set of assignments with a common domain and codomain. Let $X$ be a team with codomain $A$, and let $F \colon X \to \mathcal{P}(A) \setminus \{\emptyset\}$ be a function. We denote by $X[A/x]$ the modified team $\{s(a/x) \mid s \in X, a \in A\}$, and by $X[F/x]$ the team $\{s(a/x) \mid s \in X, a \in F(s)\}$. Let $\mathfrak{A}$ be a $\tau$-structure and $X$ a team with codomain $A$, then we say that $X$ is a team of $\mathfrak{A}$.

**Definition 2.** *Let $\mathfrak{A}$ be a $\tau$-structure and $X$ a team of $\mathfrak{A}$. The satisfaction relation $\models_X$ for first-order logic is defined as follows:*

$$\mathfrak{A} \models_X x = y \Leftrightarrow \text{for all } s \in X : s(x) = s(y)$$
$$\mathfrak{A} \models_X x \neq y \Leftrightarrow \text{for all } s \in X : s(x) \neq s(y)$$
$$\mathfrak{A} \models_X R(\boldsymbol{x}) \Leftrightarrow \text{for all } s \in X : s(\boldsymbol{x}) \in R^{\mathfrak{A}}$$
$$\mathfrak{A} \models_X \neg R(\boldsymbol{x}) \Leftrightarrow \text{for all } s \in X : s(\boldsymbol{x}) \notin R^{\mathfrak{A}}$$
$$\mathfrak{A} \models_X (\psi \wedge \theta) \Leftrightarrow \mathfrak{A} \models_X \psi \text{ and } \mathfrak{A} \models_X \theta$$
$$\mathfrak{A} \models_X (\psi \vee \theta) \Leftrightarrow \mathfrak{A} \models_Y \psi \text{ and } \mathfrak{A} \models_Z \theta \text{ for some } Y, Z \subseteq X \text{ s.t. } Y \cup Z = X$$
$$\mathfrak{A} \models_X \forall x\psi \Leftrightarrow \mathfrak{A} \models_{X[A/x]} \psi$$
$$\mathfrak{A} \models_X \exists x\psi \Leftrightarrow \mathfrak{A} \models_{X[F/x]} \psi \text{ holds for some } F \colon X \to \mathcal{P}(A) \setminus \{\emptyset\}.$$

*Multiteams* are multiset analogues of teams. Below we give a short introduction to multiteam semantics, as defined by Durand et al. [3], adjusted to the notation used later in this paper.

**Definition 3.** *A multiset is a function $\mathcal{A} \colon A \to \mathbb{N}$. The set $\{a \in A \mid \mathcal{A}(a) \geq 1\}$ is the set of elements of the multiset $\mathcal{A}$, and $\mathcal{A}(a)$ is the multiplicity of the element $a$. A multiteam is a multiset $\mathcal{X} \colon X \to \mathbb{N}$ where $X$ is a team. The domain (codomain, resp.) of $\mathcal{X}$ is defined as the domain (codomain, resp.) of $X$.*

For a multiset $\mathcal{A}$, we define the *canonical set representative* $[\mathcal{A}]_{\text{cset}}$ of $\mathcal{A}$ by

$$[\mathcal{A}]_{\text{cset}} := \{ (a, i) \mid a \in A, i \in \mathbb{N}, \, 0 < i \leq \mathcal{A}(a) \}.$$

We say that a multiset $\mathcal{A}$ is a submultiset of a multiset $\mathcal{B}$, and write $\mathcal{A} \subseteq \mathcal{B}$, if and only if $[\mathcal{A}]_{\mathrm{cset}} \subseteq [\mathcal{B}]_{\mathrm{cset}}$. We write $\mathcal{A} = \mathcal{B}$ if and only if both $\mathcal{A} \subseteq \mathcal{B}$ and $\mathcal{B} \subseteq \mathcal{A}$ hold. The *disjoint union* $\mathcal{A} \uplus \mathcal{B}$ of $\mathcal{A}$ and $\mathcal{B}$ is the function $A \cup B \to \mathbb{N}$ defined by

$$\mathcal{A} \uplus \mathcal{B}(s) := \begin{cases} \mathcal{A}(s) + \mathcal{B}(s) & \text{if } s \in A \text{ and } s \in B, \\ \mathcal{A}(s) & \text{if } s \in A \text{ and } s \notin B, \\ \mathcal{B}(s) & \text{if } s \notin A \text{ and } s \in B. \end{cases}$$

We write $|\mathcal{A}|$ to denote the size of $\mathcal{A}$, i.e., $|\mathcal{A}| := \sum_{a \in A} \mathcal{A}(a)$. Let $\mathcal{X}$ be a multiteam, $A$ a finite set, and $F: [\mathcal{X}]_{\mathrm{cset}} \to \mathcal{P}(A) \setminus \emptyset$ a function. We denote by $\mathcal{X}[A/x]$ the modified multiteam defined as

$$\biguplus_{s \in X} \biguplus_{a \in A} \{(s(a/x), \mathcal{X}(s))\}.$$

By $\mathcal{X}[F/x]$ we denote the multiteam defined as

$$\biguplus_{s \in X} \biguplus_{1 \le i \le \mathcal{X}(s)} \{(s(b/x), 1) \mid b \in F((s, i))\}.$$

A multiteam $\mathcal{X}$ *over* $\mathfrak{A}$ is a multiteam with codomain $A$. We are now ready to define multiteam semantics for first-order logic. In the semantical clauses below, we use the lax semantics for existential quantifier and strict semantics for disjunction as defined by Durand et. al. [3].

**Definition 4 (Multiteam semantics).** *Let $\mathfrak{A}$ be a $\tau$-structure and $\mathcal{X}$ a multiteam over $\mathfrak{A}$. The satisfaction relation $\models_{\mathcal{X}}$ is defined as follows:*

$\mathfrak{A} \models_{\mathcal{X}} x = y \Leftrightarrow$ *for all $s \in X$: if $\mathcal{X}(s) \ge 1$ then $s(x) = s(y)$*

$\mathfrak{A} \models_{\mathcal{X}} x \ne y \Leftrightarrow$ *for all $s \in X$: if $\mathcal{X}(s) \ge 1$ then $s(x) \ne s(y)$*

$\mathfrak{A} \models_{\mathcal{X}} R(\boldsymbol{x}) \Leftrightarrow$ *for all $s \in X$: if $\mathcal{X}(s) \ge 1$ then $s(\boldsymbol{x}) \in R^{\mathfrak{A}}$*

$\mathfrak{A} \models_{\mathcal{X}} \neg R(\boldsymbol{x}) \Leftrightarrow$ *for all $s \in X$: if $\mathcal{X}(s) \ge 1$ then $s(\boldsymbol{x}) \notin R^{\mathfrak{A}}$*

$\mathfrak{A} \models_{\mathcal{X}} (\psi \wedge \theta) \Leftrightarrow \mathfrak{A} \models_{\mathcal{X}} \psi$ *and* $\mathfrak{A} \models_{\mathcal{X}} \theta$

$\mathfrak{A} \models_{\mathcal{X}} (\psi \vee \theta) \Leftrightarrow \mathfrak{A} \models_{\mathcal{Y}} \psi$ *and* $\mathfrak{A} \models_{\mathcal{Z}} \theta$ *for some multisets*
$\qquad\qquad \mathcal{Y}, \mathcal{Z} \subseteq \mathcal{X}$ *s.t. $\mathcal{X} = \mathcal{Y} \uplus \mathcal{Z}$.*

$\mathfrak{A} \models_{\mathcal{X}} \forall x \psi \Leftrightarrow \mathfrak{A} \models_{\mathcal{X}[A/x]} \psi$

$\mathfrak{A} \models_{\mathcal{X}} \exists x \psi \Leftrightarrow \mathfrak{A} \models_{\mathcal{X}[F/x]} \psi$ *holds for some function*
$\qquad\qquad F: [\mathcal{X}]_{\mathrm{cset}} \to \mathcal{P}(A) \setminus \emptyset$.

Using the counting measure, a multiteam $\mathcal{X}$ can be seen as a probability distribution over $X$; let $p_{\mathcal{X}}$ denote the distribution defined as follows:

$$p_{\mathcal{X}}(s) := \frac{\mathcal{X}(s)}{\sum_{t \in X} \mathcal{X}(t)}.$$

Conversely, every probability distribution $p$ over a team $X$ can be seen as a class $\mathcal{C}(p)$ of multiteams with that distribution as its counting measure:

$$\mathcal{C}(p) := \{\mathcal{X} \mid p_{\mathcal{X}} = p\}.$$

Teams in $\mathcal{C}(p)$ can be seen as discrete approximations of the probability distribution $p$. In the section below we abandon the discrete approach and device team based logics that take probability distributions of teams as primitive. Intuitively, the semantics of these probabilistic logics is defined such that satisfaction of formulae with respect to probabilistic teams and their *large enough* discrete approximations coincide.

## 3.2    Probabilistic Teams

Let $D$ be a finite set of variables, $A$ a finite set, and $X$ a finite set of assignments from $D$ to $A$. A *probabilistic team* $\mathbb{X}$ is a distribution $\mathbb{X} \colon X \to \mathbb{Q}_{[0,1]}$. We call $D$ and $A$ the variable domain and value domain of $\mathbb{X}$, respectively. Let $\mathfrak{A}$ be a $\tau$-structure and $\mathbb{X}$ a probabilistic team such that the domain of $\mathfrak{A}$ is the value domain of $\mathbb{X}$. Then we say that $\mathbb{X}$ is a probabilistic team of $\mathfrak{A}$. In the following, we will define two notations $\mathbb{X}[A/x]$ and $\mathbb{X}[F/x]$, similar to $\mathcal{X}[A/x]$ and $\mathcal{X}[F/x]$ of the previous section, in order to define the semantics of the universal and existential quantification of variables. Their intuition is depicted in Fig. 1.

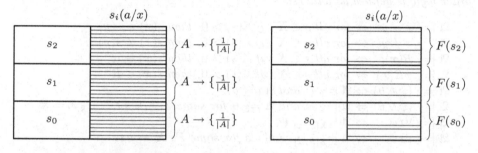

**Fig. 1.** Intuition of universal quantification of $x$ (i.e., the set $\mathbb{X}[A/x]$) is depicted on the left side. The intuition of existential quantification of $x$ (i.e., the set $\mathbb{X}[F/x]$) is depicted of the right side. The height of a box labelled by an assignment corresponds to the assignments probability. E.g., on left the probability of $s_0$ is $\frac{1}{3}$ whereas the probability of $s_0(a/x)$ (for any $a \in A$) is $\frac{1}{3|A|}$.

Let $\mathbb{X} \colon X \to \mathbb{Q}_{[0,1]}$ be a probabilistic team, $A$ a finite set, $p_A$ the set of all probability distributions $d \colon A \to \mathbb{Q}_{[0,1]}$, and $F \colon X \to p_A$ a function. We denote by $\mathbb{X}[A/x]$ the probabilistic team $X[A/x] \to \mathbb{Q}_{[0,1]}$ such that

$$\mathbb{X}[A/x](s(a/x)) = \sum_{\substack{t \subseteq X \\ t(a/x)=s(a/x)}} \mathbb{X}(t) \cdot \frac{1}{|A|},$$

for each $a \in A$ and $s \in X$. Note that if $x$ is a fresh variable then the righthand side of the above equation is simply $\mathbb{X}(s) \cdot \frac{1}{|A|}$. By $\mathbb{X}[F/x]$ we denote the probabilistic team $X[A/x] \to \mathbb{Q}_{[0,1]}$ defined such that

$$\mathbb{X}[F/x](s(a/x)) = \sum_{\substack{t \in X \\ t(a/x)=s(a/x)}} \mathbb{X}(t) \cdot F(t)(a),$$

for each $a \in A$ and $s \in X$. Again, if $x$ is a fresh variable, $\sum$ can be dropped from the above equation.

Let $\mathbb{X} \colon X \to \mathbb{Q}_{[0,1]}$ and $\mathbb{Y} \colon Y \to \mathbb{Q}_{[0,1]}$ be probabilistic teams with common variable and value domains, and let $k \in \mathbb{Q}_{[0,1]}$ be a rational number. We denote by $\mathbb{X} \sqcup_k \mathbb{Y}$ the $k$-scaled union of $\mathbb{X}$ and $\mathbb{Y}$, that is, the probabilistic team $\mathbb{X} \sqcup_k \mathbb{Y} \colon X \cup Y \to \mathbb{Q}_{[0,1]}$ defined such that for each $s \in X \cup Y$,

$$(\mathbb{X} \sqcup_k \mathbb{Y})(s) := \begin{cases} k \cdot \mathbb{X}(s) + (1-k) \cdot \mathbb{Y}(s) & \text{if } s \in X \text{ and } s \in Y, \\ k \cdot \mathbb{X}(s) & \text{if } s \in X \text{ and } s \notin Y, \\ (1-k) \cdot \mathbb{Y}(s) & \text{if } s \in Y \text{ and } s \notin X. \end{cases}$$

We may now define probabilistic team semantics for first-order formulae.

**Definition 5.** *Let $\mathfrak{A}$ be a probabilistic $\tau$-structure over a finite domain $A$, and $\mathbb{X} \colon X \to \mathbb{Q}_{[0,1]}$ a probabilistic team of $\mathfrak{A}$. The satisfaction relation $\models_\mathbb{X}$ for first-order logic is defined as follows:*

$\mathfrak{A} \models_\mathbb{X} x = y \Leftrightarrow$ *for all* $s \in X$: *if* $\mathbb{X}(s) > 0$, *then* $s(x) = s(y)$

$\mathfrak{A} \models_\mathbb{X} x \neq y \Leftrightarrow$ *for all* $s \in X$: *if* $\mathbb{X}(s) > 0$, *then* $s(x) \neq s(y)$

$\mathfrak{A} \models_\mathbb{X} R(\boldsymbol{x}) \Leftrightarrow$ *for all* $s \in X$: *if* $\mathbb{X}(s) > 0$, *then* $s(\boldsymbol{x}) \in R^\mathfrak{A}$

$\mathfrak{A} \models_\mathbb{X} \neg R(\boldsymbol{x}) \Leftrightarrow$ *for all* $s \in X$: *if* $\mathbb{X}(s) > 0$, *then* $s(\boldsymbol{x}) \notin R^\mathfrak{A}$

$\mathfrak{A} \models_\mathbb{X} (\psi \wedge \theta) \Leftrightarrow \mathfrak{A} \models_\mathbb{X} \psi$ *and* $\mathfrak{A} \models_\mathbb{X} \theta$

$\mathfrak{A} \models_\mathbb{X} (\psi \vee \theta) \Leftrightarrow \mathfrak{A} \models_\mathbb{Y} \psi$ *and* $\mathfrak{A} \models_\mathbb{Z} \theta$ *for some* $\mathbb{Y}, \mathbb{Z}, k$ *s.t.* $\mathbb{Y} \sqcup_k \mathbb{Z} = \mathbb{X}$

$\mathfrak{A} \models_\mathbb{X} \forall x \psi \Leftrightarrow \mathfrak{A} \models_{\mathbb{X}[A/x]} \psi$

$\mathfrak{A} \models_\mathbb{X} \exists x \psi \Leftrightarrow \mathfrak{A} \models_{\mathbb{X}[F/x]} \psi$ *holds for some* $F \colon X \to p_A$.

Next we define the semantics of probabilistic atoms considered in this paper: marginal identity and probabilistic independence atom. They were first introduced in the context of multiteam semantics in [3]. We define $|\mathbb{X}_{\boldsymbol{x}=\boldsymbol{a}}|$ where $\boldsymbol{x}$ is a tuple of variables and $\boldsymbol{a}$ a tuple of values, as the rational

$$|\mathbb{X}_{\boldsymbol{x}=\boldsymbol{a}}| := \sum_{\substack{s(\boldsymbol{x})=\boldsymbol{a} \\ s \in X}} \mathbb{X}(s).$$

If $\phi$ is some first-order formula, then $|\mathbb{X}_\phi|$ is defined analogously as the total sum of weights of those assignments in $X$ that satisfy $\phi$.

If $\boldsymbol{x}, \boldsymbol{y}$ are variable sequences of length $k$, then $\boldsymbol{x} \approx \boldsymbol{y}$ is a *marginal identity atom* with the following semantics:

$$\mathfrak{A} \models_\mathbb{X} \boldsymbol{x} \approx \boldsymbol{y} \Leftrightarrow |\mathbb{X}_{\boldsymbol{x}=\boldsymbol{a}}| = |\mathbb{X}_{\boldsymbol{y}=\boldsymbol{a}}| \text{ for each } \boldsymbol{a} \in A^k \tag{1}$$

Note that the equality $|\mathbb{X}_{\boldsymbol{x}=\boldsymbol{a}}| = |\mathbb{X}_{\boldsymbol{y}=\boldsymbol{a}}|$ in (1) can be equivalently replaced with $|\mathbb{X}_{\boldsymbol{x}=\boldsymbol{a}}| \leq |\mathbb{X}_{\boldsymbol{y}=\boldsymbol{a}}|$ since the tuples $\boldsymbol{a}$ range over $A^k$. Due to this alternative formulation, marginal identity atoms were in [3] called probabilistic inclusion atoms.

If $x, y, z$ are variable sequences, then $y \perp\!\!\!\perp_x z$ is a *probabilistic conditional independence atom* with the satisfaction relation defined as

$$\mathfrak{A} \models_X y \perp\!\!\!\perp_x z \tag{2}$$

if for all $s \colon \mathrm{Var}(xyz) \to A$ it holds that

$$|\mathbb{X}_{xy=s(xy)}| \cdot |\mathbb{X}_{xz=s(xz)}| = |\mathbb{X}_{xyz=s(xyz)}| \cdot |\mathbb{X}_{x=s(x)}|.$$

The logic $\mathsf{FO}(\perp\!\!\!\perp_c, \approx)$ is now defined as the extension of $\mathsf{FO}$ with marginal identity and probabilistic conditional independence atoms. The following two examples demonstrate the expressivity of $\mathsf{FO}(\perp\!\!\!\perp_c, \approx)$.

*Example 3.* The formula $\forall y x \approx y$ states that the probabilities for $x$ are uniformly distributed over all value sequences of length $|x|$.

*Example 4.* We define a formula $\phi(x) := \exists \alpha \beta \psi(x, \alpha, \beta)$ which expresses that the weight of a predicate $P(x)$ is at least two times that of a predicate $Q(x)$ in a probabilistic team over $x$. The subformula $\psi$ in $\phi$ is given as

$$\psi := x\alpha \approx x\beta \land \alpha = 0 \leftrightarrow \beta \neq 0 \land \exists \gamma_P \gamma_Q \theta(x, \alpha, \beta, \gamma_P \gamma_Q), \text{ where} \tag{3}$$

$$\theta := \big((P(x) \land \alpha = 0) \leftrightarrow \gamma_P = 0\big) \land Q(x) \to \gamma_Q = 0 \land \gamma_P \approx \gamma_Q \tag{4}$$

Now $\mathfrak{A} \models_X \phi(x) \iff |\mathbb{X}_{P(x)}| \geq 2 \cdot |\mathbb{X}_{Q(x)}|$ for any $\mathbb{X} \colon X \to \mathbb{Q}_{[0,1]}$ where $\alpha$, $\beta$, $\gamma_P$, and $\gamma_Q$ are not in the variable domain of $\mathbb{X}$. The first two conjuncts in (3) indicate that the values of $\alpha$ must be chosen so that $\frac{1}{2} \cdot |\mathbb{Y}_{P(x)}| = |\mathbb{Y}_{P(x) \land \alpha = 0}|$. Where $\mathbb{Y}$ denotes the team obtained form $\mathbb{X}$ by evaluating the quantifiers $\exists \alpha \beta$. The first conjunct in (4) implies that $|\mathbb{Z}_{P(x) \land \alpha = 0}| = |\mathbb{Z}_{\gamma_P = 0}|$ and the second that $|\mathbb{Z}_{Q(x)}| \leq |\mathbb{Z}_{\gamma_Q = 0}|$, where $\mathbb{Z}$ is team obtained from $\mathbb{Y}$ by evaluating the quantifiers $\exists \gamma_P \gamma_Q$. The third conjunct in (4) then indicates that $|\mathbb{Z}_{\gamma_P = 0}| = |\mathbb{Z}_{\gamma_Q = 0}|$. Put together, we have that

$$|\mathbb{X}_{Q(x)}| \overset{*}{=} |\mathbb{Z}_{Q(x)}| \leq |\mathbb{Z}_{\gamma_Q = 0}| = |\mathbb{Z}_{\gamma_P = 0}| = |\mathbb{Z}_{P(x) \land \alpha = 0}|$$

$$\overset{*}{=} |\mathbb{Y}_{P(x) \land \alpha = 0}| = \frac{1}{2} |\mathbb{Y}_{P(x)}| \overset{*}{=} \frac{1}{2} |\mathbb{X}_{P(x)}|.$$

The equations $\overset{*}{=}$ follow from the fact that quantification of fresh variables do not change the distribution of assignments with respect to the old variables.

Our next example relates probabilistic conditional independence atoms and marginal identity atoms to Bayesian networks. A Bayesian network is a directed acyclic graph whose nodes represent random variables and edges represent dependency relations between these random variables. The applicability of Bayesian networks is grounded in the notion of conditional independence as the conditional independence relations encoded in the topology of such a network enable a factorization of the underlying joint probability distribution. Next we survey the possibility of refining Bayesian networks with information obtained from $\mathsf{FO}(\perp\!\!\!\perp_c, \approx)$ formulae.

*Example 5.* Consider the Bayesian network $\mathbb{G}$ in Fig. 2 that models beliefs about house safety using four Boolean random variables. We note that the awakening of `guard` or `alarm` is conditioned upon both the presence of `thief` and `cat`. Furthermore, `cat` depends on `thief`, and `guard` and `alarm` are independent given `thief` and `cat`. From the network we obtain that the joint probability distribution for these variables can be factorized as

$$P(t, c, g, a) = P(t) \cdot P(c \mid t) \cdot P(g \mid t, c) \cdot P(a \mid t, c) \tag{5}$$

where, e.g., $t$ abbreviates either `thief` $= T$ or `thief` $= F$, and $P(c \mid t)$ is the probability of $c$ given $t$. The joint probability distribution (i.e., a team $\mathbb{X}$) can hence be stored as in Fig. 2.

Let $t, c, g, a$ now refer to random variables `thief, cat, guard, alarm`. The dependence structure of a Bayesian network is characterized by the so-called local directed Markov property stating that each variable is conditionally independent of its non-descendants given its parents. For our network $\mathbb{G}$ the only non-trivial independence given by this property is $g \perp\!\!\!\perp_{tc} a$. Hence a probabilistic team $\mathbb{X}$ over $t, c, g, a$ factorizes according to (5) iff $\mathbb{X}$ satisfies $g \perp\!\!\!\perp_{tc} a$. In this situation knowledge on various $\mathsf{FO}(\perp\!\!\!\perp_c, \approx)$ formulae can further improve the decomposition of the joint probability distribution. Assume we have information suggesting that we may safely assume an $\mathsf{FO}(\perp\!\!\!\perp_c, \approx)$ formula $\phi$ on $\mathbb{X}$:

- $\phi := t = F \rightarrow g = F$ indicates that `guard` never raises alert in absence of `thief`. In this case the two bottom rows of the conditional probability distribution for `guard` become superfluous.
- $\phi := tca \approx tcg$ indicates that `alarm` and `guard` have the same reliability for any given value of `thief` and `cat`. Consequently, the conditional distributions for `alarm` and `guard` are equal and one of the them can be removed.
- $\phi := \exists x (tcg \approx tcx \wedge tcga \perp\!\!\!\perp y \wedge x = T \leftrightarrow ay = TT)$ entails that `guard` is of a factor $P(y = T)$ less sensitive to raise alert than `alarm` for any given `thief`

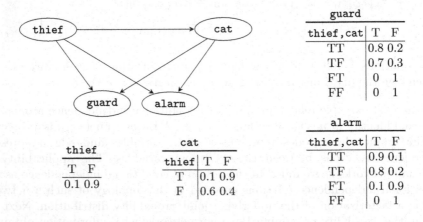

| guard | | |
|---|---|---|
| thief,cat | T | F |
| TT | 0.8 | 0.2 |
| TF | 0.7 | 0.3 |
| FT | 0 | 1 |
| FF | 0 | 1 |

| thief | |
|---|---|
| T | F |
| 0.1 | 0.9 |

| cat | | |
|---|---|---|
| thief | T | F |
| T | 0.1 | 0.9 |
| F | 0.6 | 0.4 |

| alarm | | |
|---|---|---|
| thief,cat | T | F |
| TT | 0.9 | 0.1 |
| TF | 0.8 | 0.2 |
| FT | 0.1 | 0.9 |
| FF | 0 | 1 |

**Fig. 2.** Bayesian network $\mathbb{G}$ and its related conditional distributions

and `cat`. The formula introduces a fresh free variable $y$, independent of any random variable in $\mathbb{G}$, and such that the probability of $ay = TT$ equals the probability of $g = T$ given $tc$. The latter property is expressed by introducing an auxiliary distribution for $x$. In this case it suffices to store the conditional probability table for `alarm` and the probability $P(y = T)$.

Next we connect probabilistic teams to multiteams. Denote by Prob the mapping that transforms a multiteam to its corresponding probabilistic team, i.e., given a multiteam $\mathcal{X}$, $\mathrm{Prob}(\mathcal{X})$ is the probabilistic team $\mathbb{X} \colon X \to \mathbb{Q}_{[0,1]}$ such that

$$\mathbb{X}(s) = \frac{\mathcal{X}(s)}{\sum_{s' \in X} \mathcal{X}(s')}.$$

It follows from the definitions that Prob preserves the truth condition for marginal identity and probabilistic independence atoms.

**Proposition 1.** *Let $\phi$ be a marginal identity or a probabilistic independence atom, let $\mathcal{X}$ be a multiteam of a structure $\mathfrak{A}$, and let $\mathbb{X}$ be a probabilistic team of $\mathfrak{A}$ such that $\mathbb{X} = \mathrm{Prob}(\mathcal{X})$. Then $\mathfrak{A} \models_{\mathcal{X}} \phi \iff \mathfrak{A} \models_{\mathbb{X}} \phi$.*

The restriction of a team $X$ to $V$ is defined as $X \upharpoonright V = \{s \upharpoonright V \mid s \in X\}$ where $s \upharpoonright V$ denotes the restriction of the assignment $s$ to $V$. The restriction of a probabilistic team $\mathbb{X}$ to $V$ is then defined as the probabilistic team $Q \colon X \upharpoonright V \to \mathbb{Q}_{[0,1]}$ where

$$Q(s) = \sum_{s' \upharpoonright V = s} P(s').$$

The following locality property indicates that satisfaction of $\phi \in \mathsf{FO}(\perp\!\!\!\perp_{\mathrm{c}}, \approx)$ is determined by the restriction of a probabilistic team to the free variables of $\phi$. The set of *free variables* $\mathrm{Fr}(\phi)$ of a formula $\phi \in \mathsf{FO}(\perp\!\!\!\perp_{\mathrm{c}}, \approx)$ is defined recursively as in first-order logic with the addition that for probabilistic independence and marginal identity atoms $\phi$, $\mathrm{Fr}(\phi)$ consists of all variables that appear in $\phi$.

**Proposition 2 (Locality).** *Let $\phi(\boldsymbol{x}) \in \mathsf{FO}(\perp\!\!\!\perp_{\mathrm{c}}, \approx)$ be a formula with free variables from $\boldsymbol{x} = (x_1, \ldots, x_n)$. Then for all structures $\mathfrak{A}$ and probabilistic teams $\mathbb{X} \colon X \to \mathbb{Q}_{[0,1]}$ where $\{x_1, \ldots, x_n\} \subseteq V \subseteq \mathrm{Dom}(X)$, $\mathfrak{A} \models_{\mathbb{X}} \phi \iff \mathfrak{A} \models_{\mathbb{X} \upharpoonright V} \phi$.*

*Proof.* For first-order atoms the claim is immediate. Furthermore, it is easy to check that the same holds for the atoms $\boldsymbol{x} \approx \boldsymbol{y}$ and $\boldsymbol{y} \perp\!\!\!\perp_{\boldsymbol{x}} \boldsymbol{z}$ (for multiteam semantics this has been discussed in [3]).

Assume then that $\phi := \psi \lor \theta$, and that the claim holds for $\psi$ and $\theta$. Note first that for any probabilistic teams $\mathbb{X}$ and $\mathbb{Y}$ with common variable and value domains a simple calculation shows that

$$(\mathbb{X} \sqcup_k \mathbb{Y}) \upharpoonright V = \mathbb{X} \upharpoonright V \sqcup_k \mathbb{Y} \upharpoonright V, \tag{6}$$

Suppose that $\mathfrak{A} \models_{\mathbb{X}} \phi$. Then there are $k$, $\mathbb{Y}$, and $\mathbb{Z}$ such that $\mathbb{X} = \mathbb{Y} \sqcup_k \mathbb{Z}$, $\mathfrak{A} \models_{\mathbb{Y}} \psi$, and $\mathfrak{A} \models_{\mathbb{Z}} \theta$. By the induction assumption, it holds that $\mathfrak{A} \models_{\mathbb{Y} \upharpoonright V} \psi$ and $\mathfrak{A} \models_{\mathbb{Z} \upharpoonright V} \theta$. Now by (6), $\mathfrak{A} \models_{\mathbb{X} \upharpoonright V} \phi$. The converse implication is proved analogously. The proof is similar for the cases $\phi := \exists x \psi$ and $\phi := \forall x \psi$.    $\square$

## 4   Translation from FO($\perp\!\!\!\perp_c$, $\approx$) to ESOf$_\mathbb{Q}$

In this section, we show that any formula in FO($\perp\!\!\!\perp_c$, $\approx$) can be equivalently expressed as a sentence of ESOf$_\mathbb{Q}$ that has exactly one free function variable for encoding probabilistic teams. The following lemma will be used to facilitate the translation. This lemma has been shown by Durand et al. [3] for multiteams and accordingly, by Proposition 1, it holds for probabilistic teams as well. The lemma entails that each probabilistic independence atom in $\phi \in$ FO($\perp\!\!\!\perp_c$, $\approx$) can be assumed to be either of the form $y \perp\!\!\!\perp_x z$ or of the form $y \perp\!\!\!\perp_x y$ for pairwise disjoint tuples $x, y, z$.

**Lemma 1** [3]. *Let $\mathfrak{A}$ be a structure and $\mathbb{X}$ a probabilistic team over $\mathfrak{A}$. Then*

*(i)* $\mathfrak{A} \models_\mathbb{X} y \perp\!\!\!\perp_x z \quad\Leftrightarrow\quad \mathfrak{A} \models_\mathbb{X} (y \setminus x \perp\!\!\!\perp_x z \setminus x)$,
*(ii)* $\mathfrak{A} \models_\mathbb{X} y \perp\!\!\!\perp_x z \quad\Leftrightarrow\quad \mathfrak{A} \models_\mathbb{X} (y \setminus z \perp\!\!\!\perp_x z \setminus y) \wedge (y \cap z \perp\!\!\!\perp_x y \cap z)$.

**Theorem 1.** *For every formula $\phi(x) \in$ FO($\perp\!\!\!\perp_c$, $\approx$) with free variables from $x = (x_1, \ldots, x_n)$ there exists a formula $\phi^*(f) \in$ ESOf$_\mathbb{Q}$ with exactly one free function variable $f$ such that for all structures $\mathfrak{A}$ and nonempty probabilistic teams $\mathbb{X}: X \to \mathbb{Q}_{[0,1]}$,*

$$\mathfrak{A} \models_\mathbb{X} \phi(x) \iff (\mathfrak{A}, f_\mathbb{X}) \models \phi^*(f),$$

*where $f_\mathbb{X}: A^n \to \mathbb{Q}_{[0,1]}$ is the probability distribution such that $f_\mathbb{X}(s(x)) = \mathbb{X}(s)$ for all $s \in X$.*

*Proof.* We give a compositional translation $^*$ from FO($\perp\!\!\!\perp_c$, $\approx$) to ESOf$_\mathbb{Q}$. For a subsequence $x_i$ of $x$, we denote by $x_i^c$ a sequence $x \setminus x_i$, and by $x(y/x_i)$ a sequence obtained from $x$ by replacing $x_i$ pointwise with $y$.

If $\phi(x)$ is of the form $R(x_0)$, then $\phi^*(f) := \forall x (f(x) = 0 \vee R(x_0))$.

If $\phi(x)$ is of the form $\neg R(x_0)$, then $\phi^*(f) := \forall x (f(x) = 0 \vee \neg R(x_0))$.

If $\phi(x)$ is $x_0 \approx x_1$, then $\phi^*(f) := \forall z\, \text{SUM}_{x_0^c} f(x(z/x_0)) = \text{SUM}_{x_1^c} f(x(z/x_1))$.

If $\phi(x)$ is $x_1 \perp\!\!\!\perp_{x_0} x_2$ where $x_0, x_1, x_2$ are disjoint, then $\phi^*(f) := \forall x_0 x_1 x_2$
$$\text{SUM}_{(x_0 x_1)^c} f(x) \times \text{SUM}_{(x_0 x_2)^c} f(x) = \text{SUM}_{(x_0 x_1 x_2)^c} f(x) \times \text{SUM}_{x_0^c} f(x).$$

If $\phi(x)$ is of the form $x_1 \perp\!\!\!\perp_{x_0} x_1$ where $x_0, x_1$ are disjoint, then
$$\phi^*(f) := \forall x_0 x_1 (\text{SUM}_{(x_0 x_1)^c} f(x) = 0 \vee \text{SUM}_{(x_0 x_1)^c} f(x) = \text{SUM}_{x_0^c} f(x)).$$

If $\phi(x)$ is of the form $\psi_0(x) \wedge \psi_1(x)$, then $\phi^*(f) := \psi_0^*(f) \wedge \psi_1^*(f)$.

If $\phi(x)$ is of the form $\psi_0(x) \vee \psi_1(x)$, then $\phi^*(f) := \psi_0^*(f) \vee \psi_1^*(f)$

$$\vee\, \Big( \exists pghk \big(\forall x \forall y (y = l \vee y = r \vee (p(y) = 0 \wedge k(x,y) = 0)) \tag{7}$$

$$\wedge\, \forall x (k(x,l) = g(x) \times p(l) \wedge k(x,r) = h(x) \times p(r)) \tag{8}$$

$$\wedge\, \forall x \, (\text{SUM}_y k(x,y) = f(x)) \wedge \psi_0^*(g) \wedge \psi_1^*(h)) \Big). \tag{9}$$

If $\phi(\boldsymbol{x})$ is $\exists y\psi(\boldsymbol{x}, y)$, then $\phi^*(f) := \exists g\big((\forall\boldsymbol{x}\, \mathrm{SUM}_y g(\boldsymbol{x}, y) = f(\boldsymbol{x})) \wedge \psi^*(g)\big)$.

If $\phi(\boldsymbol{x})$ is of the form $\forall y\psi(\boldsymbol{x}, y)$, then $\phi^*(f) :=$

$$\exists g\big(\forall\boldsymbol{x}(\forall y\forall z g(\boldsymbol{x}, y) = g(\boldsymbol{x}, z) \wedge \mathrm{SUM}_y g(\boldsymbol{x}, y) = f(\boldsymbol{x})) \wedge \psi^*(g)\big).$$

The claim now follows via a straightforward induction on the structure of the formula. The cases for first-order and dependency atoms, and likewise for conjunctions, follow directly from the semantical clauses.

The case for disjunctions requires a bit more care. First note that $l$ (left) and $r$ (right) denote distinct constant symbols than can be defined by $\exists l \exists r\, l \neq r$ in the beginning of the translation $*$. Recall that a probabilistic team $\mathbb{X}$ satisfies a disjunction $(\phi \vee \psi)$ if and only if $\mathbb{X}$ satisfies either $\phi$ or $\psi$, or there exists two nonempty probabilistic teams $\mathbb{Y}$ and $\mathbb{Z}$ and a ratio $q \in \mathbb{Q}_{[0,1]}$ such that $\mathbb{Y}$ satisfies $\phi$, $\mathbb{Z}$ satisfies $\psi$, and, for each assignment $s$, it holds that $\mathbb{X}(s) = q \cdot \mathbb{Y}(s) + (1 - q) \cdot \mathbb{Z}(s)$. In the translation, we encode the value of $q$ by $p(l)$ and $(1 - q)$ by $p(r)$. Line (7) expresses that $p$ is such a function. We use $k(s(\boldsymbol{x}), l)$ and $k(s(\boldsymbol{x}), r)$ to encode the values of $q \cdot \mathbb{Y}(s)$ and $(1 - q) \cdot \mathbb{Z}(s)$, respectively. Lines (7) and (8) together express that $k$ is such a function. Finally, the first part of line (9) expresses that $\forall s : \mathbb{X}(s) = q \cdot \mathbb{Y}(s) + (1 - q) \cdot \mathbb{Z}(s)$, whereas the latter part expresses that $\mathbb{Y}$ satisfies $\phi$, $\mathbb{Z}$ satisfies $\psi$.

The cases for the quantifiers follow directly by the semantical clauses.    $\square$

# 5 Translation from $\mathsf{ESOf}_{\mathbb{Q}}$ to $\mathsf{FO}(\perp\!\!\!\perp_c, \approx)$

In this section, we construct a translation from $\mathsf{ESOf}_{\mathbb{Q}}$ to $\mathsf{FO}(\perp\!\!\!\perp_c, \approx)$. The proof utilises the observation that independence atoms and marginal identity atoms can be used to express multiplication and SUM in $\mathbb{Q}_{[0,1]}$, respectively. The translation then relates $\mathsf{ESOf}_{\mathbb{Q}}$ sentences in a certain normal form, presented in Lemma 3, to open $\mathsf{FO}(\perp\!\!\!\perp_c, \approx)$ formulae. Before this, we start by stating a lemma which expresses that existential quantification of a constant probability distribution $d$ can be characterised in $\mathsf{FO}(\perp\!\!\!\perp_c, \approx)$. Given a probabilistic team $\mathbb{X} \colon X \to \mathbb{Q}_{[0,1]}$, a tuple $\boldsymbol{x} = (x_1, \ldots, x_n)$ of fresh variables, and a probability distribution $d \colon A^n \to \mathbb{Q}_{[0,1]}$, we denote by $\mathbb{X}[d/\boldsymbol{x}]$ the probabilistic team $\mathbb{Y}$ where $\mathbb{Y}(s(\boldsymbol{a}/\boldsymbol{x})) = \mathbb{X}(s) \cdot d(\boldsymbol{a})$ for all $s \in X$.

**Lemma 2.** *Let* $\phi(\boldsymbol{x}) := \exists \boldsymbol{y}(\boldsymbol{x} \perp\!\!\!\perp \boldsymbol{y} \wedge \psi(\boldsymbol{x}, \boldsymbol{y}))$ *be a* $\mathsf{FO}(\perp\!\!\!\perp_c, \approx)$-*formula with free variables from* $\boldsymbol{x} = (x_1, \ldots, x_n)$. *Then for all structures* $\mathfrak{A}$ *and probabilistic teams* $\mathbb{X} \colon X \to \mathbb{Q}_{[0,1]}$ *where* $\{x_1, \ldots, x_n\} \subseteq \mathrm{Dom}(X)$,

$$\mathfrak{A} \models_{\mathbb{X}} \phi \iff \mathfrak{A} \models_{\mathbb{X}[d/\boldsymbol{y}]} \psi \text{ for some } d \colon A^{|\boldsymbol{y}|} \to \mathbb{Q}_{[0,1]}.$$

*Proof.* By the locality principle (Proposition 2) $\mathfrak{A} \models_{\mathbb{X}} \phi$ if and only if $\mathfrak{A} \models_{\mathbb{X}\restriction\{x_1, \ldots, x_n\}} \phi$. Likewise it is straightforward to check that, for $d \colon A^{|\boldsymbol{y}|} \to \mathbb{Q}_{[0,1]}$

$$\mathfrak{A} \models_{\mathbb{X}[d/\boldsymbol{y}]} \psi \text{ if and only if } \mathfrak{A} \models_{\mathbb{X}\restriction\{x_1, \ldots, x_n\}[d/\boldsymbol{y}]} \psi,$$

since $\mathbb{X}[d/\boldsymbol{y}] \restriction \{x_1, \ldots, x_n, \boldsymbol{y}\} = \mathbb{X} \restriction \{x_1, \ldots, x_n\}[d/\boldsymbol{y}]$. Accordingly, we may assume without loss of generality, that $\mathrm{Dom}(X) = \{x_1, \ldots, x_n\}$.

Now $\mathfrak{A} \models_X \phi$ iff there is a function $F \colon X \to p_A$ such that $\mathfrak{A} \models_Y \boldsymbol{x} \perp\!\!\!\perp \boldsymbol{y} \wedge \psi(\boldsymbol{x}, \boldsymbol{y})$ where $\mathbb{Y} := \mathbb{X}[F/\boldsymbol{y}]$. Furthermore,

$$\mathfrak{A} \models_Y \boldsymbol{x} \perp\!\!\!\perp \boldsymbol{y} \text{ iff } |\mathbb{Y}_{\boldsymbol{x}\boldsymbol{y}=s(\boldsymbol{x})\boldsymbol{a}}| = |\mathbb{Y}_{\boldsymbol{x}=s(\boldsymbol{x})}| \cdot |\mathbb{Y}_{\boldsymbol{y}=\boldsymbol{a}}| \text{ for all } s \in X \text{ and } \boldsymbol{a} \in A^n.$$

Since $\mathrm{Dom}(X) = \{x_1, \ldots, x_n\}$, the right-hand side of the above is equivalent to

$$\mathbb{X}(s) \cdot F(s)(\boldsymbol{a}) = \mathbb{X}(s) \cdot |\mathbb{Y}_{\boldsymbol{y}=\boldsymbol{a}}| \text{ for all } s \in X \text{ and } \boldsymbol{a} \in A^n.$$

This is equivalent with saying that $\mathbb{X}[F/\boldsymbol{y}] = \mathbb{X}[d/\boldsymbol{y}]$ for some distribution $d \colon A^n \to \mathbb{Q}_{[0,1]}$. $\qquad\square$

Before proceeding to the translation, we construct the following normal form for ESOf$_\mathbb{Q}$ sentences.

**Lemma 3.** *Every ESOf$_\mathbb{Q}$ sentence $\phi$ is equivalent to a sentence $\phi^*$ of the form $\exists \boldsymbol{f} \forall \boldsymbol{x} \theta$, where $\theta$ is quantifier-free and such that its second sort identity atoms are of the form $f_i(\boldsymbol{uv}) = f_j(\boldsymbol{u}) \times f_k(\boldsymbol{v})$ or $f_i(\boldsymbol{u}) = \mathrm{SUM}_v f_j(\boldsymbol{uv})$ for distinct $f_i, f_j, f_k$ such that at most one of them is not quantified.*

*Proof.* First we define for each second sort term $i(\boldsymbol{x})$ a special formula $\theta_i$ defined recursively using fresh function symbols $f_i$ as follows:

- If $i(\boldsymbol{u})$ is $g(\boldsymbol{u})$ where $g$ is a function symbol, then $\theta_i$ is defined as $f_i(\boldsymbol{u}) = g(\boldsymbol{u})$. (We may intepret $g(\boldsymbol{u})$ as $\mathrm{SUM}_\emptyset g(\boldsymbol{u})$).
- If $i(\boldsymbol{uv})$ is $j(\boldsymbol{u}) \times k(\boldsymbol{v})$, then $\theta_i$ is defined as $\theta_j \wedge \theta_k \wedge f_i(\boldsymbol{uv}) = f_j(\boldsymbol{u}) \times f_k(\boldsymbol{v})$.
- If $i(\boldsymbol{u})$ is $\mathrm{SUM}_v j(\boldsymbol{uv})$, then $\theta_i$ is defined as $\theta_j \wedge f_i(\boldsymbol{u}) = \mathrm{SUM}_v f_j(\boldsymbol{uv})$.

The translation $\phi \mapsto \phi^*$ then proceeds recursively on the structure of $\phi$.

(i) If $\phi$ is $i(\boldsymbol{u}) = j(\boldsymbol{v})$, then $\phi^*$ is defined as $\exists \boldsymbol{f}(f_i(\boldsymbol{u}) = f_j(\boldsymbol{v}) \wedge \theta_i \wedge \theta_j)$ where $\boldsymbol{f}$ is lists the function symbols $f_k$ for each subterm $k$ of $i$ or $j$. If $\phi$ is $i(\boldsymbol{u}) \neq j(\boldsymbol{v})$, the translation is analogous.
(ii) If $\phi$ is an atom or negated atom of the first sort, then $\phi^* := \phi$.
(iii) If $\phi$ is $\psi_0 \circ \psi_1$ where $\circ \in \{\vee, \wedge\}$, $\psi_0^*$ is $\exists \boldsymbol{f}_0 \forall \boldsymbol{x}_0 \theta_0$, and $\psi_1^*$ is $\exists \boldsymbol{f}_1 \forall \boldsymbol{x}_1 \theta_1$, then $\phi_1^*$ is defined as $\exists \boldsymbol{f}_0 \boldsymbol{f}_1 \forall \boldsymbol{x}_0 \boldsymbol{x}_1 (\theta_0 \circ \theta_1)$.
(iv) If $\phi$ is $\exists y \psi$ where $\psi^*$ is $\exists \boldsymbol{f} \forall \boldsymbol{x} \theta$, then $\phi^*$ is defined as $\exists g \exists \boldsymbol{f} \forall \boldsymbol{x} \forall y (g(y) = 0 \vee \theta)$.
(v) If $\phi$ is $\forall y \psi$ where $\psi^*$ is $\exists \boldsymbol{f} \forall \boldsymbol{x} \theta$, then $\phi^*$ is defined as

$$\exists \boldsymbol{f}^* \exists \boldsymbol{f}_{\mathrm{id}} \exists d \forall y y' \forall \boldsymbol{x} (d(y) = d(y') \wedge \bigwedge_{f^* \in \boldsymbol{f}^*} \mathrm{SUM}_{\boldsymbol{x}} f^*(y, \boldsymbol{x}) = d(y) \wedge \theta^*)$$

where $\boldsymbol{f}^*$ is obtained from $\boldsymbol{f}$ by replacing each $f$ from $\boldsymbol{f}$ with $f^*$ such that $\mathrm{ar}(f^*) = \mathrm{ar}(f) + 1$, $\boldsymbol{f}_{\mathrm{id}}$ introduces new function symbol for each multiplication in $\theta$, and $\theta^*$ is obtained by replacing all second sort identities $\alpha$ of the form $f_i(\boldsymbol{uv}) = f_j(\boldsymbol{u}) \times f_k(\boldsymbol{v})$ with

$$f_\alpha(y, \boldsymbol{uv}) = d(y) \times f_i^*(y, \boldsymbol{uv}) \wedge f_\alpha(y, \boldsymbol{uv}) = f_j^*(y, \boldsymbol{u}) \times f_k^*(y, \boldsymbol{v})$$

and $f_i(\boldsymbol{u}) = \mathrm{SUM}_v f_j(\boldsymbol{uv})$ with $f_i^*(y, \boldsymbol{u}) = \mathrm{SUM}_v f_j^*(y, \boldsymbol{uv})$

(vi) If $\phi$ is $\exists f \psi$ where $\psi^*$ is $\exists \boldsymbol{f} \forall \boldsymbol{x} \theta$, then $\phi^*$ is defined as $\exists f \psi^*$.

It is straightforward to check that $\phi^*$ is of the correct form and equivalent to $\phi$. What happens in (v) is that instead of guessing for all $y$ some distribution $f_y$ with arity $\mathrm{ar}(f)$, we guess a single distribution $f^*$ with arity $\mathrm{ar}(f) + 1$ such that $f^*(y, \boldsymbol{u}) = \frac{1}{|A|} \cdot f_y(\boldsymbol{u})$ where $A$ is the underlying domain of the structure. This is described by the existential quantification of a unary uniform distribution $d$ such that for all fixed $y$, $\mathrm{SUM}_{\boldsymbol{u}} f^*(y, \boldsymbol{u})$ is $d(y)$. Then note that $f_y(\boldsymbol{u}) = g_y(\boldsymbol{u}') \cdot h_y(\boldsymbol{u}'')$ iff $\frac{1}{|A|} \cdot f^*(y, \boldsymbol{u}) = g^*(y, \boldsymbol{u}') \cdot h^*(y, \boldsymbol{u}'')$ iff $d(y) \cdot f^*(y, \boldsymbol{u}) = g^*(y, \boldsymbol{u}') \cdot h^*(y, \boldsymbol{u}'')$. For identities over SUM, the reasoning is analogous. $\qquad\square$

**Theorem 2.** *Let $\phi(p) \in \mathsf{ESOf}_\mathbb{Q}$ be a sentence of the form $\exists \boldsymbol{f} \forall \boldsymbol{x} \theta$ where $\theta$ is a quantifier-free $\mathsf{FOf}_\mathbb{Q}$ formula in which each second sort equality atom is of the form $f_i(\boldsymbol{x}_i) = f_j(\boldsymbol{x}_j) \times f_k(\boldsymbol{x}_k)$ or $f_i(\boldsymbol{x}_i) = \mathrm{SUM}_{\boldsymbol{x}_k} f_j(\boldsymbol{x}_k \boldsymbol{x}_j)$ for distinct $f_i, f_j, f_k$ from $\{f_1, \ldots, f_n\} \cup \{p\}$. Then there is a formula $\Phi \in \mathsf{FO}(\perp\!\!\!\perp_c, \approx)$ such that for all structures $\mathfrak{A}$ and probabilistic teams $\mathbb{X} := p^{\mathfrak{A}}$,*

$$\mathfrak{A} \models_{\mathbb{X}} \Phi \iff (\mathfrak{A}, p) \models \phi.$$

*Proof.* We define $\Phi$ as

$$\Phi := \forall \boldsymbol{x} \exists \boldsymbol{y}_1 \ldots \boldsymbol{y}_n (\Theta \wedge \Psi)$$

where $\boldsymbol{x} = (x_1, \ldots, x_m)$, $\boldsymbol{y}_i$ are sequences of variables of length $\mathrm{ar}(f_i)$, $\Theta$ is a compositional translation from $\theta$, and

$$\Psi := \bigwedge_{i=1}^{n} \boldsymbol{x} \boldsymbol{y}_1 \ldots \boldsymbol{y}_{i-1} \perp\!\!\!\perp \boldsymbol{y}_i. \tag{10}$$

By Lemma 2 it suffices to show that for all distributions $f_1, \ldots, f_n$, subsets $M \subseteq A^m$, and probabilistic teams $\mathbb{Y} = \mathbb{X}[M/\boldsymbol{x}][f_1/\boldsymbol{y}_1] \ldots [f_n/\boldsymbol{y}_n]$,

$$\mathfrak{A} \models_{\mathbb{Y}} \Theta \text{ iff } (\mathfrak{A}, p, f_1, \ldots, f_n) \models \theta(\boldsymbol{a}) \text{ for all } \boldsymbol{a} \in M. \tag{11}$$

We show the claim by structural induction on the construction of $\Theta$.

1. If $\theta$ is an atom of the first sort, it clearly suffices to let $\Theta = \theta$.
2. Assume $\theta$ is of the form $f_i(\boldsymbol{x}_i) = f_j(\boldsymbol{x}_j) \times f_k(\boldsymbol{x}_k)$. Then $\Theta$ is defined as

$$\Theta := \exists \alpha \beta \Big( (\alpha = 0 \leftrightarrow \boldsymbol{x}_i = \boldsymbol{y}_i) \wedge (\beta = 0 \leftrightarrow \boldsymbol{x}_j \boldsymbol{x}_k = \boldsymbol{y}_j \boldsymbol{y}_k) \wedge \boldsymbol{x} \alpha \approx \boldsymbol{x} \beta \Big).$$

Assume that $(\mathfrak{A}, p, f_1, \ldots, f_n) \models \theta(\boldsymbol{a})$ for any given $\boldsymbol{a} \in M$. Then we have $f_i(\boldsymbol{a}_i) = f_j(\boldsymbol{a}_j) \cdot f_k(\boldsymbol{a}_k)$. We define functions $F_\alpha, F_\beta \colon \mathbb{Y} \to \{0, 1\}$ so that $F_\alpha(s) = 0$ iff $s(\boldsymbol{x}_i) = s(\boldsymbol{y}_i)$, and $F_\beta(s) = 0$ iff $s(\boldsymbol{x}_j \boldsymbol{x}_k) = s(\boldsymbol{x}_j \boldsymbol{x}_k)$. It suffices to show that $\mathfrak{A} \models_{\mathbb{Z}} \boldsymbol{x} \alpha \approx \boldsymbol{x} \beta$ where $\mathbb{Z} = \mathbb{Y}[F_\alpha/\alpha][F_\beta/\beta]$. By the construction of $\mathbb{Z}$, we have $|\mathbb{Z}_{\boldsymbol{x}\alpha = \boldsymbol{a}0}| = |\mathbb{Z}_{\boldsymbol{x}\boldsymbol{y}_i = \boldsymbol{a}\boldsymbol{a}_i}| = |\mathbb{Y}_{\boldsymbol{x}=\boldsymbol{a}}| \cdot f_i(\boldsymbol{a}_i)$. Similarly, and using the hypothesis, we have $|\mathbb{Z}_{\boldsymbol{x}\beta = \boldsymbol{a}0}| = |\mathbb{Z}_{\boldsymbol{x}\boldsymbol{y}_j\boldsymbol{y}_k = \boldsymbol{a}\boldsymbol{a}_j\boldsymbol{a}_k}| = |\mathbb{Y}_{\boldsymbol{x}=\boldsymbol{a}}| \cdot f_j(\boldsymbol{a}_j) \cdot f_k(\boldsymbol{a}_k) = |\mathbb{Y}_{\boldsymbol{x}=\boldsymbol{a}}| \cdot f_i(\boldsymbol{a}_i)$. Furthermore, since we have $|\mathbb{Z}_{\boldsymbol{x}\alpha = \boldsymbol{a}1}| = |\mathbb{Y}_{\boldsymbol{x}=\boldsymbol{a}}| \cdot (1 - f_i(\boldsymbol{a}_i)) = |\mathbb{Z}_{\boldsymbol{x}\beta = \boldsymbol{a}1}|$, it follows that $\mathfrak{A} \models_{\mathbb{Y}} \Theta$.

Assume $\mathfrak{A} \models_{\mathbb{Y}} \Theta$, and let $\mathbb{Z}$ be the extension of $\mathbb{Y}$ to $\alpha, \beta$ where $\mathbb{Z}_{\alpha=0} = \mathbb{Z}_{x_i=y_i}$ and $\mathbb{Z}_{\beta=0} = \mathbb{Z}_{x_j x_k = y_j y_k}$. Then $\mathfrak{A} \models_{\mathbb{Z}} x\alpha \approx x\beta$ since $|\mathbb{Y}_{x=a}| \cdot f_i(a_i) = |\mathbb{Y}_{x=a}| \cdot |\mathbb{Y}_{y_i=a_i}| = |\mathbb{Y}_{xy_i=aa_i}| = |\mathbb{Y}_{xx_i=ay_i}| = |\mathbb{Z}_{x\alpha=a0}| = |\mathbb{Z}_{x\beta=a0}| = |\mathbb{Y}_{xx_j x_k=ay_j y_k}| = |\mathbb{Y}_{xy_j y_k=aa_j a_k}| = |\mathbb{Y}_{x=a}| \cdot |\mathbb{Y}_{y_j=a_j}| \cdot |\mathbb{Y}_{y_k=a_k}| = |\mathbb{Y}_{x=a}| \cdot f_j(a_j) \cdot f_k(a_k)$ for all $a \in M$.

3. Assume $\theta$ is of the form $f_i(x_i) = \text{SUM}_{x_k} f_j(x_k x_j)$. We define $\Theta$ as

$$\Theta := \exists \alpha \beta \big( (\alpha = 0 \leftrightarrow x_i = y_i) \wedge (\beta = 0 \leftrightarrow x_j = y_j) \wedge x\alpha \approx x\beta \big).$$

Assume that $(\mathfrak{A}, p, f_1, \ldots, f_n) \models \theta(a)$ for any given $a \in M$. Then $f_i(a_i) = \text{SUM}_{x_k} f_j(x_k a_j)$. We define functions $F_\alpha, F_\beta \colon Y \to \{0, 1\}$ such that $F_\alpha(s) = 0$ iff $s(x_i) = s(y_i)$, and $F_\beta(s) = 0$ iff $s(x_j) = s(y_j)$. Then $\mathfrak{A} \models_{\mathbb{Z}} x\alpha \approx x\beta$ because $|\mathbb{Z}_{x\alpha=a0}| = |\mathbb{Y}_{xx_i=ay_i}| = |\mathbb{Y}_{xy_i=aa_i}| = |\mathbb{Y}_{x=a}| \cdot f_i(a_i) = |\mathbb{Y}_{x=a}| \cdot \text{SUM}_{x_k} f_j(x_k a_j) = |\mathbb{Y}_{x=a}| \cdot |\mathbb{Y}_{y_j=a_j}| = |\mathbb{Y}_{xy_j=aa_j}| = |\mathbb{Y}_{xx_j=ay_j}| = |\mathbb{Z}_{x\beta=a0}|$. Furthermore, since $|\mathbb{Z}_{x\alpha=a1}| = |\mathbb{Z}_{x\beta=a1}|$ it follows that $\mathfrak{A} \models_{\mathbb{Y}} \Theta$. Assume that $\mathfrak{A} \models_{\mathbb{Y}} \Theta$, and let $\mathbb{Z}$ be the extension of $\mathbb{Y}$ to $\alpha, \beta$ where $\mathbb{Z}_{\alpha=0} = \mathbb{Z}_{x_i=y_i}$ and $\mathbb{Z}_{\beta=0} = \mathbb{Z}_{x_j=y_j}$. Analogously to the previous case, we obtain $\mathfrak{A} \models_{\mathbb{Z}} x\alpha \approx x\beta$ since $|\mathbb{Y}_{x=a}| \cdot f_i(a_i) = |\mathbb{Z}_{x\alpha=a0}| = |\mathbb{Z}_{x\beta=a0}| = |\mathbb{Y}_{xy_j=aa_j}| = |\mathbb{Y}_{x=a}| \cdot |\mathbb{Y}_{y_j=a_j}| = |\mathbb{Y}_{x=a}| \cdot \text{SUM}_{x_k} f_j(a_j)$ for all $a \in M$.

4. Assume $\theta$ is $\theta_0 \wedge \theta_1$. Then we let $\Theta := \Theta_0 \wedge \Theta_1$, and the claim follows by a straightforward argument.

5. Assume $\theta$ is $\theta_0 \vee \theta_1$. Then we let

$$\Theta := \exists z \Big( z \perp\!\!\!\perp_x z \wedge (\Theta_0 \wedge z = 0) \vee (\Theta_1 \wedge \neg z = 0) \Big).$$

Assume $(\mathfrak{A}, p, f_1, \ldots, f_n) \models \theta_0 \vee \theta_1$ for all $a \in M$. Then we find $M_0 \cup M_1 = M$, $M_0 \cap M_1 = \emptyset$, such that $(\mathfrak{A}, p, f_1, \ldots, f_n) \models \theta_i$ for all $a \in M_i$. We define $F : Y \to p_A$ so that $F_z(s) = c_i$ if $s(x) \in M_i$; by $c_i$ we denote the distribution

$$c_i(a) := \begin{cases} 1 & \text{if } a = i, \\ 0 & \text{otherwise.} \end{cases}$$

Letting $\mathbb{Z}_i = \mathbb{X}[M_i/x][f_1/y_1] \ldots [f_n/y_n][c_i/z]$, it follows that $\mathbb{Z} = \mathbb{Y}[F/z] = \mathbb{Z}_0 \sqcup_k \mathbb{Z}_1$ for $k = \frac{M_0}{M}$. By the induction hypothesis $\mathfrak{A} \models_{\mathbb{Z}_i} \Theta_i$, and accordingly $\mathfrak{A} \models_{\mathbb{Z}_i} \Theta_0 \wedge z_i$. Since $\mathfrak{A} \models_{\mathbb{Z}} z \perp\!\!\!\perp_x z$, we obtain by Proposition 2 that $\mathfrak{A} \models_{\mathbb{Y}} \Theta$. Assume $\mathfrak{A} \models_{\mathbb{Y}} \Theta$, and let $F : Y \to p_A$ be such that $\mathfrak{A} \models_{\mathbb{Z}} z \perp\!\!\!\perp_x z \wedge ((\Theta_0 \wedge z = 0) \vee (\Theta_1 \wedge \neg z = 0))$ for $\mathbb{Z} = \mathbb{Y}[F/z]$. Consequently, $\mathfrak{A} \models_{\mathbb{Z}_0'} \Theta_0$ and $\mathfrak{A} \models_{\mathbb{Z}_1'} \Theta_1$ where $k\mathbb{Z}_0' = \mathbb{Z}_{z=0}$ and $(1-k)\mathbb{Z}_1' = \mathbb{Z}_{z=1}$ for $k = |\mathbb{Z}_{z=0}|$. Since $\mathbb{Z}$ satisfies $z \perp\!\!\!\perp_x z$, we have furthermore that either $\mathbb{Z}_{x=a} = \mathbb{Z}_{xz=a0}$ or $\mathbb{Z}_{x=a} = \mathbb{Z}_{xz=a1}$ for all $a \in M$. This entails that $\mathbb{Z}_{z=0} = \mathbb{Z}_{x \in M_0}$ for some $M_0 \subseteq M$. Therefore, $\mathbb{Z}_0' = \frac{|M|}{|M_0|}(\mathbb{X}[M/x][f_1/y_1] \ldots [f_n/y_n])_{x \in M_0} = \mathbb{X}[M_0/x][f_1/y_1] \ldots [f_n/y_n]$. By the induction hypothesis, we then obtain $(\mathfrak{A}, p, f_1, \ldots, f_n) \models \theta_0$ for all $a \in M_0$, and by analogous reasoning that $(\mathfrak{A}, p, f_1, \ldots, f_n) \models \theta_1$ for all $a \in M \setminus M_0$. Consequently, $(\mathfrak{A}, p, f_1, \ldots, f_n) \models \theta$ for all $a \in M$ which concludes the proof. $\qquad \square$

# 6 Complexity of FO($\approx$) in Multiteams vs. Probabilistic Teams

One of the fundamental results in logics in team semantics state that, in contrast to dependence and independence logics that correspond to existential second-order logic (accordingly, NP), the expressivity of inclusion logic equals only that of positive greatest fixed-point logic and thus PTIME over finite ordered models [6,7,20]. In this section, we consider the complexity of FO($\approx$) that can be thought of as a probabilistic variant of inclusion logic. We present a formula $\phi \in$ FO($\approx$) which captures an NP-complete property of multiteams (the example works under both strict and lax semantics introduced by Durand et al. [3]). The possibility of expressing similar properties in probabilistic teams is left open. It is worth noting that our reduction is similar to the ones presented for quantifier-free dependence and independence logic formulae under team semantics [2,17] (see also the recent survey on complexity aspects of logics in team semantics [4]).

The following example relates FO($\approx$) to the exact cover problem, a well-known NP-complete problem [9]. Given a collection $S$ of subsets of a set $A$, an *exact cover* is a subcollection $S^*$ of $S$ such that each element in $A$ is contained in exactly one subset in $S^*$.

| Multiteam $\mathcal{X}$ | | | | | Probabilistic team X | | | | | | |
|---|---|---|---|---|---|---|---|---|---|---|---|
| element | set | left | right | $\mathcal{X}(s)$ | element | set | left | right | X($s$) | Y | Z |
| 0 | $S_1$ | 1 | 2 | 1 | 0 | $S_1$ | 1 | 2 | 1/10 | 1/2 | 1/2 |
| 0 | $S_1$ | 2 | 3 | 1 | 0 | $S_1$ | 2 | 1 | 1/10 | 1/2 | 1/2 |
| 0 | $S_1$ | 3 | 1 | 1 | 0 | $S_2$ | 2 | 3 | 1/10 | 1/2 | 1/2 |
| 0 | $S_2$ | 2 | 2 | 1 | 0 | $S_2$ | 3 | 2 | 1/10 | 1/2 | 1/2 |
| 0 | $S_3$ | 1 | 3 | 1 | 0 | $S_3$ | 3 | 1 | 1/10 | 1/2 | 1/2 |
| 0 | $S_3$ | 3 | 4 | 1 | 0 | $S_3$ | 1 | 3 | 1/10 | 1/2 | 1/2 |
| 0 | $S_3$ | 4 | 1 | 1 | 1 | 0 | 0 | 0 | 1/10 | | 1 |
| 1 | 0 | 0 | 0 | 1 | 2 | 0 | 0 | 0 | 1/10 | | 1 |
| 2 | 0 | 0 | 0 | 1 | 3 | 0 | 0 | 0 | 1/10 | | 1 |
| 3 | 0 | 0 | 0 | 1 | 4 | 0 | 0 | 0 | 1/10 | | 1 |
| 4 | 0 | 0 | 0 | 1 | | | | | | | |

**Fig. 3.** A multiteam $\mathcal{X}$ and a probabilistic team X

*Example 6.* Consider an exact cover problem over $A = \{1,2,3,4\}$ and $S = \{S_1 = \{1,2,3\}, S_2 = \{2\}, S_4 = \{1,3,4\}\}$. We construct a multiteam $\mathcal{X}$ as follows. The multiteam $\mathcal{X}$, depicted in Fig. 3, is a constant function mapping all assignments to 1. For each element $i$ of a subset $S_j$, we create an assignment that maps element to 0, set to $s_j$, left to $i$, and right to the next element in $S_j$ (under some ordering). Also, if $S_j = \{i\}$, then right is mapped to $i$. In our example case these assignments appear above the solid line of the multiteam $\mathcal{X}$ in Fig. 3. Furthermore, for each element $i$ of $A$ we create an assignment that maps element to $i$ and all other variables to 0. The answer to the exact cover problem is then positive iff $\mathcal{X}$ satisfies

$$\phi := \mathtt{set} \neq 0 \lor (\mathtt{element} \approx \mathtt{left} \land \mathtt{set}, \mathtt{right} \approx \mathtt{set}, \mathtt{left}). \tag{12}$$

Note that since $\phi$ consists only of variables and connectives, we do not need to concern structures; we write $\mathcal{X} \models \phi$ instead of $\mathfrak{A} \models_{\mathcal{X}} \phi$. Now $\mathcal{X} \models \phi$ if and only if $\mathcal{Z} \models \mathtt{set} \neq 0$ and $\mathcal{Y} \models \mathtt{element} \approx \mathtt{left} \land \mathtt{set}, \mathtt{right} \approx \mathtt{set}, \mathtt{left}$, for some $\mathcal{Z}, \mathcal{Y}$ such that $\mathcal{Z} \uplus \mathcal{Y} = \mathcal{X}$. Note that any subset of the assignments above the solid line in Fig. 3 satisfy $\mathtt{set} \neq 0$ and could be a priori assigned to $\mathcal{Z}$. Note also that all of the assignments below the solid line must be assigned to the team $\mathcal{Y}$. Henceforth, the conjunct $\mathtt{element} \approx \mathtt{left}$ forces to select assignments from above the solid line to $\mathcal{Y}$ exactly one assignment for each element of $A$. Then $\mathtt{set}, \mathtt{right} \approx \mathtt{set}, \mathtt{left}$ enforces that this selection either subsumes a subset $S_i$ or does not intersect it at all. In the example case, we can select the segments that corresponds to sets $S_1$ and $S_2$.

The same reduction does not work for probabilistic teams. The probabilistic team X in Fig. 3 corresponds to the exact cover problem defined over $A = \{1, 2, 3\}$ and $\mathcal{S} = \{S_1 = \{1, 2\}, S_2 = \{2, 3\}, S_4 = \{3, 1\}\}$. This instance does not admit an exact cover. However, for satisfaction of (12) by X, taking half weights of the upper part for Y and all the remaining weights for Z, we have $\mathfrak{A} \models_{\mathrm{Y}} \mathtt{set} \neq 0$ and $\mathfrak{A} \models_{\mathrm{Z}} \mathtt{element} \approx \mathtt{left} \land \mathtt{set}, \mathtt{right} \approx \mathtt{set}, \mathtt{left}$ where $\mathbb{X} = \mathbb{Y} \sqcup_k \mathbb{Z}$ for $k = \frac{3}{10}$.

It is straightforward to generalise the previous example to obtain the following result.

**Corollary 1.** *Data complexity of the quantifier-free fragment of* $\mathsf{FO}(\approx)$ *under multiteam semantics is NP-hard. This remains true for very simple fragments as* $\mathtt{set} \neq 0 \lor (\mathtt{element} \approx \mathtt{left} \land \mathtt{set}, \mathtt{right} \approx \mathtt{set}, \mathtt{left})$ *is such a formula for which model checking is hard for NP.*

The obvious brute force algorithm gives inclusion to NP.

**Theorem 3.** *Data complexities of* $\mathsf{FO}(\approx)$ *and the quantifier-free fragment of* $\mathsf{FO}(\approx)$ *under multiteam semantics are NP-complete.*

## 7    Conclusion

In this article, we have initiated a systematic study of probabilistic team semantics. Some features of our semantics have been discussed in the literature but the logic $\mathsf{FO}(\perp\!\!\!\perp_c, \approx)$ has not been studied before in the probabilistic framework. Probabilistic logics with team semantics have already been applied in the context of so-called Bell's Inequalities of quantum mechanics [15]. On the other hand, our work is in part motivated by the study of implication problems of database and probabilistic dependencies. Independence logic has recently been used to give a finite axiomatisation for the implication problem of independence atoms (i.e., EMVD's) and inclusion dependencies [12]. It is an interesting open question to apply our probabilistic logic to analyse the implication problem of conditional independence statements whose exact complexity is still open [11, 21].

**Acknowledgements.** The second author was supported by grant 3711702 of the Marsden Fund. The third author was supported by grant 308712 of the Academy of Finland. This work was supported in part by the joint grant by the DAAD (57348395) and the Academy of Finland (308099). We also thank the anonymous referees for their helpful suggestions.

# References

1. Corander, J., Hyttinen, A., Kontinen, J., Pensar, J., Väänänen, J.: A logical approach to context-specific independence. In: Väänänen, J., Hirvonen, Å., de Queiroz, R. (eds.) WoLLIC 2016. LNCS, vol. 9803, pp. 165–182. Springer, Heidelberg (2016). https://doi.org/10.1007/978-3-662-52921-8_11
2. Durand, A., Kontinen, J., de Rugy-Altherre, N., Väänänen, J.: Tractability frontier of data complexity in team semantics. In: Proceedings of GandALF 2015 (2015)
3. Durand, A., Hannula, M., Kontinen, J., Meier, A., Virtema, J.: Approximation and dependence via multiteam semantics. In: Gyssens, M., Simari, G. (eds.) FoIKS 2016. LNCS, vol. 9616, pp. 271–291. Springer, Cham (2016). https://doi.org/10.1007/978-3-319-30024-5_15
4. Durand, A., Kontinen, J., Vollmer, H.: Expressivity and complexity of dependence logic. In: Abramsky, S., Kontinen, J., Väänänen, J., Vollmer, H. (eds.) Dependence Logic: Theory and Applications, pp. 5–32. Springer, Cham (2016). https://doi.org/10.1007/978-3-319-31803-5_2
5. Galliani, P.: Probabilistic dependence logic. Manuscript (2008)
6. Galliani, P.: Inclusion and exclusion dependencies in team semantics - on some logics of imperfect information. Ann. Pure Appl. Log. **163**(1), 68–84 (2012)
7. Galliani, P., Hella, L.: Inclusion logic and fixed point logic. In: Proceedings of the CSL, pp. 281–295 (2013)
8. Galliani, P., Mann, A.L.: Lottery semantics: a compositional semantics for probabilistic first-order logic with imperfect information. Stud. Log. **101**(2), 293–322 (2013)
9. Garey, M.R., Johnson, D.S.: Computers and Intractability; A Guide to the Theory of NP-Completeness. W. H. Freeman & Co., New York (1990)
10. Grädel, E., Väänänen, J.A.: Dependence and independence. Stud. Log. **101**(2), 399–410 (2013)
11. Gyssens, M., Niepert, M., Gucht, D.V.: On the completeness of the semigraphoid axioms for deriving arbitrary from saturated conditional independence statements. Inf. Process. Lett. **114**(11), 628–633 (2014)
12. Hannula, M., Kontinen, J.: A finite axiomatization of conditional independence and inclusion dependencies. Inf. Comput. **249**, 121–137 (2016)
13. Hannula, M., Kontinen, J., Link, S.: On the finite and general implication problems of independence atoms and keys. J. Comput. Syst. Sci. **82**(5), 856–877 (2016)
14. Hodges, W.: Compositional semantics for a language of imperfect information. Log. J. IGPL **5**(4), 539–563 (1997). Electronic
15. Hyttinen, T., Paolini, G., Väänänen, J.: Quantum team logic and Bell's inequalities. Rev. Symb. Log., 1–21 (2015). FirstView
16. Hyttinen, T., Paolini, G., Väänänen, J.: A logic for arguing about probabilities in measure teams. Arch. Math. Log. **56**(5–6), 475–489 (2017)
17. Kontinen, J.: Coherence and computational complexity of quantifier-free dependence logic formulas. Stud. Log. **101**(2), 267–291 (2013)

18. Kontinen, J., Link, S., Väänänen, J.: Independence in database relations. In: Libkin, L., Kohlenbach, U., de Queiroz, R. (eds.) WoLLIC 2013. LNCS, vol. 8071, pp. 179–193. Springer, Heidelberg (2013). https://doi.org/10.1007/978-3-642-39992-3_17
19. Sevenster, M., Sandu, G.: Equilibrium semantics of languages of imperfect information. Ann. Pure Appl. Log. **161**(5), 618–631 (2010)
20. Väänänen, J.: Dependence Logic - A New Approach to Independence Friendly Logic. London Mathematical Society Student Texts, vol. 70. Cambridge University Press, Cambridge (2007)
21. Wong, S.K.M., Butz, C.J., Wu, D.: On the implication problem for probabilistic conditional independency. IEEE Trans. Syst. Man Cybern. Part A Syst. Hum. **30**(6), 785–805 (2000)

# Strategic Dialogical Argumentation Using Multi-criteria Decision Making with Application to Epistemic and Emotional Aspects of Arguments

Emmanuel Hadoux[1]([✉]), Anthony Hunter[1], and Jean-Baptiste Corrégé[2]

[1] Department of Computer Science, University College London, London, UK
{e.hadoux,anthony.hunter}@ucl.ac.uk
[2] LIMSI, CNRS, Université Paris-Saclay, 91405 Orsay, France
jean-baptiste.correge@limsi.fr

**Abstract.** Participants in dialogical argumentation often make strategic choices of move, for example to maximize the probability that they will persuade the other opponents. Multiple dimensions of information about the other agents (*e.g.*, the belief and likely emotional response that the other agents might have in the arguments) might be used to make this strategic choice. To support this, we present a framework with implementation for multi-criteria decision making for strategic argumentation. We provide methods to improve the computational viability of the framework, and analyze these methods theoretically and empirically. We finally present decision rules supported by the psychology literature and evidence using human experiments.

## 1 Introduction

In dialogical argumentation, a proponent can use strategic choices of argument when arguing with an opponent. In particular, when the number of moves is limited, the proponent needs to choose arguments that are more likely to be effective rather than exhaustively presenting all arguments. Consider for example, a doctor trying to persuade a patient to give up smoking. The doctor cannot expect the patient to have a discussion with hundreds of arguments and counterarguments being presented. Rather, the doctor has to think of what arguments and counterargument the patient believes, what arguments may have an emotional impact on the patient, etc., and then the doctor has to choose a line of argumentation that may be concluded with a relatively small number of arguments being presented by either side.

Most proposals for dialogical argumentation focus on protocols (*e.g.*, [1–4]) with strategies being under-developed. See [5] for a review of strategies in multi-agent argumentation. Strategies in argumentation have been analyzed using game theory (*e.g.*, [6,7]), but these are more concerned with issues of manipulation rather than persuasion. There are also proposals for using probability

© Springer International Publishing AG, part of Springer Nature 2018
F. Ferrarotti and S. Woltran (Eds.): FoIKS 2018, LNCS 10833, pp. 207–224, 2018.
https://doi.org/10.1007/978-3-319-90050-6_12

theory to, for instance, select a move based on what an agent believes the other is aware of [8], or, approximately predict the argument an opponent might put forward based on an history [9]. The problem can also be viewed as a probabilistic finite state machine, and generalized to POMDPs when there is uncertainty on the internal state of the opponent [10]. In [11], a planning system is used by the persuader to optimize choice of arguments based on belief in premises. But, none of these developments have systematically harnessed established notions in decision theory for maximizing the outcome of a dialogue.

To address this, Hadoux and Hunter [12] propose a general framework for representing persuasion dialogues as a decision tree, and for using decision rules such as MaxiMin for selecting moves. This is useful if we can focus on one dimension for modelling a user, such as her belief in the arguments, but it does not allow us to take into account multiple dimensions, and yet, multiple dimensions are often desirable. For instance, a user may want to maximize both the belief and appeal in an argument. In this paper, we will present a general framework for representing persuasion dialogues as a decision tree, and use multi-criteria decision making for computing an optimal policy. We will illustrate the use of these multiple dimensions by considering belief in arguments, and the emotional response evoked by arguments. For the latter, we draw on an established results from psychology for modelling emotional response in terms of valence (*i.e.*, polarity), arousal (*i.e.*, intensity) and dominance (*i.e.*, degree of feeling in control) invoked by an argument.

We proceed as follows: we review basic definitions for dialogical argumentation in Sect. 2; then in Sect. 3 we take emotional effect of arguments into account. We review decision trees and multi-criteria decision making for modelling argumentation dialogues in Sect. 4. We instantiate the multi-criteria decision making theory on multi-dimensional problems with emotions in Sect. 5. In Sect. 6 we specify size-reduction features to improve space efficiency and present some theoretical results concerning them. Sections 7 and 8 present both computational empirical results concerning the implementation and results on human experiments to validate our choice of decision rules. Finally, we discuss our contributions in Sect. 9.

## 2    Preliminaries

A *persuader* (the proponent) has a dialogue with a *persuadee* (the opponent) to make her believe (or disbelieve) some combination of arguments as a goal (*e.g.*, to do more exercise or to eat healthier food). We see that normally getting a persuadee to believe arguments is a prerequisite in the persuasion process.

For the sake of simplicity, in this paper, we deal with two agents and a singleton persuasion goal (*i.e.*, an individual argument as goal). However, our work can be extended to more agents and goals as long as only one persuader is involved. Building upon Dung's [13] abstract argumentation, a dialogue concerns an argument graph $G$ without self-attacks where $\mathsf{Args}(G)$ is the set of arguments in $G$, and $\mathsf{Attacks}(G)$ is the set of attack relations in $G$. We do not consider self-attacks in this work as we are concerned with applications where we assume participants do not present self-contradictory statements. For real applications, this restriction is often not important.

More formally, a *persuasion dialogue* is a sequence of moves $D = [m_1, \ldots, m_h]$. In this work, a move consists in positing an argument $A \in \mathsf{Args}(G)$. The attacks to and from this argument in relation to the arguments already posited come from the original graph. The parameter $h$ is the *horizon* of the debate, *i.e.*, the maximum number of moves that can be played. It is justified by the need to keep the persuadee engaged. A shorter debate (*i.e.*, a smaller value for $h$) gives more chance to keep the persuadee in the debate until the end. However, it also lowers the number of ways to make a valid point.

Each odd (resp. even) move in the dialogue is a persuader (resp. persuadee) move. However, the persuadee moves are played with respect to the arguments she believes, in reaction to the persuader positing an argument. Therefore, an efficient strategy needs to take into account the possible subsets of arguments the persuadee believes. Indeed, an agent is unlikely to posit arguments she does not have faith in. To that end, the persuader keeps and updates a *belief model* of the persuadee and uses it in her decision process. We use the epistemic approach to probabilistic argumentation [14–17], defining a model as an assignment in the unit interval to each argument where for an argument $A$, $B(A) > 0.5$ represents $A$ is believed to some degree, $B(A) = 0.5$ represents $A$ is neither believed nor disbelieved, and $B(A) < 0.5$ represents $A$ is disbelieved to some degree.

## 3    Taking Emotion into Account

In addition to belief, the emotions invoked by arguments are important to take into account since they affect the way the argument is perceived by the persuadee. Emotions are the result of how an individual appraises a stimulus [18]. According to [19], appraisal is a cognitive process composed of a number of checks aimed at categorizing a stimulus: is it relevant, what does it imply, do I have the potential to cope and is it socially significant?

This process and the various patterns of checks generate different cognitive responses and coping strategies. These strategies in turn affect the way information is processed [20]. For example, guilt leads to the use of active strategies focused on repairing the wrong made, whereas shame leads to the use of more passive strategies focused on the self. Combined with gain-loss framing [21], the emotion conveyed by an argument can be used to increase the persuasiveness of this argument. Duhachek et al. [20] developed a study in which they tested different argument configurations, varying the emotional tone of the argument (guilt v. shame) and the framing of the argument (gain v. loss). The results showed that a positively-framed message associated with guilt ("What you have to gain by drinking responsibly") is processed more fluently than a negatively-framed message associated with guilt ("What you have to lose by not drinking responsibly").

While Ekman [22] considered only 6 basic emotions (anger, disgust, fear, happiness, sadness and surprise), the definition and characterization of emotions

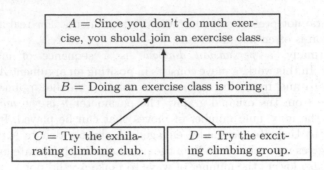

A = Since you don't do much exercise, you should join an exercise class.

B = Doing an exercise class is boring.

C = Try the exhilarating climbing club.

D = Try the exciting climbing group.

**Fig. 1.** Example of an argument graph.

has been widely discussed in psychology. Emotions in argumentation have also been investigated recently using logic and sets of discrete emotions (see, *e.g.*, [23–25]).

In this paper, we propose to focus on affective norm as used in the database built by Bradley and Lang [26]. These capture the emotional response to specific words in three dimensions: arousal (ranging from excited to calm), valence (pleasant to unpleasant), and dominance (from being in control to being dominated). For example, for valence scores, *leukemia* and *murder* are low and *sunshine* and *lovable* are high; for arousal scores, *grain* and *dull* are low and *lover* and *terrorism* are high; and for dominance scores, *dementia* and *earthquake* are low, and *smile* and *completion* are high. There are a number of databases for affective norms, and they have been used in diverse studies of emotion, behaviour, and language processing.

In this work, we draw on this psychological research into affective norms to evaluate the emotion invoked by particular choices of word in an argument. We determine an emotional scoring of arguments taken from a recent effective norm database that has nearly 14 thousand words [27]. Each word in the database has been scored by around 20 participants using crowdsourcing. Scores are also given according to gender, age group, and educational background.

By determining the emotion likely to be invoked by different candidates for a posit, strategic choices can be made by the persuader. To illustrate, consider the argument graph given in Fig. 1. Suppose the persuader wants to persuade the persuadee with argument $A$. If the other agent does not believe $A$ and believes $B$, the persuader can posit either $C$ or $D$ as counterarguments to $B$. By taking into account the score for affective norms for words in the arguments, the persuader can determine a three-dimensional score for each of $C$ and $D$ according to the gender, age group, and educational background of the persuadee, or on the whole population, and thereby make a choice of which of $C$ and $D$ to present.

The literature has focused essentially on valence and arousal, and demonstrated that these two dimensions interact with each other [28–30]. Eder and Rothermund [28], in particular, showed that words with a positive valence were treated faster when their arousal level was low than when it was high. Conversely, words with a negative valence were treated faster when their arousal level was high. This means that negative valence combined with high arousal allows for a more efficient cognitive processing than negative valence with low arousal, and conversely for positive valence. In this work, we are dealing with superficial interactions limited to the exchange of several arguments. They do not necessarily mean that the persuadee puts a lot of effort into processing the arguments. So following the psychology literature, we aim at using arguments that will be treated faster and thereby have more impact on the persuadee.

Psychology classically considers arousal as an interval reflecting the intensity of the stimulus and ranging from null to extreme, *i.e.*, from 0 to a positive value. In this case, an argument with a low arousal level should be treated more fluently. However, the affective norm considers arousal as a bipolar scale ranging from calmness to excitation, *i.e.*, from $-1$ to 1. In this case, calmness does not correspond to a null intensity of arousal but rather to a positive value on a parallel scale. In other words, in classical psychology, there is a scale from 0 to $n$ for degree of calmness with $n$ being the maximum calmness, and there is a scale from 0 to $n$ for degree of excitation with $n$ being the maximum excitation. Therefore, the middle point in the bipolar scale (*i.e.*, 0) corresponds to a state of unarousal (*i.e.*, it corresponds to 0 on each of the classical scales). As we use the affective norm databases in this paper [26,27], understanding this correspondence is important for the decision rules we present. So instead of minimizing the arousal, we are looking to neutralize it and thus select arguments with an arousal value as close to the midpoint of the bipolar scale as possible. Note, that the values in the affective norm databases are strictly positive but are meant to be rescaled into the $[-1,1]$ interval.

# 4 Decision Making for Dialogues

In order to get the persuadee to accept the persuasion goal, the persuader has to posit the right sequence of arguments with respect to the persuadee.

## 4.1 Decision Trees

Recently, Hadoux and Hunter [12] proposed a framework able to compute an optimal policy by taking into account every possible sequence of arguments using a *decision tree*. A decision tree represents all the possible combinations of decisions and outcomes of a sequential decision-making problem. In a problem with two agents, a path from the root to any leaf crosses alternatively nodes associated with the proponent (called *decision nodes* in this work) and nodes associated with the opponent (called *chance nodes* or *nature nodes*). In the case of a dialogue represented as a decision tree, a path is one possible permutation of the argument set, *i.e.*, one possible complete dialogue between the two agents. If horizon $h$ is smaller than the number of arguments, every execution (and thus path) is at most of length $h$. In this case, it is a permutation of a subset of the argument set. An edge between any two nodes $n$ and $n'$ in the tree is the decision that has to be taken by the corresponding agent in order to transition from node $n$ to node $n'$. Solving a problem modelled as a decision tree amounts to computing a *policy*, an action to perform (*i.e.*, an argument to posit) in each possible state of the dialogue.

However, Hadoux and Hunter [12] evaluate branches by averaging the values and using mono-criterion decision rules. In order, to handle multiple dimensions such as belief and emotion, we evaluate branches using multi-criteria decision making (see next subsection).

Note, for this paper, we assume that the opponent is not using a model of the proponent. Rather, she is selecting what she deems as the best arguments according to what she believes and regards as a strong emotional effect. This means we assume that the opponent is not behaving stochastically nor strategically, in particular not adversarially.

This is a reasonable assumption for some applications such as where the opponent is being co-operative or at least not being competitive. Consider for example, a proponent being a doctor trying to persuade a patient to eat more healthily. The doctor is thinking strategically because she wants to persuade the patient, whereas the patient is not trying to persuade the doctor nor trying to resist the doctor. Rather she is just playing counter-arguments that she for example believes. In future work, we will investigate how both the proponent and opponent can have a model of each other, and use these to play strategically against each other.

## 4.2    Multi-criteria Decision Making

In order to take into account several dimensions as a solution of a decision problem, we apply multi-criteria decision making. In this work, we use the traditional notion of *Pareto optimality* to compare multi-dimension solutions.

**Definition 1** *(Pareto optimality). A solution (i.e., a multi-dimension value of a leaf node) $x = (x_1, \ldots, x_n)$ **dominates** a solution $y = (y_1, \ldots, y_n)$ iff $\forall i \in \{1, \ldots, n\}, x_i \succeq y_i$ and $\exists j \in \{1, \ldots, n\}$ s.t. $x_j \succ y_j$ where $\succ$ denotes the preference operator.*

*A solution $x$ is **Pareto optimal** if no solution $y$ dominates it. The **Pareto front** is the set of all Pareto optimal solutions.*

Unfortunately, computing the Pareto front is a very costly operation because each solution has to be compared, in the worst case scenario, to all the other ones. One might use aggregation functions in order to reduce the problem to a mono-criterion decision making problem on the aggregated criterion. However, doing so reduces the number of Pareto optimal solutions that can be considered. Using for instance the Weighted Average function implies that only the solutions located on the convex envelope of the Pareto front can be found. Indeed, let $x^1 = (1, 3), x^2 = (3, 1)$ and $x^3 = (1.5, 1.5)$ be three Pareto optimal solutions. No weights $w_1$ and $w_2$ exist such that $w_1 * x_1^3 + w_2 * x_2^3 > w_1 * x_1^i + w_2 * x_2^i$ with $i \in \{1, 2\}$.

Fortunately, in this work, the number of solutions to compare in each node in order to find the Pareto optimal ones is at most equal to the number of arguments. It can therefore be computed easily.

# 5    Dimensions of the Dialogue Problem

In this paper, we illustrate the use of multi-criteria decision making with four dimensions which we explain below: the valuation of the dialogue, the belief in the goal, the aggregated valence and the aggregated arousal for the dialogue. Therefore, each solution in the multi-criteria decision making problem is a vector with four dimensions.

## 5.1    Valuation

The valuation of a dialogue is a real value $v \in [0, 1]$ representing how desirable this execution is with respect to the persuasion goal of the persuader. Therefore, they are computed only for the persuader, from her point of view.

For the sake of simplicity, in this paper, the value $v_i$ of dialogue $i$ is a value of 1 if the goal has been posited in dialogue $i$ or 0 otherwise. This function can be replaced to take into account several goals and interactions between them (*e.g.*, synergies). Note that Dung's [13] dialectical semantics can also be used. For instance, the value of the goal can be 1 if it is in the grounded extension, 0 otherwise.

Also, this value can be non-binary. Gradual valuations can be used, taking into account the interactions between arguments in the graph (*e.g.*, [31]) or argument strength (*e.g.*, [32,33]).

## 5.2    Belief

Starting from an initial value for each argument, the belief has to be updated at each step depending on the arguments played. The ambivalent method as proposed by Hunter [34] allows for belief in an argument to increase when it has been posited, and no attacker of it is believed (*i.e.*, when $\forall(B, A) \in$ Attacks$(G), B_{i-1}(B) \leq 0.5$). In this work, we use a modification of the ambivalent method that is equivalent but faster to compute (defined below). The updated belief in $A$ (*i.e.*, $B_i(A)$) is the original belief (*i.e.*, $B_{i-1}(A)$) plus $k$ times the belief in its complement (*i.e.*, $1 - B_{i-1}(A)$). The $k$ coefficient is a value in the unit interval that allows for only part of the belief to be transferred and thereby for modelling agents who do not completely belief a proposition when posited, and do not completely disbelieve a proposition when it is defeated. In addition, belief in each attackee $C$ of $A$ is reduced to $k \times B_{i-1}(C)$.

**Definition 2** *(Fast ambivalent method). At step $i$ in the dialogue, $B_i$ is generated from $B_{i-1}$ as follows if $D(i) = A$ and $\forall(B, A) \in$ Attacks$(G), B_{i-1}(B) \leq 0.5$:*

1. $B_i(A) = B_{i-1}(A) + k \times (1 - B_{i-1}(A))$,
2. $\forall C$ s.t. $(A, C) \in \mathsf{Attacks}(G), B_i(C) = k \times B_{i-1}(C)$

Whilst we use the ambivalent method in this paper, it can be replaced by any update method (see [34] for more methods). The aim of this flexibility is to model different kinds of persuadee with different kinds of behaviours, some of which are not rational.

## 5.3    Affective Norm

We now consider how we can harness the resources for affective norms in multi-criteria decision making for persuasion. The values for valence and arousal are given for singleton words and are not considered as part of a sentence. As we deal with complete arguments, we thus first need to aggregate the values to have a valence and an arousal for an argument and for a sequence of arguments. As we have seen, valence and arousal interact in a specific way. Following our discussion of the psychology literature in Sect. 3, in this paper we aggregate the values for an argument by taking the minimum valence and the maximum arousal across all words of this argument.

*Example 1.* Consider the arguments A1 = "Smoking causes lung cancer" and A2 = "Smoking causes serious disease", the aggregated affective norms are as follows. So A2 is more arousing and less pleasant, and hence indicates it would be a better argument against smoking than A1.

| Word/Argument | Arousal | Valence |
| --- | --- | --- |
| Smoke | 5 | 3.44 |
| Causes | 3.48 | 5.14 |
| Lung | 2.64 | 4.84 |
| Cancer | 5.14 | 1.9 |
| Serious | 4.05 | 5.88 |
| Disease | 5.5 | 1.68 |
| A1 | 5.14 | 1.9 |
| A2 | 5.5 | 1.68 |

Aggregating scores for valence and arousal of the keywords in the argument as the score for valence and arousal of the argument follows widespread use of keywords in text to provide the semantics of the text. This method is only meant as a simple proposal for initiating the consideration of affective norms in argumentation. By drawing on developments in affective computing (see, *e.g.*, [35]), including sentiment analysis, we could obtain a deeper understanding of the affective nature of phrase (*e.g.*, taking the use of negation into account). In this work, we aggregate across the sequence of arguments using the minimum value over each dimension.

**Table 1.** Decision rules for each dimension where $x_v$ is the valuation, $x_b$ the belief, $x_{v'}$ the valence and $x_a$ the arousal

| Dim. $(x_v, x_b, x_{v'}, x_a)$ | $x^1 \in X$ is preferred iff |
|---|---|
| Valuation | $x_v^1 = \arg\max_{x' \in X} x_v'$ |
| Belief | $x_b^1 = \arg\max_{x' \in X} x_b'$ |
| Affective norm if: | |
| $\forall x^i \in X, x_{v'}^i > 0$ | $x_a^1 = \arg\min_{x' \in X} |x_a'|$ |
| $\forall x^i \in X, x_{v'}^i < 0$ | $x_a^1 = \arg\max_{x' \in X} x_a'$ |
| Mixed valence | $x_a^1 = \arg\max_{x' \in X} x_a'$ |

## 5.4 Comparing Dimensions

In order to calculate the Pareto front, we need to compare each dimension for each solution $x$ in the set of solutions $X$. For this, we need to define the preference function for each dimension. They are all summarized in Table 1.

*Valuation and beliefs.* Both the valuation and the belief are real valued dimensions. Comparing them for two solutions is straightforward as we want to maximize them in this work. Note that it depends on the aim of the dialogue for the persuader. In another situation, we might want to minimize the belief (for instance, to discredit a political opponent).

*Affective norm.* Because of the interactions between them, we treat the two affective norm dimensions (valence and arousal) as a pair of dimensions. We need to have different sets of rules if we want to manage different situations. If, for a given argument, all the possible words have a positive valence, we shall neutralize the arousal and select the word with an arousal value close to the mean. Conversely, if all the possible words have a negative valence, we shall maximize the arousal and select the word with the highest arousal value. When the possible words have either positive or negative valence, we shall apply the rule corresponding to the negative valence. Indeed, the literature shows that there is a "positive-negative asymmetry in evaluation" [36,37]. This means that negative stimuli are treated more fluently than positive stimuli with a comparable arousal value.

Note that, in practice, when different arguments are considered, they will more likely fall under the "mixed valence" condition. However, in some situations, we want to compare arguments that have the same meaning in order to choose which one is better phrased depending on the application and the persuadee. In this case, the arguments are only differing by a few words (synonyms). Therefore, the "only positive valence" and "only negative valence" conditions are important. Once the version of the argument (out of those with the same meaning) is chosen, it is then compared with the other unrelated arguments.

## 5.5   Selection Method

In order to compute an optimal policy we need to start from the leaves of the tree and recursively compute the Pareto optimal solutions in the decision nodes. However, a deterministic policy only gives one action to perform in each possible state. Therefore, when several incomparable Pareto optimal solutions are valid in a state, we need to carefully pick one.

This choice depends on the strategy the persuader wants to apply. Indeed, in a one-shot situation, when there is only one dialogue, the persuader may want to maximize the belief at all cost, meaning without any consideration to the emotions induced by the dialogue. In this case, we pick the argument with the maximum belief amongst the argument in the Pareto front. On the other hand, when several dialogues are planned (for instance, in a doctor/patient situation), the persuader might want to sacrifice the belief in order to leave a good impression in the first dialogues, in the hope of increasing the efficiency of the future dialogues.

## 6   Size-Reducing Constraints

The low number of Pareto optimal solutions for each dialogue can be handled efficiently. However, the computational difficulty comes from the large number of possible dialogues. In the most general case where we allow the arguments to occur several times in the dialogue without a bounded horizon, this number is infinite. To reduce it, we consider three size-reducing constraints that can be independently used or combined:

**Constraint 1** no repetition of arguments in the dialogue,
**Constraint 2** no direct attacker of the goal is allowed as a proponent move,
**Constraint 3** only relevant arguments can be played.

A relevant argument is the first one of a dialogue or any argument connected to the ones already posited.

### 6.1   Theoretical Results

We now consider the theoretical benefits of size-reducing constraints by identifying the theoretical numbers of dialogues $n$ depending on the different constraints applied. In the following, $a$ is the number of arguments, $h$ the horizon and $k$ the number of direct attackers to the goal argument. We make the assumptions that $h < k < a$, for Propositions 1 to 5, and that $h < a - k$, for Proposition 3, to ensure that the dialogues are of size $h$ in any situation. Without these assumptions the number of dialogues of size $h$ is $n' \leq n$.

We start by giving the naive constraint which allows any argument to be used at each step of the dialogue.

**Proposition 1** *(Naive constraint). In the general case, the number of dialogues is $n = a^h$, i.e., $a$ choices at each of the $h$ steps.*

We consider constraint 1 and constraints 1 and 2 together.

**Proposition 2** *(No repetition constraint). When arguments cannot be repeated in the dialogue, $n = \frac{a!}{(a-h)!}$, i.e., $a \times (a-1) \times \ldots \times (a-h+1)$.*

**Proposition 3** *(No attacking arguments + no repetition). In this case, the proponent cannot play arguments that directly attack her goal argument:*

$$n = \sum_{i=0}^{\lfloor \frac{h}{2} \rfloor} \binom{\lfloor \frac{h}{2} \rfloor}{i} \times \frac{(a-k)!}{(a-k-\lceil \frac{h}{2} \rceil - i)!} \times \frac{k!}{(k-(\lfloor \frac{h}{2} \rfloor - i))!} \ .$$

*Proof* (Outline). For horizon $h = 3$, the numbers of possible choices at each step are (depending on the opponent playing a direct attacker of the goal or not):

$$n = (a-k) \times k \times (a-k-1)$$
$$+ (a-k) \times (a-k-1) \times (a-k-2)$$
$$n = 1 \times \frac{(a-k)!}{(a-k-2-0)!} \times \frac{k!}{(k-(1-0))!}$$
$$+ 1 \times \frac{(a-k)!}{(a-k-2-1)!} \times \frac{k!}{(k-(1-1))!}$$
$$n = \sum_{i=0}^{1} \binom{1}{i} \times \frac{(a-k)!}{(a-k-2-i)!} \times \frac{k!}{(k-(1-i))!} \ .$$

For horizon $h = 4$,

$$n = (a-k) \times (a-k-1) \times k \times (k-1)$$
$$+ 2 \times (a-k) \times (a-k-1) \times (a-k-2) \times k$$
$$+ (a-k) \times (a-k-1) \times (a-k-2) \times (a-k-3)$$
$$n = 1 \times \frac{(a-k)!}{(a-k-2-0)!} \times \frac{k!}{(k-(2-0))!}$$
$$+ 2 \times \frac{(a-k)!}{(a-k-2-1)!} \times \frac{k!}{(k-(2-1))!}$$
$$+ 1 \times \frac{(a-k)!}{(a-k-2-2)!} \times \frac{k!}{(k-(2-2))!}$$
$$n = \sum_{i=0}^{2} \binom{2}{i} \times \frac{(a-k)!}{(a-k-2-i)!} \times \frac{k!}{(k-(2-i))!} \ .$$

We can see the general expression from the examples.

The following result shows that we get improvement from the use of the constraints considered in the results above.

**Proposition 4.** *Given values for the number of arguments a, the horizon h, and the number of direct attackers to the goal argument k, if $n_1$ is the number of dialogues obtained by proposition 1, $n_2$ is the number of dialogues obtained by proposition 2, and $n_3$ is the number of dialogues obtained by proposition 3, then $n_1 \geq n_2$ and $n_2 \geq n_3$.*

In Table 2, we show the percentage of reduction in using the constraints as calculated by Propositions 1, 2, and 3.

**Table 2.** The fraction of all dialogues (as calculated by Proposition 1) obtained by using constraint 1 (*i.e.*, no repetition constraint) or constraint 1 and 2 (*i.e.*, no attacking arguments and no repetition), and where $h = 10$ and $k = 15$.

| Constraint | Number of arguments | | | | |
|---|---|---|---|---|---|
| | 30 | 40 | 50 | 60 | 70 |
| 1 | 0.184 | 0.293 | 0.381 | 0.452 | 0.509 |
| 1 + 2 | 0.004 | 0.023 | 0.058 | 0.101 | 0.146 |

**Table 3.** Number of nodes for a 7-argument graph

| # arcs removed | 0 | 5 | 10 | 15 |
|---|---|---|---|---|
| # nodes | | 2372 | 1182 | 319 | 28 |

We now consider the third size-reducing constraint which states that only relevant arguments can be played. The number of dialogues using this constraint is highly dependent on the structure of the graph, and so we proceed by considering the worst case scenario, which is when the graph is a complete graph, and best case scenario, which is when the graph is a chain of arguments.

**Proposition 5** *(Relevant arguments constraint) (Worst case). The number of dialogues is the same as in Proposition 2 (if we consider the no repetition constraint at the same time). (Best case) The number of dialogues is $n = a - (h - 1)$, i.e., one possible dialogue for each possible starting point leading to a sequence of length h.*

Table 3 shows the number of nodes in the decision tree generated from a 7-argument graph, with the "relevant arguments" and "no repetition" constraints applied. The top values represent the number of arcs removed from the complete graph where 0 denotes the complete graph and 15 a chain. We can see that the number of nodes in the tree exponentially decreases. Also note that the "no goal direct attackers" constraint is not applied here as it is trivial in the case of the complete graph. Indeed, in this case the only dialogues are of size 2, the goal argument for the proponent and any of the remaining arguments for the opponent. The proponent cannot play at step 3 without attacking her goal.

# 7    Computational Evaluation

In order to study the computational efficiency of our method, we use an argument graph on the topic of the annual flu vaccination for hospital staff, developed with healthcare professionals. It contains 35 arguments including a persuasion goal for taking the vaccine and various counterarguments. Some examples of arguments are: "NHS staff can transmit infections to the patients." (pro-vaccine), "The flu vaccine weakens the immunitary system." (anti-vaccine) and "The flu vaccine is useless because the strain is guessed." (anti-vaccine).

Note that, the creation of the argument graph is context dependent. In some cases, information is easily available and in others we need to rely on experts. Detailed explanations on how we can model a domain for behaviour change applications can be found in [38].

We also add synonym arguments (arguments with same meaning but different wording) for 15 of the arguments in the graph, carrying the same meaning but using different words and so different values for the affective norm. The final graph has thus 50 arguments[1]. Figure 2 depicts the graph without the synonym arguments. We can see that the graph is not a tree, it contains cycles and multiple paths from nodes to the root, making it a non-trivial example. The experiments have been run on an Intel i5-6600 at 3.30 GHz with 8 GB of RAM.

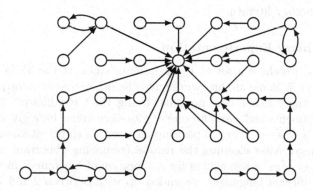

**Fig. 2.** Argument graph without synonym arguments

Using different affective norm values gives, as expected, different optimal sequences of arguments for each player. For instance, using the norm associated with older people yields the sequence with the following argument names: "annualvaccine notconcerned strongsense nocare cantransmit dontworry nodirect" while using the norm associated to younger people gives: "annualvaccine nocare strongsense dontworry caninfect noface2face nodirect".

---

[1] The code, the graph and the mapping to the actual arguments can be found at https://github.com/ComputationalPersuasion/stardec.

**Table 4.** Computation time for horizons 1 to 8 (in sec)

| 1 | 2 | 3 | 4 | 5 | 6 | 7 | 8 |
|------|------|------|------|------|---|----|-----|
| 0.08 | 0.08 | 0.08 | 0.12 | 0.26 | 4 | 28 | 597 |

Table 4 shows the computation time from the creation of the tree to the computation of an optimal policy, with constraints 1 to 3 enabled, for horizons from 1 to 8. As we can see, the time grows exponentially with the horizon. However, we argue that 8 is a good length for the horizon as it allows several exchanges of arguments between both agents without incurring a too high risk of disengagement from the persuadee. Note that most of the time is spent on creating the tree. Using methods such as Branch-and-bound can highly improve the computation time.

## 8    Study with Participants

The aim of this empirical study is to investigate the computational viability of evaluating emotion and belief associated with an argument by an opponent and using this to determine the best policy for the proponent. The purpose is also to validate the choices of decision rules (described in Table 1) when instantiating with the psychology literature.

### 8.1    Preliminary Experimentation

As a first step, we chose a set of 13 arguments amongst the 35 from the same graph as in Sect. 7. Some are pro arguments the other are counterarguments. We crowdsourced the creation of synonyms. Using the Crowdflower[2] platform, we gave all 13 arguments and asked for one or more synonyms for a given word in the argument. This was run using 25 participants, with a sufficient knowledge of the English language. After cleaning the results (removing abberrant answers such as "planetary system" when asking for a synonym of "mercury" in a vaccine, or answers in a different language), we ended up with between 2 and 7 alternative words, depending on the argument.

### 8.2    Participants, Material and Procedure

We recruited 100 participants via the Prolific[3] platform. The only screening criterion we used was the language of participants which we limited to English. We presented each of the 13 arguments considered in the preliminary experiment to each participant. For each argument, we gave the synonyms obtained in the preliminary experiment in the form of a menu, and asked the participant to select the synonym she deems the best at "conveying its message". We were therefore asking each participant which was the best version of each argument.

---

[2] https://www.crowdflower.com.
[3] https://www.prolific.ac.

## 8.3   Results

Before collating the results, we removed some arguments and participants from further consideration as follows. We removed two arguments where the choice of word was highly constrained by the domain ("complications" cannot be replaced with *e.g.*, "problems" when talking about unfortunate consequences of a vaccine, and the word "injection" is almost never used when "vaccine" can be picked). We removed the 12 participants choosing the wrong answer for these two arguments. We also removed a third argument because the set of synonyms was almost the same as for another argument, leaving us with 10 arguments.

We applied our set of rules to the same set of arguments with the same sets of synonyms. We compared the results with the answers given by the participants. Our set of rules (Table 1) gives us the most chosen word for 8 arguments out of 10 and the second most chosen for the remaining 2. It means that these rules (the second half of Table 1) approximate efficiently the relation the majority of our participants have with emotions induced by the arguments.

**Table 5.** Cumulative score for the prediction of the answers

| 9 | 7 | 6 | 5 | 3 | 1 |
|------|-------|-------|-------|-------|------|
| 1.1% | 13.2% | 36.3% | 52.7% | 95.6% | 100% |

Note that while we accurately represent the choice of the majority for each argument, only a few participants are part of the majority for all arguments at the same time. Table 5 shows the cumulative sum of good predictions when analyzing the individual participant's answers. Each percentage is the percentage of the participants we have managed to predict correctly at least $x$ answers. For instance, for $x = 9$, 1.1% means that we have correctly predicted at least 9 choices out of 10 for 1.1% of the participants. Interestingly, our method predicted correctly more than half the answers for more than half of the population: 52.7% for 5 or more answers.

This user experiment has two conclusions. First it shows that the psychology literature reflects the choices made by the participants. Second it demonstrates that we can transform the psychological principles into logical and mathematical formulae and predict the choices with good results.

## 9   Conclusion

In this paper, we have shown how decision-theoretic methods for multi-criteria decision making can be used to identify an optimal policy for dialogical argumentation. We have presented a framework for modelling a proponent and opponent in a dialogue, and for handling multiple criteria such as the degree the opponent believes an argument, and the degree of valence and arousal, that could be evoked by the argument in the opponent. Our hypotheses are supported by the psychological literature and backed by user experiments. These are only indicative of the dimensions that might be used in an application. In future work, we intend to develop the treatment of emotion in the framework as the topic has received little attention in the computational argumentation literature. Exceptions are [39] which provide rules for specifying scenarios where empathy is given or received, and [40] which investigates relationships between emotions that participants feel during a debate (measured physiologically) and arguments. In contrast, affective computing has put emotion at the centre of the relationship between users and computing systems [41].

**Acknowledgements.** This research is part funded by EPSRC Project EP/N008294/1 (Framework for Computational Persuasion).

# References

1. Prakken, H.: Coherence and flexibility in dialogue games for argumentation. J. Log. Comput. **15**(6), 1009–1040 (2005)
2. Prakken, H.: Formal sytems for persuasion dialogue. Knowl. Eng. Rev. **21**(2), 163–188 (2006)
3. Fan, X., Toni, F.: Assumption-based argumentation dialogues. In: Proceedings of IJCAI 2011, pp. 198–203 (2011)
4. Caminada, M., Podlaszewski, M.: Grounded semantics as persuasion dialogue. In: Proceedings of COMMA 2012, pp. 478–485 (2012)
5. Thimm, M.: Strategic argumentation in multi-agent systems. Kunstliche Intelligenz **28**, 159–168 (2014)
6. Rahwan, I., Larson, K.: Pareto optimality in abstract argumentation. In: Proceedings of AAAI 2008, pp. 150–155 (2008)
7. Fan, X., Toni, F.: Mechanism design for argumentation-based persuasion. In: Proceedings of COMMA 2012, pp. 322–333 (2012)
8. Rienstra, T., Thimm, M., Oren, N.: Opponent models with uncertainty for strategic argumentation. In: Proceedings of IJCAI 2013, pp. 332–338 (2013)
9. Hadjinikolis, C., Siantos, Y., Modgil, S., Black, E., McBurney, P.: Opponent modelling in persuasion dialogues. In: Proceedings of IJCAI 2013, pp. 164–170 (2013)
10. Hadoux, E., Beynier, A., Maudet, N., Weng, P., Hunter, A.: Optimization of probabilistic argumentation with Markov decision models. In: Proceedings of IJCAI 2015, pp. 2004–2010 (2015)
11. Black, E., Coles, A., Bernardini, S.: Automated planning of simple persuasion dialogues. In: Bulling, N., van der Torre, L., Villata, S., Jamroga, W., Vasconcelos, W. (eds.) CLIMA 2014. LNCS (LNAI), vol. 8624, pp. 87–104. Springer, Cham (2014). https://doi.org/10.1007/978-3-319-09764-0_6
12. Hadoux, E., Hunter, A.: Strategic sequences of arguments for persuasion using decision trees. In: Proceedings of AAAI 2017 (2017)
13. Dung, P.: On the acceptability of arguments and its fundamental role in nonmonotonic reasoning, logic programming, and n-person games. Artif. Intell. **77**, 321–357 (1995)
14. Thimm, M.: A probabilistic semantics for abstract argumentation. In: Proceedings of ECAI 2012, pp. 750–755 (2012)

15. Hunter, A.: A probabilistic approach to modelling uncertain logical arguments. Int. J. Approx. Reason. **54**(1), 47–81 (2013)
16. Hunter, A., Thimm, M.: Probabilistic argumentation with incomplete information. In: Proceedings of ECAI 2014, pp. 1033–1034 (2014)
17. Baroni, P., Giacomin, M., Vicig, P.: On rationality conditions for epistemic probabilities in abstract argumentation. In: Proceedings of COMMA 2014, pp. 121–132 (2014)
18. Lazarus, R.S.: Progress on a cognitive-motivational-relational theory of emotion. Am. psychol. **46**(8), 819 (1991)
19. Scherer, K.R.: Appraisal considered as a process of multilevel sequential checking. Apprais. Process. Emot.: Theory, Methods, Res. **92**(120), 57 (2001)
20. Duhachek, A., Agrawal, N., Han, D.: Guilt versus shame: coping, fluency, and framing in the effectiveness of responsible drinking messages. J. Mark. Res. **49**(6), 928–941 (2012)
21. Tversky, A., Kahneman, D.: The framing of decisions and the psychology of choice. Science **211**(4481), 453–458 (1981)
22. Ekman, P.: An argument for basic emotions. Cognit. Emot. **6**(3–4), 169–200 (1992)
23. Fulladoza Dalibón, S., Martinez, D., Simari, G.: Emotion-directed argument awareness for autonomous agent reasoning. Inteligencia Artificial. Revista Iberoamericana de Inteligencia Artificial **15**(50), 30–45 (2012)
24. Lloyd-Kelly, M., Wyner, A.: Arguing about emotion. In: Ardissono, L., Kuflik, T. (eds.) UMAP 2011. LNCS, vol. 7138, pp. 355–367. Springer, Heidelberg (2012). https://doi.org/10.1007/978-3-642-28509-7_33
25. Nawwab, F., Dunne, P., Bench-Capon, T.: Exploring the role of emotions in rational decision making. In: COMMA, pp. 367–378 (2010)
26. Bradley, M., Lang, P.: Affective norms for English words (ANEW): Instruction manual and affective ratings. Technical report, The Center for Research in Psychophysiology, University of Florida (1999)
27. Warriner, A., Kuperman, V., Brysbaert, M.: Norms of valence, arousal, and dominance for 13,915 English lemmas. Behav. Res. Methods **45**(4), 1191–1207 (2013)
28. Eder, A.B., Rothermund, K.: Automatic influence of arousal information on evaluative processing: valence-arousal interactions in an affective Simon task. Cognit. Emot. **24**(6), 1053–1061 (2010)
29. Jefferies, L.N., Smilek, D., Eich, E., Enns, J.T.: Emotional valence and arousal interact in attentional control. Psychol. Sci. **19**(3), 290–295 (2008)
30. Robinson, M.D.: Watch out! that could be dangerous: valence-arousal interactions in evaluative processing. Personal. Soc. Psychol. Bull. **30**(11), 1472–1484 (2004)
31. Cayrol, C., Lagasquie-Schiex, M.C.: Gradual valuation for bipolar argumentation frameworks. In: Godo, L. (ed.) ECSQARU 2005. LNCS (LNAI), vol. 3571, pp. 366–377. Springer, Heidelberg (2005). https://doi.org/10.1007/11518655_32
32. Amgoud, L., Ben-Naim, J.: Axiomatic foundations of acceptability semantics. In: Proceedings of KR 2016 (2016)
33. Bonzon, E., Delobelle, J., Konieczny, S., Maudet, N.: A comparative study of ranking-based semantics for abstract argumentation. In: Proceedings of AAAI 2016, pp. 014 020 (2016)
34. Hunter, A.: Modelling the persuadee in asymmetric argumentation dialogues for persuasion. In: Proceedings of IJCAI 2015, pp. 3055–3061 (2015)
35. Mohammad, S.: Sentiment analysis: detecting valence, emotions, and other affectual states from text. In: Emotion Management, pp. 201–238. Elsevier (2016)

36. Peeters, G., Czapinski, J.: Positive-negative asymmetry in evaluations: the distinction between affective and informational negativity effects. Eur. Rev. Soc. Psychol. **1**(1), 33–60 (1990)
37. Baumeister, R.F., Bratslavsky, E., Finkenauer, C., Vohs, K.D.: Bad is stronger than good. Rev. Gen. Psychol. **5**(4), 323–370 (2001)
38. Chalaguine, L., Hadoux, E., Hamilton, F., Hayward, A., Hunter, A., Polberg, S., Potts, H.W.W.: Domain modelling in computational persuasion for behaviour change in healthcare. CoRR abs/1802.10054 (2018)
39. Martinovski, B., Mao, W.: Emotion as an argumentation engine: modeling the role of emotion in negotiation. Group Decis. Negot. **18**, 235–259 (2009)
40. Benlamine, S., Chaouachi, M., Villata, S., Cabrio, E., Gandon, C.F.F.: Emotions in argumentation: an empirical evaluation. In: Proceedings of IJCAI 2015, pp. 156–163 (2015)
41. Calvo, R., D'Mello, S.: Affect detection: an interdisciplinary review of models, methods, and their applications. IEEE Trans. Aff. Comput. **1**(1), 18–37 (2010)

# First-Order Definable Counting-Only Queries

Jelle Hellings[1]($\boxtimes$), Marc Gyssens[1], Dirk Van Gucht[2], and Yuqing Wu[3]

[1] Hasselt University, Martelarenlaan 42, 3500 Hasselt, Belgium
jelle.hellings@uhasselt.be
[2] Indiana University, 150 S. Woodlawn Avenue, Bloomington, IN 47405, USA
[3] Pomona College, 185 E 6th Street, Claremont, CA 91711, USA

**Abstract.** For several practical queries on bags of sets of objects, the answer does not depend on the precise composition of these sets, but only on the *number* of sets to which each object belongs. This is the case $k = 1$ for the more general situation where the query answer only depends on the number of sets to which each *group* of at most $k$ objects belongs. We call such queries $k$-counting-only. Here, we focus on $k$-SyCALC, $k$-counting-only queries that are first-order definable. As $k$-SyCALC is semantically defined, however, it is not surprising that it is already undecidable whether a first-order query is in 1-SyCALC. Therefore, we introduce SimpleCALC-$k$, a syntactically defined (strict) fragment of $k$-SyCALC. It turns out that many practical queries in $k$-SyCALC can already be expressed in SimpleCALC-$k$. We prove that the $k$-counting-only queries form a non-collapsing hierarchy: for every $k$, there exist $(k+1)$-counting-only queries that are not $k$-counting-only. This result specializes to both SimpleCALC-$k$ and $k$-SyCALC. Finally, we establish a strong dichotomy between 1-SyCALC and SimpleCALC-$k$ on the one hand and 2-SyCALC on the other hand by showing that satisfiability, validity, query containment, and query equivalence are decidable for the former two languages, but not for the latter one.

## 1 Introduction

Often, (parts of) queries can be viewed as operating on a bag of sets, or, equivalently, on transaction databases [8], bipartite graphs, or binary many-to-many relations. As an example, consider the bag-of-sets dataset of Fig. 1, *left*, in which each set represents a course and contains the students taking that course. This bag of sets can alternatively be interpreted as the *bipartite graph*, shown in Fig. 1, *right*. Many practical queries on bags of sets turn out to be *counting-only*: in order to answer them, it is not necessary to know to which sets each object belongs, but only to *how many* sets each object belongs. As examples, consider the queries 'return students who take at least 2 courses', expressed by

$$Q_1 = \{\langle x \rangle \mid \text{count}(x) \geq 2\},$$

This material is based on work supported by the National Science Foundation under Grant No. NSF 1438990.

**Fig. 1.** *Left*, a bag-of-sets dataset. *Right*, same dataset represented as bipartite graph.

and 'return pairs of students who take the same number of courses', expressed by

$$Q_2 = \{\langle x, y \rangle \mid (x \neq y) \wedge \text{count}(x) = \text{count}(y)\}.$$

In the above expressions, "count$(\cdot)$" counts the number of sets (here, courses) to which the argument (here, a student) belongs. Clearly, one need not know which courses each student takes to answer $Q_1$ or $Q_2$, but only *how many* courses each student takes. Next, consider the queries 'return pairs of distinct students which take a common course', expressed by

$$Q_3 = \{\langle x, y \rangle \mid (x \neq y) \wedge \text{count}(x, y) \geq 1\},$$

and 'return pairs of distinct students which take the same courses', expressed by

$$Q_4 = \{\langle x, y \rangle \mid (x \neq y) \wedge \text{count}(x, y) = \text{count}(x) \wedge \text{count}(x, y) = \text{count}(y)\}.$$

Notice that $Q_3$ is a basic intersection query and $Q_4$ is a basic equivalence query. Both can be answered by counting not only *(i)* how many courses each student takes, but also *(ii)* how many courses each *pair* of students share. For $k \geq 0$, we call a query *$k$-counting-only* if it can be answered by only counting to how many sets each *group* of at most $k$ objects belongs. Hence, $Q_1$ and $Q_2$ are 1-counting-only, while $Q_3$ and $Q_4$ are 2-counting-only. Similarly, the Boolean query 'does there exist a course taken by 3 students', expressed by

$$Q_5 = \{\langle \rangle \mid \exists x \exists y \exists z \, ((x \neq y \wedge x \neq z \wedge y \neq z) \wedge \text{count}(x, y, z) \geq 1)\},$$

is 3-counting-only. In contrast, the Boolean query 'there are at least 3 courses', expressed by

$$Q_6 = \{\langle \rangle \mid \text{count}() \geq 3\}.$$

can already be answered at the scheme level, and is therefore 0-counting-only.

Observe that the counting-only queries $Q_3$ and $Q_4$ only differ in the use of the *generalized quantifiers* 'takes some' versus 'takes all and only'. Similar familiar families of counting-only queries can be formulated using other generalized quantifiers such as 'takes only', 'takes all', 'takes no', 'takes at least $k$', and 'takes all but $k$'. Such queries are not only of relevance in the study of generalized quantifiers [4,19], but also play an obvious central role in the *frequent itemset*

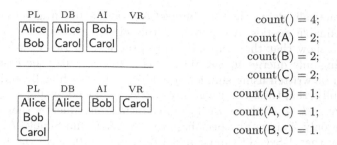

| PL | DB | AI | VR |
|---|---|---|---|
| Alice | Alice | Bob | |
| Bob | Carol | Carol | |

$$count() = 4;$$
$$count(A) = 2;$$
$$count(B) = 2;$$
$$count(C) = 2;$$
$$count(A, B) = 1;$$
$$count(A, C) = 1;$$
$$count(B, C) = 1.$$

**Fig. 2.** *Left,* Bags of sets $S_1$ (top) and $S_2$ (bottom), both assigning students to four courses. *Right,* Count-information shared between $S_1$ and $S_2$.

*problem* [8]. In essence, bag-of-set-like data models and counting-only queries can also be found in the *differential constraints* of Sayrafi et al. [17], *citation analysis and bibliometrics* [5], the *symmetric Boolean functions* of Quine [11,16], *finite set combinatorics* [2], and the *data spaces* of Fletcher et al. [7], either explicitly or implicitly.

A more formal way to capture the notion of $k$-counting-only query is that such queries cannot distinguish between bags of sets which share the same up-to-$k$ counting information. Consider, e.g., the bags of sets $S_1$ and $S_2$ of Fig. 2. Clearly, $S_1$ and $S_2$ agree on all up-to-2 counting information, but disagree on count(Alice, Bob, Carol). Hence, $Q_1$–$Q_4$ and $Q_6$ yield the same result on $S_1$ and $S_2$, whereas $Q_5$, which is 3-counting-only, evaluates to `false` on $S_1$ and `true` on $S_2$.

Finally, notice that the concept of counting-only query applies to more general data models than the bag-of-sets model. Consider, e.g., a database with a student-course relation $SC$ and a department-course relation $DC$, with the obvious meaning. On this database, query

$$P = \{\langle x, y \rangle \mid count(\{z \mid SC(x, z) \wedge DC(y, z)\}) = count(\{z \mid SC(x, z)\})\}$$

returns student-department pairs in which the student only takes courses offered by that department. This query, conceptually similar to $Q_4$ above, certainly has a counting-only flavor.

Motivated by the above, we believe that the class of counting-only queries deserves a broader understanding. Our notion of $k$-counting-only queries, $k \geq 0$, significantly generalizes the notion of counting-only queries of Gyssens et al. [11], which only corresponds with our case $k = 1$.

As many interesting counting-only queries are first-order definable, including $Q_1$ and $Q_3$–$Q_6$, we study more specifically the class of first-order definable counting-only queries on the bags-of-sets data model. To do so, we use (a variation of) the two-sorted first-order logic SyCALC of Gyssens et al. In this logic, we have object variables, set name variables, and a set-membership relation relating objects and set names. Our main results are as follows:

1. We semantically define the class of $k$-counting-only queries, and show that they include many practically relevant first-order-definable queries.

2. We syntactically define the class SimpleCALC-$k$, $k \geq 0$, a fragment of the first-order-definable queries. All queries in this class turn out to be $k$-counting-only. We show that they capture many practical queries in $k$-SyCALC, the $k$-counting-only queries in SyCALC. This is in particular the case for those that can be written using simple "count($\cdot$)" terms, such as $Q_1$ and $Q_3$–$Q_6$.

3. We establish that the $k$-counting-only queries form a non-collapsing hierarchy: for every $k$, $k \geq 0$, there are $(k+1)$-counting-only queries that are not $k$-counting-only. This result specializes to $k$-SyCALC and SimpleCALC-$k$.

4. We show that 1-SyCALC and SimpleCALC-$k$, $k \geq 0$, have the finite model property and use that to prove that satisfiability (and, hence, validity, query containment, and query equivalence) is decidable for these classes. We also establish that satisfiability is NEXPTIME-hard for SimpleCALC-$k$. In contrast, satisfiability for 2-SyCALC is shown to be undecidable. Hence, there is a strong dichotomy between 1-SyCALC and SimpleCALC-$k$, $k \geq 0$, on the one hand and 2-SyCALC on the other hand. Moreover, the decidability of 1-SyCALC and SimpleCALC-$k$, $k \geq 0$, sets them apart from many other fragments of first-order logic. In particular, this result identifies a large "well-behaved" fragment of first-order logic in which many practical queries can be expressed, and other than the usual classes of "well-behaved" first-order queries such as the conjunctive queries, the monadic first-order logic, and the two-variable fragments of first-order logic [1,3,9,10,14].

## 2   Bags of Sets and Counting-Only Queries

Let $\mathcal{D}$ and $\mathcal{N}$ be two disjoint infinitely enumerable domains of objects and names. We represent finite bags of finite sets by structures, as follows:

**Definition 2.1.** *A structure* $\mathbf{S}$ *is a pair* $\mathbf{S} = (\mathbf{N}, \gamma)$, *with* $\mathbf{N} \subset \mathcal{N}$ *a finite set of set names and* $\gamma \subset \mathcal{D} \times \mathbf{N}$ *a finite* set-membership *relation. For* $\text{N} \in \mathbf{N}$, $\text{objects}(\text{N}; \mathbf{S}) = \{\text{o} \mid (\text{o}, \text{N}) \in \gamma\}$ *is the set of objects that are a member of the set named* $\text{N}$. *We write* $\text{adom}(\mathbf{S}) = \bigcup_{\text{N} \in \mathcal{N}} \text{objects}(\text{N}; \mathbf{S})$ *for the* active domain *of* $\mathbf{S}$. *If* $\text{A} \subseteq \mathcal{D}$, *then* $\mathbf{S}|_\text{A}$ *denotes the structure* $(\mathbf{N}, \gamma \cap (\text{A} \times \mathbf{N}))$.

Structures explicitly define the set $\mathbf{N}$ of set names they use, whereas objects are only defined via the set-membership function $\gamma$. In this way, $\mathbf{N}$ allows the representation of empty sets:

*Example 2.2.* The bag-of-sets dataset of Fig. 1 is represented by the structure $\mathbf{S}_1 = (\mathbf{N}, \gamma)$ with $\mathbf{N} = \{\text{PL}, \text{DB}, \text{AI}\}$ and $\gamma = \{(\text{Alice}, \text{PL}), (\text{Bob}, \text{PL}), (\text{Alice}, \text{DB}), (\text{Bob}, \text{DB}), (\text{Carol}, \text{DB}), (\text{Dan}, \text{AI})\}$. If we were to add course VR to $\mathbf{N}$ without changing $\gamma$, this would mean that VR is offered but no student takes it.

A *query* $q$ maps a structure to a relation of fixed arity over objects. We write $[\![q]\!]_\mathbf{S}$ to denote the *evaluation* of $q$ on structure $\mathbf{S}$. If the arity of $q$ is 0, then $q$ is *Boolean*. The only two relations of arity 0, $\emptyset$ and $\{\langle\rangle\}$, represent `false` and `true`, respectively. In the Introduction, we showed that many queries on bags of sets cannot distinguish structures with the same up-to-$k$ count information, for some $k$, $k \geq 0$. We formalize this next:

**Definition 2.3.** *Let* $\mathbf{S} = (\mathbf{N}, \gamma)$ *be a structure and* $\mathrm{I} \subset \mathcal{D}$ *a finite set of objects, often referred to as an* itemset. *The* cover *of* $\mathrm{I}$ *in* $\mathbf{S}$ *is defined by* $\mathrm{cover}(\mathrm{I}; \mathbf{S}) = \{\mathrm{N} \mid (\mathrm{N} \in \mathbf{N}) \wedge (\mathrm{I} \subseteq \mathrm{objects}(\mathrm{N}; \mathbf{S}))\}$. *The* support *of* $\mathrm{I}$ *in* $\mathbf{S}$ *is defined by* $[\![\mathrm{count}(\mathrm{I})]\!]_{\mathbf{S}} = |\mathrm{cover}(\mathrm{I}; \mathbf{S})|$. *Structures* $\mathbf{S}_1$ *and* $\mathbf{S}_2$ *are* exactly-$k$-counting-equivalent *if* $[\![\mathrm{count}(\mathrm{I})]\!]_{\mathbf{S}_1} = [\![\mathrm{count}(\mathrm{I})]\!]_{\mathbf{S}_2}$ *for every itemset* $\mathrm{I}$ *with* $|\mathrm{I}| = k$. *Structures* $\mathbf{S}_1$ *and* $\mathbf{S}_2$ *are* $k$-counting-equivalent *if they are exactly-$j$-counting-equivalent for all* $j$, $0 \leq j \leq k$.[1]

Structures are exactly-0-counting-equivalent if they have the same number of set names. Hence, for all $k$, $k \geq 0$, $k$-counting-equivalent structures have the same number of set names.

*Example 2.4.* Consider the structures $\mathbf{S}_1$ and $\mathbf{S}_2$ in Fig. 2. Both have four set names representing courses. In both $\mathbf{S}_1$ and $\mathbf{S}_2$, each student takes two courses, and each pair of distinct students shares one common course. Since the itemset $\{\mathrm{Alice}, \mathrm{Bob}, \mathrm{Carol}\}$ has no cover in $\mathbf{S}_1$, but is covered by PL in $\mathbf{S}_2$, we conclude that $\mathbf{S}_1$ and $\mathbf{S}_2$ are 2-counting-equivalent, but not 3-counting-equivalent.

We are now ready to define $k$-counting-only queries:

**Definition 2.5.** *A query $q$ is* $k$-counting-only *if, for every pair of $k$-counting-equivalent structures* $\mathbf{S}_1$ *and* $\mathbf{S}_2$, *we have* $[\![q]\!]_{\mathbf{S}_1} = [\![q]\!]_{\mathbf{S}_2}$. *A query is* counting-only *if there exists $k$, $k \geq 0$, such that the query is $k$-counting-only.*[2]

*Example 2.6.* As mentioned in the Introduction, $\mathsf{Q}_1$ and $\mathsf{Q}_2$ are 1-counting-only, $\mathsf{Q}_3$ and $\mathsf{Q}_4$ are 2-counting-only, $\mathsf{Q}_5$ is 3-counting-only, and $\mathsf{Q}_6$ is 0-counting-only. Query $\mathsf{Q}_5$ is not 2-counting-only, since, on the 2-counting-equivalent structures $\mathbf{S}_1$ and $\mathbf{S}_2$ in Fig. 2, it returns different results. Notice that $\mathsf{Q}_2$ involves pairs of objects despite being 1-counting-only. To illustrate that this generalizes, consider

$$\mathsf{Q}_7 = \{\langle\rangle \mid \exists x \exists y_1 \exists y_2 \ (x \neq y_1) \wedge (x \neq y_2) \wedge (y_1 \neq y_2) \wedge$$
$$\mathrm{count}(y_1) = \mathrm{count}(x, y_1) \wedge \mathrm{count}(y_2) = \mathrm{count}(x, y_2) \wedge$$
$$\mathrm{count}(x) = \mathrm{count}(x, y_1) + \mathrm{count}(x, y_2) - \mathrm{count}(x, y_1, y_2)\}.$$

On the student-courses examples, $\mathsf{Q}_7$ returns **true** if there is a student who takes exactly the courses taken by a pair of distinct other students combined. Clearly, it is 3-counting-only. However, $\mathsf{Q}_7$ is also 2-counting-only, as it is equivalent to

$$\mathsf{Q}_7' = \{\langle\rangle \mid \exists x \exists y_1 \exists y_2 \ (x \neq y_1) \wedge (x \neq y_2) \wedge (y_1 \neq y_2) \wedge$$
$$\mathrm{count}(y_1) = \mathrm{count}(x, y_1) \wedge \mathrm{count}(y_2) = \mathrm{count}(x, y_2) \wedge$$
$$\mathrm{count}(x) = \mathrm{count}(x, y_1) + \mathrm{count}(x, y_2) - \mathrm{count}(y_1, y_2)\}.$$

So, some 2-counting-only queries can be used to reason on more than two objects.

---

[1] Gyssens et al. [11] use the tem *incidence* to refer to the support of a single object, and *incidence-equivalence* to refer to 1-counting-equivalence.

[2] Gyssens et al. [11] use the term *counting-only* to denote the first-order definable queries that are 1-counting-only.

We now show that $k$-counting information can be used to express the existence of any set-membership relation between at most $k$ objects. To do so, we use the notion of *generalized support*, borrowed from Calders and Goethals [6].

**Definition 2.7.** *The* generalized cover *of itemsets* $I$ *and* $E$ *in structure* $\mathbf{S} = (\mathbf{N}, \gamma)$ *is defined by* $\mathrm{gcover}(I; E; \mathbf{S}) = \{ \mathrm{N} \mid (\mathrm{N} \in \mathbf{N}) \wedge (I \subseteq \mathrm{objects}(\mathrm{N}; \mathbf{S})) \wedge (\mathrm{objects}(\mathrm{N}; \mathbf{S}) \cap E = \emptyset) \}$ *and the* generalized support *of* $I$ *and* $E$ *in* $\mathbf{S}$ *is defined by* $[\![\mathrm{gcount}(I; E)]\!]_{\mathbf{S}} = |\mathrm{gcover}(I; E; \mathbf{S})|$.

Observe that $I \cap E \neq \emptyset$ implies that $\mathrm{gcover}(I; E; \mathbf{S}) = \emptyset$ and $[\![\mathrm{gcount}(I; E)]\!]_{\mathbf{S}} = 0$. Using the inclusion-exclusion principle [6], we can show that generalized-support terms $[\![\mathrm{gcount}(I; E)]\!]_{\mathbf{S}}$ are fully expressible using $|I \cup E|$-support terms only:

**Proposition 2.8.** *Let* $\mathbf{S}_1$ *and* $\mathbf{S}_2$ *be* $k$*-counting-equivalent structures and let* $I, E$ *be itemsets with* $|I \cup E| \leq k$. *We have* $[\![\mathrm{gcount}(I; E)]\!]_{\mathbf{S}_1} = [\![\mathrm{gcount}(I; E)]\!]_{\mathbf{S}_2}$.

Allowing basic $\mathrm{gcount}(\cdot)$ terms[3] of the form $\mathrm{gcount}(\mathcal{X}; \mathcal{Y}) \sim c$, with $\mathcal{X}$ and $\mathcal{Y}$ sets of object variables, "$\sim$" a comparison, and $c$ a constant, often simplifies the expression of counting-only queries.

*Example 2.9.* Since $\mathrm{count}(\mathcal{X}) = \mathrm{gcount}(\mathcal{X}; \emptyset)$, $\mathsf{Q}_1$, $\mathsf{Q}_3$, $\mathsf{Q}_5$, and $\mathsf{Q}_6$ can be expressed with basic $\mathrm{gcount}(\cdot)$ terms. Query $\mathsf{Q}_2$ cannot be rewritten with basic $\mathrm{gcount}(\cdot)$ terms, because it is not first-order definable [15] (see also Proposition 5.3). Query $\mathsf{Q}_4$ is equivalent to $\mathsf{Q}_4' = \{ \langle x, y \rangle \mid (x \neq y) \wedge \mathrm{gcount}(x; y) = 0 \wedge \mathrm{gcount}(y; x) = 0 \}$. Finally, $\mathsf{Q}_7$ and $\mathsf{Q}_7'$ are equivalent to

$$\mathsf{Q}_7'' = \{ \langle \rangle \mid \exists x \exists y_1 \exists y_2 \ (x \neq y_1) \wedge (x \neq y_2) \wedge (y_1 \neq y_2) \wedge$$
$$\mathrm{gcount}(x; y_1, y_2) = 0 \wedge \mathrm{gcount}(y_1; x) = 0 \wedge \mathrm{gcount}(y_2; x) = 0 \}.$$

## 3   A First-Order Logic for Bag-of-Sets Structures

We now study the relationships between counting-only queries and first-order definable queries. To query bag-of-sets structures, we use a two-sorted variant of first-order logic denoted SyCALC, based on the work of Gyssens et al. [11].[4] *Partial* SyCALC *formulae* are defined by the grammar

$$e := \Gamma(x, X) \mid x = y \mid X = Y \mid e \vee e \mid \neg e \mid \exists x \ e \mid \exists X \ e,$$

in which the lowercase variables $x$ and $y$ represent objects and the uppercase variables $X$ and $Y$ denote set names. We also allow the usual shorthands.

As to the semantics of a partial SyCALC formula $e$, let $\mathbf{S} = (\mathbf{N}, \gamma)$ be a structure, $\nu_{\mathcal{D}}$ a mapping from object variables to objects in $\mathcal{D}$, and $\nu_{\mathbf{N}}$ a mapping from

---

[3] These play a central role in the normal form of 1-counting-only first-order definable queries of Gyssens et al. [11]: **gteq**$(\mathrm{o}, c)$ corresponds to $[\![\mathrm{gcount}(\mathrm{o}; \emptyset)]\!]_{\mathbf{S}} \geq c$ and **cogteq**$(\mathrm{o}, c)$ to $[\![\mathrm{gcount}(\emptyset; \mathrm{o})]\!]_{\mathbf{S}} \geq |\mathbf{N}| - c$.

[4] Gyssens et al. [11] disallow object comparisons ($x = y$ in the grammar).

set name variables to set names in $\mathbf{N}$. We define the relationship $(\mathbf{S}, \nu_D, \nu_\mathbf{N}) \vDash e$, with all free variables of $e$ in the union of the domains of $\nu_D$ and $\nu_\mathbf{N}$, as follows:

$(\mathbf{S}, \nu_D, \nu_\mathbf{N}) \vDash \Gamma(x, X)$ if $(\nu_D(x), \nu_\mathbf{N}(X)) \in \gamma$;
$(\mathbf{S}, \nu_D, \nu_\mathbf{N}) \vDash x = y$    if $\nu_D(x) = \nu_D(y)$;
$(\mathbf{S}, \nu_D, \nu_\mathbf{N}) \vDash X = Y$    if $\nu_\mathbf{N}(X) = \nu_\mathbf{N}(Y)$;
$(\mathbf{S}, \nu_D, \nu_\mathbf{N}) \vDash e_1 \vee e_2$ if $(\mathbf{S}, \nu_D, \nu_\mathbf{N}) \vDash e_1$ or $(\mathbf{S}, \nu_D, \nu_\mathbf{N}) \vDash e_2$;
$(\mathbf{S}, \nu_D, \nu_\mathbf{N}) \vDash \neg e$    if $(\mathbf{S}, \nu_D, \nu_\mathbf{N}) \nvDash e$;
$(\mathbf{S}, \nu_D, \nu_\mathbf{N}) \vDash \exists x\ e$   if there exists $o \in \mathcal{D}$ with $(\mathbf{S}, \nu_D[x \mapsto o], \nu_\mathbf{N}) \vDash e$;
$(\mathbf{S}, \nu_D, \nu_\mathbf{N}) \vDash \exists X\ e$   if there exists $N \in \mathbf{N}$ with $(\mathbf{S}, \nu_D, \nu_\mathbf{N}[X \mapsto N]) \vDash e$.

Above, $M[\alpha \mapsto \beta]$ denotes $M$ modified by mapping $\alpha$ to $\beta$.

Let $e$ be a partial SyCALC formula with free object variables $x_1, \ldots, x_m$ and free set name variables $X_1, \ldots, X_n$, and let $\mathbf{S} = (\mathbf{N}, \gamma)$ be a structure. We define the *evaluation* of $e$ on $\mathbf{S}$ by $[\![e]\!]_\mathbf{S} = \{\langle o_1, \ldots, o_m, N_1, \ldots, N_n \rangle \mid (\mathbf{S}, \nu_D, \nu_\mathbf{N}) \vDash e\}$ in which $\nu_D = \{x_1 \mapsto o_1, \ldots, x_m \mapsto o_m\}$ and $\nu_\mathbf{N} = \{X_1 \mapsto N_1, \ldots, X_n \mapsto N_n\}$. A *SyCALC query* is a partial SyCALC formula without free set name variables.[5]

*Example 3.1.* Queries $Q_1$ and $Q_3$–$Q_7$ are all expressible in SyCALC:

$$Q_1 = \{\langle x \rangle \mid \exists X_1 \exists X_2\, ((X_1 \neq X_2) \wedge \Gamma(x, X_1) \wedge \Gamma(x, X_2))\};$$
$$Q_3 = \{\langle x, y \rangle \mid (x \neq y) \wedge \exists X\, (\Gamma(x, X) \wedge \Gamma(y, X))\};$$
$$Q_4 = \{\langle x, y \rangle \mid (x \neq y) \wedge \forall X\, (\Gamma(x, X) \iff \Gamma(y, X))\};$$
$$Q_5 = \{\langle\rangle \mid \exists X \exists x \exists y \exists z\, ((x \neq y) \wedge (x \neq z) \wedge (y \neq z) \wedge$$
$$\Gamma(x, X) \wedge \Gamma(y, X) \wedge \Gamma(z, X))\};$$
$$Q_6 = \{\langle\rangle \mid \exists X_1 \exists X_2 \exists X_3\, ((X_1 \neq X_2) \wedge (X_1 \neq X_3) \wedge (X_2 \neq X_3))\};$$
$$Q_7 = \{\langle\rangle \mid \exists x \exists y_1 \exists y_2\, ((x \neq y_1) \wedge (x \neq y_2) \wedge (y_1 \neq y_2) \wedge$$
$$(\forall X\, (\Gamma(x, X) \iff (\Gamma(y_1, X) \vee \Gamma(y_2, X)))))\}.$$

Not all counting-only queries are in SyCALC. An example is the 1-counting-only query $Q_2$ [15] (see also Proposition 5.3). Also, not all SyCALC queries are counting-only. To show this, we must exhibit a SyCALC query $Q$ and, for every $k$, $k \geq 0$, a pair of $k$-counting-equivalent structures $\mathbf{S}_{1,k}$ and $\mathbf{S}_{2,k}$, such that $Q$ can distinguish $\mathbf{S}_{1,k}$ and $\mathbf{S}_{2,k}$. To do so, we generalize the ideas underlying Example 2.4:

**Proposition 3.2.** *Let $A$ be a finite nonempty itemset, and $\mathbf{S}_{1,A}$ and $\mathbf{S}_{2,A}$ structures respectively representing the bags of sets $\{T \mid T \subseteq A \text{ and } \text{even}(|A - T|)\}$ and $\{T \mid T \subseteq A \text{ and } \text{odd}(|A - T|)\}$. We have the following:*

*(i) $\mathbf{S}_{1,A}$ is $(|A| - 1)$-counting-equivalent to $\mathbf{S}_{2,A}$.*
*(ii) $\mathbf{S}_{1,A}$ is not exactly-$|A|$-counting-equivalent to $\mathbf{S}_{2,A}$.*
*(iii) Only one of the structures has a set name to which no objects are related.*

---

[5] We also write a SyCALC query $e$ as $\{\langle x_1, \ldots, x_m \rangle \mid e\}$ to show the free object variables and their order explicitly.

*Proof.* Statement (ii) follows from the observation that only the itemset A has $|A|$ objects, and only $\mathbf{S}_1$ has a set name that covers this itemset. Statement (iii) follows from the observation that $\emptyset$ is represented only in $\mathbf{S}_1$—if even($|A|$)—or only in $\mathbf{S}_2$—if odd($|A|$). We now turn to Statement (i). Let $k = |A|$ and $I \subsetneq A$ an itemset with $|I| = m$. We must prove that $[\![\mathrm{count}(I)]\!]\mathbf{S}_1 = [\![\mathrm{count}(I)]\!]\mathbf{S}_2$. Consider any itemset T with $I \subseteq T \subseteq A$. Let $|T| = n$. As T contains the objects of I, there remain $n - m$ unconstrained objects in $A - I$. Hence, there are exactly $\binom{k-m}{n-m}$ of such sets T. Thus,

$$[\![\mathrm{count}(I)]\!]\mathbf{S}_1 = \sum_{\substack{m \leq n \leq k, \\ \mathrm{even}(k-n)}} \binom{k-m}{n-m} = \sum_{\substack{0 \leq j \leq k-m, \\ \mathrm{even}(k-m-j)}} \binom{k-m}{j} = 2^{k-m-1}$$

$$= \sum_{\substack{0 \leq j \leq k-m, \\ \mathrm{odd}(k-m-j)}} \binom{k-m}{j} = \sum_{\substack{m \leq n \leq k, \\ \mathrm{odd}(k-n)}} \binom{k-m}{n-m} = [\![\mathrm{count}(I)]\!]\mathbf{S}_2,$$

completing the proof. □

Using Proposition 3.2, we can now prove the following:

**Proposition 3.3.** *Not all Boolean SyCALC queries are counting-only.*

*Proof.* For all $k$, $k \geq 0$, let $A_k \subset \mathcal{D}$ be a set of objects with $|A_k| = k + 1$, and let $\mathbf{S}_{1,A_k}$ and $\mathbf{S}_{2,A_k}$ be as in Proposition 3.2. We see that the Boolean SyCALC query

$$Q_8 = \{\langle\rangle \mid \exists X \forall x \; (\exists Y \; (\Gamma(x, Y)) \implies \Gamma(x, X))\}$$

cannot be counting-only, since $[\![Q_8]\!]\mathbf{S}_{1,A_k} = \mathbf{true}$ and $[\![Q_8]\!]\mathbf{S}_{2,A_k} = \mathbf{false}$. □

Even though not all counting-only queries are in SyCALC and vice versa, there is a strong connection between both: all basic $\mathrm{gcount}(\cdot)$ terms are expressible in SyCALC. E.g., $\mathrm{gcount}(\mathcal{X}; \mathcal{Y}) \geq c$ is expressed by

$$\exists Z_1 \ldots \exists Z_c \left( \bigwedge_{1 \leq i < j \leq c} (Z_i \neq Z_j) \wedge \bigwedge_{x \in \mathcal{X}} (\Gamma(x, Z_1) \wedge \cdots \wedge \Gamma(x, Z_c)) \wedge \right.$$
$$\left. \bigwedge_{y \in \mathcal{Y}} (\neg\Gamma(y, Z_1) \wedge \cdots \wedge \neg\Gamma(y, Z_c)) \right).$$

## 4   QuineCALC and SimpleCALC

In Sect. 3, we studied the counting-only SyCALC queries, a *semantic* fragment of SyCALC. The observation that the SyCALC expression for $\mathrm{gcount}(\mathcal{X}; \mathcal{Y}) \geq c$ above, which can be used to express most queries we have seen up till now, does not use object quantification inspires us to define the following *syntactic* fragments of SyCALC:

**Definition 4.1.** *QuineCALC*[6] *consist of all SyCALC queries that do not use object quantification. SimpleCALC consists of all queries that are built from QuineCALC queries using disjunction, negation, and object quantification.*

---

[6] Gyssens et al. [11] introduced the single-object-variable fragment of QuineCALC as a first-order query language that provides a conservative extension of the symmetric Boolean functions of Quine [16], hence the name.

For $k \geq 0$, $k$-SyCALC denotes the $k$-counting-only SyCALC queries; Quine-CALC-$k$ denotes the QuineCALC queries with at most $k$ free object variables; and SimpleCALC-$k$ denotes the SimpleCALC queries built from QuineCALC-$k$ queries.

By definition, all queries expressible using basic gcount($\cdot$) terms only, such as $Q_1$ and $Q_3$–$Q_7$, are in SimpleCALC. We will show next that all SimpleCALC-$k$ queries are $k$-counting-only. To do so, we need

**Definition 4.2.** *Let $\mathbf{S}_1 = (\mathbf{N}_1, \gamma_1)$ and $\mathbf{S}_2 = (\mathbf{N}_2, \gamma_2)$ be structures, and let I be an itemset. Set names $N_1 \in \mathbf{N}_1$ and $N_2 \in \mathbf{N}_2$ are I-equivalent if objects($N_1$; $\mathbf{S}_1$) $\cap$ I = objects($N_2$; $\mathbf{S}_2$) $\cap$ I. A bijection $b : \mathbf{N}_1 \to \mathbf{N}_2$ is an I-preserving mapping if, for all $N \in \mathbf{N}_1$, N and $b(N)$ are I-equivalent.*

We can now give an alternative characterization of $k$-counting equivalence:

**Lemma 4.3.** *Let $\mathbf{S}_1 = (\mathbf{N}_1, \gamma_1)$ and $\mathbf{S}_2 = (\mathbf{N}_2, \gamma_2)$ be structures. Then, $\mathbf{S}_1$ and $\mathbf{S}_2$ are $k$-counting-equivalent if and only if, for every itemset I, $|I| \leq k$, there exists an I-preserving mapping $b : \mathbf{N}_1 \to \mathbf{N}_2$.*

Using Lemma 4.3, a straightforward structural induction argument on partial QuineCALC formulae—partial SyCALC formula without object quantification—yields the following:

**Lemma 4.4.** *Let $e$ be a partial QuineCALC formula with $k$ free object variables. For every pair of $k$-counting-equivalent structures $\mathbf{S}_1 = (\mathbf{N}_1, \gamma_1)$, $\mathbf{S}_2 = (\mathbf{N}_2, \gamma_2)$, every mapping $\nu_{\mathcal{D}}$ from free object variables in $e$ to an itemset $I \subset \mathcal{D}$ with $|I| \leq k$, every mapping $\nu_{\mathbf{N}_1}$ from free set name variables in $e$ to $\mathbf{N}_1$, and every I-preserving mapping $b$ from $\mathbf{S}_1$ to $\mathbf{S}_2$, $(\mathbf{S}_1, \nu_{\mathcal{D}}, \nu_{\mathbf{N}_1}) \vDash e \iff (\mathbf{S}_2, \nu_{\mathcal{D}}, b \circ \nu_{\mathbf{N}_1}) \vDash e$.*

Lemma 4.4 implies that QuineCALC-$k$ queries are $k$-counting-only. To extend this to SimpleCALC-$k$, it suffices to show that

**Proposition 4.5.** *$k$-SyCALC is closed under disjunction, negation, and object quantification.*

**Corollary 4.6.** *All QuineCALC-$k$ and SimpleCALC-$k$ queries are in $k$-SyCALC.*

# 5 Counting-Only Hierarchies

We now have four hierarchies of counting-only queries, for $k \geq 0$: $k$-counting-only queries, $k$-SyCALC, QuineCALC-$k$, and SimpleCALC-$k$. We show that all four hierarchies are non-collapsing:

**Theorem 5.1.** *Let $k \geq 0$*

*(i) Every $k$-counting-only query is also $(k+1)$-counting-only.*
*(ii) There is QuineCALC-$(k+1)$ query which is not $k$-counting-only.*
*(iii) There is a Boolean SimpleCALC-$(k+1)$ query which is not $k$-counting-only.*

*Proof.* Statement (i) follows immediately from the definition. For Statements (ii) and (iii), let $\mathbf{S}_{1,A}$ and $\mathbf{S}_{2,A}$ be the structures of Proposition 3.2 with $|A| = k+1$. These structures are $k$-counting-equivalent, but not $(k+1)$-counting-equivalent. For Statement (ii), we consider $e = \exists X \left( \bigwedge_{1 \leq i \leq k+1} \Gamma(x_i, X) \right)$, which is a $(k+1)$-counting-only QuineCALC-$(k+1)$ query by Corollary 4.6. Let $t$ be a $(k+1)$-tuple containing each value of A once. Then, $t \in [\![e]\!]_{\mathbf{S}_1}$, but $t \notin [\![e]\!]_{\mathbf{S}_2}$. Hence, $e$ is not $k$-counting-only. For Statement (iii), we construct from $e$ the Boolean SimpleCALC-$(k+1)$ query $e' = \exists x_1 \ldots x_{k+1} \left( \left( \bigwedge_{1 \leq j < j' \leq k+1} (x_j \neq x_{j'}) \right) \wedge e(x_1, \ldots, x_{k+1}) \right)$ Then, $[\![e']\!]_{\mathbf{S}_1} = \texttt{true}$ and $[\![e']\!]_{\mathbf{S}_2} = \texttt{false}$. Hence, $e'$ is not $k$-counting-only.  □

Statement (iii) can be interpreted as the Boolean version of Statement (ii). Since QuineCALC-$k$ and SimpleCALC-$k$ queries are also $k$-SyCALC queries as well as $k$-counting queries, Theorem 5.1 extends to all four hierarchies.

We now proceed by comparing the fragments *mutually*. The 0-counting-only fragments have straightforward relationships:

**Proposition 5.2.** *The languages 0-SyCALC, SimpleCALC-0, and QuineCALC-0 all express exactly the same set of queries.*

We have already argued that the 1-counting-only query $\mathsf{Q}_2$ is not first-order definable [15]. Also the 0-counting-only query

$$\mathsf{Q}_9 = \{\langle\rangle \mid \text{count}() \text{ is } even\}$$

is not first-order definable. Consequently, we have:

**Proposition 5.3.** *There is a Boolean 0-counting-only query not expressible in SyCALC.*

By Proposition 5.3 and Theorem 5.1 (i), $\mathsf{Q}_9$ also witnesses that, for all $k$, $k \geq 0$, there is a Boolean $k$-counting-only queries not expressible in $k$-SyCALC.

Due to QuineCALC queries not allowing object quantification, all Boolean QuineCALC queries are in QuineCALC-0. Hence, no Boolean query that is $k$-counting-only, $k \geq 1$, but not $(k-1)$-counting-only is expressible in QuineCALC-$k$. Hence, it only remains to establish a separation between $k$-SyCALC and Simple-CALC-$k$. We first deal with the special case $k = 1$.

**Proposition 5.4.** *There is a Boolean 1-SyCALC query not expressible in SimpleCALC-1.*

*Proof.* The Boolean 1-SyCALC query

$$\mathsf{Q}_{10} = \{\langle\rangle \mid \exists x \exists y \, ((x \neq y) \wedge \exists X \exists Y \, (\Gamma(x, X) \wedge \Gamma(y, Y)))\},$$

which queries for structures with an active domain of at least two objects, is 1-counting-only but not expressible in SimpleCALC-1.  □

To establish the separation between $k$-SyCALC and SimpleCALC-$k$, $k \geq 2$, we exhibit a 2-SyCALC query, which is not 1-counting-only, that is not expressible in SimpleCALC. Thereto, let

$$\texttt{set-ids} =| \ \forall X \exists x \ (\Gamma(x, X) \wedge \neg \exists Y \ ((X \neq Y) \wedge \Gamma(x, Y)))$$

be the Boolean query specifying that each set in a bag of sets has a distinct identifying object. We first prove that $\texttt{set-ids}$ is in 2-SyCALC, but not in 1-SyCALC, despite it using only a single object variable.

**Proposition 5.5.** *Query* $\texttt{set-ids}$ *is 2-counting-only, but not 1-counting-only.*

*Proof.* Let $o_1, o_2 \in \mathcal{D}$ and $N_1, N_2 \in \mathcal{N}$. Let $\mathbf{S}_1 = (\{N_1, N_2\}, \{(o_1, N_1), (o_2, N_2)\})$ and $\mathbf{S}_2 = (\{N_1, N_2\}, \{(o_1, N_1), (o_2, N_1)\})$. Since $\mathbf{S}_1$ and $\mathbf{S}_2$ are 1-counting-equivalent, while $[\![\texttt{set-ids}]\!]_{\mathbf{S}_1} = \texttt{true}$ and $[\![\texttt{set-ids}]\!]_{\mathbf{S}_2} = \texttt{false}$, $\texttt{set-ids}$ is not 1-counting-only. For a structure $\mathbf{S} = (\mathbf{N}, \gamma)$ with $|\mathbf{N}| = n$, $[\![\texttt{set-ids}]\!]_{\mathbf{S}} = \texttt{true}$ if and only if there exist $o_1, \dots, o_n \in \text{adom}(\mathbf{S})$ such that, for all $i$, $1 \leq i \leq n$, $[\![\text{count}(o_i)]\!]_{\mathbf{S}} = 1$ and, for all $i, j$, $1 \leq i < j \leq n$, $[\![\text{count}(o_i, o_j)]\!]_{\mathbf{S}} = 0$. By Proposition 2.8, $\texttt{set-ids}$ is 2-counting-only. $\square$

Observe that $\texttt{set-ids}$ can only evaluate to $\texttt{true}$ on a structure if the size of its active domain is lowerbounded by the number of set names in the structure. This contradicts $\texttt{set-ids}$ being expressible in SimpleCALC provided we can prove that whenever a SimpleCALC query evaluates to $\texttt{true}$ on some structure, it also evaluates to $\texttt{true}$ on some structure for which the size of the active domain is upperbounded by a function of the size of the query only. Thereto, we start with QuineCALC queries. If a QuineCALC query returns on some structure the tuple $t$, we can intuitively reduce the number of active-domain objects in that structure to the number of object variables in the query without compromising that $t$ is returned, because all object variables are free. In order to substantiate this intuition, we introduce the notion of *active-domain preservation*:

**Definition 5.6.** *Let* $\mathbf{S} = (\mathbf{N}, \gamma)$ *be a structure and* $I$ *an itemset. A bijection* $m : \mathcal{D} \to \mathcal{D}$ *is* active-domain preserving *for* $\mathbf{S}$ *and* $I$ *if it is the identity on* $\text{adom}(\mathbf{S}|_I)$, *and maps objects to* $\mathcal{D} - \text{adom}(\mathbf{S}|_I)$ *only if they are in* $\mathcal{D} - \text{adom}(\mathbf{S})$.

Notice that $m$ is not necessarily the identity on all of $I$.

For QuineCALC queries with $k$ (free) object variables, we can use active-domain preservation to state in a precise way that, for our purposes, we can restrict the active domain of structures to $k$ objects:

**Proposition 5.7.** *Let* $e$ *be a partial QuineCALC formula with* $k$ *object variables. For every structure* $\mathbf{S} = (\mathbf{N}, \gamma)$, *mapping* $\nu_{\mathcal{D}}$ *from object variables in* $e$ *to an itemset* $I \subset \mathcal{D}$ *with* $|I| \leq k$, *mapping* $\nu_{\mathbf{N}}$ *from free set name variables in* $e$ *to* $\mathbf{N}$, *and active-domain preserving mapping* $m$ *for* $\mathbf{S}$ *and* $I$, $(\mathbf{S}, \nu_{\mathcal{D}}, \nu_{\mathbf{N}}) \vDash e \iff (\mathbf{S}|_I, m \circ \nu_{\mathcal{D}}, \nu_{\mathbf{N}}) \vDash e$.

To generalize Proposition 5.7 to SimpleCALC, we need to take into account object quantification:

**Definition 5.8.** *Let $e$ be a SimpleCALC query. We denote the* object variable count *of $e$ by* vars$(e)$. *If $e$ is a QuineCALC query with $k$ (free) object variables, then* vars$(e) = k$; *if $e \equiv \neg e'$ or $e \equiv \exists x \; e'$, then* vars$(e) = $ vars$(e')$; *and if $e \equiv e_1 \vee e_2$, then* vars$(e) = $ vars$(e_1) + $ vars$(e_2)$.

**Proposition 5.9.** *Let $e$ be a SimpleCALC query with $k$ free object variables, $\mathbf{S} = (\mathbf{N}, \gamma)$ a structure, and $\nu_{\mathcal{D}}$ a mapping from free object variables in $e$ to an itemset $I \subset \mathcal{D}$ with $|I| \leq k$. There exists an itemset $V$ with $I \subseteq V$ and $|V| \leq$ vars$(e)$ such that, for every itemset $W$ with $V \subseteq W$ and active-domain preserving mapping $m$ for $\mathbf{S}$ and $W$, we have $(\mathbf{S}, \nu_{\mathcal{D}}, \emptyset) \vDash e$ if and only if $(\mathbf{S}|_W, m \circ \nu_{\mathcal{D}}, \emptyset) \vDash e$.*

We can now prove that `set-ids` is not expressible in SimpleCALC:

**Proposition 5.10.** *The query `set-ids` is not expressible in SimpleCALC.*

*Proof.* Assume there exists a (Boolean) SimpleCALC query $e$ such that, for every structure $\mathbf{S}$, $[\![e]\!]_{\mathbf{S}} = [\![\text{set-ids}]\!]_{\mathbf{S}}$. Let $n = $ vars$(e) + 1$, $\{o_0, \ldots, o_n\}$ an itemset, and $\mathbf{N} = \{N_0, \ldots, N_n\} \subset \mathcal{N}$. Let $\mathbf{S}_{n+1} = (\mathbf{N}, \{(o_i, N_i) \mid 0 \leq i \leq n + 1\})$, and $\mathbf{S}_n = (\mathbf{N}, \{(o_i, N_i) \mid 1 \leq i \leq n\})$. Hence, $\mathbf{S}_n = \mathbf{S}_{n+1}|_W$ with $W = \{o_1, \ldots, o_n\}$. By construction, $[\![e]\!]_{\mathbf{S}_{n+1}} \neq \emptyset$ and $[\![e]\!]_{\mathbf{S}_n} = \emptyset$. By Proposition 5.9, however, $[\![e]\!]_{\mathbf{S}_{n+1}} = \emptyset \iff [\![e]\!]_{\mathbf{S}_n} = \emptyset$, a contradiction. Hence, `set-ids` is not expressible in Simple-CALC. $\qquad\square$

**Corollary 5.11.** *There is a Boolean 2-SyCALC query not expressible in Simple-CALC.*

# 6    Dichotomy for Satisfiability-Related Decision Problems

We study the decidability of satisfiability, validity, query containment, and query equivalence for the query languages we introduced. We first observe the following:

**Lemma 6.1.** *Let $L$ be $k$-SyCALC or SimpleCALC-$k$, and $p_1$ and $p_2$ two decision problems chosen from satisfiability, validity, query containment, and query equivalence. Then $p_1$ is decidable for $L$ if and only if $p_2$ is decidable for $L$.*

Because of Lemma 6.1, we only study the satisfiability problem in more detail.

## 6.1    Satisfiability of SimpleCALC is Decidable

To prove that satisfiability is decidable for queries in SimpleCALC, we show that this language has the *finite model property*: a query is satisfiable if and only if it is satisfiable in a structure of which the size (in terms of the number of set names and active domain objects) is uniformly bounded in terms of the size of the query. Proposition 5.9 gives an upperbound on the required number of active domain objects. To also obtain an upperbound on the required number of set names, we consider that SyCALC is essentially a two-sorted variant of first-order logic. Intuitively, this puts severe restrictions to the ability of SyCALC and SimpleCALC to count. We formalize this intuition next.

**Definition 6.2.** *Let $k, d \geq 0$. Structures $\mathbf{S}_1 = (\mathbf{N}_1, \gamma_1)$ and $\mathbf{S}_2 = (\mathbf{N}_2, \gamma_2)$ are $d$-partial $k$-counting-equivalent if, for every pair of itemsets $I$ and $E$ with $|I \cup E| \leq k$, either*

*(i) $[\![\text{gcount}(I; E)]\!]_{\mathbf{S}_1} = [\![\text{gcount}(I; E)]\!]_{\mathbf{S}_2} \leq d$; or*
*(ii) $d < [\![\text{gcount}(I; E)]\!]_{\mathbf{S}_1} < |\mathbf{N}_1| - d$ and $d < [\![\text{gcount}(I; E)]\!]_{\mathbf{S}_2} < |\mathbf{N}_2| - d$; or*
*(iii) $|\mathbf{N}_1| - [\![\text{gcount}(I; E)]\!]_{\mathbf{S}_1} = |\mathbf{N}_2| - [\![\text{gcount}(I; E)]\!]_{\mathbf{S}_2} \leq d$.*

Even though partial counting-equivalence is a weaker condition than counting-equivalence, it is nevertheless sufficient to establish the indistinguishability of two structures by a SyCALC query if we know its set name quantifier depth:

**Lemma 6.3.** *Let $e$ be a SyCALC query with set name quantifier depth $d$, and let $\mathbf{S}_1$ and $\mathbf{S}_2$ be $d$-partial $k$-counting-equivalent structures with $k = |\text{adom}(\mathbf{S}_1)| = |\text{adom}(\mathbf{S}_2)|$. Then $[\![e]\!]_{\mathbf{S}_1} = [\![e]\!]_{\mathbf{S}_2}$.*

Lemma 6.3 can be proved using an Ehrenfeucht-Fraïssé game in which the Spoiler can play up to $d$ set names and an arbitrary number of objects. We now use this lemma to prove the following upperbound:

**Proposition 6.4.** *Let $\mathbf{S} = (\mathbf{N}, \gamma)$ be a structure with $|\text{adom}(\mathbf{S})| = k$, and let $d \geq 0$. There exists a structure $\mathbf{S}' = (\mathbf{N}', \gamma')$ with $|\mathbf{N}'| \leq (d+1) \cdot 2^k$ such that $\mathbf{S}$ and $\mathbf{S}'$ are $d$-partial $k$-counting-equivalent structures.*

*Proof (Sketch).* Initially, $\mathbf{S}'$ is empty. Then, for every itemset $I$ of $\mathbf{S}$, we add $\min(d+1, [\![\text{gcount}(I; \text{adom}(\mathbf{S}) - I)]\!]_{\mathbf{S}})$ relation names to $\mathbf{N}'$ and associate each of them in $\gamma'$ with precisely all elements of $I$. By construction, $|\mathbf{N}'| \leq (d+1) \cdot 2^k$. It is then verified that $\mathbf{S}$ and $\mathbf{S}'$ are $d$-partial $k$-counting-equivalent. $\qquad\square$

Combining Propositions 5.9 and 6.4 proves that SimpleCALC has the finite model property and that the size of these finite models is uniformly upperbounded by an exponential function of the query size. Hence, the satisfiability problem is decidable. Using a reduction involving monadic first-order logic (over structures with only unary relations), for which satisfiability is NEXPTIME-complete [3,14], we can also prove a lowerbound on the complexity of the satisfiability problem:

**Theorem 6.5.** *Satisfiability is decidable for SimpleCALC queries, and is NEXP-TIME-hard for SimpleCALC-$k$ query, $k \geq 2$.*

*Proof (Sketch).* Let $S = (\mathcal{M}; X_1, \ldots, X_n)$ be a first-order structure over domain $\mathcal{M}$ with unary predicates $X_1, \ldots, X_n$ and $\varphi$ a first-order logic formula over $S$ without free variables. We encode the first-order structure $S$ into bag-of-sets structure. To do so, we represent the unary predicates $X_1, \ldots, X_n$ by set names $N_1, \ldots, N_n$. In SimpleCALC, we cannot freely use set name quantification, however. We solve this by associating to each set name $N_i$ a unique identifying object $o_i$, $1 \leq i \leq n$. The domain element of $\mathcal{M}$ are represented by objects distinct from $o_1, \ldots, o_n$, and translate predicate membership tests into $\mathrm{count}(\cdot, \cdot)$ terms. In summary, we encode $S$ by a structure $\mathbf{S} = (\mathbf{N}, \gamma)$ with $\mathbf{N} = \{N_1, \ldots, N_n\}$ and $\gamma = \{(o_1, N_1), \ldots, (o_n, N_n)\} \cup \{(m, N_i) \mid m \in \mathcal{M} \wedge X_i(m)\}$, in which $m$ is the object representing $m$. We now translate $\varphi$ to the expression $e$ given by

$$\mathrm{count}() = n \wedge \exists y_1 \ldots \exists y_n \left( \tau(\varphi) \wedge \left( \bigwedge_{1 \leq i \leq n} \mathrm{count}(y_i) = 1 \right) \wedge \right.$$
$$\left. \left( \bigwedge_{1 \leq i < j \leq n} \mathrm{count}(y_i, y_j) = 0 \right) \right),$$

in which $\tau(\varphi)$ is the translation of $\varphi$ obtained by replacing all subformula $\exists y\, \varphi'$ by $\exists y\, (\bigwedge_{1 \leq i \leq n} (y \neq y_i) \wedge \tau(\varphi'(y)))$ and all terms of the form $X_i(b)$ by $\mathrm{count}(b, y_i) = 1$. Using Lemma 6.10, one can prove that the resulting Boolean formula $e$ is in SimpleCALC-2, and that $e$ is satisfiable if and only if the monadic first-order logic formula $\varphi$ is satisfiable. □

## 6.2  Satisfiability of 1-SyCALC is Decidable

By Propositions 5.2, the decidability of the satisfiability problem for 0-SyCALC follows from the decidability of the satisfiability problem for SimpleCALC-1. This does not extend to 1-SyCALC, unfortunately, but we can still prove that the satisfiability problem for 1-SyCALC is decidable. Again, we show that the finite model property holds. First, we put an upperbound on the number of set names.

**Proposition 6.6.** *Let $d \geq 0$, and let $\mathbf{S} = (\mathbf{N}, \gamma)$ be a structure. There exists a structure $\mathbf{S}' = (\mathbf{N}', \gamma')$ with $|\mathbf{N}'| \leq 2d + 1$ such that $\mathbf{S}$ and $\mathbf{S}'$ are $d$-partial 1-counting-equivalent structures.*

*Proof.* If $|\mathbf{N}| \leq 2d + 1$, we put $\mathbf{S}' = \mathbf{S}$, and Proposition 6.6 trivially holds. Otherwise, let $\mathbf{N}' = \{N_1, \ldots, N_{2d+1}\}$ and

$$\gamma' = \{(o, N_i) \mid ([\![\mathrm{count}(o)]\!]_{\mathbf{S}} \leq d) \wedge (1 \leq i \leq [\![\mathrm{count}(o)]\!]_{\mathbf{S}})\} \cup$$
$$\{(o, N_i) \mid (d < ([\![\mathrm{count}(o)]\!]_{\mathbf{S}}) < |\mathbf{N}| - d) \wedge (1 \leq i \leq d + 1)\} \cup$$
$$\{(o, N_i) \mid (|\mathbf{N}| - d \leq [\![\mathrm{count}(o)]\!]_{\mathbf{S}}) \wedge (1 \leq i \leq 2d + 1 - (|\mathbf{N}| - [\![\mathrm{count}(o)]\!]_{\mathbf{S}}))\}.$$

Using that, for $o \in \mathcal{D}$ and $\mathbf{S}'' = (\mathbf{N}'', \gamma'')$ any structure, $[\![\mathrm{gcount}(o; \emptyset)]\!]_{\mathbf{S}''} = [\![\mathrm{count}(o)]\!]_{\mathbf{S}''}$ and $[\![\mathrm{gcount}(\emptyset; o)]\!]_{\mathbf{S}''} = |\mathbf{N}''| - [\![\mathrm{count}(o)]\!]_{\mathbf{S}''}$, we can verify that $\mathbf{S}$ and $\mathbf{S}'$ are $d$-partial 1-counting-equivalent structures. □

Next, we put an upper bound on the number of objects.

**Proposition 6.7.** *Let $e$ be a 1-SyCALC query with set name quantifier depth $d$ and object quantifier depth $r$, and let $\mathbf{S} = (\mathbf{N}, \gamma)$ be a structure. Then, $[\![e]\!]_{\mathbf{S}} \neq \emptyset$ if and only if there exists a structure $\mathbf{S}' = (\mathbf{N}', \gamma')$ with $|\mathbf{N}'| \leq 2d + 1$, $|\mathrm{adom}(\mathbf{S}')| \leq r(2d + 1)$, and $[\![e]\!]_{\mathbf{S}'} \neq \emptyset$.*

*Proof (Sketch).* By Proposition 6.6, we may assume without loss of generality that $|\mathbf{N}| \leq 2d + 1$. Let $\mathbf{N}' = \{N_1, \ldots, N_{|\mathbf{N}|}\}$ and $I_i = \{o \mid [\![\text{count}(o)]\!]_\mathbf{S} = i\}$, $1 \leq i \leq |\mathbf{N}|$. Since $\mathbf{S}$ and $\mathbf{S}'' = (\mathbf{N}', \gamma'')$ where $\gamma'' = \{(o, N_j) \mid (1 \leq j \leq i \leq |\mathbf{N}|) \wedge (o \in I_i)\}$ are 1-counting-equivalent, $[\![e]\!]_{\mathbf{S}''} = [\![e]\!]_\mathbf{S}$. Choose $P_i \subseteq I_i$ such that $|P_i| = \min(|I_i|, r)$, $1 \leq i \leq |\mathbf{N}|$, and let $\mathbf{S}' = (\mathbf{N}', \gamma')$ where $\gamma' = \{(o, N_j) \mid (1 \leq j \leq i \leq |\mathbf{N}|) \wedge (o \in P_i)\}$. We can show that $e$ cannot distinguish between $\mathbf{S}'$ and $\mathbf{S}$ using an Ehrenfeucht-Fraïssé game in which the Spoiler can play up to $r$ objects and an arbitrary number of set names. $\qquad \square$

Propositions 6.6 and 6.7 combined prove that 1-SyCALC has the finite model property and that the size of these finite models is uniformly upperbounded by a polynomial function of the query size. Hence,

**Theorem 6.8.** *The satisfiability problem is decidable for* 1-SyCALC *queries.*

## 6.3   Satisfiability of 2-SyCALC is Undecidable

To prove undecidability of satisfiability for 2-SyCALC, we reduce satisfiability of standard first-order logic queries on undirected unlabeled graphs without self-loops, a well-known undecidable problem,[7] to satisfiability of the strict fragment of 2-SyCALC that does not allow object comparisons (of the form $x = y$).

An *undirected unlabeled graph without self-loops*, or *graph*, for short, is a pair $\mathbf{G} = (\mathbf{V}, \mathbf{E})$ in which $\mathbf{V}$ is a set of nodes and $\mathbf{E} \subseteq \mathbf{V} \times \mathbf{V}$ is an antireflexive and symmetric edge relation. On such graphs we consider standard first-order logic formulae of the form $e := x_1 = x_2 \mid \mathbf{E}(x_1, x_2) \mid e \vee e \mid \neg e \mid \exists x\, e$, in which $x_1$, $x_2$, and $x$ are node variables. We write $[\![e]\!]_\mathbf{G}$ to denote the evaluation of $e$ on $\mathbf{G}$.

We define the encoding of $\mathbf{G} = (\mathbf{V}, \mathbf{E})$ as the structure $\text{enc}(\mathbf{G}) = (\mathbf{N}, \gamma)$ where $\mathbf{N} = \mathbf{V}$ and $\gamma = \{(\{x_1, x_2\}, x_1), (\{x_1, x_2\}, x_2) \mid (x_1, x_2) \in \mathbf{E}\} \cup \{(\{x\}, x) \mid x \in \mathbf{V}\}$. The active domain consists of node-pair sets, representing the edges of $\mathbf{G}$, and singleton node sets, serving as distinctive identifying objects. Each node pair set has a support of 2, identifying the end-points of the edge represented. The structure $\text{enc}(\mathbf{G})$ always satisfies the following Boolean SyCALC query:

$$\texttt{enc-graph} = \texttt{set-ids} \wedge \forall x \exists X_1 \exists X_2\, (((X_1 \neq X_2) \wedge \Gamma(x, X_1) \wedge \Gamma(x, X_2)) \Rightarrow$$
$$\forall Y\, ((X_1 \neq Y) \wedge (X_2 \neq Y) \Rightarrow \neg\Gamma(x, Y))).$$

If $\nu$ converts node variables in a first-order logic formula on graphs $\varphi$, then the corresponding translation $\tau(\varphi)_\nu$ into a SyCALC query is defined as follows:

$$\tau(x_1 = x_2)_\nu \equiv \nu(x_1) = \nu(x_2);$$
$$\tau(\mathbf{E}(x_1, x_2))_\nu \equiv (\nu(x_1) \neq \nu(x_2)) \wedge \exists x\, (\Gamma(x, \nu(x_1)) \wedge \Gamma(x, \nu(x_2)));$$
$$\tau(e_1 \vee e_2)_\nu \equiv \tau(e_1)_\nu \vee \tau(e_2)_\nu;$$
$$\tau(\neg e)_\nu \equiv \neg\tau(e)_\nu;$$
$$\tau(\exists x\, e)_\nu \equiv \exists X\, \tau(e)_{\nu[x \mapsto X]},$$

---

[7] We have no direct reference, but if we use a straightforward encoding from binary relations to undirected unlabeled graphs without self-loops, we can rely on Trakhtenbrot's Theorem [15, Theorem 9.2].

with $X$ a fresh set name variable. We define the encoding of a *Boolean* first-order logic formula on graphs $\varphi$ in SyCALC as $\text{enc}(\varphi) = \text{enc-graph} \land \tau(\varphi)_\emptyset$. Obviously,

**Lemma 6.9.** *Let* $\mathbf{G}$ *be a graph and let* $\varphi$ *be a Boolean first-order logic formula on graphs. Then,* $\llbracket \varphi \rrbracket_\mathbf{G} = \llbracket \text{enc}(\varphi) \rrbracket_{\text{enc}(\mathbf{G})}$.

Next, we prove that, for any first-order Boolean logic formula $\varphi$ on graphs, $\text{enc}(\varphi)$ is a Boolean 2-SyCALC query. We do so by proving that 2-counting-equivalent structures satisfying the Boolean 2-SyCALC query set-ids must be isomorphic.

**Lemma 6.10.** *If* $\mathbf{S}_1$ *and* $\mathbf{S}_2$ *are structures that are 2-counting-equivalent, and* $\llbracket \text{set-ids} \rrbracket_{\mathbf{S}_1} = \llbracket \text{set-ids} \rrbracket_{\mathbf{S}_2} = \text{true}$, *then* $\mathbf{S}_1$ *and* $\mathbf{S}_2$ *are isomorphic.*

**Corollary 6.11.** *If* $\varphi$ *is a Boolean first-order logic formula on graphs, then* $\text{enc}(\varphi)$ *is a 2-SyCALC query.*

Now, let $\mathbf{S}$ be a structure for which $\llbracket \text{enc}(\varphi) \rrbracket_\mathbf{S} \neq \emptyset$, with $\varphi$ a Boolean first-order logic formula. For the last step in our reduction, we must find a graph $\mathbf{G_S}$ such that $\llbracket \varphi \rrbracket_{\mathbf{G_S}} \neq \emptyset$. Ideally, we would like that, up to isomorphism, $\text{enc}(\mathbf{G_S}) = \mathbf{S}$, but that can unfortunately not be guaranteed. Nevertheless, we can construct a graph $\mathbf{G_S}$ for which $\llbracket \varphi \rrbracket_{\mathbf{G_S}} \neq \emptyset$:

**Lemma 6.12.** *Let* $\varphi$ *be a Boolean first-order logic formula on graphs. If there exists a structure* $\mathbf{S}$ *satisfying* $\text{enc}(\varphi)$, *then we can construct from* $\mathbf{S}$ *a graph satisfying* $\varphi$.

Using Lemmas 6.9 and 6.12, we conclude the following:

**Theorem 6.13.** *The satisfiability problem is undecidable for* 2-*SyCALC queries.*

# 7   Conclusion and Discussion

In this paper, we studied so-called counting-only queries on bag-of-sets data, which can be answered by only counting the occurrence of itemsets of objects. In particular, we identified and studied the syntactic counting-only fragments QuineCALC and SimpleCALC of first-order logic. These query languages can express many practically relevant queries other than the usual classes of "well-behaved" first-order queries—such as the conjunctive queries, the monadic first-order logic, and the two-variable fragments of first-order logic—while, at the same time, still being simple enough for satisfiability, validity, query containment, and query equivalence to be decidable. We have summarized our findings in Fig. 3.

| First-order definable queries (SyCALC) $Q_8$ | | | |
|---|---|---|---|
| QuineCALC | SimpleCALC | Counting-only SyCALC | Counting-only queries |
| $\vdots$ | $\vdots$ | $\vdots$ | $\vdots$ |
| QuineCALC-3 | SimpleCALC-3 $Q_5$ | 3-SyCALC | 3-counting-only queries |
| QuineCALC-2 $Q_3, Q_4$ | SimpleCALC-2 $Q_7$ | 2-SyCALC set-ids | 2-counting-only queries |
| QuineCALC-1 $Q_1$ | SimpleCALC-1 | 1-SyCALC $Q_{10}$ | 1-counting-only queries $Q_2$ |
| QuineCALC-0 ≡ SimpleCALC-0 ≡ 0-SyCALC $Q_6$ | | | 0-counting-only queries $Q_9$ |

**Fig. 3.** Main relationships between the query languages considered. The counting-only languages are highlighted in light gray, and the first-order definable languages in dark gray. A language to the left and/or below another language, is less expressive than the latter. Separate boxes also indicate strict separation in expressive power. The example queries $Q_1$–$Q_6$ (Introduction), $Q_7$ (Example 2.6), $Q_8$ (Proof of Proposition 3.3), $Q_9$ (Proof of Proposition 5.3), and $Q_{10}$ (Proof of Proposition 5.4) are added to the smallest language in which they can be expressed. The medium-dark gray area indicates the first-order definable counting-only queries for which satisfiability is not decidable.

We have identified several directions for future research:

1. In this paper, we have studied the formal aspect of counting-only first-order queries, but we have not yet studied practical issues such as query evaluation. Since the queries we study are all first-order queries, we can, off course, borrow standard techniques from first-order logic for their evaluation. One may wonder, however, if some of the more restricted classes considered in this paper allow for more efficient query evaluation, for example by using specialized counting-only index structures.
   As an example, consider queries using *generalized count-term predicates*, which are all expressible in SimpleCALC. Queries based on generalized count-term predicates provide a direct connection to an underlying frequent itemset problems, which can be exploited to further optimize query equivalence. A good example of such a technique is the FP-tree, used by the FP-Growth Algorithm, which can be used as an index to quickly find candidate sets of up-to-$k$-objects that have a minimum count [6, 12], and prune away all other sets of up-to-$k$-objects without any counting. Due to these implementation optimization opportunities and the prevalence of counting-only queries, we believe that the evaluation of these simple counting-only queries and their relationship to frequent itemset mining deserves a deeper understanding.

2. In the Introduction, we have already mentioned that the bag-of-sets data model and the notion of counting-only query can easily be generalized, e.g., to a model with relations between more than two disjoint domains. Therefore, it is only natural to wonder if the concepts we developed generalize to a richer data model without giving up on the well-behaved nature of SimpleCALC.

3. From a more theoretical perspective, there are several open problems for further investigation. For example, the precise complexity of the decision problems for SimpleCALC-$k$, $k \geq 0$, remains open. Crucial in pinpointing an exact upperbound is finding the exact upperbound on the complexity of model checking. We also want to study the decidability of whether a given $(k+1)$-counting-only query is also $k$-counting-only.

4. Counting is only one type of measure that can be used to define practical queries on bag-of-sets data, and we have seen that taking counting into account leads to naturally definable and well-behaved query languages. Many other practical types of measure exist [18], hence it is only natural to ask if these measures can be captured in an encompassing framework that leads, for each measure, to naturally definable and well-behaved query languages.

5. As we have shown in this paper, not all counting-only queries are first-order definable. To express some of these queries, one might consider augmenting first-order logic with non-first-order definable counting-based quantifiers [13]. We believe that it is worthwhile to study whether one can construct such query languages while, at the same time, retain the well-behaved nature of SimpleCALC.

# References

1. Abiteboul, S., Hull, R., Vianu, V. (eds.): Foundations of Databases: The Logical Level. Addison-Wesley, Reading (1995)
2. Anderson, I.: Combinatorics of Finite Sets. Dover Publications, Mineola (2011)
3. Bachmair, L., Ganzinger, H., Waldmann, U.: Set constraints are the monadic class. In: Proceedings of the 8th Annual IEEE Symposium on Logic in Computer Science, pp. 75–83 (1993)
4. Badia, A., Van Gucht, D., Gyssens, M.: Querying with generalized quantifiers. In: Ramakrishnan, R. (ed.) Applications of Logic Databases. SECS, vol. 296, pp. 235–258. Springer, Boston (1995). https://doi.org/10.1007/978-1-4615-2207-2_11
5. Bayer, A.E., Smart, J.C., McLaughlin, G.W.: Mapping intellectual structure of a scientific subfield through author cocitations. J. Am. Soc. Inf. Sci. Tech. **41**(6), 444–452 (1990)
6. Calders, T., Goethals, B.: Non-derivable itemset mining. Data Min. Knowl. Discov. **14**(1), 171–206 (2007)
7. Fletcher, G.H.L., Van Den Bussche, J., Van Gucht, D., Vansummeren, S.: Towards a theory of search queries. ACM Trans. Database Syst. **35**(4), 28:1–28:33 (2010)
8. Goethals, B.: Survey on frequent pattern mining. Technical report, University of Helsinki (2003)
9. Grädel, E., Otto, M.: On logics with two variables. Theor. Comput. Sci. **224**(1–2), 73–113 (1999)
10. Grohe, M.: Finite variable logics in descriptive complexity theory. Bull. Symb. Log. **4**, 345–398 (1998)

11. Gyssens, M., Paredaens, J., Van Gucht, D., Wijsen, J., Wu, Y.: An approach towards the study of symmetric queries. Proc. VLDB Endow. **7**(1), 25–36 (2013)
12. Han, J., Pei, J., Yin, Y., Mao, R.: Mining frequent patterns without candidate generation: a frequent-pattern tree approach. Data Min. Knowl. Discov. **8**(1), 53–87 (2004)
13. Kuske, D., Schweikardt, N.: First-order logic with counting. In: 32nd Annual ACM/IEEE Symposium on Logic in Computer Science, pp. 1–12 (2017)
14. Lewis, H.R.: Complexity results for classes of quantificational formulas. J. Comput. Syst. Sci. **21**(3), 317–353 (1980)
15. Libkin, L.: Elements of Finite Model Theory. Springer, Heidelberg (2004). https://doi.org/10.1007/978-3-662-07003-1
16. Quine, W.V.: Selected Logic Papers. Harvard University Press, Cambridge (1995)
17. Sayrafi, B., Van Gucht, D.: Differential constraints. In: Proceedings of the 24th Symposium on Principles of Database Systems, pp. 348–357. ACM (2005)
18. Sayrafi, B., Van Gucht, D., Gyssens, M.: Measures in databases and data mining. Technical report TR602, Indiana University (2004). https://www.cs.indiana.edu/cgi-bin/techreports/TRNNN.cgi?trnum=TR602
19. Väänänen, J.: Generalized quantifiers, an introduction. In: Väänänen, J. (ed.) ESSLLI 1997. LNCS, vol. 1754, pp. 1–17. Springer, Heidelberg (1999). https://doi.org/10.1007/3-540-46583-9_1

# The Power of Tarski's Relation Algebra
# on Trees

Jelle Hellings[1][(✉)], Yuqing Wu[2], Marc Gyssens[1], and Dirk Van Gucht[3]

[1] Hasselt University, Martelarenlaan 42, 3500 Hasselt, Belgium
jelle.hellings@uhasselt.be
[2] Pomona College, 185 E 6th Street, Claremont, CA 91711, USA
[3] Indiana University, 150 S. Woodlawn Avenue, Bloomington, IN 47405, USA

**Abstract.** Fragments of Tarski's relation algebra form the basis of many versatile graph and tree query languages including the regular path queries, XPath, and SPARQL. Surprisingly, however, a systematic study of the relative expressive power of relation algebra fragments on trees has not yet been undertaken. Our approach is to start from a basic fragment which only allows composition and union. We then study how the expressive power of the query language changes if we add diversity, converse, projections, coprojections, intersections, and/or difference, both for path queries and Boolean queries. For path queries, we found that adding intersection and difference yields more expressive power for some fragments, while adding one of the other operators always yields more expressive power. For Boolean queries, we obtain a similar picture for the relative expressive power, except for a few fragments where adding converse or projection yields no more expressive power. One challenging problem remains open, however, for both path and Boolean queries: does adding difference yields more expressive power to fragments containing at least diversity, coprojections, and intersection?

## 1 Introduction

Trees can be used to model data that has a hierarchical or nested structure including taxonomies, organizational charts, documents, genealogies, and file and directory structures. It is therefore not surprising that tree data models have been continuously studied since the 1960s [5, 9, 25]. Modern query languages for querying tree data have a heavy reliance on navigating the tree structure. Prime examples of this are XPath [4, 6, 7, 22] and the various JSON query languages [19]. At its core, this navigation can be captured by fragments of Tarski's relation algebra [24]. Consequently, tree querying based on fragments of the relation algebra has already been studied in great detail (e.g. [3, 16, 17, 26]). Unfortunately, these studies only covered some very basic fragments of the relation algebra, and a comprehensive study of all relation algebra fragments has not yet been undertaken.

This material is based on work supported by the National Science Foundation under Grant No. NSF 1438990.

F. Ferrarotti and S. Woltran (Eds.): FoIKS 2018, LNCS 10833, pp. 244–264, 2018.
https://doi.org/10.1007/978-3-319-90050-6_14

In this work, we undertake such a comprehensive study by investigating the relative expressive power of fragments of the relation algebra with respect to both path queries and Boolean queries. Concretely, the basic relation algebra fragment $\mathcal{N}()$ we start from only allows the constants empty-set and identity ($\emptyset$ and id), edge labels, and the operators composition and union ($\circ$ and $\cup$). This fragment allows for basic querying based on navigating alongside the parent-child axis and corresponds with the first-order fragment of the regular path queries (RPQs) [8]. We study how the expressive power changes if we add the remaining relation algebra constants and operators. This includes adding converse ($^{-1}$) which enables navigation alongside the child-parent axis, yielding the first-order fragment of the 2RPQs [1]. We also add projections ($\pi_1$ and $\pi_2$) which enable simultaneous navigation alongside several branches in the tree, yielding the first-order fragment of the nested RPQs [2]. As it turns out, the first-order fragments of the RPQs, 2RPQs, and nested RPQs are rather weak on trees. To increase their expressive power, we consider adding diversity (di) and intersection ($\cap$). The diversity constant evaluates to all pairs of distinct nodes and combined with intersection this constant can be used to, e.g., construct all pairs of distinct siblings. This enables branching and counting queries, even on unlabeled structures. Finally, we study adding negation in the form of coprojections ($\overline{\pi}_1$ and $\overline{\pi}_2$) and difference ($-$). All the above notations that are at the basis of this study can be found in Sect. 2.

Unfortunately, the relative simplicity of the tree data model turns out to be a curse rather than a blessing: compared to the graph data model [10–12,24], this simplicity makes it much more difficult to establish separation results using strong brute-force methods. Consequently, the study on trees forces us to search for deeper methods to reach our goals. Therefore, we believe that our study not only gives insight in the expressive power of the relation algebra and its fragments, but also contributes to a better understanding of the fundamental differences between graph data models and tree data models. The main contribution presented in this paper is the introduction of several properties that can be used to categorize relation algebra fragments according to their expressive power. This in turn yields several separation results on trees:

1. *Recognizing branches and siblings.* The language $\mathcal{N}()$ can only query trees by navigating alongside a single path from ancestor to descendant. Consequently, no query in $\mathcal{N}()$ can distinguish between chains and trees. Other query languages support recognizing branching up to a certain degree, and we can classify these languages accordingly. To do so, we introduce a notion called *k-subtree reductions* in Sect. 3. Languages that are closed under *k*-subtree-reduction steps allow the removal of a child of a node that is structurally equivalent to at least *k* other children of that node without changing the outcome of Boolean queries. First, the query language $\mathcal{N}(^{-1}, \pi, \overline{\pi}, \cap)$ is 1-*subtree-reducible* and, consequently, can only recognize siblings if they are not structurally equivalent. Next, query languages $\mathcal{N}(\mathcal{F})$ with di $\in \mathcal{F}$ and $\cap \notin \mathcal{F}$ are 2-*subtree-reducible* and can, in very limited circumstances, distinguish up to two structurally equivalent children of a node. Finally the

full relation algebra is *3-subtree-reducible*, and query languages $\mathcal{N}(\mathcal{F})$ with $\{^{-1}, -\} \subseteq \mathcal{F}$ or $\{\mathrm{di}, \cap\} \subseteq \mathcal{F}$ can always distinguish between nodes that have one, two, or at least three structurally equivalent children.

2. *Local queries versus non-local queries.* Queries in $\mathcal{N}(\mathcal{F})$ with $\mathcal{F} \subseteq \{^{-1}, \pi, \overline{\pi}, \cap, -\}$ yield node pairs $(m, n)$ such that one can navigate between $m$ and $n$ by traversing a number of edges, with the number depending only on the length of the query. Hence, we call these query languages *local*. Diversity is intrinsically *non-local*. From this observation, it follows that languages with diversity are not path-equivalent to local query languages. This can be strengthened towards Boolean inequivalence, as diversity can, in many cases, be used to express non-local properties on which trees and chains can be distinguished. We do so in Sect. 4 by exploiting the fact that many properties on which trees and chains can be distinguished are non-local and rely on a limited form of counting. A simple example of this are chain queries of the form "are there $k$ edges in the chain labeled with edge-label $\ell$".

3. *Downward queries versus non-downward queries.* Queries in $\mathcal{N}(\mathcal{F})$ with $\mathcal{F} \subseteq \{\pi, \overline{\pi}, \cap, -\}$ yield node pairs $(m, n)$ such that one can navigate from $m$ to $n$ by traversing along a sequence of parent-child axes. Hence, we call these query languages *downward* [16,17]. We observe that these downward query languages are all 1-subtree-reducible, which puts an upper bound on their expressive power. Diversity and the converse operator are *non-downward* in nature. Based on this observation, it follows that languages with diversity or converse are not path-equivalent to downward query languages.

4. *Monotonicity.* A query language is *monotone* if, for every query $q$, every graph $\mathcal{G}$, and every graph $\mathcal{G}'$ obtained by adding nodes and edges to $\mathcal{G}$, we have $[\![q]\!]_{\mathcal{G}} \subseteq [\![q]\!]_{\mathcal{G}'}$. One the one hand, one can show that the query language $\mathcal{N}(\mathrm{di}, {}^{-1}, \pi, \cap)$ is monotone [16,17]. On the other hand, the query languages $\mathcal{N}(\mathcal{F})$ with $\overline{\pi} \in \mathcal{F}$ are *non-monotone*. For example, we only need coprojections to construct a Boolean query that puts an upper bound on the length of a chain. Such queries are not monotone and consequently not expressible in $\mathcal{N}(\mathrm{di}, {}^{-1}, \pi, \cap)$.

In Fig. 1, we visualize the above categorization, which yields an initial classification of the expressive power of the query languages we study on trees. It does not provide all details, however, which we will start to unravel in this paper, mainly in Sects. 3 and 4. For an index on how specific results are proven, we refer the reader to Fig. 12.

Some separation results are obtained through brute-force methods, which we will show in Sect. 5. Besides separation results, we also establish collapse results in this paper. In Sect. 6, we obtain these by introducing a notion called condition tree queries for the local relation algebra fragments. They prove to be a powerful tool to show that intersection never adds expressive power beyond the ability to express projections. We also use this tool to establish limitations on the expressive power of projections in Boolean queries.

What remains open is whether adding difference to the fragments containing diversity, coprojections (and hence also projections), and intersection yields a

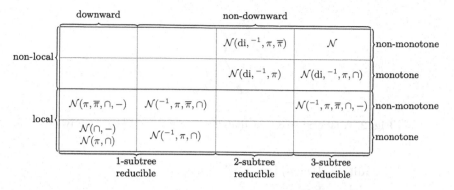

**Fig. 1.** Initial classification of the relative expressive power of fragments of the relation algebra with respect to path queries on labeled trees. In each box, the largest fragment(s) that satisfy the classification of that particular box are included. The more to the right and to the top a certain box is situated, the stronger the expressiveness of the corresponding fragment(s) become.

collapse or separation, even in the presence of converse. We claim this a very challenging open case, and we consider identifying it as the third major contribution of this paper. We discuss this open case in Sect. 8, in which we also discuss other directions for future research.

## 2    Preliminaries[1]

A *graph* is a triple $\mathcal{G} = (\mathcal{V}, \Sigma, \mathbf{E})$, with $\mathcal{V}$ a finite set of nodes, $\Sigma$ a finite set of labels, and $\mathbf{E} : \Sigma \to 2^{\mathcal{V} \times \mathcal{V}}$ a function mapping labels to edge relations. We denote by $\mathcal{E}$ the union of all edge relations. If $|\Sigma| = 1$, $\mathcal{G}$ is *unlabeled*. A *tree* $\mathcal{T} = (\mathcal{V}, \Sigma, \mathbf{E})$ is a connected acyclic graph in which one node, the *root*, has no incoming edges, and all other nodes have one incoming edge. In an edge $(m, n) \in \mathcal{E}$, $m$ is the *parent* of $n$, and $n$ a *child* of $m$. A *chain* is a tree in which all nodes have at most one child.

In this paper, we limit our study to queries on trees and chains. A query $q$ maps a tree to a set of node pairs. We write $[\![q]\!]_{\mathcal{T}}$ to denote the *evaluation* of $q$ on tree $\mathcal{T}$. We can interpret a query $q$ literally as a *path query*, or, alternatively, as a *Boolean query*, in which case **True** stands for $[\![q]\!]_{\mathcal{T}} \neq \emptyset$.

The syntax of a *relation algebra* expression is given by

$$e := \emptyset \mid \mathrm{id} \mid \mathrm{di} \mid \ell \mid e^{-1} \mid \pi_j[e] \mid \overline{\pi}_j[e] \mid e \circ e \mid e \cup e \mid e \cap e \mid e - e,$$

where $\ell \in \Sigma$ and $j \in \{1, 2\}$. Its evaluation on a tree $\mathcal{T} = (\mathcal{V}, \Sigma, \mathbf{E})$ is defined by

$$[\![\emptyset]\!]_{\mathcal{T}} = \emptyset;$$
$$[\![\mathrm{id}]\!]_{\mathcal{T}} = \{(m, m) \mid m \in \mathcal{V}\};$$

---

[1] Our formalization of graphs, the relation algebra, and equivalence notions is adapted from concepts used by Fletcher et al. [10,11].

**Fig. 2.** A labeled tree that matches $\pi_1[\ell] \circ \ell \circ \pi_1[\ell] \circ \ell$ exactly.

$$\llbracket \text{di} \rrbracket_T = \{(m,n) \mid m,n \in \mathcal{V} \wedge m \neq n\};$$
$$\llbracket \ell \rrbracket_T = \mathbf{E}(\ell);$$
$$\llbracket e^{-1} \rrbracket_T = \{(n,m) \mid (m,n) \in \llbracket e \rrbracket_T\};$$
$$\llbracket \pi_1[e] \rrbracket_T = \{(m,m) \mid \exists n \, (m,n) \in \llbracket e \rrbracket_T\};$$
$$\llbracket \pi_2[e] \rrbracket_T = \{(n,n) \mid \exists m \, (m,n) \in \llbracket e \rrbracket_T\};$$
$$\llbracket \overline{\pi}_j[e] \rrbracket_T = \llbracket \text{id} \rrbracket_T - \llbracket \pi_j[e] \rrbracket_T;$$
$$\llbracket e_1 \circ e_2 \rrbracket_T = \{(m,n) \mid \exists z \, ((m,z) \in \llbracket e_1 \rrbracket_T \wedge (z,n) \in \llbracket e_2 \rrbracket_T)\};$$
$$\llbracket e_1 \oplus e_2 \rrbracket_T = \llbracket e_1 \rrbracket_T \oplus \llbracket e_2 \rrbracket_T \quad (\text{with } \oplus \in \{\cup, \cap, -\}).$$

Notice that it suffices to consider converse $(^{-1})$ at the level of labels only. If an expression always evaluates to a subset of id, as is the case for projections and coprojections, then it is called a *node expression*.

*Example 1.* Consider the labeled tree in Fig. 2. The expression $e = \pi_1[\ell] \circ \ell \circ \pi_1[\ell] \circ \ell$ matches this tree structure, and will return the node pair $(m,n)$. The expressions $(\ell^{-1} \circ \ell) \cap \text{di}$ and $(\ell^{-1} \circ \ell) - \text{id}$ both return pairs of siblings in the tree.

For $k > 0$, we write $\mathcal{E}^k$ to represent $k$-fold composition of $\mathcal{E}$ and $\mathcal{E}^{-k}$ for its converse, we use $\mathcal{E}^0$ to denote id, $[\mathcal{E}]^+$ to denote the *descendant-axis* defined by $[\mathcal{E}]^+ = \bigcup_{k>0} \mathcal{E}^k$, and $[\mathcal{E}^{-1}]^+$ to denote the *ancestor-axis* defined by $[\mathcal{E}^{-1}]^+ = \bigcup_{k>0} \mathcal{E}^{-k}$. Given $\mathcal{F} \subseteq \{\text{di}, ^{-1}, \pi, \overline{\pi}, \cap, -\}$, $\mathcal{N}(\mathcal{F})$ denotes the relation algebra fragment in which only the atoms $\emptyset$, $\ell \in \Sigma$, and id, the operators $\circ$ and $\cup$, and all operators in $\mathcal{F}$ are allowed. In the above, we used $\pi$ as shorthand for $\pi_1$ and $\pi_2$, and $\overline{\pi}$ as shorthand for $\overline{\pi}_1$ and $\overline{\pi}_2$.

Let $q_1$ and $q_2$ be expressions. We say that $q_1$ and $q_2$ are *path-equivalent*, denoted by $q_1 \equiv_{\text{path}} q_2$, if, for every tree $T$, $\llbracket q_1 \rrbracket_T = \llbracket q_2 \rrbracket_T$ and are *Boolean-equivalent*, denoted by $q_1 \equiv_{\text{bool}} q_2$, if, for every tree $T$, $\llbracket q_1 \rrbracket_T \neq \emptyset \iff \llbracket q_2 \rrbracket_T \neq \emptyset$. Let $z \in \{\text{path}, \text{bool}\}$. We say that the class of expressions $\mathcal{L}_1$ is *z-subsumed* by the class of expressions $\mathcal{L}_2$, denoted by $\mathcal{L}_1 \preceq_z \mathcal{L}_2$, if every expression in $\mathcal{L}_1$ is $z$-equivalent to an expression in $\mathcal{L}_2$. In this connection, the following rewrite rules can be used to express operators using other operators:

$$\pi_1[e] = \pi_2[e^{-1}] = \overline{\pi}_j[\overline{\pi}_1[e]] = (e \circ e^{-1}) \cap \text{id} = (e \circ (\text{di} \cup \text{id})) \cap \text{id} \ (j \in \{1,2\});$$
$$\pi_2[e] = \pi_1[e^{-1}] = \overline{\pi}_j[\overline{\pi}_2[e]] = (e^{-1} \circ e) \cap \text{id} = ((\text{di} \cup \text{id}) \circ e) \cap \text{id} \ (j \in \{1,2\});$$
$$\overline{\pi}_1[e] = \overline{\pi}_2[e^{-1}] = \text{id} - \pi_1[e];$$
$$\overline{\pi}_2[e] = \overline{\pi}_1[e^{-1}] = \text{id} - \pi_2[e];$$
$$e_1 \cap e_2 = e_1 - (e_1 - e_2).$$

For $\mathcal{F} \subseteq \{\text{di}, ^{-1}, \pi, \overline{\pi}, \cap, -\}$, $\overline{\mathcal{F}}$ denotes the closure of $\mathcal{F}$ under the rules above.[2]

*Example 2.* The equivalence $e_1 \cap e_2 \equiv_{\text{path}} e_1 - (e_1 - e_2)$ is well-known. Hence, also $e_1 \cap e_2 \equiv_{\text{bool}} e_1 - (e_1 - e_2)$. We also have $\pi_1[\ell] \equiv_{\text{bool}} \ell \equiv_{\text{bool}} \pi_2[\ell]$, but $\pi_1[\ell] \not\equiv_{\text{path}} \ell$ and $\ell \not\equiv_{\text{path}} \pi_2[\ell]$. Finally, let $e$ be the expression as in Example 1. We have $e \equiv_{\text{path}} \ell_1 \circ \ell_1^{-1} \circ \ell_2 \circ \ell_3 \circ \ell_3^{-1} \circ \ell_4$.

## 3   Subtree Reductions

Most relation algebra fragments are able to detect obvious labeled branching in trees.

*Example 3.* Consider the expressions $e_1 = (\ell_1)^{-1} \circ \ell_2$ and $e_2 = \pi_1[\ell_1] \circ \pi_1[\ell_2]$, which are Boolean-equivalent. Clearly, for any tree $\mathcal{T}$ we have $[\![e_i]\!]_{\mathcal{T}} \neq \emptyset$, $i \in \{1,2\}$ only if $\mathcal{T}$ has a node with at least two children, one reachable via an edge labeled $\ell_1$ and another via an edge labeled $\ell_2$.

Detecting branches in the situation above, where a single node has several structurally distinct branches, is relatively simple. Next, we look at which language fragments are able to detect branching if all branches are structurally identical. As a first step towards this goal, we derive limitations on the expressive power of relation algebra fragments, taking advantage of the simple structure of trees. Thereto, we introduce *subtree-reduction steps*.

Let $k > 0$. A *$k$-subtree-reduction step* on tree $\mathcal{T} = (\mathcal{V}, \Sigma, \mathbf{E})$ consists of first finding different nodes $m, n_1, \ldots, n_{k+1} \in \mathcal{V}$ and an edge label $\ell \in \Sigma$ such that $(m, n_1), \ldots, (m, n_{k+1}) \in \mathbf{E}(\ell)$ and the subtrees rooted at $n_1, \ldots, n_{k+1}$ are isomorphic, and then picking a node $n_i$, $1 \leq i \leq k+1$, and removing the subtree rooted at $n_i$.

**Definition 4.** *We say that a tree is $k$-subtree-reducible if we can apply a $k$-subtree-reduction step.*[3]

*Example 5.* Consider the unlabeled trees $\mathcal{T}_1$, $\mathcal{T}_2$, and $\mathcal{T}_3$ in Fig. 3. The tree $\mathcal{T}_1$ can be obtained by a 1-subtree-reduction step on $\mathcal{T}_2$ and $\mathcal{T}_2$ can be obtained

---

[2] The basic atoms and operators, $\emptyset$, $\ell \in \Sigma$, id, $\circ$, and $\cup$ are left implicit because they are assumed to be present in every fragment.

[3] The 1-subtree reductions bear a close relationship to the F+B-index and the F&B-index used for indexing the structure of tree data [20].

**Fig. 3.** Trees $T_1$, $T_2$, and tree $T_3$ from Example 5 and the proof of Proposition 7.

by a 2-subtree-reduction step on $T_3$. Consequently, $T_1$ can also be obtained by two 1-subtree-reduction steps on $T_3$. Hence, $T_2$ is 1-subtree-reducible and $T_3$ is 1-subtree-reducible and 2-subtree-reducible.

We now exhibit conditions under which the result of a relation algebra expression is invariant under subtree reduction at the Boolean level.

**Proposition 6.** *Let $\mathcal{F} \subseteq \{\mathrm{di}, {}^{-1}, \pi, \overline{\pi}, \cap, -\}$, $e$ an expression in $\mathcal{N}(\mathcal{F})$, $T$ a tree, and $T'$ obtained from $T$ by a $k$-subtree-reduction step. Each of the following conditions separately implies $[\![e]\!]_T \neq \emptyset \iff [\![e]\!]_{T'} \neq \emptyset$:*

   *(i) $k \geq 3$;*
   *(ii) $k = 2$ and $\cap \notin \overline{\mathcal{F}}$; and*
   *(iii) $k = 1$ and $\{\mathrm{di}, -\} \cap \mathcal{F} = \emptyset$.*

*Proof (sketch).* Using $k$-pebble games [13,14,21], we can see that $[\![q]\!]_T \neq \emptyset \iff [\![q]\!]_{T'} \neq \emptyset$ if $q$ is a query in FO$[k]$, which is first-order logic restricted to $k$ variables. Since the relation algebra and FO[3] path-subsume each other [12,24], (i) follows. In Statement (ii), $\mathcal{F} \subseteq \{\mathrm{di}, {}^{-1}, \pi, \overline{\pi}\}$. Hence, by a result of Hellings et al. [18, Theorem 6.1], (ii) also follows.[4] To prove (iii), let $T = (\mathcal{V}, \Sigma, \mathbf{E})$ and $T' = (\mathcal{V}', \Sigma', \mathbf{E}')$. Let $n_1, n_2 \in \mathcal{V}$ be the siblings in $T$ such that $T'$ is obtained from $T$ by eliminating the subtree rooted at $n_2$. Let $\mathcal{V}_1$ and $\mathcal{V}_2$ be the nodes in the subtrees of $T$ rooted at $n_1$ and $n_2$, respectively, and let $b : \mathcal{V}_1 \to \mathcal{V}_2$ be a bijection establishing that these subtrees are isomorphic. Let $g$ be the identity on $\mathcal{V} - (\mathcal{V}_1 \cup \mathcal{V}_2)$, and let $f = b \cup b^{-1} \cup g$. Since $f$ is an automorphism of $T$, we have, for $m, n \in \mathcal{V}$, $(m, n) \in [\![e]\!]_T \iff (f(m), f(n)) \in [\![e]\!]_T$. By induction on the length of $e$, one can prove that, if $(m, n) \in \mathcal{V}_1 \times \mathcal{V}_2$ or $(m, n) \in \mathcal{V}_2 \times \mathcal{V}_1$, then $(m, n) \in [\![e]\!]_T \implies (f(m), n) \in [\![e]\!]_T$. Since $f = f^{-1}$, it then also follows that, if $(m, n) \in \mathcal{V}_1 \times \mathcal{V}_2$ or $(m, n) \in \mathcal{V}_2 \times \mathcal{V}_1$, then $(m, n) \in [\![e]\!]_T \implies (m, f(n)) \in [\![e]\!]_T$. A final induction on the length of $e$ then yields that, for $m', n' \in \mathcal{V}'$, $(m', n') \in [\![e]\!]_T \iff (m', n') \in [\![e]\!]_{T'}$. Hence, $[\![e]\!]_T \neq \emptyset \iff [\![e]\!]_{T'} \neq \emptyset$, $\qquad\square$

From the limitations imposed by Proposition 6 on the Boolean expressive power of the fragments considered, we deduce the following separation results:

**Proposition 7.** *Already on unlabeled trees, we have $\mathcal{N}(\mathrm{di}) \not\preceq_{\mathrm{bool}} \mathcal{N}({}^{-1}, \pi, \overline{\pi}, \cap)$, $\mathcal{N}({}^{-1}, -) \not\preceq_{\mathrm{bool}} \mathcal{N}({}^{-1}, \pi, \overline{\pi}, \cap)$, and $\mathcal{N}(\mathrm{di}, \cap) \not\preceq_{\mathrm{bool}} \mathcal{N}(\mathrm{di}, {}^{-1}, \pi, \overline{\pi})$.*

*Proof.* Consider the unlabeled trees $T_1$, $T_2$, and $T_3$ in Example 5. Since $T_1$ can be obtained by a 1-subtree-reduction on $T_2$, we have, by Proposition 6(iii), that,

---

[4] Notice that in the formalism of Hellings et al. [18], projection is considered to be a standard operator.

for every $e$ in $\mathcal{N}(^{-1}, \pi, \overline{\pi}, \cap)$, $[\![e]\!]_{T_2} \neq \emptyset \iff [\![e]\!]_{T_1} \neq \emptyset$. Now consider $e_1 = \mathcal{E} \circ \mathrm{di} \circ \mathrm{di} \circ \mathcal{E}$ in $\mathcal{N}(\mathrm{di})$ and $e_2 = (\mathcal{E}^{-1} \circ \mathcal{E}) - \mathrm{id}$ in $\mathcal{N}(^{-1}, -)$. We have $[\![e_1]\!]_{T_2} \neq \emptyset$ and $[\![e_2]\!]_{T_2} \neq \emptyset$, while $[\![e_1]\!]_{T_1} = [\![e_2]\!]_{T_1} = \emptyset$, establishing the first and second separations. Since $T_2$ can be obtained by a 2-subtree-reduction on $T_3$, we have, by Proposition 6(ii), that, for every $e$ in $\mathcal{N}(\mathrm{di}, {}^{-1}, \pi, \overline{\pi})$, $[\![e]\!]_{T_3} \neq \emptyset \iff [\![e]\!]_{T_2} \neq \emptyset$. Now consider $e_3 = (((\mathrm{di} \circ \mathcal{E}) \cap \mathrm{di}) \circ ((\mathrm{di} \circ \mathcal{E}) \cap \mathrm{di})) \cap \mathrm{di}$ in $\mathcal{N}(\mathrm{di}, \cap)$. We have $[\![e_3]\!]_{T_3} \neq \emptyset$, while $[\![e_3]\!]_{T_2} = \emptyset$, establishing the third separation. $\qquad \square$

The proof of Proposition 7 relies on languages being able to distinguish at least one, two, or three structurally equivalent children of a node. To do so, the proof uses minimal languages that satisfy the conditions of Proposition 6. Hence, the classification provided by $k$-subtree-reductions is strict.

# 4    The Power of Diversity

Relation algebra expressions without diversity can only inspect a local neighborhood around a given node. With respect to path queries, this puts obvious limitations on the expressive power of language fragments that do not contain diversity. With respect to Boolean queries, the situation is more subtle. To study this in more detail, we first define the notion of locality:

**Definition 8.** *Given a tree, and disregarding the direction of its edges, the distance between two nodes is the number of edges on the unique shortest path between them. A query $q$ is* local *if there exists $k \geq 0$ such that, for every tree $T$, and for all nodes $m$ and $n$, $(m, n) \in [\![q]\!]_T \iff (m, n) \in [\![q]\!]_{T'}$, with $T'$ the smallest subtree of $T$ containing all nodes at distance at most $k$ from the nearest common ancestor of $m$ and $n$.*

By an induction on their length, it can be shown that all expressions in $\mathcal{N}(^{-1}, \pi, \overline{\pi}, \cap, -)$ are local.

## 4.1    Adding Diversity to Local Fragments

As already noticed, diversity always adds power to a local relation algebra fragment at the path level, as it can construct non-local relation algebra expressions. We can also use this property to our advantage to prove that diversity often adds expressive power at the Boolean level, too.

**Proposition 9.** *Already on unlabeled trees, $\mathcal{N}(\mathrm{di}, \cap) \npreceq_{\mathrm{bool}} \mathcal{N}(^{-1}, \pi, \overline{\pi}, \cap, -)$.*

*Proof.* By the rewrite rules at the end of Sect. 2, $\mathcal{N}(\mathrm{di}, \pi, \cap) \preceq_{\mathrm{path}} \mathcal{N}(\mathrm{di}, \cap)$. Consider the expression $e = P_{2, \neg r} \circ \mathrm{di} \circ P_{2, \neg r}$ in which $P_{2, \neg r} = \pi_2[\mathcal{E}] \circ P_2$, $P_2 = \pi_1[S_2]$, and $S_2 = (\mathcal{E} \circ \mathrm{di}) \cap \mathcal{E}$. The expression $e$ selects node pairs among distinct non-root nodes such that each node in the pair has at least two distinct children. Now, assume there exists an expression $e'$ in $\mathcal{N}(^{-1}, \pi, \overline{\pi}, \cap, -)$ such that $e \equiv_{\mathrm{bool}} e'$. Since $e'$ is local, we know there exists $k \geq 0$ such that $e'$

**Fig. 4.** Trees $T$ and $T'$ in the proof of Proposition 9. The symbol ⤳ represents a chain of $k$ edges, with $k$ as in that proof.

**Fig. 5.** Chains $C$ and $C'$ in the proof of Proposition 10. The symbol ⤳ represents a chain of $2k$ edges all labeled $\ell'$, with $k$ as in that proof.

satisfies Definition 8. Now consider the trees $T$ and $T'$ shown in Fig. 4. Clearly, $[\![e]\!]_T \supseteq \{(m_1, m_2)\} \neq \emptyset$ and $[\![e]\!]_{T'} = \emptyset$. By $e \equiv_{\mathrm{bool}} e'$, we must have $[\![e']\!]_T \neq \emptyset$. Let $(m, n) \in [\![e']\!]_T$. Since every subtree of $T$ containing all nodes at distance at most $k$ from some given node is contained in a subtree of $T$ that is isomorphic to $T'$, we may conclude that $[\![e']\!]_{T'} \neq \emptyset$. However, $[\![e]\!]_{T'} = \emptyset$, contradicting $e \equiv_{\mathrm{bool}} e'$. Hence, no expression in $\mathcal{N}(^{-1}, \pi, \overline{\pi}, \cap, -)$ is Boolean-equivalent to $e$. □

We can use a similar locality argument for two more separations:

**Proposition 10.** *Already on chains, we have* $\mathcal{N}(\mathrm{di}, {}^{-1}) \not\preceq_{\mathrm{bool}} \mathcal{N}(^{-1}, \pi, \overline{\pi}, \cap, -)$ *and* $\mathcal{N}(\mathrm{di}, \pi) \not\preceq_{\mathrm{bool}} \mathcal{N}(^{-1}, \pi, \overline{\pi}, \cap, -)$.

*Proof.* Consider the path-equivalent expressions $e_1 = (\ell \circ \ell^{-1}) \circ \mathrm{di} \circ (\ell \circ \ell^{-1})$ in $\mathcal{N}(\mathrm{di}, {}^{-1})$ and $e_2 = \pi_1[\ell] \circ \mathrm{di} \circ \pi_1[\ell]$ in $\mathcal{N}(\mathrm{di}, \pi)$, and let $e$ be either $e_1$ or $e_2$. Now, assume there exists an expression $e'$ in $\mathcal{N}(^{-1}, \pi, \overline{\pi}, \cap, -)$ such that $e \equiv_{\mathrm{bool}} e'$. Since $e'$ is local, we know there exists $k \geq 0$ such that $e'$ satisfies Definition 8. Now consider the chains $C$ and $C'$ shown in Fig. 5. Clearly, $[\![e]\!]_C \supseteq \{(m_1, m_2)\} \neq \emptyset$. Hence, $[\![e']\!]_C \neq \emptyset$. By $e \equiv_{\mathrm{bool}} e'$, we must have $[\![e']\!]_T \neq \emptyset$. Let $(m, n) \in [\![e']\!]_T$. Notice that every subchain of $C$ containing all nodes at distance at most $k$ from some given node is a subchain of $C$ of length at most $2k$. Since each such subchain of $C$ is isomorphic to some subchain of $C'$, we may conclude that $[\![e']\!]_{C'} \neq \emptyset$. However, $[\![e]\!]_{C'} = \emptyset$, contradicting $e \equiv_{\mathrm{bool}} e'$. Hence, no expression in $\mathcal{N}(^{-1}, \pi, \overline{\pi}, \cap, -)$ is Boolean-equivalent to $e$. □

Observe that the separation $\mathcal{N}(\mathrm{di}, \cap) \not\preceq_{\mathrm{bool}} \mathcal{N}(^{-1}, \pi, \overline{\pi}, \cap, -)$ also holds on chains, because the expression $e_3 = (\ell \circ \mathrm{di} \cap \mathrm{id}) \circ \mathrm{di} \circ (\ell \circ \mathrm{di} \cap \mathrm{id})$ is path-equivalent to $e_1$ and $e_2$ in the proof of Proposition 10.

## 4.2  Adding Other Operators to Non-local Fragments

The erratic behavior of diversity in the non-local relation algebra fragments on trees (allowing one to jump from any node to any other node in a tree) makes studying the expressive power of these fragments inherently difficult. Luckily, we can obtain several separation results by studying these fragments on chains.

For local expressions on chains, we have the following:

**Lemma 11.** *Let* $\mathcal{F} \subseteq \{^{-1}, \pi, \overline{\pi}, \cap, -\}$, *and* $e$ *be a union-free expression in* $\mathcal{N}(\mathcal{F})$.[5] *There exists* $k \geq 0$ *such that, for every chain* $\mathcal{C}$, $[\![e]\!]_{\mathcal{C}} \subseteq [\![\mathcal{E}^k]\!]_{\mathcal{C}}$ *or* $[\![e]\!]_{\mathcal{C}} \subseteq [\![\mathcal{E}^{-k}]\!]_{\mathcal{C}}$.

Lemma 11 simplifies the reasoning about local expressions on chains. In addition, diversity on chains can be expressed using the ancestor axis and the descendant axis, as $\mathrm{di} = [\mathcal{E}]^+ \cup [\mathcal{E}^{-1}]^+$. While the descendant and ancestor axes are not operators of the fragments considered in this paper, we can still use them in intermediate steps to rewrite expressions that contain di. This in turn allows us to simplify projection terms that contain di, as we show next.

**Lemma 12.** *Let* $\mathcal{F} \subseteq \{\mathrm{di}, ^{-1}, \pi\}$ *and* $\pi_j[e]$, $j \in \{1, 2\}$, *be an expression in* $\mathcal{N}(\mathcal{F})$. *There exists a finite set* $S$ *of expressions of the form* $\pi_1[\mathcal{E}^v] \circ \pi_2[\mathcal{E}^w]$, $v, w \geq 0$, *such that, on unlabeled chains,* $\pi_j[e] \equiv_{\mathrm{path}} \bigcup S$.

*Proof.* We have $\mathrm{di} \equiv_{\mathrm{path}} [\mathcal{E}]^+ \cup [\mathcal{E}^{-1}]^+$. We also have $\pi_2[e] \equiv_{\mathrm{path}} \pi_1[e^{-1}]$. Hence, every projection expression $\pi_j[e]$, $j \in \{1, 2\}$, can be written as a union of expressions of the form $\pi_1[e']$ in which $e'$ is built over the atoms id, $\mathcal{E}$, $\mathcal{E}^{-1}$, $[\mathcal{E}]^+$, and $[\mathcal{E}^{-1}]^+$, using the operators $\circ$ and $\pi_1$.[6] We shall call such expressions $e'$ *normal* in the remainder of this proof. So, it remains to show that Lemma 12 holds for expressions $\pi_1[e']$, with $e'$ normal. We do this by structural induction on $e'$. We have the following base cases:

$$\pi_1[\mathrm{id}] \equiv_{\mathrm{path}} \mathrm{id} \equiv_{\mathrm{path}} \pi_1[\mathcal{E}^0] \circ \pi_2[\mathcal{E}^0];$$
$$\pi_1[\mathcal{E}] \equiv_{\mathrm{path}} \pi_1[[\mathcal{E}]^+] \equiv_{\mathrm{path}} \pi_1[\mathcal{E}^1] \circ \pi_2[\mathcal{E}^0];$$
$$\pi_1[\mathcal{E}^{-1}] \equiv_{\mathrm{path}} \pi_1[[\mathcal{E}^{-1}]^+] \equiv_{\mathrm{path}} \pi_1[\mathcal{E}^0] \circ \pi_2[\mathcal{E}^1].$$

Now, assume that Lemma 12 holds for expressions $\pi_1[e'']$, with $e''$ a normal expression containing at most $i$ operators, $i \geq 0$, and let $e = \pi_1[e']$ with $e'$ a normal expression containing $i + 1$ operators. Then either $e' = \pi_1[e'_1]$ or $e' = e'_1 \circ e'_2$, with $e'_1$ and $e'_2$ normal expressions containing at most $i$ operators. In the first case, $e \equiv_{\mathrm{path}} \pi_1[e'_1]$, and Lemma 12 holds for $e$ by the induction hypothesis. In the second case, we have that $e = \pi_1[e'_1 \circ e'_2] \equiv_{\mathrm{path}} \pi_1[e'_1 \circ \pi_1[e'_2]]$. By the induction hypothesis, $e'_2$ is path-equivalent to a finite union of expressions of the form $\pi_1[\mathcal{E}^{v_2}] \circ \pi_2[\mathcal{E}^{w_2}]$, $v_2, w_2 \geq 0$. For $e'_1$, we distinguish again two cases:

1. Expression $e'_1 = \pi_1[e''_1]$, with $e''_1$ again a normal expression containing at most $i$ operators. Hence, by the induction hypothesis, $e'_1$ is path-equivalent to a finite union of expressions of the form $\pi_1[\mathcal{E}^{v_1}] \circ \pi_2[\mathcal{E}^{w_1}]$, $v_1, w_1 \geq 0$. It now suffices to observe that

---

[5] Observe that, in relation algebra expressions, unions can always be pushed out to the outermost level.

[6] Recall from Sect. 2 that we need to consider converse only at the level of edges.

$$\pi_1[\mathcal{E}^{v_1}] \circ \pi_2[\mathcal{E}^{w_1}] \circ \pi_1[\mathcal{E}^{v_1}] \circ \pi_2[\mathcal{E}^{w_1}] \equiv_{\text{path}} \pi_1[\mathcal{E}^{\max(v_1,v_2)}] \circ \pi_2[\mathcal{E}^{\max(w_1,w_2)}]$$

to conclude that Lemma 12 holds for $e$.

2. In the other case, we can assume without loss of generality that $e_1'$ is an atom. Hence, it suffices to observe that, for $v, w \geq 0$,

$$\pi_1[\text{id} \circ (\pi_1[\mathcal{E}^v] \circ \pi_2[\mathcal{E}^w])] \equiv_{\text{path}} \pi_1[\mathcal{E}^v] \circ \pi_2[\mathcal{E}^w];$$
$$\pi_1[\mathcal{E} \circ (\pi_1[\mathcal{E}^v] \circ \pi_2[\mathcal{E}^w])] \equiv_{\text{path}} \pi_1[\mathcal{E}^{v+1}] \circ \pi_2[\mathcal{E}^{\max(0,w-1)}];$$
$$\pi_1[\mathcal{E}^{-1} \circ (\pi_1[\mathcal{E}^v] \circ \pi_2[\mathcal{E}^w])] \equiv_{\text{path}} \pi_1[\mathcal{E}^{\max(0,v-1)}] \circ \pi_2[\mathcal{E}^{w+1}];$$
$$\pi_1[[\mathcal{E}]^+ \circ (\pi_1[\mathcal{E}^v] \circ \pi_2[\mathcal{E}^w])] \equiv_{\text{path}} \bigcup_{1 \leq i \leq \max(1,w)} \pi_1[\mathcal{E}^{v+i}] \circ \pi_2[\mathcal{E}^{\max(0,w-i)}];$$
$$\pi_1[[\mathcal{E}^{-1}]^+ \circ (\pi_1[\mathcal{E}^v] \circ \pi_2[\mathcal{E}^w])] \equiv_{\text{path}} \bigcup_{1 \leq i \leq \max(1,v)} \pi_1[\mathcal{E}^{\max(0,v-i)}] \circ \pi_2[\mathcal{E}^{w+i}].$$

to conclude that Lemma 12 holds for $e$ in this case, too. □

*Example 13.* Consider the expression $e = \pi_1[\text{di} \circ \mathcal{E} \circ \mathcal{E}]$. We have

$$e \equiv_{\text{path}} \pi_1[[\mathcal{E}]^+ \circ \pi_1[\mathcal{E}^2] \circ \pi_2[\mathcal{E}^0]] \cup \pi_1[[\mathcal{E}^{-1}]^+ \circ \pi_1[\mathcal{E}^2] \circ \pi_2[\mathcal{E}^0]]$$
$$\equiv_{\text{path}} \pi_1[\pi_1[\mathcal{E}^3] \circ \pi_2[\mathcal{E}^0]] \cup \pi_1[\pi_1[\mathcal{E}^1] \circ \pi_2[\mathcal{E}^1]] \cup \pi_1[\pi_1[\mathcal{E}^0] \circ \pi_2[\mathcal{E}^2]]$$
$$\equiv_{\text{path}} \pi_1[\mathcal{E}^3] \circ \pi_2[\mathcal{E}^0] \cup \pi_1[\mathcal{E}^1] \circ \pi_2[\mathcal{E}^1] \cup \pi_1[\mathcal{E}^0] \circ \pi_2[\mathcal{E}^2].$$

As Example 13 shows, we can use Lemma 12 to partially eliminate diversity from non-local expressions on unlabeled chains, and then use locality-based arguments on subexpressions to establish the following separations:

**Proposition 14.** *Already on unlabeled chains, $\mathcal{N}(\text{di}, \cap) \not\leq_{\text{path}} \mathcal{N}(\text{di}, {}^{-1}, \pi)$, $\mathcal{N}({}^{-1}) \not\leq_{\text{path}} \mathcal{N}(\text{di}, \pi)$, and $\mathcal{N}(\pi) \not\leq_{\text{path}} \mathcal{N}(\text{di})$.*

*Proof.* Consider the expression $e = (\text{di} \circ \mathcal{E}) \cap \text{di}$ in $\mathcal{N}(\text{di}, \cap)$. On a chain, this expression yields all pairs of distinct non-root nodes that are not edges. Now, assume there exists an expression $e'$ in $\mathcal{N}(\text{di}, {}^{-1}, \pi)$ such that, on unlabeled chains, $e \equiv_{\text{path}} e'$. Since $e$ is non-local, $e'$ must be non-local, too, hence, it must contain diversity. Using Lemma 12, we can rewrite $e'$ into a union of terms each of which is a composition of units of the form id, di, $\mathcal{E}$, $\mathcal{E}^{-1}$, $\pi_1[\mathcal{E}^v]$, or $\pi_2[\mathcal{E}^w]$, $v, w \geq 0$. Let $t = t_1 \circ \cdots \circ t_n$ be such a term in which at least one unit is diversity (di). Since on chains $\text{di} \equiv_{\text{path}} [\mathcal{E}]^+ \cup [\mathcal{E}^{-1}]^+$, $t$ is path-equivalent to the infinite union $\bigcup_{k_1,\ldots,k_n \neq 0} t_{1k_1} \circ \cdots \circ t_{nk_n}$ in which $t_{ik_i} = t_i$ if $t_i \neq \text{di}$ and $t_{ik_i} = \mathcal{E}^{k_i}$ if $t_i = \text{di}$, $1 \leq i \leq n$. For a term $t_{1k_1} \circ \cdots \circ t_{nk_n}$ in this infinite union, we define $\exp(t_{1k_1} \circ \cdots \circ t_{nk_n}) = \sum_{1 \leq i \leq n} \exp(t_{ik_i})$, where $\exp(t_{ik_i}) = 1$ if $t_{ik_i} = \mathcal{E}$; $\exp(t_{ik_i}) = -1$ if $t_{ik_i} = \mathcal{E}^{-1}$; $\exp(t_{ik_i}) = k_i$ if $t_{ik_i} = \mathcal{E}^{k_i}$; and $\exp(t_{ik_i}) = 0$ otherwise. Since $t$ contains at least one diversity unit, the set $\{\exp(t_{1k_1} \circ \cdots \circ t_{nk_n}) \mid k_1,\ldots,k_n \neq 0\}$ covers all integer numbers with at most one exception (there is exactly one exception if $t$ contains exactly one diversity unit). We can therefore choose a term $t' = t_{1k_1} \circ \cdots \circ t_{nk_n}$ for which $\exp(t') = 0$ or $\exp(t') = 1$. Now, choose an unlabeled chain $\mathcal{C}$ which is sufficiently long to ensure that for the local expression $t'$ in $\mathcal{N}({}^{-1}, \pi)$, $[\![t']\!]_\mathcal{C} \neq \emptyset$. Then, $[\![t']\!]_\mathcal{C}$

$$\mathcal{T}:$$

**Fig. 6.** The unlabeled tree $\mathcal{T}$ in the proof of Proposition 15.

contains either an identical node pair (if $\exp(t') = 0$) or an edge (if $\exp(t') = 1$). Hence, by construction, $[\![e']\!]_C$ contains either an identical node pair or an edge, contradicting $e \equiv_{\text{path}} e'$. Hence, no expression in $\mathcal{N}(\text{di}, {}^{-1}, \pi)$ is path-equivalent to $e$.

Using similar arguments, we can prove that $\mathcal{E}^{-1}$ cannot be expressed in $\mathcal{N}(\text{di}, \pi)$ and that $\pi_1[\mathcal{E}]$ and $\pi_2[\mathcal{E}]$ cannot be expressed in $\mathcal{N}(\text{di})$ to establish the other two statements of Proposition 14. $\qquad\square$

## 5  Brute-Force Results

Using a brute-force approach in the style of Fletcher et al. [10], we establish several separations, both at the path and Boolean levels. At the core of these brute-force results is the observation than one can effectively compute the set of query results obtainable by queries in some relation algebra fragment $\mathcal{N}(\mathcal{F})$, $\mathcal{F} \subseteq \{\text{di}, {}^{-1}, \pi, \overline{\pi}, \cap, -\}$, on a given graph. We refer to Fletcher et al. [10] and Hellings [15] for further details.

For path separations between languages $\mathcal{L}_1$ and $\mathcal{L}_2$, we may conclude that $\mathcal{L}_1 \not\leq_{\text{path}} \mathcal{L}_2$ if there exists a query $q$ in $\mathcal{L}_1$ and a tree $\mathcal{T}$ such that no query in $\mathcal{L}_2$ evaluates to $[\![q]\!]_\mathcal{T}$. Using this approach, we prove the following.

**Proposition 15.** *Already on unlabeled trees, we have* $\mathcal{N}({}^{-1}) \not\leq_{\text{path}} \mathcal{N}(\text{di}, \pi, \overline{\pi})$ *and* $\mathcal{N}(\pi) \not\leq_{\text{path}} \mathcal{N}({}^{-1})$.

*Proof.* Consider the expressions $e_1 = \mathcal{E}^{-1}$ and $e_2 = \pi_1[\mathcal{E}] \circ \pi_2[\mathcal{E}]$, and let $\mathcal{T}$ be the tree in Fig. 6. An exhaustive search reveals that no expression in $\mathcal{N}(\text{di}, \pi, \overline{\pi})$ evaluates to $[\![e_1]\!]_\mathcal{T}$ and no expression in $\mathcal{N}({}^{-1})$ evaluates to $[\![e_2]\!]_\mathcal{T}$. $\qquad\square$

At the Boolean level, the key notion in the brute-force approach is the ability to *distinguish* a pair of trees. We say that a query $q$ distinguishes a pair of trees $\mathcal{T}_1$ and $\mathcal{T}_2$ if $[\![q]\!]_{\mathcal{T}_1} = \emptyset$ and $[\![q]\!]_{\mathcal{T}_2} \neq \emptyset$, or vice versa. Given two languages $\mathcal{L}_1$ and $\mathcal{L}_2$, we may conclude that $\mathcal{L}_1 \not\leq_{\text{bool}} \mathcal{L}_2$ if we can find a query $q$ in $\mathcal{L}_1$ and a pair of trees $\mathcal{T}_1$ and $\mathcal{T}_2$, indistinguishable by any query in $\mathcal{L}_2$, but distinguishable by $q$. Using this approach, we prove the following.

**Proposition 16.** *Already on unlabeled trees, we have* $\mathcal{N}(\text{di}, {}^{-1}) \not\leq_{\text{bool}} \mathcal{N}(\text{di})$, $\mathcal{N}(\text{di}, \pi) \not\leq_{\text{bool}} \mathcal{N}(\text{di})$, $\mathcal{N}(\text{di}, {}^{-1}, \cap) \not\leq_{\text{bool}} \mathcal{N}(\text{di}, \pi, \overline{\pi}, \cap, -)$, *and* $\mathcal{N}(\text{di}, \pi) \not\leq_{\text{bool}} \mathcal{N}(\text{di}, {}^{-1})$.

*Proof.* Consider the following four expressions:

$$e_1 = (\mathcal{E}^{-2} \circ \mathcal{E}) \circ \text{di} \circ (\mathcal{E}^{-1} \circ \mathcal{E}^2);$$
$$e_2 = (\mathcal{E} \circ \pi_1[\mathcal{E}]) \circ \text{di} \circ (\pi_2[\mathcal{E}] \circ \mathcal{E});$$

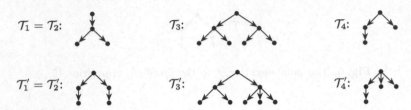

**Fig. 7.** Pairs of unlabeled trees $(\mathcal{T}_i, \mathcal{T}_i')$, $1 \le i \le 4$, in the proof of Proposition 16.

$$e_3 = ((( \mathcal{E}^{-1} \circ \mathcal{E}) \cap \mathrm{di}) \circ (( \mathcal{E}^{-1} \circ \mathcal{E}) \cap \mathrm{di})) \cap \mathrm{di};$$

$$e_4 = (\mathcal{E}^2 \circ \mathcal{E}^{-1}) \circ \mathrm{di} \circ \pi_1[\mathcal{E}^{-1} \circ \mathcal{E}^2] \circ \mathrm{di} \circ \pi_1[\mathcal{E}^{-1} \circ \mathcal{E}^2] \circ \mathrm{di} \circ (\mathcal{E} \circ \mathcal{E}^{-2}),$$

and let $(\mathcal{T}_i, \mathcal{T}_i')$, $1 \le i \le 4$, be the trees in Fig. 7. We have $[\![e_i]\!]_{\mathcal{T}_i} = \emptyset$ and $[\![e_i]\!]_{\mathcal{T}_i'} \ne \emptyset$, and $[\![e_2]\!]_{\mathcal{T}_1} = \emptyset$ and $[\![e_1]\!]_{\mathcal{T}_1'} \ne \emptyset$. Observe that $e_4$ is in $\mathcal{N}(\mathrm{di}, {}^{-1}, \pi)$, but, by Proposition 34, $e_4$ is Boolean-equivalent to an expression in $\mathcal{N}(\mathrm{di}, \pi)$. An exhaustive search reveals that no expression in $\mathcal{N}(\mathrm{di})$ can distinguish $\mathcal{T}_1 = \mathcal{T}_2$ from $\mathcal{T}_1' = \mathcal{T}_2'$; no expression in $\mathcal{N}(\mathrm{di}, \pi, \bar{\pi}, \cap, -)$ can distinguish $\mathcal{T}_3$ from $\mathcal{T}_3'$; and no expression in $\mathcal{N}(\mathrm{di}, {}^{-1})$ can distinguish $\mathcal{T}_4$ from $\mathcal{T}_4'$. □

## 6   Collapse Results

In Sects. 3, 4, and 5, we focused on separation results. Here, we focus on collapse results. The key tool to prove these are what we call *condition tree queries*, a generalization of the tree queries of Wu et al. [26], which were used to prove Proposition 30 (see Sect. 7 on related work).

### 6.1   Condition Tree Queries

We first define *condition tree queries* syntactically and semantically:

**Definition 17.** *A* condition tree query *is a tuple* $\mathcal{Q} = (\mathcal{T}, C, \mathsf{s}, \mathsf{t}, \gamma)$, *where* $\mathcal{T} = (V, \Sigma, \mathbf{E})$ *is a tree,* $C$ *is a set of node expressions that represent node conditions,* $\mathsf{s} \in V$ *is the* source *node,* $\mathsf{t} \in V$ *is the* target *node, and* $\gamma \subseteq V \times C$ *is the* node-condition *relation. We write* $\gamma(n)$ *to denote the set* $\{c \mid (n, c) \in \gamma\}$.

*Let* $\mathcal{T}' = (V', \Sigma, \mathbf{E}')$ *be a tree. Then,* $[\![\mathcal{Q}]\!]_{\mathcal{T}'}$ *consists of all the node pairs* $(m, n) \in V' \times V'$ *for which there exists a mapping* $f : V \to V'$ *satisfying the following conditions:*

*(i)* $f(\mathsf{s}) = m$ *and* $f(\mathsf{t}) = n$;
*(ii) for all* $v \in V$ *and* $c \in \gamma(v)$, $(f(v), f(v)) \in [\![c]\!]_{\mathcal{T}'}$; *and*
*(iii) for all* $\ell \in \Sigma$ *and* $(v, w) \in \mathbf{E}(\ell)$, $(f(v), f(w)) \in \mathbf{E}'(\ell)$.

We slightly extend Definition 17 to allow the *empty condition tree* where $V = \emptyset$ and $\mathsf{s}$ and $\mathsf{t}$ have some null value. On every tree, the empty condition tree evaluates to the empty set.

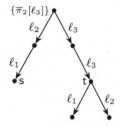

**Fig. 8.** The condition tree query of Example 18.

*Example 18.* The condition tree query $Q$ in Fig. 8 selects a node pair $(s, t)$ if the following tree traversal steps are all successful: (1) from $s$, go up via two edges labeled $\ell_1$ and $\ell_2$; (2) check if the node where we have arrived satisfies the condition $\overline{\pi}_2[\ell_3]$; (3) from there, go down via two edges labeled $\ell_3$, after which we arrive at $t$; and (4) check if $t$ has outgoing edges labeled $\ell_1$ and $\ell_2$. The condition tree query $Q$ is path-equivalent to the expression $\ell_1^{-1} \circ \ell_2^{-1} \circ \overline{\pi}_2[\ell_3] \circ \ell_3 \circ \ell_3 \circ \pi_1[\ell_1] \circ \pi_1[\ell_2]$, in $\mathcal{N}(^{-1}, \overline{\pi})$.

In the remainder of this subsection, we formalize the relationship between condition tree queries and relation algebra expressions exhibited in Example 18. Thereto, let $\mathcal{F} \subseteq \{^{-1}, \pi, \overline{\pi}\}$, and let $\mathbf{Q}_{\text{tree}}(\mathcal{F})$ be the class of all condition tree queries in which node conditions are restricted to union-free expressions in $\mathcal{N}(\mathcal{F})$. We claim that, for $\overline{\mathcal{F}} = \{^{-1}, \pi\}$ or $\overline{\mathcal{F}} = \{^{-1}, \pi, \overline{\pi}\}$, $\mathbf{Q}_{\text{tree}}(\mathcal{F})$ and the class of all union-free expressions in $\mathcal{N}(\mathcal{F})$ path-subsume each other.

Using a straightforward rewriting argument, we can show the following:

**Proposition 19.** *Let $\mathcal{F} \subseteq \{^{-1}, \pi, \overline{\pi}\}$, and $e$ be a union-free expression in $\mathcal{N}(\mathcal{F})$. There exists a condition tree query $Q$ in $\mathbf{Q}_{\text{tree}}(\mathcal{F})$ such that $e \equiv_{\text{path}} Q$.*

For the translation in the other direction, we introduce *up-down queries*:

**Definition 20.** *An* up-down query *is a condition tree query $Q = (T, C, s, t, \gamma)$ in which all edges of $T$ are on the unique path from $s$ to $t$ not taking into account the direction of the edges.*

*Example 21.* An up-down query can look like a chain if the target node is an ancestor of the source node, or vice versa, as illustrated by Fig. 9, *left*. This up-down query is path-equivalent to $\overline{\pi}_2[\ell_3] \circ \ell_2^{-1} \circ \ell_1^{-1}$. The condition tree query in the *middle* is not up-down, but is path-equivalent to the up-down tree query on the *right*. Observe that the *right* query is obtained by pushing the parts of the tree traversal described by the *middle* query that are not on the path from source to target into node conditions. The *middle* and *right* queries are path-equivalent to $\pi_1[\ell_2 \circ \overline{\pi}_2[\ell_3]] \circ \ell_1^{-1} \circ \pi_2[\ell_3] \circ \ell_2 \circ \pi_1[\ell_2] \circ \ell_1$.

As illustrated in Example 21, we can rewrite a condition tree query to an up-down query by pushing into node conditions those parts of the condition tree query not on the path from source to target:

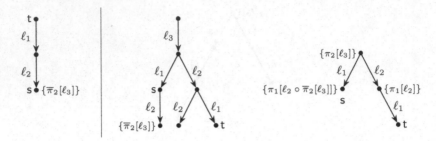

**Fig. 9.** The condition tree query on the *left* is up-down. The condition tree query in the *middle* is not, but this query is path-equivalent to the up-down query on the right.

**Lemma 22.** *Let* $\{\pi\} \subseteq \overline{\mathcal{F}} \subseteq \{^{-1}, \overline{\pi}, \pi\}$, *and* $\mathcal{Q}$ *be a condition tree query in* $\mathbf{Q}_{\text{tree}}(\mathcal{F})$. *There exists an up-down query* $\mathcal{Q}'$ *in* $\mathbf{Q}_{\text{tree}}(\mathcal{F})$ *such that* $\mathcal{Q} \equiv_{\text{path}} \mathcal{Q}'$.

As also illustrated in Example 21, an up-down query can be translated straightforwardly into a path-equivalent relation algebra expression, provided we have the converse operator $(^{-1})$ at our disposal:

**Lemma 23.** *Let* $\{^{-1}\} \subseteq \mathcal{F} \subseteq \{^{-1}, \overline{\pi}, \pi\}$, *and* $\mathcal{Q}$ *be an up-down query in* $\mathbf{Q}_{\text{tree}}(\mathcal{F})$. *There exists a union-free expression* $e$ *in* $\mathcal{N}(\mathcal{F})$ *such that* $\mathcal{Q} \equiv_{\text{path}} e$.

Finally, combining Lemmas 22 and 23 yields the following:

**Proposition 24.** *Let* $\{^{-1}, \pi\} \subseteq \overline{\mathcal{F}} \subseteq \{^{-1}, \pi, \overline{\pi}\}$, *and* $\mathcal{Q}$ *be a condition tree query in* $\mathbf{Q}_{\text{tree}}(\mathcal{F})$. *There exists a union-free expression in* $\mathcal{N}(\mathcal{F})$ *such that* $\mathcal{Q} \equiv_{\text{path}} e$.

### 6.2  Adding Intersection to Local Fragments

Hellings et al. [16,17] already proved that adding intersection to local relation algebra fragments not containing the converse operator (the *downward* relation algebra fragments) never increases their expressive power (Proposition 31). Here, we show that this result actually holds for *all* local relation algebra fragments. As a first step, consider the following example:

*Example 25.* Suppose we want to compute the intersection of the two up-down queries in Fig. 10, *left*. Since the two up-down queries have different heights, a pair of nodes of a tree can only be in the result of the intersection of the two queries on that tree if the children of the root of the second query are mapped to the same node. Hence, we can replace the second up-down query by the one shown in the *middle*. Since both queries now have the same shape and corresponding edges have the same label, the intersection is easily obtained by merging the node conditions, resulting in the up-down query on the *right*.

We now generalize Example 25:

**Proposition 26.** *Let* $\{\pi\} \subseteq \overline{\mathcal{F}} \subseteq \{^{-1}, \pi, \overline{\pi}\}$, *and* $\mathcal{Q}_1$ *and* $\mathcal{Q}_2$ *be condition tree queries in* $\mathbf{Q}_{\text{tree}}(\mathcal{F})$. *There exists a condition tree query* $\mathcal{Q}$ *in* $\mathbf{Q}_{\text{tree}}(\mathcal{F})$ *such that, for every tree* $\mathcal{T}$, $[\![\mathcal{Q}]\!]_{\mathcal{T}} = [\![\mathcal{Q}_1]\!]_{\mathcal{T}} \cap [\![\mathcal{Q}_2]\!]_{\mathcal{T}}$.

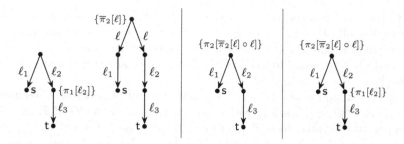

**Fig. 10.** The step-wise computation of the intersection of the two up-down queries on the *left* eventually results in the up-down query on the *right*.

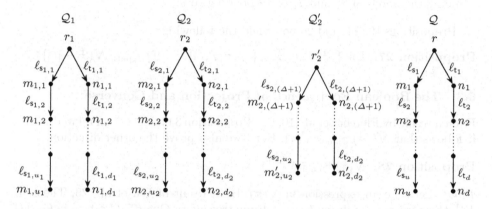

**Fig. 11.** Up-down queries $\mathcal{Q}_1$, $\mathcal{Q}_2$, $\mathcal{Q}'_2$ and $\mathcal{Q}$ in the proof of Proposition 26.

*Proof (sketch).* By Lemma 22, we may assume that $\mathcal{Q}_1 = (\mathcal{T}_1, C_1, s_1, t_1, \gamma_1)$ and $\mathcal{Q}_2 = (\mathcal{T}_2, C_2, s_2, t_2, \gamma_2)$ are up-down queries as in Fig. 11. Let $\mathcal{T}'$ be an arbitrary tree. If $u_2 - d_2 \neq u_1 - d_1$, then, obviously $[\mathcal{Q}_1]_{\mathcal{T}'} \cap [\mathcal{Q}_2]_{\mathcal{T}'} = \emptyset$. Thus, assume $u_2 - d_2 = u_1 - d_1$, or, equivalently, $u_2 - u_1 = d_2 - d_1$. We distinguish two cases:

1. $u_1 \neq u_2$. By symmetry, assume $u_2 > u_1$. We write $\Delta = u_2 - u_1 = d_2 - d_1$. To find a pair of nodes of $\mathcal{T}'$ common to $[\mathcal{Q}_1]_{\mathcal{T}'}$ and $[\mathcal{Q}_2]_{\mathcal{T}'}$, it is imperative that for all $i$, $1 \leq i \leq \Delta$, $m_{2,i}$ and $n_{2,i}$ are mapped to the same node of $\mathcal{T}$. Hence, if for some $i$, $1 \leq i \leq \Delta$, $\ell_{s_{2,i}} \neq \ell_{t_{2,i}}$, $[\mathcal{Q}_1]_{\mathcal{T}'} \cap [\mathcal{Q}_2]_{\mathcal{T}'} = \emptyset$. Thus, assume for all $i$, $1 \leq i \leq \Delta$, that $\ell_{s_{2,i}} = \ell_{t_{2,i}}$. Then, $[\mathcal{Q}_1]_{\mathcal{T}'} \cap [\mathcal{Q}_2]_{\mathcal{T}'} = [\mathcal{Q}_1]_{\mathcal{T}'} \cap [\mathcal{Q}'_2]_{\mathcal{T}'}$, where $\mathcal{Q}'_2 = (\mathcal{T}'_2, C'_2, s'_2, t'_2, \gamma'_2)$ is as in Fig. 11, with

$$\gamma'_2(r'_2) = \pi_2[\gamma_2(r_2) \circ \ell_{s_{2,1}} \circ \gamma_2(m_{2,1}) \circ \gamma_2(n_{2,1}) \circ \cdots \circ \ell_{s_{2,\Delta}} \circ \gamma_2(m_{2,\Delta}) \circ \gamma_2(n_{2,\Delta})],$$

in which $\gamma_2(v)$ is a shorthand for the composition of the node expressions in $\gamma(v)$.[7] For all other nodes $v'$ of $T_2'$, $\gamma_2'(v') = \gamma_2(v)$, $v$ being the node of $T_2$ corresponding to $v'$. Notice that the left (an hence also the right) branches of $\mathcal{Q}_1$ and $\mathcal{Q}_2'$ have equal length, which allows us to apply the next case on $\mathcal{Q}_1$ and $\mathcal{Q}_2'$.

2. $u_1 = u_2 = u$, and hence $d_1 = d_2 = d$. To find a pair of nodes of $T'$ common to $[\![\mathcal{Q}_1]\!]_{T'}$ and $[\![\mathcal{Q}_2]\!]_{T'}$, it is imperative that corresponding nodes of $T_1$ and $T_2$ are mapped to the same node of $T'$. Hence, if for some $i$, $1 \le i \le u$, $\ell_{s_{1,i}} \ne \ell_{s_{2,i}}$, or for some $j$, $1 \le j \le d$, $\ell_{t_{1,i}} \ne \ell_{t_{2,i}}$, $[\![\mathcal{Q}_1]\!]_{T'} \cap [\![\mathcal{Q}_2]\!]_{T'} = \emptyset$. Thus, assume for all $i$, $1 \le i \le u$, that $\ell_{s_{1,i}} = \ell_{s_{2,i}} = \ell_{s_i}$, and, for all $j$, $1 \le j \le d$, that $\ell_{t_{1,i}} = \ell_{t_{2,i}} = \ell_{t_i}$. Then, $[\![\mathcal{Q}_1]\!]_{T'} \cap [\![\mathcal{Q}_2]\!]_{T'} = [\![\mathcal{Q}]\!]_{T'}$, where $\mathcal{Q} = (T, C_1 \cup C_2, \mathsf{s}, \mathsf{t}, \gamma)$ is as in Fig. 11, where, for all nodes $v$ of $T$, $\gamma(v) = \gamma_1(v_1) \circ \gamma_2(v_2)$, $v_1$ and $v_2$ being the nodes of $T_1$ and $T_2$ corresponding to $v$.    □

Propositions 19, 24, and 26 now yield the following:

**Proposition 27.** *For* $\{^{-1}, \pi\} \subseteq \overline{\mathcal{F}} \subseteq \{^{-1}, \pi, \overline{\pi}, \cap\}$, $\mathcal{N}(\mathcal{F}) \preceq_{\mathrm{path}} \mathcal{N}(\mathcal{F} - \{\cap\})$.

### 6.3   The Boolean Equivalence of Projection and Converse

From a result by Fletcher et al. [10,11] (Proposition 34 in Sect. 7 on related work), it follows that $\mathcal{N}(^{-1}) \preceq_{\mathrm{bool}} \mathcal{N}(\pi)$. Here, we also prove the other direction:

**Proposition 28.** $\mathcal{N}(\pi) \preceq_{\mathrm{bool}} \mathcal{N}(^{-1})$.

*Proof.* Let $e$ be an expression in $\mathcal{N}(\pi)$. By a result of Wu et al. [26, Theorem 4.1], there exists a condition-free condition tree query $\mathcal{Q} = (T, C, \mathsf{s}, \mathsf{t}, \gamma)$ in $\mathbf{Q}_{\mathrm{tree}}()$ such that $e \equiv_{\mathrm{path}} \mathcal{Q}$.[8] Let $r$ be the root of $T$, and $\mathcal{Q}_r = (T, C, r, r, \gamma)$. Obviously, $\mathcal{Q} \equiv_{\mathrm{bool}} \mathcal{Q}_r$. Because the target node is now the root of $T$, the translation from $\mathcal{Q}_r$ to a path-equivalent up-down query (Lemma 22) only requires the first projection. Hence, there exists an up-down query $\mathcal{Q}_r' = (T', C', r', r', \gamma')$ in $\mathbf{Q}_{\mathrm{tree}}(\pi_1)$ such that $\mathcal{Q}_r \equiv_{\mathrm{path}} \mathcal{Q}_r'$. Since source and target coincide in $T'$, $r'$ is necessarily the only node of $T'$. Hence, $\mathcal{Q}_r'$ is path equivalent to the composition of the node expressions in $\gamma(r')$, which is in $\mathcal{N}(\pi_1)$. Now, a projection expression in $\mathcal{N}(\pi_1)$ can always be rewritten in the form $\pi_1[e] = \pi_1[\ell_1 \circ \pi_1[e_1] \circ \cdots \ell_n \circ \pi_1[e_n]]$, with $e_1, \ldots, e_n$ in $\mathcal{N}(\pi_1)$, which is equivalent to $e \circ \ell_n^{-1} \circ \cdots \circ \ell_1^{-1}$. By applying this rewriting top-down, we conclude that $\mathcal{N}(\pi_1) \preceq_{\mathrm{path}} \mathcal{N}(^{-1})$.    □

Hence, $\mathcal{N}(\pi)$ and $\mathcal{N}(^{-1})$ are Boolean-equivalent in expressive power.

---

[7] Observe that the composition of node expressions is associative and that this composition is path-equivalent to the intersection of node expressions.

[8] Recall that the tree queries in Wu et al. [26] are essentially the same as the condition-free condition tree queries in this paper.

# 7   Related Work

Results on node-labeled trees are usually straightforward to translate to the edge-labeled trees we use. Benedikt et al. [3] studied path-equivalence of $\mathcal{N}(^{-1}, \pi)$ and its fragments on labeled trees:

**Proposition 29** ([3, **Proposition 2.1**]). *For $\mathcal{F}_1, \mathcal{F}_2 \subseteq \{^{-1}, \pi\}$, $\mathcal{N}(\mathcal{F}_1) \preceq_{\text{path}} \mathcal{N}(\mathcal{F}_2) \Longleftrightarrow \mathcal{F}_1 \subseteq \mathcal{F}_2$.*

Where applicable, we generalize Proposition 29 to Boolean separation, in Sect. 5. Wu et al. [26] proved a collapse result for relation algebra fragments with intersection:[9]

**Proposition 30** ([26, **Theorem 4.1**]). *Both $\mathcal{N}(^{-1}, \pi, \cap) \preceq_{\text{path}} \mathcal{N}(^{-1}, \pi)$ and $\mathcal{N}(^{-1}, \pi, \cap) \preceq_{\text{path}} \mathcal{N}(^{-1}, \cap)$.*

In Sect. 6, we generalize Proposition 30 to also include coprojections.

Finally, Hellings et al. [16,17] studied the relative expressiveness of the fragments of $\mathcal{N}(\pi, \overline{\pi}, \cap, -)$,[10] and obtained the following results which are used in this study:

**Proposition 31** ([16, **Theorem 3**]). *For $\mathcal{F} \subseteq \{\pi, \overline{\pi}, \cap, -\}$, $\mathcal{N}(\mathcal{F}) \preceq_{\text{path}} \mathcal{N}(\mathcal{F} - \{\cap, -\})$.*

**Proposition 32** ([17, **Proposition 10**]). *On unlabeled chains, $\mathcal{N}(\text{di}) \npreceq_{\text{path}} \mathcal{N}(\pi, \overline{\pi}, \cap, -)$ and $\mathcal{N}(^{-1}) \npreceq_{\text{path}} \mathcal{N}(\pi, \overline{\pi}, \cap, -)$.*

**Proposition 33** ([17, **Propositions 19 and 21**]). *We have $\mathcal{N}(\pi) \npreceq_{\text{bool}} \mathcal{N}()$, $\mathcal{N}(^{-1}) \npreceq_{\text{bool}} \mathcal{N}()$, and $\mathcal{N}(\overline{\pi}) \npreceq_{\text{bool}} \mathcal{N}(\text{di}, ^{-1}, \pi, \cap)$.*

The graph query results of Fletcher et al. [10,11] include many separation results of which the proofs do not specialize to trees. They also proved a collapse result, that automatically does hold on trees:

**Proposition 34** ([11, **Proposition 4.2**]). *Let $\mathcal{F} \subseteq \{\text{di}, ^{-1}, \pi, \overline{\pi}\}$. On labeled and unlabeled graphs, we have $\mathcal{N}(\mathcal{F} \cup \{^{-1}\}) \preceq_{\text{bool}} \mathcal{N}(\mathcal{F} \cup \{\pi\})$.*

Several other well-known expressiveness results are known in the context of Conditional XPath and Navigational XPath [6,22,23], which are strongly related to the relation algebra. Unfortunately, these results are proved with respect to the sibling-ordered tree data model, and do not apply to our unordered tree data model. We observe that on chains, no sibling relation exists. Hence, the separation results we have proved on chains translate to separation results in the sibling-ordered tree data model.

---

[9] Strictly speaking, they deal with union-free expressions, but since unions can always be pushed out to the outermost level, this is not a real restriction.

[10] These are generally referred to as the *downward* fragments of the relation algebra.

| | | Boolean semantics | | | | | | Path semantics | | | | | |
|---|---|---|---|---|---|---|---|---|---|---|---|---|---|
| | | di | $^{-1}$ | $\pi$ | $\overline{\pi}$ | $\cap$ | $-$ | di | $^{-1}$ | $\pi$ | $\overline{\pi}$ | $\cap$ | $-$ |
| Local queries / Downward queries | $\mathcal{N}()$ | 7 ✗ | 33 ✗ | 33 ✗ | 33 ✗ | 31 ✓ | 31 ✓ | 32 ✗ | 29 ✗ | 29 ✗ | 33 ✗ | 31 ✓ | 31 ✓ |
| Local queries / Downward queries | $\mathcal{N}(\cap)$ | 7 ✗ | 33 ✗ | 33 ✗ | 33 ✗ | | 31 ✓ | 32 ✗ | 33 ✗ | 33 ✗ | 33 ✗ | | 31 ✓ |
| Local queries / Downward queries | $\mathcal{N}(\cap, -)$ | 33 ✗ | 33 ✗ | 33 ✗ | 33 ✗ | | | 33 ✗ | 33 ✗ | 33 ✗ | 33 ✗ | | |
| Local queries / Downward queries | $\mathcal{N}(\pi)$ | 7 ✗ | 34 ✓ | | 33 ✗ | 31 ✓ | 33 ✗ | 32 ✗ | 29 ✗ | | 33 ✗ | 31 ✓ | 33 ✗ |
| Local queries / Downward queries | $\mathcal{N}(\pi, \cap)$ | 7 ✗ | 28 ✓ | | 33 ✗ | | 33 ✗ | 32 ✗ | 32 ✗ | | 33 ✗ | | 33 ✗ |
| Local queries / Downward queries | $\mathcal{N}(\pi, \overline{\pi})$ | 7 ✗ | 34 ✓ | | | 31 ✓ | 31 ✓ | 32 ✗ | 32 ✗ | | | 31 ✓ | 31 ✓ |
| Local queries / Downward queries | $\mathcal{N}(\pi, \overline{\pi}, \cap)$ | 7 ✗ | 27 ✓ | | | | 31 ✓ | 32 ✗ | 32 ✗ | | | | 31 ✓ |
| Local queries / Downward queries | $\mathcal{N}(\pi, \overline{\pi}, \cap, -)$ | 7 ✗ | 7 ✗ | | | | | 32 ✗ | 32 ✗ | | | | |
| Local queries | $\mathcal{N}(^{-1})$ | 7 ✗ | | 28 ✓ | 33 ✗ | 28 ✓ | 33 ✗ | 32 ✗ | | 29 ✗ | 33 ✗ | 15 ✗ | 33 ✗ |
| Local queries | $\mathcal{N}(^{-1}, \pi)$ | 7 ✗ | | | 33 ✗ | 30 ✓ | 33 ✗ | 32 ✗ | | | 33 ✗ | 30 ✓ | 33 ✗ |
| Local queries | $\mathcal{N}(^{-1}, \pi, \cap)$ | 7 ✗ | | | 33 ✗ | | 33 ✗ | 32 ✗ | | | 33 ✗ | | 33 ✗ |
| Local queries | $\mathcal{N}(^{-1}, \pi, \overline{\pi})$ | 7 ✗ | | | | 27 ✓ | 7 ✗ | 32 ✗ | | | | 27 ✓ | 7 ✗ |
| Local queries | $\mathcal{N}(^{-1}, \pi, \overline{\pi}, \cap)$ | 7 ✗ | | | | | 7 ✗ | 32 ✗ | | | | | 7 ✗ |
| Local queries | $\mathcal{N}(^{-1}, \pi, \overline{\pi}, \cap, -)$ | 9 ✗ | | | | | | 32 ✗ | | | | | |
| | $\mathcal{N}(\mathrm{di})$ | | 10 ✗ | 10 ✗ | 33 ✗ | 7 ✗ | 33 ✗ | | 10 ✗ | 10 ✗ | 33 ✗ | 7 ✗ | 33 ✗ |
| | $\mathcal{N}(\mathrm{di}, \pi)$ | | 34 ✓ | | 33 ✗ | 7 ✗ | 33 ✗ | | 14 ✗ | | 33 ✗ | 7 ✗ | 33 ✗ |
| | $\mathcal{N}(\mathrm{di}, \pi, \cap)$ | | 16 ✗ | | 33 ✗ | | 33 ✗ | | 16 ✗ | | 33 ✗ | | 33 ✗ |
| | $\mathcal{N}(\mathrm{di}, \pi, \overline{\pi})$ | | 34 ✓ | | | 7 ✗ | 7 ✗ | | 15 ✗ | | | 7 ✗ | 7 ✗ |
| | $\mathcal{N}(\mathrm{di}, \pi, \overline{\pi}, \cap)$ | | 16 ✗ | | | | ? | | 16 ✗ | | | | ? |
| | $\mathcal{N}(\mathrm{di}, \pi, \overline{\pi}, \cap, -)$ | | 16 ✗ | | | | | | 16 ✗ | | | | |
| | $\mathcal{N}(\mathrm{di}, ^{-1})$ | | | 16 ✗ | 33 ✗ | 7 ✗ | 33 ✗ | | | 16 ✗ | 33 ✗ | 7 ✗ | 33 ✗ |
| | $\mathcal{N}(\mathrm{di}, ^{-1}, \pi)$ | | | | 33 ✗ | 7 ✗ | 33 ✗ | | | | 33 ✗ | 7 ✗ | 33 ✗ |
| | $\mathcal{N}(\mathrm{di}, ^{-1}, \pi, \cap)$ | | | | 33 ✗ | | 33 ✗ | | | | 33 ✗ | | 33 ✗ |
| | $\mathcal{N}(\mathrm{di}, ^{-1}, \pi, \overline{\pi})$ | | | | | 7 ✗ | 7 ✗ | | | | | 7 ✗ | 7 ✗ |
| | $\mathcal{N}(\mathrm{di}, ^{-1}, \pi, \overline{\pi}, \cap)$ | | | | | | ? | | | | | | ? |
| | $\mathcal{N}(\mathrm{di}, ^{-1}, \pi, \overline{\pi}, \cap, -)$ | | | | | | | | | | | | |

**Fig. 12.** Index to the separation and collapse results discussed in this paper. Let $(\mathcal{N}(\mathcal{F}), op)$ be a field in the "z semantics" part of the table, $z \in \{\text{bool}, \text{path}\}$. A check mark ✓ in the field $(\mathcal{N}(\mathcal{F}), op)$ means that $\mathcal{N}(\mathcal{F} \cup \{op\}) \preceq_z \mathcal{N}(\mathcal{F})$. A cross ✗ in the field $(\mathcal{N}(\mathcal{F}), op)$ means that $\mathcal{N}(\mathcal{F} \cup \{op\}) \npreceq_z \mathcal{N}(\mathcal{F})$. Finally, a question mark ? indicates an open problem.

# 8 Conclusion and Future Work

In this paper, we settled the relative expressive power of queries in fragments of the relation algebra when used to query trees. A summary of our results can be found in Fig. 12. To compensate for the limited flexibility of the tree data model, compared to the graph data model, we needed to develop several new techniques to make this study feasible. For the local fragments, i.e., fragments of $\mathcal{N}(^{-1}, \pi, \overline{\pi}, \cap, -)$, we provided a complete characterization of their relative expressive power, and with respect to the non-local fragments, only one challenging problem remains open:

*Problem 35.* Let $\{\mathrm{di}, \overline{\pi}, \cap\} \subseteq \mathcal{F} \subseteq \{\mathrm{di}, ^{-1}, \pi, \overline{\pi}, \cap\}$ and let $z \in \{\text{bool}, \text{path}\}$. Do we have $\mathcal{N}(\mathcal{F} \cup \{-\}) \preceq_z \mathcal{N}(\mathcal{F})$ or not?

The difficulties in solving this open problem are manifold. For example, consider the language $\mathcal{N}(\mathrm{di}, ^{-1}, \pi, \overline{\pi}, \cap)$. In this fairly rich query language, there are several instances of expressions for which one can express the complement. For $k > 0$, we have, e.g., $\overline{\mathcal{E}^{-k}} \equiv_{\text{path}} (\mathcal{E}^{-k} \circ \mathrm{di}) \cup (\overline{\pi}_1[\mathcal{E}^{-k}] \circ \text{all})$. Unfortunately, we have not been able yet to express complement in every instance or been able to prove that expressing the complement is impossible in some instances.

Additional difficulties arise from the fact that we can prove that a possible separation between $\mathcal{N}(\mathrm{di}, ^{-1}, \pi, \bar{\pi}, \cap)$ and $\mathcal{N}(\mathrm{di}, ^{-1}, \pi, \bar{\pi}, \cap, -)$ cannot be established on a single pair of trees, ruling out the applicability of brute-force techniques and many techniques developed in our work. Hence, we definitely face a challenging open problem, which we hope to solve in the future.

Another interesting direction for future work is augmenting the relation algebra with operators beyond the expressive power of FO[3]. Possible candidates would be an iteration construct such as an ancestor-descendant axis, or the more general and powerful Kleene-star transitive closure operator.

# References

1. Barceló, P.: Querying graph databases. In: Proceedings 32nd Symposium on Principles of Database Systems, pp. 175–188. ACM (2013)
2. Barceló, P., Pérez, J., Reutter, J.L.: Relative expressiveness of nested regular expressions. In: Proceedings of 6th Alberto Mendelzon International Workshop on Foundations of Data Management, pp. 180–195. CEUR Workshop Proceedings (2012)
3. Benedikt, M., Fan, W., Kuper, G.: Structural properties of XPath fragments. Theor. Comput. Sci. **336**(1), 3–31 (2005)
4. Benedikt, M., Koch, C.: XPath leashed. ACM Comput. Surv. **41**(1), 3:1–3:54 (2009)
5. Bray, T., Paoli, J., Sperberg-McQueen, C.M., Maler, E., Yergeau, F., Cowan, J.: Extensible Markup Language (XML) 1.1 (Second Edition). W3C Recommendation, W3C (2006). http://www.w3.org/TR/2006/REC-xml11-20060816
6. ten Cate, B.: The expressivity of XPath with transitive closure. In: Proceedings of 25th Symposium on Principles of Database Systems, pp. 328–337. ACM (2006)
7. Clark, J., DeRose, S.: XML Path Language (XPath) Version 1.0. W3C Recommendation, W3C (1999). http://www.w3.org/TR/1999/REC-xpath-19991116
8. Cruz, I.F., Mendelzon, A.O., Wood, P.T.: A graphical query language supporting recursion. In: Proceedings of 1987 ACM SIGMOD International Conference on Management of Data, pp. 323–330. ACM, New York (1987)
9. Ecma International: The JSON data interchange format, 1st Edition (2013). http://www.ecma-international.org/publications/standards/Ecma-404.htm
10. Fletcher, G.H.L., Gyssens, M., Leinders, D., Van den Bussche, J., Van Gucht, D., Vansummeren, S., Wu, Y.: Relative expressive power of navigational querying on graphs. In: Proceedings of 14th International Conference on Database Theory, pp. 197–207. ACM (2011)
11. Fletcher, G.H.L., Gyssens, M., Leinders, D., Surinx, D., Van den Bussche, J., Van Gucht, D., Vansummeren, S., Wu, Y.: Relative expressive power of navigational querying on graphs. Inform. Sci. **298**, 390–406 (2015)
12. Givant, S.: The calculus of relations as a foundation for mathematics. J. Autom. Reason. **37**(4), 277–322 (2006)
13. Grädel, E., Otto, M.: On logics with two variables. Theor. Comput. Sci. **224**(1–2), 73–113 (1999)
14. Grohe, M.: Finite variable logics in descriptive complexity theory. Bull. Symb. Logic **4**, 345–398 (1998)

15. Hellings, J.: On Tarski's Relation Algebra: querying trees and chains and the semi-join algebra. Ph.D. thesis, Hasselt University and Transnational University of Limburg (2018)
16. Hellings, J., Gyssens, M., Wu, Y., Van Gucht, D., Van den Bussche, J., Vansummeren, S., Fletcher, G.H.L.: Relative expressive power of downward fragments of navigational query languages on trees and chains. In: Proceedings of 15th Symposium on Database Programming Languages, pp. 59–68 (2015)
17. Hellings, J., Gyssens, M., Wu, Y., Van Gucht, D., Van den Bussche, J., Vansummeren, S., Fletcher, G.H.L.: Comparing downward fragments of the relational calculus with transitive closure on trees. Technical report. Hasselt University (2018). https://arxiv.org/abs/1803.01390
18. Hellings, J., Pilachowski, C.L., Van Gucht, D., Gyssens, M., Wu, Y.: From relation algebra to semi-join algebra: an approach for graph query optimization. In: Proceedings of 16th International Symposium on Database Programming Languages, pp. 5:1–5:10 (2017)
19. Hidders, J., Paredaens, J., Van den Bussche, J.: J-logic: logical foundations for JSON querying. In: Proceedings of 36th Symposium on Principles of Database Systems, pp. 137–149 (2017)
20. Kaushik, R., Bohannon, P., Naughton, J.F., Korth, H.F.: Covering indexes for branching path queries. In: Proceedings of 2002 ACM SIGMOD International Conference on Management of Data, pp. 133–144. ACM (2002)
21. Libkin, L.: Elements of Finite Model Theory. Springer, Heidelberg (2004). https://doi.org/10.1007/978-3-662-07003-1
22. Marx, M.: Conditional XPath. ACM Trans. Database Syst. **30**(4), 929–959 (2005)
23. Marx, M., de Rijke, M.: Semantic characterizations of navigational XPath. SIGMOD Rec. **34**(2), 41–46 (2005)
24. Tarski, A.: On the calculus of relations. J. Symb. Log. **6**(3), 73–89 (1941)
25. Tsichritzis, D.C., Lochovsky, F.H.: Hierarchical data-base management: a survey. ACM Comput. Surv. **8**(1), 105–123 (1976)
26. Wu, Y., Van Gucht, D., Gyssens, M., Paredaens, J.: A study of a positive fragment of path queries: expressiveness, normal form and minimization. Comput. J. **54**(7), 1091–1118 (2011)

# Improving the Performance of the k Rare Class Nearest Neighbor Classifier by the Ranking of Point Patterns

Zsolt László⬤, Levente Török⬤, and György Kovács$^{(\boxtimes)}$⬤

Analytical Minds Ltd., Budapest, Hungary
zsolt.laszlo_92@yahoo.com, toroklev@gmail.com, gyuriofkovacs@gmail.com

**Abstract.** In most real life applications of classification, samples are imbalanced. Usually, this is due to the difficulty of data collection. Large margin, or instance based classifiers suffer a lot from sparsity of samples close to the dichotomy. In this work, we propose an improvement to a recent technique developed for rare class classification. The experimental results show a definite performance gain.

**Keywords:** kNN classification · Rare class classification
Imbalanced learning · Probability smoothing · Point pattern ranking

## 1 Introduction

Classification is one of the most widely researched problems of machine learning with plenty of applications in various fields of science. Contrarily to the ideal case, real world applications usually come with imbalanced data. The umbrella term *imbalanced* refers to various issues related to the distribution of the data. Globally – due to the rare nature of a phenomenon or the high costs of sampling – some classes may be underrepresented in the training set. Local imbalancedness is related to the non-uniform sampling of the classes: some parts of the manifold representing a class may be hard or expensive to sample. Even a well sampled and globally balanced dataset may become locally imbalanced and reflect issues related to non-uniform sampling when possibly non-linear feature transforms are applied. Detailed overviews on imbalanced learning can be found in [1–3].

One specific class of imbalancedness called rare-class classification is characterized by relatively small datasets with the positive class having extremely low number of samples. Due to their simplicity and the ease of interpretation, instance based methods (like the k Nearest Neighbors classifier – kNN) are widely used on these small, sparse and imbalanced datasets. One particular field of application is medicine as many diseases and degenerations constitute small portions of the populations. Detailed overviews on the significance of instance based learning in medical decision support can be found in [4,5]. Despite its simplicity, improvements of kNN classification addressing the issues of imbalanced learning are still being developed [6–10].

© Springer International Publishing AG, part of Springer Nature 2018
F. Ferrarotti and S. Woltran (Eds.): FoIKS 2018, LNCS 10833, pp. 265–283, 2018.
https://doi.org/10.1007/978-3-319-90050-6_15

In the case of imbalanced and/or sparse data accuracy is rarely used as a measure of performance, as the incorrect classification of the low number of positive samples may still lead to extraordinarily accurate classification results. The goal is usually to maximize the sensitivity of the classifier, namely, achieve the best true positive rate (like diseased entities in medicine) at various levels of false positive rate. The most commonly used measure to characterize this kind of performance is the *Area Under Curve* (AUC), referring to the area under the *Receiver Operating Characteristic* (ROC) curve. This measure quantifies how sensitive a classifier is as the false positive rate is varied.

In this paper a new approach is proposed to improve the performance of the recently published algorithm k Rare Class Nearest Neighbors (kRNN) [9]. Experiments on real datasets are carried out and based on the results we can conclude that the proposed technique truly improves the performance of classification in various senses. We also highlight that the proposed method can be integrated into other variants of the kNN classifier to improve performance.

The paper is organized as follows. In Sect. 2 we give a brief overview on the related work, and a short introduction is given to the kRNN technique in Sect. 3. In Sect. 4 the proposed method is described, experiments and results are presented in Sect. 5, and finally, conclusions are drawn in Sect. 6.

## 2    Related Work

Many techniques have been developed to address the various issues of imbalanced learning. Regarding the imbalanced number of samples, following the categorization of [9], the major types are *re-sampling based methods*, *cost-sensitive learning techniques* and *learning algorithm specific solutions*.

Re-sampling techniques try to fix inter-class imbalancedness by randomly or heuristically over-sampling the minority class or undersampling the majority class. Some widely used heuristics are *Adaptive Synthetic Sampling Approach* (ADASYN) [11] and *Synthetic Minority Over-sampling* (SMOTE) [12]. Further approaches can be found in [13,14] with recent Python implementations in [10].

Cost-sensitive learning techniques set higher costs for incorrectly classifying elements of the rare class. Generality-oriented learning techniques, like decision trees (DT) [15] and support vector machines (SVM) [16] can naturally implement cost-sensitive learning by incorporating the cost information into the loss-function or information measure they work with. Generally, any classifier can be turned into a cost-sensitive classifier by using the MetaCost approach [17] (available in the commonly used WEKA [18] framework) or boosting [19] for the minority class. The cost can be global (setting the same cost for the misclassification of positive vectors) or instance based, assigining different cost to different vectors [20]. With cost-sensitive learning the main challange is finding the right cost for misclassifying some particular classes or samples. One common choice is using the positive-negative ratio as the global cost of incorrect classification of positive samples [9].

The third strategy is adjusting the induction bias of particular learning techniques to better cape with imbalanced data. The first results adjusting the induction of decision trees to compensate for the minority class come from the late 80s [21]. Recent results incorporate the confidence of a rule in the information gain of C4.5 [22] and propose the Hellinger distance as a skew insensitive measure to improve the generalization of the minority class [23]. Genetic algorithms are combined with decision trees in [24,25] to improve classification performance on imbalanced data, and a kernel based approach was introduced in [26]. Techniques for directly adjusting the induction bias of the specificity based kNN algorithm were introduced in [8] by introducing a training phase where positive samples were generalized to the neighbouring regions. In [7] class confidence is estimated in the training phase for each sample, while [6,9] directly adjusts the class probability estimated from the local neighborhood.

Comparative studies on the performance of cost-sensitive learning and oversampling [27,28] show no general advantage on either side, however, the combination of the two is able to outperform both of them [29]. In a recent study comparing the performance of specificity-oriented (nearest neighbor techniques, Support Vector Machines) and generality-oriented (C4.5, Naive Bayes, Multi-Layer Perceptron and Radial Basis Function based neural networks) algorithms for imbalanced learning, it was found that kNN can achieve more accurate results for local regions where positives are underrepresented.

Despite its simplicity, kNN classification can be improved in many ways. Some studies proposed to extract prototypes [30–32], select the size of the queries dynamically [33,34], or utilize the distances in the classification rule [35–38]. Recently the main focus was improving the performance of kNN on imbalanced datasets [6–8]. The most recent result inspiring this work is the *k Rare Class Nearest Neighbors* (kRNN) technique [9], which was shown to give superior results in comparison with other variants of kNN, generality-oriented techniques and oversampling based approaches. kRNN gives a Laplace-smoothing based probability estimation for the posterior probabilities [39], incorporating the information on the number of positive and negative instances in the local neighborhood and in the entire population to bias the probability estimates towards the positive class.

We have found that kRNN (just like kNN) assigns the same probabilities to various point configurations in the feature space. In regular kNN, when the classes are supposed to be balanced and uniformly sampled, this issue is not relevant. However, in imbalanced learning problems, when the sensitivity is to be maximized, real advances can be achieved by ranking these configurations based on local features and adjusting the probability estimates according to the ranking. Our contributions to the field:

1. We propose a new probability estimator based on the kRNN technique and taking into account the local features of the decision neighborhoods.
2. Proved performance improvement over kRNN.
3. As a conclusion, (2) supports the validity of (1).

## 3  A Brief Introduction to the k Rare Class Nearest Neighbor (kRNN) Algorithm

### 3.1  Notations

In the rest of the paper the following notations are used: scalar values and vectors are denoted by normal and boldface typesetting, respectively, like $p, n \in \mathbb{Z}$ and $\mathbf{t} \in \mathbb{R}^D$. Sets are denoted by calligraphic typesetting, like $\mathcal{N} \subset \mathbb{Z}$. All over the paper we suppose that there is a training set of $D$ dimensional vectors $\mathbf{x}_i \in \mathbb{R}^D$, $i = 1, \ldots, N$, with corresponding labels $y_i \in \{+, -\}$, $i = 1, \ldots, N$, where $+$ refers to the positive (rare) class. Furthermore, all over the paper the number of positive and negative training vectors is denoted by $N_+$ and $N_-$, respectively.

Given a query instance $\mathbf{t}$ in a k(R)NN classification scenario, the set of closest vectors in the training set is called the *decision neighborhood*. A decision neighborhood consist of $k$ vectors in classical kNN and $k' \geq k$ vectors in kRNN. We use the term *point configuration* referring to a particular set of vectors, mainly a given query vector and the instances in its decision neighborhood. Note that many query points may lead to the same decision neighborhood, but the point configurations within these neighborhoods are the same only if the query points are the same. By *spatial features* of point configurations we refer to any quantitative figures that can be extracted from a set of vectors. Mostly, we will work with spatial features of point configurations.

### 3.2  The k Rare Class Nearest Neighbor Algorithm

Before elaborating the details of the proposed probability estimator, we give a brief introduction to the operation of the kRNN algorithm.

When one of the classes is highly under-sampled, the main issue with the classical kNN algorithm is that it is likely to find only negative samples in the neighborhood of the hypothetical separating hyperplane. In these cases the probability of a test point coming from the negative class becomes strictly 1. This property of the classical kNN classification schema highly reduces the sensitivity of the algorithm, as no threshold on probabilities will make these samples turn into positive, even if they are extremely close to the hypothetical separating hyperplane. Based on three principles, the kRNN classifier tries to resolve the issues of imbalanced datasets by design:

1. Using a dynamic query size by increasing the decision neighborhood of a test point until the following two conditions hold:
   (a) the neighborhood contains at least $k$ positive samples;
   (b) the neighborhood reaches a positive-negative border.
   In this way, the decision neighborhood always contains at least 1 positive sample, thus the estimated probability of the negative class will never be exactly 1.
2. Supposing that the distribution of positive labels in some neighborhood follows a binomial distribution, one can construct confidence intervals on the

estimated proportion of the labels. Particularly, the probability (proportion) of positive samples can be estimated as $\hat{q} = \dfrac{N_+}{N}$, with the confidence interval on the real value $q^*$ as

$$q^* \in [L^{lower}_{glob}(\hat{q}, N, \alpha), L^{upper}_{glob}(\hat{q}, N, \alpha)], \tag{1}$$

$$L^{lower}_{glob}(\hat{q}, N, \alpha) = \hat{q} - z_{\alpha/2}\sqrt{\hat{q}(1-\hat{q})/N}, \tag{2}$$

$$L^{upper}_{glob}(\hat{q}, N, \alpha) = \hat{q} + z_{\alpha/2}\sqrt{\hat{q}(1-\hat{q})/N}. \tag{3}$$

where $z_{\alpha/2}$ denotes the z-score of the normal distribution corresponding to the confidence level $(1 - \alpha)$, and $\alpha$ is the significance level specified by the user. For small sample size, the confidence interval needs to be corrected for underestimation [9]: let $n$, $p$ and $r = n + p$ denote the number of negative and positive samples and the size of a decision neighborhood. Then, $\hat{q} = \dfrac{p}{r}$ and for the real value $q^*$ one gets

$$q^* \in [L^{lower}_{small}(\hat{q}, r, \alpha), L^{upper}_{small}(\hat{q}, r, \alpha)], \tag{4}$$

$$L^{lower}_{small}(\hat{q}, r, \alpha) = \frac{\hat{q} + z^2_{\alpha/2}/(2r) - z_{\alpha/2}\sqrt{\hat{q}(1-\hat{q})/r + z^2_{\alpha/2}/(4r^2)}}{1 + z^2_{\alpha/2}/r}, \tag{5}$$

$$L^{upper}_{small}(\hat{q}, r, \alpha) = \frac{\hat{q} + z^2_{\alpha/2}/(2r) + z_{\alpha/2}\sqrt{\hat{q}(1-\hat{q})/r + z^2_{\alpha/2}/(4r^2)}}{1 + z^2_{\alpha/2}/r}. \tag{6}$$

Again, $\alpha$ is the user specified significance level of the confidence interval.

3. Given a local neighborhood, the estimated probability of the positive class is determined by Laplacian smoothing:

$$\mathbb{P}(+|\mathbf{t}) = \frac{p + \frac{1}{N}}{p + \gamma n + \frac{2}{N}}, \tag{7}$$

where $\mathbf{t}$ is the test vector, and $p$, $n$ denote the number of positive and negative samples in the decision neighborhood around $\mathbf{t}$. Note that due to the second constraint of the dynamic query $p > k$ is possible. The factor $\gamma$ depends on the confidence of the local proportion estimate compared to the global one. Particularly,

$$\gamma = \begin{cases} 1 & , \text{if } L^{lower}_{small}(p/r, r, \alpha_s) \leq L^{upper}_{global}(N_+/N, N, \alpha_g), \\ \dfrac{nN_+}{pN_-} & , \text{otherwise}, \end{cases} \tag{8}$$

where $\alpha_s$ and $\alpha_g$ denote the significance levels of the local (small) and global proportion estimations. In practice, both significance levels are set to 0.1. The $\gamma$ factor is responsible to bias the probability estimation towards the positive class if the local proportion of positive samples seems to be significantly higher than the global proportion of positive vectors.

The kRNN technique was shown to give superior performance compared to various competing classification techniques. For a more detailed description of kRNN see [9].

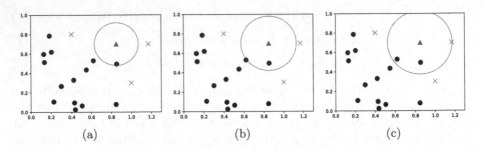

(a)                              (b)                              (c)

**Fig. 1.** Illustration of the operation of kRNN (black dots, red crosses and green triangle denote the samples of the negative and positive classes, and the test vector, respectively): (a) decision neighborhood with classical kNN at $k = 1$; (b) decision neighborhood with classical kNN at $k = 2$; (c) decision neighborhood with kRNN at $k = 1$ or classical kNN at $k = 3$. (Color figure online)

### 3.3 Demonstrating the Operation of kRNN

For a visual illustration of the operation of the method, see Fig. 1. In the subfigures, one can see a classification problem where the positive class is highly undersampled compared to the negative class. With a classical kNN at $k = 1$, the decision neighborhood is depicted in Fig. 1(a) by blue circle, and one can observe $\mathbb{P}(+|t) = 0$, as no positive sample resides inside the decision neighborhood. Similarly, with $k = 2$, the decision neighborhood contains only two negative samples (Fig. 1(b)), leading to $\mathbb{P}(+|t) = 0$. Figure 1(c) illustrates the decision neighborhood with the classical kNN technique at $k = 3$, and the decision neighborhood with kRNN at $k = 1$. With classical kNN the posterior probability becomes $\mathbb{P}(+|t) = 1/3$. Distance weighted kNN variants [36,37] assign a weight to each neighbor which is inversely proportional to its distance from the test point. These variants will give $\mathbb{P}(+|t) < 1/3$, as the negative vectors are closer to the test vector than the positive instance. With kNN the estimated positive probability becomes $\mathbb{P}(+|t) = 1/3$, while kRNN gives $\mathbb{P}(+|t) \simeq 1/3$, where $\simeq$ is due to the implicit probability smoothing. However, while the static query size of kNN cannot ensure that there is at least one positive sample in the decision neighborhood, the dynamic query of the kRNN technique guarantees this.

## 4    The Proposed Method

In this section the details of the proposed improvements are elaborated.

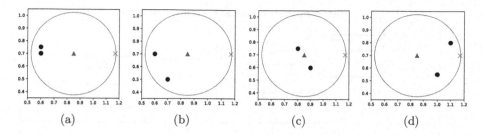

**Fig. 2.** Configurations to which the same posterior probability is assigned by kRNN. Green triangle, black dots and red crosses represent the test vectors, the negative samples and the positive samples, respectively. (Color figure online)

## 4.1   Ranking of Point Configurations

The kRNN technique was reported to give superior results compared to other techniques on real datasets, especially in terms of the AUC score. Noting that the AUC measure is invariant to monotonic transformations of the estimated probabilities, we can conclude that the ranking of posterior probability estimates is more accurate than that of other techniques. From Eq. (7), one can readily see that the positive posterior probability estimate of kRNN depends only on the number of positive and negative samples in the decision neighborhood: $\mathbb{P}(+|\mathbf{t}) = \mathbb{P}(+|p(\mathbf{t}), n(\mathbf{t}))$. Thus, kRNN assigns the same probability to the various point configurations in Fig. 2, even though the common sense suggests that the test vector in Fig. 2(a) should have somewhat higher positive posterior probability, than the test points in the configurations in Fig. 2(b), (c) and (d). Our expectation is that the performance of kRNN could be increased by breaking up the equal probability levels of point configurations with the same number of positive and negative instances in the decision neighborhoods. Put in another way, the high performance of kRNN suggests that the ordering of kRNN based probability estimates is generally good, thus, these probability estimates should be used as baselines for an adjusted probability estimate taking into consideration spatial features of the point patterns in the decision neighborhoods.

For a visual illustration, in Fig. 3(a) we have plotted the probability levels corresponding to some $p$ and $n$ combinations on a hypothetical dataset consisting of 40 positive and 200 negative vectors. The goal is to break up the equal probabilities of decision neighborhoods with the same $p$ and $n$ cardinality based on some local features of the point configurations, leading to bands of probability estimates like the illustration in Fig. 3(b). Consequently, we look for the adjusted positive probability estimate in the form

$$\mathbb{P}'(+|\mathbf{t}) - \max\{\min\{\mathbb{P}(+|\mathbf{t}) + (R(\mathbf{t}, \mathcal{N}_+, \mathcal{N}_-) - 1/2)\, w, 1\}, 0\}, \qquad (9)$$

where $w \in \mathbb{R}^+$ is the non-zero width of the bands and $R : \mathbb{R}^D \times \mathbb{Z}^p \times \mathbb{Z}^n \to [0, 1]$ is a so-called ranking function operating on the test vector and the sets of closest positive ($\mathcal{N}_+$) and negative ($\mathcal{N}_-$) neighbors in the decision neighborhood. $R$ is expected to assign an absolute value to the point configuration in the decision

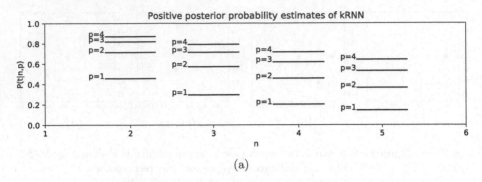

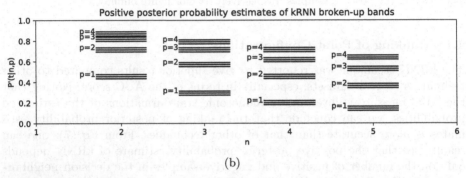

**Fig. 3.** Illustration of breaking up equal probabilities. The lines in Fig. (a) represent the probability levels assigned to decision neighborhood consisting of $n$ negative (horizontal axis) and $p$ positive samples. Using the local, spatial features extracted, these probability levels broke up into probability bands. Probability levels in the same band are related to decision neighborhoods consisting of the same number of positive and negative samples, the differences within a band are adjustments related to the spatial features of the point configurations, used to distinguish and rank situations like the ones depicted in Fig. 2.

neighborhood reflecting our preconception on the probability of the positive class for $\mathbf{t}$. In other words, given two neighborhoods with the same number of positive and negative samples, $R(\mathbf{t}, \mathcal{N}_+, \mathcal{N}_-) < R(\mathbf{t}', \mathcal{N}'_+, \mathcal{N}'_-)$, $|\mathcal{N}_+| = |\mathcal{N}'_+|$, $|\mathcal{N}_-| = |\mathcal{N}'_-|$ should reflect that $\mathbb{P}(+|\mathbf{t}) < \mathbb{P}(+|\mathbf{t}')$. The min and max operators are used to prevent exceeding the range $[0, 1]$. In practice, $w$ is a free parameter controlling the width of the probability bands. The larger $w$ is, the more likely it becomes that the bands corresponding to decision neighborhoods with different number of positive and negative instances will overlap and the ordering of pure kRNN positive probability estimates will be mixed up. If

$$w < \min_{\substack{n,n' \in \{0, N_-\} \\ p,p' \in \{0, N_+\}}} |\mathbb{P}(+|n, p) - \mathbb{P}(+|n', p')|, \tag{10}$$

then no overlap is possible, $\mathbb{P}(+|p, n) < \mathbb{P}(+|p', n')$ implies $\mathbb{P}'(+|\mathbf{t}) < \mathbb{P}'(+|\mathbf{t}')$, where $p$, $n$ and $p'$, $n'$ denote the number positive and negative samples in the decision neighborhoods of $\mathbf{t}$ and $\mathbf{t}'$, respectively. Generally, $R$ may be considered as a probability estimator, as well. The reason why we refer to it as a ranking function is that we do not expect $R$ being backed by any reasoning from probability theory. Depending on the properties of the feature space and the dissimilarity measure, $R$ may incorporate the distances and angles of the points, their distributions, $R$ may try to carry out linear separation, and any combination of these, even applying different techniques in different situations. Thus, the outcomes of the ranking functions are not expected to be comparable for different decision neighborhoods, yet they are expected to break up the probability ties around the baseline kRNN estimations.

In practice, many ranking functions can be developed depending on the expectations on the data, the feature space, or the properties of the dissimilarity measures being used. For the sake of generality, without any assumptions on the space, the manifold of the classes or the dissimilarity measure being used, we introduce three ranking functions which may be used to improve the performance of the kRNN classifier in general:

1. It is a natural assumption that the larger the minimum distance of negative samples from the test vector is, the less likely it is that the test vector is negative. Accordingly, the following ranking function seems to be a good candidate to break up probability ties:

$$R_1(\mathbf{t}, \mathcal{N}_+, \mathcal{N}_-) = \frac{\min_{\mathbf{x} \in \mathcal{N}_-} d(\mathbf{x}, \mathbf{t})}{\min_{\mathbf{x} \in \mathcal{N}_-} d(\mathbf{x}, \mathbf{t}) + \min_{\mathbf{x} \in \mathcal{N}_+} d(\mathbf{x}, \mathbf{t})}. \tag{11}$$

The denominator is used to norm the function into the range $[0, 1]$.

2. Another approach is fitting a line on a positive and a negative sample in the decision neighborhood, projecting the query point onto that line, and the position of the projection can be used to infer on the membership of the query point regarding the positive and negative class. Namely, let $\mathbf{x}_+$ and $\mathbf{x}_-$ denote a positive and a negative instance in the decision neighborhood, respectively. Then,

$$z = \frac{(\mathbf{x}_+ - \mathbf{x}_-)^T (\mathbf{t} - \mathbf{x}_+)}{\|\mathbf{x}_+ - \mathbf{x}_-\| \|\mathbf{t} - \mathbf{x}_+\|} \tag{12}$$

denotes the signed distance of $\mathbf{x}_-$ and the projection of the query point onto the line fitted to $\mathbf{x}_+$ and $\mathbf{x}_-$, with $z = 1$ if the projection falls on $\mathbf{x}_+$ and $z = 0$ if the projection falls on $\mathbf{x}_-$. Note, that $z$ can be negative or can be greater than 1.

We certainly assume that more negative the $z$ is, the more likely that the query point belongs to the negative class, the more positive $z$ is, the more likely that the query belongs to the positive class.

By aggregating this measure for all pairs of positive and negative pairs, we would have an empirical distribution on the $z$.

Unfortunately, this estimation does not take into account the natural assumption, that the confidence of a decision based on $z$ should decrease as the distance $d$ of $\mathbf{t}$ and the line fitted on $\mathbf{x}_+$ and $\mathbf{x}_-$ increases. Then, replacing $z$

by the Gaussian distribution $\mathcal{G}_{t,x_+,x_-}(z, \sqrt{d/\|x_+ - x_-\|})$, where the standard deviation increases with the square root of $d$ in units $\|x_+ - x_-\|$ to make these values comparable for various settings.

By aggregation of these individual probability density functions (pdf), we would get a more realistic estimation on the pdf of $z$,

$$p_z(z) = \sum_{\substack{x_+ \in \mathcal{N}_+ \\ x_- \in \mathcal{N}_-}} \mathcal{G}_{t,x_+,x_-}$$

The cumulative density function at $1/2$ (parameter) of this sum can result in a ranking function as

$$R_2(t, \mathcal{N}_+, \mathcal{N}_-) = \int_{-\infty}^{1/2} p_z(z)dz.$$

3. Finally, we can construct a ranking function using the density of negative samples in the query neighborhood. Supposing that the sample points are the realization of a sampling Poisson point process, the intensity of the process (inversely proportional to the density of points) is a function of the first neighbor distances [40]. Thus, the mean of the first neighbor distances of the negative samples characterizes the density of the negative samples. If the query point belongs to the negative class, we can expect that its mean distance to the negative samples should be similar. Taking the ratio of the two leads to a measure which gives 0 if the negative samples are the same and the query point differs or the query point is infinitely far from the negative samples, and gives 1 if the query point is at the same distance, or closer to the negative samples than they are to their closest neighbor.

$$R_3(t, \mathcal{N}_+, \mathcal{N}_-) = \min \left\{ 1, \frac{\sum\limits_{x \in \mathcal{N}_-} d_1(x, \mathcal{N}_-)}{\sum\limits_{x \in \mathcal{N}_-} d(t, x)} \right\}, \tag{13}$$

where $d_1$ denotes the first neighbor distance of $x$ regarding the set $\mathcal{N}_-$. Note that this ranking function does not use the positive samples at all.

We have constructed three ranking functions based on simple but meaningful principles, which can be expected to improve the probability estimations of point configurations in decision neighborhoods which have the same number of positive and negative samples. We also emphasize that all the ranking functions are based on information available in the query neighborhoods, but not utilized by the majority based kRNN decision rule.

## 4.2    Summary of the Proposed Method

The proposed, improved kRNN method is given in Algorithm 1. The technique can be summarized as a two-phase kNN algorithm. In the first phase, a raw

---

**Algorithm 1.** Classification by the improved kRNN method

---

**Input:** The training set $\mathbf{x}_i \in \mathbb{R}^D$, $i = 1, \ldots, N$, with corresponding labels $y_i \in \{+, -\}$, $i = 1, \ldots, N$; a test vector $\mathbf{t} \in \mathbb{R}^D$; the width $w$ of bands.
**Output:** $\mathbb{P}'(+|\mathbf{t})$: the positive posterior probability of $\mathbf{t}$.
  $\mathbb{P}(+|\mathbf{t}) \leftarrow$ the positive posterior probability determined by the kRNN algorithm.
  $\mathcal{N} \leftarrow$ the indices of training vectors in the decision neighborhood determined by the kRNN query.
  $\mathbb{P}'(+|\mathbf{t}) \leftarrow \max\{\min\{\mathbb{P}(+|\mathbf{t}) + (R(\mathbf{t}, \mathcal{N}) - 0.5)w, 1\}, 0\}$ where $R$ is an arbitrarily choosen ranking function.

---

probability estimation is carried out using the kRNN algorithm. In the second phase, these probability estimates are refined according to the local spatial features of the point patterns. At $w = 1$, Eq. (9) is highly similar to an ensemble-like average of the kRNN and ranking function based probability estimations. The main difference of the proposed method and averaging based ensembles is that we use kRNN as a baseline estimation, and the effect of the ranking function is always centered around a certain kRNN based probability level. According to our best knowledge, no technique like this has been proposed before.

## 5 Experiments and Results

We have carried out various tests to measure the performance of the proposed technique for imbalanced classification problems. In this section, the details of the experimental settings are presented and the results are discussed.

### 5.1 Experimental Settings

For the ease of comparison, we have used the same real-world datasets as used in [6,8,9] for testing, a summary of their characteristics is given in Table 1. The Glass, Hypothyroid, SPECT_F, Hepatitis and Vehicle datasets are downloaded from the UCI Machine Learning repository [41]; the PC1, CM1 and KC1 datasets describe problems for predicting software defects, each obtained from the NASA IV&V Facility Metrics Data Program (MDP) repository[1]. In multiclass problems one particular class was selected and classified against the others. Besides the datasets being highly imbalanced regarding the number of samples, the distribution of sample points related to the two classes is also uneven in most of the datasets. To demonstrate this, the data has been normalized by statistical standardization, and we have computed the nearest neighbor distances of sample points within the positive and negative classes. The nearest neighbor distance distribution is directly related to the hypothetical sampling rate of training vectors [40]. Differing distance distributions suggest differing, uneven sampling of the positive and negative classes. The mean of the closest neighbor distances and the p-value of Welch's t-test on the equality of means are summarized in Table 2.

---

[1] http://promise.site.uottawa.ca/SERepository/datasets-page.html.

**Table 1.** Summary of the datasets used for testing

| Dataset | Size | Num. of attributes | Classes (Pos., Neg.) | Pos:Neg |
|---------|------|--------------------|-----------------------|---------|
| Glass | 214 | 9 | (3, others) | 17:197 (7.94%) |
| Hypothyroid | 3163 | 25 | (true, false) | 151:3012 (4.77%) |
| PC1 | 1109 | 21 | (true, false) | 77:1032 (6.94%) |
| CM1 | 498 | 21 | (true, false) | 49:449 (9.84%) |
| KC1 | 2109 | 21 | (true, false) | 326:1783 (15.46%) |
| SPECT_F | 267 | 44 | (0, 1) | 55:212 (20.60%) |
| Hepatitis | 155 | 19 | (1, 2) | 32:123 (20.65%) |
| Vehicle | 846 | 18 | ('van', others) | 199:647 (23.52%) |

**Table 2.** Mean distances within classes

| Dataset | Mean pos. dist | Mean neg. dist | p-value |
|---------|----------------|----------------|---------|
| Glass | 0.96 | 0.61 | 0.8684 |
| Hypothyroid | 1.06 | 1.98 | 0.0000 |
| PC1 | 1.53 | 4.73 | 0.0017 |
| CM1 | 1.54 | 2.90 | 0.0008 |
| KC1 | 1.07 | 1.82 | 0.0000 |
| SPECT_F | 2.19 | 0.62 | 0.0000 |
| Hepatitis | 2.71 | 1.94 | 0.0001 |
| Vehicle | 0.35 | 0.50 | 0.6534 |

One can observe, that except 3 datasets, we can reject the null-hypothesis that the means are equal. Thus, besides the imbalance in the number of samples, the sampling rate of classes also seems to be different in most of the cases. Naturally, the nearest neighbor distance statistics depend on the distance used and the way the data is normalized. Accordingly, the conclusions we have drawn on the differing sampling rates are valid for the Euclidean distance with the statistical standardization of the data.

There are various metrics used to measure the performance of classifiers in binary classification problems. However, many of them are affected by the imbalanced nature of the training and test sets. We do report measures which are more-or-less independent from the number of samples in the two classes. The first measure is the already mentioned Area Under Curve (AUC), where the curve refers to the Receiver Operating Characteristic (ROC) curve [42]. AUC is an aggregated measure of how sensitive the classifier is for the positive samples at various levels of false positive rates. The two further relevant measures we used are $F_1$-score and balanced accuracy (BACC):

$$F_1 = \frac{2TP}{2TP + FP + FN}, \quad BACC = \frac{1}{2}\left(\frac{TP}{TP + FP} + \frac{TN}{TN + FN}\right), \quad (14)$$

both of them providing a composite measure for the average performance of classifiers on the positive and negative classes, with $TP$, $TN$, $FP$ and $FN$ denoting the number of true positive, true negative, false positive and false negative detections, respectively.

Zhang et al. [9] give a detailed comparison of kRNN to various classification techniques, including kNN variants, minority oversampling based approaches, generality based methods and cost-based techniques. As the primary goal of the proposed technique is to improve the kRNN itself, due to space limitations we compare the method to kRNN only. We emphasize that we used the datasets and followed the testing methodology described in [9]. In each test, shuffle cross validation is used, by shuffling the dataset 20 times, and each time using 90% for training and 10% for testing. This validation technique generates a larger number and more different test cases than k-fold or leave-one-out cross validation.

## 5.2 Results at Particular Bandwidths

Although $w$ is a free parameter of the proposed technique and optimization over $w$ could improve its performance on any given dataset, we expect that any reasonable choice should improve the performance, in general. Before examining the aggregated performance of the proposed technique as a function of $w$, we analyze its performance at some particular choices to demonstrate that gains are achieved on most of the datasets. The results at $w = 0.0001$, $w = 0.1$ and $k = 1$ (following the methodology of [9]) are compared to that of the original kRNN technique in terms of AUC in Table 3. One can observe, that in most of the cases the highest scores are related to the $R_1$ ranking function with bandwidth

**Table 3.** AUC scores at two particular $w$ bandwidths, the highest scores highlighted by boldface typesetting. The first column contains the results of the pure kRNN technique.

| Ranking | - | $R_1$ | $R_2$ | $R_3$ | $R_1$ | $R_2$ | $R_3$ |
|---|---|---|---|---|---|---|---|
| Bandwidth ($w$) | - | 0.0001 | 0.0001 | 0.0001 | 0.1 | 0.1 | 0.1 |
| Hypothyroid | **0.9485** | **0.9485** | **0.9485** | **0.9485** | 0.9471 | 0.9442 | 0.9475 |
| Glass | 0.7336 | 0.7345 | 0.7338 | **0.7340** | 0.7539 | **0.7340** | 0.7566 |
| PC1 | 0.7805 | 0.7807 | 0.7806 | 0.7806 | **0.7906** | 0.7736 | 0.7836 |
| CM1 | 0.7040 | 0.7044 | 0.7042 | 0.7041 | **0.7223** | 0.7099 | 0.7020 |
| KC1 | 0.7321 | 0.7322 | 0.7321 | 0.7321 | **0.7434** | 0.7367 | 0.7324 |
| SPECT_F | 0.7013 | 0.7015 | 0.7014 | 0.7009 | **0.7020** | 0.6927 | 0.6983 |
| Hepatitis | 0.7883 | 0.7884 | 0.7881 | 0.7886 | 0.8133 | 0.7858 | **0.8207** |
| Vehicle | 0.9400 | 0.9400 | 0.9400 | 0.9400 | 0.9397 | 0.9396 | **0.9408** |
| Mean | 0.7910 | 0.7913 | 0.7911 | 0.7911 | 0.8015 | 0.7895 | 0.7977 |

$w = 0.1$, the average gain in performance is more than 1%. One can also confirm that the improvements are present for most of the datasets.

At $w = 0.0001$, the method breaks up the ties in the probability estimations of the kRNN technique, but due to the relatively small value of $w$, the overlapping of probability bands related to different numbers of positive and negative neighbors is limited. In this case the performance gains are also small. The reason for this is that all datasets are relatively small, thus, the number of situations where the proposed technique may have a positive effect is limited. For example, if all the decision neighborhoods containing $n = 21$ negative and $p = 1$ positive instances are truly negative regions, breaking up the ties does not improve the sensitivity or the AUC score of the method. When the true label of neighborhoods containing, say, $n = 2$ and $p = 1$ negative and positive instances varies, breaking up the ties could improve the performance, but the number of situations like these might still be limited.

At larger bandwidths the probability bands tend to overlap. In these cases the ranking of probabilities related to neighborhoods of different number of positive and negative instances are affected, as well. As the results show, this may have a positive effect on the performance (up to some certain bandwidth), since the ranking function may be a good proxy on the real ranking of probabilities related to the same kRNN estimations.

## 5.3    The Aggregated Performance Measures as Functions of $w$

The mean performance measures as functions of $w$ are summarized in Table 4. Besides the already defined ranking functions we have introduced $R_m$ as the mean of the $R_1$, $R_2$ and $R_3$, incorporating the features of each previously defined functions.

Regarding the AUC scores, one can observe that the $R_1$ function provides the best results, with the highest score of 0.8224 at the bandwidth of 1.0, giving a more than 3% improvement compared to the simple kRNN technique.. For higher bandwidths, like 1.3, the performance slightly drops. The bandwidth of 1.0 may seem extremely large affecting the kRNN based probability estimates heavily. This can be explained by the nature of the ranking functions: although they are normalized to the range $[0, 1]$, the marginal results are rare, in the common situations they take values near 0.5. Thus, although the bandwidth 1.0 suggests extremely wide bands, in practice the effective bandwidth are much smaller. One can also observe that in most of the cases the $R_1$ ranking function outperforms $R_2$ and $R_3$, which shows that the spatial feature used in $R_1$ is more effective than those used in $R_2$ and $R_3$. However, the mean ranking function $R_m$ provides better results than any of its constituents at the bandwidths 0.4 and 0.7. This shows that although $R_2$ and $R_3$ give worse results than $R_1$, in general, the combination of all ranking functions by taking their mean is able to capture the features of the dataset better than any single one. The reason why $R_1$ outperformed $R_m$ at the bandwidth 1.0 is that $R_2$ and $R_3$ reach their maxima at 0.7 and 0.1, respectively; consequently, taking the mean of the ranking functions at 1.0 we can expect that $R_2$ and $R_3$ will contribute slightly worse results than

**Table 4.** Aggregated performance measures as functions of $w$, highest scores in each block are highlighted by boldface typesetting

| Method | Measure\$w$ | 0.0001 | 0.05 | 0.1 | 0.4 | 0.7 | 1.0 | 1.3 |
|---|---|---|---|---|---|---|---|---|
| kRNN | AUC | 0.7910 | 0.7910 | 0.7910 | 0.7910 | 0.7910 | 0.7910 | 0.7910 |
| kRNN + $R_1$ | | 0.7913 | 0.7985 | 0.8015 | 0.8093 | 0.8118 | **0.8224** | 0.8179 |
| kRNN + $R_2$ | | 0.7911 | 0.7898 | 0.7896 | 0.7884 | 0.7962 | 0.7961 | 0.7855 |
| kRNN + $R_3$ | | 0.7911 | 0.7955 | 0.7977 | 0.7959 | 0.7841 | 0.7794 | 0.7692 |
| kRNN + $R_m$ | | 0.7912 | 0.7963 | 0.7999 | 0.8103 | 0.8142 | 0.8211 | 0.8166 |
| kRNN | $F_1$ | 0.4961 | 0.4961 | 0.4961 | 0.4961 | 0.4961 | 0.4961 | 0.4961 |
| kRNN + $R_1$ | | 0.4961 | 0.4937 | 0.4925 | 0.4870 | 0.4765 | 0.4533 | 0.4379 |
| kRNN + $R_2$ | | 0.4961 | 0.4953 | 0.4951 | 0.4903 | 0.4850 | 0.4220 | 0.3583 |
| kRNN + $R_3$ | | 0.4961 | 0.4967 | 0.4987 | 0.5031 | 0.5023 | 0.4934 | 0.4839 |
| kRNN + $R_m$ | | 0.4961 | 0.4952 | 0.4971 | 0.5009 | **0.5034** | 0.4993 | 0.4965 |
| kRNN | BACC | 0.7577 | 0.7577 | 0.7577 | 0.7577 | 0.7577 | 0.7577 | 0.7577 |
| kRNN + $R_1$ | | 0.7577 | 0.7580 | 0.7589 | 0.7622 | 0.7610 | 0.7473 | 0.7447 |
| kRNN + $R_2$ | | 0.7577 | 0.7587 | 0.7597 | 0.7602 | 0.7592 | 0.7294 | 0.6877 |
| kRNN + $R_3$ | | 0.7577 | 0.7554 | 0.7559 | 0.7497 | 0.7466 | 0.7422 | 0.7397 |
| kRNN + $R_m$ | | 0.7577 | 0.7572 | 0.7589 | 0.7640 | 0.7656 | 0.7639 | **0.7660** |

$R_1$. This might be solved by taking weighted means of the ranking functions where the weights reflect their optimal bandwidths.

Regarding the $F_1$ and BACC measures, the $R_m$ ranking function provided the highest values at the bandwidths of 0.7 and 1.3, respectively. Note that the $F_1$ and BACC scores measure the absolute performance of the classifier, in other words, they measure the effect of the ranking functions near the 0.5 probability level. Naturally, this is a small segment of the entire probability range [0,1], thus, smaller performance gains can be expected than in the case of the AUC score.

The highest overall score at the bandwidth 1.0 may suggest that the best results are achieved by taking the average of the probability estimation provided by kRNN and the ranking functions. This is not the case. However, this is accidental: on the one hand, the corrections added by the ranking functions to the probability estimates are centered at the kRNN based probability estimates, on the other hand, ranking functions like $R_3$ cannot be interpreted as probability estimates, thus, incorporating it into an ensemble of estimators is meaningless.

## 5.4   Performance as a Function of $k$

As the summarized results in Table 5 clearly show, the proposed technique outperforms the kRNN technique at each $k$ being examined, in terms of all performance measures. Interestingly, in most of the cases $R_1$ ranking function provides the highest scores. The decreasing trends in the scores of $R_2$ and $R_3$ are related to

**Table 5.** Performance measures as functions of $k$; highest values in each block, for each $k$ are indicated by boldface typesetting

| Method | Measure | k = 1 | k = 3 | k = 5 | k = 7 |
|---|---|---|---|---|---|
| kRNN | AUC | 0.7910 | 0.8263 | 0.8225 | 0.8101 |
| kRNN + $R_1$ | | **0.8057** | **0.8403** | **0.8409** | **0.8331** |
| kRNN + $R_2$ | | 0.7869 | 0.8125 | 0.7993 | 0.7788 |
| kRNN + $R_3$ | | 0.7991 | 0.8304 | 0.8235 | 0.8125 |
| kRNN + $R_m$ | | 0.8041 | 0.8370 | 0.8347 | 0.8241 |
| kRNN | $F_1$ | 0.4961 | 0.4994 | 0.4735 | 0.4426 |
| kRNN + $R_1$ | | 0.4935 | **0.5138** | **0.4893** | **0.4542** |
| kRNN + $R_2$ | | 0.4941 | 0.4975 | 0.4742 | 0.4410 |
| kRNN + $R_3$ | | **0.5051** | 0.4988 | 0.4629 | 0.4367 |
| kRNN + $R_m$ | | 0.4972 | 0.5082 | 0.4763 | 0.4472 |
| kRNN | BACC | 0.7577 | 0.7269 | 0.7096 | 0.6898 |
| kRNN + $R_1$ | | **0.7613** | **0.7453** | **0.7232** | **0.7015** |
| kRNN + $R_2$ | | 0.7601 | 0.7272 | 0.7102 | 0.6893 |
| kRNN + $R_3$ | | 0.7571 | 0.7220 | 0.6999 | 0.6830 |
| kRNN + $R_m$ | | 0.7595 | 0.7346 | 0.7124 | 0.6939 |

the fact that unlike $R_1$, these ranking functions change as the decision neighborhoods increase, and this change seems to deteriorate the rankings. Localization of these techniques (like applying them to the closest N samples in the decision neighborhood) might improve their performance for larger $k$ values. Again, the most important score is AUC, which shows an average of 2% increase for kRNN + $R_1$ compared to pure kRNN. One can also observe that the $F_1$ and BACC scores also show improvements, especially with the $R_1$ ranking function. The reason why we didn't increase $k$ over 7 is that some databases contain low number of positive samples, like Glass having 17 positive instances only: approaching the number of positive samples by $k$ leads to meaningless situations.

## 6    Discussion and Summary

We have proposed improvements to the kRNN classifier incorporating features of the point patterns in the decision neighborhoods. The proposed technique is formulated in terms of ranking functions which express preconceptions on the classification of point patterns of the same number of positive and negative samples. We also proposed three ranking functions, two of them using only the distances of the unseen vector and the instances in the decision neighborhood. As the ranking functions are expressed in terms of the distance, the proposed technique can be applied in any problem where kRNN, and can be kernelized, as well. The effect of the proposed improvement is controlled by a free parameter:

the bandwidth. Although the bandwidth can be trained by grid search, the test results show, that most of the choices in the reasonable range of $[0, 1]$ tend to improve the performance regardless of the ranking function or the data. The proposed technique is agnostic in the sense that no assumption on the data is made. The improvement is based on the fact that the robust majority based kRNN estimator is likely to assign the same probability to highly different point patterns. The test results on various datasets clearly show that reasonable choices of the bandwidth parameter can significantly increase the performance in terms of AUC. Further steps include:

- discovering further ranking functions of general use;
- analytically finding the optimal bandwidth parameter for certain ranking functions;
- carry out further tests on datasets with various types of imbalancedness;

An open-source Python implementation of the classifier with a conventional **sklearn** interface is available at
https://github.com/gykovacs/krnn_with_spatial_features.

# References

1. He, H., Garcia, E.A.: Learning from imbalanced data. IEEE Trans. Knowl. Data Eng. **21**(9), 1263–1284 (2009)
2. He, H., Ma, Y.: Imbalanced Learning: Foundations, Algorithms, and Applications. Wiley, Hoboken (2013)
3. Chawla, N.V.: Data mining for imbalanced datasets: an overview. In: Maimon, O., Rokach, L. (eds.) Data Mining and Knowledge Discovery Handbook. Springer, Boston (2010). https://doi.org/10.1007/978-0-387-09823-4_45
4. Gagliardi, F.: Instance-based classifiers applied to medical databases: diagnosis and knowledge extraction. Artif. Intell. Med. **52**(3), 123–139 (2011)
5. Hu, L.-Y., Huang, M.-W., Ke, S.-W., Tsai, C.-F.: The distance function effect on k-nearest neighbor classification for medical datasets. SpringerPlus **5**(1), 1304 (2016)
6. Zhang, X., Li, Y.: A positive-biased nearest neighbour algorithm for imbalanced classification. In: Pei, J., Tseng, V.S., Cao, L., Motoda, H., Xu, G. (eds.) PAKDD 2013. LNCS (LNAI), vol. 7819, pp. 293–304. Springer, Heidelberg (2013). https://doi.org/10.1007/978-3-642-37456-2_25
7. Liu, W., Chawla, S.: Class confidence weighted $k$nn algorithms for imbalanced data sets. In: Huang, J.Z., Cao, L., Srivastava, J. (eds.) PAKDD 2011. LNCS (LNAI), vol. 6635, pp. 345–356. Springer, Heidelberg (2011). https://doi.org/10.1007/978-3-642-20847-8_29
8. Li, Y., Zhang, X.: Improving $k$ nearest neighbor with exemplar generalization for imbalanced classification. In: Huang, J.Z., Cao, L., Srivastava, J. (eds.) PAKDD 2011. LNCS (LNAI), vol. 6635, pp. 321–332. Springer, Heidelberg (2011). https://doi.org/10.1007/978-3-642-20847-8_27
9. Zhang, X.J., Tari, Z., Cheriet, M.: KRNN: k rare-class nearest neighbor classification. Pattern Recogn. **62**(2), 33–44 (2017)

10. Lemaitre, G., Nogueira, F., Aridas, C.K.: Imbalanced-learn: a python toolbox to tackle the curse of imbalanced datasets in machine learning. J. Mach. Learn. Res. **18**(1), 1–5 (2017)
11. He, H., Bai, Y., Garcia, E.A., Li, S.: ADASYN: adaptive synthetic sampling approach for imbalanced learning. In: Proceedings of IJCNN, pp. 1322–1328 (2008)
12. Chawla, N.V., Bowyer, K.W., Hall, L.O., Kegelmeyer, W.P.: SMOTE: synthetic minority over-sampling technique. J. Artif. Intell. Res. **16**, 321–357 (2002)
13. Alhammady, H., Ramamohanaran, K.: Using emerging patterns and decision trees in rare-class classification. In: Proceedings of Fourth IEEE International Conference on Data Mining (ICDM04), pp. 315–318. IEEE, New York (2004)
14. Liu, X.Y., Wu, J., Zhou, Z.H.: Exploratory undersampling for class-imbalance learning. IEEE Trans. Syst. Man Cybern. Part B (Cybern.) **39**(2), 539–550 (2009)
15. Lomax, S., Vadera, S.: A survey of cost-sensitive decision tree induction algorithms. ACM Comput. Surv. **45**(2), 16:1–16:35 (2013)
16. Qi, Z., Tian, Y., Shi, Y., Yu, X.: Cost-sensitive support vector machine for semi-supervised learning. Procedia Comput. Sci. **18**, 1684–1689 (2013)
17. Domingos, P.: Metacost: a general method for making classifiers cost-sensitive. In: Proceedings of the fifth ACM SIGKDD International Conference on Knowledge Discovery and Data Mining, pp. 155–164 (1999)
18. Hall, M., Frank, E., Holmes, G., Pfahringer, B., Reutemann, P., Witten, I.H.: The WEKA data mining software: an update. In: SIGKDD Explorations, vol. 11, no. 1 (2009)
19. Masnadi-Shirazi, H., Vasconcelos, N.: Cost-sensitive boosting. IEEE Trans. Pattern Anal. Mach. Intell. **33**(2), 294–309 (2011)
20. Zadrozny, B., Langford, J., Abe, N.: Cost-sensitive learning by cost-proportionate example weighting. In: Proceedings of Third IEEE International Conference on Data Mining ICDM2003, pp. 435–442. IEEE (2003)
21. Holte, R.C., Acker, L., Porter, B.W.: Concept learning and the problem of small disjunts. In: Proceedings of IJCAI, pp. 813–818 (1989)
22. Liu, W., Chawla, S., Cieslak, D., Chawla, N.: A robust decision tree algorithm for imbalanced data sets. In: Proceedings of the 2010 SIAM International Conference on Data Mining, p. 12 (2010)
23. Cieslak, D.A., Chawla, N.V.: Learning decision trees for unbalanced data. In: Daelemans, W., Goethals, B., Morik, K. (eds.) ECML PKDD 2008. LNCS (LNAI), vol. 5211, pp. 241–256. Springer, Heidelberg (2008). https://doi.org/10.1007/978-3-540-87479-9_34
24. Carvalho, D.R., Freitas, A.A.: A genetic-algorithm for discovering small-disjunct rules in data mining. Appl. Soft Comput. **2**(2), 75–88 (2002)
25. Carvalho, D., Freitas, A.: A hybrid decision tree/genetic algorithm method for data mining. Inf. Sci. **163**(1–3), 13–35 (2004)
26. Hong, X., Chen, S., Harris, C.J.: A kernel-based two-class classifier for imbalanced data sets. IEEE Trans. Neural Netw. **18**(1), 28–41 (2007)
27. Elkan, C.: The foundations of cost-sensitive learning. In: Proceedings of IJCAI 2001, pp. 973–978 (2001)
28. Weiss, G.M., McCarthy, K., Zahar, B.: Cost-sensitive learning vs. sampling: Which is best for handling unbalanced classes with unqeual error costs. In: Proceedings of ICDM, pp. 35–41 (2007)
29. Akbani, R., Kwek, S., Japkowicz, N.: Applying support vector machines to imbalanced datasets. In: Boulicaut, J.-F., Esposito, F., Giannotti, F., Pedreschi, D. (eds.) ECML 2004. LNCS (LNAI), vol. 3201, pp. 39–50. Springer, Heidelberg (2004). https://doi.org/10.1007/978-3-540-30115-8_7

30. Wilson, D.R., Martinez, T.R.: Reduction techniques for instance-based learning algorithms. Mach. Learn. **38**(3), 257–286 (2000)
31. Pekalska, E., Duin, R.P.W., Paclik, P.: Prototype selection for dissimilarity-based classifiers. Pattern Recogn. **39**(2), 189–208 (2006)
32. Huang, Y., Chiang, C., Shieh, J., Grimson, E.: Prototype optimization for nearest neighbor classification. Pattern Recogn. **35**(6), 1237–1245 (2002)
33. Wu, Y., Ianakiev, K., Govindaraju, V.: Improved k-nearest neighbor classification. Pattern Recogn. **35**(10), 2311–2318 (2002)
34. Wang, J., Neskovic, P., Cooper, L.: Neighborhood size selection in the k-nearest neighbour rule using statistical confidence. Pattern Recogn. **39**, 417–423 (2006)
35. Zhou, C.Y., Chen, Y.Q.: Improving nearest neighbor classification with cam weighted distance. Pattern Recogn. **39**(4), 635–645 (2006)
36. Gou, J., Du, L., Zhang, Y., Xiong, T.: A new distance-weighted k-nearest neighbor classifier. J. Inf. Comput. Sci. **9**(6), 1429–1436 (2012)
37. Dudani, S.A.: The distance weighted k-nearest-neighbor rule. IEEE Trans. Syst. Man Cybern. **SMC-6**(4), 325–327 (1976)
38. Yigit, H.: ABC-based distance weighted kNN algorithm. J. Exp. Theor. Artif. Intell. **27**(2), 189–198 (2015)
39. Manning, C.D., Raghavan, P., Schütze, M.: Introduction to Information Retrieval. Cambridge University Press, Cambridge (2008)
40. Moltchanov, D.: Distance distributions in random networks. Ad Hoc Netw. **10**(6), 1146–1166 (2012)
41. Bache, K., Lichman, M.: UCI machine learning repository. Technical report (2013)
42. Fawcett, T.: An introduction to ROC analysis. Pattern Recogn. Lett. **27**(8), 861–874 (2006)

# Preference Learning and Optimization for Partial Lexicographic Preference Forests over Combinatorial Domains

Xudong Liu[1]([⊠]) and Miroslaw Truszczynski[2]

[1] School of Computing, University of North Florida, Jacksonville, USA
xudong.liu@unf.edu
[2] Department of Computer Science, University of Kentucky, Lexington, USA
mirek@cs.uky.edu

**Abstract.** We study preference representation models based on partial lexicographic preference trees (PLP-trees). We propose to represent preference relations as forests of small PLP-trees (PLP-forests), and to use voting rules to aggregate orders represented by the individual trees into a single order to be taken as a model of the agent's preference relation. We show that when learned from examples, PLP-forests have better accuracy than single PLP-trees. We also show that the choice of a voting rule does not have a major effect on the aggregated order, thus rendering the problem of selecting the "right" rule less critical. Next, for the proposed PLP-forest preference models, we develop methods to compute optimal and near-optimal outcomes, the tasks that appear difficult for some other common preference models. Lastly, we compare our models with those based on decision trees, which brings up questions for future research.

## 1 Introduction

Preferences are fundamental to decision making and have been researched in areas such as knowledge representation, decision theory, social choice, and constraint satisfaction. Preferences amount to a total order or preorder on a set of *outcomes* (*alternatives*). In some settings, for instance in voting theory, the number of outcomes is small enough to allow an explicit enumeration as a method to represent preference relations. However, in other settings outcomes are specified in terms of *attributes*, each with its own *domain*, where an outcome is a tuple of values, one for each attribute. Such outcome spaces are called *combinatorial domains*. If attribute domains have at least two values, the cardinality of a combinatorial domain is exponential in the number of attributes. Consequently, explicit enumeration of preference orders, even for combinatorial domains over as few as ten attributes, is infeasible.

To represent preferences over combinatorial domains, we use languages that concisely express agent's criteria for preferring one outcome over another, thus determining preference orders on outcomes. Languages exploiting *lexicographic orders* have been especially extensively studied. They include lexicographic

© Springer International Publishing AG, part of Springer Nature 2018
F. Ferrarotti and S. Woltran (Eds.): FoIKS 2018, LNCS 10833, pp. 284–302, 2018.
https://doi.org/10.1007/978-3-319-90050-6_16

strategies [17], lexicographic preference trees [2], partial lexicographic preference trees [13] (our focus in this paper), and preference trees [6,14]. These models naturally support preference reasoning [18,19]. Most recently, Bräuning et al. [3] studied learning of preference lists, a model orthogonal to the model of PLP-trees. On the one hand, preference lists can capture preferences that cannot be captured by PLP-trees. On the other hand, preference lists cannot capture conditional importances that can naturally be modeled by PLP-trees.

Lexicographic preference models have structure that factors the agent's preference order into the importance, sometimes conditional, of attributes, and preference orders, also sometimes conditional, on values of individual attribute domains. This structure can be exploited for preference elicitation. It also provides useful insights into what is important for an agent when choosing among available outcomes. In particular, it makes it easy to compare outcomes (dominance testing) and to identify outcomes that are most preferred.

In this paper, we focus on lexicographic models given by partial lexicographic preference trees, or PLP-trees for short [13]. PLP-trees that impose strong restrictions on the structure, for instance, those with unconditional importance of attributes and unconditional preference orders on values of attribute domains, can be elicited effectively from the agents. However, in general, PLP-trees are difficult to elicit directly and have to be *learned*, that is, built from examples of pairwise comparisons or other observed expressions of the agent's preference [11]. Unrestricted PLP-trees may have size of the order of the size of the underlying combinatorial domain. Such large trees offer no advantages over explicit enumerations of preference orders. However, PLP-trees learned from a set $E$ of examples have size $O(|E|)$. This gives us control over the size of learned trees but the predictive power of trees learned from small sets of examples may be limited. Learning *forests* of small trees and using some voting aggregation method was proposed as a way to circumvent the problem. Following ideas proposed by Breiman [4], Liu and Truszczynski [11] studied learning forests of PLP-trees and used the Pairwise Majority rule (PMR) to obtain a new type of a lexicographic preference model [11].

There are two main problems with this last approach. First, the PMR does not (in general) yield an order. Second, it does not lead to any obvious algorithms for reasoning tasks other than dominance testing. For instance, it does not seem to lead to natural approaches to preference optimization, that is, computing optimal or near-optimal outcomes. In this paper, we extend the results by Liu and Truszczynski [11] by replacing the PMR with several common *voting rules*. Using *voting* rules to aggregate preference orders defined by lexicographic models has drawn significant attention lately. Lang and Xia [10] studied sequential voting protocols. Lang et al. [9] established computational properties of voting-based methods to aggregate LP-trees, and Liu and Truszczynski [12] conducted an experimental study of aggregating LP-trees by voting using SAT-based tools.

Using voting rules to aggregate forests of PLP-trees turns out to yield preference models where dominance testing is as direct as with the PMR. However, preference optimization becomes feasible, too. As there are many voting rules that could be used, and they pose different computational challenges, it is important to study whether some rules are better than others. Earlier work in the standard voting setting showed significant robustness of the aggregated order to the choice of a voting rule. Comparing several common voting rules, researchers found that, except for Plurality, these voting methods show a high consensus on the resulting aggregated preference orderings [5,15]. Our results on rank correlation in the setting when individual preferences are represented by PLP-trees over possibly large combinatorial domains also show high consensus among orders determined by the PLP-forest models, at levels consistent with those reported for the voting setting.

As long as we are interested in dominance testing only, one can build predictive models by learning decision trees.[1] We compare the quality of learned PLP-trees and forests with those of learned decision trees. Decision trees turn out to be more accurate for dominance testing. However, they have drawbacks. Decision trees do not in general represent order nor partial order relations. They do not provide any explicit information about underlying orders and so, do not provide insights into how agents whose preferences they aim to model make decisions. Lastly, they do not lend themselves easily to tasks involving preference optimization.

To summarize, our contributions are as follows. (1) We propose to model preferences by forests of PLP-trees, aggregated by voting rules. We study computational complexity of key reasoning tasks for the resulting models. (2) We demonstrate that the models we studied had higher predictive accuracy than the models given by a single PLP-tree, and by a PLP-forest with the PMR. (3) We show that for several voting rules the orders obtained by aggregating PLP-forests are quite close to each other. This alleviates the issue of selecting the "right" rule. (4) For the proposed PLP-forest preference models, we develop methods to compute optimal and near-optimal outcomes, the reasoning task that has no natural solutions under models based on the PMR. (5) We compare our models with those based on decision trees. We show that the latter are more accurate but, as noted above, have shortcomings in other aspects.

The higher accuracy of models based on decision trees on the dominance testing task does not invalidate PLP-tree based approaches, as they have important advantages noted above. Rather, they suggest an intriguing question of whether PLP-trees (forests) could be combined with decision trees (forests) retaining the best features of each approach. One possibility might be to use PLP-trees to some top-level partitioning of outcomes, with decision trees used for low-level details.

---

[1] One can also learn random forests of decision trees. In our experiments, decision trees show high accuracy and seem robust to overfitting. Thus, we do not discuss here results we obtained for random forests.

## 2    Partial Lexicographic Preference Trees and Forests

Let $\mathcal{A} = \{X_1, \ldots, X_p\}$ be a set of attributes, each attribute $X_i$ having a finite domain $D_i$. The corresponding *combinatorial domain* over $\mathcal{A}$ is the Cartesian product $CD(\mathcal{A}) = D_1 \times \ldots \times D_p$. We call elements of combinatorial domains *outcomes*.

A PLP-tree over $CD(\mathcal{A})$ is an ordered labeled tree, where: (1) every non-leaf node is labeled by some attribute from $\mathcal{A}$, say $X_i$, and by a *local preference* $>_i$, a total strict order on the corresponding domain $D_i$; (2) every non-leaf node labeled by an attribute $X_i$ has $|D_i|$ outgoing edges; (3) every leaf node is denoted by $\square$; and (4) on every path from the root to a leaf each attribute appears *at most once* as a label.

Each outcome $\alpha \in CD(\mathcal{A})$ determines in a PLP-tree $T$ its *outcome path*, $H(\alpha, T)$. It starts at the root of $T$ and proceeds downward. When at a node $d$ labeled with an attribute $X$, the path descends to the next level based on the value $\alpha(X)$ of the attribute $X$ in the outcome $\alpha$ and on the local preference order associated with $d$. Namely, if $\alpha(X)$ is the $i$-th most preferred value in this order, the path descends to the $i$-th child of $d$. We denote by $\ell^T(\alpha)$ the index of the leaf in which the outcome path $H(\alpha, T)$ ends (the leaves are indexed from left to right with integers $0, 1, \ldots$).

We say that an outcome $\alpha$ is at least as good as an outcome $\beta$ ($\alpha \succeq_T \beta$) if $\ell^T(\alpha) \leq \ell^T(\beta)$. The associated equivalence and strict order relations $\approx_T$ and $\succ_T$ are specified by the conditions $\ell^T(\alpha) = \ell^T(\beta)$ and $\ell^T(\alpha) < \ell^T(\beta)$, respectively. Preference relations modeled by PLP-trees are total preorders.

The leaves of a PLP-tree can be indexed in time $O(s(T))$, where $s(T)$ is the number of nodes in $T$, by adapting the inorder traversal to the task. After that, the value $\ell^T(\alpha)$ can be computed in time $O(h(T))$, where $h(T)$ is the height of tree $T$. Thus, assuming the indices were precomputed, all three relations can be decided in time $O(h(T))$.

To illustrate, let us consider the domain of cars described by four multi-valued attributes. The attribute *BodyType* ($B$) has three values: *minivan* ($v$), *sedan* ($s$), and *sport* ($r$). The attribute *Make* ($M$) can either have value *Honda* ($h$) or *Ford* ($f$). The *Price* ($P$) can be *low* ($l$), *medium* ($d$), or *high* ($g$). Finally, *Transmission* ($T$) can be *automatic* ($a$) or *manual* ($m$). An agent's preference order on cars from this space could be expressed by a PLP-tree $T$ in Fig. 1.

The tree tells us that *BodyType* is the most important attribute to the agent and that she prefers minivans, followed by sedans and by sport cars. Her next most important attribute is contingent upon what type of cars the agent is considering. For minivans, her most important attribute is *Make*, where she likes Honda more than Ford. Among sedans, her most important attribute is *Price*, where she prefers medium-priced cars over low-priced ones, and those over high-priced ones. She does not differentiate between sport cars; they are least preferred.

To compare a Ford sedan with a middle-range price and an automatic transmission ($\langle s, f, d, a \rangle$, in our notation) and a Honda sedan with a high-range price and a manual transmission (that is, $\langle s, h, g, m \rangle$), we traverse the tree $T$. We see

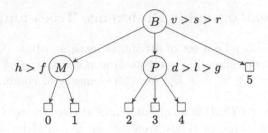

**Fig. 1.** A PLP-tree $T$ over the car domain

that the cars diverge on the node labeled by attribute $P$, and that the Ford car falls to leaf 2 and the Honda car leaf 4. Thus, the Ford car is preferred to the Honda car.

A *PLP-forest* is a finite set of PLP-trees. When extended with a voting rule to aggregate orders given by its constituent PLP-trees, a PLP-forest specifies a single preference order on the space of outcomes. In this way, PLP-forests with voting rules can be viewed as models of preference relations.

## 3    Voting in Partial Lexicographic Preference Forests

To aggregate PLP-forests we consider the voting rules Top-$k$ Clusters, Plurality, Borda, Copeland, and Maximin. In our experiments, we also consider the earlier model of PLP-forests combined with the PMR. In general, the PMR does not yield a sensible preference relation as it suffers from the Condorcet paradox [7]. Nevertheless, it performs well in dominance testing [4,11]. We consider it here as the baseline for the voting rules.

The five voting rules are *scoring* rules in the sense that, given a PLP-forest $P$, they assign to each outcome $o$ the *score* $S_r(o, P)$ (where $r$ refers to a voting rule). The scores define the preference relation $\succeq$ as follows: for outcomes $o, o'$, we have $o \succeq o'$ if and only if $S_r(o, P) \geq S_r(o', P)$. Clearly, the relation defined in this way is a total preorder[2].

The first three rules we discuss are versions of the well-known *positional scoring rules* used with total preference orders. They are adjusted here to the case of total preorders. Each tree $T$ in a PLP-forest $P$ determines the score $S_r(o, T)$ of an outcome $o$ in the preference preorder given by $T$. This score depends on the position of the preorder "cluster" containing $o$, its size, and on the number of outcomes in the clusters that are more preferred than the one containing $o$. In each case we consider, namely, Top-$k$ Clusters, Plurality and Borda the specific formula for $S_r(o, T)$ is a natural generalization of the corresponding formula for

---

[2] While the preference models we consider here represent total preorders, arguably the most important class of preference relations, we note that some studies of preference relations allow for incomparability of outcomes, which leads to preference relations models by arbitrary preorders (not necessarily total).

the standard case of total orders to total preorders. In each case, the sum of scores with respect to all trees in the forest $P$ yields the score $S_r(o, P)$.

Below we introduce the five voting rules adjusted to the setting of total preorders (they are commonly defined for strict total orders), as well as the PMR.

**Top-$k$ Clusters** (where $k$ is a positive integer): For an outcome $o$, we define $S_{tkc}(o, T) = \max\{k - \ell^T(o), 0\}$ and set

$$S_{tkc}(o, P) = \sum_{T \in P} S_{tkc}(o, T).$$

Assuming that we precomputed indices of leaves in all trees, which can be accomplished in time $O(s(P))$, where $s(P)$ denotes the number of nodes in all trees in $P$, we can compute $S_{tkc}(o, P)$, for any outcome $o$, in time $O(t(P) \cdot \max\{h(T) : T \in P\})$, where $t(P)$ is the number of trees in $P$. We note that Top Cluster ($k = 1$) is a rule similar to approval, where each tree approves all outcomes in the leftmost cluster (and only those outcomes); and Top-$k$ Cluster rules with $k > 1$ are its natural generalizations.

**Plurality:** Let $\ell_0^T$ be the set of most preferred outcomes in a PLP-tree $T$ (the set of all outcomes $o$ with $\ell^T(o) = 0$). Next, let $\Delta^T(o) = 1$ if outcome $o$ is a most preferred one in $T$, and $\Delta^T(o) = 0$, otherwise. We define the Plurality score $S_{pl}(o, P)$ by setting

$$S_{pl}(o, P) = \sum_{T \in P} \frac{\Delta^T(o)}{|\ell_0^T|}.$$

We can compute $\Delta^T(o)$ and $|\ell_0^T|$ in time $O(h(T))$. Thus, $S_{pl}(o, P)$ can be computed in time $O(t(P) \cdot \max\{h(T) : T \in P\})$.

**Borda:** Let $T$ be a PLP-tree. We define $\ell_i^T$ to be the set of all outcomes $o$ with $\ell^T(o) = i$ (the $i^{th}$ cluster in the order defined by $T$). Let $c(o)$ be the cluster containing $o$ (in our notation, $c(o) = \ell_{\ell^T(o)}^T$). We define

$$S_b(o, T) = \frac{\sum\limits_{1 \le j \le |c(o)|} (n - j - \sum\limits_{0 \le i < \ell^T(o)} |\ell_i^T|)}{|c(o)|},$$

where $n$ is the size of the combinatorial domain,[3] and set $S_b(o, P)$ as follows:

$$S_b(o, P) = \sum_{T \in P} S_b(o, T).$$

---

[3] This captures the idea that the all outcomes in the top cluster in $T$ have their score (with respect to $T$) equal to the average of $n - 1, n - 2, \ldots, n - i$ (with $i$ being the number of outcomes in the top cluster), the outcomes in the next to top cluster have their scores equal to the average of $n - i - 1, n - i - 2, \ldots, n - i - j$ (with $j$ being the number of elements in that cluster), etc.

Assuming that the sizes $|\ell_i^T|$ of clusters and the quantities $\sum\limits_{0 \le i < \ell} |\ell_i^T|)$ are pre-computed, which can be done in time $O(s(P))$, we can compute $S_b(o,T)$ in time $O(h(T))$. Consequently, $S_b(o,P)$ can be computed in time $O(t(P) \cdot \max\{h(T) : T \in P\})$.

**Copeland:** Let us define $N_P(o,o')$ to be the number of trees $T \in P$ such that $o \succ_T o'$. Informally, $N_P(o,o')$ is the number of trees that declare $o$ more preferred to $o'$. If $N_P(o,o') > N_P(o',o)$, then $o$ *wins* with $o'$ in $P$. If $N_P(o,o') < N_P(o',o)$, then $o$ *loses* to $o'$ in $P$. The Copeland score $S_{cp}(o,P)$ is given by the difference between the number of pairwise wins and the number of pairwise losses of $o$:

$$S_{cp}(o,P) = |\{o' \in C \setminus \{o\} : N_P(o,o') > N_P(o',o)\}|$$
$$- |\{o' \in C \setminus \{o\} : N_P(o,o') < N_P(o',o)\}|.$$

**Maximin:** This method (also known as the Simpson-Kramer method) is considered in several variants in which the definition of the Maximin scoring function $S_{xn}(o,P)$ may include winning votes, margins, and pairwise oppositions. In this paper, we will define it in terms of the margin for an outcome, that is, the smallest difference between the numbers of pairwise wins and pairwise losses against all opponents.

$$S_{xn}(o,P) = \min_{o' \in C \setminus \{o\}} (N_P(o,o') - N_P(o',o)).$$

Both the Copeland score and the Maximin score can be computed in time $O(n \cdot t(P) \cdot \max\{h(T) : T \in P\})$, where $n$ is the size of the combinatorial domain.

**Pairwise Majority Rule (PMR):** The PMR is not a scoring rule. We use it to decide preferences between outcomes. Specifically, given two outcomes $o$ and $o'$, $o \succ_{pm} o'$ if $N_P(o,o') > N_P(o',o)$. Thus, deciding pairwise preferences takes time $O(t(P) \cdot \max\{h(T) : T \in P\})$.

## 4    Computational Complexity

In the previous sections we listed estimates of the running time of algorithms that could be used to compute scores of the five scoring rules we consider. Here we complete the discussion by considering the complexity of the problems *SCORE*, *QUALITY*, and *OPTIMIZATION*.

*SCORE* (for a scoring rule $r$): Given a PLP-forest $P$, an outcome $o$, and a positive rational number $s$, decide whether $S_r(o,P) \ge s$.

*QUALITY* (for a scoring rule $r$): Given a PLP-forest $P$ and a positive rational number $\ell$, decide whether there is an outcome $o$ such that $S_r(o,P) \ge \ell$.

*OPTIMIZATION* (for a scoring rule $r$): Given a PLP-forest $P$, compute an outcome with the highest score (an optimal outcome).

The picture for the rules Top-$k$ Clusters, Plurality and Borda is complete. As we noted above, the *SCORE* problem for Borda is in the class P, and Lang

et al. [9] proved that the *QUALITY* and *OPTIMIZATION* problems for Borda
are NP-complete and NP-hard, respectively. The *SCORE* problem for Top-$k$
Clusters and Plurality is in P (cf. our comments in the previous section) and
the following two results show that in each case, the problems *QUALITY* and
*OPTIMIZATION* are NP-complete and NP-hard, respectively.

**Theorem 1.** *The QUALITY problem for Top Cluster is NP-complete.*

*Proof* (Sketch). Membership is obvious, as one can guess an outcome $o$ in $O(p)$
time, and verify that $S_{tc}(o, P) \geq l$ in polynomial time in the size of $P$. Hardness
is proved by reduction from MIN2SAT: Given a set $\Phi$ of $n$ 2-clauses $\{C_1, \ldots, C_n\}$
over a set of propositional variables $\{X_1, \ldots, X_p\}$, and a positive integer $g$ ($g \leq$
$n$), decide whether there is a truth assignment that satisfies at most $g$ clauses in
$\Phi$.

Specifically, let $\Phi$ be a collection of $n$ 2-clauses. For each clause in $\Phi$, say
$C = X_i \vee \neg X_j$, we create a PLP-tree $T_C$ in Fig. 2, treating propositional variables
$X_i$ as attributes with the domains $\{0_i, 1_i\}$ (the form of the tree for other types
of 2-clauses is evident from the example we selected for illustration). We also set
$l = n - g$.

A truth assignment $v$ falsifies a clause $C$ in $\Phi$ if and only if, when viewed as
an outcome, it belongs to the top cluster of the corresponding tree $T_C$. Clearly,
there is an assignment satisfying at most $g$ clauses of $\Pi$ if and only if there is an
assignment that falsifies at least $l$ clauses in $\Phi$. The latter is equivalent to the
existence of an outcome that belongs to the top cluster of at least $l$ trees $T_C$,
$C \in \Phi$, that is, an outcome $v$ such that $S_{tc}(v, P) \geq l$.                           □

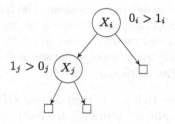

**Fig. 2.** PLP-tree

The case of the Top-$k$ Cluster rule with $k > 1$ is dealt with in the next
theorem.

**Theorem 2.** *The QUALITY problem for Top-k Clusters, where $k > 1$, is NP-complete.*

*Proof* (Sketch). The membership in NP is evident. To prove NP-hardness for
when $k > 1$, we again reduce from the MIN2SAT problem, but the construction
is different. For every clause $C \in \Phi$, say $C = X_i \vee \neg X_j \in \Phi$, we construct a

set $P_C$ of three PLP-trees shown in Fig. 3 (the construction is evident from the example we selected here for illustration).

We note that if an assignment $v$ satisfies a clause $C \in \Phi$, then we have $S_{tkc}(v, P_C) = 3 \cdot k - 4$; otherwise, we have $S_{tkc}(v, P_C) = 3 \cdot k - 3$. We now set $P = \bigcup_{C \in \Phi} P_C$ and $l = 3n(k-1) - g$. We need to show that assignment $v$ satisfies at most $g$ clauses in $\Phi$ if and only if $v$ scores at least $l$ in $P$ according to the Top-$k$ Clusters rule.

Let $v$ be an assignment satisfying $g'$ clauses in $\Phi$. Then, $S_{tkc}(v, P) = g'(3 \cdot k - 4) + (n - g')(3 \cdot k - 3) = 3n(k-1) - g'$. Thus, as required, there is an assignment $v$ that satisfies at most $g$ clauses if and only if there is an outcome with the score at least $l$. $\qquad\square$

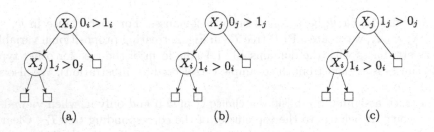

**Fig. 3.** Set $P_C$ of PLP-trees for clause $C = X_i \vee \neg X_j$

**Theorem 3.** *The QUALITY problem for Plurality is NP-complete.*

*Proof* (Sketch). The membership in NP is clear. The NP-hardness can be proved by reduction from MIN2SAT. For each clause in $\Phi$, we create a PLP-tree $T_C$ as in the proof of Theorem 1, and we set $l = (n-g)/2^{p-2}$. One can show that there is a truth assignment satisfying at most $g$ clauses in $\Phi$ if and only if there exists an outcome whose Plurality score is at least $l$. $\qquad\square$

Theorems 2 and 3 show that the corresponding *OPTIMIZATION* problems for Top-$k$ Cluster, $k \geq 1$, and for Plurality are NP-hard.

The *SCORE*, *QUALITY* and *OPTIMIZATION* problems for Copeland and Maximin were studied by Lang et al. [9]. These results are partial and not tight. We studied the complexity of these problems for the scoring rules Top-$k$ Clusters, Plurality and Borda. Our results are complete and tight. We summarize all these results in Table 1. Completing the complexity picture for Copeland and Maximin remains a challenging open problem.

## 5    Experiments and Results

PLP-trees and forests are difficult to elicit from users directly. In practical settings they have to be learned from *examples*, that is, pairs $(o, o')$ of outcomes,

**Table 1.** Computational complexity results

|  | *SCORE* | *QUALITY* | *OPTIMIZATION* |
|---|---|---|---|
| Top-$k$ clusters | P | NPC (Theorems 1 and 2) | NPH |
| Plurality | P | NPC (Theorem 3) | NPH |
| Borda | P | NPC (cf. [9]) | NPH |
| Copeland | #PH (cf. [9]) | ? | ? |
| Maximin | ? | coNPH (cf. [9]) | coNPH |

where $o$ is strictly preferred to $o'$ in the preference order we are trying to elicit (model). A method to learn PLP-trees was proposed by Liu and Truszczynski [11]. They also applied it learn PLP-forests and aggregate them with the PMR. In this paper, we extend this work to the case when learned PLP-forests (forests of learned PLP-trees) are aggregated by means of voting rules.

In our main results, we evaluate the ability of PLP-forests extended with voting rules to approximate preference orders arising in practical settings. Further, we compare in this respect PLP-forest models with models based on decision trees, develop for PLP-forests effective techniques to compute optimal or near optimal outcomes, and study the effect of the choice of a specific voting rule on the quality of the preference model.

## 5.1  Datasets and Experimental Set-up

We implemented the scoring rules discussed above as order aggregators for PLP-forests and experimented with them on the twelve preferential datasets used before by Liu and Truszczynski [11].[4] Their key characteristics are given in Table 2. The third column gives the number of pairs of outcomes from the corresponding domain with the first outcome being strictly better than the second one. As mentioned earlier, we refer to such pairs as examples.

The PLP-forest learning procedure works as follows. For each of the datasets, we randomly partition the set of examples $\mathcal{E}$, generating a training set of 70% of $\mathcal{E}$ and use the rest 30% as the testing set. In the training phase, we use the *greedy learning heuristic* [11] to learn a PLP-forest of a given number of PLP-trees, each of which is learned from $M$ (a parameter) examples selected with replacement and uniformly at random from the training set. In the testing phase, the trees in the learned PLP-forest are aggregated using the seven voting methods, Top Cluster, Top-2 Clusters, Top-3 Clusters, Plurality, Borda, Copeland and Maximin, to predict testing examples and to compute the social welfare rankings. We repeat this procedure 20 times for each dataset.

We recall that the greedy heuristic algorithm to learn a PLP-tree [11] takes as input the set $\mathcal{E}$ of examples, the set $\mathcal{A}$ of attributes, and a node $n$. The algorithm labels $n$ with an attribute $X$ and picks the preference order of elements

---

[4] The datasets are available at https://www.unf.edu/~N01237497/preflearnlib.php.

**Table 2.** Preference datasets in the preference learning library

| Dataset | #Attributes | #Outcomes | #Examples |
|---|---|---|---|
| Breast Cancer Wisconsin (BCW) | 9 | 270 | 9,009 |
| Car Evaluation (CE) | 6 | 1,728 | 682,721 |
| Credit Approval (CA) | 10 | 520 | 66,079 |
| German Credit (GC) | 10 | 914 | 172,368 |
| Ionosphere (IN) | 10 | 118 | 3,472 |
| Mammographic Mass (MM) | 5 | 62 | 792 |
| Mushroom (MS) | 10 | 184 | 8,448 |
| Nursery (NS) | 8 | 1,266 | 548,064 |
| SPECT Heart (SH) | 10 | 115 | 3,196 |
| Tic Tac Toe (TTT) | 9 | 958 | 207,832 |
| Vehicle (VH) | 10 | 455 | 76,713 |
| Wine (WN) | 10 | 177 | 10,322 |

in the domain of $X$ so that to maximize the number of examples in $\mathcal{E}$ *correctly* decided by $X$ and this domain order. For each value in the domain of $X$, the algorithm generates a child node of $n$ for which the algorithm recursively repeats with updated inputs: $\mathcal{E}'$, $\mathcal{A}'$ and $n'$, where $\mathcal{E}'$ is obtained from $\mathcal{E}$ excluding the examples decided at node $n$, $\mathcal{A}' = \mathcal{A}\setminus\{X\}$, and $n'$ is a child node of $n$. The algorithm stops and returns at a node where either $\mathcal{E}$ or $\mathcal{A}$ becomes empty.

The following three subsections present our experimental results. The first one concerns the task of predicting new preferences. For this task, we compute and report average *accuracy* results, where the accuracy is defined as the number of examples in the testing set that are in agreement with the learned model divided by the size of the testing set.

In the next subsection, we discuss computing optimal outcomes for PLP-forests using the Top-$k$ Clusters rules. We show that the problem can be reduced to the weighted partial MAXSAT problem [1]. This allows one to use the MAXSAT solver *toulbar2* [8] to solve them.

Finally, we consider the effect of the choice of a scoring rule on the preference order. To this end, we calculate the Spearman's rho [15] for Top Cluster, Top-2 Clusters, Top-3 Clusters, Plurality, Borda and Maximin, all against Copeland. This allows us to quantify the similarity between orders generated by different rules.

## 5.2   Preference Prediction Results

We focus on PLP-forests of trees learned from *small* sets of examples. This supports fast learning and leads to small constituent PLP-trees. In our experiments we learned PLP-trees from samples of 50, 100 and 200 examples. The results, averaged over all datasets for the Top-2 Clusters rule, are shown in

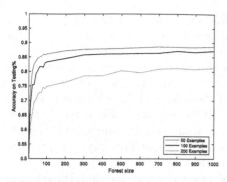

(a) Mean testing accuracy across all datasets for PLP-forests applying Top-2 Clusters, where every member tree is trained using random samples of sizes 50, 100 and 200.

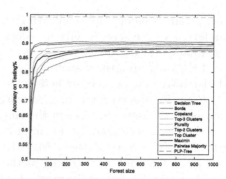

(b) Mean testing accuracy across all datasets for decision trees, PLP-forests applying voting rules and PLP-trees.

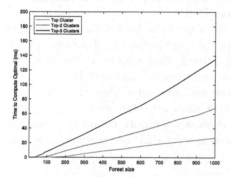

(c) Mean time across all datasets computing optimal outcomes using Toulbar2 for PLP-forests applying Top Cluster, Top-2 Clusters and Top-3 Clusters.

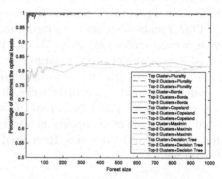

(d) Mean results across all datasets evaluating optimal outcomes for PLP-forests applying Top Cluster, Top-2 Clusters and Top-3 Clusters, against other voting rules and decision trees.

**Fig. 4.** Preference learning and optimization results for PLP-forests

Fig. 4a. They show that the testing accuracy is better when smaller PLP-trees are learned. We saw similar behavior for other scoring rules and so omitted the results from Fig. 4a. Based on these experiments, we now restrict our discussion to PLP-forests with trees learned from samples of size 50.

In Fig. 4b, we present the mean learning curves over all datasets for all 8 rules, where each curve shows how testing results (accuracy percentages) change with the PLP-forest size (the number of trees in the forest). We also show there the results for learning a single PLP-tree and a single decision tree using the whole training set (70% of $\mathcal{E}$). Decision trees in our experiments are classification trees trained using labeled instances, where an instance consists of two outcomes and has a binary label, 1 (0) indicating the first outcome is (is not, resp.) strictly preferred to the second. Given a decision tree $D$ and two outcomes $o$, $o'$, the dominance testing query asks if it is true that $o$ is strictly preferred to $o'$ in $D$. In testing, to answer such a query for two outcomes, they are input into a decision tree. If the tree predicts 1, we answer *yes* to the query; otherwise, *no*.

First, we observe that independently of the rule used the PLP-forest models across all datasets outperform the single PLP-tree model. This is most notable for the Borda rule, with a 4% improvement from 87% for single PLP-trees to 91% for PLP-forests. Pairwise Majority used by Liu and Truszczynski [11] turns out to be the worst aggregating method overall.

Moreover, looking at the results for 1000-tree forests, we see that, these forests have high accuracy of about 89–91%, on the testing datasets, depending on the voting rule. This provides strong evidence for the adequacy of the PLP-forest model to represent user preferences over practical combinatorial domains. This also demonstrates that the differences between these voting rules in predicting new preferences are not significant. In particular, the Top-3 Clusters rule finishes 90%, only a percentile point difference from Borda.

Our results also show that decision trees perform better on our datasets with accuracy of about 99%. We attribute the near-perfect performance of the decision-tree model to their large size (cf. Table 3) that enables classifying with high-granularity whether one outcome is preferred to another. However, the decision-tree model has drawbacks. It does not guarantee that the relation it determines is an order or a partial order, it does not offer clear explanations what factors affect comparisons, and it does not support computing optimal and near-optimal outcomes. In each of these aspects PLP-forest models have an advantage.

**Table 3.** Size comparison of PLP-trees and decision trees learned from the training data (70% of $\mathcal{E}$)

| Dataset | BCW | CE | CA | GC | IN | MM | MS | NS | SH | TTT | VH | WN |
|---|---|---|---|---|---|---|---|---|---|---|---|---|
| Decision tree | 188.8 | 683.0 | 897.2 | 2003.0 | 116.0 | 58 | 27.4 | 681.0 | 73.6 | 564.2 | 1549.0 | 36.2 |
| PLP-tree | 25.7 | 109.5 | 81.1 | 190.0 | 30.6 | 10.0 | 16.3 | 116.9 | 19.0 | 115.2 | 105.4 | 14.6 |
| Ratio | 7.6 | 6.2 | 11.1 | 10.5 | 3.8 | 5.8 | 1.7 | 5.8 | 3.9 | 4.9 | 14.7 | 2.5 |

## 5.3   Preference Optimization Results

PLP-forests with scoring rules allow for effective optimal outcome computation. We show it here for orders obtained by using Top, Top-2 and Top-3 Clusters rule to aggregate orders defined by individual PLP-trees in a PLP-forest.

For every dataset, we learn PLP-forests of up to 1000 PLP-trees. To compute the optimal outcome in each forest (under Top, Top-2 or Top-3 Clusters rule), we encode the problem as an instance of the weighted partial MAXSAT problem [1] and use *toolbar2* [8] to solve it. A weighted partial MAXSAT instance $\Phi$ consists of two parts $\Phi_h$ and $\Phi_s$, where $\Phi_h$, called *hard constraints*, is a collection of clauses, and $\Phi_s$, called *soft constraints*, is a collection of weighted clauses. If $\Phi_h$ is over-constrained and thus unsatisfiable, there is no solution to $\Phi$. Otherwise, the solution to $\Phi$ is a truth assignment $v$ that satisfies $\Phi_h$ and maximizes the sum of the weights of the clauses satisfied by $v$. We now briefly discuss the encoding for the case of binary attributes, which extends in a straightforward way to the general case of multi-valued attributes.

The encoding consists of two main steps and assumes that we are using the Top-$k$ Clusters rule for aggregation. First, given a PLP-forest $P = \{T_1, \ldots, T_m\}$, we build a collection $\Psi = \{(B_1^1, k), \ldots, (B_k^1, 1), \ldots, (B_1^m, k), \ldots, (B_k^m, 1)\}$ of term-weight pairs. Each term $B_j^i$ is the conjunction of literals $x$ or $\neg x$, where $x$'s are the names of the attributes labeling the nodes on the path in the tree $T_i$ from its root to the leaf $\ell_j$. If the path follows to the left child of the node labeled by $x$, the term $B_j^i$ includes the literal $x$, otherwise, it includes the literal $\neg x$. This collection of terms can be built in time that is linear in the size of the input. One can show that the winning outcome for $P$ with respect to the Top-$k$ Clusters rule is precisely the truth assignment with the maximum sum of weights of those terms in $\Psi$ that it satisfies (and conversely).

Second, we translate $\Psi$ to an equivalent weighted partial MAXSAT instance $\Phi$ of two parts $\Phi_s$ and $\Phi_h$. Given $\Psi = \{(B_1, w_1), \ldots, (B_N, w_N)\}$, we build in linear time $\Phi_s = \{(c_1, w_1), \ldots, (c_N, w_N)\}$ where every $c_i$ is a new atom, and $\Phi_h = \{CNF(B_i \leftrightarrow c_i) : (B_i, w_i) \in \Psi\}$ where $CNF$ denotes the set of clauses of a given formula. One can show that the truth assignment with the maximum sum of weights of satisfied terms in $\Psi$ is precisely the truth assignment that satisfies all clauses in $\Phi_h$ and for which the sum of weights of clauses in $\Phi_s$ that it satisfies is maximum (and the converse holds, too).

Average computational time spent on searching for optimal outcomes for all datasets is shown in Fig. 4c. We see that, for any dataset and for any forest size up to 1000, a weighted partial MAXSAT instance encoding preference optimization can be solved within 0.2 s.

The reductions are straightforward for the Top-$k$ Clusters rules. It is not clear how to extend them to other scoring rules. Instead, we show that optimal outcomes computed for the three of the Top-$k$ Clusters rules are close to optimal for orders obtained for other rules. Specifically, for every optimal outcome computed based on Top-$k$ Clusters rule ($k = 1, 2, 3$) and every dataset, we randomly select 1000 outcomes and check how well the optimal outcome compares to them, when other voting rules (Plurality, Borda, Copeland and Maximin) are used. Average percentiles of the number of outcomes "beaten" by the optimal one are shown in Fig. 4d. We note that, when forests are big, the optimal outcomes based on the three Top-$k$ Clusters rules are either very likely optimal (when the percentiles are exactly 100%) or very likely near-optimal (when the percentiles are not 100% but very close to), for all other voting rules. This is desirable because it shows that computing optimal outcomes for orders determined by Top-$k$ Clusters rules, which we demonstrated to be computationally feasible, are likely optimal or near-optimal for rules where methods to optimize preferences are not straightforward. For decision trees, the results show that outcomes optimal for Top-$k$ Rules are further from optimal but still within the top 20% of outcomes according to the decision-tree model.

## 5.4   Rank Correlation Results

In the standard voting setting, the rankings generated by different voting rules are quite close to each other [5,15]. For the setting of combinatorial domain setting, when preference orders are given as PLP-forests (with scoring rules as aggregators), the results we discussed in the previous sections suggest that here, too, the choice of a voting rule does not affect the order significantly (all rules result in models of similar accuracy and outcomes highly preferred for one rule are highly preferred for other).

Specifically, we empirically studied the correlation to orders determined by the Copeland rule of orders determined by the other scoring rules we studied. As suggested in previous work on measuring rank correlation [5,15,16], we used the Spearman's rho (denoted by $\rho$) as the rank correlation coefficient. Given two total orders $L_1$ and $L_2$ of outcomes in $C$, we define

$$\rho(L_1, L_2) = 1 - \frac{6 \cdot \sum_{1 \leq i \leq n} (i - D_2(L_1(i)))^2}{n \cdot (n^2 - 1)},$$

where $i$ is the rank value between 1 and $n$, and $D_2(o)$ is the rank of outcome $o$ in $L_2$. The value of $\rho(L_1, L_2)$ is in between $-1$ and 1, both inclusive. When $L_1$ and $L_2$ order $C$ exactly the same, we have $\rho(L_1, L_2) = 1$. If $\rho(L_1, L_2) = -1$, it means $L_1$ and $L_2$ reversely order $C$. Furthermore, the closer the value to 0, the weaker the correlation between $L_1$ and $L_2$.

Our results (cf. Table 4) suggest that Borda-generated orders have a very high degree of consensus with those generated by Copeland, and that Plurality and Top Cluster lead to orders with the lowest degrees of agreement. Nevertheless, in all cases the Spearman's rho has high values, similar to those obtained for strict preference orders over non-combinatorial domains with few outcomes [5,15,16].

## 6   Conclusions and Future Work

We proposed to use PLP-forests extended with a voting rule as a model of preference relations. We considered five voting rules, Top-$k$ Clusters, Borda, Plurality, Copeland and Maximin, all adjusted to the case of total preorders. We studied the complexity of three key preference reasoning problems arising in this setting: *SCORE*, *QUALITY* and *OPTIMIZATION*. For Top-$k$ Clusters, Borda and Plurality, our results, together with those obtained earlier in the literature, provide a complete picture. In all cases, the *SCORE* problem is in P, the *QUALITY* problem is NP-complete and the *OPTIMIZATION* problem is NP-hard. For the Copeland and Maximin rules, investigated by Lang et al. [9],

**Table 4.** Mean and standard deviation of the Spearman's rho results for voting rules against Copeland across all datasets in learning PLP-forests of size 1000

| Dataset | Borda | Top-3 | Top-2 | Maximin | Plurality | Top |
|---------|-------|-------|-------|---------|-----------|-----|
| BCW | 0.9616 | 0.8405 | 0.8456 | 0.8310 | 0.8288 | 0.8196 |
| CE | 0.7741 | 0.5532 | 0.5384 | 0.4716 | 0.4591 | 0.4665 |
| CA | 0.9847 | 0.9413 | 0.9354 | 0.9435 | 0.9260 | 0.9277 |
| GC | 0.9898 | 0.9159 | 0.9108 | 0.9165 | 0.9088 | 0.8742 |
| IN | 0.9240 | 0.9867 | 0.9786 | 0.9823 | 0.9763 | 0.9706 |
| MM | 0.8678 | 0.9331 | 0.9234 | 0.9109 | 0.9005 | 0.9054 |
| MS | 0.9712 | 0.9353 | 0.9115 | 0.9433 | 0.9025 | 0.8898 |
| NS | 0.9939 | 0.9908 | 0.9851 | 0.9766 | 0.9768 | 0.9806 |
| SH | 0.9729 | 0.9968 | 0.9810 | 0.9786 | 0.9747 | 0.9785 |
| TTT | 0.9900 | 0.9916 | 0.9841 | 0.9931 | 0.9847 | 0.9531 |
| VH | 0.9691 | 0.8612 | 0.8346 | 0.8588 | 0.8573 | 0.7958 |
| WN | 0.9937 | 0.9740 | 0.9266 | 0.9101 | 0.9090 | 0.9015 |
| Mean | **0.9494** | 0.9100 | 0.8963 | 0.8930 | 0.8837 | 0.8719 |
| SD | **0.0632** | 0.1181 | 0.1182 | 0.1358 | 0.1364 | 0.1347 |

only some results are known. However, they suggest the two rules may be more demanding computationally.

We studied our PLP-forest models experimentally. Our results showed that using these voting rules for preferential datasets generated from real-world classification datasets yields models reflecting underlying preference relations with high accuracy, exceeding that of PLP-forest models utilizing the Pairwise Majority rule.

We also studied the correlation among the orders given by different PLP-forest models, extending to the setting of "votes" over combinatorial domains several earlier studies in the standard voting setting with a small number of alternatives. We found that when compared to the model given by PLP-forests with Copeland as an aggregator, all models showed high levels of correlation, similar to those reported in the literature for the standard voting setting. Our results suggest that using rules such as Borda or Top-3 clusters (the two closest to Copeland) produces orders representative for all those that can be obtained by combining a PLP-forest with a scoring rule.

For the Top-$k$ Clusters rule, we developed methods to compute optimal outcomes for orders they determine given a PLP-forest. Our experiments for when $k = 1, 2, 3$ showed that the methods are computationally feasible. They also show that optimal outcomes computed for the Top-$k$ Clusters rules are near optimal for orders determined by all other scoring rules.

Our results suggest that PLP-forest preference models with scoring rules as aggregators, especially Top-$k$ Clusters and Borda, have many attractive features.

They can be learned so that to reflect underlying true preference relation with high accuracy. They represent well orders that result from using other scoring rules. Lastly, they support fast methods for computing optimal outcomes and these outcomes are likely to be near optimal for orders given by other scoring rules.

We also compare our PLP-forest models with the decision tree approach. The decision trees learned from examples can approximate underlying orders with higher accuracy (as high as 99% in our experiments). However, they do have drawbacks not present in PLP-forest models. First, unlike in the case of the PLP-forests, the relation defined by decision trees is not guaranteed to be a total order (not even a partial order). Second, decision trees do not provide any clear insights into key factors determining the underlying preference relations. In contrast, the PLP-tree and PLP-forest models yield information about attributes most significant for determining the preference order. For the PLP-tree model, it is the attribute that labels the root, for the PLP-forest model, the attributes appearing most frequently as the labels of the roots of its trees. Lastly they do not offer effective ways to solve optimization tasks (finding optimal or near optimal outcomes) while, as we show, PLP-tree and forest models do. These drawbacks of decision trees make PLP-forests, despite their lower accuracy, an attractive preference model for use in applications.

Our results provide evidence of low effect of the choice of a voting rule when aggregating preference orders determined by trees in a PLP-forest on the final preference order. Clearly, the strength of this observation is has to be quantified by the range of the data sets we considered. Expanding the scope of experiments to other domains implied by practice, as well as to randomly generated ones is a goal for future research. It will provide a more detailed understanding of sensitivity of the model to the choice of a voting rule.

Improving the accuracy of the PLP-forest model is the main challenge for future work. There seem to be two natural directions. First, one can explore a possibility of combining the PLP-forest and decision-tree models, for instance, by using decision trees at leaf nodes of PLP-trees for comparison tests of outcomes in the corresponding clusters. Second, one can investigate other PLP-tree learning algorithms, possibly developing methods to find trees that best fit with given sets of examples, rather than to use heuristics, as we do now. Another promising direction is to extend the work of Bräuning et al. [3]. First, one can generalize the concept of a preference list to the tree of preference lists. In this way one can expand the ability of the preference list model to handle conditional preferences. Second, similarly as we do in this work considering PLP-forests, that is, collections of PLP-trees, one can study collections of preference list models.

**Acknowledgments.** The work of the second author was supported by the NSF grant IIS-1618783.

# References

1. Ansótegui, C., Bonet, M.L., Levy, J.: A new algorithm for weighted partial MaxSAT. In: Fox, M., Poole, D. (eds.) Proceedings of the 24th AAAI Conference on Artificial Intelligence, AAAI 2010. AAAI Press (2010)
2. Booth, R., Chevaleyre, Y., Lang, J., Mengin, J., Sombattheera, C.: Learning conditionally lexicographic preference relations. In: ECAI, pp. 269–274 (2010)
3. Bräuning, M., Hüllermeier, E., Keller, T., Glaum, M.: Lexicographic preferences for predictive modeling of human decision making: a new machine learning method with an application in accounting. Eur. J. Oper. Res. **258**(1), 295–306 (2017)
4. Breiman, L.: Random forests. Mach. Learn. **45**(1), 5–32 (2001)
5. Felsenthal, D.S., Maoz, Z., Rapoport, A.: An empirical evaluation of six voting procedures: do they really make any difference? Br. J. Polit. Sci. **23**(01), 1–27 (1993)
6. Fraser, N.M.: Ordinal preference representations. Theor. Decis. **36**(1), 45–67 (1994)
7. Gehrlein, W.V.: Condorcet's paradox and the likelihood of its occurrence: different perspectives on balanced preferences. Theor. Decis. **52**(2), 171–199 (2002)
8. Hurley, B., O'Sullivan, B., Allouche, D., Katsirelos, G., Schiex, T., Zytnicki, M., De Givry, S.: Multi-language evaluation of exact solvers in graphical model discrete optimization. Constraints **21**(3), 413–434 (2016)
9. Lang, J., Mengin, J., Xia, L.: Aggregating conditionally lexicographic preferences on multi-issue domains. In: Milano, M. (ed.) CP 2012. LNCS, pp. 973–987. Springer, Heidelberg (2012). https://doi.org/10.1007/978-3-642-33558-7_69
10. Lang, J., Xia, L.: Sequential composition of voting rules in multi-issue domains. Math. Soc. Sci. **57**(3), 304–324 (2009)
11. Liu, X., Truszczynski, M.: Learning partial lexicographic preference trees and forests over multi-valued attributes. In: Proceedings of the 2nd Global Conference on Artificial Intelligence (GCAI 2016). EPiC Series in Computing, vol. 41, pp. 314–328. EasyChair (2016)
12. Liu, X., Truszczynski, M.: Aggregating conditionally lexicographic preferences using answer set programming solvers. In: Perny, P., Pirlot, M., Tsoukiàs, A. (eds.) ADT 2013. LNCS (LNAI), vol. 8176, pp. 244–258. Springer, Heidelberg (2013). https://doi.org/10.1007/978-3-642-41575-3_19
13. Liu, X., Truszczynski, M.: Learning partial lexicographic preference trees over combinatorial domains. In: Proceedings of the 29th AAAI Conference on Artificial Intelligence (AAAI), pp. 1539–1545. AAAI Press (2015)
14. Liu, X., Truszczynski, M.: Reasoning with preference trees over combinatorial domains. In: Walsh, T. (ed.) ADT 2015. LNCS (LNAI), vol. 9346, pp. 19–34. Springer, Cham (2015). https://doi.org/10.1007/978-3-319-23114-3_2
15. Mattei, N.: Empirical evaluation of voting rules with strictly ordered preference data. In: Brafman, R.I., Roberts, F.S., Tsoukiàs, A. (eds.) ADT 2011. LNCS (LNAI), vol. 6992, pp. 165–177. Springer, Heidelberg (2011). https://doi.org/10.1007/978-3-642-24873-3_13
16. Myers, J.L., Well, A., Lorch, R.F.: Research Design and Statistical Analysis. Routledge, Abingdon (2010)
17. Schmitt, M., Martignon, L.: Complexity of Lexicographic Strategies on Binary Cues. Preprint (1999)

18. Wilson, N.: Preference inference based on lexicographic models. In: Schaub, T., Friedrich, G., O'Sullivan, B. (eds.) Proceedings of the 21st European Conference on Artificial Intelligence, ECAI 2014. Frontiers in Artificial Intelligence and Applications, vol. 263, pp. 921–926. IOS Press (2014)
19. Wilson, N., George, A.: Efficient inference and computation of optimal alternatives for preference languages based on lexicographic models. In: Sierra, C. (ed.) Proceedings of the Twenty-Sixth International Joint Conference on Artificial Intelligence, IJCAI 2017, pp. 1311–1317 (2017)

# Enumeration Complexity of Poor Man's Propositional Dependence Logic

Arne Meier$^{(\boxtimes)}$ and Christian Reinbold

Leibniz Universität Hannover, Institut für Theoretische Informatik, Appelstrasse 4,
30167 Hannover, Germany
{meier,reinbold}@thi.uni-hannover.de

**Abstract.** Dependence logics are a modern family of logics of independence and dependence which mimic notions of database theory. In this paper, we aim to initiate the study of enumeration complexity in the field of dependence logics and thereby get a new point of view on enumerating answers of database queries. Consequently, as a first step, we investigate the problem of enumerating all satisfying teams of formulas from a given fragment of propositional dependence logic. We distinguish between restricting the team size by arbitrary functions and the parametrised version where the parameter is the team size. We show that a polynomial delay can be reached for polynomials and otherwise in the parametrised setting we reach FPT delay. However, the constructed enumeration algorithm with polynomial delay requires exponential space. We show that an incremental polynomial delay algorithm exists which uses polynomial space only. Negatively, we show that for the general problem without restricting the team size, an enumeration algorithm running in polynomial space cannot exist.

## 1 Introduction

Consider the simple database scheme containing a single table SMARTPHONE with attributes MANUFACTURER (M), SERIAL NUMBER (SN), MANUFACTURE DATE (MD) and BLUETOOTH SUPPORT (BS), where MANUFACTURER and SERIAL NUMBER form the primary key. Now we are interested in all possible answers of a database query on SMARTPHONE selecting entities with bluetooth support. In terms of dependence logic, a database instance $T$ conforms with the primary key condition if and only if $T \models\ =(\{M, SN\}, \{MD, BS\})$. Taking the selection of the query into consideration, we obtain the formula $=(\{M, SN\}, \{MD, BS\}) \wedge BS$ for which we would like to enumerate satisfying database instances. Since team semantics is commonly used in the area of dependence logic, we model the database instance $T$ as a team, that is, a set of assignments, such that each assignment represents a row in SMARTPHONE.

The task of enumerating all solutions of a given instance is relevant in several prominent areas, e.g., one is interested in all tuples satisfying a database query,

This work was partially supported by DFG project ME4279/1-2.

F. Ferrarotti and S. Woltran (Eds.): FoIKS 2018, LNCS 10833, pp. 303–321, 2018.
https://doi.org/10.1007/978-3-319-90050-6_17

DNA sequencings, or all answers of a web search. In enumeration complexity one is interested in outputting all solutions of a given problem instance without duplicates. Often, the algorithmic stream of solutions has to obey a specific order, in particular, on such order increasingly arranges solutions with respect to their cost. In view of this, the enumeration task (with respect to this order) outputs the cheapest solutions first. Of course, all these algorithms usually are not running in polynomial time as there often exist more than polynomially many solutions. As a result, one classifies these deterministic algorithms with respect to their *delay* [1–3]. Informally, the delay is the time which elapses between two output solutions and guarantees a continuous stream of output solutions. For instance, the class DelayP then encompasses problems for which algorithms with a polynomial delay (in the input length) exist. Another class relevant to this study is IncP, incremental P. For this class the delay of outputting the $i$th solution of an instance is polynomial in the input size *plus* the index $i$ of the solution. Consequently, problem instances exhibiting exponentially many solutions eventually possess an exponential delay whereas, in the beginning, the delay was polynomial. Some natural problems in this class are known such as enumerating all minimal triangulations [4] or some problems for matroids [5].

A prominent approach to attacking computationally hard problems is the framework of parametrised complexity by Downey and Fellows [6,7]. Essentially, one searches for a *parameter k* of a given problem such that the problem can be solved in time $f(k) \cdot n^{\mathcal{O}(1)}$ instead of $n^{f(k)}$ where $n$ is the input length and $f$ is an arbitrary recursive function. Assuming that the parameter is slowly growing or even constant, then the first kind of algorithms is seen relevant for practice. In these cases, one says that the problem is *fixed parameter tractable*, or short, in FPT. A simple example here is the propositional satisfiability problem with the parametrisation *numbers of variables*. For this problem, the straightforward brute-force algorithm already yields FPT. Recently, this framework has been adapted to the field of enumeration by Creignou et al. [8,9]. There, the authors introduced the corresponding enumeration classes DelayFPT and IncFPT and provided some characterisations of these classes.

In 2007, Väänänen introduced *dependence logic* (DL) [10] as a novel variant of Hintikka's *independence-friendly logic*. This logic builds on top of compositional team semantics which emerges from the work of Hodges [11]. In this logic, the satisfaction of formulas is interpreted on *sets of assignments*, i.e., teams, instead of a single assignment as in classical Tarski semantics. Significantly, this semantics allows for interpreting reasoning in this logic in the view of databases. Essentially, a team then is nothing different than a database: its domain of variables is the set of columns and its (team) members, that is, assignments, can be seen as rows in the table. As a result, the aforementioned dependence atoms allow for expressing key properties in databases, e.g., functional dependencies. On that account, many research from the area of databases coalesced with scientific results from logic, complexity theory and further other disciplines [12]. As a result, within the team semantics setting several different formalisms have been investigated that have counterparts in database theory: inclusion and exclusion dependencies

[13–16], functional dependence (the dependence atom $=(P, Q)$) [10], and independence [17]. Such operators will be the topic of future research connecting to the here presented investigations.

To bring the motivation full circle, the study of enumeration in dependence logic is the same as investigating the enumeration of answers of specific database queries described over some formulas in some logic. For instance, consider a dependence logic formula that specifies some database related properties such as functional or exclusion dependencies of some attributes. Now one is interested in the question whether this specification is meaningful in the sense that there exists a database which obeys these properties. This problem can be seen as the satisfiability problem in dependence logic. Further connections to database theory have been exemplified by Hannula et al. [18]. The study of database queries is a deeply studied problem and exists for several decades now. Our aim for this paper is to initiate the research on enumeration (in databases) from the perspective of dependence logic. This modern family of logics might give fresh insights into this settled problem and produce new enumeration techniques that will help at databases as well. From a computational complexity perspective, DL is well understood: most of the possible operator fragments have been classified [19, 20]. However, it turned out that model checking and satisfiability for propositional dependence logic $\mathcal{PDL}$ are already NP-complete [21, 22]. As a result, tractable enumeration of solutions in the full logic is impossible (unless P and NP coincide) and we focus on a fragment of $\mathcal{PDL}$ which we will call, for historical reasons, the Poor Man's fragment [23].

In this paper, we investigate the problem of enumerating all satisfying teams of a given Poor Man's propositional dependence logic formula. In particular, we distinguish between restricting the team size by arbitrary functions $f$ and the parametrised version where the parameter is the team size. We show that DelayP can be reached if $f$ is a polynomial in the input length and otherwise the parametrised approach leads to DelayFPT. However, the constructed DelayP enumeration algorithm requires exponential space. If one desires to eliminate this unsatisfactory space requirement, we show that this can be achieved by paying the price of an increasing delay, i.e., then an IncP algorithm can be constructed which uses polynomial space only. Here, we show, on the downside, that for the general problem without restricting the team size an enumeration algorithm running in polynomial space cannot exist.

Proofs omitted for space reasons can be found in the technical report [24].

## 2    Preliminaries

Further, the underlying machine concept will be RAMs as we require data structures with logarithmic costs for standard operations. A detailed description of the RAM computation model may be found in [25]. The space occupied by a RAM is given by the total amount of used registers, provided that the content of each register is polynomially bounded in the size of the input. Furthermore, we will follow the notation of Durand et al. [26], Creignou et al. [8] and Schmidt [2].

The complexity classes of interest are P and NP (over the RAM model which is equivalent to the standard model over Turing machines in this setting).

*Team-Based Propositional Logic.* Let $\mathcal{V}$ be a (countably infinite) set of variables. The class of all *Poor Man's Propositional formulas* $\mathcal{PL}^-$ is derived via the grammar

$$\varphi ::= x \mid \neg x \mid 0 \mid 1 \mid \varphi \wedge \varphi,$$

where $x \in \mathcal{V}$. The set of all variables occurring in a propositional formula $\varphi$ is denoted by $\mathrm{Var}(\varphi)$.

Now we will specify the notion of teams and its interpretation on propositional formulas. An *assignment* over $\mathcal{V}$ is a mapping $s\colon \mathcal{V} \to \{0,1\}$. We set $2^{\mathcal{V}} := \{s : s \text{ assignment over } \mathcal{V}\}$. A *team* $T$ over $\mathcal{V}$ is a subset $T \subseteq 2^{\mathcal{V}}$. Consequently, the set of all teams over $\mathcal{V}$ is denoted by $\mathcal{P}\left(2^{\mathcal{V}}\right)$. If $X$ is a subset of $\mathcal{V}$, we set $T\big|_X := \left\{s\big|_X : s \in T\right\}$, where $s\big|_X$ is the restriction of $s$ on $X$. If $T$ has cardinality $k \in \mathbb{N}$, we say that $T$ is a *$k$-Team*. If $\varphi$ is a formula, then a team (assignment) over $\mathrm{Var}(\varphi)$ is called a *team (assignment) for $\varphi$*.

A *team-based propositional formula* $\varphi$ is constructed by the rule set of $\mathcal{PL}^-$ with the extension $\varphi ::= {=}(P, Q)$, where $P, Q$ are sets of arbitrary variables. We write $=(x_1, x_2, \ldots, x_n)$ as a shorthand for $=(\{x_1, x_2, \ldots, x_{n-1}\}, \{x_n\})$ and set $\mathcal{PDL}^- := \mathcal{PL}^-({=}(\cdot))$ for the formulas of *Poor Man's Propositional Dependence Logic*.

**Definition 1 (Satisfaction).** *Let $\varphi$ be a team-based propositional formula and $T$ be a team for $\varphi$. We define $T \models \varphi$ inductively by*

$$
\begin{aligned}
T &\models x & &:\Leftrightarrow s(x) = 1 \quad \forall s \in T, \\
T &\models \neg x & &:\Leftrightarrow s(x) = 0 \quad \forall s \in T, \\
T &\models 1 & &:\Leftrightarrow \mathit{true}, \\
T &\models 0 & &:\Leftrightarrow T = \emptyset, \\
T &\models \varphi \wedge \psi & &:\Leftrightarrow T \models \varphi \text{ and } T \models \psi, \\
T &\models {=}(P, Q) & &:\Leftrightarrow \forall s, t \in T : s\big|_P = t\big|_P \Rightarrow s\big|_Q = t\big|_Q
\end{aligned}
$$

*We say that $T$ satisfies $\varphi$ iff $T \models \varphi$ holds.*

Note that we have $T \models (x \wedge \neg x)$ iff $T = \emptyset$. This observation motivates the definition for $T \models 0$. Observe that the evaluation in classical propositional logic occurs as the special case of evaluating singletons in team-based propositional logic.

**Definition 2 (Downward closure).** *A team-based propositional formula $\varphi$ is called* downward closed, *if for every team $T$ we have that $T \models \varphi \Rightarrow \forall S \subseteq T : S \models \varphi$. An operator $\circ$ of arity $k$ is called* downward closed, *if $\circ(\varphi_1, \ldots, \varphi_k)$ is downward closed for all downward closed formulas $\varphi_i$, $i = 1, \ldots, k$. A class $\phi$ of team-based propositional formulas is called* downward closed, *if all formulas in $\phi$ are downward closed.*

The following lemma then is straightforward to prove.

**Lemma 1.** *All atoms and operators in $\mathcal{PDL}^-$ are downward closed. In particular, $\mathcal{PDL}^-$ is downward closed.*

*Enumeration Problems.* Let $\Sigma$ be a finite alphabet and $(S, \leq)$ a partially ordered set of possible solutions. An *enumeration problem* is a triple $E = (Q, \text{Sol}, \leq)$ such that (i) $Q \subset \Sigma^*$ is a decidable language and (ii) $\text{Sol} \colon Q \to \mathcal{P}(S)$ is a computable function. For an element $x \in Q$ we call $x$ an *instance* and $\text{Sol}(x)$ its set of *solutions*. If $\leq$ is the trivial poset given by $x \leq y :\Leftrightarrow x = y$, we omit it and write $E = (Q, \text{Sol})$. Analogously, we write $x < y$ for $x \leq y$ and $x \neq y$.

**Definition 3 (Enumeration algorithm).** *Let $E = (Q, \text{Sol}, \leq)$ be an enumeration problem. A deterministic algorithm $\mathcal{A}$ is an enumeration algorithm for $E$ if $\mathcal{A}$ terminates for every input $x \in Q$, outputs the set $\text{Sol}(x)$ without duplicates and for every $s, t \in \text{Sol}(x)$ with $s < t$ the solution $s$ is outputted before $t$.*

**Definition 4 (Delay).** *Let $\mathcal{A}$ be an enumeration algorithm for the enumeration problem $E = (Q, \text{Sol}, \leq)$ and $x \in Q$. The $i$-th delay of $\mathcal{A}$ is defined as the elapsed time between outputting the $i$-th and $(i+1)$-th solution of $\text{Sol}(x)$, where the $0$-th and $(|\text{Sol}(x)| + 1)$-st delay are considered to happen at the start and the end of the computation respectively. The $0$-th delay is called* precomputation phase *and the $(|\text{Sol}(x)| + 1)$-st delay is called* postcomputation phase.

**Definition 5.** *Let $E = (Q, \text{Sol}, \leq)$ be an enumeration problem and $\mathcal{A}$ be an enumeration algorithm for $E$. $\mathcal{A}$ is*

1. *an* IncP*-algorithm if there exists a polynomial $p$ such that the $i$-th delay on input $x \in Q$ is bounded by $p(|x| + i)$.*
2. *a* DelayP*-algorithm if there exists a polynomial $p$ such that all delays on input $x \in Q$ are bounded by $p(|x|)$.*
3. *a* DelaySpaceP*-algorithm if it is a* DelayP*-algorithm using polynomial amount of space with respect to the size of the input.*

For ease of notation, we define the classes DelayP (IncP, DelaySpaceP) as the class of all enumeration problems admitting a DelayP- (IncP, DelaySpaceP)-algorithm. Now we introduce the parametrised version of enumeration problems. The extensions are similar to those when extending P to FPT. We follow Creignou et al. [8].

**Definition 6 (Parametrised enumeration problem).** *An enumeration problem $(Q, \text{Sol}, \leq)$ together with a polynomial time computable parametrisation $\kappa \colon \Sigma^* \to \mathbb{N}$ is called a parametrised enumeration problem $E = (Q, \kappa, \text{Sol}, \leq)$. As before, if $\leq$ is omitted, we assume $\leq$ to be trivial.*

**Definition 7.** *Let $\mathcal{A}$ be an enumeration algorithm for a parametrised enumeration problem $E = (Q, \kappa, \text{Sol}, \leq)$. If there exist a polynomial $p$ and a computable function $f \colon \mathbb{N} \to \mathbb{N}$ such that the $i$-th delay on input $x \in Q$ is bounded by*

308    A. Meier and C. Reinbold

$f(\kappa(x)) \cdot p(|x| + i)$, *then* $\mathcal{A}$ *is an* IncFPT-*algorithm. We call* $\mathcal{A}$ *a* DelayFPT-*algorithm if all delays on input* $x \in Q$ *are bounded by* $f(\kappa(x)) \cdot p(|x|)$. *The class* IncFPT *contains all enumeration problems that admit an* IncFPT-*algorithm. The class* DelayFPT *is defined analogously.*

*Group Action.* The following section provides a compact introduction in group actions on sets. For a deeper introduction see, for instance, Rotman's textbook [27].

**Definition 8 (Group action).** *Let* $G$ *be a group with identity element* $e$ *and* $X$ *be a set. A* group action *of* $G$ *on* $X$, *denoted by* $G \circlearrowright X$, *is a mapping* $G \times X \to X$, $(g, x) \mapsto gx$, *with*

1. $ex = x \quad \forall x \in X$
2. $(gh)x = g(hx) \quad \forall g, h \in G, \ x \in X.$

Now observe the following. Let $G$ be a group and $X$ a set. The mapping $(g, h) \mapsto gh$ for $g, h \in G$ defines a group action of $G$ on itself. A group action $G \circlearrowright X$ induces a group action of $G$ on $\mathcal{P}(X)$ by $gS := \{gs : s \in S\}$ for all $g \in G$, $S \subseteq X$. Note that this group action preserves the cardinality of sets.

**Definition 9 (Orbit).** *Let* $G \circlearrowright X$ *be a group action and* $x \in X$. *Then the* orbit *of* $x$ *is given by* $Gx := \{gx : g \in G\} \subseteq X$.

**Proposition 1** ([27]). *Let* $G \circlearrowright X$ *be a group action and* $x, y \in X$. *Then either* $Gx = Gy$ *or* $Gx \cap Gy = \emptyset$. *Consequently the orbits of* $G \circlearrowright X$ *partition the set* $X$.

**Definition 10 (Stabiliser).** *Let* $G \circlearrowright X$ *be a group action and* $x \in X$. *The* stabilizer subgroup *of* $x$ *is given by* $G_x := \{g \in G : gx = x\}$ *and indeed is a subgroup of* $G$.

**Proposition 2 (Orbit-Stabiliser theorem,** [27, Theorem 3.19]**).** *Let* $G$ *be a finite group acting on a set* $X$. *Let* $x \in X$. *Then the mapping* $gG_x \mapsto gx$ *is a bijection from* $G/G_x$ *to* $Gx$. *In particular, we have that* $|Gx| \cdot |G_x| = |G|$.

**Proposition 3 (Cauchy-Frobenius lemma,** [27, Theorem 3.22]**).** *Let* $G$ *be a finite group acting on a set* $X$. *Then the amount of orbits is given by* $\frac{1}{|G|} \sum_{g \in G} |\{x \in X : gx = x\}|$.

## 3   Results

In this section, we investigate the complexity of enumerating all satisfying teams for various fragments of team-based propositional logic. After introducing the problem ENUMTEAM and its parametrised version P-ENUMTEAM we develop two enumeration algorithms for $\mathcal{PDL}^-$, either guaranteeing polynomial delay or incremental delay in polynomial space.

**Problem 1.** Let $\Phi$ be a class of team-based propositional formulas and $f \colon \mathbb{N} \to \mathbb{N}$ be a computable function. Then we define $\text{ENUMTEAM}(\Phi, f) := (\Phi, \text{Sol})$ where

$$\text{Sol}(\varphi) := \left\{ \emptyset \neq T \in \mathcal{P}\left(2^{\text{Var}(\varphi)}\right) : T \models \varphi, |T| \leq f(|\varphi|) \right\} \quad \text{for } \varphi \in \Phi.$$

As we are interested in non-empty teams as solutions, we excluded the $\emptyset$ from the set of all solutions. Nevertheless, formally by the *empty team property*, it always holds that $\emptyset \models \varphi$.

**Problem 2.** Let $\Phi$ be a class of team-based propositional formulas and $f \colon \mathbb{N} \to \mathbb{N}$ a computable function. Then P-$\text{ENUMTEAM}(\phi) := (\Phi \times \mathbb{N}, \kappa, \text{Sol})$ where $\kappa((\varphi, k)) := k$ and

$$\text{Sol}((\varphi, k)) := \left\{ \emptyset \neq T \in \mathcal{P}\left(2^{\text{Var}(\varphi)}\right) : T \models \varphi, |T| \leq k \right\} \quad \text{for } (\varphi, k) \in \Phi \times \mathbb{N}.$$

We write $\text{ENUMTEAM}(\Phi)$ for $\text{ENUMTEAM}(\Phi, n \mapsto 2^n)$. Since $|T| \leq 2^{|\varphi|}$ holds for every team $T$ for $\varphi$, we effectively eliminate the cardinality constraint. As we shall see, the order in which the teams are outputted plays an important role in the following reasoning. There are two natural orders on teams to consider.

**Definition 11 (Order of cardinality).** *Let $R, S$ be two teams. Then we define a partial order on the set of all teams by $R \leq_{size} S :\Leftrightarrow |R| < |S|$ or $R = S$.*

When a formula $\varphi$ is given, we assume to have a total order $\leq$ on $2^{\text{Var}(\varphi)}$ such that comparing two elements is possible in $\mathcal{O}(|\text{Var}(\varphi)|)$ and iterating over the set of all assignments is feasible with delay $\mathcal{O}(|\text{Var}(\varphi)|)$. When interpreting each assignment as a binary encoded integer, we obtain an appropriate order on $2^{\text{Var}(\varphi)}$ by translating the order on $\mathbb{N}_0$. If necessary, one could demand that adjacent assignments differ in only one place by using the order induced by the Gray code. Now we are able to define the second order.

**Definition 12 (Lexicogr. order).** *Let $R = \{r_1, \ldots, r_n\}$ and $S = \{s_1, \ldots, s_m\}$ be two teams such that $r_1 < \cdots < r_n$ and $s_1 < \cdots < s_m$. Let $i$ be the maximum over all $j \in \mathbb{N}_0$ such that $j \leq \min(n, m)$, $r_\ell = s_\ell$ for all $\ell \in \{1, \ldots, j\}$. Then we define a partial order on $\mathcal{P}\left(2^{Var(\varphi)}\right)$ by*

$$R \leq_{lex} S :\Leftrightarrow \begin{cases} n \leq m, & i = \min(n, m) \\ r_{i+1} < s_{i+1}, & else. \end{cases}$$

Observe that the lexicographical order is a total order that does not extend the order of cardinality. For example, we have $\{00, 01, 10\} <_{\text{lex}} \{00, 10\}$ when assignments are ordered according to their integer representation.

**Problem 3.** Let $\Phi$ be a class of team-based propositional formulas and $f \colon \mathbb{N} \to \mathbb{N}$ be a computable function. We define $\text{ENUMTEAMSIZE}(\Phi, f) := (\Phi, \text{Sol}, \leq_{\text{size}})$ with Sol as in Problem 1. P-$\text{ENUMTEAMSIZE}$ is defined accordingly.

### 3.1   Enumeration in Poor Man's Propositional Dependence Logic

Now, we start with the task of enumerating satisfying teams for the fragment $\mathcal{PDL}^-$, i.e., Poor Man's Propositional Logic. The delay of the resulting algorithm is polynomial regarding the size of the input and the maximal size of an outputted teams. As teams may grow exponentially large according to the input size, the delay will not be polynomial in the classical sense of DelayP. As a result, we proceed to DelayFPT and set the maximal cardinality of outputted teams as the parameter. Note that the drawback of having a polynomial delay in the output is minor. When following algorithms process the outputted teams, they have to input them first, requiring at least linear time in the output size.

In fact, we will see that we cannot obtain a DelayP-algorithm when the output is sorted by cardinality. This sorting, however, is an inherent characteristic of our algorithm as satisfying teams of cardinality $k$ are constructed by analysing those of cardinality $k - 1$.

Before diving into details, we would like to introduce some notation used in this section. Let $\varphi \in \mathcal{PDL}^-$ be fixed, $k \in \mathbb{N}_0$,

$$n := |\mathrm{Var}(\varphi)|,$$
$$\mathcal{T}_k := \left\{ T \in \mathcal{P}\left( 2^{\mathrm{Var}(\varphi)} \right) : T \models \varphi, |T| = k \right\},$$
$$\mathcal{T}_k^0 := \{ T \in \mathcal{T}_k : (\forall x \in \mathrm{Var}(\varphi) : x \mapsto 0) \in T \},$$
$$t_k := |\mathcal{T}_k|,$$
$$t_k^0 := |\mathcal{T}_k^0|.$$

An assignment $s \in 2^{\mathrm{Var}(\varphi)}$ is depicted as a sequence of 0 and 1, precisely: $s = s(x_1)s(x_2)\ldots s(x_n)$.

*Example 1.* For $\varphi := \ =(x_1, x_2)$ we have: $n = 2$ and consequently

$$\mathcal{T}_2 = \{\{00, 10\}, \{00, 11\}, \{01, 10\}, \{01, 11\}\},$$
$$\mathcal{T}_2^0 = \{\{00, 10\}, \{00, 11\}\},$$
$$\mathcal{T}_3 = \mathcal{T}_3^0 = \emptyset.$$

Note that formulas of the form $\varphi \equiv \left( \bigwedge_{x \in I} x \right) \wedge \left( \bigwedge_{x \in J} \neg x \right) \wedge \left( \bigwedge_{\ell \in L} =(P_\ell, Q_\ell) \right)$ can be simplified w.l.o.g. to

$$\varphi' := \bigwedge_{\ell \in L} =(P_\ell', Q_\ell') \quad \text{with} \quad P_\ell' := P_\ell \setminus (I \cup J), \ Q_\ell' := Q_\ell \setminus (I \cup J). \qquad (\star)$$

Then all satisfying teams for $\varphi$ can be recovered by extending those for $\varphi'$. For instance, the formula

$$x_3 \wedge =(\{x_1\}, \{x_2, x_3\}) \wedge =(\{x_4\}, \{x_2, x_3\})$$

may be reduced to $=(x_1, x_2) \wedge =(x_4, x_2)$. The team $\{00-0, 00-1\}$ satisfies the latter formula ('$-$' indicates the missing $x_3$) and is extended to $\{0010, 0011\}$ in order to satisfy the former one.

**The Group Action of Flipping Bits.** By the semantics of $=(\cdot)$ we see that flipping the bit at a fixed position in all assignments of a team $T$ is an invariant for $T \models =(P,Q)$. For example, the teams $\{00, 10\}$ and $\{00, 11\}$ satisfy $=(x_1, x_2)$. The remaining 2-teams satisfying the formula are given by $\{01, 11\}$ and $\{01, 10\}$. Note that these teams may be constructed from the previous ones by flipping the value of $x_2$. Accordingly, it would be enough to compute the satisfying teams $\{00, 10\}$ and $\{00, 11\}$, constructing the other 2-teams by flipping bits. The concept of computing a minor set of satisfying $k$-Teams and constructing the remaining ones by flipping bits is the main concept of our algorithm for ensuring FPT-delay.

By identifying each assignment $s$ with the vector $(s(x_1), \ldots, s(x_n))$ we obtain a bijection of sets $\mathbb{F}_2^n \leftrightarrow 2^{\mathrm{Var}(\varphi)}$. We will switch between interpreting an element as an assignment or an $\mathbb{F}_2$-vector as necessary, leading to expressions like $s + t$ for assignments $s$ and $t$. Those may seem confusing at first, but become obvious when interpreting $s$ and $t$ as vectors. Vice versa, we will consider $\mathbb{F}_2$-vectors as assignments that may be contained in a team. When both notations are to be used, this is indicated by taking $s \in \mathbb{F}_2^n \cong 2^{\mathrm{Var}(\varphi)}$ instead of simply writing $s \in \mathbb{F}_2^n$ or $s \in 2^{\mathrm{Var}(\varphi)}$.

**Definition 13 (Group action of flipping bits).** *By the observation after Definition 8 the group action of $(\mathbb{F}_2^n, +)$ on itself induces a group action of $\mathbb{F}_2^n$ on $\mathcal{P}(\mathbb{F}_2^n)$. On that account we obtain a group action $\mathbb{F}_2^n \circlearrowright \mathcal{P}\left(2^{\mathrm{Var}(\varphi)}\right)$, called group action of flipping bits.*

Let $e_i$ be the $i$-th standard vector of $\mathbb{F}_2^n$. Then the operation of $e_i$ on $\mathcal{P}\left(2^{\mathrm{Var}(\varphi)}\right)$ corresponds to flipping the value for $x_i$ in each assignment of a team.

**Theorem 1.** *Let $k \in \mathbb{N}$. The restriction of $\mathbb{F}_2^n \circlearrowright \mathcal{P}(\mathbb{F}_2^n)$ on $\mathcal{T}_k$ yields a group action $\mathbb{F}_2^n \circlearrowright \mathcal{T}_k$.*

*Proof.* As the axioms of group actions still hold on a subset of $\mathcal{P}(\mathbb{F}_2^n)$, it remains to show that $zT \in \mathcal{T}_k \quad \forall z \in \mathbb{F}_2^n, T \in \mathcal{T}_k$. Let $z \in \mathbb{F}_2^n$ and $T \in \mathcal{T}_k$. By the remark following Definition 8 we have $|zT| = k$. Let $P \subseteq \mathrm{Var}(\varphi)$ and $s, t \in 2^{\mathrm{Var}(\varphi)}$. If $s', t' \in 2^{\mathrm{Var}(\varphi)}$ arise from $s, t$ by flipping the value for a variable $x_i$, then obviously $s|_P = t|_P \Leftrightarrow s'|_P = t'|_P$. It follows that $T \models =(P,Q) \Leftrightarrow zT \models =(P,Q)$ for all $P, Q \subseteq \mathrm{Var}(\varphi)$. When assuming that $\varphi$ has the form of $(\star)$, it clearly holds that $zT \models \varphi$ because of $T \models \varphi$. This proves $zT \in \mathcal{T}_k$. ∎

**Lemma 2.** *Let $T \in \mathcal{T}_k$, $k \in \mathbb{N}$. Then, we have that $\mathbb{F}_2^n T \cap \mathcal{T}_k^0 \neq \emptyset$. For this reason $\mathcal{T}_k^0$ contains a representative systems for the orbits of $\mathbb{F}_2^n \circlearrowright \mathcal{T}_k$.*

*Proof.* Take $s \in T \subseteq 2^{\mathrm{Var}(\varphi)} \cong \mathbb{F}_2^n$. Then $sT \in \mathcal{T}_k^0$ because of $z + z = \vec{0}$ for all $z \in \mathbb{F}_2^n$ ∎

The previous lemma states that we can compute $\mathcal{T}_k$ from $\mathcal{T}_k^0$ by generating orbits. Next we want to present and analyse an algorithm for enumerating those orbits. The results are given in Theorem 2.

**Definition 14.** *Let* $\vec{0} \neq s = (s_1, \ldots, s_n) \in \mathbb{F}_2^n$ *and* $\mathcal{B} \subseteq \mathbb{F}_2^n \setminus \{\vec{0}\}$. *Then we define* $\mathrm{last}(s) := \max\{i \in \{1, \ldots, n\} : s_i = 1\}$, *and* $\mathrm{last}(\mathcal{B}) := \{\mathrm{last}(s) : s \in \mathcal{B}\}$.

**Definition 15.** *Let* $\mathcal{B}$ *be a subset of* $\mathbb{F}_2^n$. *Then the subspace generated by* $\mathcal{B}$ *is defined by* $\mathrm{span}(\mathcal{B}) := \{b_1 + \cdots + b_r : r \in \mathbb{N}_0, \ b_i \in \mathcal{B} \ \forall i \in \{1, \ldots, r\}\}$.

**Lemma 3.** *Let* $U$ *be a subspace of the* $\mathbb{F}_2$*-vector space* $\mathbb{F}_2^n$. *Let* $\mathcal{B} \subseteq U \setminus \{\vec{0}\}$ *be a maximal subset with*

$$b \neq b' \Rightarrow \mathrm{last}(b) \neq \mathrm{last}(b') \quad \forall b, b' \in \mathcal{B}. \tag{1}$$

*Then* $\mathcal{B}$ *is a basis for* $U$.

*Proof.* First we show that any set $A \subseteq U \setminus \{\vec{0}\}$ satisfying (1) is linearly independent. We conduct an induction over $|A|$. For $|A| = 1$ the claim is obvious. Because of (1) there exists an element $a_0 \in A$ with $\mathrm{last}(a_0) > \mathrm{last}(a)$ for all $a_0 \neq a \in A$. When considering the $\mathrm{last}(a_0)$-th component, clearly the equation

$$a_0 = \sum_{a_0 \neq a \in A} \lambda_a a, \quad \lambda_a \in \mathbb{F}_2$$

has no solution. As $A \setminus \{a_0\}$ is linearly independent by induction hypothesis, it follows that A is linearly independent.

Now assume that $\mathcal{B}$ does not generate $U$. We take an element $s \in U \setminus \mathrm{span}(\mathcal{B})$ with minimal $\mathrm{last}(s)$. As $\mathcal{B}$ is a maximal subset fulfilling (1), we have that $\mathrm{last}(b) = \mathrm{last}(s)$ for a suitable element $b \in \mathcal{B}$. But then $s - b \in U \setminus \mathrm{span}(\mathcal{B})$ with $\mathrm{last}(s - b) < \mathrm{last}(s)$ contradicts the minimality of $s$.

**Theorem 2.** *Let* $T \in \mathcal{T}_k$, $k \in \mathbb{N}$. *Then* $\mathbb{F}_2^n T$ *can be enumerated with delay* $\mathcal{O}(k^3 n)$.

*Proof.* W.l.o.g. let $T \in \mathcal{T}_k^0$. Otherwise, consider the team $zT$ with an arbitrary $z \in T$. Note that $T$ may have a nontrivial stabilizer subgroup so that duplicates occur when simply applying each $z \in \mathbb{F}_2^n$ to $T$. However, Proposition 2 states that we can enumerate the orbit of $T$ without duplicates when applying a representative system for $\mathbb{F}_2^n/(\mathbb{F}_2^n)_T$.

When taking $\mathbb{F}_2^n$ as a vector space over $\mathbb{F}_2$, the subspaces of $\mathbb{F}_2^n$ correspond to the subgroups of $(\mathbb{F}_2^n, +)$. In view of this any basis for a complement of the stabilizer subgroup $(\mathbb{F}_2^n)_T$ of $T$ in $\mathbb{F}_2^n$ generates a representative system for $\mathbb{F}_2^n/(\mathbb{F}_2^n)_T$.

Take a basis $\mathcal{B}$ of $(\mathbb{F}_2^n)_T$ as in Lemma 3. Set $\mathcal{C} := \{e_i : i \in \{1, \ldots, n\} \setminus \mathrm{last}(\mathcal{B})\}$, where $e_i$ denotes the $i$-th standard vector of $\mathbb{F}_2^n$. By construction of $\mathcal{C}$ we can arrange the elements of $\mathcal{B} \cup \mathcal{C}$ so that the matrix containing these elements as columns has triangular shape with 1-entries on its diagonal. Consequently $\mathcal{B} \cup \mathcal{C}$ is a basis for $\mathbb{F}_2^n$ and $\mathcal{C}$ is a basis for a complement of $(\mathbb{F}_2^n)_T$. Now it remains to construct $\mathcal{B}$ as desired. For $s \in 2^{\mathrm{Var}(\varphi)} \cong \mathbb{F}_2^n$ we have

$$s \in (\mathbb{F}_2^n)_T \Rightarrow sT = T \Rightarrow s = s + \vec{0} \in T.$$

---

**Algorithm 1.** Enumerating orbits

---

**Input**: A team $T$ with $\vec{0} \in T$
**Output**: The orbit $\mathbb{F}_2^n T$ of $T$ where each outputted team is sorted

```
1  Blast ← ∅;                                    /* Assume that Blast is sorted */
2  for 0̄ ≠ s ∈ T do                              /* < k iterations */
3  |  if last(s) ∈ Blast then continue;          /* O(n) */
4  |  failed ← false;
5  |  for t ∈ T do                               /* ≤ k iterations */
6  |  |  if s + t ∉ T then failed ← true;        /* O(kn) */
7  |  if not failed then Blast ← Blast ∪ {last(s)};  /* O(n) */
8  Clast ← {1,...,n} \ Blast;                     /* O(n) */
9  for s ∈ span({eᵢ : i ∈ Clast}) do
10 |  Compute sT;                                 /* O(kn) */
11 |  Sort sT;                                    /* O(kn log k) */
12 |  output sT;
```

---

As a result, we can compute $(\mathbb{F}_2^n)_T$ by checking $sT = T$ for $|T| = k$ elements in $\mathbb{F}_2^n$. In fact it is enough to check $sT \subseteq T$ as we have $|sT| = |T|$. We obtain $\mathcal{B}$ by inserting each element of $(\mathbb{F}_2^n)_T \setminus \{\vec{0}\}$ preserving (1) into $\mathcal{B}$. This shows that Algorithm 1 outputs $\mathbb{F}_2^n T$ without duplicates. The delay is dominated by the precomputation phase (lines 1 to 8), which is $\mathcal{O}(k^3 n)$. Note that we sort the $k$ assignments of each team in ascending order before returning it.

Finally we would like to relate $t_k$ to $t_k^0$. The larger the quotient $t_k/t_k^0$, the more computation costs are saved by generating orbits instead of computing $\mathcal{T}_k$ immediately.

**Theorem 3.** *Let $k \in \mathbb{N}$ with $t_k \neq 0$. Then, we have that $t_k/t_k^0 = 2^n/k$.*

*Proof.* Because of $t_k \neq 0$ and Lemma 2 it follows that $t_k^0 \neq 0$. For this reason we can choose $T \in \mathcal{T}_k^0$. We claim

$$|\mathbb{F}_2^n T \cap \mathcal{T}_k^0| = \frac{k}{|(\mathbb{F}_2^n)_T|}. \tag{2}$$

For any $s \in 2^{\mathrm{Var}(\varphi)} \cong \mathbb{F}_2^n$ we have that

$$sT \in \mathcal{T}_k^0 \Leftrightarrow \exists t \in T : s + t = \vec{0} \Leftrightarrow \exists t \in T : s = t \Leftrightarrow s \in T. \tag{3}$$

Consequently we have $\mathbb{F}_2^n T \cap \mathcal{T}_k^0 = \{sT : s \in T\} =: TT$. Let $r, s \in T$. Both elements yield the same team $rT = sT$ iff $s \in r(\mathbb{F}_2^n)_T$ so that for any fixed $r \in T$ we find exactly $|r(\mathbb{F}_2^n)_T| = |(\mathbb{F}_2^n)_T|$ ways of expressing $rT$ in the form of $sT$, where $s \in T$ by (3). When iterating over the $k$ elements $sT$, $s \in T$, each team in $TT$ is counted $|(\mathbb{F}_2^n)_T|$ times. It follows that

$$|TT| = \frac{k}{|(\mathbb{F}_2^n)_T|},$$

proving (2).

By Lemma 2 we find a representative system $R \subseteq \mathcal{T}_k^0$ for the orbits of $\mathbb{F}_2^n \circlearrowleft \mathcal{T}_k$. With Eq. (2) and the Orbit-Stabilizer theorem (see Proposition 2) we obtain

$$t_k = \sum_{T \in R} |\mathbb{F}_2^n T| \qquad \text{(by Proposition 1)}$$

$$= \sum_{T \in \mathcal{T}_k^0} \frac{|\mathbb{F}_2^n T|}{|\mathbb{F}_2^n T \cap \mathcal{T}_k^0|}$$

$$= \sum_{T \in \mathcal{T}_k^0} \frac{|(\mathbb{F}_2^n)_T|}{k} \cdot |\mathbb{F}_2^n T| \qquad \text{(by (2))}$$

$$= \sum_{T \in \mathcal{T}_k^0} \frac{|(\mathbb{F}_2^n)_T|}{k} \cdot \frac{2^n}{|(\mathbb{F}_2^n)_T|} \qquad \text{(by Proposition 2)}$$

$$= \frac{2^n}{k} \sum_{T \in \mathcal{T}_k^0} 1$$

$$= \frac{2^n}{k} t_k^0.$$

**Constructing $\mathcal{T}_k^0$.** Now that we are able to construct all satisfying $k$-teams from a representative system, the next step is the construction of $\mathcal{T}_k^0$. For this purpose the concept of coherence will prove useful.

**Definition 16** ([28, Definition 3.1]). *Let $\phi$ be a team-based propositional formula. Then $\phi$ is $k$-coherent iff for all teams $T$ we have that*

$$T \models \phi \Leftrightarrow R \models \phi \, \forall R \subseteq T \text{ with } |R| = k.$$

**Proposition 4** ([28, Proposition 3.3]). *The atom $=(\cdot)$ is 2-coherent.*

**Proposition 5** ([28, Proposition 3.4]). *If $\phi$, $\psi$ are $k$-coherent then $\phi \wedge \psi$ is $k$-coherent.*

Let $T = \{s_1, \ldots, s_k\}$ be a team with $s_1 < \cdots < s_k$, $k \geq 2$. Then write $T_{\text{red}}^1 := \{s_1, \ldots, s_{k-1}\}$, $T_{\text{red}}^2 := \{s_1, \ldots, s_{k-2}, s_k\}$, $\max(T) := s_k$. The following lemma provides a powerful tool for constructing the sets $\mathcal{T}_k^0$.

**Lemma 4.** *Let $T$ be as above and $k := |T| \geq 3$. Then the following are equivalent:*

*1. $T \in \mathcal{T}_k^0$,*
*2. $T_{\text{red}}^1, T_{\text{red}}^2 \in \mathcal{T}_{k-1}^0$ and $\{\vec{0}, s_{k-1} + s_k\} \in \mathcal{T}_2^0$.*

---

**Algorithm 2.** Constructing $\mathcal{T}_k^0$

---

**Input:** $k \in \mathbb{N}$, $k \geq 2$
**Dependencies:** If $k > 2$: $\mathcal{D}_2[\{\vec{0}\}]$, $\mathcal{D}_{k-1}$ of the previous iteration
**Result:** $\mathcal{T}_k^0$

```
1  𝒯ₖ⁰ ← ∅, 𝒟ₖ ← new Map(Team, List(Assignment));
2  if k = 2 then
3  |    𝒟₂[{0⃗}] ← ∅;
4  |    for 0⃗ ≠ s ∈ 2^Var(φ) do                          /* ≤ 2ⁿ iterations */
5  |    |    if {0⃗, s} ⊨ φ then                           /* 𝒪(|φ|) */
6  |    |    |    𝒟₂[{0⃗}] ← 𝒟₂[{0⃗}] ∪ {s};                /* 𝒪(n) */
7  |    |    |    𝒯₂⁰ ← 𝒯₂⁰ ∪ {0⃗, s};                     /* 𝒪(n) */
8  else
9  |    for (T, L) ∈ 𝒟ₖ₋₁ do
10 |    |    for r ∈ L do                                 /* t⁰ₖ₋₁ iterations */
11 |    |    |    T' ← T ∪ {r}, 𝒟ₖ[T'] ← ∅;
12 |    |    |    for s ∈ L with s > r do                  /* ≤ 2ⁿ iterations */
13 |    |    |    |    if r + s ∈ 𝒟₂[{0⃗}] then             /* 𝒪(n) */
14 |    |    |    |    |    𝒟ₖ[T'] ← 𝒟ₖ[T'] ∪ {s};         /* 𝒪(kn) */
15 |    |    |    |    |    𝒯ₖ⁰ ← 𝒯ₖ⁰ ∪ {T' ∪ {s}};        /* 𝒪(kn) */
```

---

Algorithm 2 computes the sets $\mathcal{T}_k^0$ by exploiting the previous lemma. In order to ensure fast list operations, we manage teams in tries [29, Chap. 6.3]. Since any team of cardinality $k$ may be described by $kn$ bits, the standard list operations as searching, insertion and deletion are realised in $\mathcal{O}(kn)$. We organise satisfying teams such that all teams of cardinality $k$ which only differ in their maximal assignment are described by a list $\mathcal{D}_k[T']$, where $T'$ is the team containing the common $k - 1$ smaller assignments. It suffices to store the maximal assignment of each team $T$ described in $\mathcal{D}_k[T']$ since $T$ may be recovered by $T'$ and $\max(T)$. Hence $\mathcal{D}_k$ becomes a collection of lists indexed by teams of cardinality $k - 1$. The following lemma states the correct construction of $\mathcal{D}_k$ in Algorithm 2.

**Lemma 5.** *Let $k \geq 2$. For $T \in \mathcal{T}_k^0$ we have that $\max(T) \in \mathcal{D}_k[T_{\mathrm{red}}^1]$. Vice versa, if $s \in \mathcal{D}_k[T]$, then it follows that $T \cup \{s\} \in \mathcal{T}_k^0$ and $s > \max(T)$.*

**Corollary 1.** *Algorithm 2 correctly constructs the sets $\mathcal{T}_k^0$ and it requires time $t_{k-1}^0 \cdot 2^n \cdot \mathcal{O}(k|\varphi|)$ on input $k \in \mathbb{N}$.*

Although by Corollary 1 Algorithm 2 does not perform in polynomial time on input $k \subset \mathbb{N}$, we can ensure polynomial delay when distributing its execution over the process of outputting all satisfying teams of cardinality $k - 1$. For this reason we investigate the costs of computing $\mathcal{T}_k^0$ divided by $t_{k-1}$. With Corollary 1 and $k - 1 = \frac{t_{k-1}^0 \cdot 2^n}{t_{k-1}}$, which is a transformation of the equation in Theorem 3, we obtain

---

**Algorithm 3.** Enumerating satisfying teams in $\mathcal{PDL}^-$, ordered by cardinality

---

**Input**: A team-based propositional formula $\varphi$ as in Equation $(\star)$, $k \in \mathbb{N}$
**Output**: All teams $T$ for $\varphi$ with $T \models \varphi$, $1 \leq |T| \leq k$

1   $\mathcal{T}_1^0 \leftarrow \{\{\vec{0}\}\}$;
2   **for** $\ell = 2, \ldots, k+1$ **do**
3      **simultaneously**
4         **while** $\mathcal{T}_{\ell-1}^0 \neq \emptyset$ **do**
5            Choose $T \in \mathcal{T}_{\ell-1}^0$;
6            **for** $T' \in \mathbb{F}_2^n T$ (Algorithm 1) **do output** $T'$ and $\mathcal{T}_{\ell-1}^0 \leftarrow \mathcal{T}_{\ell-1}^0 \setminus \{T'\}$ ;
7      **simultaneously** Compute $\mathcal{T}_\ell^0$ by Algorithm 2;
8      **if** $\mathcal{T}_\ell^0 = \emptyset$ **then break**;

---

$$\frac{\text{computationCosts}(\mathcal{T}_k^0)}{t_{k-1}} = \frac{t_{k-1}^0 \cdot 2^n \cdot \mathcal{O}(k|\varphi|)}{t_{k-1}} = (k-1) \cdot \mathcal{O}(k|\varphi|) = \mathcal{O}(k^2|\varphi|).$$

Since the delay of generating the orbits $\mathbb{F}_2^n T$ is $\mathcal{O}(k^3 n)$ by Theorem 2, the overall delay of Algorithm 3 is bounded by $\mathcal{O}(k^3|\varphi|)$. Note that the cost of removing elements in $\mathcal{T}_k^0$, which is $\mathcal{O}(kn)$, is contained in $\mathcal{O}(k^3|\varphi|)$. Proposition 1 and Lemma 2 witness a correct enumeration of Algorithm 2 without duplicates. In practise, we interleave both computation strands by executing $k$ iterations of the loop at line 12 in Algorithm 2 whenever a team is outputted. Finally, we conclude.

**Theorem 4.** *1.* P-ENUMTEAMSIZE($\mathcal{PDL}^-$) $\in$ DelayFPT,
*2.* ENUMTEAMSIZE($\mathcal{PDL}^-, f$) $\in$ DelayP *for any poly. time computable function* $f \in n^{\mathcal{O}(1)}$.

**Consequences of Sorting by Cardinality.** In the previous section we have seen that the restriction on polynomial teams is sufficient to obtain a DelayP-algorithm for $\mathcal{PDL}^-$. As we will see in this section, the restriction is not only sufficient, but also necessary when the output is sorted by its cardinality. Consequently, the algorithm presented above is optimal regarding output size.

**Lemma 6.** *Let* $k \geq 2$ *and* $\varphi(x_1, \ldots, x_k) := \bigwedge_{i=1}^{k-1} =(x_i, x_k) \in \mathcal{PDL}^-$. *Then for any team* $T \neq \emptyset$ *with* $T \models \varphi$ *and* $|T| \geq 3$ *we have that* $\left| T|_{\{x_k\}} \right| = 1$.

**Theorem 5.** *Let $f$ be a polynomial time computable function. Then we have that* ENUMTEAMSIZE($\mathcal{PDL}^-, f$) $\in$ DelayP *if and only if* $f \in n^{\mathcal{O}(1)}$.

*Proof.* "$\Leftarrow$": immediately follows from Theorem 4.
"$\Rightarrow$": Let $f \notin n^{\mathcal{O}(1)}$. Assume that ENUMTEAMSIZE($\mathcal{PDL}^-, f$) $\in$ DelayP holds via an algorithm with a delay bounded by $n^c$, $c \in \mathbb{N}$. Then there exists $k \in \mathbb{N}$ such that $z := \min\{f(k), 2^{k-1}\} > 4^c \cdot k^c \geq k \geq 3$. Let $\varphi$ be as in Lemma 6.

Obviously, there exist teams $T_0, T_1 \in \mathcal{T}_z$ with $s(x_k) = i$ for all $s \in T_i$, $i \in \{0, 1\}$. Since the elements in $\mathcal{T}_z$ have to be outputted in succession and $\left| T \right|_{\{x_k\}} = 1$ for any $T \in \mathcal{T}_z$, we can choose $T_0$ and $T_1$ such that both teams are outputted in consecutive order. However, both teams differ in at least $z$ bits describing the evaluation at $x_k$. For this reason the delay is at least $z > (4k)^c \geq (|\varphi|)^c$, contradicting that the delay is bounded by $n^c$.

**Corollary 2.** ENUMTEAMSIZE($\mathcal{PDL}^-$) $\notin$ DelayP.

The trick of examining the symmetric difference of consecutive teams gives rise to the previous theorem. Unfortunately this trick cannot be applied to arbitrary orders and certainly fails for the lexicographical order. In order to prove this claim, consider Theorem 6 with $S = 2^{\mathrm{Var}(\varphi)}$, $X = \{T \in \mathcal{P}\left(2^{\mathrm{Var}(\varphi)}\right) : T \models \varphi\}$.

**Theorem 6.** Let $S = \{s_1, \ldots, s_n\}$ be a finite totally ordered set and $X \subseteq \mathcal{P}(S)$ be a downward closed set, meaning $T \in X \Rightarrow R \in X \; \forall R \subseteq T$. When $X$ is ordered lexicographically in respect with the order on $S$, the symmetric difference $\triangle$ between two consecutive elements in $X$ is at most 3.

## 3.2   Limiting Memory Space

Next we examine the memory usage of Algorithm 3. Throughout the execution, $\mathcal{D}_2[\{\vec{0}\}]$, $\mathcal{D}_k$ and $\mathcal{T}_k^0$ have to be saved. However the size of those lists increases exponentially when raising the size of the outputted teams or the amount of variables occurring in the formula $\varphi$. In general, Algorithm 3 requires space $\mathcal{O}(2^{2^n})$, and $\mathcal{O}(2^n)$ when fixing the parameter $k$. In fact, any algorithm that saves a representative system for the orbits of $\mathbb{F}_2^n \circlearrowleft \mathcal{T}_k$ cannot perform in polynomial space by the following theorem. For this reason we have to discard the group action of flipping bits when limiting memory space to polynomial sizes.

**Theorem 7.** Let $1 \neq k \in \mathbb{N}$ and $n \in \mathbb{N}$. We set $\varphi := \, =(x_1, x_2, \ldots, x_n)$. Then the amount of orbits of $\mathbb{F}_2^n \circlearrowleft \mathcal{T}_k$ is not polynomial in $n$.

In the previous sections we had to limit the cardinality of outputted teams for obtaining polynomial delay. As the following theorem shows, this measure is necessary as well when demanding polynomial space.

**Theorem 8.** Let $\Phi$ be any fragment of team-based propositional logic and $f$ be a function with $f \notin n^{\mathcal{O}(1)}$ such that for any $n \in \mathbb{N}$ there exists a formula $\varphi_n \in \Phi$ in $n$ variables with at least $2^{f(n)}$ satisfying teams. Then it follows that ENUMTEAM($\Phi$) cannot be enumerated in polynomial space.

**Corollary 3.** The problem ENUMTEAM($\mathcal{PDL}^-$) cannot be enumerated in polynomial space.

---

**Algorithm 4.** Enumerating satisfying teams in polynomial space, ordered by cardinality

---

**Input**: A team-based propositional formula $\varphi$ as in Equation $(\star)$
**Output**: All teams $T$ for $\varphi$ with $T \models \varphi$, $1 \leq |T| \leq f(|\varphi|)$

1  **for** $k = 1, \ldots, f(|\varphi|)$ **do**
2  $\quad$ $T \leftarrow \{s_{\text{first}}\}$;
3  $\quad$ **while true do**
4  $\quad\quad$ **if** $|T| = k$ and $T \models \varphi$ **then output** $T$;
5  $\quad\quad$ $s \leftarrow \max(T)$;
6  $\quad\quad$ **if** $|T| < k$ and $T \models \varphi$ and $s \in$ hasNext **then** $T \leftarrow T \cup \{\text{next}(s)\}$ ;
7  $\quad\quad$ **else if** $s \in$ hasNext **then** $T \leftarrow T \setminus \{s\} \cup \{\text{next}(s)\}$ ;
8  $\quad\quad$ **else if** —T— ¿ 1 **then**
9  $\quad\quad\quad$ $\mid$ $T \leftarrow T \setminus \{s\}$, $s \leftarrow \max(T)$, $T \leftarrow T \setminus \{s\} \cup \{\text{next}(s)\}$;
10 $\quad\quad$ **else break**;

---

We now present an algorithm enumerating $\textsc{EnumTeamSize}(\mathcal{PDL}^-, f)$ for any $f \in n^{\mathcal{O}(1)}$ in polynomial space. Compared to Algorithm 3, it saves memory space by recomputing the satisfying teams of lower cardinality instead of storing them in a list. As a downside we have to accept incremental delays.

Then, we define a unary relation hasNext on $2^{\text{Var}(\varphi)}$ by $s \in$ hasNext if and only if $\exists t \in 2^{\text{Var}(\varphi)} : s < t$. For any $s \in$ hasNext let $\text{next}(s)$ be the unambiguous assignment such that $s < \text{next}(s)$ holds but $s < t < \text{next}(s)$ does not hold for any assignment $t$. We denote the smallest element in $2^{\text{Var}(\varphi)}$ by $s_{\text{first}}$. The largest element is denoted by $s_{\text{last}}$. As already mentioned when defining the lexicographical order, we assume that hasNext, next and $s_{\text{first}}$ may be determined in $\mathcal{O}(n)$ time.

**Theorem 9.** *Let* $f \in n^{\mathcal{O}(1)}$ *be a polynomial time computable function. Then Algorithm 4 is an* IncP-*algorithm for* $\textsc{EnumTeamSize}(\mathcal{PDL}^-, f)$ *which performs in polynomial space.*

## 4   Conclusion

In this paper we have shown that the task of enumerating all satisfying teams of a given propositional dependence logic formula without split junction is a hard task when sorting the output by its cardinality, i.e., only for polynomially sized teams, we constructed a DelayP algorithm. In the unrestricted cases, we showed that the problem is in DelayFPT when the parameter is chosen to be the team size. Further, we explained that the algorithm is optimal regarding its output size and pointed out that any algorithm saving a representative system for the orbits of $\mathbb{F}_2^n \circlearrowleft \mathcal{T}_k$ cannot perform in polynomial space.

Furthermore, we want to point out that allowing for split junction (and accordingly talking about full $\mathcal{PDL}$) will not yield any DelayFPT or DelayP algorithms in our setting unless P = NP.

Lastly, we would like to mention that the algorithms enumerating orbits and the satisfying teams, respectively, can be modified such that satisfying teams for formulas of the form $\varphi_1 \lor \varphi_2 \lor \cdots \lor \varphi_r$ with $r \in \mathbb{N}$, $\varphi_i \in \mathcal{PDL}^-$ can be enumerated, where $\lor$ is the classical disjunction. The idea is to merge the outputs $\mathrm{Sol}(\varphi_i)$, $i \in \{1, \ldots, r\}$, which is possible in polynomial delay if the output for each $\varphi_i$ is pre-sorted according to a total order.

By now, we presented an algorithm that sorts the output by cardinality. It remains open to identify the enumeration complexity of Poor Man's Propositional Dependence Logic when other orders, e.g., the lexicographical order, are considered. Besides, one can investigate the conjunction free fragment of $\mathcal{PDL}$, permitting the split junction operator but no conjunction operator. Similarly to the Poor Man's fragment, one can assume that the group action of flipping bits is an invariant for satisfying teams when formulas are simplified properly. Nonetheless, the 2-coherence property is lost so that the algorithm for constructing the sets $T_k^0$ fails.

Finally, we want to close with some questions. Are there exact connections or translations to concrete fragments of SQL or relational algebra (relational calculus)? Currently, propositional dependence logic can be understood as relational algebra on a finite (and two valued) domain. Do the presented enumeration algorithms mirror or even improve known algorithmic tasks in database theory? Are there better fragments or extensions of $\mathcal{PDL}^-$ with a broader significance for practice?

**Acknowledgements.** We thank the anonymous referees for their valuable comments.

# References

1. Johnson, D.S., Yannakakis, M., Papadimitriou, C.H.: On generating all maximal independent sets. Inf. Process. Lett. **27**(3), 119–123 (1988)
2. Schmidt, J.: Enumeration: algorithms and complexity. Master's thesis, Leibniz Universität Hannover & Université de la Méditerranée Aix-Marseille II (2009). https://www.thi.uni-hannover.de/fileadmin/forschung/arbeiten/schmidt-da.pdf
3. Strozecki, Y.: Enumeration complexity and matroid decomposition. Ph.D. thesis, Université Paris Diderot – Paris 7 (2010). http://www.prism.uvsq.fr/~ystr/these_strozecki
4. Carmeli, N., Kenig, B., Kimelfeld, B.: Efficiently enumerating minimal triangulations. In: Sallinger, E., den Bussche, J.V., Geerts, F. (eds.) Proceedings of the 36th ACM SIGMOD-SIGACT-SIGAI Symposium on Principles of Database Systems, PODS 2017, Chicago, IL, USA, 14–19 May 2017, pp. 273–287. ACM (2017)
5. Khachiyan, L.G., Boros, E., Elbassioni, K.M., Gurvich, V., Makino, K.: On the complexity of some enumeration problems for matroids. SIAM J. Discret. Math. **19**(4), 966–984 (2005)
6. Downey, R.G., Fellows, M.R.: Fundamentals of Parameterized Complexity. Texts in Computer Science. Springer, London (2013). https://doi.org/10.1007/978-1-4471-5559-1
7. Downey, R.G., Fellows, M.R.: Parameterized Complexity. Monographs in Computer Science. Springer, New York (1999). https://doi.org/10.1007/978-1-4612-0515-9

8. Creignou, N., Meier, A., Müller, J., Schmidt, J., Vollmer, H.: Paradigms for parameterized enumeration. Theory Comput. Syst. **60**(4), 737–758 (2017)
9. Creignou, N., Ktari, R., Meier, A., Müller, J.-S., Olive, F., Vollmer, H.: Parameterized enumeration for modification problems. In: Dediu, A.-H., Formenti, E., Martín-Vide, C., Truthe, B. (eds.) LATA 2015. LNCS, vol. 8977, pp. 524–536. Springer, Cham (2015). https://doi.org/10.1007/978-3-319-15579-1_41
10. Väänänen, J.: Dependence Logic. Cambridge University Press, Cambridge (2007)
11. Hodges, W.: Compositional semantics for a language of imperfect information. Logic J. IGPL **5**(4), 539–563 (1997)
12. Abramsky, S., Kontinen, J., Väänänen, J.A., Vollmer, H.: Dependence logic: theory and applications (dagstuhl seminar 13071). Dagstuhl Rep. **3**(2), 45–54 (2013)
13. Fagin, R.: A normal form for relational databases that is based on domains and keys. ACM Trans. Database Syst. **6**(3), 387–415 (1981)
14. Casanova, M.A., Fagin, R., Papadimitriou, C.H.: Inclusion dependencies and their interaction with functional dependencies. J. Comput. Syst. Sci. **28**(1), 29–59 (1984)
15. Casanova, M.A., Vidal, V.M.P.: Towards a sound view integration methodology. In: Proceedings of the 2nd ACM SIGACT-SIGMOD Symposium on Principles of Database Systems, PODS 1983, pp. 36–47. ACM, New York (1983)
16. Galliani, P.: Inclusion and exclusion dependencies in team semantics – on some logics of imperfect information. Ann. Pure Appl. Logic **163**(1), 68–84 (2012)
17. Grädel, E., Väänänen, J.A.: Dependence and independence. Stud. Logica **101**(2), 399–410 (2013)
18. Hannula, M., Kontinen, J., Virtema, J.: Polyteam semantics. CoRR abs/1704.02158 (2017)
19. Hannula, M., Kontinen, J., Virtema, J., Vollmer, H.: Complexity of propositional logics in team semantics. CoRR, extended version of [30] abs/1504.06135 (2015)
20. Hella, L., Kuusisto, A., Meier, A., Virtema, J.: Model checking and validity in propositional and modal inclusion logics. CoRR abs/1609.06951 (2016)
21. Ebbing, J., Lohmann, P.: Complexity of model checking for modal dependence logic. In: Bieliková, M., Friedrich, G., Gottlob, G., Katzenbeisser, S., Turán, G. (eds.) SOFSEM 2012. LNCS, vol. 7147, pp. 226–237. Springer, Heidelberg (2012). https://doi.org/10.1007/978-3-642-27660-6_19
22. Lohmann, P., Vollmer, H.: Complexity results for modal dependence logic. Stud. Logica **101**(2), 343–366 (2013)
23. Hemaspaandra, E.: The complexity of poor man's logic. J. Logic Comput. **11**(4), 609–622 (2001)
24. Meier, A., Reinbold, C.: Enumeration complexity of poor man's propositional dependence logic. CoRR abs/1704.03292 (2017)
25. van Emde Boas, P.: Machine models and simulations. In: Leeuwen, J.V. (ed.) Algorithms and Complexity. Handbook of Theoretical Computer Science, pp. 1–66. Elsevier, Amsterdam (1990)
26. Durand, A., Kontinen, J., Vollmer, H.: Expressivity and complexity of dependence logic. In: Abramsky, S., Kontinen, J., Väänänen, J., Vollmer, H. (eds.) Dependence Logic: Theory and Applications, pp. 5–32. Birkhäuser (2016). https://doi.org/10.1007/978-3-319-31803-5_2
27. Rotman, J.J.: An Introduction to the Theory of Groups. Graduate Texts in Mathematics, vol. 148. Springer, Heidelberg (1995). https://doi.org/10.1007/978-1-4612-4176-8
28. Kontinen, J.: Coherence and computational complexity of quantifier-free dependence logic formulas. Stud. Logica **101**(2), 267–291 (2013)

29. Knuth, D.: The Art of Computer Programming, Volume 3: Sorting and Searching, 2nd edn. Addison-Wesley, Boston (1998)
30. Hannula, M., Kontinen, J., Virtema, J., Vollmer, H.: Complexity of propositional independence and inclusion logic. In: Italiano, G.F., Pighizzini, G., Sannella, D.T. (eds.) MFCS 2015. LNCS, vol. 9234, pp. 269–280. Springer, Heidelberg (2015). https://doi.org/10.1007/978-3-662-48057-1_21

# Refining Semantic Matching for Job Recruitment: An Application of Formal Concept Analysis

Gábor Rácz, Attila Sali$^{(\boxtimes)}$, and Klaus-Dieter Schewe

Alfréd Rényi Institute of Mathematics, Hungarian Academy of Sciences, Budapest P.O.B.127, 1364, Hungary
gabee33@gmail.com, sali.attila@renyi.mta.hu, kd.schewe@acm.org

**Abstract.** A profile describes a set of skills a person may have or a set of skills required for a particular job. Profile matching aims to determine how well the given profile fits the requested profile. Skills are organized into ontologies that form a lattice by the specialization relation. Matching functions were defined based on filters of the lattice generated by the profiles. In the present paper the ontology lattice is extended by additional information in form of so called extra edges that represent some kind of quantifiable relationship between skills. This allows refinement of profile matching based on these relations between skills. However, that may introduce directed cycles and lattice structure is lost. We show a construction of weighted directed acyclic graphs that gets rid of the cycles, and then present a way to use formal concept analysis to gain back the lattice structure and the ability to apply filters. We also give sharp estimates how the sizes of the original ontology lattice and our new constructions relate.

## 1 Introduction

A profile describes a set of properties and profile matching is concerned with the problem to determine how well a given profile fits to a requested one. Profile matching appears in many application areas such as matching applicants for job requirements, matching buyers' requirements with goods advertised such as used cars, etc.

An early idea of profile matching was considering profiles as sets of unrelated items. Then one tries to measure the similarity or distance of sets. Several ways of definition of distances of sets were introduced, such as Jaccard or Sørensen-Dice measures [13] turned out to be useful in ecological applications. However, skills or properties included in profiles are usually not totally unrelated items, implications or dependencies exist between them and need to be taken into

The research of the first author of this paper has been partly supported by the Austrian Ministry for Transport, Innovation and Technology, the Federal Ministry of Science, Research and Economy, and the Province of Upper Austria in the frame of the COMET center SCCH.

© Springer International Publishing AG, part of Springer Nature 2018
F. Ferrarotti and S. Woltran (Eds.): FoIKS 2018, LNCS 10833, pp. 322–339, 2018.
https://doi.org/10.1007/978-3-319-90050-6_18

account. For example, in the human resources area several taxonomies for skills, competences and education such us DISCO [1], ISCED [2] and ISCO [3] have been set up. These taxonomies organize the individual properties into a lattice structure. Popov and Jebelean [18] proposed defining an asymmetric matching measure on the basis of filters in such lattices.

Besides the subsumption relations of the ontology lattice other "horizontal" relations between skills exist. The existence of some skills imply that the applicant may have some other skills with certain probabilities, or of some (not complete) proficiency level. For example, we may reasonably assume that knowledge of Java implies knowledge of NetBeans up to a grade of 0.7 or with probability 0.7. This kind of interdependencies were exploited in [19]. The idea is that a job application is considered better than another one for a given offer profile even if they match equally using filter methods, if the first one has more skills implied in the "fractional" way that match the offer, than the second application has. In this way we get a refinement of the matching hierarchy given by previous methods.

The subsumption hierarchy of the ontology of skills was considered as a directed graph with edge weights 1. A lattice filter generated by a profile corresponded to the set of nodes reachable from the profile's nodes in the directed graph. Then extra edges were added with weights representing the probability/grade of the implication between skills or properties. This introduced the possibility of directed cycles. Filters of application profiles are replaced by nodes reachable in the extended graph from the profile's nodes. For each vertex $x$ reached a probability/grade was assigned, the largest probability/weight of a path from the profile's nodes to $x$. Path probability/weight was defined as the product of probabilities of edges of the path. This process resulted in a set of nodes, which we call *derived skills*, with grades between zero and one, so it was natural interpreting it as a fuzzy set. It was proved that it's a fuzzy filter as defined in [11,14].

In the present paper we provide a construction that gets rid of directed cycles caused by the extra edges. In doing so we show that all matching results that can be obtained by exploiting extra edges can also be obtained from an extended lattice without such extra edges. That is, the theory of profile matching remains within the filter-based approach that we developed in [17], which underlines the power and universality of this theory. In particular, we emphasised how to obtain the lattices underlying the matching theory from knowledge bases that define concepts used in job and candidate profiles. These knowledge bases are grounded in description logics, so the lattice extensions provide also feedback for fine-tuning the knowledge representation, whereas weighted extra-edges are not supported in the knowledge bases. Furthermore, we also showed in [17] that under mild plausibility constraints on human-defined matchings appropriate weights can be defined such that the filter-based matchings preserve the human-defined rankings, which further enables linear optimization to synchronize matchings with human expertise.

The extension is done by extending the ontology lattice by new nodes and weighting of the nodes. The result is a directed acyclic graph, whose structure reflects the different possible path lengths between nodes of the ontology lattice. A directed acyclic graph naturally represents a poset, however that is not a lattice in general. In order to gain back the lattice structure formal concept analysis is used.

While extension of applications by skills derived using extra edges is natural, as employers may benefit from these skills, it is not so clear whether the offer profiles should be extended. On one hand, profiles should be handled uniformly, since a profile could represent both, application, as well as offer. On the other hand, if offers are also extended with derived skills, then it may happen that an application scores high match by having only these derived skills, not the ones in the original offer. This situation may not be so advantageous. In the present paper we discuss both scenarios, the latter one is treated by applying different weighting functions for applications and offers.

The paper is organized as follows. Section 2 introduces the basic concepts and definitions, furthermore the matching functions studied. Section 3 deals with the construction of directed extension graph and formal concept lattice. We also give node weightings that preserve the weights of fuzzy filters assuming that offers are also extended with derived skills. Section 4 discusses related extremal problems, that is how the sizes of the constructed structures relate to the size of the original ontology lattice. We show that our obtained bounds are sharp. Section 5 contains the analysis when offers are not extended by derived skills, just by those that are reachable via lattice (ontology) edges. In order to preserve the weights of fuzzy filters we have to give different node weights for offers from the weights of applications. Section 6 surveys related results, while Sect. 7 is a summary.

## 2    Semantic Matching

Semantic matching has various application areas from dating applications to online product searching tools. We approach the problem from the field of human resources, namely we search for the best fitting application for a given job.

Formally, let $S = \{s_1, \ldots, s_n\}$ be a set of skills. A job offer $O = \{o_1, \ldots, o_k\}$ is a subset of $S$ that contains the skills that are required for the job. An application $A = \{a_1, \ldots, a_l\}$ is also a subset of $S$ that represents skills of the applicant. Our task is to find the most suitable applicant for a given job. Let $match :$ $\mathcal{P}(S) \times \mathcal{P}(S) \rightarrow [0,1]$ be a matching function that determines how well an application fits to a job offer. If we know the matching function, then finding the most suitable applicant is a maximum search over the matching values.

Let $\preceq$ be a specialization relation over the skills such that for all $s, s' \in S$ : $s \preceq s'$ iff $s$ is a specialization of $s'$ or $s'$ is more general skill than $s$. This relation is reflexive, antisymmetric and transitive, so it defines a partial order, a hierarchy over elements of $S$. Let us suppose that $\mathcal{L} = (S, \preceq)$ is an ontology lattice, i.e. for each pair of skills has infimum (greatest lower bound) and supremum (least upper bound). Note, that we can always add a top (respectively a bottom) element to the skills that everybody (nobody) possesses.

We can extend the lattice with additional information in form of so called extra edges that represent some kind of quantifiable relationship between skills. However, these edges can form cycles in the hierarchy therefore we use directed graphs to handle them instead of the lattice structure [19].

Let $G = (V, E)$ be a directed graph where $V = S$ and $E = E_{lat} \cup E_{ext}$ is a set of lattice edges and extra edges such that for two nodes $v_i, v_j \in V$ : $(v_i, v_j) \in E_{lat}$ iff $v_i \preceq v_j$ and $(v_i, v_j) \in E_{ext}$ iff there is an extra edge between $v_i$ and $v_j$. Let $w_{edge} : E \to [0, 1]$ be an edge weighting function such that for all $e_{lat} \in E_{lat} : w_{edge}(e_{lat}) = 1$ and for all $e_{ext} \in E_{ext} : w_{edge}(e_{ext}) \in (0, 1)$ that represents the strength of the relationship between start and end node of the edge. Let $p_F(x, v)$ denote the set of directed paths from node $x$ to node $v$ using edges of a subset $F \subseteq E$ of edge set $E$ of $G$.

We can define a matching function of an application $A$ to an offer $O$ using the graph in the following way. First, we define function $ext$ to extend the application and the offer with all the skills that are available from them via directed path in $G$. For an arbitrary set of skills $X \subseteq S$ and a subset $F \subseteq E$ of edges, let $ext_F(X) = \{(v, \gamma_v) \mid v \in V$ and $\exists x \in X : |p_F(x, v)| \geq 1$ and $\gamma_v = max_{x' \in X, p \in p_F(x', v)} length(p)\}$ where length of a path $p = (v_1, \ldots, v_n)$ is the product of the edge weights on $p$, i.e. $length(p) = \prod_{i=1}^{n-1} w_{edge}((v_i, v_{i+1}))$.

It was shown that the extended sets are fuzzy filters [14] in $\mathcal{L} = (S, \preceq)$, i.e. for a set of skills $X$ and for all $t \in [0, 1] : ext_E(X)_t = \{x \in X \mid \gamma_x \geq t\}$ is filter in $\mathcal{L}$.

It perfectly makes sense to use lattice edges to extend applications and offers as lattice edges describe specialization relation between skills. Namely if an applicant possesses a special skill then he or she must possess the more general skills as well. However extra edges are used in the extension as well to get more selective matching functions that help differentiate applications.

Let us call nodes in $ext_E(X) \setminus ext_{E_{lat}}(X)$ *derived* nodes for a set $X \subseteq S$ of skills. We investigate two approaches or philosophies when extending profiles using the extra edges. The first one is *symmetric*, that is the case when offers and applications are treated in the same way. In this case we use extension function $ext_E$ for both, offers $O$ and applications $A$. The advantage is that we only have to apply one weighting function and the proof of equivalence of different representations is simpler than that of the other case. There is a disadvantage, though. If offers are also extended with derived skills, then an application may obtain high matching value just having those skills. However, it is not really advantageous for an employer, as required skills are not in the application.

The second approach called the *strict approach* is when offers are only extended with non-derived nodes, that is $ext_E$ is used for applications but $ext_{E_{lat}}$ is used for offers. This is the approach of [19]. The disadvantage of this case is that different weighting functions have to be applied for applications and offers, consequently the proofs of equivalences are more complicated. However, the point of view of employers is better represented in the second way. An application has to have good matching in target skills to score high, and the derived skills can be used to rank applications scoring equally otherwise. Note, that $ext_{E_{lat}}(X)$ is exactly the set of nodes contained in the lattice filter generated by $X$ in the ontology lattice $(S, \preceq)$.

We adapted the profile matching function proposed by Popov and Jebelean et al. [18] to fuzzy sets in [19]. We use the same function here except the different approaches in extension of offers. So, let the matching value of $A$ to $O$ be

$$match_{sym}(A, O) = \frac{\|ext_E(A) \cap ext_E(O)\|}{\|ext_E(O)\|} \tag{1}$$

in case of the symmetric approach, and

$$match(A, O) = \frac{\|ext_E(A) \cap ext_{E_{lat}}(O)\|}{\|ext_{E_{lat}}(O)\|} \tag{2}$$

in case of the strict approach. For two fuzzy sets $f, g$ of $S$ and for a skill $s \in S$ let $(f \cap g)(s) := \min\{f(s), g(s)\}$, and $\|f\| := \sum_{(v,\gamma_v) \in f} \gamma_v$, i.e. $\| \cdot \|$ denotes sigma cardinality and intersection is defined as the $min$ t-norm. Note, that other cardinality and intersection functions can be applied in the same way [11,23].

Let $w_{node} : V \to [0, 1]$ be a node weighting function that assigns 1 to every nodes and let $w_{fset} : \mathbb{F}_S \to [0, 1]$ be a weighting function for fuzzy sets such that for a fuzzy set $f$ let $w_{fset}(f) = \sum_{(v,\gamma_v) \in f} \gamma_v = \sum_{(v,\gamma_v) \in f} \gamma_v \cdot w_{node}(v)$ where $\mathbb{F}_S$ denotes all fuzzy sets of $S$. Note, that $w_{node}$ is defined only to unify the notations in the rest of the paper. With this weighting functions, the matching value of $A$ to $O$ can be given as

$$match_{sym}(A, O) = \frac{w_{fset}(ext_E(A) \cap ext_E(O))}{w_{fset}(ext_E(O))} \tag{3}$$

and

$$match(A, O) = \frac{w_{fset}(ext_E(A) \cap ext_{E_{lat}}(O))}{w_{fset}(ext_{E_{lat}}(O))}, \tag{4}$$

respectively.

## 3    Lattice Enlargement

In this section, we present a graph transformation method to eliminate extra edges from extended lattices preserving symmetric matching values of applications to offers, and then we use formal concept analysis to restore lattice properties in the transformed graphs.

### 3.1    Extension Graph

Let $G = (V, E)$ be a directed graph with $w_{edge}, w_{node}$ weighting functions as defined above and $c_{ij}$ be the weight of the longest path from $v_i$ to $v_j$ where

$v_i, v_j \in V$ are two nodes. Let $v_{i_1 j}, \ldots v_{i_k j}$ be the nodes from where $v_j$ is available via directed path such that $c_{i_1 j} \leq \cdots \leq c_{i_k j}$. Let $c^{j_1}, \ldots, c^{j_l}$ denote the different values among $c_{i_1 j}, \ldots, c_{i_k j}$, i.e. $c^{j_1} < \cdots < c^{j_l}$.

For all $c^{j_1} \ldots c^{j_l}$, add new nodes $V_j = \{v_{j_1}, \ldots, v_{j_l}\}$ (for simplicity let $v_{j_l} = v_j$) to $V$ and add new lattice edges from $v_{j_l}$ to $v_{j_{l-1}}$, $\ldots$, from $v_{j_2}$ to $v_{j_1}$, and from $v_{j_1}$ to the top to $E$. The new edges forms a directed path from $v_j$ to the top. Let $q_j = (v_{j_l}, \ldots, v_{j_1}, top)$ denote that path. Assign weight $w_{j_k} = c^{j_k} - c^{j_{k-1}}$ to $v_{j_k}$ ($k = 1, \ldots, l$) where $c^{j_0} = 0$. Note, that $\sum_{k=1}^{l} w_{j_k} = 1$ as it is a telescoping sum. If the length of the longest path from $v_i$ to $v_j$ was $c^{j_k}$, then add a new lattice edge from $v_i$ to $v_{j_k}$. Finally, remove all extra edges from the graph. Let $G' = ext(\mathcal{L}, E_{ext}) = (V', E')$ denote the modified graph, called extension graph, and $w'_{node}$ denote the modified node weighting function.

New nodes of $V_j$ and new edges of $q_j$ can be considered as an extension of $v_j$ to a chain because there do not start edges from intermediate nodes to other chains so out-degrees of intermediate nodes are always one. We call $v_j$ the base node of the chain. Base nodes of such chains are nodes of $\mathcal{L}$, and $G$ as well.

Let $q_j$ and $q_k$ be two chains with base nodes $v_j$ and $v_k$, respectively. Then, an edge from $q_j$ to $q_k$ in $G'$ can go

- from $v_j$ to $v_k$ and then it represents a directed path in $G$ from $v_j$ to $v_k$ containing lattice edges only;
- from $v_j$ to an intermediate node $v_i$ of $q_k$ and then it represents a directed path $p_{v_j v_k}$ of $G$ from $v_j$ to $v_k$ such that $length(p_{v_j v_k}) = \sum_{s=1}^{i} w'_{node}(v_s)$ if $q_k = (v_{k_l}, \ldots, v_{s+1}, v_s, v_{s-1}, \ldots, v_1, top)$.

Note, that lattice edges in $G$ are acyclic so the corresponding edges in $G'$ are acyclic as well, and newly added edges start from base nodes of chains only. So $G'$ is an acyclic graph.

Figure 1 shows an example of the construction of $G'$. There is the original graph, called $G$, on the left. Blue (solid) edges represent lattice edges and orange (dashed) edges with numbers on them represent extra edges and their weights. There is the extension graph, called $G'$, on the right where green edges represent the newly added edges, and numbers in the top right corners of nodes are weights of the nodes.

As it can be seen, for example, node $A$ of $G$ has been transformed into the chain $q_A = (A, A_1, Top)$ since $A$ is available via lattice edges (i.e. via maximum length paths) from $B, C, Bottom$ and it is available from $D$ via the path $p_{DA} = (D, C, A)$ whose length is 0.8 and $A$ is not available from any other nodes. Therefore $A_1$ got the weight 0.8 and $A$ got the weight 0.2.

**Lemma 3.1.** *Let $G = (V, E)$ be a directed graph extending the lattice $\mathcal{L} = (S, \preceq)$ with extra edges, $w_{fset}$ be the fuzzy set weighting function, $G' = ext(\mathcal{L}, E_{ext}) = (V', E')$ be the extension graph, and $w'_{fset}$ be the modified weighting function. Let $O \subseteq S$ be an offer and $A \subseteq S$ be an application. Then,*

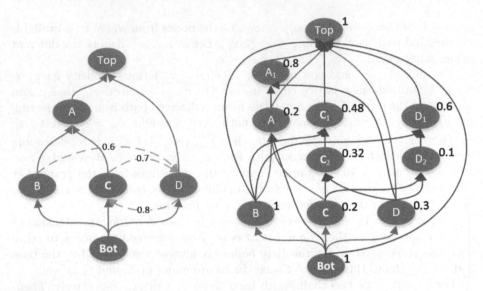

**Fig. 1.** Lattice with extra edges and the generated extension graph (Color figure online)

$$match_{sym}(A, O) = \frac{w_{fset}(ext_E(A) \cap ext_E(O))}{w_{fset}(ext_E(O))} = \frac{w'_{fset}(ext_{E'}(A) \cap ext_{E'}(O))}{w'_{fset}(ext_{E'}(O))}.$$

$$(5)$$

*Proof.* Let $u \in G'$ and let $q_z = (z_l, \dots, z_1, top)$ be the node chain with base node $z \in G$ that contains $u$, i.e. $z_l = z$ and $u = z_i$ for some $i \in [1..l]$. First, we will show for an arbitrary $X \subseteq S$ that $u \in ext_{E'}(X)$ iff $z \in ext_E(X)$.

If $u \in ext_{E'}(X)$, then there is a node $a \in X \subseteq V'$ and a directed path $q_{au} = (x_1, \dots, x_i, x_{i+1}, \dots x_n)$ from $a$ to $u$ in $G'$ where $x_1 = a$ and $x_n = u$. If $a = z$ then $z \in ext_E(X)$. Otherwise let $x_{i+1}$ be the first node of $q_{au}$ that is an intermediate node of $q_z$ as well. Such node must exist because edges between chains can start from base nodes only and we cannot reach $u$ from $a$ otherwise. Then for $j \in [1..i]$: $x_j, x_{j+1}$ are nodes of $G$, and $(x_j, x_{j+1})$ edges of $q_{au}$ represent directed paths containing lattice edges only in $G$. Therefore there is a $p_{az} = (x_1, \dots, x_i, z)$ path in $G$ from $a = x_1$ to $z$ such that $length(p_{az}) = \sum_{s=1}^{k} w'_{node}(z_s)$. It means $z \in ext_E(X)$ in this case as well.

On the other hand, if $z \in ext_E(X)$ with grade $\gamma_z$, then there is a node $b \in X$ and a maximal length path $p_{bz}$ from $b$ to $z$ in $G$ such that $length(p_{bz}) = \gamma_z$. In that case, there is an edge from $b$ to $z_r$ in $G'$ for some $r \in [1..l]$ such that $\sum_{s=1}^{r} w'_{node}(z_r) = length(p_{bv})$ and $z_r, z_{r-1}, z_1 \in ext_{E'}(X)$.

Consequently, $ext_{E'}(A) \cap ext_{E'}(O)$ contains fragments of chains generated from base nodes that are available from both $A$ and $O$ in $G$. Sum of node weights in a fragment equals to the minimum of the lengths of the maximal length paths starting from $A$ or $O$ ending in the base node of the chain. Thus, $w_{fset}(ext_E(A) \cap ext_E(O)) = w'_{fset}(ext_{E'}(A) \cap ext_{E'}(O))$ and $w_{fset}(ext_E(O)) = w'_{fset}(ext_{E'}(O))$, i.e. Eq. (5) holds.  □

Note, that $G'$ is acyclic by its construction but does not necessarily define a lattice. Therefore, we build a concept lattice from $G'$ in which matching values of applications to offers will also be preserved.

## 3.2 Concept Lattice

First, we define a formal context and formal concepts based on $G'$. Let $(V_1', V_2', T')$ be a formal *context*, where $V_1' = V_2' = V'$ and $(v_i, v_j) \in T'$ iff $v_j$ is available from $v_i$ via directed path supposing that the relation is reflexive. Consider the element of $V_1'$ as start points and the element of $V_2'$ as end points of directed paths in $G'$. Let $I \subseteq V_1'$ and $J \subseteq V_2'$ and let us define their dual sets $I^{D_s}$ and $J^{D_e}$ as follows:

$$I^{D_s} = \{b \in V_2' \mid (a, b) \in T' \text{ for all } a \in I\}$$
$$J^{D_e} = \{a \in V_1' \mid (a, b) \in T' \text{ for all } b \in J\}$$

A *concept* of the context $(V_1', V_2', T')$ is a pair $\langle I, J \rangle$ such that $I \subseteq V_1'$, $J \subseteq V_2'$ and $I^{D_s} = J$, $J^{D_e} = I$. $I$ is called an *extent* of $\langle I, J \rangle$, and $J$ is called an *intent* of $\langle I, J \rangle$.

**Table 1.** Formal context $(V_1', V_2', T')$

|      | Bot | B | C | C1 | C2 | D | D1 | D2 | A | A1 | Top |
|------|-----|---|---|----|----|----|----|----|----|----|-----|
| Bot  | X   | X | X | X  | X  | X | X  | X  | X | X  | X   |
| B    |     | X |   | X  |    | X |    |    | X | X  | X   |
| C    |     |   | X | X  | X  |   | X  | X  | X | X  | X   |
| C1   |     |   |   | X  |    |   |    |    |   |    | X   |
| C2   |     |   |   | X  | X  |   |    |    |   |    | X   |
| D    |     |   |   | X  | X  | X | X  | X  |   | X  | X   |
| D1   |     |   |   |    |    |   | X  |    |   |    | X   |
| D2   |     |   |   |    |    |   | X  | X  |   |    | X   |
| A    |     |   |   |    |    |   |    |    | X | X  | X   |
| A1   |     |   |   |    |    |   |    |    |   | X  | X   |
| Top  |     |   |   |    |    |   |    |    |   |    | X   |

Table 1 shows the formal context $(V_1', V_2', T')$ that was generated based on graph $G'$ of Fig. 1. Labels of rows and columns represent the elements of $V_1'$ and the elements of $V_2'$, respectively. There is an $X$ in row $i$ column $j$ if $(i, j) \in T'$, i.e. $j$ is available from $i$ via directed path in $G'$.

**Lemma 3.2.** *If $G'$ is an acyclic graph, then*

(1) *For every concept $\langle I, J \rangle$ of the context $(V_1', V_2', T')$: $I \cap J = \{v\}$ for some $v \in V'$ or $I \cap J = \emptyset$*

(2) *For every $v \in V'$: there is a concept $\langle I_v, J_v \rangle$ in the context $(V_1', V_2', T')$ such that $I_v \cap J_v = \{v\}$.*

*Proof.*

(1) Indirectly, suppose that for a concept $\langle I, J \rangle$ of $(V_1', V_2', T')$ and for two different nodes $u, v \in V'$: $u, v \in (I \cap J)$ holds. In this case $(u, v) \in T'$ and $(v, u) \in T'$ hold as well. It would mean that there is a cycle in $G'$ which is a contradiction as $G'$ is acyclic.

(2) For a node $v \in V'$ let $J_v = \{v\}^{D_s}$ be the set of all nodes that are available from $v$ via directed path (including $v$ itself). Let $I_v = J_v^{D_e}$, then $v \in I_v$. If $I_v = \{v\}$, then $\langle I_v, J_v \rangle$ is the concept we are looking for.

Otherwise, suppose that for a node $u$ such that $u \neq v$: $u \in I_v = J_v^{D_e} = (\{v\}^{D_s})^{D_e}$. That means $(u, v) \in T'$, i.e. $v$ is available from $u$. As $T'$ is a transitive relation $\{v\}^{D_s} \subseteq \{u, v\}^{D_s}$. However $\{u, v\}^{D_s} \subseteq \{v\}^{D_s}$ because $\{u, v\}^{D_s}$ cannot contain such node that is not available from all nodes of $\{u, v\}$. Following this construction we can get that if $J_v^{D_e} = I_v = \{u_1, \ldots, u_i, v\}$, then $I_v^{D_s} = \{u_1, \ldots, u_i, v\}^{D_s} = \{v\}^{D_s} = J_v$. Therefore $\langle \{u_1, \ldots, u_i, v\}, \{v\}^{D_s} \rangle$ is a concept such that $\{u_1, \ldots, u_i, v\} \cap \{v\}^{D_s} = \{v\}$. $\square$

Let $\mathcal{B}(V_1', V_2', T')$ be the set of all formal concepts in the context, and $\leq$ be a subconcept-superconcept order over the concepts such that for any $\langle A_1, B_1 \rangle$, $\langle A_2, B_2 \rangle \in \mathcal{B}(V_1', V_2', T')$ : $\langle A_1, B_1 \rangle \leq \langle A_2, B_2 \rangle$, iff $A_1 \subseteq A_2$ (or, iff $B_2 \subseteq B_1$). $(\mathcal{B}(V_1', V_2', T'), \leq)$ is called *concept lattice* [10] and let $cl((\mathcal{L}, E_{ext}))$ denote the concept lattice obtained from the extension graph $ext(\mathcal{L}, E_{ext})$.

Figure 2[1] shows concept lattice of the context $(V_1', V_2', T')$ from Table 1. Concepts $\langle I_v, J_v \rangle$ where $I_v \cap J_v = \{v\}$ are labeled with $v$. For example, $\langle I_{C_2}, J_{C_2} \rangle = \langle \{Bot, C, C_2, D\}, \{C_2, C_1, Top\} \rangle$. But, concepts $\langle I, J \rangle$ such that $I \cap J = \emptyset$ are unlabeled like the $\langle \{Bot, B, C\}, \{A, A_1, C_1, D_1, Top\} \rangle$ parent of concepts $B$ and $C$. Another, larger example is the ontology on Fig. 3 with added extra edges from [19].

It is worth mentioning that the concept lattice $cl((\mathcal{L}, E_{ext}))$ generated from ontology $\mathcal{L}$ endowed with extra edges $E_{ext}$ coincides with the Dedekind-McNeille completion [8] of the poset obtained as transitive closure of acyclic directed graph $ext(\mathcal{L}, E_{ext})$. Indeed, the collection of upper bounds of a subset $S$ of elements of the poset is exactly the collection of the vertices reachable from the vertices of $S$ via directed paths in the directed graph. We use the concept lattice formulation for two reasons. First, a direct construction is obtained skipping the step of constructing the poset from the directed graph $ext(\mathcal{L}, E_{ext})$. Second, the concept lattice structure allows us to define node weights properly.

An offer $O = \{o_1, \ldots, o_k\} \subseteq S = V \subseteq V'$ generates a filter $F_O \subseteq \mathcal{B}(V_1', V_2', T')$ in the concept lattice such that $F_O = \{\langle I, J \rangle \mid \exists \langle I_o, J_o \rangle \leq \langle I, J \rangle$ such that $I_o \cap J_o = \{o\}$ for some $o \in O\}$. Similarly, an application $A$ generates a filter $F_A$ in the concept lattice.

---

[1] The concept lattices were generated using the Concept Explorer tool. Web page: http://conexp.sourceforge.net/.

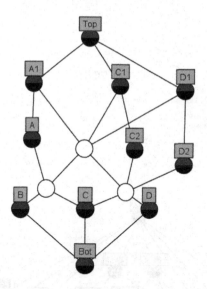

**Fig. 2.** Concept lattice of context $(V_1', V_2', T')$

Let $w_{con} : \mathcal{B}(V_1', V_2', T') \rightarrow [0, 1]$ be a concept weighting function such that for a concept $\langle I, J \rangle$ of $\mathcal{B}(V_1', V_2', T')$:

$$w_{con}(\langle I, J \rangle) = \begin{cases} w_{node}'(v) & \text{if } I \cap J = \{v\} \text{ for some } v \in V', \\ 0 & \text{otherwise.} \end{cases}$$

Let $w_{fil}$ be a filter weighting function such that for a filter $F \in \mathcal{P}(\mathcal{B}(V_1', V_2', T'))$: $w_{fil}(F) = \sum_{\langle I, J \rangle \in F} w_{con}(\langle I, J \rangle)$.

**Theorem 3.1.** *Let $G = (V, E)$ be a directed graph extending the lattice $\mathcal{L} = (S, \preceq)$ with extra edges and $cl((\mathcal{L}, E_{ext})) = (\mathcal{B}(V_1', V_2', T'), \leq)$ be the concept lattice constructed from $G$ and $w_{fil}$ be the filter weighting function. Let $O \subseteq S$ be an offer and $A \subseteq S$ be an application. Then,*

$$match_{sym}(A, O) = \frac{w_{fil}(F_A \cap F_O)}{w_{fil}(F_O)}. \tag{6}$$

*Proof.* Based on Lemma 3.1 it is enough to prove that

$$\frac{w_{fil}(F_A \cap F_O)}{w_{fil}(F_O)} = \frac{w_{fset}'(ext_{E'}(A) \cap ext_{E'}(O))}{w_{fset}'(ext_{E'}(O))} \tag{7}$$

Let $\langle I_u, J_u \rangle$ and $\langle I_v, J_v \rangle$ be two concepts such that $I_u \cap J_u = \{u\}$ and $I_v \cap J_v = \{v\}$ where $u, v \in V'$, i.e. $u$ and $v$ are nodes of $G'$ that is generated from $G$ as defined above. First, we will show that $\langle I_u, J_u \rangle \leq \langle I_v, J_v \rangle$ iff there is a directed path from $u$ to $v$ in $G'$.

If $\langle I_u, J_u \rangle \leq \langle I_v, J_v \rangle$, then $J_v \subseteq J_u$. But $u \in I_u$ and $v \in J_v \subseteq J_u$, and therefore $(u, v) \in T'$, i.e. there is a directed path from $u$ to $v$ in $G'$. On the other

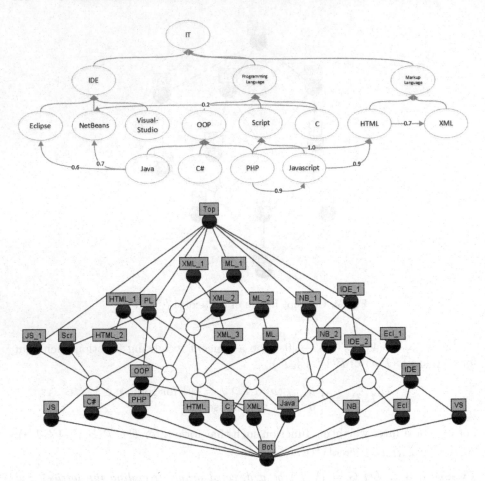

**Fig. 3.** Ontology with extra edges and the corresponding concept lattice

hand, if there is a directed path from $u$ to $v$ in $G'$, then $(u, v) \in T'$ therefore $v \in J_u = \{x \mid (u, x) \in T'\}$. However if $v$ is available from $u$, then all nodes that are available from $v$, i.e. elements of $J_v$ are also available from $u$ as $T'$ is a transitive relation. So $J_v \subseteq J_u$, but then $\langle I_u, J_u \rangle \leq \langle I_v, J_v \rangle$. It means that if $v \in ext_{E'}(O)$, then $\langle I_v, J_v \rangle \in F_O$ and if $\langle I_u, J_u \rangle \in F_O$, then $u \in ext_{E'}(O)$ and the same holds for $ext_{E'}(A)$ and $F_A$.

Since $w_{con}$ assigns the same weights to concepts of $F_A$ and $F_O$ in form of $\langle I_v, J_v \rangle$ where $v \in V'$ as $w'_{node}$ assigns to $v$ and $w_{con}$ assigns 0 to any other concepts therefore $w_{fil}$ sums up the same values as $w'_{fset}$, so Eq. (7) holds.  $\square$

## 4   Extremal Problems

It is a natural question how the size of the original ontology lattice $\mathcal{L} = (S, \preceq)$ relates to the sizes of the extension graph $ext(\mathcal{L}, E_{ext})$ and the concept lattice $cl((\mathcal{L}, E_{ext}))$ obtained from $ext((\mathcal{L}, E_{ext}))$. First, let us consider $ext(\mathcal{L}, E_{ext})$.

**Proposition 4.1.** *Let $\mathcal{L} = (S, \preceq)$ be an ontology lattice of $n + 2$ nodes. Then for $G' = ext(\mathcal{L}, E_{ext}) = (V', E')$ we have $|V'| \leq n^2 + 2$. Furthermore, this estimate is sharp, that is for every positive integer $n$ there exists ontology $\mathcal{L}_n = (S_n, \preceq)$ and set of extra edges $E_{ext}$ such that $ext(\mathcal{L}_n, E_{ext})$ has $n^2 + 2$ vertices.*

*Proof.* Let the nodes of $\mathcal{L} = (S, \preceq)$ be $v_0, v_1, \ldots, v_n, v_{n+1}$ with $v_0 = bottom$ and $v_{n+1} = top$. Then clearly there is no directed path from $v_i$ $i > 0$ to $v_0$ in $\mathcal{L} \cup E_{ext}$, and the maximum weight path from any node $v_i$ $i > 0$ to $v_{n+1}$ is of weight 1, so no new nodes are generated from top and bottom. For $v_j$ $0 < j < n + 1$ there can be at most $n$ distinct $c^{j_1}, \ldots, c^{j_l}$ values ($l \leq n$) that there exists a maximum weight path to $v_j$ of weight $c^{j_m}$, as these paths could come from nodes $v_i$ $i \in \{0, 1, \ldots, n\} \setminus \{j\}$ only.

On the other hand, let $\mathcal{L}_c = (S, \preceq)$ be defined as $v_1, \ldots, v_n$ be pairwise incomparable elements, furthermore let $E_{ext}^c = \{(v_i, v_{i+1}) : i = 1, 2, \ldots n\}$ where $i + 1$ is meant modulo $n$. Let the weight of each extra edge in $E_{ext}^c$ be a fixed $0 < p < 1$ value. $\mathcal{L}_c \cup E_{ext}^c$ is shown on Fig. 4. The maximum weight path from $v_i$ to $v_j$ has weight $p^{j-i}$ if $1 \leq i < j \leq n$, while the weight is $p^{n-1-(j-i)}$ if $1 \leq j < i \leq n$, finally the weight is 1 for $i = 0 < j \leq n$. Thus, each node $v_j$ $1 \leq j \leq n$ has exactly $n$ different maximum weight path going into it, so $ext(\mathcal{L}_c, E_{ext}^c)$ has exactly $n^2 + 2$ nodes.                                    □

Our next goal is to bound the size of concept lattice $cl((\mathcal{L}, E_{ext}))$. The main question is how many "dummy" vertices are generated, that is concepts $\langle I, J \rangle$ such that $I \cap J = \emptyset$.

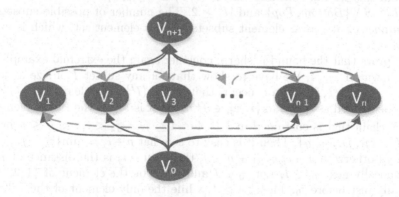

**Fig. 4.** Extremal example

**Theorem 4.1.** *Let $\mathcal{L} = (S, \preceq)$ be an ontology lattice of $n + 2$ nodes. Then for a set $E_{ext}$ of extra edges $|cl((\mathcal{L}, E_{ext}))| \leq 2^n + n^2 - n + 1$ and this estimate is sharp, that is there exist $\mathcal{L}_n = (S_n, \preceq)$ and and set of extra edges $E_{ext}$ such that $|cl((\mathcal{L}_n, E_{ext}))| = 2^n + n^2 - n + 1$.*

*Proof.* It is enough to prove that the number of concepts $\langle I, J \rangle$ such that $I \cap J = \emptyset$ is at most $2^n - n - 1$ to establish the upper bound by Lemma 3.2 and by Proposition 4.1. Indeed, Lemma 3.2 tells us that there is a concept corresponding to each element of $ext(\mathcal{L}_c, E_{ext}^c)$ and the other concepts $\langle I, J \rangle$ of $cl((\mathcal{L}, E_{ext}))$ have the property $I \cap J = \emptyset$.

Let $v_{j_i}$ be a vertex of $ext(\mathcal{L}_c, E_{ext}^c)$ such that $v_{j_i}$ is in the chain with base node $v_j$ and $v_{j_i} \neq v_j$ furthermore assume that $i$ is maximal with respect to $v_{j_i} \in I$ for some set of nodes of $ext(\mathcal{L}_c, E_{ext}^c)$. The nodes reachable from $v_{j_i}$ via directed paths are $\{v_{j_i}, v_{j_{i-1}}, \ldots, v_{j_1}, Top\}$, thus $I^{D_s} \subseteq \{v_{j_i}, v_{j_{i-1}}, \ldots, v_{j_1}, Top\}$. This implies that $(I^{D_s})^{D_e} \supseteq \{v_{j_i}, v_{j_{i-1}}, \ldots, v_{j_1}, Top\}^{D_e} \ni v_j$. However, $v_j \notin I$ by the maximality of $i$, so $(I^{D_s})^{D_e} \neq I$, that is $I$ cannot be the extent of a concept of $cl((\mathcal{L}, E_{ext}))$. Suppose now that $\langle I, J \rangle$ is a concept and $v_{j_i} \in I$ as well as $v_{k_e} \in I$ for some $j \neq k$ so that neither $v_{j_i}$ nor $v_{k_e}$ is the base node of its chain. Then $I^{D_s} \subseteq \{v_{j_i}, v_{j_{i-1}}, \ldots, v_1, Top\} \cap \{v_{k_e}, v_{k_{e-1}}, \ldots, v_{k_1}, Top\} = \{Top\}$, so $I = \{Top\}^{D_e} = S$, that is $\langle I, J \rangle = \langle I_{Top}, J_{Top} \rangle$, i.e., $I \cap J = \{Top\}$. So we may assume that if $\langle I, J \rangle$ is a concept and $v_{j_i} \in I$ for some non-base node of a chain of $ext(\mathcal{L}_c, E_{ext}^c)$, then $I$ does not contain non-base element of any other chain. Let $i$ be minimal such that $v_{j_i} \in I$, where $v_{j_0}$ is understood to be $Top$. We claim that $(I^{D_s}) = \{v_{j_i}, v_{j_{i-1}}, \ldots, v_{j_1}, Top\}$. Indeed, we have $J = I^{D_s}$ and $I = J^{D_e}$. Let $\ell$ be maximal so that $v_{j_\ell} \in J$, then $J = \{v_{j_\ell}, v_{j_{\ell-1}}, \ldots v_{j_1}, Top\}$, since if there is a directed path from a node $x$ to $v_{j_\ell}$, then there is a path to any $v_{j_t}$ for $\ell > t$, as well. Also, if $J = \{v_{j_\ell}, v_{j_{\ell-1}}, \ldots v_{j_1}, Top\}$, then for any node $x$, there is a directed path from $x$ to every node in $J$ iff there is a directed path from $x$ to $v_{j_\ell}$, since $J$ itself forms a directed path from $v_{j_\ell}$ to $Top$. Now, by $I = J^{D_e}$ we have that $v_{j_i} = v_{j_\ell}$ and $\langle I, J \rangle = \langle I_{j_i}, J_{j_i} \rangle$.

From this we can conclude that if $\langle I, J \rangle$ is a concept such that $I \cap J = \emptyset$, then $I \subset S \setminus \{Bottom, Top\}$ and $|I| \geq 2$. The number of possible subsets $I$ is the number of at least 2 element subsets of an $n$-element set, which is exactly $2^n - n - 1$.

To prove that the bound is sharp, consider again the extremal example $\mathcal{L}_c \cup E_{ext}^c$ shown on Fig. 4. We have to show that for any subset $I$ of size at least 2 of $\{v_1, \ldots, v_n\}$, $\langle I, I^{D_s} \rangle$ is a concept, that is $I = (I^{D_s})^{D_e}$. Clearly, $I \subseteq (I^{D_s})^{D_e}$. Let $i_j$ be defined as $i_j = \max\{i : v_{j_i} \in I^{D_s}\}$, that is $v_{j_{i_j}}$ is the lowest element of the $j^{\text{th}}$ chain that is contained in $I^{D_s}$. Let $1 \leq j_1 < j_2 < \ldots < j_t \leq n$ be such that $I = \{j_1, j_2, \ldots, j_t\}$. Then it is easy to see that $n - i_j = \min\{j_k - j : j_k > j\}$ if $j < j_t$, otherwise $n - i_j = j_1 + n - j$, that is $n - i_j$ is the distance of $j$ from the cyclically next $j_k \in I$. Let $j_0 \notin I$ and let $j'$ be the element of $\{1, 2, \ldots, n\}$ cyclically just before $j_0$. Then $i_{j'} > 1$, while the only element of the $j'^{\text{th}}$ chain that is an endvertex of a directed path from $v_{j_0}$ is $v_{j'_1}$, so $v_{j_0} \notin (I^{D_s})^{D_e}$. □

Another interesting question could be how the average or expected size of extension graph and the concept lattice relates to the size of the original ontology lattice. This is the topic of further investigations. The first task is finding a reasonable probability distribution for the extra edges.

## 5  Strict Approach

As it was mentioned above, extra edges can be used based on different philosophies when extending offers. In this section, we show that strict matching values of applications to offers can also be preserved in the extension graph and in the concept lattice.

### 5.1  Preserving Strict Matching in Extension Graph

The main problem of preserving strict matching values in the extension graph is if extra edges are used to extend the offer, then extra nodes might appear in the extended offer whose weights are greater then 0. However, to address this problem, special node weighting functions can be defined depending on the offers.

For an offer $O$ let $w_{node}^O$ be a node weighting function that preserves the weights of the nodes that are available from $O$ via lattice edges in $G$, and the nodes that were generated from such nodes in $G'$, and it assigns 0 to the other nodes, i.e. for a node $v \in V'$ let

$$w_{node}^O(v) = \begin{cases} w'_{node}(v) & \text{if } \exists v_j \in ext_{E_{lat}}(O) : v \in V_j, \\ 0 & \text{otherwise.} \end{cases}$$

Let $w_{fset}^O$ be a fuzzy set weighting function that uses $w_{node}^O$, so for a fuzzy set $f$ let $w_{fset}^O(f) = \sum_{(v,\gamma_v) \in f} \gamma_v \cdot w_{node}^O(v)$. Note, that computing $w_{node}^O$ is a preprocessing step that has to be done once for all offers, and then $w_{node}^O$ can be reused to calculate matching values of applications to the given offer.

With these weighting function a similar result can be shown as in Lemma 3.1.

**Lemma 5.1.** *Let* $G = (V, E)$ *be a directed graph extending the lattice* $\mathcal{L} = (S, \preceq)$ *with extra edges,* $w_{fset}$ *be the fuzzy set weighting function,* $G' = ext(\mathcal{L}, E_{ext}) = (V', E')$ *be the extension graph, and* $w'_{fset}$ *be the modified weighting function. Let* $O \subseteq S$ *be an offer with* $w_{node}^O$ *and* $w_{fset}^O$ *node and fuzzy set weighting functions, respectively and let* $A \subseteq S$ *be an application. Then,*

$$match(A, O) = \frac{w_{fset}(ext_E(A) \cap ext_{E_{lat}}(O))}{w_{fset}(ext_{E_{lat}}(O))} = \frac{w_{fset}^O(ext_{E'}(A) \cap ext_{E'}(O))}{w_{fset}^O(ext_{E'}(O))}$$

$$(8)$$

*Proof.* The proof is analogous to Lemma 3.1's. However, $ext_{E'}(A) \cap ext_{E'}(O)$ may contain chain fragment $(v_{y_k}, \ldots, v_{y_1})$ of a chain $q_y = \{v_{y_l}, \ldots, v_{y_1}, top\}$ with base node $v_y$ where $v_y$ is only available from $O$ via extra edges in $G$, i.e.

$v_y \in ext_E(O) \setminus ext_{E_{lat}}(O)$. But $w^O_{node}$ assigns 0 to such $v_{y_k}, \ldots, v_{y_l}$ nodes by definition. In addition, $G'$ contains lattice edges only, so $ext_{E'}(A)$ and $ext_{E'}(O)$ are crisps sets, so grades of their elements are always 1. Therefore $w^O_{fset}(ext_{E'}(A) \cap ext_{E'}(O)) = \sum_{u \in ext_{E'}(A) \cap ext_{E'}(O)} w^O_{node}(u) = w_{fset}(ext_E(A) \cap ext_{E_{lat}}(O))$ and analogously, $w_{fset}(ext_{E_{lat}}(O)) = w^O_{fset}(ext_{E'}(O))$. Thus Eq. (8) holds as well. □

## 5.2   Preserving String Matching in Concept Lattice

The same issue appears if we want to preserve strict matching values of applications to offers in the concept lattice as we solved in case of the extension graph, namely extended offer might contain new nodes with weight greater than 0. However, the offer specific weighting functions solve this issue as well.

We extend $w^O_{node}$ to be able to use it for concepts. So, let $w^O_{con}$ be a concept weighting function generated by an offer $O$ such that for a concept $\langle I, J \rangle$:

$$w^O_{con}(\langle I, J \rangle) = \begin{cases} w_{con}(\langle I, J \rangle) & \text{if } I \cap J = \{v\} \text{ such that } \exists v_j \in ext_{E_{lat}}(O) : v \in V_j, \\ 0 & \text{otherwise.} \end{cases}$$

Let $w^O_{fil}$ be the filter weighting function based on $w^O_{con}$, i.e. for a filter $F \in \mathcal{P}(\mathcal{B}(V'_1, V'_2, T'))$: $w^O_{fil}(F) = \sum_{\langle I, J \rangle \in F} w^O_{con}(\langle I, J \rangle)$.

With these weighting functions, we can prove the following theorem similarly to Theorem 3.1.

**Theorem 5.1.** *Let $G = (V, E)$ be a directed graph extending the lattice $\mathcal{L} = (S, \preceq)$ with extra edges and $cl((\mathcal{L}, E_{ext})) = (\mathcal{B}(V'_1, V'_2, T'), \leq)$ be the concept lattice constructed from $G$ and $w_{fil}$ be the filter weighting function. Let $O \subseteq S$ be an offer with $w^O_{con}$ and $w^O_{fil}$ concept and filter weighting functions, respectively and let $A \subseteq S$ be an application. Then,*

$$match(A, O) = \frac{w^O_{fil}(F_A \cap F_O)}{w^O_{fil}(F_O)} \tag{9}$$

*Proof.* Analogously to Theorem 3.1's proof and based on Lemma 3.1 it is enough to prove that

$$\frac{w^O_{fil}(F_A \cap F_O)}{w^O_{fil}(F_O)} = \frac{w^O_{fset}(ext_{E'}(A) \cap ext_{E'}(O))}{w^O_{fset}(ext_{E'}(O))}. \tag{10}$$

However, $F_A$ and $F_O$ contain concepts for all nodes of $ext_{E'}(A)$ and $ext_{E'}(O)$ respectively. But $w^O_{con}$ assigns 0 to such $\langle I_v, J_v \rangle$ concepts where $v \in V'$ is not contained in any chain whose base was available from $O$ in $G$ using lattice edges only. Therefore $w^O_{fil}$ sums up the same values as $w^O_{fset}$, i.e. Eq. (10) holds as well. □

# 6    Related Work

The aim of profile matching is to find the most fitting candidates to given profiles. Due to its various applications areas, it has become a widely investigated topic recently. Profiles can be represented as sets of elements and then numerous set similarity measures [5], such as Jaccard or Sørensen-Dice, are applicable to compute matching values.

There exist methods assuming that elements of profiles are organized into a hierarchy or ontology. For example, Lau and Sure [12] proposed an ontology based skill management system for eliciting employee skills and searching for experts within an insurance company. Ragone et al. [20] investigated peer-to-peer e-market place of used cars and presented a fuzzy extension of Datalog to match sellers and buyers based on required and offered properties of cars.

Di Noia et al. [7] placed matchmaking on a consistent theoretical foundation using description logic. They defined matchmaking as information retrieval task where demands and supplies are expressed using the same semi-structured data in form of advertisement and task results are ranked lists of those supplies best fulfilling the demands. Popov and Jebelean et al. [18] used filters in the ontology hierarchy lattice to represent profiles and defined matching function based on the filters.

We also assumed a structure among elements of profiles. We supposed this structure is an ontology that fulfills lattice properties as well and similarly to Popov's proposal we also represented profiles with filters. However, we extended the ontology lattice with extra edges to capture such relationships that subsumptions cannot express. Then we showed how these edges are usable to refine the ontology.

There are several methodologies to learn ontologies from unstructured texts or semi-structured data [4, 21]. Besides identifying concepts, discovering relationships between the concepts is a crucial part of ontology construction and refinement. Text-To-Onto [16] uses statistical, data mining, and pattern-based approaches over text corpus to extract taxonomic and non-taxonomic relations. In [22], various similarity measures were introduced between semi-structured Wikipedia infoboxes and then SVMs and Markov Logic Networks were used to detect subsumptions between infobox-classes.

We presented a method to refine ontology based on extra edges that represent some sort of quantifiable relationship between skills. These relationships can be given by domain experts, computed from statistics, or resulted by data mining techniques. For example, in [24] the authors used association rules and latent semantic indexing over job offers to detect relationships between competencies. In our method we defined profile extensions and weighting functions as well to preserve matching values of profiles computed from edge weights.

Formal concept analysis (FCA) [9] is also used to build and maintain formal ontologies. For example, Cimiano et al. [6] presented a method of automatic acquisition of concept hierarchies from a text corpus based on FCA. In [15], the authors used FCA to revise ontology when new knowledge was added to it.

In our method we used FCA to restore lattice properties after added new nodes and edges to it based on extra edges. However as we focused on preserving matching values of profiles during the transformations, we adapted our profile weighting functions to the modified ontology lattice as well.

## 7   Summary

In this paper we investigated how ontology lattices can be extended by additional information and used for semantic matching. We focused on the field of human resources and defined matching functions to find the most suitable applicant to a job offer, however, our results are applicable in other fields as well.

First, profiles of job applications and offers were represented as filters in an ontology lattice of skills that was built based on specialization relations between skills. Then, the ontology lattice got extended by additional information in form of extra edges describing quantifiable relations between the skills. A directed graph was built from the lattice endowed with extra edges to handle directed cycles that the new edges might have introduced and matching functions were defined based on reachable, or derived, nodes from profiles' nodes.

Two approaches were presented to extend profiles with derived nodes. In the first one, the offer and the applications were all extended, since the same profile can describe an application and an offer as well and these cases should be handled uniformly. In the second approach, only the applications were extended to help the employer differentiate better among the applicants.

We presented a method that eliminates directed cycles from the graph. It constructed an extension graph by adding node chains to the original lattice based on directed paths between nodes in the directed graph and node weights got also modified as part of the construction. An extension graph is a directed acyclic graph and therefore a poset but it is not necessary a lattice. Formal concept analysis was used to extend the poset into a concept lattice so that filters of this lattice could be used to calculate matching values. Different node weightings were used to preserve the original matching values in the two approaches.

Comparisons of the sizes of the ontology lattice and the generated acyclic directed graph, as well as the concept lattice were given.

## References

1. European Dictionary of Skills And Competences. http://www.disco-tools.eu
2. International Standard Classification of Education. http://www.uis.unesco.org/Education/Pages/international-standard-classification-of-education.aspx
3. International Standard Classification of Occupations (2008)
4. Buitelaar, P., Cimiano, P., Magnini, B.: Ontology learning from text: an overview. Ontol. Learn. Text: Methods Eval. Appl. **123**, 3–12 (2005)
5. Choi, S.S., Cha, S.H., Tappert, C.C.: A survey of binary similarity and distance measures. J. Systemics Cybern. Inf. **8**(1), 43–48 (2010)
6. Cimiano, P., Hotho, A., Staab, S.: Learning concept hierarchies from text corpora using formal concept analysis. J. Artif. Intell. Res. (JAIR) **24**(1), 305–339 (2005)

7. Di Noia, T., Di Sciascio, E., Donini, F.M.: Semantic matchmaking as non-monotonic reasoning: a description logic approach. J. Artif. Intell. Res. (JAIR), **29**, 269–307 (2007)
8. Ganter, B., Kuznetsov, S.O.: Stepwise construction of the Dedekind-MacNeille completion. In: Mugnier, M.-L., Chein, M. (eds.) ICCS-ConceptStruct 1998. LNCS, vol. 1453, pp. 295–302. Springer, Heidelberg (1998). https://doi.org/10.1007/BFb0054922
9. Ganter, B., Stumme, G., Wille, R. (eds.): Formal Concept Analysis. LNCS (LNAI), vol. 3626. Springer, Heidelberg (2005). https://doi.org/10.1007/978-3-540-31881-1
10. Ganter, B., Wille, R.: Formal Concept Analysis: Mathematical Foundations. Springer Science & Business Media, Heidelberg (2012)
11. Hájek, P.: Mathematics of Fuzzy Logic. Kluwer Academic Publishers, Dordrecht (1998)
12. Lau, T., Sure, Y.: Introducing ontology-based skills management at a large insurance company. In: Proceedings of the Modellierung, pp. 123–134 (2002)
13. Levandowsky, M., Winter, D.: Distance between sets. Nature **234**(5), 34–35 (1971)
14. Liu, L., Li, K.: Fuzzy filters of bl-algebras. Inf. Sci. **173**(1), 141–154 (2005)
15. Looser, D., Ma, H., Schewe, K.D.: Using formal concept analysis for ontology maintenance in human resource recruitment. In: Proceedings of the Ninth Asia-Pacific Conference on Conceptual Modelling, Vol. 143, pp. 61–68. Australian Computer Society Inc. (2013)
16. Maedche, A., Volz, R.: The ontology extraction & maintenance framework text-to-onto. In: Proceedings of the Workshop on Integrating Data Mining and Knowledge Management, USA, pp. 1–12 (2001)
17. Martínez Gil, J., Paoletti, A.L., Rácz, G., Sali, A., Schewe, K.D.: Accurate and efficient profile matching in knowledge bases (2017, submitted for publication)
18. Popov, N., Jebelean, T.: Semantic matching for job search engines–a logical approach. Technical report 13-02, Research Institute for Symbolic Computation. JKU Linz (2013)
19. Rácz, G., Sali, A., Schewe, K.-D.: Semantic matching strategies for job recruitment: a comparison of new and known approaches. In: Gyssens, M., Simari, G. (eds.) FoIKS 2016. LNCS, vol. 9616, pp. 149–168. Springer, Cham (2016). https://doi.org/10.1007/978-3-319-30024-5_9
20. Ragone, A., Straccia, U., Di Noia, T., Di Sciascio, E., Donini, F.M.: Fuzzy matchmaking in e-marketplaces of peer entities using Datalog. Fuzzy Sets Syst. **160**(2), 251–268 (2009)
21. Shamsfard, M., Barforoush, A.A.: The state of the art in ontology learning: a framework for comparison. Knowl. Eng. Rev. **18**(4), 293–316 (2003)
22. Wu, F., Weld, D.S.: Automatically refining the wikipedia infobox ontology. In: Proceedings of the 17th International Conference on World Wide Web, pp. 635–644. ACM (2008)
23. Wygralak, M.: Cardinalities of Fuzzy Sets. Springer, Heidelberg (2003)
24. Ziebarth, S., Malzahn, N., Hoppe, H.U.: Using data mining techniques to support the creation of competence ontologies. In: AIED, pp. 223–230 (2009)

# OntoDebug: Interactive Ontology Debugging Plug-in for Protégé

Konstantin Schekotihin[✉], Patrick Rodler[iD], and Wolfgang Schmid

Alpen-Adria-Universität, Klagenfurt, Austria
{konstantin.schekotihin,patrick.rodler,wolfgang.schmid}@aau.at

**Abstract.** Applications of semantic systems require their users to design ontologies that correctly formalize knowledge about a domain. In many cases factors such as insufficient understanding of a knowledge representation language, problems concerning modeling techniques and granularity, or inability to foresee all implications of formulated axioms result in faulty ontologies.

Debugging tools help to localize faults in ontologies by finding explanations of discrepancies between the actual ontology and the intended one. In this paper we present OntoDebug – a plug-in for the currently most popular open-source ontology editor Protégé – that implements an interactive approach to ontology debugging. Given a faulty ontology and a specification of requirements to the intended ontology, encoded as a set of test cases, our tool finds a set of faulty axioms explaining the problem. In case the user provides a set of test cases that does not allow for the computation of a unique explanation, OntoDebug is able to collect the missing information by asking the user a sequence of automatically generated questions.

## 1 Introduction

Broad application of semantic systems requires the existence of tools allowing for an efficient and intuitive localization of faults in the underlying ontologies. The main reason for such erroneous ontological definitions is that for humans it is generally hard to formulate correct logical descriptions [6], even if they have some experience with the used knowledge representation language [18,25]. In order to solve the fault localization problem a number of ontology debugging approaches were suggested over time aiming to explain inconsistency of an ontology or unsatisfiability of its classes [3,5,8,27].

Most of the approaches are derived from the Model-Based Diagnosis (MBD) techniques such as [10,19] in which a fault is revealed by comparison of expected and observed states of a system. Similarly [22], in case of ontology debugging these approaches investigate discrepancies between user requirements to the intended ontology, such as consistency, satisfiability of certain classes, entailment or non-entailment of axioms, etc., and observations made for the current version of an ontology. If some discrepancies are found, e.g. the developed ontology is inconsistent, then a fault is detected and the debugger is called to localize one or more faulty axioms, called diagnosis, that explain the observed behavior.

© Springer International Publishing AG, part of Springer Nature 2018
F. Ferrarotti and S. Woltran (Eds.): FoIKS 2018, LNCS 10833, pp. 340–359, 2018.
https://doi.org/10.1007/978-3-319-90050-6_19

The fault localization is usually implemented using various search techniques. One differentiates between glass-box and black-box approaches [16]. *Glass-box* methods, such as [1, 16, 26] introduce significant modifications to general-purpose description logic reasoners with the goal to use available internal information for a fast computation of diagnoses. In contrast, *black-box* approaches [3,5,8] are not dependent on the underlying reasoning algorithms. They use a reasoner as an oracle to check if some set of axioms is consistent and/or coherent.[1] Therefore such approaches can immediately benefit from the most recent advances in reasoning algorithms as well as use reasoners specifically designed and tuned for the developed ontology. As various evaluations indicate, glass-box approaches might show better performance in comparison to black-box ones. However, in [4] the authors demonstrate that these gains lay within the same order of magnitude and, therefore, are not significant.

Existing ontology development environments, such as Protégé [15], Swoop [9] or ORE [12], use various fault localization methods allowing for the debugging of ontologies. For instance, in Swoop both black-box and glass-box approaches [16] were used to find a justification why some class is unsatisfiable. These justifications, also called minimal conflict sets, are irreducible sets of axioms that entail unsatisfiability of the class. To increase the understandability of its explanations, Swoop generated quasi-natural language descriptions out of the identified axioms, which were then presented to the user. ORE uses a sound but incomplete variant of the same black-box algorithm for computation of justifications as in Swoop. This trade-off results in a significant speed-up in a number of cases, but incompleteness might result in situations where some faults cannot be found by the debugger. Finally, Protégé uses an implementation of the black-box algorithms presented in [8] to search for justifications of ontology entailments. The main advantage of this approach is that it can simplify axioms in justifications by computing their laconic versions [5]. The latter comprise only those parts of axioms which are essential for the derivation of the selected entailment. In addition, the same algorithm can be used to find explanations for the inconsistency of an ontology. However, these explanations are represented by collections of justifications, which must be analyzed manually by the user in order to find a correct repair.

Since in the general case there might exist an exponential number of explanations for a fault in an ontology, an interactive debugger was suggested in [28]. If the available information about a fault in an ontology is insufficient to localize the fault and multiple diagnoses are returned by the debugger, the interactive algorithm tries to acquire this missing information by asking a user a number of questions: Whether some axiom must be or must not be entailed by the intended ontology. Given answers of the user, the debugger recomputes the set of diagnoses and, if the fault is not yet revealed, asks additional questions.

---

[1] An ontology $\mathcal{O}$ is *coherent* iff there do not exist any unsatisfiable classes in $\mathcal{O}$. A class $X$ is *unsatisfiable* in an ontology $\mathcal{O}$ iff, for each interpretation $\mathcal{I}$ of $\mathcal{O}$, $X^{\mathcal{I}} = \emptyset$. See also [17, Definitions 1 and 2].

*Contributions.* In this paper we present OntoDebug – an interactive ontology debugger for Protégé – which is available in the standard plug-ins repository of Protégé and can be installed directly in the editor. Our interactive debugger builds on the ideas of the tools listed above and improves on them as follows:

- OntoDebug implements a number of black-box algorithms suggested for ontology debugging over the recent decade [3,5,29,30].[2] The best debugging performance of the plug-in for various ontologies is achieved in combination with modern reasoners available in Protégé, such as Pellet [31] or Hermit [14].
- The debugging process is user centric. By using the interactive techniques suggested in [28] and further improved in [20,21,23] our approach requires the user only to use her domain knowledge to answer questions about axioms of the intended ontology. As opposed to the existing approaches the user is not required to manually define, analyze and compare various explanations and/or justifications.
- The plug-in enables test-driven ontology development. OntoDebug supports definition of test cases, which capture requirements of the user to the intended ontology. In particular, the user can define axioms which must be entailments or non-entailments of the intended ontology. OntoDebug automatically verifies the test cases and starts a debugging session if at least one of them does not hold.
- Versatile parametrization of various algorithm combinations. For any debugging computation task the plug-in offers a number of algorithms that work best in different settings. Selection and proper parametrization of appropriate algorithms can help to significantly reduce the delays of OntoDebug between two queries.
- Repair interface enabling non-intrusive modifications of the ontology. While defining a correct repair, a user can introduce and test various modifications of faulty axioms on a virtual copy of the ontology. All modifications will be applied only when the user is satisfied with the obtained result.

The paper is organized as follows. In Sect. 2 we provide a brief introduction to the theoretical background of interactive ontology debugging. The architecture and the user interface of OntoDebug are presented in Sect. 3. Section 4 describes the possible settings of the plug-in and gives some hints on how to appropriately configure the tool for different purposes of application. Finally, we conclude in Sect. 5.

## 2   Interactive Ontology Debugging

Approaches to ontology debugging, such as those described in the previous section, are aiming at finding explanations of various discrepancies between the current $\mathcal{O}$ and the intended ontology $\mathcal{O}^*$. Examples of such discrepancies

---

[2] The source code and documentation is available at https://git-ainf.aau.at/inter active-KB-debugging/debugger.

include an inconsistency of $\mathcal{O}$, unsatisfiability of its classes, presence (absence) of unwanted (expected) entailments, etc. Ontology debuggers can help their users by automatically finding sets of logical axioms in $\mathcal{O}$ that must be changed in order to allow for the definition of the intended ontology $\mathcal{O}^*$.

*Example 1 (Simple ontology).* Consider the ontology with the terminology $\mathcal{T}$:

$$\{ax_1 : A \sqsubseteq B, \qquad ax_2 : B \sqsubseteq C, \qquad ax_3 : C \sqsubseteq D, \qquad ax_4 : D \sqsubseteq R\}$$

and assertions $\mathcal{A} : \{A(w), A(v)\}$. Let the user explicitly declare all axioms in $\mathcal{A}$ as correct (which at the same time means that all axioms in $\mathcal{T}$ are considered potentially faulty). In this case we say that $\mathcal{B} := \mathcal{A}$ is the specified *background knowledge* [20, Sect. 3.2] for the debugging session and $\mathcal{O} := \mathcal{T}$ is the ontology to be debugged. The implication of this is that faults are only sought within $\mathcal{O}$ in the "context" of $\mathcal{B}$, i.e. all the requirements to the intended ontology $\mathcal{O}^*$ such as consistency and fulfillment of test cases must hold for the union $\mathcal{O}^* \cup \mathcal{B}$. Finally, the user specifies test cases to check whether $\mathcal{O}$ corresponds to the intended ontology $\mathcal{O}^*$. Let the test cases define that $\mathcal{O}^* \cup \mathcal{B}$ entails (i) none of the axioms in the collection of *negative test cases* $N = \{R(w)\}$, i.e. $\mathcal{O}^* \cup \mathcal{B} \not\models n \; \forall n \in N$, and (ii) each axiom in the collection of *positive test cases* $P = \{B(v)\}$, i.e. $\mathcal{O}^* \cup \mathcal{B} \models p \; \forall p \in P$.

Since $\mathcal{O} \cup \mathcal{B}$ given in the example entails $R(w)$, some axioms in $\mathcal{O}$ must be modified in order to obtain $\mathcal{O}^*$. The only irreducible set of axioms in $\mathcal{O}$, called a *minimal conflict set* or a *justification* in the literature, that violates the user requirements is $CS : \{ax_1, ax_2, ax_3, ax_4\}$. In order to fulfill the requirements provided in the sets $P$ and $N$ the user must modify or remove at least one of the axioms $ax_i \in CS$. Consequently, there are four minimal repair strategies, called *minimal diagnoses*:

$$\mathcal{D}_1 : [ax_1] \quad \mathcal{D}_2 : [ax_2] \quad \mathcal{D}_3 : [ax_3] \quad \mathcal{D}_4 : [ax_4] \tag{1}$$

□

Note, the specification of a background theory $\mathcal{B}$ as well as of the test cases $P$ and $N$ allows the debugger to stay focused on the possibly incorrect statements and might significantly reduce the runtime of search procedures.

The presence of more than one diagnosis indicates that the information provided by the user to the debugger is insufficient for localization of the real cause of the problem. Therefore, the user must either select the correct diagnosis manually or provide more information, e.g. by extending the set $N$ or declaring more axioms as correct moving them from the ontology $\mathcal{O}$ to the background knowledge $\mathcal{B}$.

*Example 2.* Assume that in Example 1 the user adds a negative test case $B(w)$. Given the sets $N = \{R(w), B(w)\}$ and $P = \{B(v)\}$, the debugger will return only one diagnosis $\mathcal{D}_1$, which explains the fault in $\mathcal{O}$. That is, $\mathcal{O} \cup \mathcal{B} \models B(w)$ because of $ax_1 \in \mathcal{O}$ and an assertion $A(w) \in \mathcal{B}$. □

However, the application of diagnosis $\mathcal{D}_1$ results in a new ontology $\mathcal{O}_1 :=$ $\mathcal{O} \setminus \mathcal{D}_1$ that, along with $\mathcal{B}$, does not entail $B(v)$ as required by the set of positive test cases. Consequently, $\mathcal{O}_1$ must be extended with some set of axioms $EX$ such that $\mathcal{O}_1 \cup EX$ fulfills all requirements to $\mathcal{O}^*$. Of course, the intended set $EX$ is unknown to the debugger and possibly some complex learning methods must be used to obtain it. One solution [20, Proposition 3.5] to this problem is to approximate $EX$ with the set of positive test cases $P$, which comprises all necessary entailments of $\mathcal{O}^*$. In our example the ontology $\mathcal{O}_1 \cup P$ satisfies all test cases. Hence, in order to specify $\mathcal{O}^*$ the user must extend the ontology $\mathcal{O}_1$ with the assertion $B(v)$ or axioms entailing $B(v)$.

**Definition 1 (Diagnosis Problem Instance (DPI)).** *Let $\mathcal{O}$ be an ontology (including possibly faulty axioms) and $\mathcal{B}$ be a background theory (including correct axioms) where $\mathcal{O} \cap \mathcal{B} = \emptyset$, and let $\mathcal{O}^*$ denote the (unknown) intended ontology. Moreover, let $P$ and $N$ be sets of axioms where each $p \in P$ must and each $n \in N$ must not be entailed by $\mathcal{O}^* \cup \mathcal{B}$, respectively. Then, the tuple $\langle \mathcal{O}, \mathcal{B}, P, N \rangle$ is called a diagnosis problem instance (DPI).*

**Definition 2 (Diagnosis).** *Let $\langle \mathcal{O}, \mathcal{B}, P, N \rangle$ be a DPI. Then, a set of axioms $\mathcal{D} \subseteq \mathcal{O}$ is a diagnosis iff both of the following conditions hold:*

1. *$(\mathcal{O} \setminus \mathcal{D}) \cup P \cup \mathcal{B}$ is consistent (coherent, if required)*
2. *$(\mathcal{O} \setminus \mathcal{D}) \cup P \cup \mathcal{B} \not\models n$ for all $n \in N$*

*A diagnosis $\mathcal{D}$ is minimal iff there is no $\mathcal{D}' \subset \mathcal{D}$ such that $\mathcal{D}'$ is a diagnosis.*

Note that, following [10,19], in our approach we focus on the computation of minimal diagnoses $\mathcal{D}_i$ only, since they suggest the smallest possible changes of a faulty ontology. That is, each axiom $ax_j \in \mathcal{D}_i$ is faulty and must be modified, whereas each axiom $ax_k \in \mathcal{O} \setminus \mathcal{D}_i$ is correct and its alteration is redundant.

Computation of diagnoses for ontologies can be accomplished by means of various algorithms. Some of them compute diagnoses directly [29], whereas others [3,8,20,27] find diagnoses using *conflict sets*. In many practical scenarios these sets allow for an efficient restriction of the search space, which in turn causes a good performance of debugging approaches.

**Definition 3 (Conflict Set).** *Given a DPI $\langle \mathcal{O}, \mathcal{B}, P, N \rangle$, a set of axioms $CS \subseteq \mathcal{O}$ is a conflict set iff at least one of the following conditions holds:*

1. *$CS \cup P \cup \mathcal{B}$ is inconsistent (incoherent)*
2. *$CS \cup P \cup \mathcal{B} \models n$ for some $n \in N$.*

*A conflict set $CS$ is minimal iff there is no conflict set $CS'$ where $CS' \subset CS$.*

The conflict-based approaches use the property shown in [19], which states that a (minimal) diagnosis is a (minimal) hitting set of all minimal conflict sets.

*Example 3.* Reconsider Example 1 presented above, in which the ontology debugger returns four minimal diagnoses $\{\mathcal{D}_1, \ldots, \mathcal{D}_4\}$. In this case the user must modify the DPI by specifying more test cases and allowing the debugger to narrow its search and to find the correct diagnosis. Users might have various strategies for finding these missing test cases. One of them is to compare the entailments of the repaired ontologies $\mathcal{O}_i^* := (\mathcal{O} \setminus \mathcal{D}_i) \cup P$ (along with the background knowledge $\mathcal{B}$) that result from the application of the different diagnoses $\mathcal{D}_i$. In our example all the four thus obtained ontologies have, among others, the following class assertion entailments regarding the individual $w$, that can be computed using instantiation algorithms of a description logic reasoner [14,31]:

$$\mathcal{O}_1^* : \emptyset \quad \mathcal{O}_2^* : \{B(w)\} \quad \mathcal{O}_3^* : \{B(w), C(w)\} \quad \mathcal{O}_4^* : \{B(w), C(w), D(w)\} \tag{2}$$

Any assertion $B(w)$, $C(w)$, or $D(w)$ can be used as a test case allowing for the discrimination between the diagnoses. For instance, assume the user extends the input DPI $\langle \mathcal{T}, \{A(v), A(w)\}, \{B(v)\}, \{R(w)\}\rangle$ with a positive test case $D(w)$. For the resulting new DPI $\langle \mathcal{T}, \{A(v), A(w)\}, \{B(v), D(w)\}, \{R(w)\}\rangle$ the debugger can find only the single minimal diagnosis $\mathcal{D}_4 = [ax_4]$. In fact, all other minimal diagnoses for the input DPI, namely $\mathcal{D}_1 = [ax_1]$, $\mathcal{D}_2 = [ax_2]$ and $\mathcal{D}_3 = [ax_3]$, are no longer diagnoses for the new DPI. That is, for $i \in \{1, 2, 3\}$, the assumption that $ax_i$ is the only faulty axiom in $\mathcal{O}$ conflicts with the new positive test case $D(w)$. Because each $\mathcal{O}_i^* \cup \mathcal{B}$ for $i \in \{1, 2, 3\}$ includes the axiom $ax_4 : D \sqsubseteq R$ which causes the unwanted entailment $R(w) \in N$ once the necessary entailment $D(w)$ is added. However, since $ax_4$ is the only axiom in $\mathcal{O}$ that can cause the entailment $R(w)$ given $D(w)$, it follows that $ax_4$ must be faulty given the new DPI. In other words, all diagnoses for the new DPI must include $ax_4$, which is why $\mathcal{D}_4$ is the only minimal repair remaining. □

An *interactive debugger* [20,28] automates the process described in the example and suggests its user good possible test cases. The user in this case must only provide the correct classification of the suggested axioms to either $P$ or $N$. In particular, we model the user as a query-answering oracle as follows:

**Definition 4 (Oracle).** *Let* **Ax** *be a set of axioms and* $ans : \mathbf{Ax} \to \{P, N\}$ *a function which assigns axioms in* **Ax** *to either the positive or the negative test cases. Then, we call* $ans$ *an oracle wrt. the intended ontology* $\mathcal{O}^*$*, iff for* $ax \in \mathbf{Ax}$ *both of the following conditions hold:*

$$ans(ax) = P \quad \Longrightarrow \quad \mathcal{O}^* \cup \mathcal{B} \models ax \tag{3}$$

$$ans(ax) = N \quad \Longrightarrow \quad \mathcal{O}^* \cup \mathcal{B} \not\models ax \tag{4}$$

The implications in Eqs. (3) and (4) signify that the oracle classifies each axiom based on the intended ontology $\mathcal{O}^*$. The oracle function $ans$ can be either total or partial. In the former case the oracle can be seen as a *full domain expert* for $\mathcal{O}^*$ (able to label all asked axioms as $P$ or $N$), in the latter as a *partial domain expert* (possibly not able to label all asked axioms as $P$ or $N$). Note, in case of a full domain expert, the implications in Eqs. (3) and (4) become bi-implications, telling that exactly all axioms in **Ax** entailed by $\mathcal{O}^*$ (along with $\mathcal{B}$) are assigned to $P$ and exactly all that are not entailed are added to $N$.

A query is a set of axioms $Q$ that guarantees the elimination of at least one diagnosis given any answer of a full domain expert. More formally, letting $Q_{ans}^P := \{q \in Q \mid ans(q) = P\}$ and $Q_{ans}^N := \{q \in Q \mid ans(q) = N\}$ denote the subsets of $Q$ assigned to $P$ and $N$ by an oracle $ans$, respectively, we define:

**Definition 5 (Query).** *Let $\langle \mathcal{O}, \mathcal{B}, P, N \rangle$ be a DPI, $\mathbf{D}$ be a set of diagnoses for this DPI, and $Q$ be a set of axioms. Then we call $Q$ a query for $\mathbf{D}$ iff, for any classification $Q_{ans}^P, Q_{ans}^N$ of the axioms in $Q$ of a full domain expert oracle $ans$, at least one diagnosis in $\mathbf{D}$ is no longer a diagnosis for the new DPI $\langle \mathcal{O}, \mathcal{B}, P \cup Q_{ans}^P, N \cup Q_{ans}^N \rangle$.*

Computation of queries can be done by different algorithms. These usually rely on the concept of a *query partition*, a unique partitioning $\langle \mathbf{D^P}, \mathbf{D^N}, \mathbf{D^\emptyset} \rangle$ of the (known) diagnoses $\mathbf{D}$ into three sets based on a given set of axioms $Q$:

- $\mathbf{D^P}$ includes all diagnoses in $\mathbf{D}$ that predict an all-positive classification of the oracle $ans$ for $Q$, i.e. $Q_{ans}^P = Q$ (and thus $Q_{ans}^N = \emptyset$)
- $\mathbf{D^N}$ includes all diagnoses in $\mathbf{D}$ that predict a some-negative classification of the oracle $ans$ for $Q$, i.e. $Q_{ans}^N \supset \emptyset$ (and thus $Q_{ans}^P \subset Q$),
- $\mathbf{D^\emptyset}$ includes all diagnoses in $\mathbf{D} \setminus (\mathbf{D^P} \cup \mathbf{D^N})$.

Formally, a diagnosis $\mathcal{D}_i$ *predicts*

(a) an all-positive,
(b) a some-negative

classification of the oracle $ans$ for $Q$, respectively, iff for the ontology $\mathcal{O}_i^* = (\mathcal{O} \setminus \mathcal{D}_i) \cup P$ it holds that

- $\mathcal{O}_i^* \cup \mathcal{B} \models Q$ for (a),
- $\mathcal{O}_i^* \cup \mathcal{B} \cup Q \models n$ for some $n \in N$ or is inconsistent (incoherent) for (b).

Given the notion of a query partition, we have:

**Proposition 1.** *A set of axioms $Q$ is a query for $\mathbf{D}$ as per Definition 5 whenever both sets $\mathbf{D^P}$ and $\mathbf{D^N}$ in the query partition of $Q$ are non-empty.*

Besides being useful for query verification (as per Proposition 1), a query partition also enables the estimation of the quality of a query. A brute force query computation algorithm suggested in [28], for instance, exploits query partitions in that it investigates query partition candidates by enumerating all subsets of the set $\mathbf{D}$. For each candidate the algorithm checks whether there exists a set of axioms which is a query according to Definition 5. Given a *query selection measure* [21] that maps any query partition to a real number (expressing the goodness of the partition), more sophisticated algorithms can be used. For example, in [28] the authors adopted the Complete Karmarkar-Karp algorithm [11] to efficiently find a query partition that maximizes the expected information gain after a user answers the query [10]. Further performance improvements can be achieved by minimizing the number of reasoner calls required to compute a query. Thus, the approach presented in [23] first constructs a query prototype that optimizes the given measure using only implicit information provided by the set of diagnoses $\mathbf{D}$. The reasoner is then only called optionally for the one already optimized prototype to achieve further enhancements wrt. additional query quality metrics such as easy understandability of sentences in the query.

Note also that the evaluation of query selection measures is often based on additional information about possibly faulty axioms [20, Sect. 4.6], e.g. by defining for every such axiom its probability of being faulty. In [28] such probabilities are computed by analyzing axioms and estimating how well a user can understand them. This estimation might be accomplished using some user profile, which assesses for every syntactic feature of a knowledge representation language, e.g. boolean connectives or property restrictions in OWL2, a probability for the user to use this feature in a wrong way. Such a profile can be either established manually by the user or generated automatically by analyzing past debugging sessions of that user. Moreover, a user profile can be refined by incorporating the user's contentual expertise and possibly some axiom provenance information [20]. For instance, in a medical ontology, for a dermatologist the probability of making content-related mistakes using the classes *Melanoma*, *Eczema* or *Acne* will usually be rather small, and lower than for a, say, oculist using these terms.

*Example 4.* Let us sketch the *query generation and selection* by means of the entropy-based quality measure proposed in [10] for our Example 1. Recall that we had four minimal diagnoses $\mathbf{D} = \{\mathcal{D}_1, \ldots, \mathcal{D}_4\}$ for this DPI, given by Eq. (1), and therefore four respective ontologies $\mathcal{O}_i^* = (\mathcal{O} \setminus \mathcal{D}_i) \cup P$ resulting from the application of the diagnoses $\mathcal{D}_i$ to the ontology $\mathcal{O}$. Assume that a user profile based on syntactical axiom structure, as discussed above, is used to assess the fault likeliness of axioms $ax_i$ in $\mathcal{O}$. In this case, since all axioms share the same structure (including only the logical connective $\sqsubseteq$) and each $\mathcal{D}_i \in \mathbf{D}$ includes exactly one axiom, it can be easily derived that all diagnoses in $\mathbf{D}$ have the same probability 0.25 (normalized over $\mathbf{D}$). Since the entropy-based query selection measure is optimized if the sum of diagnoses probabilities in the query partition set $\mathbf{D^P}$ is equal to the sum of diagnoses probabilities in the query partition set $\mathbf{D^N}$ [28], the query selection will in this case favor queries including two of the four diagnoses in each of the sets $\mathbf{D^P}$ and $\mathbf{D^N}$. Let the reasoner used for query computation (be configured in a way to) compute exactly the entailments for the ontologies $\mathcal{O}_i^*$ (along with $\mathcal{B}$) given in Eq. (2), and let the adopted query computation algorithm be similar to the one suggested in [20, Chap. 8]. Then, the explored query candidates are sets of common (reasoner) entailments of some ontologies out of $[\mathcal{O}_1^* \cup \mathcal{B}, \ldots, \mathcal{O}_4^* \cup \mathcal{B}]$, e.g. $\mathcal{Q}_1 := \{B(w), C(w)\}$ is a *generated candidate* because it is entailed by both ontologies in $\{\mathcal{O}_3^* \cup \mathcal{B}, \mathcal{O}_4^* \cup \mathcal{B}\}$. In other words, if the oracle *ans* says that some element(s) of $\mathcal{Q}_1$ must not be entailed, (at least) diagnoses $\mathcal{D}_3, \mathcal{D}_4$ are no longer diagnoses for the new DPI, i.e. $\mathcal{D}_3, \mathcal{D}_4 \in \mathbf{D^P}$. In contrast, if all elements of $\mathcal{Q}_1$ must be entailed according to *ans*,

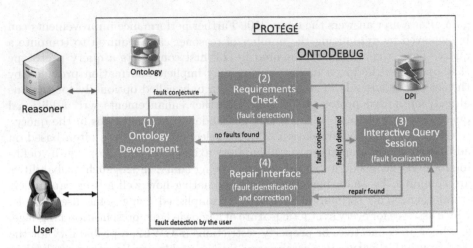

**Fig. 1.** Ontology evolution using OntoDebug

then $\mathcal{D}_1, \mathcal{D}_2$ are no diagnoses for the new DPI as both $\mathcal{O}_1^* \cup \mathcal{B}, \mathcal{O}_2^* \cup \mathcal{B}$ do not allow for the addition of the postulated entailment $C(w) \in Q_1$ without violating some other required criteria, in this case the negative test case $R(w)$. Hence, $\mathcal{D}_1, \mathcal{D}_2 \in \mathbf{D}^{\mathbf{N}}$. The obtained query partition for $Q_1$ is thus $\langle \{\mathcal{D}_3, \mathcal{D}_4\}, \{\mathcal{D}_1, \mathcal{D}_2\}, \emptyset \rangle$; since both $\mathbf{D}^{\mathbf{P}}$ and $\mathbf{D}^{\mathbf{N}}$ are non-empty sets, $Q_1$ is in fact a *verified query* conforming to Definition 5 (cf. Proposition 1). Using the reasoner, similarly as described, for *candidate generation* and *query verification* leads to a pool of queries, from which the best wrt. the entropy measure is selected. In this case, $Q_1$ turns out to be the optimal choice (with even the best theoretical entropy value, as explained above). However, as a final *query minimality check* [20, Sect. 8.3] yields that $Q_1' = \{C(w)\}$ has exactly the same query partition and thus entropy measure as $Q_1$, but comprises fewer sentences (less effort for the user), the minimized optimal query $Q_1'$ is finally presented to the interacting user.     □

## 3   OntoDebug Protégé Plug-in

In diagnosis literature [32] one distinguishes between various diagnostic goals, namely *fault detection* (is there a fault?), *fault localization* (where is the fault?) as well as *fault identification* (what is the fault?) *and correction*. OntoDebug assists the user regarding all these tasks. In particular, the ontology evolution using OntoDebug can be characterized as a reiteration of four main phases, shown in Fig. 1: (1) ontology development, (2) fault detection, (3) fault localization, (4) fault identification and correction. We next explicate all four stages.[3]

---

[3] Please note that our OntoDebug Plug-In is still in the development phase and that changes regarding its described look & feel or functionality enhancements might still be incorporated in the future.

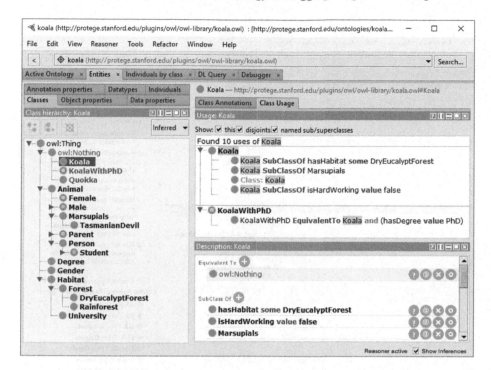

**Fig. 2.** Koala ontology in Protégé

*(1) Ontology Development.* In this stage a user formulates, modifies or deletes axioms with the goal of expressing the intended ontology. In addition, a user might i.e. browse the ontology, use some visualization plug-ins offered by Protégé or call a reasoner. For instance, by invoking the reasoner a user can verify consistency of the ontology and satisfiability of its classes, check axioms inferred by classification and realization services, or – in conjunction with a Protégé Explanation Plug-In – compute justifications [5] for certain inferences.

When analyzing the manually defined and inferred axioms, i.e. the semantics, of the present ontology, a user might have doubts about their correctness. The reasons for these doubts might be explicit or implicit. In the first case a *user might directly detect the presence of a fault*, e.g., by observing that the ontology is inconsistent, incoherent, or has entailments which are obviously incorrect. In such a situation, the fault detection is already accomplished by the user who can now directly commence the fault localization, see stage (3) below.

*Example 5.* Consider a Koala ontology[4] which was created for educational purposes and illustrates common problems occurring in cases where users do not completely understand the knowledge representation language they are using. Due to mistakes made while developing the ontology, a reasoner recognizes three

---

[4] This ontology can be loaded from bookmarks in `Open from URL...` menu of Protégé.

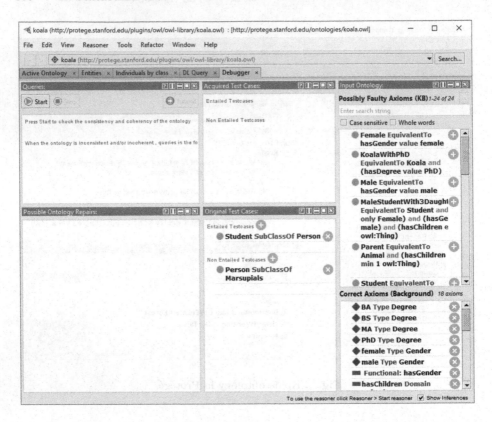

**Fig. 3.** Interactive debugging session in OntoDebug (DPI specification)

subclasses of the *Marsupials* class, namely *Koala*, *KoalaWithPhD*, and *Quokka*, as unsatisfiable classes and Protégé labels them in red (see Fig. 2). In fact, the user erroneously used one of the two properties *isHardWorking* and *hasDegree* to describe each of the three classes listed above. Since the domains of these properties are restricted to a *Person* class, the reasoner derives that *Koala*, *KoalaWithPhD*, and *Quokka* are subclasses of the class *Person*. However, the ontology comprises an axiom stating that the classes of marsupials and persons are disjoint, which results in an unsatisfiability of the three discussed classes. Since in this case the user is able to detect the presence of a fault directly in the editor, she can immediately start an interactive debugging session in the debugger tab.                                                                                    □

In the second – implicit – case, the user might only conjecture that something is wrong, i.e. the faultiness of the ontology is not obvious. For example, the user might find that over time, after multiple modifications, some of the ontology axioms are hard to understand, relations between them are unclear, or their entailments are not comprehensible. Therefore, similarly to the scenario discussed in Example 1, the user might want to verify such axioms by formulating a *fault conjecture*, which can be defined as test cases in OntoDebug, see stage (2) below.

*(2) Fault Detection.* This stage is where OntoDebug first comes into play. To use it for fault detection, the user can simply open the debugger tab in Protégé and specify a DPI based on the ontology $\mathcal{O}$ at hand. In particular, the user interface of OntoDebug allows its users to move correct axioms to the background theory which enables OntoDebug to focus just on the relevant ontology parts. If in Example 5 the user wants to focus on class axioms only, then she should move all assertions and property restrictions from the list of Possibly Faulty Axioms to the list of Correct Axioms in the Input Ontology view. In addition, the user might specify positive test cases $P$, which describe desired entailments, as well as negative test cases $N$ that correspond to non-desired entailments. In Fig. 3 both lists, which are shown in the Original Test Cases view, comprise one axiom. The positive test case states that ontology axioms must allow for an entailment "a student is a person" and the negative one asserts that "a person is a marsupial" must not be entailed.

Given the final DPI $\langle \mathcal{O}, \mathcal{B}, P, N \rangle$, the verification of ontology consistency (coherency) and execution of the test cases can be triggered by the "Start" button. If no faults are present, i.e. the user's fault conjecture is unjustified, OntoDebug informs the user about this fact whereupon the user can continue with the ontology development. Otherwise, i.e. if the ontology is inconsistent (incoherent) or the evaluation of at least one test case is unsuccessful, OntoDebug automatically invokes the diagnoses computation as well as query generation and selection engines to provide the user with a first question, thereby initializing the fault localization process.

*(3) Fault Localization.* OntoDebug localizes faults in an ontology by executing an *interactive query session*, a snapshot of which is presented in Fig. 4. During this process, the user gets queries about desired entailments and non-entailments of the intended ontology in the Queries view.

For instance, in the second iteration of the query session, shown in Fig. 4, the user is asked whether "a Koala with PhD is a Koala" and "a Koala with PhD is a Person" must or must not be entailed by the intended ontology. In our case, using the common knowledge about koalas, the user classifies positively the first axiom and negatively the second, as indicated by corresponding buttons. The "Submit" button instructs OntoDebug to construct a new DPI in which the first axiom is added to the list of positive test cases and the second to the list of negative ones. The answers of the user provided during the query session are shown in the Acquired Test Cases view. In our example, the query asked in the first iteration of the session, namely "a Koala is a Marsupial" was answered positively and the corresponding axiom was added to the list of Entailed Testcases.

In case the user misclassified an axiom and wants to backtrack, she can simply remove this axiom from the Acquired Test Cases lists. OntoDebug will automatically recompute the diagnoses and suggest a new query.

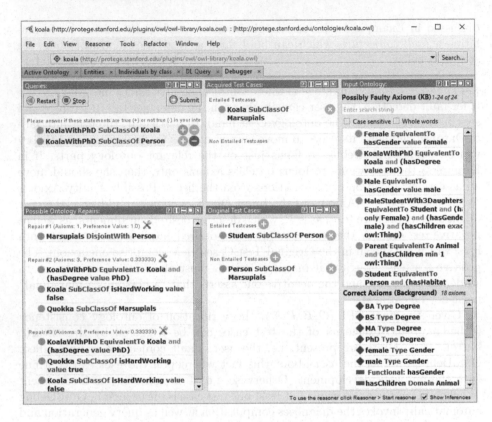

**Fig. 4.** Interactive ontology debugging session in OntoDebug (during query session)

Note, a handy feature of the automatic query suggestion implemented by OntoDebug is the guaranteed avoidance of any incompatibilities regarding the acquired test cases, independent of the provided user answers. By contrast, in the same way as faults might creep in during the development of the ontology itself, inconsistencies between test cases might arise when they are specified manually.

Also, the user is not required to be a full domain expert (cf. Sect. 2) wrt. the intended ontology, i.e. not every axiom in a shown query must be classified positively or negatively. In fact, simply not marking an axiom by $(+)$ or $(-)$ means "unknown", which is handled in a way that the respective axiom is neither added to $P$ (Entailed Test Cases) nor to $N$ (Non Entailed Test Cases). Since OntoDebug currently focuses on queries for the full expert case, the implication of answering the query partially might be a weaker discrimination among the possible repairs. It is a future research topic to develop methods for query computation and optimization in case of interaction with a partial domain expert.

Acquisition of test cases allows OntoDebug to restrict the set of minimal diagnoses **D** (cf. Sect. 2) shown in the Possible Ontology Repairs view. Consecutive query answering enables the final determination of the (single) semantically correct minimal diagnosis, i.e. the proper minimally invasive repair for the ontology $\mathcal{O}$. Any other minimal diagnosis has a (proven) wrong semantics [20]. Also, OntoDebug presents the current repairs to the user in a best-first order, e.g., most probable or minimum cardinality first. Besides, the already computed minimal conflict sets are constantly refined by OntoDebug and can be displayed on demand. These represent minimal faulty sub-ontologies, i.e. justifications for non-desired entailments or inconsistency/incoherency. Analysis of minimal conflicts can help the user to gain further insight into the problems in the ontology or to make better sense of the shown repairs.

We emphasize that a "manual" analysis of conflict sets and repairs as an approach to fault localization might be tedious (exponentially many repair candidates), error-prone [5] and mentally (over)straining [2] and thus often not viable. As opposed to this, in OntoDebug the user is **not required** to analyze

- why exactly *the input ontology* is faulty, or
- which entailments (axioms) do or do not hold, or why certain entailments do or do not hold, *in the faulty input ontology.*

All the user is **required** to do is answering questions about whether specific statements should be true or not true *in the intended ontology.*

Given the answers, OntoDebug will return which axioms must be repaired in the faulty input ontology. The event of just *one remaining repair* or *the commitment of the user to one (of multiple) repair(s)* marks the transition between the fault localization (3) and the fault identification stage (4).

*(4) Fault Identification.* For the purpose of fault identification, OntoDebug provides a separate *repair interface* presented in Fig. 5. This interface comes i.a. with the functionality of enabling a per-axiom modification or deletion, using Protégé's built-in editor. Moreover, the user can analyze the faults caused by exactly this particular axiom by considering explanations generated by the debugger. The latter feature is supposed to give the user a hint of how the axiom contributes to the faults and what to change in the axiom in order to obtain a correct ontology. In our example, Explanation 1 comprises all axioms that are relevant to the axiom describing the *Quokka* class, which is selected in the Repair view above. Analysis of these axioms elucidates that a *Quokka* is a *Marsupial* (axiom 5) and a *Person* (axioms 2 and 4) simultaneously. However, since *Marsupial* and *Person* are disjoint classes (axiom 1), the *Quokka* class is unsatisfiable.

Furthermore, the repair interface lets the user check at any time whether all faults (conflict sets) in the original ontology are already resolved or not. To do so, the user just needs to select the "OK" button and check the default OntoDebug tab. In case any of the previous faults remain or some new faults are introduced by modifications done in the repair interface, the debugger will automatically start a new interactive session. Otherwise, OntoDebug informs the user that the ontology is correct.

Once the user obtains a fault-free ontology, the performed modifications can be stored and all acquired test cases moved to the permanent ones. In this way

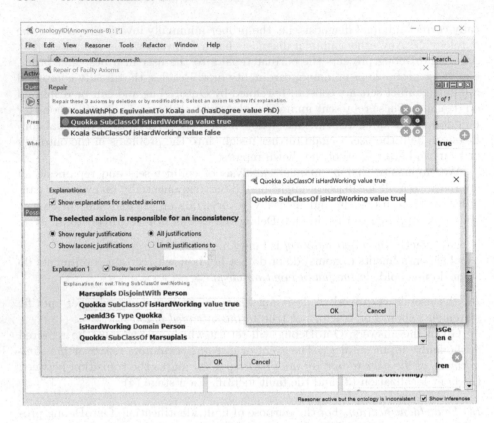

**Fig. 5.** Interactive ontology debugging session in OntoDebug (repair interface)

our debugger enables a continuous acquisition and maintenance of test cases, which is very important for quality assurance in the ontology development process. Finally, the user can continue to

(a) the ontology development stage (1) by starting the described ontology evolution loop anew, or
(b) the fault detection stage (2), if new fault conjectures, i.e. test cases, arise after the repair session, e.g. in case the user feels that some parts of the ontology were not tested well enough.

As a final remark, note that OntoDebug does not focus on the validation of the entire ontology, but rather pursues a symptom-driven fault repair. That is, once a deficiency, e.g. an inconsistency or a violation of a test case, of the developed ontology becomes evident, OntoDebug assists in restoring the ontology's correctness in terms of the *given or already acquired test cases*. It is a future work topic to develop strategies for test case suggestion given an ontology that *is* compatible with the specified criteria. Such strategies could, for instance, be guided by logical counterparts to code smells from the field of software debugging such as OWL antipatterns [25] or common modeling mistakes [18].

# 4    Settings and Hints for Proper Configuration

To ensure the best performance for various ontologies OntoDebug allows its users to use different combinations of algorithms for the computation of minimal conflict sets and diagnoses as well as for the generation and selection of queries.

The Fault Localization view of the plug-in settings, shown in Fig. 6, comprises selectors and parameters of the algorithms related to diagnoses computation tasks. OntoDebug offers three algorithms for the identification of minimal conflict sets that have different properties. QuickXPlain [7] is a default divide-and-conquer conflict searcher that guarantees stable performance in cases when reasoning tasks for an ontology can be performed rather fast. MergeXPlain [30] is an extension of QuickXPlain that works best when an ontology comprises a number of non-intersecting minimal conflicts. In such situations, this algorithm can find multiple conflicts at once and can be easily parallelized on multi-core architectures. Finally, Progression [13] is an algorithm designed for situations when reasoning for the ontology is hard. This algorithm starts with a smaller subset of axioms and extends it until a conflict is acquired. Then, the obtained set of axioms is minimized. However, on simpler ontologies with fewer faults it shows a slower performance than QuickXPlain.

Computation of diagnoses in OntoDebug can be done using two algorithms, namely HS-Tree [19] (default) and Inv-HS-Tree [29]. The first algorithm implements a breadth-first or uniform-cost search for diagnoses via the computation of minimal conflict sets. HS-Tree is the best choice if an ontology comprises a small number of minimal conflicts with only a few axioms each. This case can be met in practice when a user tests the developed version of an ontology regularly for incompatibility with the specified requirements. The second algorithm, Inv-HS-Tree, computes diagnoses directly and does not rely on the computation of conflict sets. As a consequence, this diagnosis engine can leverage a linear-space depth-first search method which comes, however, at the cost of not guaranteeing a best-first computation of the minimal diagnoses. Therefore, the user should prefer this algorithm if the ontology comprises large numbers of high-cardinality faults, like in cases of ontologies output by automatic alignment approaches. In ontology development scenarios the performance of this algorithm tends to be inferior to HS-Tree.

Furthermore, this tab allows to select the preference measure for the diagnosis computation, such as cardinality of diagnoses, probability, or no preference (equal costs). At the moment, our framework by default ranks diagnoses that comprise fewer axioms higher, reflecting the situation where no bias concerning the fault probability of axioms in the ontology is given. That is, the minimally invasive solutions are presented to the user first. The probability-based measures and the specification of respective user profiles are implemented in the back-end, but the user interface is still in work.

The Query Computation view allows the user to choose the query selection measure out of Entropy [10], Split-in-Half [28] and Dynamic Risk (which is called RIO in the original publication [24]). The first strategy prefers queries that yield a maximal information gain given an answer of the user. The second one always

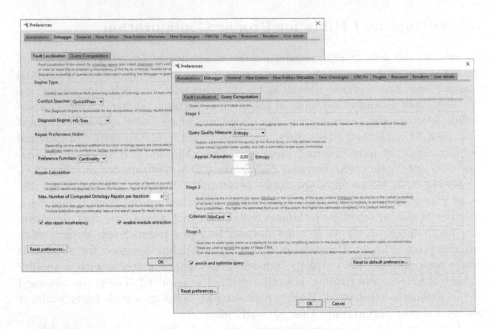

**Fig. 6.** Preferences views of OntoDebug

selects queries which ensure that a half of the (known) diagnoses of the current DPI are no longer diagnoses of the next DPI, regardless of the user's answer. Dynamic Risk is a parameterized measure that is automatically adapted by reinforcement learning based on the diagnoses elimination performance achieved. It combines the two previous measures to find the golden mean between the stability of Split-in-Half and the ability of Entropy to make risky decisions, where "risky" refers to the exploitation of possibly vague or misleading prior probabilities.

Finally, a user can specify the preferences for queries in terms of their cardinality (MinCard), overall syntactical complexity of the axioms used in the query (MinSum), and the complexity of the most syntactically complex axiom in a query (MinMax). Furthermore, the user can decide whether queries must be enriched by computing additional entailments. This feature is recommended since it can significantly improve the understandability of queries, but should be avoided if the computation of entailments is hard.

## 5    Conclusions

In this paper we presented OntoDebug – an interactive ontology debugging plug-in for Protégé. Our approach implements all tasks relevant to fault detection, localization and repair. The interactive debugging technique significantly reduces the burden of fault localization by hiding analysis and comparison of different fault explanations behind a query interface. The user of OntoDebug is only required to use her domain knowledge to answer questions of the debugger regarding entailments and non-entailments of the intended ontology. Finally, the possibility to define and maintain test cases and automatically acquire new ones in the course of a debugging session makes it possible for the first time to apply a test-driven methodology for ontology development and thus to improve the quality of the final ontology.

# References

1. Baader, F., Peñaloza, R.: Axiom pinpointing in general tableaux. J. Log. Comput. **20**(1), 5–34 (2010)
2. Ceraso, J., Provitera, A.: Sources of error in syllogistic reasoning. Cogn. Psychol. **2**(4), 400–410 (1971)
3. Friedrich, G., Shchekotykhin, K.: A general diagnosis method for ontologies. In: Gil, Y., Motta, E., Benjamins, V.R., Musen, M.A. (eds.) ISWC 2005. LNCS, vol. 3729, pp. 232–246. Springer, Heidelberg (2005). https://doi.org/10.1007/11574620_19
4. Horridge, M.: Justification based explanation in ontologies. Ph.D. thesis, University of Manchester (2011)
5. Horridge, M., Parsia, B., Sattler, U.: Laconic and precise justifications in OWL. In: Sheth, A., Staab, S., Dean, M., Paolucci, M., Maynard, D., Finin, T., Thirunarayan, K. (eds.) ISWC 2008. LNCS, vol. 5318, pp. 323–338. Springer, Heidelberg (2008). https://doi.org/10.1007/978-3-540-88564-1_21
6. Johnson-Laird, P.N.: Deductive reasoning. Annu. Rev. Psychol. **50**, 109–135 (1999)
7. Junker, U.: QUICKXPLAIN: preferred explanations and relaxations for over-constrained problems. In: AAAI 2004, vol. 3, pp. 167–172 (2004)
8. Kalyanpur, A., Parsia, B., Horridge, M., Sirin, E.: Finding all justifications of OWL DL entailments. In: Aberer, K., et al. (eds.) ASWC/ISWC -2007. LNCS, vol. 4825, pp. 267–280. Springer, Heidelberg (2007). https://doi.org/10.1007/978-3-540-76298-0_20
9. Kalyanpur, A., Parsia, B., Sirin, E., Grau, B.C., Hendler, J.A.: Swoop: a web ontology editing browser. J. Web Semant. **4**(2), 144–153 (2006)
10. de Kleer, J., Williams, B.C.: Diagnosing multiple faults. Artif. Intell. **32**(1), 97–130 (1987)
11. Korf, R.E.: A complete anytime algorithm for number partitioning. Artif. Intell. **106**(2), 181–203 (1998)
12. Lehmann, J., Bühmann, L.: ORE - a tool for repairing and enriching knowledge bases. In: Patel-Schneider, P.F., Pan, Y., Hitzler, P., Mika, P., Zhang, L., Pan, J.Z., Horrocks, I., Glimm, B. (eds.) ISWC 2010. LNCS, vol. 6497, pp. 177–193. Springer, Heidelberg (2010). https://doi.org/10.1007/978-3-642-17749-1_12
13. Marques-Silva, J., Janota, M., Belov, A.: Minimal sets over monotone predicates in Boolean formulae. In: Sharygina, N., Veith, H. (eds.) CAV 2013. LNCS, vol. 8044, pp. 592–607. Springer, Heidelberg (2013). https://doi.org/10.1007/978-3-642-39799-8_39
14. Motik, B., Shearer, R., Horrocks, I.: Hypertableau reasoning for description logics. J. Artif. Intell. Res. **36**, 165–228 (2009)
15. Musen, M.A., The Protégé Team: The protégé project: a look back and a look forward. AI Matters **1**(4), 4–12 (2015)

16. Parsia, B., Sirin, E., Kalyanpur, A.: Debugging OWL ontologies. In: Proceedings of 14th international conference on WWW, pp. 633–640. ACM (2005)
17. Qi, G., Hunter, A.: Measuring incoherence in description logic-based ontologies. In: Aberer, K., et al. (eds.) ASWC/ISWC -2007. LNCS, vol. 4825, pp. 381–394. Springer, Heidelberg (2007). https://doi.org/10.1007/978-3-540-76298-0_28
18. Rector, A., Drummond, N., Horridge, M., Rogers, J., Knublauch, H., Stevens, R., Wang, H., Wroe, C.: OWL pizzas: practical experience of teaching OWL-DL: common errors & common patterns. In: Motta, E., Shadbolt, N.R., Stutt, A., Gibbins, N. (eds.) EKAW 2004. LNCS, vol. 3257, pp. 63–81. Springer, Heidelberg (2004). https://doi.org/10.1007/978-3-540-30202-5_5
19. Reiter, R.: A Theory of diagnosis from first principles. Artif. Intell. **32**(1), 57–95 (1987)
20. Rodler, P.: Interactive debugging of knowledge bases. Ph.D. thesis, Alpen-Adria Universität Klagenfurt (2015). http://arxiv.org/pdf/1605.05950v1.pdf
21. Rodler, P.: On active learning strategies for sequential diagnosis. In: 28th International Workshop on Principles of Diagnosis (DX 2017). Kalpa Publications in Computing, vol. 4, pp. 264–283. EasyChair (2018). https://easychair.org/publications/paper/zHgj
22. Rodler, P., Schekotihin, K.: Reducing model-based diagnosis to knowledge base debugging. In: 28th International Workshop on Principles of Diagnosis (DX 2017). Kalpa Publications in Computing, vol. 4, pp. 284–296. EasyChair (2018). https://easychair.org/publications/paper/3g9Q
23. Rodler, P., Schmid, W., Schekotihin, K.: Inexpensive cost-optimized measurement proposal for sequential model-based diagnosis. In: 28th International Workshop on Principles of Diagnosis (DX 2017). Kalpa Publications in Computing, vol. 4, pp. 200–218. EasyChair (2018). https://easychair.org/publications/paper/HhPf
24. Rodler, P., Shchekotykhin, K., Fleiss, P., Friedrich, G.: RIO: minimizing user interaction in ontology debugging. In: Faber, W., Lembo, D. (eds.) RR 2013. LNCS, vol. 7994, pp. 153–167. Springer, Heidelberg (2013). https://doi.org/10.1007/978-3-642-39666-3_12
25. Roussey, C., Corcho, O., Vilches-Blázquez, L.M.: A catalogue of OWL ontology antipatterns. In: International Conference on Knowledge Capture, pp. 205–206. ACM, Redondo Beach (2009)
26. Schlobach, S., Cornet, R.: Non-standard reasoning services for the debugging of description logic terminologies. In: IJCAI-2003, Proceedings of 18th International Joint Conference on Artificial Intelligence, Acapulco, Mexico, 9–15 August 2003, pp. 355–362. Morgan Kaufmann (2003)
27. Schlobach, S., Huang, Z., Cornet, R., Harmelen, F.: Debugging incoherent terminologies. J. Autom. Reason. **39**(3), 317–349 (2007)
28. Shchekotykhin, K.M., Friedrich, G., Fleiss, P., Rodler, P.: Interactive ontology debugging: two query strategies for efficient fault localization. J. Web Semat. **12**, 88–103 (2012)
29. Shchekotykhin, K.M., Friedrich, G., Rodler, P., Fleiss, P.: Sequential diagnosis of high cardinality faults in knowledge-bases by direct diagnosis generation. In: ECAI 2014–21st European Conference on Artificial Intelligence. Frontiers in Artificial Intelligence and Applications, vol. 263, pp. 813–818. IOS Press (2014)

30. Shchekotykhin, K.M., Jannach, D., Schmitz, T.: Mergexplain: fast computation of multiple conflicts for diagnosis. In: Proceedings of 24th International Joint Conference on Artificial Intelligence, IJCAI 2015, Buenos Aires, Argentina, 25–31 July 2015, pp. 3221–3228. AAAI Press (2015)
31. Sirin, E., Parsia, B., Grau, B.C., Kalyanpur, A., Katz, Y.: Pellet: a practical OWL-DL reasoner. Web Semant.: Sci. Serv. Agents World Wide Web **5**(2), 51–53 (2007)
32. Struss, P.: Model-based problem solving. In: Handbook of Knowledge Representation, Foundations of Artificial Intelligence, vol. 3, pp. 395–465. Elsevier (2008)

# A Framework for Comparing Query Languages in Their Ability to Express Boolean Queries

Dimitri Surinx[1(✉)], Jan Van den Bussche[1], and Dirk Van Gucht[2]

[1] Hasselt University, Hasselt, Belgium
{dimitri.surinx,jan.vandenbussche}@uhasselt.be
[2] Indiana University, Bloomington, IN, USA
vgucht@cs.indiana.edu

**Abstract.** We identify three basic modalities for expressing boolean queries using the expressions of a query language: nonemptiness, emptiness, and containment. For the class of first-order queries, these three modalities have exactly the same expressive power. For other classes of queries, e.g., expressed in weaker query languages, the modalities may differ in expressiveness. We propose a framework for studying the expressive power of boolean query modalities. Along one dimension, one may work within a fixed query language and compare the three modalities, e.g., we can compare a fixed query language $\mathcal{F}$ under emptiness to $\mathcal{F}$ under nonemptiness. Here, we identify crucial query features that enable us to go from one modality to another. Furthermore, we identify semantical properties that reflect the lack of these query features to establish separations. Along a second dimension, one may fix a modality and compare different query languages. This second dimension is the one that has already received quite some attention in the literature, whereas in this paper we emphasize the first dimension. Combining both dimensions, it is interesting to compare the expressive power of a weak query language using a strong modality, against that of a seemingly stronger query language but perhaps using a weaker modality. We present some initial results within this theme. As an important auxiliary result, we establish a preservation theorem for monotone containments of conjunctive queries.

## 1 Introduction

When a relational database is queried, the result is normally a relation. Some queries, however, only require a yes/no answer; such queries are often called *boolean queries*. We may ask, for example, "is student 14753 enrolled in course c209?" Also, every integrity constraint is essentially a boolean query. Another application of boolean queries is given by SQL conditions, as used in updates and triggers, or in if-then-else statements of SQL/PSM (PL/SQL) programs.

In the theory of database query languages and in finite model theory [1–4], it is standard practice to express boolean queries under what we call the

F. Ferrarotti and S. Woltran (Eds.): FoIKS 2018, LNCS 10833, pp. 360–378, 2018.
https://doi.org/10.1007/978-3-319-90050-6_20

*nonemptiness modality.* Under this modality, boolean queries are expressed in the form $e \neq \emptyset$ where $e$ is a query expression in some query language. For example, under the nonemptiness modality, the above boolean query "is student 14753 enrolled in course c209?" is expressed by the nonemptiness of the query "give all students with id 14753 that are enrolled in course c209". The nonemptiness modality is used in practice in the query language SPARQL. In that language, the result of a boolean query ASK $P$ is true if and only if the corresponding query SELECT $*$ $P$ has a nonempty result. Another example of the nonemptiness modality in practice is given by SQL conditions of the form EXISTS $(Q)$.

Sometimes, however, an integrity constraint is more naturally expressed by a query that looks for violations; then the constraint holds if the query returns no answers. So, here we use the *emptiness* modality rather than nonemptiness. For example, to express the integrity constraint that students can be enrolled in at most ten courses, we write a query retrieving all students enrolled in more than ten courses. The query must return an empty result; otherwise an error is raised. SQL conditions of the form NOT EXISTS $(Q)$, instrumental in formulating nonmonotone queries, obviously use the emptiness modality.

Yet another natural modality is *containment* of the form $e_1 \subseteq e_2$, where $e_1$ and $e_2$ are two query expressions. This boolean query returns true on a database $D$ if $e_1(D)$ is a subset of $e_2(D)$.[1] For example, the integrity constraint "every student taking course c209 should have passed course c106" is naturally expressed by $e_1 \subseteq e_2$, where $e_1$ is the query retrieving all students taking c209 and $e_2$ is the query retrieving all students that passed c106. An embedded tuple-generating dependency [1,6] can be regarded as the containment of two conjunctive queries. Similarly, an equality-generating dependency can be regarded as the containment of a conjunctive query in the query returning all identical pairs of data elements.

This brings us to the main motivation of this paper: by using the containment modality, one can use a weaker query language, such as conjunctive queries, and still be able to express integrity constraints that would not be expressible in the language using, say, the nonemptiness modality. A weaker language is easier to use and queries can be executed more efficiently. We find it an intriguing question how different modalities compare to each other, under different circumstances depending on the query language at hand. Furthermore, one may want to compare the expressiveness of different query languages across different modalities for expressing boolean queries. Moreover, we can observe that the emptiness modality is simply the negation of the nonemptiness modality. Inspired by this, we are interested in understanding under what circumstances the containment

---

[1] In this paper, $e_1 \subseteq e_2$ stands for a boolean query which, in general, may return true on some databases and return false on the other databases. Thus $e_1 \subseteq e_2$ as considered in this paper should not be misconstrued as an instance of the famous query containment problem [1,5], where the task would be to verify statically if $e_1(D)$ is a subset of $e_2(D)$ on *every* database $D$. Indeed, if $e_1$ is contained in $e_2$ in this latter sense, then the boolean query $e_1 \subseteq e_2$ is trivial as it returns true on every database.

modality is closed under negation, or under other boolean connectives such as conjunction.

We can illustrate the above questions using well-known simple examples.

*Example 1.* A referential integrity constraint (inclusion dependency) is clearly expressible by a containment of conjunctive queries (CQs), but not by the nonemptiness of a CQ. This is simply because CQs are monotone, whereas an inclusion dependency is not. On the other hand it is neither expressible by the emptiness of a CQ, because such boolean queries are antimonotone whereas again inclusion dependencies are not.

For another example, a key constraint (functional dependency, FD) is again not monotone, so again not expressible by the nonemptiness of a monotone query. An FD is, however, naturally expressed by the *emptiness* of a CQ with nonequalities. For example, a relation $R(A, B, C)$ satisfies the FD $A \to B$ if and only if the result of

$$() \gets R(x, y_1, z_1), R(x, y_2, z_2), y_1 \neq y_2$$

is empty. An FD is also expressible as a containment of two CQs. For example, the above FD holds if and only if the containment

$$(x, y_1, y_2) \gets R(x, y_1, z_1), R(x, y_2, z_2) \quad \subseteq \quad (x, y, y) \gets R(x, y, z)$$

is satisfied.                                                                                        □

In this paper, we attack the above questions from several angles. We begin by comparing the three basic modalities: emptiness, nonemptiness, containment, in the general context of an arbitrary query language. In such a context it is possible to formulate sufficient conditions for, say, emptiness queries to be convertible to nonemptiness queries, or nonemptiness queries to be convertible to containment queries. For example, if we have a sufficiently powerful query language that can express cylindrification and complementation, such as full first-order logic, then it does not really matter which boolean query modality one uses. Conversely, we also formulate some general properties of query languages, like monotonicity or additivity, that preclude the conversion of one modality into another.

Our second angle is to consider a range of specific query languages and characterize how the different modalities compare to each other, for each language in this range. It would be very natural to do this for Codd's relational algebra, where we obtain a range of fragments by varying the allowed operations. For example, we may allow attribute renaming or not, or we may allow set difference or not. While such an investigation remains to be done, in this paper, we have opted to work with the algebra of *binary relations*. This algebra can be seen as a more controlled setting of the relational algebra, and also serves as a well-established and adopted formalization of graph query languages [7–14]. We will completely characterize how the different boolean query modalities compare for each fragment of the algebra of binary relations. Apart from this algebra, we will also look at the popular class of conjunctive queries under the light of the three boolean query modalities.

Our third angle is to investigate how the expressiveness of two different query languages can be compared when using a different modality for each language. One can, for example, compare a stronger language under the weak emptiness modality, to a weak language under the stronger containment modality. The FD example in Example 1 clearly follows this pattern. In this theme we offer a general preservation theorem for monotone containments of CQs: these boolean queries are exactly the nonemptiness CQs. Using this result, and earlier results on the nonexpressibility of certain nonemptiness queries [15], we can show separations between the nonemptiness modality and the containment modality for different fragments of the algebra of binary relations. There remain some open problems in this theme, which we will summarize.

Finally, we look at the question of when a class of boolean queries is closed under conjunction, or under negation. Especially the question of closure under conjunction for boolean queries expressed as containments is very interesting with some open problems remaining.

Several proofs have been omitted due to space limitations, and will be included in a following journal publication.

*Previous Work.* In our previous work we have compared the expressive power of fragments of the algebra of binary relations under the nonemptiness modality [15–17] and under the containment modality [18]. The present paper is complementary in that it emphasizes the comparison of different boolean query modalities, for fixed fragments or across fragments.

## 2    Preliminaries

A database schema $S$ is a finite nonempty set of relation names. Every relation name $R$ is assigned an arity, which is a natural number. Assuming some fixed infinite universe of data elements $V$, an instance $I$ of a relation name $R$ of arity $k$ is a finite $k$-ary relation on $V$, i.e., a subset of $V^k = V \times \cdots \times V$ ($k$ times). More generally, an instance $I$ of a database schema $S$ assigns to each $R \in S$ an instance of $R$, denoted by $I(R)$. The active domain of an instance $I$, denoted by $\mathrm{adom}(I)$, is the set of all data elements from $V$ that occur in $I$. For technical reasons we exclude the *empty instance*, i.e., one of the relations in $I$ must be nonempty. Thus, $\mathrm{adom}(I)$ is never empty.

For a natural number $k$, a $k$-ary query over a database schema $S$ is a function that maps each instance $I$ of $S$ to a $k$-ary relation on $\mathrm{adom}(I)$. We require queries to be generic [1]. A query $q$ is generic if for any permutation $f$ of the universe $V$, and any instance $I$, we have $q(f(I)) = f(q(I))$.

We assume familiarity with the standard relational query languages such as first-order logic, relational algebra, conjunctive queries [1].

## 2.1   Tests, Cylindrification, Complementation

Let $q_1$ and $q_2$ be queries over a common database schema. We define the query $(q_1$ if $q_2)$ as follows:

$$(q_1 \text{ if } q_2)(I) = \begin{cases} q_1(I) & \text{if } q_2(I) \neq \emptyset; \\ \emptyset & \text{otherwise.} \end{cases}$$

Naturally, we say that a family $\mathcal{F}$ of queries over a common database schema is *closed under tests* if for any two queries $q_1$ and $q_2$ in $\mathcal{F}$, the query $(q_1$ if $q_2)$ is also in $\mathcal{F}$.

*Cylindrification* is an operation on relations that, like projection, corresponds to existential quantification, but, unlike projection, does not reduce the arity of the relation [19,20]. We introduce an abstraction of this operation as follows. For any natural number $k$ and query $q$, we define the *$k$-ary cylindrification of* $q$, denoted by $\gamma_k(q)$, as follows:

$$\gamma_k(q)(I) = \begin{cases} \text{adom}(I)^k & \text{if } q(I) \neq \emptyset; \\ \emptyset & \text{otherwise.} \end{cases}$$

We say that a family $\mathcal{F}$ of queries over a common database schema is *closed under $k$-ary cylindrification* $(k \geq 1)$ if for any query $q \in \mathcal{F}$, the query $\gamma_k(q)$ is also in $\mathcal{F}$.

*Example 2.* Let $S$ be a schema with two ternary relations $R$ and $T$, and let $q$ be the 3-ary query that maps any instance $I$ over $S$ to $I(R) - I(T)$. Then, $\gamma_1(q)$ is the unary query that maps any instance $I$ over $S$ to $\text{adom}(I)$ if $I(R) \nsubseteq I(T)$ and to $\emptyset$ otherwise. $\qquad\square$

For a $k$-ary query $q$, the *complement* of $q$, denoted by $q^c$, is defined by $q^c(I) = \text{adom}(I)^k - q(I)$ (set difference). We say that a family $\mathcal{F}$ of queries over a common database schema is *closed under $k$-complementation* if for any query $q \in \mathcal{F}$ of arity $k$, the query $q^c$ is also in $\mathcal{F}$.

Finally, we say that a family $\mathcal{F}$ of queries over a common database schema is *closed under set difference* if for any two queries $q_1, q_2 \in \mathcal{F}$ of the same arity, the query $q$ that maps instances $I$ onto $q_1(I) - q_2(I)$ is also in $\mathcal{F}$.

## 2.2   Navigational Graph Query Languages

Some of the results in this paper concern graph databases, corresponding with the case where the database schema $S$ is restricted to only binary relation names. Any instance $I$ of $S$ can be considered as a graph, where the elements of the active domain are considered as nodes, the pairs in the binary relations are directed edges, and the relation names are edge labels.

The most basic language we consider for expressing binary queries over graphs is the algebra $\mathcal{N}_S$. The expressions of this algebra are built recursively from the relation names in $S$ and the primitives $\emptyset$ and id, using the operators composition $(e_1 \circ e_2)$ and union $(e_1 \cup e_2)$. Semantically, each expression denotes a query in the following way.

$$id(G) = \{(m,m) \mid m \in \text{adom}(G)\}$$
$$R(G) = G(R) \qquad \text{for relation name } R \in S$$
$$\emptyset(G) = \emptyset$$
$$e_1 \circ e_2(G) = \{(m,n) \mid \exists p : (m,p) \in e_1(G) \wedge (p,n) \in e_2(G)\}$$
$$e_1 \cup e_2(G) = e_1(G) \cup e_2(G).$$

Although the assumption of a basic language is a point of discussion, it can be argued that our choice of basic language is not unreasonable [18].

The basic algebra $\mathcal{N}_S$ can be extended by adding some of the following features: the primitives diversity (di), and the full relation (all); and the operators converse $(e^{-1})$, intersection $(e_1 \cap e_2)$, set difference $(e_1 - e_2)$, projections $(\pi_1(e)$ and $\pi_2(e))$, coprojections $(\overline{\pi}_1(e)$ and $\overline{\pi}_2(e))$, and transitive closure $(e^+)$. We refer to the operators in the basic algebra as *basic features*; we refer to the extensions as *nonbasic features*. The semantics of the extensions are as follows:

$$di(G) = \{(m,n) \mid m,n \in \text{adom}(G) \wedge m \neq n\}$$
$$all(G) = \{(m,n) \mid m,n \in \text{adom}(G)\}$$
$$e^{-1}(G) = \{(m,n) \mid (n,m) \in e(G)\}$$
$$e_1 \cap e_2(G) = e_1(G) \cap e_2(G)$$
$$e_1 - e_2(G) = e_1(G) - e_2(G)$$
$$\pi_1(e)(G) = \{(m,m) \mid m \in \text{adom}(G) \wedge \exists n : (m,n) \in e(G)\}$$
$$\pi_2(e)(G) = \{(m,m) \mid m \in \text{adom}(G) \wedge \exists n : (n,m) \in e(G)\}$$
$$\overline{\pi}_1(e)(G) = \{(m,m) \mid m \in \text{adom}(G) \wedge \neg\exists n : (m,n) \in e(G)\}$$
$$\overline{\pi}_2(e)(G) = \{(m,m) \mid m \in \text{adom}(G) \wedge \neg\exists n : (n,m) \in e(G)\}$$
$$e^+(G) = \text{the transitive closure of } e(G).$$

All the above operators are well-established in so-called "navigational" graph querying [10–14].

A *fragment* is any set $F$ of nonbasic features, in which we either take both projections $\pi_1$ and $\pi_2$ or none of them, and the same for coprojection.[2]

If $F$ is a fragment, we denote by $\mathcal{N}_S(F)$ the language obtained by adding the features in $F$ to $\mathcal{N}_S$. For example, $\mathcal{N}_S(\cap)$ denotes the extension with intersection, and $\mathcal{N}_S(\cap, \pi)$ denotes the extension with intersection and both projections. We will omit the subscript $S$ in $\mathcal{N}_S(F)$ when the precise database schema is not of importance.

---

[2] Some of our results can be refined to fragments containing just one of the two projections or coprojections, but for others this remains a technical open problem [21].

Various interdependencies exist between the nonbasic features [12]:

$$\text{all} = \text{di} \cup \text{id}$$
$$\text{di} = \text{all} - \text{id}$$
$$e_1 \cap e_2 = e_1 - (e_1 - e_2)$$
$$\pi_1(e) = (e \circ e^{-1}) \cap \text{id} = (e \circ \text{all}) \cap \text{id} = \pi_1(\pi_1(e)) = \pi_2(e^{-1})$$
$$\pi_2(e) = (e^{-1} \circ e) \cap \text{id} = (\text{all} \circ e) \cap \text{id} = \pi_2(\pi_2(e)) = \pi_1(e^{-1})$$
$$\overline{\pi}_1(e) = \text{id} - \pi_1(e)$$
$$\overline{\pi}_2(e) = \text{id} - \pi_2(e)$$

For example, by the third equation, when we add difference, we get intersection for free. The closure of a fragment $F$ by the above equations is denoted by $\overline{F}$. For example, $\overline{\{-, \text{di}\}} = \{-, \text{di}, \text{all}, \cap, \pi, \overline{\pi}\}$. Clearly $F$ and $\overline{F}$ are equivalent in expressive power. This closure notation will be used extensively in what follows.

## 3   Boolean Query Modalities

A *boolean query* over a database schema $S$ is a mapping from instances of $S$ to $\{true, false\}$. As argued in the Introduction, boolean queries can be naturally expressed in terms of the emptiness, or the nonemptiness, of an ordinary query, or by the containment of the results of two queries. Using these three base modalities we can associate an array of boolean query families to any family of queries $\mathcal{F}$ on a common database schema $S$:

| family of boolean queries expressible in the form | with |
|---|---|---|
| $\mathcal{F}^{=\emptyset}$ | $q = \emptyset$ | $q \in \mathcal{F}$ |
| $\mathcal{F}^{\neq\emptyset}$ | $q \neq \emptyset$ | $q \in \mathcal{F}$ |
| $\mathcal{F}^{\subseteq}$ | $q_1 \subseteq q_2$ | $q_1, q_2 \in \mathcal{F}$ |

For $\mathcal{F}^{\subseteq}$, it is understood that only two queries of the same arity can form a containment boolean query.

When working in the algebra of binary relations, for any fragment $F$ of nonbasic features, we abbreviate $\mathcal{N}(F)^{=\emptyset}$, $\mathcal{N}(F)^{\neq\emptyset}$ and $\mathcal{N}(F)^{\subseteq}$ by $F^{=\emptyset}$, $F^{\neq\emptyset}$ and $F^{\subseteq}$, respectively.

Obviously, these are by no means the only way to express boolean queries. We could, for example, allow boolean connectives within a family of boolean queries. Indeed, we can consider boolean queries of the form $q_1 \neq \emptyset \wedge \ldots \wedge q_n \neq \emptyset$ where $q_i \neq \emptyset \in \mathcal{F}^{\neq\emptyset}$ where $i = 1, \ldots, n$. Furthermore, we could even combine two different families of boolean queries by using boolean connectives. For example, we can consider boolean queries of the form $q_1 \neq \emptyset \wedge q_2 \subseteq q_3$ where $q_1 \neq \emptyset \in \mathcal{F}^{\neq\emptyset}$ and $q_2 \subseteq q_3 \in F^{\subseteq}$. Our goal in this paper is to propose a framework along which we can investigate and compare different ways of expressing boolean queries.

## 4    Comparing the Modalities

The goal of this section is to compare $\mathcal{F}^{=\emptyset}$, $\mathcal{F}^{\neq\emptyset}$ and $\mathcal{F}^{\subseteq}$, for a fixed family of queries (modeling a query language) $\mathcal{F}$. Formally, this amounts to making six comparisons, but we can immediately get one of them out of the way by noting that $\mathcal{F}^{=\emptyset}$ is the negation of $\mathcal{F}^{\neq\emptyset}$.

Formally, for a boolean query $q$, we define its negation $\neg q$ naturally as $(\neg q)(I) = \neg q(I)$, where $\neg true = false$ and $\neg false = true$. For a family of boolean queries $\mathcal{A}$, we define its negation $\neg\mathcal{A}$ as $\{\neg q \mid q \in \mathcal{A}\}$.

Now clearly $\mathcal{A} \subseteq \mathcal{B}$ if and only if $\neg\mathcal{A} \subseteq \neg\mathcal{B}$. Hence, we only have to investigate whether $\mathcal{F}^{=\emptyset} \subseteq \mathcal{F}^{\neq\emptyset}$; the other direction $\mathcal{F}^{\neq\emptyset} \subseteq \mathcal{F}^{=\emptyset}$ then directly follows. This amounts to investigating when the emptiness modality is *closed under negation*. Formally, a family $\mathcal{B}$ of boolean queries is called closed under negation if $\neg\mathcal{B} \subseteq \mathcal{B}$ (or, equivalently, $\mathcal{B} \subseteq \neg\mathcal{B}$). Note that we define closure under negation semantically, it thus applies to any family of boolean queries, so it is not a syntactic definition as it would apply to a query language. (e.g., formulas that do not use certain operators or connectives like difference or logical negation)

We first identify query features that enable the expression of one base modality in terms of another one. We also identify general properties that reflect the absence of these query features, notably, the properties of monotonicity and additivity. We then observe how these properties indeed prevent going from one modality to another.

The announced query features are summarized in the following theorem. We leave out the comparison $\mathcal{F}^{\subseteq} \subseteq \mathcal{F}^{\neq\emptyset}$, since we know of no other general way of going from containment to nonemptiness than via emptiness $\mathcal{F}^{\subseteq} \subseteq \mathcal{F}^{=\emptyset} \subseteq \mathcal{F}^{\neq\emptyset}$. This leaves four comparisons, dealt with in the following theorem. We refer to the notions introduced in Sect. 2.1.

**Theorem 1.** *Let $\mathcal{F}$ be a family of queries.*

1. $\mathcal{F}^{\subseteq} \subseteq \mathcal{F}^{=\emptyset}$ *if $\mathcal{F}$ is closed under set difference ($-$).*
2. $\mathcal{F}^{=\emptyset} \subseteq \mathcal{F}^{\neq\emptyset}$ *if there exists $k$ such that $\mathcal{F}$ is closed under*
   - *$k$-ary complementation, and*
   - *$k$-ary cylindrification.*
3. $\mathcal{F}^{\neq\emptyset} \subseteq \mathcal{F}^{\subseteq}$ *if*
   - *$\mathcal{F}$ contains a never-empty query (one that returns nonempty on every instance), and*
   - *$\mathcal{F}$ is closed under tests, or $\mathcal{F}$ is closed under $k$-ary cylindrification for some $k$.*
4. $\mathcal{F}^{=\emptyset} \subseteq \mathcal{F}^{\subseteq}$ *if $\mathcal{F}$ contains the* empty *query which always outputs the empty relation.*

*Proof.* 1. $q_1 \sqsubseteq q_2$ is expressed by $q_1 - q_2 = \emptyset$.
2. $q = \emptyset$ is expressed by $\gamma_k(q)^c \neq \emptyset$.
3. Let $p$ be a never-empty query. Then $q \neq \emptyset$ is expressed by $p \subseteq (p \text{ if } q)$ as well as by $\gamma_k(p) \subseteq \gamma_k(q)$.
4. $q = \emptyset$ is expressed by $q \subseteq$ empty.    $\square$

Obviously, the above theorem only provides sufficient conditions under which we can go from one modality to another. Since the conditions hold for any general family $\mathcal{F}$, we cannot expect the literal converses of these statements to hold in general. Indeed, one could always concoct an artificial family $\mathcal{F}$ that is not closed under set difference but for which $\mathcal{F}^{\subseteq} \subseteq \mathcal{F}^{=\emptyset}$.

*Example 3.* Over a schema with two unary relation names $R$ and $S$, let $\mathcal{F}$ be the set of queries

$$\text{if } C \text{ then } e_1 \text{ else } e_2$$

with $C$ finite boolean combinations of expressions $h_i \subseteq h_j$ and $e_1, e_2, h_i, h_j$ in $\{\emptyset, R, S, R \cup S\}$. It can be verified that $\mathcal{F}^{\subseteq} \subseteq \mathcal{F}^{=\emptyset}$, and that $\mathcal{F}$ is not closed under difference.                                                                □

Our approach to still find a kind of converse of Theorem 1, is to come up with general semantic properties of the queries in a family that would prevent the sufficient conditions to hold. We can then proceed to show that the different modalities become incomparable under these properties.

More concretely, we can observe two main themes in the sufficient conditions: *negation*, in the forms of set difference and complementation, and *global access to the database*, in the forms of cylindrification and tests. A well-known semantic property of queries that runs counter to negation is *monotonicity*. Global access is an intuitive notion. As a formal property that intuitively prevents global access, we propose *additivity*.

## 4.1   Monotonicity

A query $q$ is *monotone* if $I \subseteq J$ implies $q(I) \subseteq q(J)$, where $I \subseteq J$ means that $I(R) \subseteq J(R)$ for each relation name $R$. In Theorem 1, we have seen that closure under complementation or set difference, which typically destroys monotonicity, is instrumental for the emptiness modality to be closed under negation, as well as the containment modality to be subsumed by emptiness. We next show that both fail under monotonicity.

The first failure is the strongest:

**Lemma 1.** *Let* MON *denote the family of monotone queries. The only boolean queries in* $\mathrm{MON}^{=\emptyset} \cap \mathrm{MON}^{\neq\emptyset}$ *are the constant* true *and* false *queries.*

As a corollary, we obtain:

**Proposition 1.** *Let* $\mathcal{F}$ *be a family of monotone queries. As soon as* $\mathcal{F}^{=\emptyset}$ *contains a non-constant query,* $\mathcal{F}^{=\emptyset} \not\subseteq \mathcal{F}^{\neq\emptyset}$.

This also implies that for any monotone family of queries $\mathcal{F}$ that contains the empty query, we have $\mathcal{F}^{\subseteq} \not\subseteq \mathcal{F}^{\neq\emptyset}$, since $\mathcal{A}^{=\emptyset} \subseteq \mathcal{A}^{\subseteq}$ for any family of queries $\mathcal{A}$ that contains the empty query. We will apply Proposition 1 to conjunctive queries in Sect. 4.3.

We next turn to the failure of going from containment to emptiness. Whenever $q$ is monotone, the boolean query $q = \emptyset$ is antimonotone (meaning that if

$q(I)$ = false and $I \subseteq J$, also $q(J)$ = false). However, a boolean containment query is typically not antimonotone. The following straightforward result gives two examples.

**Proposition 2.** *Let $\mathcal{F}$ be a family of monotone queries over a database schema $S$.*

1. *If $S$ contains two distinct relation names $R$ and $T$ of the same arity, and the two queries $R$ and $T$ belong to $\mathcal{F}$, then $\mathcal{F}^{\subseteq} \not\subseteq \mathcal{F}^{=\emptyset}$. This is shown by the boolean query $R \subseteq T$.*
2. *If $R$ is a binary relation name in $S$ and the two queries $R \circ R$ and $R$ belong to $\mathcal{F}$, then $\mathcal{F}^{\subseteq} \not\subseteq \mathcal{F}^{=\emptyset}$.*

## 4.2   Additivity

A query $q$ is *additive* if for any two instances $I$ and $J$ such that adom($I$) and adom($J$) are disjoint, $q(I \cup J) = q(I) \cup q(J)$. Additive queries (also known as "queries distributing over components") have been recently singled out as a family of queries that are well amenable to distributed computation [22]. Indeed, additivity means that a query can be separately computed on each connected component, after which all the subresults can simply be combined by union to obtain the final result.

Both cylindrification and tests run counter to additivity. For example, just computing adom($I$) × adom($I$) is not additive. Also tests of the form ($q_1$ if $q_2$) are not additive, since testing if $q_2$ is nonempty takes part in the entire instance, across connected components. We have seen that cylindrification (together with complementation) can be used to close the emptiness modality under negation; moreover, cylindrification or tests suffice to move from nonemptiness to containment. We next show that this all fails under additivity.

The following lemma is of a similar nature as Lemma 1.

**Lemma 2.** *Let $\mathrm{ADD}$ denote the family of additive queries. The only boolean queries in $\mathrm{ADD}^{\neq\emptyset} \cap \mathrm{ADD}^{\subseteq}$ are the constant* true *and* false *queries.*

As a corollary, we obtain:

**Proposition 3.** *Let $\mathcal{F}$ be a family of additive queries.*

1. *As soon as $\mathcal{F}^{\subseteq}$ contains a non-constant query, $\mathcal{F}^{\subseteq} \not\subseteq \mathcal{F}^{\neq\emptyset}$.*
2. *As soon as $\mathcal{F}^{\neq\emptyset}$ contains a non-constant query, $\mathcal{F}^{\neq\emptyset} \not\subseteq \mathcal{F}^{\subseteq}$ and $\mathcal{F}^{=\emptyset} \not\subseteq \mathcal{F}^{\neq\emptyset}$.*

Additivity and monotonicity are orthogonal properties. For example, the additive queries are closed under set difference. Thus, additive queries may involve negation and need not be monotone. On the other hand, computing the Cartesian product of two relations is monotone but not additive.

### 4.3   Conjunctive Queries

In this brief section we compare the three base modalities for the popular languages CQ (conjunctive queries) and UCQ (unions of conjunctive queries). The result is that nonemptiness is strictly subsumed by containment, and that all other pairs of modalities are incomparable.

**Theorem 2.** *Let $\mathcal{F}$ be* CQ *or* UCQ. *Then*

1. $\mathcal{F}^{\subseteq} \not\subseteq \mathcal{F}^{=\emptyset}$ *and* $\mathcal{F}^{=\emptyset} \not\subseteq \mathcal{F}^{\subseteq}$.
2. $\mathcal{F}^{=\emptyset} \not\subseteq \mathcal{F}^{\neq\emptyset}$.
3. $\mathcal{F}^{\neq\emptyset} \subseteq \mathcal{F}^{\subseteq}$.
4. $\mathcal{F}^{\subseteq} \not\subseteq \mathcal{F}^{\neq\emptyset}$.

*Proof.* 1. Consider the instance $Z$ where $Z(R) = \{(1,\ldots,1)\}$ for each relation $R$. Every query in $\mathcal{F}^{\subseteq}$ returns true on $Z$, whereas every query in $\mathcal{F}^{=\emptyset}$ returns false.
2. By Proposition 1.
3. By Theorem 1(3). Indeed, a CQ with an empty body is never empty. CQs and UCQs are also closed under tests. Indeed, let $q_1$ and $q_2$ be UCQs. Then ($q_1$ if $q_2$) is expressed by the UCQ consisting of the following rules. Take a rule $r$ of $q_1$ and a rule $s$ of $q_2$. Produce the rule obtained from $r$ by conjoining to the body a variable-renamed copy of the body of $s$. If $q_1$ has $n$ rules and $q_2$ has $m$ rules, we obtain $nm$ rules. In particular, if $q_1$ and $q_2$ are CQs, we obtain a single rule so again a CQ.
4. Let $R$ be a relation name in the database schema, and consider the two queries

$$q_1(x,y) \leftarrow R(x,\_,\ldots,\_), R(y,\_,\ldots,\_)$$
$$q_2(x,x) \leftarrow R(x,\_,\ldots,\_).$$

Here, the underscores stand for fresh nondistinguished variables (Prolog notation). Then $q_1 \subseteq q_2$ returns true on an instance $I$ iff the first column of $R(I)$ holds at most one distinct element. This boolean query is not monotone and thus not in $\mathcal{F}^{\neq\emptyset}$.    $\square$

*Remark 1.* In the proof of Theorem 2(4) we make convenient use of repeated variables in the head. For the version of CQs where this is disallowed, the result can still be proven by using

$$q_1(x_1,\ldots,x_k) \leftarrow R(x_1,\ldots,x_k)$$
$$q_2(x_1,\ldots,x_k) \leftarrow R(x_1,\ldots,x_k), R(x_k,\_,\ldots,\_).$$

This does not work if $R$ is unary; if there are two different relation names $R$ and $T$, we can use

$$q_1(x) \leftarrow R(x,\_,\ldots,\_)$$
$$q_2(x) \leftarrow T(x,\_,\ldots,\_).$$

These arguments only fail when the database schema consists of just one single unary relation name, and we cannot use repeated variables in the head. In this extreme case, both $CQ^{\subseteq}$ and $CQ^{\neq\emptyset}$ consist only of the constant true query, so the subsumption becomes trivial.                                                                □

## 4.4   Navigational Graph Query Languages

In this section we compare the three base modalities for the navigational graph query languages introduced in the Preliminaries.

The results are summarized in the following theorem. This theorem can be seen as a version of our earlier Theorem 1, specialized to navigational graph query language fragments. However, now, every statement is a *characterization*, showing that the sufficient condition is also necessary for subsumption to hold. Particularly satisfying is that, with a few exceptions, almost the entire theorem can be proven from the general results given earlier.

**Theorem 3.** *Let $F$ be a fragment.*

1. $F^{\subseteq} \subseteq F^{=\emptyset}$ *if and only if* $- \in F$.
2. $F^{=\emptyset} \subseteq F^{\neq\emptyset}$ *if and only if all* $\in \overline{F}$ *and* $(- \in F$ *or* $\overline{\pi} \in \overline{F})$.
3. $F^{\neq\emptyset} \subseteq F^{\subseteq}$ *if and only if all* $\in \overline{F}$.
4. $F^{\subseteq} \subseteq F^{\neq\emptyset}$ *if and only if all* $\in \overline{F}$ *and* $- \in F$.

Notice that Theorem 3 no longer contains an adapted version for Theorem 1(4). This is because the empty query is in $\mathcal{N}(F)$ for any fragment $F$ by definition, whence $F^{=\emptyset} \subseteq F^{\subseteq}$ always holds. Instead, we now do provide in item 4 an explicit characterization for when the subsumption from containment to nonemptiness holds.

In every part of the above theorem, the if-direction is proven by showing that $\mathcal{N}(F)$ fulfills the conditions of Theorem 1.

To prove the only-if directions of the theorem, we will exhibit inexpressibility results.

For the first part of the theorem, it is sufficient to show that $F^{\subseteq}$ is not subsumed by $F^{=\emptyset}$ for every fragment $F$ without set difference. Thereto we introduce NoDiff, the largest fragment without set difference, which is defined as $\{\text{di}, ^{-1}, \cap, \overline{\pi}, ^{+}\}$. The following lemma establishes the first part of the theorem by exhibiting, for every fragment $F$, a boolean query in $F^{\subseteq}$ but not in NoDiff$^{=\emptyset}$.

**Lemma 3.** *Let $R$ be a relation schema in $S$. Then the boolean query "$R$ is transitive", formally, $R \circ R \subseteq R$, is neither in NoDiff$^{=\emptyset}$ nor in NoDiff$^{\neq\emptyset}$.*

The only-if directions of the remaining parts of the theorem all revolve around the fragment NoAll $= \{^{-1}, -, ^{+}\}$, the largest fragment without the full relation all. This fragment lacks the only two features (di and all) that allow to jump from one connected component to another. Hence we obtain the following:

**Additivity Lemma.** *Every binary-relation query in $\mathcal{N}(\text{NoAll})$ is additive.*

This lemma can be proven directly but also follows from the additivity of connected stratified Datalog [22].

The Additivity Lemma allows an easy proof for the second and third parts of the theorem, as we next demonstrate. Also the proofs of several later results hinge upon additivity.

For the second part, we must prove that $F^{=\emptyset}$ is not subsumed by $F^{\neq\emptyset}$ for any fragment $F$ without all, as well as any fragment having neither difference nor coprojection. The latter case is clear. Indeed, difference and coprojection are the only two nonmonotone operators. Thus $\mathcal{N}(F)$ is monotone, whence Proposition 1 proves the result.

For a fragment $F$ without all but possibly with difference or coprojection, we have that $\mathcal{N}(F)$ is additive. Hence, Proposition 3 establishes the second as well as the third parts when all $\notin F$.

Finally, for the fourth part, we must prove that $F^{\subseteq}$ is not subsumed by $F^{\neq\emptyset}$ for any fragment $F$ without all or without set difference. The case without set difference already follows from Lemma 3. The case without all already follows from the second part.

**Regular Path Queries.** The fragment $\{^+\}$ corresponds to a well known family of graph queries called regular path queries (RPQ) [23]. Theorem 3 directly tells us that $\mathrm{RPQ}^{=\emptyset} \not\subseteq \mathrm{RPQ}^{\neq\emptyset}$, $\mathrm{RPQ}^{\subseteq} \not\subseteq \mathrm{RPQ}^{=\emptyset}$ and $\mathrm{RPQ}^{\subseteq} \not\subseteq \mathrm{RPQ}^{\neq\emptyset}$.

## 5   Cross-Language Comparisons

In the previous section, we have compared different modalities within a given family of queries (query language). Dually, one may investigate how different query languages compare for a given modality. In the context of navigational graph query languages, we have already done this research [15,18].

The next step, then, is to see how different query languages relate when using different modalities. In this paper, we investigate how $F_1^{\neq\emptyset}$ compares to $F_2^{\subseteq}$, for different navigational graph query language fragments $F_1$ and $F_2$. This question is interesting especially since nonemptiness is the standard modality for expressing boolean queries, and containment is a fundamentally different but also very natural modality. Then it is interesting to try to understand to what extent the containment modality, using some language $F_2$, can be used to express nonemptiness queries using some other language $F_1$.

*Example 4.* For a positive example, consider the query $R^2 \circ R^{-1} \circ R^2 \neq \emptyset$ in $\{^{-1}\}^{\neq\emptyset}$. This query is expressed by all $\subseteq$ all $\circ \pi_1(R^2 \circ \pi_2(\pi_1(R^2) \circ R)) \circ$ all in $\{\pi, \text{all}\}^{\subseteq}$. For a negative example, we can show that $R^2 \circ R^{-1} \circ R^2 \neq \emptyset$ is not in $\{\text{all}\}^{\subseteq}$.                                                                 □

Whenever we can move from $F_1$ to $F_2$ staying with the nonemptiness modality, i.e., $F_1^{\neq\emptyset} \subseteq F_2^{\neq\emptyset}$, and moreover, we can switch from nonemptiness to containment within $F_2$, i.e., $F_2^{\neq\emptyset} \subseteq F_2^{\subseteq}$, we obviously obtain $F_1^{\neq\emptyset} \subseteq F_2^{\subseteq}$ by transitivity. Actually, our conjecture is that nothing else can happen:

*Conjecture 1.* Let $F_1$ and $F_2$ be fragments. If $F_1^{\neq\emptyset} \subseteq F_2^{\subseteq}$, then $F_2^{\neq\emptyset} \subseteq F_2^{\subseteq}$ and $F_1^{\neq\emptyset} \subseteq F_2^{\neq\emptyset}$.

We can prove large parts of this conjecture; the only open case revolves around the fragments $F_1 = \{\pi\}$ and $F_2 \subseteq \{\text{di}, \text{all}, {}^{-1}, +\}$. In particular, if one could show that

$$\{\pi\}^{\neq\emptyset} \not\subseteq \{\text{di}, {}^{-1}, +\}^{\subseteq}$$

then Conjecture 1 would be entirely resolved.

It is sufficient to prove the conjecture under the following two assumptions:

- If $F_2^{\neq\emptyset} \not\subseteq F_2^{\subseteq}$, our proof of Theorem 3(3) actually implies $\mathcal{N}^{\neq\emptyset} \not\subseteq F_2^{\subseteq}$ (recall that $\mathcal{N}$ is the most basic fragment). Hence, certainly $F_1^{\neq\emptyset} \not\subseteq F_2^{\subseteq}$, so the conjecture is void in this case. Thus, we may assume that $F_2^{\neq\emptyset} \subseteq F_2^{\subseteq}$, i.e., that all is present in $F_2$.
- If moreover $-$ is in $F_2$, then $F_2^{\subseteq} = F_2^{\neq\emptyset}$, and the conjecture becomes trivial again. Thus, we may assume that $-$ is not in $F_2$.

Under the above assumptions we propose to prove the conjecture by its contrapositive. So we assume $F_1^{\neq\emptyset} \not\subseteq F_2^{\neq\emptyset}$ and try to establish $F_1^{\neq\emptyset} \not\subseteq F_2^{\subseteq}$. Now the given $F_1^{\neq\emptyset} \not\subseteq F_2^{\neq\emptyset}$ has been precisely characterized in our previous work [15]. We refer to the paper [15], which shows that $F_1^{\neq\emptyset} \not\subseteq F_2^{\neq\emptyset}$ can only happen in the following cases:

**Intersection, difference, diversity, or coprojection:** One of these features is in $\overline{F}_1$ but not in $\overline{F}_2$.

**Transitive closure:** Transitive closure is in $\overline{F}_1$ but not in $\overline{F}_2$, and either the database schema has at least two relation names, or $\overline{F}_1$ contains at least one of $\cap$, $\overline{\pi}$ or ${}^{-1}$.

**Converse:** Converse is in $\overline{F}_1$ but not in $\overline{F}_2$, and
 (a) $\cap$ is in $\overline{F}_1$;
 (b) $+$ is in $\overline{F}_1$; or
 (c) $F_1 \subseteq \{{}^{-1}, \text{di}, \text{all}, \pi, \overline{\pi}\}$ and $F_2 \subseteq \{\text{all}, \text{di}, +\}$.

**Projection:** Projection is in $\overline{F}_1$ but not in $\overline{F}_2$.

We can deal completely with all cases, except for projection, which we will discuss last.

**Intersection.** The largest fragment for $F_2$ we need to consider is NoInt $= \{\text{di}, \overline{\pi}, {}^{-1}, +\}$ ("no intersection"). We can show that the query $R \cap \text{id} \neq \emptyset$ ("the graph has self-loops") is not in NoInt$^{\subseteq}$.

**Difference.** We can show that $R^2 - R \neq \emptyset$ ("the graph is not transitive") is not in NoDiff$^{\subseteq}$.

**Diversity.** We can show that $\text{di} \neq \emptyset$ ("the graph has at least two nodes") is not in $\{\text{all}, {}^{-1}, \overline{\pi}, \cap, +\}^{\subseteq}$.

**Coprojection.** We can show that $\overline{\pi}_1(R) \neq \emptyset$ ("the graph has at least one sink node") is not in $\{\text{di}, {}^{-1}, \cap, +\}^{\subseteq}$.

**Transitive closure.** From our earlier work we know that $F_1^{\neq\emptyset}$ can express some query not expressible in first-order logic (FO), whereas $F_2^{\subseteq}$ is clearly subsumed by FO.

**Converse.** The largest fragment without converse is NoConv $= \{\mathsf{di}, \pi, ^+, -\}$. Since NoConv has both all and $-$, we have NoConv$^{\neq\emptyset} = $ NoConv$^{\subseteq}$. Now in case (a), we already know [16, Proposition 6.6] that the query $(R^2 \circ R^{-1} \circ R) \cap R \neq \emptyset$ is not in NoConv$^{\neq\emptyset}$. In case (b), we already know [15, Proposition 5.4] that $R^2 \circ (R \circ R^{-1})^+ \circ R^2 \neq \emptyset$ is not in NoConv$^{\neq\emptyset}$. To settle case (c), we can show that $R^2 \circ R^{-1} \circ R^2 \neq \emptyset$ is not in $\{\mathsf{di}, ^+\}^{\subseteq}$.

**A Preservation Result.** In the case of projection, the largest fragment for $F_2$ we need to consider is $\{\mathsf{di}, ^{-1}, ^+\}$. We would like to show that $\{\pi\}^{\neq\emptyset} \not\subseteq \{\mathsf{di}, ^{-1}, ^+\}^{\subseteq}$.

We already know [16] that there are queries in $\{\pi\}^{\neq\emptyset}$ but not in $\{\mathsf{di}, ^{-1}, ^+\}^{\neq\emptyset}$. Furthermore, note that queries in $\{\pi\}^{\neq\emptyset}$ are always monotone. Hence, if we could show that monotone queries in $\{\mathsf{di}, ^{-1}, ^+\}^{\subseteq}$ are always in $\{\mathsf{di}, ^{-1}, ^+\}^{\neq\emptyset}$, the conjecture would be proved.

Note that such a result would fit the profile of a preservation theorem since it gives a syntactical characterization for a semantical property (here monotonicity). Preservation theorems have been studied intensively in model theory, finite model theory and database theory [24–29].

We can give a partial answer in the form of the following preservation result, which we believe to be interesting in its own right. In the following Theorem, the conjunctive queries need not be safe. (A CQ is safe if all variables in its head are present in its body). This is important for the application to graph queries in the corollary; to express all we need an unsafe CQ.

**Theorem 4.** *Let $Q_1$ and $Q_2$ be conjunctive queries so that the boolean containment query $Q_1 \subseteq Q_2$ is monotone. Then $Q_1 \subseteq Q_2$ is also expressible as a nonemptiness query $P \neq \emptyset$, where $P$ is a conjunctive query. Moreover, the body of $P$ can be taken so that it is part of the body of $Q_2$.*

**Corollary 1.** $\{\pi\}^{\neq\emptyset} \not\subseteq F_2^{\subseteq}$, *where $F_2$ is the union-free fragment of $\{\mathsf{all}, ^{-1}\}$.*

*Proof.* Path queries expressed in the union-free fragment of $\mathcal{N}(\mathsf{all}, ^{-1})$ are expressible as conjunctive queries. As mentioned above, we know there exists a (monotone) boolean query $Q$ in $\{\pi\}^{\neq\emptyset}$ that is not in $\{\mathsf{all}, ^{-1}\}^{\neq\emptyset}$. If $Q$ would be in $\{\mathsf{all}, ^{-1}\}^{\subseteq}$, the above Theorem would imply $Q$ in $\{\mathsf{all}, ^{-1}\}^{\neq\emptyset}$, a contradiction. □

It is an interesting challenge to try to extend Theorem 4 to unions of CQs, CQs with nonequalities, and perhaps even recursive (Datalog) programs.

## 6   Closure Under Boolean Connectives

In Sect. 4 we already observed that the question whether $\mathcal{F}^{=\emptyset}$ is subsumed by $\mathcal{F}^{\neq\emptyset}$ is equivalent to whether $\mathcal{F}^{\neq\emptyset}$ is closed under negation. One may now also wonder about the logical negation of $\mathcal{F}^{\subseteq}$. It turns out, however, that $\mathcal{F}^{\subseteq}$ is seldom closed under negation. For navigational graph query language fragments $F$, we have closure under negation of $F^{\subseteq}$ only if both all and $-$ are in $\overline{F}$. When $\mathcal{F}$ is the family of conjunctive queries, or unions of conjunctive queries, $\mathcal{F}^{\subseteq}$ is again not closed under negation. We omit the details.

Closure under conjunction is more interesting. Since we often enforce a set (conjunction) of integrity constraints, or specify logical theories consisting of sets of axioms, it is a natural question to ask if such conjunctions can be written as single boolean queries in the same language.

We begin this investigation for our navigational graph query language fragments. Under the emptiness modality, closure under conjunction is trivial, since $(q_1 = \emptyset) \wedge (q_2 = \emptyset)$ is equivalent to $q_1 \cup q_2 = \emptyset$.

Under the nonemptiness modality, we have the following.

**Theorem 5.** *Let $F$ be a fragment. Then $F^{\neq\emptyset}$ is closed under conjunction if and only if either* all $\in \overline{F}$, *or the database schema $S$ consists of a single binary relation name and $F \subseteq \{^+\}$.*

*Proof.* If $\overline{F}$ has all, then we can directly express $(e_1 \neq \emptyset) \wedge (e_2 \neq \emptyset)$ by $e_1 \circ$ all $\circ e_2 \neq \emptyset$. If $F \subseteq \{^+\}$ and $S$ is a singleton $\{R\}$, the language $\mathcal{N}(F)$ is very simple and $F^{\neq\emptyset}$ is easily seen to be closed under conjunction.

For the only-if direction, first assume $\overline{F}$ does not have all and $S$ contains at least two relation names, say $R$ and $T$. Now by the Additivity Lemma, the boolean query $R \neq \emptyset \wedge T \neq \emptyset$ is not in NoAll$^{\neq\emptyset}$.

The other possibility is that $\overline{F}$ does not have all and $F \not\subseteq \{^+\}$. Then $\overline{F}$ must contain at least one of the features converse, projection, or intersection. Using intersection, we can show that $R^2 \cap R \neq \emptyset \wedge R^3 \cap R \neq \emptyset$ is not in NoAll$^{\neq\emptyset}$.

Using converse, we can show that $R^2 \circ R^{-1} \circ R^3 \neq \emptyset \wedge R^3 \circ R^{-1} \circ R^2 \neq \emptyset$ is not in NoAll$^{\neq\emptyset}$. This result also covers the case with projection. Indeed, both conjuncts are in $\{^{-1}\}^{\neq\emptyset}$, which is subsumed by $\{\pi\}^{\neq\emptyset}$ [16]. Hence, the lemma also gives a conjunction of $\{\pi\}^{\neq\emptyset}$ queries that is not in NoAll$^{\neq\emptyset}$. $\square$

Turning to the containment modality, we can only offer the general observation that $F^{\subseteq}$ is closed under conjunction whenever $F$ has set difference. Indeed, we can express $e_1 \subseteq e_2 \wedge e_3 \subseteq e_4$ as $(e_1 - e_2) \cup (e_3 - e_4) \subseteq \emptyset$.

At this point we have not been able to prove the converse direction, although we conjecture that set difference in $F$ is indeed necessary for $F^{\subseteq}$ to be closed under conjunction. Two partial results we could prove are that $R^3 \subseteq$ id $\wedge R^2 \subseteq R$ is not in $\{di, ^{-1}, ^+\}^{\subseteq}$, and that $R^3 \subseteq \emptyset \wedge R^2 \subseteq R$ is not in $\{\cap, \pi, ^{-1}, ^+\}^{\subseteq}$. The difficulty here is to extend this allowing coprojection.

**Conjunctive Queries.** Under nonemptiness, both CQ and UCQ are closed under conjunction, using the same construction as the one used to express tests (proof of Theorem 2).

Under emptiness, note that a family of emptiness queries is closed under conjunction if and only if the corresponding family of nonemptiness queries is closed under *disjunction*. This is clearly the case for UCQ nonemptiness queries. For CQs this happens only rarely:

**Theorem 6.** *Let $S$ be a database schema. Then, $CQ_S^{\neq\emptyset}$ is closed under disjunction if and only if $S$ only contains at most two unary relations and no other $n$-ary relation names with $n \geq 2$.*

Finally, we consider CQs under containment. Here closure under conjunction happens only in the most trivial setting.

**Theorem 7.** *Let $S$ be a database schema. Then, $CQ_S^{\subseteq}$ is closed under conjunction if and only if $S$ only contains one unary relation and no other $n$-ary relation names with $n \geq 2$.*

The question whether UCQs under the containment modality are closed under conjunction is still open.

# 7     Discussion and Conclusion

Observe that the closure under conjunction of the containment modality subsumes the *equality* modality $q_1 = q_2$, which is equivalent to $q_1 \subseteq q_2 \wedge q_2 \subseteq q_1$, as well as to $q_1 \cup q_2 \subseteq q_1 \cap q_2$. Conversely, equality always subsumes containment for any family closed under union, since $q_1 \subseteq q_2$ if and only if $q_1 \cup q_2 = q_2$.

More generally, it becomes clear that there is an infinitude of modalities one may consider. A general definition of what constitutes a boolean-query modality may be found in the formal notion of *generalized quantifier* [30,31]. The affinity of generalized quantifiers to natural language constructs makes them interesting as query language constructs. For example, for two relations $R$ and $S$, Barwise and Cooper consider the boolean query $R \cap S \neq \emptyset$. This query can be stated as "some tuple in $R$ belongs to $S$". Correspondingly, the modality $e_1 \cap e_2 \neq \emptyset$ states the language construct "some $e_1$ are $e_2$". Obviously, most query languages are closed under intersection, so that this modality is subsumed by the nonemptiness modality. But again one may investigate whether the presence of intersection is actually necessary.

Questions of the same nature as the ones studied here have also been studied by logicians interested in generalized quantifiers. For example, Hella et al. [32] showed that for every finite set of generalized quantifier there is a more powerful one (by moving to more or higher-arity relations).

Obviously, the value of singling out certain generalized quantifiers for investigation in a study such as ours will depend on their naturalness as query language constructs. We believe that (non)emptiness and containment are among the most fundamental modalities. It would be too large of a project to provide a complete picture for all relevant boolean query families. Our goal in this paper has been to provide a framework that helps to investigate such matters. We hope we have also provided some interesting results that fit into this framework.

# References

1. Abiteboul, S., Hull, R., Vianu, V.: Foundations of Databases. Addison-Wesley, Boston (1995)
2. Ebbinghaus, H.D., Flum, J.: Finite Model Theory, 2nd edn. Springer, Heidelberg (1999). https://doi.org/10.1007/3-540-28788-4
3. Libkin, L.: Elements of Finite Model Theory. Springer, Heidelberg (2004). https://doi.org/10.1007/978-3-662-07003-1
4. Kolaitis, P.: On the expressive power of logics on finite models. In: Grädel, E., Kolaitis, P.G., Libkin, L., Marx, M., Spencer, J., Vardi, M.Y., Venema, Y., Weinstein, S. (eds.) Finite Model Theory and Its Applications. Springer, Heidelberg (2007). https://doi.org/10.1007/3-540-68804-8_2
5. Chandra, A., Merlin, P.: Optimal implementation of conjunctive queries in relational data bases. In: Proceedings 9th ACM Symposium on the Theory of Computing, pp. 77–90. ACM (1977)
6. Beeri, C., Vardi, M.: A proof procedure for data dependencies. J. ACM **31**(4), 718–741 (1984)
7. Angles, R., Gutierrez, C.: Survey of graph database models. ACM Comput. Surv. **40**(1), 1 (2008)
8. Wood, P.: Query languages for graph databases. SIGMOD Rec. **41**(1), 50–60 (2012)
9. Barceló, P.: Querying graph databases. In: Proceedings 32nd ACM Symposium on Principles of Databases, pp. 175–188. ACM (2013)
10. Marx, M., de Rijke, M.: Semantic characterizations of navigational XPath. SIGMOD Rec. **34**(2), 41–46 (2005)
11. ten Cate, B., Marx, M.: Navigational XPath: calculus and algebra. SIGMOD Rec. **36**(2), 19–26 (2007)
12. Fletcher, G., Gyssens, M., Leinders, D., Van den Bussche, J., Van Gucht, D., Vansummeren, S., Wu, Y.: Relative expressive power of navigational querying on graphs. In: Proceedings 14th International Conference on Database Theory (2011)
13. Libkin, L., Martens, W., Vrgoč, D.: Quering graph databases with XPath. In: Proceedings 16th International Conference on Database Theory. ACM (2013)
14. Angles, R., Barceló, P., Rios, G.: A practical query language for graph DBs. In: Bravo, L., Lenzerini, M. (eds.) Proceedings 7th Alberto Mendelzon International Workshop on Foundations of Data Management. CEUR Workshop Proceedings, vol. 1087 (2013)
15. Surinx, D., Fletcher, G., Gyssens, M., Leinders, D., Van den Bussche, J., Van Gucht, D., Vansummeren, S., Wu, Y.: Relative expressive power of navigational querying on graphs using transitive closure. Log. J. IGPL **23**(5), 759–788 (2015)
16. Fletcher, G., Gyssens, M., Leinders, D., Surinx, D., Van den Bussche, J., Van Gucht, D., Vansummeren, S., Wu, Y.: Relative expressive power of navigational querying on graphs. Inf. Sci. **298**, 390–406 (2015)
17. Fletcher, G., Gyssens, M., Leinders, D., Van den Bussche, J., Van Gucht, D., Vansummeren, S., Wu, Y.: The impact of transitive closure on the expressiveness of navigational query languages on unlabeled graphs. Ann. Math. Artif. Intell. **73**(1–2), 167–203 (2015)
18. Surinx, D., Van den Bussche, J., Van Gucht, D.: The primitivity of operators in the algebra of binary relations under conjunctions of containments. In: Proceedings 32nd Annual ACM/IEEE Symposium on Logic in Computer Science. IEEE Computer Society Press (2017)

19. Imielinski, T., Lipski, W.: The relational model of data and cylindric algebras. J. Comput. Syst. Sci. **28**, 80–102 (1984)
20. Van den Bussche, J.: Applications of Alfred Tarski's ideas in database theory. In: Fribourg, L. (ed.) CSL 2001. LNCS, vol. 2142, pp. 20–37. Springer, Heidelberg (2001). https://doi.org/10.1007/3-540-44802-0_2
21. Surinx, D.: A framework for comparing query languages in their ability to express boolean queries. Ph.D. thesis, Hasselt University (2017). http://dsurinx.be/phd.pdf
22. Ameloot, T., Ketsman, B., Neven, F., Zinn, D.: Weaker forms of monotonicity for declarative networking: a more fine-grained answer to the CALM-conjecture. ACM Trans. Database Syst. **40**(4), 21 (2016)
23. Cruz, I., Mendelzon, A., Wood, P.: A graphical query language supporting recursion. In: Dayal, U., Traiger, I. (eds.) Proceedings of the ACM SIGMOD 1987 Annual Conference. SIGMOD Record, vol. 16, no. 3, pp. 323–330. ACM Press (1987)
24. Chang, C., Keisler, H.: Model Theory, 3rd edn. North-Holland, Amsterdam (1990)
25. Benedikt, M., Leblay, J., ten Cate, B., Tsamoura, E.: Generating Plans from Proofs: The Interpolation-Based Approach to Query Reformulation. Morgan & Claypool, San Rafael (2016)
26. Rossman, B.: Homomorphism preservation theorems. J. ACM **55**(3), 15 (2008)
27. Gurevich, Y.: Toward logic tailored for computational complexity. In: Börger, E., Oberschelp, W., Richter, M.M., Schinzel, B., Thomas, W. (eds.) Computation and Proof Theory. LNM, vol. 1104, pp. 175–216. Springer, Heidelberg (1984). https://doi.org/10.1007/BFb0099486
28. Ajtai, M., Gurevich, Y.: Monotone versus positive. J. ACM **34**(4), 1004–1015 (1987)
29. Stolboushkin, A.: Finitely monotone properties. In: Proceedings 10th Annual IEEE Symposium on Logic in Computer Science, pp. 324–330 (1995)
30. Barwise, J., Cooper, R.: Generalized quantifiers and natural language. Linguist. Philos. **4**(2), 159–219 (1981)
31. Badia, A.: Quantifiers in Action. ADS, vol. 37. Springer, Boston, MA (2009). https://doi.org/10.1007/978-0-387-09564-6
32. Hella, L., Luosto, K., Väänänen, J.: The hierarchy theorem for generalized quantifiers. J. Symb. Log. **61**(3), 802–817 (1996)

# A Generalized Iterative Scaling Algorithm for Maximum Entropy Model Computations Respecting Probabilistic Independencies

Marco Wilhelm[1]([✉]), Gabriele Kern-Isberner[1], Marc Finthammer[2], and Christoph Beierle[2]

[1] Department of Computer Science, TU Dortmund, Dortmund, Germany
marco.wilhelm@tu-dortmund.de
[2] Department of Computer Science, University of Hagen, Hagen, Germany

**Abstract.** Maximum entropy distributions serve as favorable models for commonsense reasoning based on probabilistic conditional knowledge bases. Computing these distributions requires solving high-dimensional convex optimization problems, especially if the conditionals are composed of first-order formulas. In this paper, we propose a highly optimized variant of generalized iterative scaling for computing maximum entropy distributions. As a novel feature, our improved algorithm is able to take probabilistic independencies into account that are established by the principle of maximum entropy. This allows for exploiting the logical information given by the knowledge base, represented as weighted conditional impact systems, in a very condensed way.

## 1 Introduction

In recent years, *relational probabilistic programming* [1,2] gained in importance due to its expressive power when modeling uncertain knowledge about properties of and interactions among individual objects. Notably, sophisticated *weighted first-order model counting* techniques [3] play an important part in contributing to the tractability of this research area. Many approaches, however, rely on one or more of the following unfavorable restrictions: The probability of each ground atom (≙ random variable) has to be known, ground atoms are assumed to be stochastically independent, or probabilities may be assigned to first-order *sentences*, i.e. closed formulas, only. The *maximum entropy methodology* (MaxEnt) [4,5] in combination with probabilistic first-order conditionals under the aggregating semantics overcomes all these restrictions but lacks attention due to missing efficient reasoning techniques.

In this paper, we show how probabilistic independencies can be used to speed up the computation of maximum entropy distributions. For this, we formulate a sufficient condition for probabilistic independence at maximum entropy based on the logical structure of the underlying knowledge base, and we introduce a very

© Springer International Publishing AG, part of Springer Nature 2018
F. Ferrarotti and S. Woltran (Eds.): FoIKS 2018, LNCS 10833, pp. 379–399, 2018.
https://doi.org/10.1007/978-3-319-90050-6_21

condensed representation of this logical structure in terms of *weighted conditional impact systems* (WCI systems). The main contribution of this paper is the presentation of our algorithm iGIS which essentially extends existing approaches used to compute MaxEmnt distributions, mainly [6], by exploiting these WCI systems and therefore the probabilistic independencies.

Formally, we build upon a probabilistic language which allows for expressing uncertain knowledge by *probabilistic conditionals* of the form $(B|A)[p]$, meaning that $B$ follows from $A$ with probability $p$, where $A$ and $B$ are first-order formulas (that may contain free variables). The *aggregating semantics* [7] attributes a formal interpretation to these conditionals by combining stochastic and subjective aspects of probabilities (probabilities of type 1 and type 2 according to Halpern [8]), and without making any independence assumptions. Because of this generous representation of probabilistic knowledge, no distinct probability distribution as a model is predetermined. For reasoning tasks, however, it is favorable to choose such a single model. The one which fits best to commonsense reasoning and which is in the focus of this paper is provided by the *principle of maximum entropy* [4,9]. Determining this maximum entropy distribution requires solving a complex optimization problem, which is the (computational) bottleneck of the MaxEnt approach. A common way of calculating the MaxEnt distribution is based on the *generalized iterative scaling* (GIS) algorithm [10] which starts from a uniform probability distribution and adjusts the single probabilities while iterating over the set of possible worlds. As this set is typically large (exponential in the number of ground atoms), iterative scaling in its primitive version is intractable for the first-order case. In [6], an optimized version of GIS was presented which works on equivalence classes of possible worlds that share the same *conditional impact* on the knowledge base (so-called *weighted conditional impacts* or WCIs for short). However, the runtime of this algorithm still depends on the domain size. Here, we further optimize this approach by also taking probabilistic independencies and identically distributed parts of the MaxEnt distribution into account that arise from the logical structure of the underlying knowledge. Instead of adjusting the whole set of probabilities, our novel algorithm iGIS adjusts the marginal probabilities induced by these independencies, only. Notably, the independencies do not have to be considered during the modeling process (like in graphical models such as Bayesian networks or Markov random fields [11]) but appear implicitly by the definition of the MaxEnt distribution. In order to represent the logical structure of the knowledge in such a way that one can benefit from the independencies, we introduce the concept of *weighted conditional impact systems* which generalize the idea of WCIs. Our algorithm iGIS then iterates over these WCI systems instead of simple WCIs. In a first empirical analysis we show that the runtime of iGIS is entirely independent of the domain size in some cases. This happens if the domain elements that are not explicitly mentioned in the knowledge base behave interchangeably, i.e., if they have the same impact on the MaxEnt distribution. In general, our algorithm iGIS is at least as fast as the algorithm in [6], as the latter can be reproduced as a special instance of iGIS.

The rest of the paper is organized as follows: After briefly recalling the basics of the aggregating semantics and maximum entropy reasoning, we motivate the study of probabilistic independencies at maximum entropy and formulate a sufficient condition for their appearance. Then, we introduce weighted conditional impact systems as a basis for our generalized iterative scaling algorithm which is presented in the subsequent section. Finally, we give some empirical results and conclude. All proofs can be found in the Appendix.

## 2    Preliminaries

As a background language we consider a function-free first order language FOL over the signature $\Sigma = (\mathsf{Pred}, \mathsf{Const})$ consisting of a finite set of predicates Pred and a finite set of constants Const. Formulas in FOL are built in the usual way using the connectives $\wedge$ (conjunction), $\vee$ (disjunction), $\neg$ (negation), and the quantifiers $\forall X.$ (universal quantification) and $\exists X.$ (existential quantification). In order to increase readability, we sometimes abbreviate conjunctions $A \wedge B$ with $AB$, tautologies $A \vee \neg A$ with $\top$, and negations $\neg A$ with $\overline{A}$ for formulas $A, B \in$ FOL. Further, $\models$ denotes the classical entailment relation, and $\equiv$ the equivalence relation on formulas in FOL.

Let $P/n \in$ Pred be a predicate of arity $n$, and let $c_1, \ldots, c_n \in$ Const.[1] Then, $P(c_1, \ldots, c_n)$ is called a *ground atom*. The set of all possible ground atoms is denoted with $\mathcal{G}_\Sigma$. If a formula $A$ is either a ground atom or its negation, $A$ is called a *ground literal*. $\mathsf{Lit}(\mathcal{G})$ denotes the set of all ground literals derived from $\mathcal{G} \subseteq \mathcal{G}_\Sigma$. Every formula $A \in$ FOL can be grounded by substituting each free variable in $A$ with a constant and by executing all quantifications (over the finite domain). For example, $(R(a,a) \vee P(a)) \wedge (R(b,a) \vee P(b)) \wedge (R(c,a) \vee P(c))$ is a proper ground instance of $A = \forall X.(R(X,Y) \vee P(X))$ if $\mathsf{Const} = \{a, b, c\}$. In particular, ground formulas are *closed*, i.e., they do not contain free variables. The set of all proper ground instances of a formula $A$ is denoted with $\mathsf{Grnd}(A)$. Hence, in the previous example one has $|\mathsf{Grnd}(A)| = 3$.

A *conditional* $(B|A)[p]$ with $A, B \in$ FOL and $p \in [0,1]$ is a formal representation of the statement "If $A$ holds, then $B$ follows with probability $p$". We explicitly allow $A$ and $B$ to contain free variables. A ground instance of a conditional $(B|A)[p]$ is obtained by grounding $A$ and $B$ such that free variables occurring in both $A$ and $B$ are substituted with the same constant. For example, $(R(a,b)|P(a))[p]$ and $(R(a,a)|P(a))[p]$ are proper ground instances of $(R(X,Y)|P(X))[p]$ if $a, b \in$ Const, but $(R(a,b)|P(b))[p]$ is not. The set of all proper ground instances of a conditional $r$ is also denoted with $\mathsf{Grnd}(r)$. A finite (ordered) set of conditionals is called a *knowledge base*.

*Example 1 (Knowledge Base $\mathcal{R}_{bfp}$).* We consider the following knowledge base as a running example: Let $\Sigma = (\mathsf{Pred}, \mathsf{Const})$ with

$$\mathsf{Pred} = \{\mathsf{Bird}/1, \mathsf{Flies}/1, \mathsf{Penguin}/1\}, \qquad \mathsf{tweety} \in \mathsf{Const},$$

---

[1] In this paper, predicate and variable names will always begin with an uppercase letter and constant names with a lowercase letter.

where the predicates shall express that an individual is a bird, that it is able to fly, and that it is a penguin, respectively. The knowledge base $\mathcal{R}_{\text{bfp}} = \{r_1, \ldots, r_4\}$,

$$r_1 = (\text{Flies}(X)|\text{Bird}(X))[0.9],$$
$$r_2 = (\neg\text{Flies}(X)|\text{Penguin}(X))[0.99],$$
$$r_3 = (\text{Bird}(X)|\text{Penguin}(X))[1],$$
$$r_4 = (\text{Penguin}(\text{tweety})|\top)[1],$$

states that (1) birds are able to fly with a probability of 0.9, (2) penguins are very unlikely to fly (as no one has ever seen a flying penguin), say, with probability 0.99, (3) every penguin is a bird (by definition), and (4) the individual Tweety is a penguin.

The probabilistic interpretations of conditionals are given by probability distributions over possible worlds. Here, a *possible world* $\omega$ is a complete conjunction of ground literals, i.e., every ground atom occurs in a possible world exactly once, either negated or positive. The set of all possible worlds is denoted with $\Omega$. Further, $\Omega_{\mathcal{G}}$ denotes the set of all complete conjunctions that can be built using only the subset of ground atoms $\mathcal{G} \subseteq \mathcal{G}_{\Sigma}$. We call these conjunctions *partial* possible worlds. Probability distributions $\mathcal{P} : \Omega \to [0,1]$ are extended to closed formulas $A \in \text{FOL}$ by defining $\mathcal{P}(A) = \sum_{\omega \models A} \mathcal{P}(\omega)$. The *aggregating semantics* [7] further extends $\mathcal{P}$ to conditionals and resembles the definition of a conditional probability by summing up the probabilities of all respective ground instances.

**Definition 1 (Aggregating Semantics).** *Let* $\mathcal{P} : \Omega \to [0,1]$ *be a probability distribution, and let* $r = (B|A)[p]$ *be a conditional.* $\mathcal{P}$ *is a* model *of* $r$, *written* $\mathcal{P} \models r$, *iff*

$$\frac{\sum_{(B'|A')[p] \in \text{Grnd}(r)} \mathcal{P}(A'B')}{\sum_{(B'|A')[p] \in \text{Grnd}(r)} \mathcal{P}(A')} = p \tag{1}$$

*and* $\sum_{(B'|A')[p] \in \text{Grnd}(r)} \mathcal{P}(A') > 0$. $\mathcal{P}$ *is a model of a knowledge base* $\mathcal{R}$ *iff* $\mathcal{P} \models r$ *for all* $r \in \mathcal{R}$.

If the formulas $A$ and $B$ of the conditional $r = (B|A)[p]$ in Definition 1 are closed already, the fraction in (1) reduces to the standard conditional probability $\mathcal{P}(AB)/\mathcal{P}(A)$ since $|\text{Grnd}(r)| = 1$. Further, if $\mathcal{P}$ assigns the probability 1 to a single possible world $\omega$ and 0 to all the others, Eq. (1) reduces to the purely statistical claim that the fraction of ground instances $(B'|A')[p] \in \text{Grnd}(r)$ that are *verified* in $\omega$ ($\omega \models A'B'$) compared to those that are *applicable* in $\omega$ ($\omega \models A'$) equals $p$.

A knowledge base $\mathcal{R}$ that has a model is called *consistent*. Consistent knowledge bases usually have many models. For reasoning tasks, it is favorable to select a certain model among them. The one which fits best to commonsense according to [4,9] and which is in the focus of this paper is provided by the *principle of maximum entropy*. This *maximum entropy distribution (MaxEnt distribution)* $\mathcal{P}_{\mathcal{R}}^{\text{ME}}$ is the unique distribution that models $\mathcal{R}$ while maximizing the entropy $\mathcal{H}(\mathcal{P}) = -\sum_{\omega \in \Omega} \mathcal{P}(\omega) \log \mathcal{P}(\omega)$, which is a measure of indifference in $\mathcal{P}$. Computing the MaxEnt distribution requires solving a convex optimization problem in a $|\Omega|$-dimensional space, which is typically very large (exponential in the number of ground atoms, where the number of ground atoms itself grows polynomially depending on the number of constants and the arity of the predicates). Therefore, sophisticated solvers are needed for this task in order to stay tractable, i.e. for not suffering under an exponential blow-up. In [6], a generalized iterative scaling approach is presented, which is based on building equivalence classes of possible worlds in order to speed up calculations. We extend and improve upon this approach by also taking probabilistic independencies of the MaxEnt distribution into account.

## 3    Motivating the Study of Probabilistic Independencies

Independence properties are important in order to decompose probability distributions into smaller parts that are computationally easier to handle. However, they are difficult to unveil in a first-order setting. Before we formulate a criterion for probabilistic independence at maximum entropy, we give an intuition to it by the aid of the knowledge base $\mathcal{R}_{\mathrm{bfp}}$ from Example 1.

It is a well-known result (cf. [5]) that the MaxEnt probabilities of two distinct possible worlds do not differ if for all conditionals $r_i \in \mathcal{R}$ the two possible worlds *verify* and *falsify* the same number of ground instances of $r_i$, where the number of verifications is defined by

$$\mathsf{ver}_i(\omega) = |\{(B|A)[p] \in \mathsf{Grnd}(r_i) \mid \omega \models AB\}|$$

and the number of falsifications is defined by

$$\mathsf{fal}_i(\omega) = |\{(B|A)[p] \in \mathsf{Grnd}(r_i) \mid \omega \models A\overline{B}\}|.$$

The functions $\mathsf{ver}_i$ and $\mathsf{fal}_i$ are known as *counting functions* (cf. [12,13]). For example, if we consider a knowledge base $\mathcal{R}$ which consists of the single conditional $r_1 = (\mathsf{Flies}(X)|\mathsf{Bird}(X))[0.9]$ only (cf. Example 1), the possible worlds in which both the number of flying birds ($\mathsf{ver}_1(\omega)$) and the number of non-flying birds ($\mathsf{fal}_1(\omega)$) are the same also have the same MaxEnt probability. This fact motivates the investigation of *conditional impacts*, i.e. tuples $(\mathsf{ver}_i(\omega), \mathsf{fal}_i(\omega))$ for $\omega \in \Omega$ and $r_i \in \mathcal{R}$, as abstractions of possible worlds that are convenient for maximum entropy reasoning. In preparation of WCI systems, we will further breakdown the notion of these conditional impacts. For instance, in order to calculate the counting functions with respect to $r_1 = (\mathsf{Flies}(X)|\mathsf{Bird}(X))[0.9]$, it is admissible to disassemble the possible worlds into several partial possible worlds: As every constant $c \in \mathsf{Const}$ leads to a different ground instance $r_1(c) = (\mathsf{Flies}(c)|\mathsf{Bird}(c))[0.9]$ of $r_1$ whose verification resp. falsification depends on the truth values of the ground atoms concerning the constant $c$ only, the possible worlds can be disassembled into those partial possible worlds dealing with only one constant. For example, the possible world

$$\omega = \ldots \text{Bird}(c) \wedge \text{Flies}(c) \wedge \text{Penguin}(c) \wedge \text{Bird}(d) \wedge \overline{\text{Flies}(d)} \wedge \text{Penguin}(d) \ldots$$

can be written as the conjunction of

$$\omega_c = \text{Bird}(c) \wedge \text{Flies}(c) \wedge \text{Penguin}(c), \qquad \omega_d = \text{Bird}(d) \wedge \overline{\text{Flies}(d)} \wedge \text{Penguin}(d),$$

and the remaining ground literals in $\omega$, whereby the evaluation of $r_1(c)$ depends on $\omega_c$ only. Analogously, the evaluation of $r_1(d) = (\text{Flies}(d)|\text{Bird}(d))[0.9]$ depends on $\omega_d$ only. This motivates the definition of conditional impacts of partial possible worlds, and if the decomposition of the possible worlds into their parts is chosen appropriately, the conditional impacts of the partial possible worlds reassemble to the conditional impacts of the whole possible worlds by componentwise addition (cf. Proposition 2). Moreover, the decomposition carries over to the MaxEnt probabilities themselves, and one obtains, in this particular case,

$$\mathcal{P}_{\mathcal{R}}^{\text{ME}}(\omega) = \ldots \mathcal{P}_{\mathcal{R}}^{\text{ME}}(\omega_c) \cdot \mathcal{P}_{\mathcal{R}}^{\text{ME}}(\omega_d) \ldots$$

As our algorithm iGIS, which we will present later on (cf. Fig. 1), calculates MaxEnt distributions iteratively by adjusting marginal probabilities (here $\mathcal{P}_{\mathcal{R}}^{\text{ME}}(\omega_c), \mathcal{P}_{\mathcal{R}}^{\text{ME}}(\omega_d), \ldots$) instead of the probabilities $\mathcal{P}_{\mathcal{R}}^{\text{ME}}(\omega)$ themselves, this observation alone means a reduction from about[2] $2^{3 \cdot |\text{Const}|}$ to about $|\text{Const}| \cdot 2^3$ many adjustments per iteration step for the present knowledge base and also for the knowledge base $\mathcal{R}_{\text{bfp}}$ from Example 1 (note that 3 is the number of the unary predicates in the signature). Furthermore, for $\mathcal{R}_{\text{bfp}}$, the marginal distributions on the sets of partial possible worlds $\Omega_{\mathcal{G}_c}$ with $\mathcal{G}_c = \{\text{Bird}(c), \text{Flies}(c), \text{Penguin}(c)\}$ for $c \in \text{Const} \setminus \{\text{tweety}\}$ are identical since the conditional impacts of the partial possible worlds defined over these sets $\mathcal{G}_c$ are the same. More precisely, for every partial possible world $\omega_c \in \mathcal{G}_c$ with $c \neq \text{tweety}$ there is a partial possible world $\omega_d' \in \mathcal{G}_d$ with $d \neq \text{tweety}$ that has the same conditional impact. Only the constant tweety is exceptional, since there are partial possible worlds in $\mathcal{G}_{\text{tweety}}$ that verify the conditional $r_4 = (\text{Penguin}(\text{tweety})|\top)[1]$ (for example, $\omega_{\text{tweety}} = \text{Bird}(\text{tweety}) \wedge \overline{\text{Flies}(\text{tweety})} \wedge \text{Penguin}(\text{tweety}))$, but no partial possible world in any $\mathcal{G}_c$ with $c \neq \text{tweety}$ verifies $r_4$. The fact that some parts of the maximum entropy distribution are identically distributed can also be considered by our algorithm iGIS which further reduces the number of necessary adjustments. Actually, only one of the identically distributed parts has to be adjusted which leads to a further reduction from about $|\text{Const}| \cdot 2^3$ to about $2 \cdot 2^3$ many adjustments per iteration step for the knowledge base $\mathcal{R}_{\text{bfp}}$. As a quintessence, if all the constants that do not explicitly occur in a knowledge base $\mathcal{R}$ are interchangeable, the costs of computing $\mathcal{P}_{\mathcal{R}}^{\text{ME}}$ are mostly independent of the domain size. In the following, we provide a formal basis for these deliberations.

---

[2] Actually, the numbers of adjustment steps are smaller in both cases since we group (partial) possible worlds with the same conditional impact together (*weighted* conditional impacts) and filter out "impossible" worlds beforehand.

# 4   Independence Criterion for MaxEnt Distributions

We formulate a sufficient condition for probabilistic independence under maximum entropy (Proposition 1) which is based on the logical structure of the underlying knowledge base. While our former approach in [14] is on a purely syntactical level, our novel deliberations here are semantically driven (cf. Eq. (2)) and therefore able to unveil independencies disguised by superfluous syntax. We first refine the definition of a knowledge base to the following sense.

**Definition 2 (Knowledge Base Decomposition).** *A ground knowledge base is an (ordered) set of finitely many sets, each consisting of finitely many ground conditionals. The distinct ground knowledge base* $\mathcal{R}_G = \{\mathsf{Grnd}(r_1), \ldots, \mathsf{Grnd}(r_n)\}$ *is called the* grounding *of the knowledge base* $\mathcal{R} = \{r_1, \ldots, r_n\}$.

*A set* $\mathfrak{R} = \{\mathcal{R}_G^1, \ldots, \mathcal{R}_G^k\}$ *of k ground knowledge bases* $\mathcal{R}_G^j = \{R_1^j, \ldots, R_n^j\}$, $j = 1, \ldots, k$, *is called a* decomposition *of* $\mathcal{R}$ *iff* $\dot{\cup}_{j=1,\ldots,k}\ R_i^j = \mathsf{Grnd}(r_i)$ *for* $i = 1, \ldots, n$, *where* $\dot{\cup}$ *is the disjoint union.*

Obviously, $\{\mathcal{R}_G\}$ is a decomposition of $\mathcal{R}$, i.e., every knowledge base has at least one decomposition. A non-trivial decomposition of a knowledge base is shown in the following example.

*Example 2 (Running Example Cont'd).* A decomposition of the knowledge base $\mathcal{R}_{\text{bfp}}$ from Example 1 is given by $\mathfrak{R}_{\text{bfp}} = \{\mathcal{R}_G^c \mid c \in \mathsf{Const}, \mathcal{R}_G^c = \{R_1^c, \ldots, R_4^c\}\}$,

$$\mathcal{R}_1^c = \{(\mathsf{Flies}(c)|\mathsf{Bird}(c)[0.9]\}, \qquad c \in \mathsf{Const},$$
$$\mathcal{R}_2^c = \{(\neg\mathsf{Flies}(c)|\mathsf{Penguin}(c)[0.99]\}, \qquad c \in \mathsf{Const},$$
$$\mathcal{R}_3^c = \{(\mathsf{Bird}(c)|\mathsf{Penguin}(c)[1]\}, \qquad c \in \mathsf{Const},$$
$$\mathcal{R}_4^c = \emptyset, \qquad c \in \mathsf{Const} \setminus \{\mathsf{tweety}\},$$
$$\mathcal{R}_4^{\text{tweety}} = \{(\mathsf{Penguin}(\mathsf{tweety})|\top)[1]\}.$$

In the decomposition $\mathfrak{R}_{\text{bfp}}$ the ground instances of the conditionals in $\mathcal{R}_{\text{bfp}}$ are separated by the constants in $\mathsf{Const}$ and are consolidated into the several sets $\mathcal{R}_G^c$. As there are no ground instances of conditional $r_4$ concerning constants other than $\mathsf{tweety}$, $\mathcal{R}_4^c = \emptyset$ for $c \neq \mathsf{tweety}$.

Certain decompositions correspond to so-called *syntax partitions* (specific partitions of $\mathcal{G}_\Sigma$) and lead to probabilistic independencies of the MaxEnt distribution $\mathcal{P}_{\mathcal{R}}^{\mathsf{ME}}$ as we will see next. Beforehand, we give some convenient notations.

For a finite set of ground conditionals $R_G$ and a ground formula $C \in \mathsf{FOL}$ we generalize the counting functions by

$$\mathsf{ver}_{R_G}(C) = |\{(B|A)[p] \in R_G \mid C \models AB\}|,$$
$$\mathsf{fal}_{R_G}(C) = |\{(B|A)[p] \in R_G \mid C \models A\overline{B}\}|.$$

Note that $\mathsf{ver}_{\mathsf{Grnd}(r_i)}(\omega) = \mathsf{ver}_i(\omega)$ and $\mathsf{fal}_{\mathsf{Grnd}(r_i)}(\omega) = \mathsf{fal}_i(\omega)$ for $\omega \in \Omega$ in coincidence with the standard definition of counting functions. Further, we define

$$\omega_{\mathcal{G}} = \bigwedge_{\substack{L \in \mathsf{Lit}(\mathcal{G}), \\ \omega \models L}} L, \qquad \omega \in \Omega, \quad \mathcal{G} \subseteq \mathcal{G}_\Sigma.$$

$w_\mathcal{G}$ coincides with $w$ except for the ground literals that are not in $\mathcal{G}$ and, thus, do not occur in $w_\mathcal{G}$. If $\{\mathcal{G}_1, \ldots, \mathcal{G}_k\}$ is a partition of $\mathcal{G}_\Sigma$, then $w \equiv \bigwedge_{j=1}^k w_{\mathcal{G}_j}$ holds.

**Definition 3 (Syntax Partition).** *Let $\mathcal{R} = \{r_1, \ldots, r_n\}$ be a knowledge base, and let $\mathfrak{G} = \{\mathcal{G}_1, \ldots, \mathcal{G}_k\}$ be a partition of $\mathcal{G}_\Sigma$. $\mathfrak{G}$ is called a* syntax partition *for $\mathcal{R}$ if there is a decomposition $\mathfrak{R} = \{\mathcal{R}_G^1, \ldots, \mathcal{R}_G^k\}$ of $\mathcal{R}$ such that for all $w \in \Omega$,*

$$\mathsf{ver}_i(w) = \sum_{j=1}^k \mathsf{ver}_{R_i^j}(w_{\mathcal{G}_j}), \quad \mathsf{fal}_i(w) = \sum_{j=1}^k \mathsf{fal}_{R_i^j}(w_{\mathcal{G}_j}), \quad i = 1, \ldots, n. \quad (2)$$

*We call the decomposition $\mathfrak{R}$ a $\mathfrak{G}$-respecting decomposition in this case.*

Note that a syntax partition needs the semantic condition (2) to induce an effective decomposition of possible worlds. A non-trivial syntax partition respecting decomposition dismembers $\mathcal{R}$ into "smaller" ground knowledge bases while preserving all the logical information that is needed for MaxEnt calculations. Typical cases where knowledge bases have non-trivial syntax partitions are the following:

1. There are knowledge bases $\mathcal{R}_1, \mathcal{R}_2$ such that $\mathcal{R}_1 \dot\cup \mathcal{R}_2 = \mathcal{R}$ and $\mathcal{R}_1, \mathcal{R}_2$ do not share any ground atoms[3] (cf. Example 3). In other words, the knowledge base $\mathcal{R}$ splits into the syntactically independent knowledge bases $\mathcal{R}_1$ and $\mathcal{R}_2$.
2. There are sets of ground conditionals $R_i^1, R_i^2$ such that $R_i^1 \dot\cup R_i^2 = \mathsf{Grnd}(r_i)$ for $i = 1, \ldots, n$, and the sets of ground conditionals $\bigcup_{i=1}^n R_i^1$ and $\bigcup_{i=1}^n R_i^2$ do not share any ground atoms (cf. Example 4). In other words, the ground instances of the conditionals split into syntactically independent sets.

*Example 3.* Let $\Sigma = (\{A/1, B/1, C/1\}, \mathsf{Const})$, and let $p_1, p_2 \in [0, 1]$. We consider $\mathcal{R}_{\mathrm{sp}} = \{r_1, r_2\}$ with $r_1 = (B(X)|A(X))[p_1]$ and $r_2 = (C(X)|\top)[p_2]\}$. It is obvious that $\mathfrak{G} = \{\mathcal{G}_1, \mathcal{G}_2\}$ with $\mathcal{G}_1 = \{A(a) \mid a \in \mathsf{Const}\} \cup \{B(a) \mid a \in \mathsf{Const}\}$ and $\mathcal{G}_2 = \{C(a) \mid a \in \mathsf{Const}\}$ is a syntax partition for $\mathcal{R}_{\mathrm{sp}}$ as $\mathfrak{R} = \{\{R_1^1, R_2^1\}, \{R_1^2, R_2^2\}\}$,

$$R_1^1 = \{(B(a)|A(a))[p_1] \mid a \in \mathsf{Const}\}, \qquad R_2^1 = \emptyset,$$
$$R_1^2 = \emptyset, \qquad\qquad\qquad\qquad R_2^2 = \{(C(a)|\top)[p_2] \mid a \in \mathsf{Const}\},$$

is a $\mathfrak{G}$-respecting decomposition of $\mathcal{R}$. However, the partition $\mathfrak{G}' = \{\mathcal{G}_1', \mathcal{G}_2'\}$ of $\mathcal{G}_\Sigma$ with $\mathcal{G}_1' = \{A(a) \mid a \in \mathsf{Const}\}$ and $\mathcal{G}_2' = \{B(a) \mid a \in \mathsf{Const}\} \cup \{C(a) \mid a \in \mathsf{Const}\}$ is not a syntax partition for $\mathcal{R}$ as, for instance,

$$\mathsf{ver}_{\mathsf{Grnd}(r_1)}(w_{\mathcal{G}_1'}) = 0 < |\mathsf{Const}| = \mathsf{ver}_{\mathsf{Grnd}(r_1)}(w)$$

for $w = \left(\bigwedge_{a \in \mathsf{Const}} A(a)\right) \wedge \left(\bigwedge_{a \in \mathsf{Const}} B(a)\right)$. Hence, there is no $R \subseteq \mathsf{Grnd}(r_1)$ with

$$\mathsf{ver}_R(w_{\mathcal{G}_1'}) = \mathsf{ver}_{\mathsf{Grnd}(r_1)}(w).$$

---

[3] We say that $\mathcal{R}_1$ and $\mathcal{R}_2$ share a ground atom $A \in \mathcal{G}_\Sigma$ if there are $r_1 \in \mathcal{R}_1$ and $r_2 \in \mathcal{R}_2$ with ground instances $r_1' \in \mathsf{Grnd}(r_1)$ and $r_2' \in \mathsf{Grnd}(r_2)$ that both contain the ground atom $A$.

Note that the syntax partition $\mathfrak{G}$ is not "optimal", since the more fine-grained partition $\mathfrak{G}_2 = \{\mathcal{G}_a \mid a \in \mathsf{Const}\} \cup \{\mathcal{G}'_a \mid a \in \mathsf{Const}\}$ with $G_a = \{A(a), B(a)\}$ and $G'_a = \{C(a)\}$ is also a syntax partition for $\mathcal{R}$ (cf. also Example 4).

*Example 4 (Running Example Cont'd).* We recall the knowledge base $\mathcal{R}_{\mathrm{bfp}}$ from Example 1. $\mathfrak{G}_{\mathrm{bfp}} = \{\mathcal{G}_c \mid c \in \mathsf{Const}\}$ with $\mathcal{G}_c = \{\mathsf{Bird}(c), \mathsf{Flies}(c), \mathsf{Penguin}(c)\}$ is a syntax partition for $\mathcal{R}$, as $\mathfrak{R}_{\mathrm{bfp}}$ from Example 2 is a $\mathfrak{G}_{\mathrm{bfp}}$-respecting decomposition of $\mathcal{R}_{\mathrm{bfp}}$: For $i = 1, 2, 3$, let $r_i^c \in \mathsf{Grnd}(r_i)$ be the ground instance of $r_i \in \mathcal{R}_{\mathrm{bfp}}$ which is obtained by substituting the free variable $X$ in $r_i$ with the constant $c \in \mathsf{Const}$. Then, for all $c, d \in \mathsf{Const}$ and for all $\omega \in \Omega$,

$$\mathsf{ver}_{\{r_i^c\}}(\omega_{\mathcal{G}_d}) = \begin{cases} \mathsf{ver}_{\{r_i^c\}}(\omega), & d = c \\ 0, & d \neq c \end{cases}.$$

Hence, $\mathsf{ver}_i(\omega) = \sum_{c \in \mathsf{Const}} \mathsf{ver}_{\{r_i^c\}}(\omega) = \sum_{c \in \mathsf{Const}} \mathsf{ver}_{\{r_i^c\}}(\omega_{\mathcal{G}_c}) = \sum_{c \in \mathsf{Const}} \mathsf{ver}_{R_i^c}(\omega_{\mathcal{G}_c})$ as necessary. Further, $\mathsf{ver}_{R_4^c}(\omega) = \mathsf{ver}_{R_4^c}(\omega_{\mathcal{G}_c}) = 0$ for all constants $c \neq \mathsf{tweety}$ as $R_4^c$ is empty in this case, and $\mathsf{ver}_4(\omega) = \mathsf{ver}_{R_4^{\mathsf{tweety}}}(\omega_{\mathcal{G}_{\mathsf{tweety}}})$ holds. Analogous calculations show $\mathsf{fal}_i(\omega) = \sum_{c \in \mathsf{Const}} \mathsf{fal}_{R_i^c}(\omega_{\mathcal{G}_c})$ for $i = 1, \dots, 4$ for all $\omega \in \Omega$.

The next proposition finally shows that a syntax partition $\mathfrak{G} = \{\mathcal{G}_1, \dots, \mathcal{G}_k\}$ serves as a basis for decomposing MaxEnt distributions into independent parts, i.e., all the MaxEnt probabilities $\mathcal{P}_{\mathcal{R}}^{\mathsf{ME}}(\omega)$ can be factorized into marginal probabilities $\mathcal{P}_{\mathcal{R}}^{\mathsf{ME}}(\omega_{\mathcal{G}_j})$ over $\mathcal{G}_j$, $j = 1, \dots, k$, and reassembled as a joint probability over $\bigcup_{j=1}^k \mathcal{G}_j \ (= \mathcal{G}_{\Sigma})$.

**Proposition 1.** *Let $\mathcal{R}$ be a consistent knowledge base, and let $\{\mathcal{G}_1, \dots, \mathcal{G}_k\}$ be a syntax partition for $\mathcal{R}$. For all $\omega \in \Omega$,*

$$\mathcal{P}_{\mathcal{R}}^{\mathsf{ME}}(\omega) = \prod_{j=1}^k \mathcal{P}_{\mathcal{R}}^{\mathsf{ME}}(\omega_{\mathcal{G}_j}). \tag{3}$$

*Example 5 (Running Example Cont'd).* Since $\mathcal{R}_{\mathrm{bfp}}$ from Example 1 is consistent and $\mathfrak{G}_{\mathrm{bfp}} = \{\mathcal{G}_c \mid c \in \mathsf{Const}\}$ with $\mathcal{G}_c = \{\mathsf{Bird}(c), \mathsf{Flies}(c), \mathsf{Penguin}(c)\}$ is a syntax partition for $\mathcal{R}_{\mathrm{bfp}}$ (cf. Example 4), the MaxEnt distribution $\mathcal{P}_{\mathcal{R}_{\mathrm{bfp}}}^{\mathsf{ME}}$ satisfies

$$\mathcal{P}_{\mathcal{R}_{\mathrm{bfp}}}^{\mathsf{ME}}(\omega) = \prod_{c \in \mathsf{Const}} \mathcal{P}_{\mathcal{R}_{\mathrm{bfp}}}^{\mathsf{ME}}(\omega_{\mathcal{G}_c}).$$

Moreover, the sets $\mathcal{G}_c, \mathcal{G}_d$ for $c, d \neq \mathsf{tweety}$ are even identically distributed. To see this, consider the bijection $\beta . \Omega_{\mathcal{G}_c} \to \Omega_{\mathcal{G}_d}$ which simply replaces the constant $c$ with the constant $d$ whenever $c$ occurs. Then, $\mathcal{P}_{\mathcal{R}_{\mathrm{bfp}}}^{\mathsf{ME}}(\omega_{\mathcal{G}_d}) = \mathcal{P}_{\mathcal{R}_{\mathrm{bfp}}}^{\mathsf{ME}}(\beta(\omega_{\mathcal{G}_c}))$ for all $\omega_{\mathcal{G}_d} \in \Omega_{\mathcal{G}_d}$.[4] Hence, in order to determine the MaxEnt distribution $\mathcal{P}_{\mathcal{R}_{\mathrm{bfp}}}^{\mathsf{ME}}$, only

---

[4] Consider the bijection $\beta : \Omega_{\mathcal{G}_c} \to \Omega_{\mathcal{G}_d}$ which simply replaces the constant $c$ with the constant $d$ whenever $c$ occurs.

the probabilities $\mathcal{P}_{\mathcal{R}_{\text{bfp}}}^{\text{ME}} (\omega_{G_{\text{tweety}}})$ for all $\omega_{G_{\text{tweety}}} \in \Omega_{\mathcal{G}_{\text{tweety}}}$ as well as the probabilities $\mathcal{P}_{\mathcal{R}_{\text{bfp}}}^{\text{ME}} (\omega_{\mathcal{G}_c})$ for all $\omega_{G_c} \in \Omega_{\mathcal{G}_c}$ for only one single constant $c \neq$ tweety are needed. At this point, we want to anticipate that our algorithm iGIS in Sect. 6 makes use of this benefit.

The fact that $\{\mathcal{G}_1, \ldots, \mathcal{G}_k\}$ is a syntax partition for $\mathcal{R}$ is a sufficient but, in general, not a necessary condition for the factorization of $\mathcal{P}_{\mathcal{R}}^{\text{ME}}$ as in Proposition 1. The main reason for this is that $\mathcal{P}_{\mathcal{R}}^{\text{ME}}$ does not only depend on the logical structure of $\mathcal{R}$ but also on the probabilities of the conditionals in $\mathcal{R}$ that are not considered by syntax partitions. However, the differentiation between independencies caused by the logical structure of $\mathcal{R}$ and those which are caused by the probabilities of $\mathcal{R}$ is desired, as the logical part of $\mathcal{R}$ can be understood as a reasoner's fundamental conception of the coherences in the world, while the probabilities are often volatile and imprecise. In this sense, independencies based on the logical structure of $\mathcal{R}$ are more essential.

## 5   Weighted Conditional Impact Systems

The generalized iterative scaling algorithm for computing maximum entropy distributions as presented in [6] works on a set of so-called *weighted conditional impacts* (WCIs; cf. [13]). Conditional impacts are, as already mentioned in Sect. 3, an abstraction of possible worlds that are characterized by their verification and falsification of conditionals. Identical conditional impacts are grouped together and are assigned a weight (their quantity). Therefore, they serve as a formal representation of equivalence classes of possible worlds. Here, we refine the set of weighted conditional impacts to a system of several sets of weighted conditional impacts (WCI system) that has its origin in a predetermined syntax partition, and which is an even more condensed representation of the possible worlds. Proposition 1 will then allow us to perform generalized iterative scaling on this WCI system.

For the rest of the paper, let

- $\mathcal{R} = \{r_1, \ldots, r_n\}$ be a knowledge base with $r_i = (B_i|A_i)[p_i]$ for $i = 1, \ldots, n$,
- $\mathfrak{G} = \{\mathcal{G}_1, \ldots, \mathcal{G}_k\}$ be a syntax partition for $\mathcal{R}$,
- $\mathfrak{R} = \{\mathcal{R}_G^j \mid j = 1, \ldots, k\}$ with $\mathcal{R}_G^j = \{R_1^j, \ldots, R_n^j\}$ be a $\mathfrak{G}$-respecting decomposition of $\mathcal{R}$.

We further differentiate the conditionals in $\mathcal{R}$ into two categories: A *deterministic conditional* $r = (B|A)[p] \in \mathcal{R}$ is a conditional with $p \in \{0, 1\}$. It prevents models of $\mathcal{R}$ from assigning a positive probability to possible worlds $\omega \in \Omega$ with

$$\text{ver}_{\text{Grnd}(r)}(\omega) > 0 \text{ if } p = 0, \quad \text{fal}_{\text{Grnd}(r)}(\omega) > 0 \text{ if } p = 1, \tag{4}$$

which is a requirement of the aggregating semantics. We call possible worlds that satisfy (4) for any deterministic conditional in $\mathcal{R}$ *null-worlds*. The set of all null-worlds is denoted with $\Omega^0$.

A *non-deterministic conditional* instead is of the form $r = (B|A)[p]$ with $p \in (0,1)$. For the rest of the paper, we assume $\mathcal{R} = \{r_1, \ldots, r_m, r_{m+1}, \ldots, r_n\}$ with $r_1, \ldots, r_m$ being non-deterministic conditionals, and $r_{m+1}, \ldots, r_n$ being deterministic. For our algorithm it will be necessary to separate out the null-worlds first, due to their different impact on the MaxEnt distribution (which is in common with the algorithm in [6]). This preprocessing step is implicitly covered by the following definition of conditional impacts.

The *conditional impact* caused by $\omega \in \Omega_{\mathcal{G}_j}$ on $\mathcal{R}_G^j$ is

$$\gamma_{\mathcal{R}_G^j}(\omega) = \begin{cases} ((\mathsf{ver}_{R_i^j}(\omega), \mathsf{fal}_{R_i^j}(\omega)))_{i=1,\ldots,m} & \text{if } (*) \text{ holds} \\ \text{undefined} & \text{otherwise} \end{cases},$$

where the condition $(*)$ is true iff

$$\mathsf{ver}_{R_i^j}(\omega) = 0 \text{ if } p_i = 0, \quad \mathsf{fal}_{R_i^j}(\omega) = 0 \text{ if } p_i = 1, \quad i = m+1, \ldots, n.$$

Note that conditional impacts leave the deterministic conditionals out except for the cases specified in condition $(*)$. As a consequence of the next proposition, the definition of conditional impacts which we use here is a refinement of the standard definition of conditional impacts according to [6].

**Proposition 2.** *Let $\mathcal{R}$ be a knowledge base, let $\mathfrak{G}$ be a syntax partition for $\mathcal{R}$, and let $\mathfrak{R}$ be a $\mathfrak{G}$-respecting decomposition of $\mathcal{R}$ as described above. If $\omega \in \Omega$ is not a null-world, then*

$$\gamma_{\mathcal{R}_G}(\omega) = ((\sum_{j=1}^{k}(\gamma_{R_i^j}(\omega_{\mathcal{G}_j})_i)_1, \sum_{j=1}^{k}(\gamma_{R_i^j}(\omega_{\mathcal{G}_j})_i)_2))_{i=1,\ldots,m}.$$

*If $\omega$ is a null-world, then $\gamma_{\mathcal{R}_G^j}(\omega_{\mathcal{G}_j})$ is undefined for at least one $j \in \{1, \ldots, k\}$.*

According to Proposition 2, conditional structures of null-worlds are not well-defined and hence excluded from the following elaboration. Apart from that, the conditional impact of each non-null-world can be broken down into the decomposition of $\mathcal{R}$ and hence is considered in the following.

A tuple $\gamma \in (\mathbb{N}_0 \times \mathbb{N}_0)^m$ is a *conditional impact* of $\mathcal{R}_G^j$ iff there is a partial possible world $\omega \in \Omega_{\mathcal{G}_j}$ with $\gamma_{\mathcal{R}_G^j}(\omega) = \gamma$. For such a $\gamma$,

$$\mathsf{wgt}_j(\gamma) = |\{\omega_{\mathcal{G}_j} \in \Omega_{\mathcal{G}_j} \mid \gamma_{R_G^j}(\omega_{\mathcal{G}_j}) = \gamma\}|$$

is the *weight* of $\gamma$, and $\mathsf{wgt}_j$ is called the *weighting function* of $\mathcal{R}_G^j$. Further, $\Gamma_j$ denotes the set of all conditional impacts of $\mathcal{R}_G^j$, and $(\Gamma_j, \mathsf{wgt}_j)$ is called the *weighted conditional impact* of $\mathcal{R}_G^j$. Weighted conditional impacts (WCIs) store the possible combinations of the numbers of verifications (ver) and falsifications (fal) of the ground conditionals in $\mathcal{R}_G^j$ and how often these combinations can be observed (wgt). To be able to trace back the total number of ground conditionals in $\mathcal{R}_G^j$, we annotate the WCIs with corresponding vectors $\eta_j = (|R_1^j|, \ldots, |R_m^j|)$. The resulting *weighted conditional impact components* form the essentials of the *weighted conditional impact systems*.

**Definition 4 (Weighted Conditional Impact System).** *Let $\mathcal{R}$ be a knowledge base, let $\mathfrak{G}$ be a syntax partition for $\mathcal{R}$, and let $\mathfrak{R}$ be a $\mathfrak{G}$-respecting decomposition of $\mathcal{R}$ as described above. A tuple $(\Gamma, \mathsf{wgt}, \boldsymbol{\eta})$ is a weighted conditional impact component of $\mathfrak{R}$ iff there is a $\mathcal{R}_G^j \in \mathfrak{R}$ with $(\Gamma_j, \mathsf{wgt}_j, \boldsymbol{\eta}_j) = (\Gamma, \mathsf{wgt}, \boldsymbol{\eta})$. For such a weighted conditional impact component $c = (\Gamma, \mathsf{wgt}, \boldsymbol{\eta})$,*

$$\mathsf{cnt}_{\mathfrak{R}}(c) = |\{\mathcal{R}_G^j \in \mathfrak{R} \mid (\Gamma_j, \mathsf{wgt}_j, \boldsymbol{\eta}_j) = c\}|$$

*is the count of $c$, and $\mathsf{cnt}_{\mathfrak{R}}$ is called the counting function of $\mathfrak{R}$. Further, $C_{\mathfrak{R}}$ denotes the set of all conditional impact components of $\mathfrak{R}$, and $(C_{\mathfrak{R}}, \mathsf{cnt}_{\mathfrak{R}})$ is called the weighted conditional impact system of $\mathfrak{R}$.*

A weighted conditional impact system (WCI system) is uniquely defined by a consistent knowledge base $\mathcal{R}$ and a syntax partition $\mathfrak{G}$ for $\mathcal{R}$ which justifies the notation $\mathfrak{G}(\mathcal{R}, \mathfrak{G})$ for the one WCI system for $\mathcal{R}$ and $\mathfrak{G}$.

*Example 6 (Running Example Cont'd).* The weighted conditional impact system for the knowledge base $\mathcal{R}_{\mathrm{bfp}}$ from Example 1 and the syntax partition $\mathfrak{G}$ from Example 4 is $\mathfrak{G}(\mathcal{R}_{\mathrm{bfp}}, \mathfrak{G}_{\mathrm{bfp}}) = (\{c_{\mathrm{tweety}}, c_c\}, \mathsf{cnt})$ with

$$c_{\mathrm{tweety}} = (\Gamma_{\mathrm{tweety}}, \mathsf{wgt}_{\mathrm{tweety}}, \boldsymbol{\eta}_{\mathrm{tweety}}), \qquad c_c = (\Gamma_c, \mathsf{wgt}_c, \boldsymbol{\eta}_c),$$

$$\mathsf{cnt}(c_{\mathrm{tweety}}) = 1, \qquad\qquad\qquad \mathsf{cnt}(c_c) = |\mathsf{Const}| - 1,$$

$$\Gamma_{\mathrm{tweety}} = \{\gamma_{\mathrm{tweety}}^1, \gamma_{\mathrm{tweety}}^2\}, \qquad\qquad \Gamma_c = \{\gamma_c^1, \ldots, \gamma_c^5\},$$

$$\gamma_{\mathrm{tweety}}^1 = \big((1,0),(0,1)\big), \qquad\qquad \gamma_c^1 = \big((1,0),(0,1)\big),$$

$$\gamma_{\mathrm{tweety}}^2 = \big((0,1),(1,0)\big), \qquad\qquad \gamma_c^2 = \big((1,0),(0,0)\big),$$

$$\gamma_c^3 = \big((0,1),(1,0)\big),$$

$$\gamma_c^4 = \big((0,1),(0,0)\big),$$

$$\gamma_c^5 = \big((0,0),(0,0)\big),$$

$$\mathsf{wgt}(\gamma_{\mathrm{tweety}}^i) = 1, \quad i = 1,2, \qquad\qquad \mathsf{wgt}(\gamma_c^i) = 1, \quad i = 1,\ldots,4,$$

$$\mathsf{wgt}(\gamma_c^5) = 2,$$

$$\boldsymbol{\eta}_{\mathrm{tweety}} = (1,1), \qquad\qquad\qquad \boldsymbol{\eta}_c = (1,1).$$

For example, the conditional impact $\gamma_{\mathrm{tweety}}^1 \in \Gamma_{\mathrm{tweety}}$ refers to the conjunction $\mathsf{Bird}(\mathrm{tweety}) \wedge \mathsf{Flies}(\mathrm{tweety}) \wedge \mathsf{Penguin}(\mathrm{tweety}) \in \Omega_{\mathcal{G}_{\mathrm{tweety}}}$ that occurs in every possible world in which Tweety is an abnormal penguin which can fly. This conjunction verifies the conditional $(\mathsf{Flies}(\mathrm{tweety})|\mathsf{Bird}(\mathrm{tweety}))[0.9] \in \mathcal{R}_1^{\mathrm{tweety}}$ but falsifies the conditional $(\neg\mathsf{Flies}(\mathrm{tweety})|\mathsf{Penguin}(\mathrm{tweety}))[0.99] \in \mathcal{R}_2^{\mathrm{tweety}}$ and indeed leads to the conditional impact $((1,0),(0,1))$. The same conditional impact occurs in $\Gamma_c$ for any $c \in \mathsf{Const}$, too, since the conjunction $\mathsf{Bird}(c) \wedge \mathsf{Flies}(c) \wedge \mathsf{Penguin}(c)$ verifies and falsifies the corresponding conditionals in $\mathcal{R}_1^c$ resp. $\mathcal{R}_2^c$.

On the other side, the conditional impact $((1,0),(0,0))$ is in $\Gamma_c$ but not in $\Gamma_{\text{tweety}}$, since the presence of this conditional impact in $\Gamma_{\text{tweety}}$ would demand that Tweety is not a penguin (as the conditional $(\neg\text{Flies(tweety)}|\text{Penguin (tweety)})[0.99]$ might not be applicable) which contradicts $(\text{Penguin(tweety)}|\top)$ $[1] \in \mathcal{R}_4^{\text{tweety}}$. As such a deterministic conditional does not exist for the constants other than Tweety (it is $\mathcal{R}_4^c = \emptyset$), the conditional impact $((1,0),(0,0))$ is in $\Gamma_c$, $c \neq \text{tweety}$.

# 6    Generalized Iterative Scaling Algorithm

We now propose our generalized iterative scaling algorithm iGIS which is an optimization of the algorithm $\text{GIS}^{\text{WCI}}$ presented in [6], since iGIS is able to propagate probabilistic independencies, in addition. The algorithm iGIS takes a weighted conditional impact system $\mathfrak{S}(\mathcal{R}, \mathfrak{G})$, the number of deterministic conditionals in $\mathcal{R}$, and the probabilities of the non-deterministic conditionals in $\mathcal{R}$ as input, and returns $|\mathcal{R}| + 1$ many real numbers determining the maximum entropy distribution $\mathcal{P}_{\mathcal{R}}^{\text{ME}}$.

iGIS is based on the idea of representing the MaxEnt distribution $\mathcal{P}_{\mathcal{R}}^{\text{ME}}$ as a Gibbs distribution [15]: Following the method of Lagrange multipliers [16], $\mathcal{P}_{\mathcal{R}}^{\text{ME}}$ is given by[5]

$$\mathcal{P}_{\mathcal{R}}^{\text{ME}}(\omega) = \begin{cases} \alpha_0 \prod_{i=1}^{m} \alpha_i^{(1-p_i)\cdot\text{ver}_i(\omega)-p_i\cdot\text{fal}_i(\omega)}, & \omega \in \Omega \setminus \Omega^0 \\ 0, & \omega \in \Omega^0 \end{cases}, \qquad (5)$$

where the non-negative real numbers $\alpha_i$, $i = 0,\ldots,n$, are exponentials of the Lagrange multipliers corresponding to the $m$ non-deterministic conditionals in $\mathcal{R}$ as well as the normalizing condition $\sum_{\omega\in\Omega} \mathcal{P}_{\mathcal{R}}^{\text{ME}}(\omega) = 1$, which together constitute the constraints on $\mathcal{P}_{\mathcal{R}}^{\text{ME}}$. The $\alpha_i$-values are the output of iGIS. For a more detailed analysis of the theoretical background of (5), we refer to [5]. Here, we want to note that if $\{\mathcal{G}_1,\ldots,\mathcal{G}_k\}$ is a syntax partition for $\mathcal{R}$, then the Gibbs representation (5) of $\mathcal{P}_{\mathcal{R}}^{\text{ME}}$ further factorizes to

$$\mathcal{P}_{\mathcal{R}}^{\text{ME}}(\omega) = \begin{cases} \alpha_0 \prod_{j=1}^{k} \prod_{i=1}^{m} \alpha_i^{(1-p_i)\cdot\text{ver}_{\mathcal{R}_i^j}(\omega_j)-p_i\cdot\text{fal}_{\mathcal{R}_i^j}(\omega_j)}, & \omega \in \Omega \setminus \Omega^0 \\ 0, & \omega \in \Omega^0 \end{cases},$$

in accordance with the independence result in Proposition 1. Hence, MaxEnt reasoning can directly be performed based on the information provided by a WCI system.

The pseudo code of iGIS is presented in Fig. 1. In Step 2, a probability distribution $\mathcal{P}$ is initialized to the uniform distribution.[6] In the main loop (Step 4),

---

[5] This representation of $\mathcal{P}_{\mathcal{R}}^{\text{ME}}$ exists except for very rare pathological cases which can be circumvented by prescient knowledge engineering.

[6] More precisely, uniform marginals of the probability distribution are considered in order to avoid iterations over the whole probability distribution.

**Input:**     - Probabilities $p_1, \ldots, p_m$ of the non-deterministic conditionals in $\mathcal{R}$
             - WCI system $\mathfrak{S}(\mathcal{R}, \mathfrak{B}) = ((c_1, \ldots, c_k), \mathrm{cnt})$ with $c_j = (\Gamma_j, \mathrm{wgt}_j, \eta_j)$
**Output:**    - Effects $\alpha_1, \ldots, \alpha_m$ and normalizing constant $\alpha_0$ according to Eq. (5)

---

1. **for i $= 1, \ldots, \hat{m}$:**
   $$\hat{\alpha}_i^{(0)} := 1 \qquad\qquad\qquad\qquad \text{(initialize normalized effects)}$$

2. **for j $= 1, \ldots, k$ for $\gamma \in \Gamma_j$:**
   $$\mathcal{P}_j^{(0)}(\gamma) := \tfrac{1}{\sum_{\gamma' \in \Gamma_j} \mathrm{wgt}_j(\gamma')} \qquad \text{(initialize uniform (marginal) probabilities)}$$

3. $l := 0 \qquad\qquad\qquad\qquad\qquad\qquad\qquad\qquad \text{(initialize iteration counter)}$

4. **repeat until** ⟨abortion condition⟩ **holds**
   (a) $l := l + 1 \qquad\qquad\qquad\qquad\qquad\qquad \text{(increase iteration counter)}$

   (b) **for j $= 1, \ldots, k$:**
   $$\delta_j^{(l)} := \sum_{\gamma \in \Gamma_j} \mathrm{wgt}_j(\gamma) \cdot \mathcal{P}_j^{(l-1)}(\gamma)$$

   **for j $= 1, \ldots, k$:**
   $$\nu_j^{(l)} := \mathrm{cnt}(c_j) \cdot \left(\delta_j^{(l)}\right)^{\mathrm{cnt}(c_j)-1} \cdot \prod_{\substack{h=1,\ldots,k \\ h \neq j}} \left(\delta_h^{(l)}\right)^{\mathrm{cnt}(c_h)}$$

   **for i $= 1, \ldots, \hat{m}$:**
   $$\beta_i^{(l)} := \frac{\hat{\varepsilon}_i}{\sum_{j=1}^{k} \nu_j^{(l)} \cdot \left(\sum_{\gamma \in \Gamma_j} \mathrm{wgt}_j(\gamma) \cdot \mathcal{P}_j^{(l-1)}(\gamma) \cdot \hat{f}_{i,j}(\gamma)\right)}$$
   $$\text{(determine scaling factors)}$$

   (c) **for i $= 1, \ldots, \hat{m}$:**
   $$\hat{\alpha}_i^{(l)} := \hat{\alpha}_i^{(l-1)} \cdot \beta_i^{(l)} \qquad\qquad\qquad \text{(scale normalized effects)}$$

   (d) **for j $= 1, \ldots, k$ for $\gamma \in \Gamma_j$:**
   $$\mathcal{P}_j'^{(l)}(\gamma) := \mathcal{P}_j^{(l-1)}(\gamma) \prod_{i=1}^{\hat{m}} (\beta_i^{(l)})^{\hat{f}_{i,j}(\gamma)} \qquad \text{(scale probabilities)}$$

   (e) **for j $= 1, \ldots, k$ for $\gamma \in \Gamma_j$:**
   $$\mathcal{P}_j^{(l)}(\gamma) := \frac{\mathcal{P}_j'^{(l)}(\gamma)}{\sum_{\gamma' \in \Gamma_j} \mathrm{wgt}_j(\gamma') \cdot \mathcal{P}_j'^{(l)}(\gamma')} \qquad\qquad \text{(normalize probabilities)}$$
   **end loop**

5. **for i $= 1, \ldots, m$:**
   $$\alpha_i := \left(\frac{\hat{\alpha}_i^{(l)}}{\hat{\alpha}_{\hat{m}}^{(l)}}\right)^{\frac{1}{G}} \qquad\qquad\qquad\qquad \text{(determine effects and)}$$

6. $\alpha_0 := \dfrac{\hat{\alpha}_{\hat{m}}^{(l)} \prod_{i=1}^{m} \alpha_i^{p_i \cdot \sum_{j=1}^{k} \mathrm{cnt}(c_j) \cdot (\eta_j)_i}}{\prod_{j=1}^{k} \left(\sum_{\gamma \in \Gamma_j} \mathrm{wgt}_j(\gamma) \prod_{i=1}^{\hat{m}} (\hat{\alpha}_i^{(l)})^{\hat{f}_{i,j}(\gamma)}\right)^{\mathrm{cnt}(c_j)}} \qquad$ (normalizing constant)

**Fig. 1.** Pseudo code of iGIS which computes $\mathcal{P}_{\mathcal{R}}^{\mathsf{ME}}$ based on a WCI system.

scaling factors $\beta_i$ depending on the input of the algorithm and the current state of $\mathcal{P}$ are determined, which are used to adjust the probability distribution $\mathcal{P}$ afterwards. This is repeatedly done until an abortion condition holds. Usually, this condition is chosen such a way that the loop aborts when the probability distribution (or the scaling factors) do not change substantially. Finally, the values $\alpha_0, \alpha_1, \ldots, \alpha_m$ are extracted from the scaling factors respectively the last state of the probability distribution. The pseudo code uses some abbreviations which we want to define in the following: $\hat{m}$ is the number of non-deterministic conditionals in $\mathcal{R}$ plus one, i.e., $\hat{m} = m + 1$. With $G$ we denote the number of all ground instances of all non-deterministic conditionals in $\mathcal{R}$, which can be derived from the input WCI system by $G = \sum_{i=1}^{m} \sum_{j=1}^{k} \mathsf{cnt}(c_j) \cdot (\eta_j)_i$. The so-called *normalized feature functions* are given by

$$\hat{f}_{i,j}(\gamma) = \frac{(\gamma_i)_1 + \big((\eta_j)_i - (\gamma_i)_1 - (\gamma_i)_2\big) \cdot p_i}{G}, \quad \hat{f}_{\hat{m},j}(\gamma) = \frac{\sum_{i=1}^{m}(\eta_j)_i}{G} - \sum_{i=1}^{m} \hat{f}_{i,j}(\gamma),$$

for $i = 1, \ldots, m$, $j = 1, \ldots, k$, and $\gamma \in \Gamma_j$. The corresponding *normalized expected values* are

$$\hat{\epsilon}_i = \frac{p_i \cdot \sum_{j=1}^{k} \mathsf{cnt}(c_j) \cdot (\eta_j)_i}{G}, i = 1, \ldots, m, \qquad \hat{\epsilon}_{\hat{m}} = 1 - \sum_{i=1}^{m} \hat{\epsilon}_i.$$

The correctness[7] of iGIS can be proven by realizing that the original algorithm GIS$^{\mathsf{WCI}}$ in [6] is correct and that our algorithm is in one-to-one correspondence to the latter. We just took advantage of the fact that many expressions of the original algorithm either factorize or decompose into sums if the independence result in Proposition 1 is applicable. In particular, the loops in the Steps 2, 4(d), and 4(e) of iGIS are executed over WCIs in the original algorithm (i.e., equivalence classes of the possible worlds in $\Omega$), while they are executed *independently* over the elements of WCI components here (i.e., equivalence classes of the *partial* possible worlds in $\Omega_{\mathcal{G}_j}$), which means a reduction from $|\Gamma|$ to $\sum_{j=1}^{k} |\Gamma_j|$ many iterations.[8] Being more precise, if for several $\Gamma_i$ it holds that the tuples $(\Gamma_i, \mathsf{wgt}_i, \eta_i)$ are componentwise equal, we iterate only over one of them and consider the count $\mathsf{cnt}((\Gamma_i, \mathsf{wgt}_i, \eta_i))$ as an exponent or as a prefactor (e.g., in the Steps 4(b) and 6). In terms of probability theory, this is possible since $\mathcal{P}_{\mathcal{R}}^{\mathsf{ME}}$ is identically distributed on the corresponding sets of atoms $\mathcal{G}_i$ in this case. As a consequence, the number of iterations within the main repeat-loop in Step 4 is independent of the domain size iff the number of components of the considered WCI system is independent of the domain size, which again is possible iff the number of *differently* distributed parts of $\mathcal{P}_{\mathcal{R}}^{\mathsf{ME}}$ is independent of the domain size. The algorithm GIS$^{\mathsf{WCI}}$ from [6] can be reproduced as an instance of iGIS by invoking iGIS on the trivial WCI system $\mathfrak{S}(\mathcal{R}, \{\mathcal{G}_\Sigma\})$. Consequently, iterations in iGIS are executed on standard WCIs in this trivial case.

---

[7] Correctness here means that $\alpha_0, \alpha_1, \ldots, \alpha_m$ can be calculated with any precision if the loop in Step 4 is executed sufficiently often.

[8] Here, $\Gamma$ is the set of all ordinary WCIs with respect to the knowledge base $\mathcal{R}$.

**Table 1.** Empirical results of applying iGIS to some example knowledge bases (abortion condition: $\delta_\beta = 0.001$).

| Set-up | | Problem size | | | | Runtimes | | |
|---|---|---|---|---|---|---|---|---|
| $\mathcal{R}$ | \|Const\| | $\|\Omega\|$ | $\|\Omega \setminus \Omega^0\|$ | $\sum_{j=1}^{k} \|\Gamma_j\|$ on $\{\mathcal{G}_\Sigma\}$ | $\sum_{j=1}^{k} \|\Gamma_j\|$ on $\mathfrak{G}$ | CONV + iGISon $\{\mathcal{G}_\Sigma\} \hat{=}$ GIS$^{\text{WCI}}$ | | iGIS on $\mathfrak{G}$ |
| $\mathcal{R}_{\text{bfp}}$ | 14 | $2^{42}$ | $\approx 2^{35}$ | 2,940 | 7 | 1.0 s | 0.9 s | <0.1 s |
| $\mathcal{R}_{\text{bfp}}$ | 16 | $2^{48}$ | $\approx 2^{40}$ | 4,692 | 7 | 1.7 s | 0.5 s | <0.1 s |
| $\mathcal{R}_{\text{bfp}}$ | 18 | $2^{54}$ | $\approx 2^{45}$ | 7,125 | 7 | 4.2 s | 0.8 s | <0.1 s |
| $\mathcal{R}_{\text{bfp}}$ | 20 | $2^{60}$ | $\approx 2^{50}$ | 10,395 | 7 | 14.7 s | 1.5 s | <0.1 s |
| $\mathcal{R}_{\text{cty}}$ | 4 + 4 | $2^{28}$ | $\approx 2^{27}$ | 3,601 | 20 | 1.4 s | 0.7 s | <0.1 s |
| $\mathcal{R}_{\text{cty}}$ | 6 + 4 | $2^{42}$ | $\approx 2^{41}$ | 23,541 | 20 | 53.7 s | 9.6 s | <0.1 s |
| $\mathcal{R}_{\text{cty}}$ | 8 + 4 | $2^{56}$ | $\approx 2^{54}$ | 91,713 | 20 | >600.0 s | 65.0 s | <0.1 s |
| $\mathcal{R}_{\text{cty}}$ | 10 + 4 | $2^{70}$ | $\approx 2^{68}$ | 266,453 | 20 | >600.0 s | 218.3 s | <0.1 s |
| $\mathcal{R}_{\text{mth}}$ | 4 | $2^{40}$ | $\approx 2^{38}$ | 75 | 6 | <0.1 s | <0.1 s | <0.1 s |
| $\mathcal{R}_{\text{mth}}$ | 10 | $2^{220}$ | $\approx 2^{216}$ | 726 | 6 | 0.2 s | <0.1 s | <0.1 s |
| $\mathcal{R}_{\text{mth}}$ | 12 | $2^{312}$ | $\approx 2^{307}$ | 1,183 | 6 | 0.2 s | <0.1 s | <0.1 s |
| $\mathcal{R}_{\text{mth}}$ | 14 | $2^{420}$ | $\approx 2^{414}$ | 1,800 | 6 | 0.3 s | <0.1 s | <0.1 s |

# 7   Empirical Results

We applied our algorithm iGIS to different knowledge bases (cf. Examples 1, 7, and 8) while varying the domain size |Const| as well as the syntax partition based on which the input WCI system is calculated. More precisely, we ran iGIS with WCI systems based on the trivial syntax partition $\{\mathcal{G}_\Sigma\}$ as input ($\hat{=}$ executing GIS$^{\text{WCI}}$ from [6]) as well as with very condensed WCI systems based on more fine-grained syntax partitions ($\mathfrak{G}_{\text{bfp}}$, $\mathfrak{G}_{\text{cty}}$, and $\mathfrak{G}_{\text{mth}}$). While the condensed WCI systems of our example knowledge bases can be determined by hand, the trivial WCI systems become very large. Actually, we extrapolated them from the condensed WCI systems with the help of an auxiliary algorithm CONV which we implemented only for this purpose. Determining the trivial WCI systems directly by the naïve approach described in Fig. 2 of [6] was far too time-consuming for our larger examples. As an abortion condition we used the accuracy threshold

$$\beta_i^{(l)} - \beta_i^{(l-1)} < 0.001, \qquad i = 1, \ldots, n. \qquad (\delta_\beta = 0.001)$$

The results are shown in Table 1. Besides the runtimes themselves, the number of iterations in the Steps 2, 4(d), and 4(e) of iGIS, namely $\sum_{j=1}^{k} |\Gamma_j|$, is given.

   As the number of iteration steps $\sum_{j=1}^{k} |\Gamma_j|$ is very low ($\leq 20$) and independent of the domain size |Const| (resp. |Person| in Example 7) for all of the example knowledge bases when using the condensed WCI systems, iGIS is able to compute the MaxEnt distributions very fast (in less than 100 ms). In contrast, the runtimes of iGIS increase significantly when using the trivial WCI systems (which corresponds to applying $\mathsf{GIS}^{\mathsf{WCI}}$ from [6]), because of the dependence of the number of iteration steps $\sum_{j=1}^{k} |\Gamma_j|$ on $|\mathsf{Const}|$ in this case. Moreover, one would need to add the runtimes of $\mathsf{CONV}$ to those of $\mathsf{iGIS}$ in order to get the total runtimes, since calculating the trivial WCI systems is expensive. To qualify these observations, we have to say that we purposely have chosen example knowledge bases that come up with very condensed WCI systems in order to illustrate the benefit of taking account of probabilistic independencies when calculating MaxEnt distributions. If a knowledge base does not have such a condensed WCI system, then, of course, $\mathsf{iGIS}$ needs the trivial one as input.

*Example 7 (Knowledge Base $\mathcal{R}_{cty}$).* We consider the knowledge base $\mathcal{R}_{cty}$ from [6] which makes use of typed constants and predicates: There is a certain number of constants of type Person and a certain number of constants of type City, namely four (City $=$ {london, paris, rome, vienna}), such that Person $\dot{\cup}$ City $=$ Const. The predicate $\mathsf{VisitsEUcity}(P, C)$ expresses that a person $P$ visits the city $C$. The predicates $\mathsf{LikesSightseeing}(P)$, $\mathsf{LivesInEurope}(P)$, and $\mathsf{LikesChurches}(P)$ express that a person $P$ likes sightseeing, lives in Europe, and likes churches, respectively. The knowledge base $\mathcal{R}_{cty}$ itself consists of the four conditionals

$$r_1 = (\mathsf{VisitsEUcity}(P, C) | \top)[0.1],$$
$$r_2 = (\mathsf{VisitsEUcity}(P, C) | \mathsf{LikesSightseeing}(P))[0.3],$$
$$r_3 = (\mathsf{VisitsEUcity}(P, C) | \mathsf{LivesInEurope}(P))[0.6],$$
$$r_4 = (\mathsf{VisitsEUcity}(P, \mathsf{rome}) | \mathsf{LikesChurches}(P) \wedge \mathsf{LikesSightseeing}(P))[1].$$

$\mathfrak{B}_{cty} = \{\mathcal{G}_c \mid c \in \mathsf{Person}\}$ with

$$\mathcal{G}_c = \{\mathsf{LikesSightseeing}(c), \mathsf{LivesInEurope}(c), \mathsf{LikesChurches}(c)\}$$
$$\cup \{\mathsf{VisitsEUcity}(c, d) \mid d \in \mathsf{City}\}$$

is a syntax partition for $\mathcal{R}_{cty}$ and the corresponding WCI system $\mathfrak{S}(\mathcal{R}_{cty}, \mathfrak{B}_{cty})$ is $(\{c\}, \mathsf{cnt})$ with $\mathsf{cnt}(c) = |\mathsf{Person}|$ and $c = (\Gamma, \mathsf{wgt}, \eta)$ such that

$$\Gamma = \Big\{ \underbrace{\big((a, b),\ c \cdot (a, b),\ d \cdot (a, b)\big)}_{=\gamma_{(a,b)}^{c,d}} \mid 0 \le a, b, \le 4,\ a + b = 4,\ c, d \in \{0, 1\} \Big\},$$

$$\mathsf{wgt}(\gamma_{(a,b)}^{c,d}) = \begin{cases} 1, & a = 0,\ c = 1 \\ 2, & (a = 4)\ \text{or}\ (a = 0,\ c = 0) \\ 5, & a = 1,\ c = 1 \\ 7, & a = 3,\ c = 1 \\ 8, & (a = 1,\ c = 0)\ \text{or}\ (a = 3,\ c = 0) \\ 9, & a = 2,\ c = 1 \\ 12, & a = 2,\ c = 0 \end{cases},$$

$$\eta = (4, 4, 4).$$

*Example 8 (Knowledge Base $\mathcal{R}_{mth}$).* Consider the knowledge base $\mathcal{R}_{mth}$ about characteristics of human beings which consists of the conditionals

$$r_1 = (\forall Y.(\mathsf{ChildOf}(Y, X) \Rightarrow \mathsf{Loves}(X, Y)) | \top)[0.9],$$
$$r_2 = (\mathsf{Mother}(X) | \mathsf{Female}(X))[0.6],$$
$$r_3 = (\mathsf{Female}(X) \wedge \exists Y.\mathsf{ChildOf}(Y, X) | \mathsf{Mother}(X))[1],$$

expressing that humans typically love all their children (with a probability of 0.9), females are mothers with probability 0.6, and mothers are females who have at least one child, respectively. As $\mathfrak{G}_{mth} = \{\mathcal{G}_c \mid c \in \mathsf{Const}\}$ with

$$\mathcal{G}_c = \{\mathsf{Female}(c), \mathsf{Mother}(c)\} \cup \{\mathsf{ChildOf}(d, c), \mathsf{Loves}(c, d) \mid d \in \mathsf{Const}\}$$

is a syntax partition for $\mathcal{R}_{mth}$, the WCI system $\mathfrak{S}(\mathcal{R}_{mth}, \mathfrak{G}_{mth}) = (\{c\}, \mathsf{cnt})$ consists of $c = (\Gamma, \mathsf{wgt}, \eta)$ with $\mathsf{cnt}(c) = |\mathsf{Const}|$ and

$$\Gamma = \{\gamma^1, \ldots, \gamma^6\},$$

$$\gamma^1 = \Big((1,0),(1,0)\Big), \qquad \mathsf{wgt}(\gamma^1) = 3^{|\mathsf{Const}|} - 2^{|\mathsf{Const}|},$$

$$\gamma^2 = \Big((0,1),(1,0)\Big), \qquad \mathsf{wgt}(\gamma^2) = 4^{|\mathsf{Const}|} - 3^{|\mathsf{Const}|},$$

$$\gamma^3 = \Big((0,1),(0,1)\Big), \qquad \mathsf{wgt}(\gamma^3) = 4^{|\mathsf{Const}|} - 3^{|\mathsf{Const}|},$$

$$\gamma^4 = \Big((0,1),(0,0)\Big), \qquad \mathsf{wgt}(\gamma^4) = 4^{|\mathsf{Const}|} - 3^{|\mathsf{Const}|},$$

$$\gamma^5 = \Big((1,0),(0,1)\Big), \qquad \mathsf{wgt}(\gamma^5) = 3^{|\mathsf{Const}|},$$

$$\gamma^6 = \Big((1,0),(0,0)\Big), \qquad \mathsf{wgt}(\gamma^6) = 3^{|\mathsf{Const}|},$$

$$\eta = (1, 1).$$

# 8   Conclusion and Future Work

We formulated a sufficient condition under which maximum entropy distributions decompose into probabilistic independent parts. This condition is based on the notion of syntax partitions which was originally introduced in [14] and is reformulated in a slightly different way here. We further utilized this result to improve the generalized scaling approach for determining maximum entropy distributions presented in [6], which results in a significant reduction of computation times in our benchmark examples.

In future work, we want to address mainly two tasks: First, we want to develop an algorithm which computes a syntax partition for a given knowledge base and the corresponding weighted conditional impact system automatically. Second, we want to extend our approach to deal with conditional independencies which would widen the application area of our improved algorithm a lot. Both are important steps towards lifted inferences at maximum entropy. A further question would be how the independence results carry over to other qualitative and quantitative frameworks for uncertain knowledge representation.

**Acknowledgements.** This research was supported by the German National Science Foundation (DFG), Research Unit FOR 1513 on Hybrid Reasoning for Intelligent Systems.

# Proofs of Results

**Proposition 1.** *Let $\mathcal{R}$ be a consistent knowledge base, and let $\{\mathcal{G}_1, \ldots, \mathcal{G}_k\}$ be a syntax partition for $\mathcal{R}$. For all $\omega \in \Omega$,*

$$\mathcal{P}_{\mathcal{R}}^{\mathsf{ME}}(\omega) = \prod_{j=1}^{k} \mathcal{P}_{\mathcal{R}}^{\mathsf{ME}}(\omega_{\mathcal{G}_j}).$$

*Proof.* We give a proof for those cases in which the representation (5) of $\mathcal{P}_{\mathcal{R}}^{\mathsf{ME}}$ exists. The normalizing constant can be written as $\alpha_0 = \sum_{\omega \in \Omega} \prod_{i=1}^{m} \alpha_i^{f_i(\omega)}$ where $f_X(C)$ abbreviates $(1 - p_i) \cdot \mathsf{ver}_X(C) - p_i \cdot \mathsf{fal}_X(C)$ for any ground formula $C \in \mathsf{FOL}$. Further, let $\mathfrak{R} = \{R_G^1, \ldots, R_G^k\}$ be a $\{\mathcal{G}_1, \ldots, \mathcal{G}_k\}$-respecting decomposition of $\mathcal{R}$ with $R_G^j = \{R_1^j, \ldots, R_n^j\}$ for $j = 1, \ldots, k$. Then, $\alpha_0 = \prod_{j=1}^{k} \alpha_0^j$ holds where $\alpha_0^j = \sum_{\omega_j \in \Omega_{\mathcal{G}_j}} \prod_{i=1}^{m} \alpha_i^{f_i(\omega_j)}$. For $\omega \in \Omega \setminus \Omega^0$, it follows that

$$\mathcal{P}_{\mathcal{R}}^{\mathsf{ME}}(\omega) = \alpha_0 \prod_{i=1}^{m} \alpha_i^{f_i(\omega)} = \alpha_0 \prod_{i=1}^{m} \prod_{j=1}^{k} \alpha_i^{f_{R_i^j}(\omega_{\mathcal{G}_j})}$$

$$= \prod_{j=1}^{k} \left[ \left( \alpha_0^j \prod_{i=1}^{m} \alpha_i^{f_{R_i^j}(\omega_{\mathcal{G}_j})} \right) \cdot \prod_{l \neq j} \underbrace{\left( \sum_{\omega_l' \in \Omega_{\mathcal{G}_l}} \alpha_0^l \prod_{i=1}^{m} \alpha_i^{f_{R_i^l}(\omega_l')} \right)}_{=1} \right]$$

$$= \prod_{j=1}^{k} \left( \sum_{\substack{\omega' \in \Omega \\ \omega' \models \omega_{\mathcal{G}_j}}} \alpha_0 \prod_{i=1}^{m} \prod_{l=1}^{k} \alpha_i^{f_{R_i^l}(\omega_{\mathcal{G}_l})} \right) = \prod_{j=1}^{k} \left( \sum_{\substack{\omega' \in \Omega \\ \omega' \models \omega_{\mathcal{G}_j}}} \alpha_0 \prod_{i=1}^{m} \alpha_i^{f_i(\omega')} \right)$$

$$= \prod_{j=1}^{k} \mathcal{P}_{\mathcal{R}}^{\mathsf{ME}}(\omega_{\mathcal{G}_j}).$$

If $\omega \in \Omega^0$, there is a deterministic conditional $r = (B|A)[p] \in \mathcal{R}$ and an index $l \in \{1, \ldots, k\}$ such that $\mathsf{ver}_{\mathsf{Grnd}(r)}(\omega_{\mathcal{G}_l}) > 0$ if $p = 0$ and $\mathsf{fal}_{\mathsf{Grnd}(r)}(\omega_{\mathcal{G}_l}) > 0$ if $p = 1$. As a consequence, every $\omega'$ with $\omega' \models \omega_{\mathcal{G}_l}$ is a null-world, and

$$\prod_{j=1}^{l_0} \mathcal{P}_{\mathcal{R}}^{\mathsf{ME}}(\omega_{\mathcal{G}_j}) = \left( \sum_{\omega' \models \omega_{\mathcal{G}_l}} \mathcal{P}_{\mathcal{R}}^{\mathsf{ME}}(\omega') \right) \cdot \prod_{j \neq l} \mathcal{P}_{\mathcal{R}}^{\mathsf{ME}}(\omega_{\mathcal{G}_j}) = 0 \cdot \prod_{j \neq l} \mathcal{P}_{\mathcal{R}}^{\mathsf{ME}}(\omega_{\mathcal{G}_j}) = 0$$

as required. $\qquad\square$

**Proposition 2.** *Let $\mathcal{R}$ be a knowledge base, let $\mathfrak{G}$ be a syntax partition for $\mathcal{R}$, and let $\mathfrak{R}$ be a $\mathfrak{G}$-respecting decomposition of $\mathcal{R}$ as described above. If $\omega \in \Omega$ is not a null-world, then*

$$\gamma_{\mathcal{R}_G}(\omega) = \left(\left(\sum_{j=1}^{k}(\gamma_{R_i^j}(\omega_{\mathcal{G}_j})_i)_1, \sum_{j=1}^{k}(\gamma_{R_i^j}(\omega_{\mathcal{G}_j})_i)_2\right)\right)_{i=1,\ldots,m}.$$

*If $\omega$ is a null-world, then $\gamma_{\mathcal{R}_G^j}(\omega_{\mathcal{G}_j})$ is undefined for at least one $j \in \{1, \ldots, k\}$.*

*Proof.* Let $\omega \in \Omega \setminus \Omega^0$. By definition, $\gamma_{\mathcal{R}_G}(\omega) = ((\mathsf{ver}_i(\omega), \mathsf{fal}_i(\omega)))_{i=1,\ldots,m}$. Since $\mathfrak{R}$ is a $\mathfrak{G}$-respecting decomposition of $\mathcal{R}$, $\mathsf{ver}_i(\omega) = \sum_{j=1}^{k} \mathsf{ver}_{R_i^j}(\omega_{\mathcal{G}_j})$ as well as $\mathsf{fal}_i(\omega) = \sum_{j=1}^{k} \mathsf{fal}_{R_i^j}(\omega_{\mathcal{G}_j})$ hold for $i = 1, \ldots, n$, and hence, in particular, this holds for $i = 1, \ldots, m$ (since $m \leq n$). By applying the definition of $\gamma_{R_i^j}(\omega_{\mathcal{G}_j})$, the proposition follows. As syntax partitions also take deterministic conditionals into account, the statement concerning null-worlds follows immediately.     □

# References

1. Getoor, L., Taskar, B. (eds.): Introduction to Statistical Relational Learning. MIT Press, Cambridge (2007)
2. Raedt, L.D., Frasconi, P., Kersting, K., Muggleton, S.H. (eds.): Probabilistic Inductive Logic Programming. Springer, Heidelberg (2008). https://doi.org/10.1007/978-3-540-78652-8
3. Van Den Broeck, G.: First-order model counting in a nutshell. In: Proceedings of the 25th International Joint Conference on Artificial Intelligence (IJCAI), pp. 4086–4089. AAAI Press (2016)
4. Paris, J.B.: The Uncertain Reasoner's Companion - A Mathematical Perspective. Cambridge University Press, Cambridge (1994)
5. Kern-Isberner, G.: Conditionals in Nonmonotonic Reasoning and Belief Revision. Springer, Heidelberg (2001). https://doi.org/10.1007/3-540-44600-1
6. Finthammer, M., Beierle, C.: A two-level approach to maximum entropy model computation for relational probabilistic logic based on weighted conditional impacts. In: Straccia, U., Calì, A. (eds.) SUM 2014. LNCS (LNAI), vol. 8720, pp. 162–175. Springer, Cham (2014). https://doi.org/10.1007/978-3-319-11508-5_14
7. Thimm, M., Kern-Isberner, G.: On probabilistic inference in relational conditional logics. Logic J. IGPL **20**(5), 872–908 (2012)
8. Halpern, J.Y.: An analysis of first-order logics of probability. Artif. Intell. **46**(3), 311–350 (1990)
9. Paris, J.B.: Common sense and maximum entropy. Synthese **117**(1), 75–93 (1999)
10. Darroch, J.N., Ratcliff, D.: Generalized iterative scaling for log-linear models. Ann. Math. Stat. **43**(5), 1470–1480 (1972)
11. Koller, D., Friedman, N.: Probabilistic Graphical Models. MIT Press, Cambridge (2009)
12. Kern-Isberner, G., Thimm, M.: A ranking semantics for first-order conditionals. In: Proceedings of the 20th European Conference on Artificial Intelligence (ECAI). FAIA, vol. 242, pp. 456–461. IOS Press (2012)

13. Finthammer, M., Beierle, C.: Using equivalences of worlds for aggregation semantics of relational conditionals. In: Glimm, B., Krüger, A. (eds.) KI 2012. LNCS (LNAI), vol. 7526, pp. 49–60. Springer, Heidelberg (2012). https://doi.org/10.1007/978-3-642-33347-7_5
14. Wilhelm, M., Kern-Isberner, G., Ecke, A.: Basic independence results for maximum entropy reasoning based on relational conditionals. In: Proceedings of the 3rd Global Conference on Artificial Intelligence (GCAI). EPiC Series in Computing, vol. 50, pp. 36–50 (2017)
15. Geman, S., Geman, D.: Stochastic relaxation, Gibbs distributions, and the Bayesian restoration of images. IEEE Trans. Pattern Anal. Mach. Intell. **6**(6), 721–741 (1984)
16. Boyd, S., Vandenberghe, L.: Convex Optimization. Cambridge University Press, Cambridge (2004)

# Author Index

Printed in the United States
By Bookmasters